FOLLIES

FOLLIES

GROTTOES & GARDEN BUILDINGS

GWYN HEADLEY
&
WIM MEULENKAMP

AURUM PRESS

First published in Great Britain in 1999

Aurum Press Ltd
25 Bedford Avenue
London WC1B 3AT

A catalogue record for this book is available from
the British Library.

ISBN 1 85410 625 2

10 9 8 7 6 5 4 3 2 1
2003   2002   2001   2000   1999

Printed in Great Britain by Butler & Tanner Ltd,
Frome

Map References
The authors have tried to provide accurate grid references but were not always in a position to do
so. Where the third and sixth digits of the grid reference are both zeros (e.g. TQ 120 240)
accuracy to within a kilometre cannot be guaranteed. The walk is good for you.
Many of the sites visited have been marked with a GPS navigational aid which is subject to a
random accuracy degradation of 100 metres under the USA's Department of Defense Selective
Availability Program.

CONTENTS

Introduction 6

SCOTLAND

WALES

ENGLAND

INTRODUCTION

A folly is a misunderstood building.

We are continually asked: What is a folly? How do we define a folly? The short and unsatisfactory answer is that we don't; it defines itself. Somewhere in these pages you will find a selection of definitions—or interpretations—of the word, but essentially the problem lies in the name. Follies are follies to us, because we do not understand them. Why spend a lifetime tunnelling under Liverpool? Why build a huge tower on a hill miles from civilization? Why create a concrete zoo in your back garden and then be forced to buy a neighbouring field to accommodate the overflow? Why be a human being? Life does not have to be logical. These builders had their reasons—we have guessed at some of them here, and we have revealed others—and in the process, inevitably, there has to be a degree of demystification.

But they retain their fascination for us. This celebration of the meretricious in architecture is a complete rewrite and reworking of *Follies: A National Trust Guide*, first published in 1986 and its revised 1990 paperback *Follies: A Guide to Rogue Architecture*, with the addition of a great deal of new material. The most obvious difference is that the book is now laid out as a gazetteer, instead of being divided into National Trust regions, as before. We have retravelled the land, checking on the many changes members of the Folly Fellowship have told us about over the years. We have unashamedly used information from the invaluable *Follies Magazine*, edited with wit, scholarship and élan by Michael Cousins, on the grounds that culling data from one issue may be plagiarism, but trawling through all 36 back issues is definitely research. We have also turned the country upside down; when we first planned the book Gwyn Headley wrote about the follies of Wales and southern England, while Wim Meulenkamp covered Scotland and the north. We have now swapped ends, to give a different perspective on each county—although, as before, we have each reluctantly allowed the other to meddle with our previously perfect text.

The original book covered England, Scotland and Wales, with the promise of Ireland to come in a future edition. In the event our friend James Howley covered the ground with far greater detail and architectural expertise than we could have hoped for in his definitive *Follies and Garden Buildings of Ireland*. In very partial recompense we have added the Isle of Man and the Channel Islands. Another benefit wrought by the change of publisher is that the photographs are new—not only that, but few of the buildings illustrated here were seen in the earlier books, with the exception of the ten best-known and best-loved follies, as chosen by the Folly Fellowship. This alone points out the breathtaking diversity of folly architecture in Great Britain.

This is the last nineteenth century book to be written in the twentieth century. We make this faintly absurd claim because nobody today would be stupid enough to embark on a project of this nature without first securing grant aid, lottery funding, heritage support or some other form of outside subvention to carry out research, travel, photography and writing. It would be sheer folly. Our perverse sense of pride at having done exactly this is completely outweighed by our incoherent rage at failing to achieve any such funding. This book has been financed by its authors, out of depressingly shallow pockets. So we cheerfully present it to you, aware that it cannot be regarded as definitive, aware that there are many flaws and omissions, aware that this is the best we can afford, all mitigated by the fact that it's the only game in town. The advantage it gives us is complete editorial independence. Although we would willingly have sold our souls for a mess of pottage no one has offered us any, so we are free to say what we like about the National Trust, Cadw, Historic Scotland, English Heritage, local councils and all the other worthy and not so worthy organisations which affect our architectural heritage. They are all handy targets for criticism, especially the National Trust which is now showing signs of emerging from its depressing 1980s obsession with tea-rooms and gifte shoppes.

However this has not been written as a peevish snipe at bureaucracy—some of our best follies have been constructed by bureaucrats—this is an enthusiastic celebration of building for pure pleasure. You will find marvels inside; they will be hard to find because the best usually is, but be assured they are here.

PRIVACY AND VISITING

Isn't it a shame? All these wonderful buildings, and you can't go and see them because they're on private ground. This is the case for the great majority of follies and garden buildings in this book. Some of course are owned by organisations such as Cadw, the National Trust, the Landmark Trust, English Heritage or are visitor attractions in their own right, and can be visited on payment of a fee. Others stand in towns, remarked on by passers-by, then ignored. There are some ways to overcome this problem. Firstly, join the Folly Fellowship*. This immediately marks you out as a person of taste and discrimination.

Then ask your Folly Fellowship regional secretary if an outing is being planned to the folly site you wish to see. If not, write enclosing a stamped addressed envelope to The Estate Office at the site. The great majority of estates will allow public access on certain days of the year, although in these increasingly security-conscious and paranoid days even requests from pillars of the community such as the President and Vice-President of the Folly Fellowship are sometimes looked on with suspicion.

A NOTE ON THE LAYOUT OF THE BOOK BY COUNTIES

The shires are the physical backbone of England; from Hampshire in the south to Yorkshire in the north they run straight and strong. The counties east and west are supported like ribs—Cornwall, Kent, Norfolk, Cumberland are all English counties, but they are not shires. It has been this way for a millennium, since before the Norman conquest, when over a period of one or two hundred years the counties of England took shape. There they stayed, through invasion, civil war, insurrection,

through the rolling up of the map of Europe, through world wars, for nine hundred years until 1972, when the map of Britain was not so much rolled up as rubbed out and redrawn. The English lost Rutland. They lost Westmorland. They were introduced to Cleveland, Tyne & Wear, Avon, Humberside and others. A thousand years of history were overwritten. Wales was awarded names even more unpronounceable to the English: Dyfed, Clwyd, Powys. No more Merioneth, no more Montgomery, no more Radnor. The Scots fared even worse. Gone were Kirkcudbrightshire, Ayrshire, Kincardineshire, Banffshire; in came Strathclyde, Borders, Grampian. The country began to sound like a television franchise. Unbelievably, there was no rioting. We are the silent people, and we have not spoken yet. What does it take? Pragmatically the Scots ignored the new, artificial divisions, like sensible member states of the European Union, and carried on using the old, time-honoured names.

In 1996 it happened all over again. Humberside was mercifully put down. Wales suddenly found itself with 21 counties instead of the eight it had held for centuries. People who had been born in Glamorgan suddenly found they were natives of the county of Rhondda Cynon Taff. Tiflis becomes Tblisi, Bombay becomes Mumbai, Upper Volta has come to Britain.

Being fuddy-duddy old reactionaries, we found it difficult to keep pace with these changes; once the barriers come down anything can happen, and it probably will. The ice is breaking up on every side. Will the current changes last a generation? Every politician keen to make a mark will now want to redraw the county boundaries. We have entered an era of continuous change, change for change's sake. We wondered how we could best address this in a county-by-county gazetteer, and decided that if people are familiar with Britain and its history at all, they will be familiar with the counties which have existed for a thousand years. So we have sited the buildings in this book in the counties in which they were built. We have given the new county in brackets after the location name. If you have any problems, contact your local authority for this month's new county name. Other collectors of

---

* 7 St Catherines Way, Fareham Hampshire PO16 8RL

geographically based data have had to address this problem (those invaluable Pevsners, as the *Buildings of Britain* series will always be known, have simply ignored all post-1972 boundary changes) and the diplomatic solution is to call the old counties as used in this book the Ceremonial Counties.

As for the people, the diversity of ancestry in these islands has exploded in the last fifty years. Some families—the Brudenells in Northamptonshire, the Giffards in Staffordshire, to name but two—have defended the same patch of land for nearly a thousand years, yet others with less resonant names can claim an even more spectacular lineage: in 1996 a DNA sample taken from a 9,000-year-old skeleton found in a Somerset cave was shown to match the DNA of a 52-year-old schoolteacher living in the next village. In any urban environment, there may be thirty different languages spoken in any one street, so the old stereotypes of county manners and peculiarities are largely obsolete. Now our formerly static population has migrated to airport departure lounges. We are bound together by the common desire to live here, in God's own country. We have all made that choice, some more recently than others.

Scholarly work on the folly has not been lacking since the 1980s, some of it in tandem with the ever-increasing interest in historic gardens: garden buildings are now acknowledged to form an integral part of the historic park (see David R. Coffin's excellent study *The English Garden: Meditation and Memorial*), and a plethora of publications has researched in depth hitherto unregarded specific building types such as lodges, icehouses and grottoes. Monographs on regional follies have appeared with a vengeance (among the weightier tomes James Howley's aforementioned study of Irish follies). The accumulated pages of eleven volumes of *Follies: the International Magazine for Follies, Grottoes and Garden Buildings* are bursting with the results of enthusiastic on the spot research and the fallout of weeks, months, years spent in archives looking up dates and builders.

The Folly Fellowship has, since its foundation in 1988, taken the lead in providing a basis for folly research and is actively involved in saving follies and garden buildings. We have to salute our fellow Trustees Andrew Plumridge, Michael Cousins and Vernon Gibberd for the splendid work they have done, and also defer to the impressive work done by the numerous members of the Committee and all the other volunteers without whom a charity like this could never have made the impact it is now having.

A sister organisation has sprung up in the Netherlands (usually such a level-headed country), the DonderbergGroep—the Foundation for Follies, Garden Ornaments and Pleasure Architecture, which among other activities also publishes a Newsletter, and has annexed Belgium in the process.

We have not been totally lazy ourselves, although of course we make little attempt at producing the more scholarly publication. Gwyn Headley published his *Architectural Follies of America* (John Wiley & Sons/ Preservation Press, New York) in 1996 and in 1995 Wim Meulenkamp took time off from writing a thousand other books to produce a guide to Dutch and Belgian follies, *Follies: Bizarre bouwwerken in Nederland en België* (Arbeiderspers, Amsterdam).

The follies themselves seem to be breeding in the undergrowth: hundreds of hitherto unnoticed buildings have emerged, and new ones have been built in an orgy of *furor architecturalis*. We are astonished at the amount of DIY follies and *jardins imaginaires* that has come to our attention. We kept up a brave face in the first two editions of this book, but rather doubted whether there was any future in these kinds of folly. So plentiful on the continent and in the United States, they appeared to be almost completely lacking in Britain, despite the supposed eccentricity and individualism of the Brit. Whole areas of Scotland turn out to be fully follied, and a town like Hastings, for example, which had no entry in the last edition, now can claim three follies. The entries for the three B's: Bath, Bristol and Brighton, have been significantly enlarged. Looking at most follies afresh has also sometimes resulted in a changed opinion: the Wrightean follies at Badminton are not so dull after all, nor are the chains of small Scottish folly towers on low hills, many carefully restored by local councils and enthusiasts. Scottish eyecatchers such as the Hundy-Mundy and the Gates of Negapatam have swelled in importance and memory.

We have lost a good folly architect in Peter Foster, but have gained many more: Diana Reynell, who has taken it upon her to restore every grotto in sight, with exciting results; Belinda Eade and Simon Verity who turn out the most splendid work, and of course Vernon Gibberd who has not only given us the astonishing grotto at Leeds Castle but seems to be unstoppable, producing folly furniture, grottoes, towers, temples, the lot. There are even new patrons straight from the eighteenth century mould: John Paul Getty in Buckinghamshire and Duncan Davidson in Northumberland for example; we heard about the latter's Gothic folly tower at Lilburn near Alnwick too late to include it in this edition.

This brings us to restoration work, an immensely difficult and taxing area. How to restore a folly? Do we leave the ivy on? All too often the job is done, but no provision is made for the upkeep of a folly or garden building, and its renewed deterioration is only a matter of time. Major folly collections have however been the subject of long bouts of restoration and consolidation: Painshill, Painswick and Stowe should be mentioned here, and 'to be Painshilled' has become something of a saying. The severely mangled Hadlow Tower however still awaits restoration at the moment of writing, as does the astonishingly grand mausoleum at Cobham Park, Kent.

The last two decades have given us some of the twentieth century's best follies: The Forbidden Corner in Yorkshire, Leeds Castle Grotto in Kent, Little Italy in Corris, and the work of the Last brothers at Corpusty. One shudders to think what the twenty-first century will have in store for us. One thing is sure—there will be follies that cannot be imagined even by the most fevered imagination. New forms of inventiveness, new forms of craftsmanship, new forms of insanity. We long to see them.

We hope to have put the record straight, to have added what was missing, to have corrected what was inaccurate. But such is the nature of the subject that we can never claim to be complete, that is one thing we have learned since 1986. Within a few moments after this book hits the bookshops, somewhere in Britain, on a cold hilltop or from some bramble bushes miles from nowhere, the battle cry 'It's Not In The Book!' will resound. And strangely enough this failure, this omission, will mean that we have succeeded—succeeded in getting people interested in the subject, interested enough to spend their valuable weekends in searching out the remnants of Great Britain's weirdest heritage: the folly.

After all this, what is the fascination? Where is the magic? There is a strange potency in small towers, peculiarly ones (like many follies) which are otherwise unremarkable but suddenly through some trick of light or quirk of nature inadvertently reveal the reason, or a reason, why they were built in that particular spot. It is as if a portal opens up and allows us to see into the mind of the builder. One example will show what may happen. In the early summer of 1988 a party of Folly Fellowship members visited the park at Glynllifon, near Caernarfon in North Wales. There was much to see and much to hear about, and the visit culminated with a walk to the Newborough Mausoleum, topping a hill three fields away. None of them knew what to expect, apart from an abandoned building which had never served its intended purpose. They were fortunate to be allowed inside, to see the plain unadorned interior. Pitch black, and so damp for so long that reasonably well-established stalactites and -mites had formed (ground floor, first floor, chapel, stair to roof, Theodoricus buried anew in a Celtic dawn), we climbed up the chill, dank stone stairs and abruptly out into the sunlit meadow which had grown untended on the roof for nearly two centuries. The building was transformed into a sudden ha-ha in the huge landscape, our own private Darien.

We hardly gazed at each other with a wild surmise, but we did stand silent. It gets us like that.

Gwyn Headley & Wim Meulenkamp, Harlech, London & Utrecht, 1999

Scotland

WESTERN
ISLES

HIGHLAND

GRAMPIAN

TAYSIDE

FIFE

CENTRAL

LOTHIAN

STRATHCLYDE

BORDER

DUMFRIES &
GALLOWAY

BORDERS

BERWICKSHIRE

Dryburgh

Wallace on the Hill (1814)
NT 591 327

John Smith, the father of the bridge-building John and Thomas Smith, was responsible for the sculpting of the huge naïve statue of Sir William Wallace in Roman garb, towering 22ft (6.7m) high on its plinth above Dryburgh. This first monument to Scotland's national hero was erected in 1814 by the Earl of Buchan, and the plinth proclaims:

> WALLACE
> *Great patriot hero*
> *Ill-requited Chief*

and an urn in front is inscribed:

> *The peerless knight of Ellerslie*
> *Who waved on Ayr's romantic shore*
> *The beamy torch of liberty*
> *And roaming round from sea to sea*
> *From glad obscure or gloomy rock*
> *His bold compatriots called to free*
> *This realm from Edward's iron yoke.*

Duns

Nisbet Pentagonal Doocot (late 18th century)
NT 797 506

South of Duns, Nisbet House has a pentagonal castellated doocot—interesting because the pentagonal plan is extremely rare in England and Wales. From the might of its three slight storeys three tiny castellations on each side lour down at the imaginary assailant; above is a stone-slated roof, topped with a ball finial.

Greenlaw

Hume Castle (1789)
NT 705 414

This eyecatcher ruin, 600ft (183m) up on Hume Craigs, is largely artificial. It was erected by Lord Marchmont in 1789, albeit on top of a genuine castle slighted by Oliver Cromwell in 1651. The Marchmont castellations were restored by the Berwickshire Civic Society in 1993 and are now open to those of the public who can face the short climb.

Mellerstain

Hundy Mundy (1778)
NY 666 376

Gloriously named, gloriously functionless, the Hundy Mundy at Mellerstain near Kelso manages to be at the same time one of Scotland's finest and least known follies. Happily, there is no indication of what Hundy Mundy could possibly mean, unless it is a Borders dialect phrase to describe any two-dimensional building with a central arch and two four-storey flanking towers with pyramidal roofs, in which case they've got it bang on. This is pure, pure folly. It was built by Robert Adam as an eyecatcher for the Hon. George Baillie and sited on a low rise 2 miles due south of the house. It's a folly held in great affection by the family—the 12th Earl of Haddington, a talented amateur jockey who raced in the 1933 Grand National, named a favourite horse Hundy Mundy. Unfortunately for us, an intervening cornfield makes it inaccessible.

Paxton Park

Entrances (1997)
NU 950 550

We have repeatedly stated that one cannot set out to build a folly. 'Folly' is a title, an honorarium, awarded by others; the builder should be the last person to accept that the construction is one. But in our knowing age there is a strange desire to build and claim the building to be folly. Shaking our heads in mild incomprehension, we record the erection of a 'new' folly in the woodlands of Paxton Park, Berwick-upon-Tweed, constructed by the artist Julia Hilton, inspired by an opening bud and titled 'Entrances'. This name suggests that it was installed as a work of art rather than as a building, but it is brick-built — 6000 unfired bricks built, torn down, fired and rebuilt — and takes the form of an arch leading nowhere, so the premise is there, even if the intent was premeditated. Once all documentation has been lost and the artist is long forgotten it may qualify as a folly, but until that time we reserve our judgement.

Spottiswoode

Spottiswoode Arches (mid-19th century)
NT 584 484

These are strange and wonderful unarchitectural entrances—tall Gothic-style pointed arches, bristling with rubble cones, mad and staring, hackles raised. One feels that the Gothic was arrived at involuntarily. But on one of the arches there are the fragmentary traces of an inscription:

Without being... enjoy it

Without knowing... how it came about ... it away
Without knowing ... behind it
Without it ...
Without being conscious of our misfortune

Grief rips through the remnants of this wailing inscription, and what can be pieced together of the story behind it supports the idea that the builder was deep in misery. Lady Scott, who built the arch and the castellated lodges near Whiteburn, was a close contemporary of Queen Victoria. Her beloved husband, Sir John, died at about the same age and time as Prince Albert, and Lady Scott developed the Miss Havisham syndrome. Like so many before and after her, she found solace in building and adorned the gate posts of her estate with mottoes and homilies, carved, alas, in temporal sandstone. The remaining vestiges of an anguished soul have weathered away— withered away, perhaps—and barely survive on these weird, alien arches. The plaque on the left-hand side is totally illegible.

Whiteburn

Castellated Cottages (1832)
NT 611 475

Castellations and screens on proletarian buildings achieved much the same popularity here in the Scottish Borders as they did in the English border counties. Two lodge cottages on the long, straight post road from Greenlaw (now the A697) were done up with battlements, apparently to serve as eyecatchers from the distant Spottiswoode House, which was built in 1832 by William

Mellerstain's Hundy Mundy

Burn but is now demolished. Fortunately, the lodges now are sufficiently strange to slow down curious motorists, who thus avoid the Gatso speed camera on the other side of the road. Mr Hollingworth, an Englishman, is delighted to live in East Clock Lodge or English Clock Lodge, where all the distances are to English towns; on the west lodge all the distances are to Scottish towns. He recalled that there used to be eagles on the gateposts and that the painted clocks gave the times of the London to Edinburgh stagecoaches; although the stop itself was a couple of miles up the road, at a former pub called the Eagle, now a private house.

PEEBLESSHIRE

Blyth Bridge

Whalebone Arch (1794)
NT 118 444

At Blyth Bridge's Netherurd House is an entrance arch made of two whalebones fixed to folly-style gate piers. As we were inspecting it we were startled by a sudden skirl of bagpipes behind us. We turned to discover two things: one, that Netherurd House is the headquarters of the Scottish Guides Association, which had chosen that day to hold a jamboree, and two, we had left the

The Whalebone Arch

handbrake of the car off and it was rapidly reversing towards the drystone flanking wall.
The house itself was built between 1791 and 1794 for William Lawson by Robert Burn. Burn was certainly enough of a folly architect to grasp this opportunity to create a small conceit, which had to be rebuilt in 1959, and perhaps it is now time for the

whalebones to be replaced. If this is the sort of thing you find exciting, you can hasten up to the far north of the country to see the whalebone arch at Latheron in Caithness, or to the Meadows, south of Edinburgh's Old Town, where there is another.

Eddlestone

Black Barony Hotel Temple (18th century)
NT 234 472

An 18th-century temple in the grounds of the hotel is now partnered by a relief map of Scotland, made in the 1970s.

Hallyards

Black Dwarf (1802)
NT 212 371

David Ritchie, who was the model for Sir Walter Scott's 1816 novel *The Black Dwarf*, is represented in a woodman's tunic, with a dagger in his belt and leaning negligently on a tall stick. The statue was sculpted by Robert Forrest, an autodidact famous for his carvings of Scott's heroes and the Wallace Monument in Lanark.
Ritchie's cottage is to the south of Hallyards. It was expressly erected for the dwarf by Sir James Nasmyth in 1802. The house does not shout 'folly' at the visitor; it has normal doors and windows, except on one side, where the dwarf's special entrance is only about 3ft (1m) high. Ritchie lived in this cottage until his death in 1811.

Peebles

Rosetta Castellated Stables (1807)
NT 244 414

At Rosetta, a manor on the northwest outskirts of Peebles, the stable block is effectively hidden behind a lavishly castellated screen. Rosetta was built in 1807 for Dr Thomas Young, physician and Egyptologist, and the house owes its name to the fact that Young helped to decipher the Rosetta Stone. The house and stables stand in good, solid condition, but the extensive grounds have been turned over to a large caravan site.

Skirling

Lord Carmichael's Figures (1920)
NT 079 395

Baron Carmichael of Skirling, the first governor of Bengal, was a pleasant if diffident man. His quixotic sense of humour manifested itself in his gift to the village: around the green is a collection of bizarre, painted, wrought-iron figures, including pigs, lizards, flowers, birds and other whimsies. The work was done after World War I by Thomas Hadden of Edinburgh, who decorated the grounds of Carmichael's house in similar fashion.

Traquair House

Bear Gates (1745)
Rustic Summerhouses (1834)
NT 244 412

At Traquair House the unused main gates are known as the Bear Gates. They were finished in 1745, and it is said that the Earl of Traquair kept them shut after the Battle of Culloden just a year later, when the last person to pass through them was Bonnie Prince Charlie. This story is perpetuated on every bottle of Traquair House Ale, a blisteringly strong beer, which is brewed at the house and which can occasionally be obtained elsewhere. Implicit in this summary is approbation of the Stuart cause. But despite the later romanticization of the Bonnie Prince, the Jacobite earl was not a wholehearted supporter, and the extent of his support was merely to promise that the Bear Gates should not be opened until the Stuarts reigned. A promise made is a promise kept, and the gates have stayed shut ever since. Today, they are kept bolted. Only a Land Rover could negotiate the grassy knoll up to them, but if you walk there you will find that the view of the house from the gates is the classic Scottish Heritage picture.

A second, less exciting story tells that the 7th Earl of Traquair closed them in 1796, on the day the last countess died, declaring that they should not be opened until a new countess came to Traquair.

The brick gate piers were built between 1737 and 1738, but it was only in 1745 that the two bears carrying the Traquair shield and the motto IUDGE NOUGHT were carved by George Jamieson from stone quarried at Penicuik.

Bear Gates at Traquair

Near the house are two pavilions with ogee roofs; the south pavilion has a painting of the Toilet of Venus on its ceiling.

Whim

Doocot (mid-18th century)
NT 213 532

There are two Whims in Scotland (there is a Whimsey in Gloucestershire), and it would be pleasant had 'whim' been adopted as the Scottish word for a folly; it has the right feel. Despite the attempt at Blair Atholl, however, the name did not catch on. Whim House, on the borders of Lothian, acquired its name through the siting of the estate by Archibald Campbell, 3rd Duke of Argyll, and here again 'whim' is used in the same context as 'folly' would be in England. Argyll bought the terrain, ominously called Blair Bogg, from his friend Thomas Cochrane in 1729. The transaction was treated as a joke between the two men—'a Comicall Bargain' was the actual term used—but the duke was bent on making the estate arable, and after 30 years' hard work and a vast outlay, there were nurseries, pleasure grounds and gardens at Whim. There was also a castellated doocot, which was designed by Lord Milton, the duke's associate, but this was truncated years ago. The story of Milton's having designed the doocot does shed some interesting light on the practice of folly building. It appears that he searched contemporary architectural pattern books for a Gothick tower as a model for the doocot. When he failed to find what he wanted, he had to resort to his own inventiveness. The house has now been taken over as a nursing home, and there is a small industrial estate carved out of the woods by the main road, just where a fine doocot might have been advantageously placed.

ROXBURGHSHIRE

Ancrum (Monteviot)

Baron's Folly (18th century)
NT 637 268
Mausoleum
NT 613 268
Waterloo Column (1815)
NT 653 263

Despite its promising name, Baron's Folly is little more than a hexagonal Gothick belvedere with sweeping views. The Mausoleum is more splendid. It is a square building, with

Romanesque arches on each façade, which enclose a lunette above two pilasters, all topped with a small dome pierced by star-shaped glass lights, now mostly broken.

The memorial on top of the 777ft (237m) high Penielheugh is a 150ft (46m) tall plain pillar with a covered viewing gallery at the top. There are 228 steps to the cone-capped top; it was erected by the Marquis of Lothian 'and his tenants' to celebrate Wellington's victory at Waterloo.

Denholm

The Text House (1900)
NT 568 184

This rather curious looking town house, which faces the village green, resembles an early effort by an untrained architect with a kit of parts—gable (one), pilasters (two), Rennie Mackintosh windows (two), bay windows (two, one on top of the other), spare windows (two), doors (two). It was the home of a Dr Haddon, who placed pithy homilies on the exterior:

> *Tak tent in time*
> *ere time be tent*
> *all was others*
> *all will be others*

The house was built in 1900 in a freestyle Arts and Crafts fashion, with the architectural elements standing rather incongruously together. Yet the good doctor was not so obsessed that he lost his

The Text House, Denholm

patrimony—nearly a century later his descendants still live happily in the house.

Right next door to the Text House is the birthplace of Sir James A.H. Murray (1837–1915), editor of the New English Dictionary.

Obelisk (1861)
NT 568 184

To the memory of the poet John Leyden.

Eckford

Watchtower (late 18th century)
NT 709 262

In Eckford churchyard a small folly seems to have lost its way and landed up among the graves. It is a 12ft (3.6m) high round towerette, castellated with arrowslit windows and with three steps leading to a door. The tower was built as a watch house, and there was to have been a guard inside to scare off any body-snatchers who might have tried to dig up a freshish cadaver for the ever-demanding dissection rooms of the medical faculties at Edinburgh University. Even in the days of cheap labour it would have been expensive to maintain a permanent watch in what is only a small village, so it is possible that the watchtower functioned like the fake alarm systems on the walls of suburban bungalows.

Ednam

Thomson Obelisk (mid-19th century)
NT 736 363

A plain stone obelisk on Ferniehill to the south of the town was built to honour James Thomson, who wrote the words to 'Rule Britannia'. There must be something in the air of Ednam, for the author of 'Abide with Me', Henry Francis Lyte, was also born here.

Melrose

Abbotsford Screen (early 19th century)
NT 593 342

Scott's View is an arch set in a wall crowned with five rough pinnacles, like squat obelisks. The view is now obscured by feral trees. This may have been the screen wall built by J. & T. Smith for Sir Walter Scott.

Teviothead

Riddell Cone (1874)
NT 407 055

The hilltop cone near Teviothead on the A7 commemorates a shepherd poet, Henry Scott Riddell.

CENTRAL

Lanrick Castle

Gartincaber

Stirling

Loch Lomond

Killearn

Dunmore

Callendar House

Falkirk

Mugdock

STIRLINGSHIRE

Callendar House

Mausoleum (1816)
NS 904 790

There is nothing of the folly here, but there is a splendid Doric colonnaded drum of a mausoleum buried in woodland that is well worth seeking out. It was built for the grieving widow of William Forbes by the leading Edinburgh architect Archibald Elliott.

Dunmore

The Pineapple (1761)
NS 889 885

At the end of the walled garden in Dunmore Park is a folly *par excellence*, a stone fruit to revitalize the palate of the most jaded architect. This gigantic reproduction of the now familiar fruit dwarfs the surrounding fruit trees and is the most singular monument to come out of the little practised art of fruit architecture.

In 1761 the 29-year-old John Murray, 4th Earl of Dunmore, had been married for two years. Perhaps it was the fact that his marriage was going sour that prompted the enormous fruit; or it may have been intended as a belated wedding present. It may have been the result of a frivolous wager, or it may have commemorated the growing of a pineapple—not the first, for they had been grown in hothouses in Scotland for nearly 30 years. The likeliest story is inevitably unsubstantiated. Many years ago the Scottish Secretary of the Folly Fellowship gave a lift to an old man who used to be a gardener on the estate. He told her that the Earl of Dunmore took his bride to Italy where they saw a similar building. (We wonder where?) He promised that on their return he would build her a replica, and here it stands.

Whatever the reason, this extraordinary building never fails to astonish. From a range of side pavilions rises an octagon with Gothick windows, the arches of which culminate in carved stone foliage. Then the actual pineapple starts, 53ft (16m) high and

Scotland's finest folly

brilliantly carved from stone. There is no need to describe it—it is a remarkably accurate rendering of a pineapple—but two centuries ago the fruit was so rare, luxurious and desirable that it made today's luxuries such as caviar, smoked salmon and champagne mundane by comparison. The pineapple was scarcely seen except by the very rich, so the stone copy must have astounded the locals—and if we narrow our eyes and place ourselves in Martian mode, imagining that we have never seen a pineapple before, it really is a most extraordinary looking object.

The building was planned and designed with the utmost care, with each of the gently curving leaves being drained separately in order to prevent frost from damaging the delicate masonry. There are two entrances—a classical loggia to the south and a Gothick doorway to the north on the upper level, leading into the second storey. The keystone above the south entrance carries the date 1761, and above this is a carved heart and the inscription FIDELIS IN ADVERSIS, commemorating the marriage in 1803 of George Murray, 5th Earl of Dunmore, to the daughter of the Duke of Hamilton. Some years ago the Landmark Trust took the building on a long lease from the National Trust for Scotland and carefully restored it for letting as a holiday home. A hermit's cave

has been reported nearby, so perhaps The Pineapple was not the only Dunmore folly. Sadly, the name of the designer of this wonderful structure has not been recorded— it is a work of genius, certainly unique and probably impossible to duplicate nowadays. Tradition ascribes it to Sir William Chambers, but he was working in London at the time it was built and it is not mentioned in his writings, as such a remarkable building surely would have been. Of course, the Dunmore family papers for 1761 are missing. Other rumours flit about—Lord Perth, a sometime owner, apparently wanted to move it to his park but was deterred when told that the dome would collapse if it was touched (we detect some fast thinking by an astute surveyor there).

Falkirk

Carron House Doocot (18th century)
NS 830 897

The doocot at Carron House, near Falkirk, just manages to insinuate itself into the folly bracket. It is octagonal, with an ogival arched entrance and an *oeil-de-boeuf* window above the door. On the second storey there is a similar course of decorative openings.

Killearn

Buchanan Obelisk (1788)
NS 521 860

In the village of Killearn, some 6 or 7 miles east of Loch Lomond, there is an enormous 100ft (30m) high obelisk, which was designed by James Craig and built in 1788 by the mason William Gray. The monument commemorates the reformist historian George Buchanan, who was born at Killearn in 1506. When the obelisk was repaired in 1850 a Latin inscription was added, celebrating his attacks on the clergy, probably for their use of Latin rather than the vulgate.

Loch Lomond

Inchmurrin Tower (1789)
NS 377 862

On an island in one of Scotland's two most famous lochs stood, and perhaps still stands, a tower designed in 1789 by James Playfair for Lord Graham, later the 3rd Duke of Montrose. It was intended to be a hunting lodge disguised as an old 'Gothic tower of strength', but we have not been able to visit Inchmurrin in Loch Lomond to find out if it still exists.

VERTIGO

Some Steep Climbs/Cliffhangers

OLD JOHN
Leicestershire

———

MOW COP
Cheshire

———

ST MICHAEL'S MOUNT
Cornwall

———

RIBER CASTLE
Derbyshire

———

HOPETON MONUMENT
Lothian

———

WHITE NANCY
Cheshire

Mugdock

Smith's Folly (18th century)
NS 558 769

A tiny octagonal folly tower, almost too small
to be noticed by anyone but village children
at play, hides on a hill in the hamlet of
Mugdock. Trimmed to half its height, it is
strenuously guarded by loose alsatians from
the nearby cottage. It would seem to have
been built as a belvedere for the
neighbouring estate of Craigend. Once it was
finely decorated with Gothick windows,
trefoils and expensively dressed stone—now
it is not.

Stirling

Wallace Monument (1859)
NS 811 958

The enormous, 220ft (67m) high Wallace
Monument dominates the town of Stirling
from its site above the bridge where, in 1297,
Scotland's national hero, Sir William
Wallace, wreaked havoc on the English. The
monument was designed by J.T. Rochead
and took ten years from 1859 to build. The
original site chosen for the monument was
Glasgow Green, but there were forcefully
expressed objections from the Edinburgh
area, so Abbey Craig, outside Stirling, was
the compromise choice. Justifying it, a
correspondent to the *Stirling Observer* in
1869 claimed it was at the geographical
centre of Scotland, an agreeable, if totally
inaccurate, sentiment.

The monument is a splendid, confident,
exuberant celebration of a tower, with
bartizans, pinnacles, rough harling, boles,
buttresses and an impressive open-worked
spire. The 15ft (4.6m) statue of Wallace by
D.W. Stephenson inside must, such is the
hero's renown in these parts, be life-size.

The reputations of national heroes are
prone to revision and deconstruction, most
often shortly after their deaths, and it is
interesting to note that at the time of writing
Wallace's genocidal inclinations are being
analysed together with his undoubted
Anglophobia, for which he is celebrated. The
debunking of myths is not a recent
development, the product of this cynical
century—the trigger for the erection of the
Wallace Monument was an article in the
North British Review in 1856 questioning the
purity of his motives.

The wedding cake wonder of Wallace's Monument

DUMFRIES & GALLOWAY

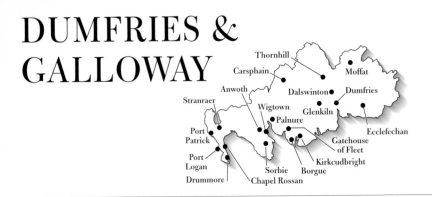

KIRKCUDBRIGHTSHIRE

Anwoth

Rutherford Obelisk (18th century)
`NX 583 564`

An obelisk to commemorate Samuel Rutherford, minister of Anwoth in the 17th century.

Borgue

Cow Palace (1901)
`NX 630 487`

At Kirkandrews, some 5 miles south of Gatehouse of Fleet, is Borgue, famous for the Cow Palace, a model dairy built in 1901 for the Manchester businessman James Brown. The Gothic buildings were designed with great care and put up at huge expense—so much so that local rumour still has it that Brown's cows were tethered with chains of silver. The central Corseyard Tower was to have been the farm's grandest feature, a water tower built as a baronial castle, but on completion it was found to be pitifully inadequate as a means of water supply. Nevertheless, it looked great.

Carsphain

Deer Obelisk (19th century)
`NX 559 940`

A cairn in Knockray Park marks the place where the last wild deer in the Scottish Lowlands was killed.

Gatehouse of Fleet

Cally House Gothic Temple (1789)
`NX 598 555`

Directly south of Gatehouse is Cally House. Here the architect and landscape gardener James Ramsey laid out the gardens in the 1780s. About 1789 he must have designed the Gothick Temple, hidden between newly planted trees and originally housing a 'farm-servant'. Now the two-storey tower is dilapidated, but it was sturdily built so it may yet survive. It is square, with corner buttresses; a flight of steps leads to a door with an uncouth arch. The castellations are quite heavy, a course of open slabs of stone, filled in with rubble.

Jubilee Clock Tower (1871)
`NX 660 568`

This starts off as a typical Scottish harled tower, with a gently battered base rising to a bartizaned upper level, at which point typicality deserted Mr Pilkington, the architect, and he went on to add the most improbable castellations, curled like phoenix flames or palmettes. There is a similar tower in Creetown, which may be by the same architect?

Glenkiln

Johnny Turner's Monument (19th century)
Sculpture Park (1950s onwards)
`NX 845 797`

The grave of the shepherd Johnny Turner is sited on remote Bishop Forest Hill, above the Glenkiln reservoir. Old Johnny was terrified of the Resurrectionists and determined not to let them get his dead body, so he hacked his own grave out of the solid rock. An inscription marks the spot. This is passing strange, but not as strange as the sculptures on this bleak, abandoned hillside. Between 1951 and 1966 the local landowner beautified the dale with sculptures by the masters of the day, Henry Moore and Jacob Epstein among them. Leaving negotiable works of art unprotected in such an unfrequented area could be seen as folly in itself, and indeed some insanely dedicated vandal did manage to decapitate one of the Moores.

After years of study, we can partly understand the motives of some of the folly builders, but we will never understand the thought processes of the wanton vandal. It took thought and forward planning, both indicators of ratiocination, to get to the right spot with the requisite tools. But why use them? Where is the gain, the satisfaction, the pleasure?

Kirkcudbright

Gazebo (19th century)
NX 685 514

This early 19th-century, circular, castellated Gothic gazebo—standing in the back garden of 10 High Street, which has a similarly styled façade—is best seen from the walk along the River Dee. Next door, the Broughton House Museum has a Japanese garden designed by the Edwardian painter E.A. Hornel.

Palnure

Kelburn Cottage Gnome Garden
(mid-20th century)
NX 455 637

If you are passing along the A75 and have a passion for gnomes, stop for a while and enjoy the excesses to be relished here.

DUMFRIESSHIRE

Dalswinton

Miller's Maggot (1810)
NX 958 858

Near Clonfeckle Farm (named after Clonfeacle in Co. Tyrone?), above Dalswinton, stands this 30ft (9m) high, round tower, which bears the following inscription:

> *This Tower erected anno 1810 is, from motives of Esteem and Gratitude, dedicated to the Revd. Dr. William Richardson of Ireland, who, having discovered the wonderful properties of the Fiorin Grass, was the first to teach others the culture and uses of this Invaluable Gift of a Beneficent Providence.*

It was erected by Patrick Miller, an Edinburgh merchant banker and one of the first men to see the possibilities of steam navigation. The beneficial uses of fiorin grass have so far eluded your researchers.

Dumfries

Camera Obscura (1836)
NX 970 760

Situated on Corbelly Hill is this intriguing and still functioning device, built from a windmill truncated in 1836 and now part of the Dumfries Museum. Walter Newall, a local architect, added a good number of decorative conceits—'Egyptian', according to one source—to pull it above the common turn of converted windmills to make an agreeable classical towerlet.

Queensbury Column (1780)
NX 970 760

By Robert Adam.

Ecclefechan

Repentance Tower or Trailtrow (1560)
NY 155 722

There is no hint of architectural fancy in this sombre building, which stands in silence but for the wind soughing through the abandoned graveyard on the hilltop. The strange names of this ancient square tower, lone and distant above Hoddom Bridge, hint

---

IN THE BEGINNING

Some Old Follies

FRESTON TOWER
Suffolk

CHATSWORTH HUNTING TOWER
Derbyshire

RUSHTON TRIANGULAR LODGE
Northamptonshire

ALFRED'S HALL
Gloucestershire

THE PEPPERPOT
Wiltshire

THE FOLLY, SETTLE
North Yorkshire

LYME CAGE
Cheshire

FAWLEY COURT SHAM RUIN
Berkshire

at a good story, and indeed there is one. It was built by John Maxwell in expiation of his betrayal to the English of 12 fellow Scots and their subsequent execution. The door lintel bears just one word, inscribed in an eerie, runic-style script: REPENTANCE. Other sources claim that it was built by John, Lord Herries as a watchtower, and that the word 'Repentance' is intended merely to draw the visitor's attention to the adjoining graveyard. It could scarcely be missed. One tombstone, its back to the bleak and lonely tower, is elegantly inscribed:

HERE LIES

CHARLES MURRAY

A NATIVE OF AFRICA

SERVANT TO M. MURRAY

OF MURRAYTHWAITE

DIED 3rd FEBRY 1776

Moffat

Colvin Fountain (1875)
`NT 085 053`

A ram perched on a crag makes this a highly visible monument by William Brodie to the sheep that turned much of the Scottish farmland into wasteland. There is a copy of the monument in the extraordinary Cement Menagerie in Branxton, Northumberland.

Thornhill

Drumlanrig Castle Rustic Summerhouses (1840)
`NX 851 996`

By Charles M'Intosh.

Column (1714)
`NX 880 955`

A column dedicated to the memory of the 2nd Duke of Queensbury who died in 1711.

WIGTOWNSHIRE

Chapel Rossan

Folly Lodge (19th century)
`NX 110 450`

The lodge, with Gothick windows, resembles an ecclesiastical building. To the west is a neo-baronial house, which is painted with colours too glossy and which is itself a little too small for it to be anything other than a folly. A mile south, at Balgown, we glimpsed between the trees a tower on the water's edge.

Drummore

Lighthouse Tombstone (19th century)
`NX 135 370`

Towards the Mull of Galloway, the village graveyard at Drummore has a curious tombstone in the shape of a lighthouse, as if Ulverston's The Hoad had crossed the Solway Firth and pupped.

Port Logan

Fish Pond House and Bath House
(19th century)
`NX 094 413`

You will almost certainly be visiting the Logan Gardens if you find yourself in this part of the world, and the Fish Pond is worth a look, with its castellated keeper's house and a castellated bath house, where ladies could change before immersing themselves in the sea-filled basin. They built them tough in those days.

Port Patrick

Bath House (19th century)
`NX 000 539`

A strange little bungalow, consisting of two linked hexagons, was possibly built to compete with the bath house at Logan House (*see above*).

Sorbie

Cruggleton Look-out (19th century)
`NX 950 473`

A 1905 postcard shows this as a short, circular, castellated, ivy-clad belvedere tower with an external staircase, but a regrettably peremptory search yielded no evidence of its survival.

Stranraer

North West Castle Hotel (19th century)
`NX 950 473`

Sir John Ross (1777–1856), of Arctic fame, wanted to build his house as a ship but didn't completely succeed. Nevertheless, he managed to convey a nautical flavour to both the inside and outside of this neo-Gothic, castellated mansion. The name of the house derives, of course, from his searches for the North West Passage.

Wigtown

Murray Obelisk (18th century)
`NX 438 555`

FIFE

FIFE

Colinsburgh

Balcarres Crag Folly (1813)
`NO 478 043`

After a spell of 21 years in India, the Hon. Robert Lindsay bought part of the Balcarres Estate in Colinsburgh from his elder brother and employed James Fisher to build him a very beautiful and visible eyecatcher on

Balcarres Crag Folly

Balcarres Crag. It is one of the most elegant, archetypal follies in Scotland: a neat sham castle with ruined arch and walls, carefully worked in the local grey-black stone, with startling white for the bold castellations and to highlight the windows and doors. There are a flagpole, arrowslits, pointed arches, a round window—everything the folly lover could want. At the bottom of the path leading to the folly is a ruined but consolidated chapel, now serving as a mausoleum for the Earls of Crawford and Balcarres. Yews add to the funereal atmosphere, and pieces of broken fluted columns complete it.

Crail

East Newhall Folly Steading
(late 18th century)
`NO 604 107`

Behind and to the side of the frowning battlemented sham castle façade of the Mains at East Newhall is a large octagonal room with floor-to-ceiling windows. Whether this is the remnant of some faltering commercial enterprise we do not know, but it would repay a visit in a couple of years.

Cupar

Preston Hall Mausoleum (1795)
`NO 394 150`

There is something of the folly about many mausoleums, which are erected to enhance dynasties and reputations in an antithesis of the humility of mortality. Here is an elegant example of pomposity pricked: a fine octagonal colonnaded temple built by Robert Mitchell for Sir John Callendar to commemorate his brother, Alexander Callendar Crichton. The dear departed was to be interred in a vault surmounted by a white marble statue, but they never got round to it:

there was no interment, no vault, no statue—just this colonnaded monument to vainglory.

Dunfermline

Pittencrieff Doocot (1770)
`NT 083 873`

Hiding in the trees by the north wall of the public park, is this well-restored and surprisingly unvandalized doocot, round and castellated like a little castle tower.

Elie

The Lady's Tower (mid-18th century)
`NT 500 994`

On the coast at Elie is The Lady's Tower, a two-storey bath house built especially for Lady Janet Anstruther of Elie House so that she could bathe unobserved. Loungers were shooed away by a servant ringing handbells. The Gothicky structure may have been built by William Adam who worked at the house in the 1740s, when he also helped to popularize the Gothick style in Scotland by supervising the building of Inveraray Castle. It has three tall arched windows and a door, a fireplace and the remnants of two upper floors, which would have bisected the windows.

Below it on the beach is an odd little stone grotto, with large slabs of stone projecting into the grotto from the roof, looking rather like an inverted hedgehog.

Further up the coast from Elie, the little battlemented tower on the links at Anstruther turns out to be a war memorial.

Falkland

Falkland House Sham Chapel (18th century)
`NO 248 074`

We were told about this and went to find it with some excitement, expecting a Scottish Tattingstone Wonder or a Steeple Lodge. But it looks far too realistically distressed to be a genuine sham. 'It is not every man that can execute a ruin…'

High Valleyfield

Woodhead Farm (late 18th century)
`NT 087 875`

Want to stay in a folly? Above the immaculate medieval town of Culross (blighted only by the approach past Longannet Power Station), Woodhead Farm B&B at Valleyfield is not so much a folly as a seaside frivolity set a mile or so inland. There is nothing exceptional about the building's structure. Enter down the drive, and you arrive in a small, plain courtyard with no sign of nonsense. But go through an arched tunnel, round the side of the house and suddenly the façade bounds into life—knapped flint in exuberant Gothick. It is the grace notes that turn it into a pretty little musical box of a house. The doorway and windows are all Gothick, surrounded by rustication akin to shellwork. The side walls have blind windows in the same style. Above the doorway on the front façade is a large quatrefoil light. All these embellishments were probably the work of a local builder who used his pattern book over-enthusiastically.

The Lady's Tower at Elie

A fragment of Mr. Bisset's wall at Leven

Kinghorn

Alexander Monument (1886)
NT 270 862

Victorian Scotland seems to have been obsessed with commemorative monuments, obelisks, towers, arches and any other structure that could be run up quickly to mark some otherwise long-forgotten event. This one is a pillar surmounted by a cross above Pettycur Bay, constructed in 1886 on the place where apparently King Alexander III had fallen over and died 500 years earlier.

Kinglassie

Blythe's Folly (1820)
NT 227 996

Inland at Kinglassie, on top of Redwells Hill, stands a late-Georgian tower, called Blythe's Folly. A rough-harled, square, four-storey building with fancy battlements, it was never completed, but still served the Home Guard as a look-out tower in World War II. Old buildings, alas, are treated like old soldiers, and it is now in danger of collapsing through neglect, so cheer yourself up with the thought that the village of Kinglassie was once called Goatmilk.

Kirkcaldy

Raith Park Look-out Tower (early 19th century)
NT 249 919

On Cormie Hill is a fat, three-storey, square belvedere, formerly used as a museum.

Leven

Shell Wall (mid-20th century)
NO 382 005

The Shell Wall in Leven is at the end of School Street, parallel with the promenade. This tiny scrap is all that remains of the only real reason to come to Leven—Walter Bisset's magnificent and sadly destroyed Shell Bus. (The only other shell bus we have heard of was at Buailedubh on South Uist, also recently crushed—perhaps the construction and destruction of shell buses is a peculiarly Scottish pastime.)

After the paean of praise awarded it in the first edition of this book, someone decided the Shell Bus had outlived its usefulness, and it was swept away to make room for an utterly nondescript bungalow. Such is progress. For 50 years the only thing that made Leven rate a mention in the guide books was the Shell Bus. Now you can visit the resort and stare at the Methil Power Station at the end of the beach instead. Don't bother asking in the Tourist Information Office—they only employ sales staff, because it's presumably too difficult to find people who know about or have an interest in the locality. But then they may give out information to visitors who could then leave without buying anything. Warming to this theme, why do Tourist Information Offices hire only callow youths, who are only vaguely aware of which part of the country they are in? Why can't they employ old codgers who have lived in the region all their lives and actually *know* what's good and what's not. Or even (shudder) local historians? Because we live in a market economy, that's why. Goodbye, old bus.

Lower Largo

Lundin Tower (1800)
NT 399 029

Lundin Tower was apparently a genuine medieval chapel, which was Gothicized and converted into a doocot in about 1800.

Mount Hill

Hopetoun Monument (1826)
NO 331 165

Human beings are far from perfect. The blind spot is a point on the back of the retina where the nerves from the eye to the brain block the reception of images. This is why it pays to look slightly away from a star in order to see it more clearly. The blind spots of the authors of this book appear to be larger than most, for despite five visits to the region we still have not seen the monument on Mount Hill, northwest of Cupar. Everyone else says it is a huge Doric column tower, which can be climbed, a monument to the 4th Earl of Hopetoun, but we are beginning to suspect a conspiracy.

Tayport

Waterloo Tower (1816)
NO 443 286

The same goes for the Waterloo Tower on Hare Law between Newport-on-Tay and Tayport as for the Hopetoun Monument (see above). It is clearly marked on the Ordnance Survey map, but we could not find it. No doubt readers will tell us if these two towers actually exist. We have our doubts.

West Wemyss

Home Farm (18th century)
NT 382 005

Along the coast, Wemyss Castle has a home farm that is castellated and ornamented with cross arrowslits. James Wyatt's nephew Lewis designed a Gothic gateway and lodge here for William Wemyss, but they were never built— perhaps the farmhouse was also his work.

JUST PASSING THROUGH
Some Follies to Stay in

THE PINEAPPLE *Stirlingshire*	ENDSLEIGH COTTAGE *Devon*
HOUSE IN THE CLOUDS *Suffolk*	CLYTHA CASTLE *Monmouth*
FIDDLEBACK COTTAGE *Cumberland*	BELMONT PARK TOWER *Kent*
LUTTRELL'S TOWER *Hampshire*	STOWE GOTHICK TEMPLE *Buckinghamshire*
EUROCLYDON HOTEL *Gloucestershire*	PETERSON'S FOLLY *Hampshire*
MRS. PETERS'S TOWER *Devon*	PIG STY FYLING OLD HALL *North Yorkshire*

GRAMPIAN

ABERDEENSHIRE

Ellon

Whitefield Farm Tower (1950)
NJ 930 310

Whitefield Farm outside Ellon has an identical white, castellated round tower to one at Stichill, near Galashiels. Perhaps there is a Scottish pattern book for folly-styled silage towers.

Harlaw

Monument (1911)
NJ 751 240

At Harlaw is a solid battered hexagonal monument with a pyramidal roof, which was erected to commemorate the 500th anniversary of the Battle of Harlaw in 1411, when the Lowlanders defeated the Highlanders. The tower was put up in 1911 in a splendid celebration of late Arts and Crafts confidence. The superb lettering, as clear today as when it was carved, reads:

> Harlaw Monument
> ERECTED BY
> THE BURGH OF
> ABERDEEN A.D.1911
> ADAM MAITLAND
> LORD PROVOST

then on the other side

> HARLAW
> JULY 24 A.D.1411

We wonder if it was as cold as 24 June 1997, which was the day we went there. It was impossible to stay and ponder longer, for the astonishing stench of liquid fertilizer from the surrounding fields drove us away.

Kintore

Toy Garden (1990)
NJ 788 154

At Gauchhill, just south of Kintore on the B977, is a toy garden. We don't mean a miniature garden—we mean a garden constructed of toys laid out in serried ranks on raked gravel. 'My landlords did it,' said a young man sitting on a bench. 'As a hobby, I suppose,' he volunteered after a minute or two. There seemed little more to say.

Laurencekirk

Johnston Tower (1812)
NO 726 692

Visible for miles around, this rocketship-shaped folly commands the high ridge of Garvock Hill above the main A90. Its size emphasizes its remoteness—when you get close, you will be surprised by how small it is. However, it takes a long time and a degree of dogged persistence to approach it. The tower stands on a rubble mound alongside a farm track that runs southwards along the crest of the hill towards a telecom installation, but the track winds so lethargically on its lengthy way up to the folly that the temptation to break off and head directly up the deceptively gentle slope is hard to resist. The casual slope becomes vertical shortly after you enter the field that houses a particularly alert and short-tempered bull. Vaulting a barbed wire fence while carrying a couple of cameras, a GPS and a laptop computer is possible, although it is seldom done for pleasure.

As we finally regained our wind at the tower, two BT engineers waved cheerily as they drove past along the track. We busied

The Johnston Tower—worth the climb?

ourselves with an inspection of the tower, which once had a plaque over the little doorway. The interior staircase appears sound, but has collapsed just short of the parapet. The raw summer sleet obscured what view there might have been over the Howe o' the Mearns to the sea. It took nearly an hour to get back down to the car, nonchalantly skirting the bull field. Surely there was a glint of taurine triumph in those tiny eyes.

The tower is said to have been built by James Farquhar MP from stones left over from the building of his house, Johnston Lodge, in Laurencekirk, and the plans are still extant. Every year during Gala Week the townspeople organize a race to the tower; one hopes the bull does not take part.

Longside

Inverquhomery Gothick Doocots
(19th century)
NK 021 464

Doocots are not the least common building type in Scotland, and perhaps we have erred on the side of generosity in including so many examples. We claim in our defence that this is where the Scots take a more pragmatic, American approach to the folly canon than do the English, who are perfectly prepared to run up a little tower on their estate for no discernible purpose. Like the Americans, the Scots have a different approach—there has to be a function, however nominal, for their architectural flight of fancy. Only when that has been established, can the imagination run free, and the well-suppressed Scottish exuberance takes wing in the building of castles, forts and palaces for birds.

No one could possibly resist the Inverquhomery Doocots, perfect if puzzling proof that farming can be charming. You walk into the mains and there they stand in a row, like three rotund chubby little guards—three circular conical roofed doocots, the big one in the middle and two lesser doocots, clearly siblings, flanking it. Why was this done? Did they build the central one first,

Tweededum, Tweedledee and their fat friend, at Inverquhomery

then discover they wanted more squab pie? Or were they conceived as a picturesque entity from the start? Whatever the reason, the effect is so whimsical and engaging that one involuntarily gasps with pleasure on first seeing them.

Methlick

Haddo House Obelisk (1816)
NJ 868 344

A plain Gibbsian obelisk to the memory of the brother of the Earl of Aberdeen, who was killed at Waterloo. We searched in vain for the alleged inscription: 'Rather you than me…'

New Deer

Culsh Memorial (1876)
NJ 881 482

The Culsh Memorial at New Deer should, by rights, be called the Fordyce Memorial, but as it stands on the Hill of Culsh the present name stuck. It was built in 1876 to the memory of William Dingwall Fordyce of Brucklay Castle, now a picturesque ruin. It is a fine tower, square for the first two storeys then octagonal, with tall arched windows at the top, the whole edifice capped by an extremely tall spire.

Fordyce was the local laird, a man untypical of his time. He was elected Liberal MP for East Aberdeenshire in 1866, and, although a large landowner himself, he quickly aroused the anger of his neighbouring landlords by championing the rights of farm-workers and labourers. He died early, at the age of 39, and the memorial plaque on the tower is unaffectedly simple and, for once, genuine in its sentiments:

> *This Tower was erected by Tenants and friends in token of their sorrow for his early death and their warm remembrance of him as a just and liberal landlord, a trustworthy Member of Parliament, and an exemplary Christian gentleman. 'No Man Liveth To Himself'.*

The tower was splendidly restored by Banff and Buchan Council in 1991, and one can now climb it. The windows are even glazed.

Old Deer

Memorial Gates (1816)
NK 973 499
Temple of Theseus (1830)
Observatory Tower (1845)
NK 975 487

The architect John Smith, who roamed these parts in the first half of the last century, was responsible for Pitfour House at Old Deer, about 7 miles from New Deer. A.A. Tait characterized Smith as 'a notable Greek Revival architect, with a moment of crisis in mid-life which turned him into the Gothic Johnny of later life'. Another source refers to him as 'Tudor Johnny'. He may also have been responsible for some of the follies at Pitfour. In 1816 James Ferguson, the owner of the estate, had the Memorial Gates erected. These pillars, topped with urns, commemorate William Pitt and Lord Melville, whom Ferguson much revered.

But the real changes at Pitfour started when old Ferguson died in 1820, and his son, the admiral, took over. The sailor centred the landscape on the Pitfour Lake—naturally enough, considering his profession. On the shore is a magnificent, crumbling Temple of Theseus, Theseus being the Athenian hero whose life was ended when he was thrown into the sea—a rather morbid choice for an admiral. It is a slightly smaller copy of the Grecian original. Inside the temple is an ice-cold plunge pool. The story goes that Admiral Ferguson used to take cold baths

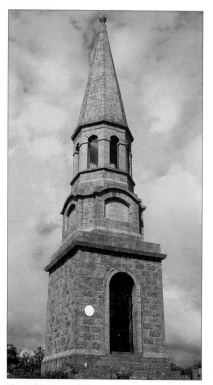

The Culsh Memorial

The scaffolding around Pitfour's Temple of Theseus now appears to be permanent

here to keep his body shipshape. Also on the lake is the ruined Gothic boathouse, its ragged outlines enhancing the beauty of decay at Pitfour. Although now genuinely ruinous, it is thought that it was originally built as a sham ruin.

The lake was intended to be the start of a most ambitious project: a canal to the sea at Peterhead, 10 miles away. Unsurprisingly, insufficient funds led to the cancellation of the project, but not before an octagonal brick tower had been erected in the Forest of Deer as a look-out point down the canal. The venture seems not to have been the obvious folly we first assumed, because cutting work did begin and there was strong local support for the project, which would have increased employment in the area. Another reason given for the building of the tower is that it was used as an observatory grandstand for the racecourse (which still exists, though it is no longer in use) laid out in the middle of the forest by the Fergusons. The Observatory Tower was restored in 1993 by Banff and Buchan Council, which is to be commended for its

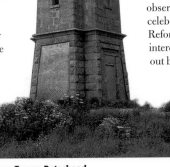

Reform Tower, Peterhead

excellent work in maintaining the county's landmarks. There are two staircases inside: a wooden one leading to the first floor and a metal spiral one climbing up the central brick staircase pillar to the octagonal top, where there is a history of the Pitfour Estate and topographs of the surrounding views. You can see the sea from here, which, given the relative flatness of the landscape, makes the concept of building a canal less absurd than we thought.

Admiral Ferguson's mausoleum was one of the Pitfour buildings that were demolished this century, as was the house. Only the mausoleum's portico survives—as a bus shelter, a pedestrian end for an admiral's last resting place.

Peterhead

Reform Tower (1832)
NK 121 447

At Meet Hill House, south of the town, work began on a five-storey observatory and belvedere to celebrate the passing of the Reform Act, but money or interest or both apparently ran out before completion. From the outside it looks reasonably finished, if a little startled by the executive housing encroaching up the hill to meet it.

Portlethen

Boswell Monument (19th century)
`NO 889 972`

Dr Johnson's biographer and companion came from the Lowlands, but for some reason it was seen fit to erect this elegant and rather charming pale grey granite tower in his memory up here in the hills south of Aberdeen. It is a round, three-storeyed tower on a plain, octagonal base, little more than a sheltered staircase, which was once topped by a series of intricate arches, which now lie scattered around the base. Given the present positive attitude to memorial towers in the north of Scotland, we hope it will not be long before it is restored to its former reflected glory.

Tarves

Prop of Ythsie (1861)
`NJ 884 315`

A small, ugly Gothic tower was built on the highest point of the Haddo Estate. 'Prop' is the local name for a tower; Ythsie is the scattering of hamlets that surround the hill. Overlooking the village of Tarves, with a fine view over central Aberdeenshire, the plain square tower was built as a tribute to George Gordon, 4th Earl of Aberdeen, an able Foreign Secretary who became a victim of the Peter Principle by being promoted beyond his level of competence to become Prime Minister; soon after, the tribulations of the

Crimean War brought about his downfall. The inscription reads:

TO GEORGE HAMILTON GORDON
FOURTH EARL OF ABERDEEN
BY HIS ATTACHED AND GRATEFUL TENANTRY
HE WAS BORN AT EDINBURGH 28 JAN 1784
AND DIED AT LONDON 14 DEC 1860

The tower has been restored, and access is free. There are 91 steps to the top (with a rope handrail), and the central stair pillar is brick. It is owned by the Haddo Estate, leased to Gordon District Council and guarded by two herds of friendly and extremely inquisitive Jersey and Friesian cows. A stile prevents any of the madder cows attempting to climb the tower for the traditional folly–bovine suicide attempt (see Curry Rivel, Somerset).

Whitehouse

Castle Forbes Dairy (early 19th century)
`NJ 620 194`

It was probably Archibald Simpson who, in the second decade of the 19th century, built the dairy at Castle Forbes, 3 miles north of Whitehouse. The dairy seems to have been intended as a serious agricultural establishment, not as the rustic bijou or Chinese trinket most dairies of the period turned out to be. Instead, it consists of a squat, round tower with castellations and three crow-stepped, gabled side pavilions tacked onto it—rather like the side pavilions at the Culzean Home Farm.

The Jersey Guard at the Prop of Ytsie

BANFFSHIRE

Aberlour

Column (1834)
NJ 278 437

The tall column originally had a ball finial on top. It subsequently collapsed. When it was rebuilt in 1888 the ball was replaced by the much heavier statue of a unicorn. It still stands.

Banff

Doune Hill Temple
Island Temple (1738)
NJ 698 637

Duff House, near Banff, suffered the same fate as Pitfour. Here the ravages of time have left only one building fully standing: a plain domed circular Temple of Venus, *sans* Venus, on the top of Doune Hill over the river in MacDuff. It was the work of William Adam, who was not concentrating hard when he dashed this one off. The temples were built for William Duff, Lord Braco and 1st Earl of Fife, but Adam had to resort to law to get Braco to pay him. Another temple and a triumphal arch on an island in the River Deveron have reverted to rubble, and so has a circular Gothick tower at the Bridge of Alva, south of the house, which was erected by the 2nd Earl, who was keen on agricultural reform.

Macduff War Memorial (1920)
NJ 704 642

A field further north than the Doune Hill Temple is a far more exciting prospect: a battlemented folly tower, which turns out to be an expensive and elaborate war memorial. We sometimes wonder if the builders of these egregious monuments ever thought of the widows of the poor bloody infantry who died for their country and of their prospects without a wage-earner in the family.

Cullen

Temple of Pomona (1822)
NJ 505 672

This sophisticated but rigidly classical monopteros is said to have been designed by James Playfair in 1788, although it was not completed until 1822, by William Robertson of Elgin for Colonel F.W. Grant. In the plinth of the rotunda is a panelled room with underfloor heating. Apart from that, it is as plain and dull a garden ornament as one could possibly hope to find.

Not knowing this beforehand, we sought permission from the estate—Cullen House itself has been divided up into flats—to see the building. On arrival in Cullen (where the butchers archaically title themselves 'fleshers'), we were directed to the estate office, presented our credentials, made our request to a representative of the factor and waited. And waited. And waited. A young man sauntered through the lobby two or three times, inspecting us curiously. After 45 minutes he returned and revealed himself to be the factor. An interrogation followed,

The Temple of Pomona, Cullen

during which we just escaped being searched for the incendiary devices, aerosol spray cans and other implements of hooliganism that middle-aged men invariably carry. Finally, reluctantly, he lent us the key, laced with warnings, to the park gate nearest the temple. 'Ye'll have tae wade across the river, mind,' he said, and the memory of a distant ancestor's smile flitted behind his frozen features. We found the temple, right by the side of the road on the way out of town. It was raining steadily. The key did not fit the lock. We returned to the estate office. It had closed for lunch. On the way to Elgin the car broke down.

Now, where did we put that spray can?

KINCARDINESHIRE

Banchory

Scolty Hill Tower (1842)
NO 679 939

Here is a demonstration of the changing attitude towards our heritage of folly towers. Unexceptional enough to be omitted from previous editions of this book, this little tower has now received the loving attention of the local Rotary Club, which landscaped the area around the tower and put up seats and a topograph, all to celebrate its 150th anniversary. Twenty-five years ago people would have been looking for an excuse to tear it down. What hit the headlines here was the reinstallation of the staircase. Not content with merely constructing a new one inside the hollow shell of the old tower, the citizens of Banchory had a steel spiral staircase made, then hired the Prince of Wales to lower it in one piece down through the top of the tower from his helicopter. Can this be true? It must be true—it was in the papers.

Fasque

Gothick Pavilion (1809)
NO 648 752

A practice peculiar to the North is the building of elaborate garden pavilions in walled gardens. A good example is the Gothic summerhouse in the walled garden at Fasque. It consists of a centre pavilion, pyramid roofed with tiny quatrefoil windows, and two flanking hexagonal towers, which carry pointed windows

The Pavilion at Fasque

and blind quatrefoils for decoration. Fasque was built between 1809 and 1820 and is attributed to John Paterson. The summerhouse is probably of the same date and architect.

Fettercairn

Jubilee Arch (1864)
NO 650 735

As at Edzell, this loyally over-decorated arch straddles the road in the middle of the village.

Stonehaven

Fetteresso Church (1850)
NO 870 864

There is a world of difference between John Paterson's worthy but rather dull mansion and summerhouse at Fasque and Fetteresso Church in

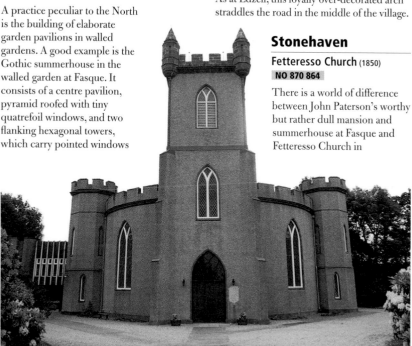

Fetteresso Church

Stonehaven. Yet this church was also designed by Paterson, and its air of frivolity owes as much to its eccentric ground plan and whitewashed exterior as to its gay turrets and overall cardboardy quality. All this convinces the visitor that the church's primary function was to be an eyecatcher from Fetteresso Castle rather than a place of worship.

Ury House Ink Bottle Lodge (1860)
`NO 870 889`

The road system within the park of Ury House, now a ruin, is bigger than that of some small countries. Having passed the Blue Lodge (which is painted green), we eventually found the delightful circular Ink Bottle Lodge with its central chimney. But we were too late—the roof has caved in, and the building has been abandoned.

MORAYSHIRE

Alves

York Tower (1827)
`NJ 163 629`

Between Elgin and Alves, off the A96, stands York Tower, which is said to have been raised on the spot where Macbeth met the three witches. The tower only commemorates the Duke of York, however, and it was built not by witchcraft but by Alexander Forteath, whose tomb is perched on unconsecrated ground hard by the tower at the edge of the hill. It is three stories high, octagonal, embattled, machicolated and decorated with blind, cruciform arrowslits. Above the locked door is an elegantly carved plaque reading

YORK TOWER

5th Jany 1827

The views would be excellent if the trees hadn't grown up around the tower.

Forres

Nelson Monument (1806)
`NJ 035 585`

In the middle of Forres, on steeply wooded Cluny Hill and overlooking the Moray Firth, is the elongated Nelson Monument, octagonal like the York Tower (see above) but dating from 1806. It was built to commemorate Trafalgar and designed by local architect Charles Stuart. A spiral stair turret, with 97 steps to the top, is buried in

The much-loved Nelson Monument, Forres

the east wall. There is a small Nelson Museum on the first floor of the tower, which was built 'to form a most agreeable object to every traveller in the country at large, a sea beacon, an excellent observatory and a commanding alarm post in the event of an enemy's approach by sea or land'.

This would appear to be the earliest Nelson monument in Britain. England was to wait a further 14 years before honouring her native son.

HIGHLAND

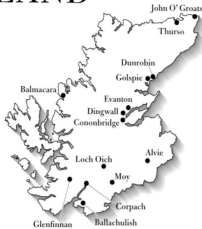

ARGYLLSHIRE

The traditional county of Argyllshire is split between two regions, Highland and Strathclyde. For the remainder of Argyllshire, see pages 50–53.

Ballachulish

Steward o' the Glens Monument
(late 18th century)
NN 080 580

An early poke at the iniquities of British justice, this sad little monument was erected to the memory of James of the Glens, who was hanged in 1752 for the murder of Colin Roy Campbell, a murder of which, naturally, he was innocent. No one knows who the murderer was; the fame of the incident owes not a little to R.L. Stevenson's description of it in *Kidnapped* (1886).

CAITHNESS

John O'Groats

Octagonal Room (20th century)
ND 378 738

Thurso has Britain's most northerly follies, but it was not always so. In the 16th century a Dutch farmer, Johan de Groot, settled about 10 miles along the coast with his seven sons. The brothers continually disputed precedence, so de Groot had an octagonal table made to settle the issue. Unfortunately,

it was too large for the farmhouse, so the farmhouse was rebuilt in an octagon to accommodate the table. The Scotticization of de Groot's name has given him posthumous worldwide fame, and today the John O'Groats Hotel continues the tradition by having an octagonal room.

Thurso

Harald's Tower (1790)
ND 135 693
Castle Lodge (1875)
ND 125 686

On the north coast of Scotland near Thurso Castle is Harald's Tower, which is not a tower at all but a sham mausoleum, erected for Sir John Sinclair (1754–1835), sometime president of the Board of Agriculture and champion of James Macpherson's claim that Ossian, the medieval Scottish poet, really existed. Harald was an Earl of Caithness, who was killed here at the end of the 12th century and from whom Sinclair believed he was descended. There seems to have been no intention to use this as a working tomb; it was merely to legitimize Sinclair's claim to distant ancestry, even if only to the gulls floating along this lonely northern shore.

The 1790 plan for the building shows a fairytale castle keep, pennants fluttering in the wind, within an encircling wall, but the present reality is worn and weird. A plaque still reads 'Burial Place of the Sinclairs of Ulster', but the place looks eternally old and almost Arabian, like a small fortress in Nizwa or Sur, with blunt pinnacles sticking erect

The bartizan turret in Thurso's fantastic castle lodge

from a circular wall, like stubby little penises.

But the most extraordinary piece of architecture in this region is the wildly fantastic Gothick of Sinclair's Thurso Castle Lodge. It is basically a square, embattled block, but the southwest corner has a taller (three-storey), square tower built out of it. Each corner has a thin, elongated bartizan turret with massively oversized crenellations; three have chimneys and the fourth, jutting out of the taller tower, was topped with a statue. The gate arch is massively top heavy, with two spidery legs supporting yet another pair of bartizan turrets, which are separated by extremely ornate battlements above machicolations with no fewer than five steps. This is a truly manic piece of Gothic Revival architecture, and the design has been attributed both to Donald Leed, the estate architect who worked at the castle in 1870–80, and to David Smith.

Howard Colvin notes an 1801 engraving by the architect A. McInnes of a proposed Washington Monument near Thurso, which was to take the form of a round castellated tower, but we do not know if it was ever realized.

INVERNESS

Alvie

Duke of Gordon's Monument (19th century)
NH 877 088

A monument on a hill just south of Aviemore, seen from the A9.

Corpach

Cameron Obelisk (early 19th century)
NN 092 770

The inscription on this obelisk, just by the road and protected by railings, is said to have been written by Sir Walter Scott. It commemorates Colonel John Cameron, who was killed at Waterloo.

Glenfinnan

Tower (1815)
NM 904 806

Glenfinnan is another Stuart rallying point, for it was here that Bonnie Prince Charlie's standard was raised and the long road that led to Derby and back to nemesis at Culloden began. The monument is accordingly substantial. Enclosed by an octagonal wall is a tall round tower with palmette battlements, surmounted by a statue of the luckless prince. The property of the National Trust for Scotland, the monument was put up in 1815 by Alexander Macdonald, and it carries inscriptions in Gaelic, English and Latin. After the 1745 rising the Highlanders became inveterate monument builders as a way of filling the void left by Bonnie Prince Charlie's flight to France. There are scores of monuments and memorials referring to Culloden and its aftermath, and a similar number of caves, cottages and cairns where Charles Edward or one of his supporters is supposed to have hidden. We have ignored most of them, but the real enthusiast can chase cairn after cairn, dotted across the countryside like obelisks in southerly regions, all commemorating the same thing.

Loch Oich

Well of Seven Heads (1812)
NN 300 995

On the Invergarry side of Loch Oich, next to the A82, stands an obelisk topped by seven heads and a hand holding a sword. The monument was raised in 1812 above the Well of the Seven Heads, and it came by its name in the wake of a clan-land killing, when seven brothers were brought to justice by having their heads chopped off. The heads were washed in the well before being put on public display. With admirable internationalism, the inscription is written in French as well as in Gaelic, English and Latin.

Moy

Mackintosh Obelisk (19th century)
NN 420 830

ROSS & CROMARTY

Balmacara

Murchison Obelisk (1863)
NG 788 786

Above Loch Alsh stands this elegant, tapering obelisk, put up in 1863 to commemorate an unrequited loyalty. Colonel Donald Murchison, factor to the Earl of Seaforth, dutifully collected the rents from the earl's estates and remitted them to the exiled lord after the Jacobite rebellion in 1745. On the earl's return, Murchison was cold-shouldered. This obelisk was an attempt to set the record straight, some hundred years later. Memories run long and deep on this part of the globe.

Cononbridge

Kinkell Pyramid (1970)
NH 554 544

When we first saw this small pyramid—almost more of a sculpture than a pyramid, with its tuning-fork top raised high—we were entranced by its stark, alien outline against the harled bartizan flourish of the restored Kinkell Castle. The owner, an eminent sculptor and keen gardener who single-handedly restored the castle, has now allowed it to be swamped with ivy, so that the once familiar pyramidal shape has metamorphosed into a strangely defined ivy bush. What we didn't realize is that it is still possible to get inside the pyramid and sit in the two facing central niches, and hear the rushing of your blood and the beating of your heart, and the background hiss of your thoughts pressing down like surface noise on an old 45 rpm record.

Dingwall

MacDonald Monument (1907)
NH 549 584

Hector Archibald MacDonald rose from the ranks to become a general, a knight and a hero of the Battle of Omdurman. This all proved too much for him to handle, and he shot himself in Paris in 1903. In his memory, subscribers erected this square 100ft (30m) high tower with a side turret. It is a large, rough stone monument, flanked by cannon, with a battered base and rope moulding around the locked Romanesque arched door. Solidly built and towering above the puny gravestones in the Mitchell cemetery, it was completed on 23 May 1907. The Saltire flies proudly from the top. The views are grandiose, and the monument is in the best tradition of folly towers.

> THIS TOWER
> WAS ERECTED
> AS A NATIONAL
> MEMORIAL TO
> MAJOR-GENERAL
> SIR HECTOR
> ARCHIBALD
> MACDONALD
> KCB • DSO • ADC
> A.D. 1907

Above the inscription are a mailed fist holding a cross and this motto:

> AIR MUIR'S AIR TIR

Dingwall Leaning Monument (1874)
NH 550 590

Last seen in a 1910 postcard, this teetering obelisk probably did not survive World War I.

Evanton

Gates of Negapatam (1790)
NH 607 697

Sir Hector Munro's folly was built to commemorate his own heroism. It is a replica of the Gates of Negapatam (now Negapattinam), an Indian stronghold he had captured from the Dutch on 12 November 1781 after a four-week siege. After 20 years of service in the Indian army, he retired in the 1780s to Novar House near Evanton in Cromarty. During the last years of his life he found time to develop Novar into a model estate, and he shared some of his fortune by paying the unemployed a penny a day to build this splendid eyecatcher on Fyrish Hill. There are three battlemented arches, the centre one taller, with ruined pillars standing

The Gates of Negapatam, one of the finest eyecatchers in Scotland

to either side. Heavy and oppressive—and very Scottish rather than Indian—it is reminiscent of Yorke's Folly in North Yorkshire in its situation, but it is much finer. The northern flanking arch, now ruined, is set a little behind the main monument, while the southern flanking arch is pushed a little forward, presumably for better optical effect when viewed from Novar House.

It is a spectacular eyecatcher; it can be seen for miles around, and indeed is best seen from a distance. The frustrating thing about the 40-minute walk to the folly is that the goal is invisible until one is four minutes away. Wrap up warm for the climb; we were numbed by the June sleet on the descent. Only on closer inspection from the top of the hill did we discover that the indefatigable Munro had constructed two further hilltop eyecatchers (there is no shortage of suitable hills in the area) due south of the Gates. Incidentally, Fyrish Hill is not a Munro—that is, a peak over 3000ft (915m) high—and it was another Hector Munro who gave his name to the term. By the time you read this, the hills to the west will bear wind farms.

SUTHERLAND

Dunrobin

The Hunting House (1723)
NC 851 012

At the seat of the Countess of Sutherland, an ancient summerhouse acquired this name for being so packed with hunting trophies.

Golspie

Sutherland Monument (1837)
NC 813 015

Above the coastal town of Golspie a gated road winds to the top of the 1300ft (396m) Beinn na Bragie, on which stands the enormous statue of the 'Great Improver', George Granville Leveson-Gower, 1st Duke of Sutherland, who was responsible for the controversial Highland Clearances in which thousands of crofters were evicted in favour of sheep. William Burn designed the pedestal in 1837, and the 30ft (9m) statue itself is by Chantrey.

Even after nearly 200 years the monument inspires fear and loathing among Highlanders, and there has been an active campaign to have the statue destroyed and replaced by a Celtic cross in memory of the evicted crofters. A resident was initially taciturn—'It's not for me to say'—but a little persuasion produced a further, 'It's for tourists,' and finally, 'I dinna ken why they put up a monument to someone everybody hated'. 'This is the single most detested symbol in the Highlands', spat a less-constrained resident. Local councillor Sandy Lindsay went on record to say: 'That man was worse than Hitler.' There was nearly a riot in 1992 when someone proposed to floodlight the monument during Gala Week in August, but the Chair of the local planning authority brought some sanity to the fevered debate: 'That monument's been there for over 100 years, and if it is going to be removed, it should be by an act of God, not for a cheap political gesture.'

LOTHIAN

The geologist Sir James Hall of Dunglass in Lothian held strong architectural opinions, although he tended towards the theoretical rather than the practical side. In 1813 he published his notorious 'Essay on Gothic Architecture', in which he sought to prove that the Gothic style derived directly from prehistoric hut dwellers, who found, so Sir James claimed, that reeds and willows could most easily be bent into common Gothic motifs. In pursuing this theory he had constructed a Willow Cathedral in 1794, a painting of which makes his case pleasantly convincing. The detached spire in the picture is uncannily reminiscent of the Cone at Barwick Park in Somerset, or even Watts Towers in Los Angeles, but as might be expected, nothing now remains of this architectural prodigy of basket weaving.

Map of Lothian showing locations: Musselburgh, East Fortune, Portobello, Amisfield Mains, Leith, Tyninghame House, Edinburgh, Aberlady, Cramond Bridge, Cockenzie, Queensferry, Broxburn, Hopetoun House, Linlithgow, Turnhouse, Haddington, Torpichen, Bilston, Dalkeith, Gifford, Harburn, West Saltoun, Carlops, Gladsmuir, Penicuik, Yorkston

Aberlady

Gosford Mausoleum (1794)
Grotto (1796)
NT 455 790

The gardens of Gosford House, on the shores of the Firth of Forth, 2 miles from Luffness, were landscaped by Allan Ramsay. One corner now contains a caravan park, although this does not impinge on the serenity of the estate. On a knoll in the woods at the end of an avenue stands the great mausoleum of the Earls of Wemyss, classical of course, with a pyramidal roof bearded with plants. The stone capping of the wall round the mausoleum is solidly laid with dovetail joints.

It is hard to resist walking round on the safe, flat top of the encircling wall, viewing the pyramid from every angle, but take heed when you are climbing down—we stepped on a mausoleum-living mouse, which squeaked so loudly that it cannot have been seriously hurt.

The mausoleum may have been designed by Robert Adam, who started work on the house in 1790, but the Wemysses may have been inspired by James Wyatt's similar but much larger and even more elaborate mausoleum in 1783 for the Earl of Darnley at Cobham in Kent. It's some distance away, but earls talk. Ramsay was planting the area surrounding the mausoleum in about 1796.

The nearby ice house, with its three-arched Gothick grotto ante-room, is probably by Ramsay himself.

Luffness Doocot (18th century)
NT 476 805

Lothian, and indeed the whole of Scotland, must have had an insatiable appetite for squab pie in the 18th and early 19th century. Almost every holding of some standing had its own doocot, and the vogue for architectural novelties during that period meant that many doocots were built as medieval watchtowers or heathen temples. There are several good examples of folly doocots in the rest of Scotland as well as a few in England, but nowhere else are there are as many splendid examples as in the Lothians.

Luffness House, east of Aberlady, has a peculiar example, which is reminiscent of a modernistic 1950s church tower. Standing in the fields south of the house, the building is

The Mausoleum of Aberlady

buttressed and two storeys high, with elongated slits for windows. A roof resting on a couple of posts makes for a third storey. Sir George Hope, the present owner of Lufness, also has a very fine beehive doocot behind the wall that borders the main road.

Bilston

Dryden Tower (mid-19th century)
NT 270 647

South of Edinburgh is Dryden Tower at Bilston. This is a proper folly—no adapted doocot but a straightforward, otiose folly tower, tall, lonely and irrelevant. It stands uncertainly in a semi-rural, semi-industrial landscape, surrounded by concrete posts and fencing, reinforced by DANGER—KEEP OUT notices, to keep out the inquisitive. For once the notices are fully justified: the two remaining pinnacles of the four that once graced the tower's graceless roof are poised to penetrate the foolhardy climber. Some consolidation restoration work has recently been carried out.

The tower may have been built in the mid-19th century by a member of the Farquhar family. The name Dryden has nothing to do with the poet as we first supposed but refers to a locality nearby. It would still be good to find out more.

Broxburn

Sloughbiggin Tower (mid-19th century)
NT 700 779

Lothian has a surprising number of major follies, with Edinburgh and its outskirts boasting more per square mile than any other urban district in Britain, London excepted. Coming in from the east on the A1 you will find this example on the Duke of Roxburghe's Broxmouth House Estate, between Broxburn and East Barns. Low, lonely and isolated, Sloughbiggin Tower is a small Victorian embattled octagonal tower with a square side turret—there must have been a ladder to access the upper level—with seven windows looking out over the coast and sea. A fireplace remains. Queen Victoria allegedly stayed at Broxmouth Hall for a week—might it have been built in honour of her visit?

Carlops

Newhall Obelisks (1810)
NT 175 566

Robert Brown of Newhall on the banks of the Esk, southwest of Penicuik, was another do-it-yourself architect. Here are two obelisks, one to the poet Allan Ramsay, who here 'recited to his distinguished and literary Patrons, as he proceeded with the Scenes of his unequalled PASTORAL COMEDY amid the Objects and Characters introduced to it'. It is signed 'R.B. 1810'. The other obelisk is dedicated to Brown's ancestor, Thomas Dunmore of Kelvinside, Glasgow.

Other acquaintances of Brown also raised monuments to Ramsay, including James Clerk of Penicuik and A. Fraser-Tytler of Woodhouselee, who erected a rustic temple to the poet and his 'Gentle Shepherd'. Woodhouselee was once owned by Alexander Crichton, and it was probably the Ramsay link that prompted Mary Crichton's Bower at Newhall, a Gothick hut some way from the house and also built by Brown.

Cockenzie and Port Seton

Hecla Grotto (1783)
NT 400 757

Cockenzie and Port Seton (the little towns have been twinned for centuries) is dominated by the twin stacks of the Cockenzie Power Station, an uncompromising manifestation of 20th-century power. The forces of uncontrollable natural power are best expressed by the fearsome volcano, fortunately unknown in these sceptered isles. Almost as rare is the garden volcano, one of the treats in the folly canon. Chambers enlarged on its supposed use as a garden ornament by the Chinese in his *Dissertation on Oriental Gardening* (1772), but the mainspring for the slight popularity volcanoes achieved in the West must be sought in those Grand Tours that reached Vesuvius. The 18th- and 19th-century traveller to Naples usually brought back one of the numerous paintings, prints and painted boxes depicting an eruption of the great volcano. Garden volcanoes mainly remained a manifestation of the *jardin Anglo-Chinois*, and as a result their provenance is almost entirely restricted to the mainland of Europe—the Tivoli Gardens in Paris boasted an erupting volcano; near Doorn in The Netherlands an entire cottage poses as a lump of volcanic rock; and the most famous of them all, the Stein, still exists, splendidly preserved, at Wörlitz in Germany.

The Cadells, iron founders and coal merchants from Cockenzie and Port Seton, aptly managed a small volcano—albeit only in name—in the garden of their Cockenzie House (now a nursing home), although perhaps their more lasting claim to fame was the first recorded use of a cat flap, which they invented in the 17th century to let the cats into the attic of the house to kill the rats. But this is about grottoes, not firsts. Behind a whalebone arch beneath the trees in the tight walled garden is a small, above-ground grotto with a shell interior. The interior decoration has largely gone, but enough of the pattern and species of shell remain for an authentic restoration to be carried out.

Built of burned stone and pumice, with tufa-covered walls, the edifice was presumably intended to simulate a recent eruption, yet it cannot be said to be a successful imitation. The builder, aware of this, reinforced the point by inscribing HECLA in a huge raised arc of letters over the whalebone arch entrance, referring to the Icelandic volcano of that name. The tufa is said to have come from the same mountain, although there is another, closer Hecla on South Uist in the Hebrides, which is the more likely source.

The Claret House is the name given to the eastern of two gazebos built into the garden walls, both having the same design—round turret, conical slate roof, exterior

Hecla Grotto, Cockenzie and Port Seton

staircase, one missing. It acquired its elegant name from the story that Mary Queen of Scots used to take a glass of claret here after playing golf at Seton House, so along with the first recorded cat flap, perhaps Cockenzie House can claim the first recorded 19th hole.

Cramond Bridge

Craigie Hall Temple (1759)
NT 171 749

We came across the Craigie Hall Temple at Cramond Bridge while we were looking for Clermiston Tower. We were lost in the country lanes behind the airport, when a squat, round building suddenly poked its head over a ridge, and a dash across a field revealed this forgotten basilica. Inside are two beautiful stone fireplaces; once there were two floors. The majestically carved coat of arms on the semicircular pediment carries the motto 'Nemo Me Impune Lacessit', and a plaque set in the wall to the right of the entrance reads:

Dum licet in rebus Iucundis
vive beatus
Vive memor quam sis aevi brevis
C : H : W : 1759

Its peculiar truncated appearance is due to the upper storey's having been removed in 1975, presumably in case it frightened the aeroplanes.

Dalkeith

Esbank Tower (1878)
NT 327 662

This is not, repeat *not* a folly, but we have included it because everyone in Edinburgh says, 'Have you seen that tower at Dalkeith?' and it's much admired, and no doubt loved, by its owners, the architects Gerry and Susan Goldwyre, who, in the late 1980s, bought a disused Victorian water tower of multicoloured brick for £8000, spent £175,000 and their own time restoring and rebuilding it, and now have a unique and startlingly wonderful eight-storey home and office. Where's the folly in that?

East Fortune

Gilmerton Screen (C.1800)
NT 549 778

A screened farm, battlemented with blind Gothic arches, can be seen at Gilmerton House opposite the Museum of Flight at East Fortune, northeast of Amisfield.

Edinburgh

Calton Hill Folly Group (early 19th century)
NT 263 742

In the early 19th century Calton Hill, one of the hills that dominate the city, was designated a Scottish Valhalla, but the first monument erected on the hill was to an all-England hero, Horatio Nelson. The Gothick observatory had already been sited here before the rest of the monuments were built, exploiting the picturesque characteristics of the hill to maximum effect. In a bid for consistency, the Nelson Monument, designed by Robert Burn and built between 1807 and 1816, was also in the Gothick style. The monument was built on a trapezoid ground plan. The walls connect four corner towers and out of the midst of what was originally intended to be a restaurant rises a tall tower, staged and embattled and expressly made to look like an upside-down telescope. Above the entrance is the date 1805 and an inscription that runs:

TO THE MEMORY OF
VICE ADMIRAL
HORATIO LORD VISCOUNT NELSON
AND OF THE GREAT VICTORY OF
TRAFALGAR
TOO DEARLY PURCHASED WITH HIS
BLOOD
THE GRATEFUL CITIZENS OF EDINBURGH
HAVE ERECTED THIS MONUMENT:
NOT TO EXPRESS THEIR UNAVAILING
SORROW FOR HIS DEATH:
NOR YET TO CELEBRATE THE MATCHLESS
GLORIES OF HIS LIFE:
BUT, BY HIS NOBLE EXAMPLE, TO TEACH
THEIR SONS
TO EMULATE WHAT THEY ADMIRE AND,
LIKE HIM, WHEN DUTY REQUIRES IT,
TO DIE FOR THEIR COUNTRY.
A. D. MDCCCV

And then, sprayed in paint on the wall below: 'ENGLISH OUT OF SCOTLAND.' Still the good citizens of Edinburgh did not tire of their patriotism. In 1822 they embarked on another project, the National Monument, which was intended to commemorate the Scottish soldiers killed in the Napoleonic Wars. The architects, C.R. Cockerel and William Playfair, came up with a rather bizarre idea: a replica of the Parthenon, harking back to Edinburgh's self-bestowed sobriquet, the Athens of the North. The designs were approved, and an appeal was launched for £42,000 to realize the building. Eventually only £16,000 was subscribed, but by then the building work had already started. By 1829 Playfair had to admit defeat, and he spoke of the National Monument as 'the pride and the poverty of Scotland'. When it was evident that no more money was forthcoming, the project was abandoned, but the half-finished, sham temple was consolidated and proclaimed as the National Monument. All that was built were 12 massive Doric columns supporting an ornamental frieze—a *memento mori* as poignant in its ruined state as the broken pillars to be seen in graveyards.

Edinburgh: the unfinished National Monument on Calton Hill

At roughly the same time as the National Monument the Playfair Monument was built. This was a scholarly mix of the Tomb of Theron at Agrigento and the Lion Tomb at Cuidos: a base with a tomb surrounded by heavy Doric pillars. It was designed by William Playfair to commemorate his uncle, Professor John Playfair.

Naturally, by 1830 it was time for Robert Burns to be immortalized. Thomas Hamilton designed him a Tholos-style temple on a base, with a sculpture group on top of the monument. A year later the philosopher Dugald Stewart, who died in 1828, was honoured with a copy of the Choragic Monument of Lysicrates, again by Playfair. A measured drawing of this by Roger Cooke won the first Folly Fellowship/Lawson-Price Measured Drawings Award in 1990.

The scramble for heritage cash from the British lottery in the 1990s will rank in retrospect as one of the less dignified episodes in the conservation of historic buildings. A minor frenzy was whipped up, with every organization scenting a Klondike opportunity. Every charity, corporation, group and gathering trawled through its remit to find some project that would qualify for Camelot cash, and Edinburgh District Council was no exception. In 1996 it applied for £37 million, not to complete the Calton Hill Monument, but to erect a 100ft (30m) viewing tower on the hilltop, complete with the obligatory visitor centre and a funicular railway. The funds were not, in the end, forthcoming.

The Calton burial ground at the foot of the hill has many delightful funerary monuments, but to describe them would carry us outside our brief.

Drummond Scrolls 1884

The gate lodge to Redford House is, for obscure reasons, called the Drummond Scrolls. It was assembled out of the spare parts of William Adam's Royal Infirmary of 1738–48, most of which was demolished in 1884. The most noticeable pieces of the lodge's preposterous ornamentation are the enormous volutes set against the wall and reaching to the top of the structure, which give it its name.

Prestonfield Ace of Clubs House

Prestonfield House, originally built in 1687 by Robert Mylne, is now a smart restaurant. The design of the once-famous Ace of Clubs gardens—supposed to have been laid out in this pattern to celebrate a famous triumph in a card game—has been overplanted, but the story lingers.

Moray House Pavilion

The entrance to Moray House in the centre of Edinburgh has a pair of stiletto piers not unlike those at Rosebery. At the back of the house is a rectangular summerhouse with rusticated doors and windows. On the façade corners are small lions holding shields in their claws, one of the shields being monogrammed 'MH'. Inside the pavilion the Act of Union between Scotland and England is said to have been signed in 1707.

Scott Monument (1840–46)

The city's famous Scott Monument, in elegant Princes Street, serves as a prelude to the equally august follies on Calton Hill— here we are treading on dangerous ground for few Scotsmen will enjoy seeing these national monuments being classed as follies. In 1836 a competition was held to choose the best design for a Scott memorial. George Meikle Kemp, an unknown architect who was nevertheless thoroughly versed in the Gothick idiom, was initially placed only third, but for some reason the competition was held again and this time Kemp carried off the first prize. His design showed a staged spire nearly 200ft (61m) high, worked open, with the whole gamut of pointed arches and pinnacles. The building of the monument took six years, 1840–46, but Kemp did not live to see it—he was accidentally drowned in the Union Canal in 1844, bereaving us of a potentially great folly architect.

Duddingston House Rotunda (1768)

We have been deprived of a 1741 prospect tower—long demolished—by William Adam at The Drum in Liberton, but a rotunda by Chambers at Duddingston House still survives.

St Bernard's Mineral Well (1789)
NT 244 743

On the banks of the Water of Leith, in Mackenzie Place, at the bottom of the hill, stands St Bernard's Mineral Well, a circular, domed classical temple, designed in 1789 by the landscape painter Alexander Nasmyth. Inside is a remarkably unvandalized statue of Hygeia by D.W. Stephenson, which replaced the earlier Coade stone statue and which is safe because the railings surrounding it are tall and sharp.

The mineral spa had been discovered in about 1760, but when Francis Garden, Lord

St Bernard's Well

Gardenstone, partook of the waters he was so gratified by the imagined effect that he had the temple erected. Gardenstone, a law lord and slightly eccentric bachelor who kept pigs in his bedroom, died a mere four years later at the unremarkable age of 72. He was buried, according to his wishes, in an unmarked grave.

Gifford

Yester House Grotto (1708)
Clock Tower Summerhouse (1970)
NT 544 671

The top of the old clock tower from Edinburgh's old Caledonian Station has been removed and re-erected in the grounds of Yester House as a fine and fanciful summerhouse, with full-moon glazed windows—inevitable really, when one considers its provenance.

Gladsmuir

Trabroun Doocot (18th century)
NT 465 743

Another in the series of ornamental doocots to be found throughout Lothian is near Trabroun Steading at Gladsmuir, 4 miles south of Gosford. The steading itself has a pend doocot, but a second one stands on its own. It takes the form of a round and castellated tower reminiscent, in its plump, bold way of the Roman tomb of Caecilia Metella on the Via Appia.

Haddington

Huntington Doocot (18th century)
NT 485 749
Nungate Doocot (18th century)
NT 517 734

As with the Traboun Doocot, the sepulchral architecture of the Via Appia comes to mind when one looks at the impressively over-architectured doocot at Huntington House, northwest of Haddington. Set on a square base is a tempietto with blind arches, pilasters and a pediment with three urns. On the other side of the roof a large vase masks a chimney, a rare feature in a doocot. The design here is nothing like the happy-go-lucky style of Luffness; it is, on the contrary, rather self-conscious.

Yet another ornamental doocot is at Haddington itself, near the Nungate bridge over the Tyne. This time the style is embattled Gothick.

Amisfield Mains (1766)
Doric Temple (1783)
NT 528 751

Amisfield House, a mile or so northeast of Haddington, was demolished in 1928, but the outbuildings remain. John Henderson built the four Doric pavilions in the corners of the large walled garden in 1783-5. One of these pavilions doubles as a doocot. Beside the Tyne is a Doric Temple, presumed to have been designed by Isaac Ware, but the best feature here is Amisfield Mains.

The commonly encountered word 'mains' derives from demesne, and it is the Scottish term for a home farm. This farm was given the full screen treatment: three bays, pyramidal gables with slim castellations and pointed arches. In all probability this is the 'castle' that Robert Mylne noted in his diary

The Amisfield Mains castellated farm eyecatcher

in 1766 as being built for the Earl of Wemyss. It is, therefore, contemporary with Mylne's tower at Blaise Castle in Avon, done for Thomas Farr.

Hopetoun Monument (1824)
NT 501 764

On the summit of 560ft (170m) Byers Hill, in the Garleton Hills north of Haddington, is a monument to General John Hope, 4th Earl of Hopetoun, who soldiered in the West Indies, Egypt and the Iberian peninsula. The monument, a slim brick tower, was erected shortly after the general's death in 1823. The foundation stone laid on 3 May 1824, and the inscription reads:

THIS

MONUMENT

WAS ERECTED TO THE MEMORY

OF

THE GREAT AND GOOD

JOHN — FOURTH EARL OF HOPETOUN

BY

HIS AFFECTIONATE AND GRATEFUL

TENANTRY

IN

EAST LOTHIAN

MDCCCXXIV

The land belonged to the Earls of Hopetoun until 1960, when it was bought by Sir James and Lady Miller, who gave it, with the tower, to East Lothian District Council in 1977. 'Anyone wishing to climb to the top of the monument is advised to take a torch,' warns a notice at the bottom of the hill. There is no mention of an oxygen cylinder, although the hill is very steep and there are 127 steps to the top of the monument, where there are eight useful topographs to help you admire the expected spectacular view.

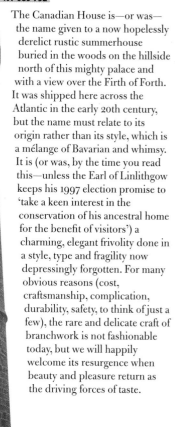

Harburn

Column and Doocot (early 19th century)
NT 045 608

Harburn House, north of Cobbinshaw Reservoir, has another splendid doocot. This is a tall, square, crenellated tower in the Gothick style and dating from the early 19th century. Also in the grounds is a column with a ball on top, commemorating a visit in 1832 by Charles X of France.

Hopetoun House

Canadian House (early 20th century)
NT 089 792

The Canadian House is—or was— the name given to a now hopelessly derelict rustic summerhouse buried in the woods on the hillside north of this mighty palace and with a view over the Firth of Forth. It was shipped here across the Atlantic in the early 20th century, but the name must relate to its origin rather than its style, which is a mélange of Bavarian and whimsy. It is (or was, by the time you read this—unless the Earl of Linlithgow keeps his 1997 election promise to 'take a keen interest in the conservation of his ancestral home for the benefit of his visitors') a charming, elegant frivolity done in a style, type and fragility now depressingly forgotten. For many obvious reasons (cost, craftsmanship, complication, durability, safety, to think of just a few), the rare and delicate craft of branchwork is not fashionable today, but we will happily welcome its resurgence when beauty and pleasure return as the driving forces of taste.

Hopetoun Monument, Haddington

Detail of the Canadian House, Hopetoun

The nearby bandstand, also approaching decay, apparently has a chance of survival.

Leith

Mylne's Mill (1686)
NT 271 767

Incongruously perched on top of a pub at the corner of Tower Street and The Shore, this round, four-storey stone tower at the end of a terrace started life as a windmill but somehow got overtaken by events and urban sprawl. Being close to the harbour, it was usurped as a signal tower in the 18th century and was decorated with battlements and quatrefoils in the early 19th century. Now, in the late 20th century, the dock area has been scrubbed, polished, sanitized and given over to cool bars and restaurants, from which the Lascar seamen who once haunted these streets would be summarily ejected. The old tower is above all this hectic change, plonked on its plinth-like pub, but we have not discovered its current use.

Linlithgow

Hope Monuments (19th century)
NT 003 790; NS 988 758

Halfway between the coast and Linlithgow is the Hope Monument, an elaborate Victorian cross on an octagonal plinth, which was erected to commemorate Brigadier-General Adrian Hope, who died at the Siege of Lucknow in 1858.

There is another Hope Monument on a golf course south of the town. This is a tall cone on a plinth, erected to commemorate the general's father, John Hope.

Musselburgh

Newhailes Grotto (1792)
NT 326 727

A mile or so west of Musselburgh is Newhailes, where another shell-lined grotto stood in the gardens of Newhailes House. This was perhaps erected when Miss Dalrymple inherited the house in 1792, shell grottoes being particularly feminine follies. The shell of the grotto remains, roofless and bare, but still boasting massive vermiculated rustication on its entrance arch. Further along through the thick, muddy undergrowth are the even scantier remains of a Tea House.

Also in the gardens is an obelisk to the memory of John Dalrymple, 2nd Earl of Stair, who died in 1747. The poor earl's life started on the wrong foot when he was rejected by his parents at the age of eight after accidentally shooting his brother.

Mylne's Mill, Leith

Newhailes Grotto

The estate has decayed slowly but surely as municipal Edinburgh has begun to eat away at its fringes, and small parcels of land have been sold off for housing , a scrap metal yard, motor repair sheds and worse. When we visited, Newhailes was just being handed over to the National Trust for Scotland after the death of Lady Dalrymple, and the house was still perfection—habitable but dilapidated, proudly and unashamedly showing its age. Now this grand old lady will be given over to the house surgeons, who will nip here and tuck there and pull up a little where the sag is too noticeable, and in a few years we will be presented with a glazed debutante, breathing a little heavily under the weight of her hidden centuries but rouged and ready to face another hundred years or so. At least, however, the depredation of the estate will surely be stopped, and encouragingly the National Trust is allowing bramble growth in the grounds in order to deter vandals.

Penicuik

Terregles Tower (1748–51)
> NT 220 597

Ramsay's Monument (1759)
> NT 224 586

Hurley Grotto (1742)
> NT 219 590

Arthur's O'on (1760)
> NT 217 594

Sir John Clerk of Penicuik was the Scottish answer to Lord Burlington. He thoroughly influenced early 18th-century building and gardening in Scotland. His manuscript poem *The Country Seat* (1727) bears witness to his Palladian leanings and prescribes the siting of mansions and gardens. Clerk took a premature dislike to the Gothick style, which was surprising because at this early date the revival had scarcely begun. At the end of his epic he exhorts:

> *From your gen'ral Rules instruction take,*
> *What Edifice to raise or Gardens make:*
> *But other are, on whom those Rules you*
> *   waste,*
> *For Goths will always have a Gothic*
> *   taste.*

This did not prevent Sir John from erecting a few follies at Penicuik, although obviously none was in the Gothick taste—he invariably chose the Roman style for his garden ornaments. Opposite the house, on a hill called Knight's Law, stands the well-turned-out Terregles Tower, a tall, circular, Roman-style, battlemented look-out tower, with open machicolations and blank windows—a very smooth building that might have been lifted out of a Poussin painting.

Aligned with the house is Ramsay's Monument, which is reached by crossing the Esk over the Centurion's Bridge (1738). The monument, a pierced obelisk over an archway, was built in 1759 by Sir John's son James a year after the death of the poet Allan Ramsay.

To the west, on the south bank of the river, is the Hurley Cove or Grotto, a clearly dangerous 130ft (40m) tunnel with a military-style, rusticated entrance. Inside is said to be a room with the inscription 'Tenebrosa Occultaque Cave' ('Beware of dark and secret things'). Clerk called the grotto:

> *a frightful cave… To those who enter,*
> *first occurs the memory of the Cumaean*
> *Sybil, for the ruinous aperture, blocked*

Ramsay's Monument, Penicuik

up with stones and briars, strikes the eye.
After some yards explorers
*stand in doubt whether they are among
the living or the dead…there comes upon
the visitor a shudder.*

The tunnel had another, rather unexpected function. According to Sir John, one could stand at one end and, by looking through the tunnel, determine the sun's diameter.

James Clerk carried on where his father left off, and in the 1760s he designed the stables back at the house. On top of the rear entrance to the stable or steading block is a replica of a Roman building, the large dome commonly known as Arthur's O'on (oven), which had been demolished in 1743 in Stirlingshire. As in so many Scottish steadings, part of the stable block doubles as a doocot.

Penicuik House is now a grand, grass-topped ruin, burned down in 1899 while tenants were renting it from the diminishingly rich Clerk family. The current owner was frostily polite, making us feel as welcome as a bridge-builder at a ferryman's convention. We were kindly but firmly turned away from the park, not without eliciting some information about a Heritage Lottery Grant application for aid and the fact that the Hurley Cove, the dark and mysterious tunnel, is still there but sorely vandalized and extremely dangerous, so much so that it is now barred and shut. Some of the follies are in separate ownership.

Portobello

Jamieson's Folly (1785)
NT 306 741

Day and night the ogre of demolition hovers over Lothian's most gloriously gimcrack folly, Portobello Tower. From 1763 onwards a certain William Jamieson developed a stretch of land along the coast west of Edinburgh and named it Portobello, and his energetic exploitation made it into a popular watering-place. The tower, which is the sole survivor of a series of buildings at Portobello built for the lawyer John Cunningham, and it originally served as a belvedere. As you are approaching the folly, several details appear genuinely medieval—and so they are: most of them came from demolished medieval churches and houses in Edinburgh. The edifice has an octagonal main tower, rusticated, with battlements and pointed blank arches, some blank through having been bricked up. A higher, square turret in the same Gothick style is attached. This joyful folly reveals its true nature as a structure built for pleasure before purpose by having the word 'LETARE'

('Rejoice') carved on the lintel. Its present condition gives cause for concern. It crouches behind a seafront amusement arcade, whose management and clientele are seldom noted for their architectural interests.

The house to the west of the tower has been extensively restored and now serves as offices, so one hopes the example will be noted by the owner of Jamieson's splendid folly tower.

Queensferry

Midhope Tower (1826)
NT 052 786

Above the House of the Binns, on top of Binns Hill, is a tall, castellated, three-storey, circular tower, an eyecatcher called Midhope Tower, which was built in 1826 to a design by Alexander Allen for Sir James Dalyell to celebrate the battle of Waterloo.

Torphichen

Doocot (early 19th century)
NS 967 726

A mysterious early 19th-century tower, octagonal with castellations, stands to the northeast of Torphichen—mysterious because we can't find out anything about it. We would love to hear from any reader who can enlighten us.

Turnhouse

Clermiston or Cammo Tower (1871)
NT 176 743

Below Corstorphine Hill stands a tall monument, which is clearly visible from aeroplanes coming into land and conveniently located at the bottom of a hill so that visitors can avoid a fatiguing climb. Clermiston or Cammo Tower is said to have been built in 1871 by William MacFie to celebrate Sir Walter Scott's centenary, and it is also claimed to have been the inspiration for Robert Louis Stevenson's *Kidnapped* (1886), another highly improbable attribution. The folly is round, banded, four storeys high and of dark brown stone, and it is topped with a corbelled and embattled parapet. For openings there are slit windows and a round-headed entrance doorway. The grille door swings open to reveal a strange mechanical device bolted to the floor.

Is this the right tower? In the Lothian volume of *Buildings of Scotland* (1978) Colin McWilliam classes it as a water tower. Why should a water tower be lower than the stables and be so far away? The ruined U-shaped stables at Cammo are very elegant, with an octagonal clock turret with 'JW i8ii' over the central arch, but they are buried in the woods a field and a half away from the tower, whose true purpose remains a mystery to us.

Tyninghame House

Obelisk (1856)
Pavilion (1970)
NT 615 798

At Tyninghame House the 1960s have left some unexpected traces about the house and grounds. The house contains several *trompe l'oeil* murals, while the garden harbours knickknacks we hoped were to come back into fashion: a battlemented Gothick pavilion and an off-the-peg Gothick arbour. Dating from a century earlier is the 1856 obelisk, which bears a laudatory inscription to Thomas Hamilton, 6th Earl of Haddington:

who at a period of the greatest national depression had foresight and energy to set the example of planting on an extensive scale and to be an active and successful promoter of agricultural improvement, and to his wife... of whose valued suggestions and assistance her husband has left an ample record.

A contemporary of the earl, who died in 1735, judged him differently: 'Hot, proud, vain and ambitious.'

West Saltoun

Saltoun Doocot (early 19th century)
NT 458 686

Southwest of Haddington, off the A6093 near Pencaitland, is the remarkable Saltoun Doocot. A miniature castle, shrouded in trees and damp and dark, it lies on the other side of the burn from the house. It would have made an excellent eyecatcher before all the trees grew up to obscure it. In all probability it was designed by Robert Burn, who worked at Saltoun between 1803 and 1804.

The doocot, which stands in a thicket of trees in the park, is a square tower with quatrefoils above the door on all four sides, rusticated pilasters and castellations, all topped by an octagonal, castellated lantern. Nothing remotely suggests functionality, yet the interior is circular and has nesting boxes. It is a sham castle eyecatcher with a practical purpose.

The monument on nearby Skimmer Hills now has nothing to show but a plinth, but on the other side of the road is a tiny, enigmatic grave marker buried in the undergrowth:

In Loving Memory of
Peter Barlas
Who Died Here
18 August 1993
Aged 44
To Those Who Loved Him
He Loved Them Back

Yorkston

Rosebery Steading (early 19th century)
NT 305 571

Rosebery, on the B6372 a mile east of Yorkston, has lost its house, but the steading is still working. Its architect could not or would not take sides in the Battle of Styles that was still raging in the early 19th century, and accordingly he crenellated the walls of the steading but hit upon rogue classicalism for the structure's centrepiece, the clock tower. There are two storeys of round arches and bizarre pointed windows, surmounted by a single pointed blank window, which leads up to the clock face. The tower culminates in an octagonal church spire with oval lights and a weather vane.

Across the road are the gate piers to the house: clustered pillars with stiletto pyramids on top. The architect must have been an amateur—a likely candidate could well have been Archibald John Primrose, 4th Earl of Rosebery, who, if he was capable of publishing a book titled *An Address to the Middle Classes on the Subject of Gymnastic Exercises*, was certainly capable of designing this monstrosity.

Saltoun Doocot

STRATHCLYDE

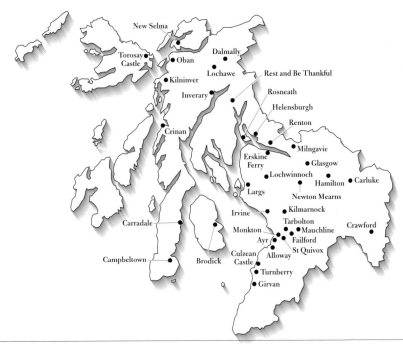

New Selma
Torosay Castle
Oban
Dalmally
Kilninver
Lochawe
Rest and Be Thankful
Inverary
Rosneath
Helensburgh
Crinan
Renton
Milngavie
Erskine Ferry
Glasgow
Lochwinnoch
Hamilton
Carluke
Largs
Newton Mearns
Irvine
Kilmarnock
Carradale
Tarbolton
Crawford
Monkton
Mauchline
Ayr
Failford
St Quivox
Campbeltown
Culzean Castle
Brodick
Alloway
Turnberry
Girvan

ARGYLLSHIRE

The traditional county of Argyllshire is split between two regions, Highland and Strathclyde. For the remainder of Argyllshire, see pages 35-36.

Campbeltown

Oatfield Grotto (late 19th century)
NR 682 178

In the garden of Oatfield House near Campbeltown, towards the Mull of Kintyre, stands a peculiar small grotto—in fact, it is little more than a large niche. The façade consists of pointed double arches and a large, open quatrefoil, all said to have been taken from Dunblane Cathedral in 1890, but it has a Georgian air.

Carradale

Torrisdale Castle Arch (early 19th century)
NR 794 364

In far away Kintyre are some more Gothicisms. The cardboard Gothick of the entrance arch to Torrisdale Castle, southwest of Carradale, is nudged towards follydom by dint of its decorations: lancet windows pierce the walls either side of a Tudor arch, above

which is a tablet with what probably are the MacAlister arms; the bartizan turrets carry arrowslits. Torrisdale was built about 1815 by James Gillespie Graham for General MacAlister.

Crinan

Duntrune Rotunda (1961)
NR 791 954

Six columns were taken from a house in Old Burlington Street, London, that was demolished in 1960. They are topped by an open ironwork dome, designed by Muriel Malcolm of Poltalloch.

Dalmally

Macintyre Monument (1859)
NN 146 261

One of the people the Duke of Argyll occasionally employed was the poet Duncan Ban MacIntyre (1724–1812), who jobbed as a forester. MacIntyre neither spoke nor wrote English, but his Gaelic poetry proved popular enough for him to live off the proceeds. His fame survived to the 19th century, and in 1859 Freemasons and Scottish Nationalists erected a monument to his memory on Beacon Hill, southwest of

Dalmally. The massive circular granite temple, a foretaste of the Albert Speer school of architecture, commands superb views over the mountains and glens.

Inveraray

Beehive Cottage (1802)
Bealachanuaran Grotto (1747)
Carloonan Doocot (1747)
Hexagon (1802)
NN 095 093
Watchtower (1747)
NN 100 105

Rather late in life, Archibald Campbell, 3rd Duke of Argyll, started turning his estates at Inveraray into a pleasance. From 1745 onwards Roger Morris built the castle that became the first major Gothick work in Scotland, and on 2 October 1747 the same architect drew up a contract for:

> *a pidgeon house to be built at the end of the back walk being a Circular building 20 f^t Diam.^r & 42 f^t high … for which he is to be paid Fourty Eight pounds Ster.*

At the same time Morris was also to:

> *build a Tower upon Duniquaick 20 f^t Sq & 45 f^t high … for the sum of Fourty Six pounds Ster.*

The whitewashed doocot still stands in a meadow. It is circular with a rusticated entrance and a conical roof with ornamental chimney. The Watchtower on Duniquoick Hill is also lasting well, providing a prominent landmark. The tower is built of rubble, with a pointed and rusticated entrance and window, and a pyramidal roof from which, after nearly two and a half centuries of harsh Scottish winters, the original staging has now almost totally weathered away. It was re-roofed in 1989.

Under the bridge by the side of the house are a pair of doorways joined by an arched tunnel with a pair of hemispherical niches, fitted with the remains of curved stone seats. No decoration, no discernible purpose, no reason.

Towards the northeast of the estate, in Glen Shira, are several Gothick farm buildings, almost all decked out as eyecatchers with pointed arches, battlements and quatrefoils. Maam Steading, designed by Robert Mylne in 1787–9, stands out from its companions. It was originally planned as a circle, not uncommon for Scottish farms, but eventually only a half-circle was realized. Blank castellated white walls end both sides of the semicircle. In the centre the barns have been given the screen treatment; castellations and pointed arches abound.

At the same time a grotto, serving as a wellhead, was built at nearby Bealachanuaran. It is a classical building, set into the hillside, with a pediment and ball on top and a large and heavily rusticated arch as an entrance. Sadly, the Gothick dairy of 1752 has been demolished.

Under the 5th Duke, John Campbell, the ornamentation of the policies (to use the Scottish word) was resumed. In 1785 a small domed icehouse, probably to Mylne's design, was built north of a plot called Cherry Park. In the late 18th and early 19th century several Gothick lodges and cottages were built on the estate, one of the prettiest being The Hexagon, a summerhouse beside the River Aray and possibly designed by Alexander Nasmyth, who at this time was also building the Belvedere Steading at Rosneath. It is a pity that one of Nasmyth's more far-flung designs was never built: a drawing shows a Gothick lighthouse tower for Innerarary harbour, complete with battlemented parapets and machicolations rising from a castellated and buttressed base. On top of the tower a small Chinese pavilion was planned.

Kilninver

Armaddy Castle Boathouse (1795)
NM 785 164

North of the peninsula, 7 miles from Kilninver and overlooking Seil Sound, is Armaddy Castle. South of the house is an 18th-century boathouse, or rather the remains of one. The façade still stands, a pointed entrance arch and cruciform arrowslits making it an excellent eyecatcher. Nearby, in the same vein of overgrown decay, is a rustic bridge with six obelisks for pylons.

Lochawe

St Conan's Church (1881)
NN 120 278

St Conan's church was built as a church, was used as a church and still functions as a church today. However, it also makes a beautiful folly. Walter Douglas Campbell came to live with his mother at Lochawe in the 19th century. Legend has it that she could not make the long drive to church at Dalmally, and so her ever-loving son built her his own church—a chapel, in fact. Nevertheless, it took six years to build, 1881–6. Even then, he appears not to have been satisfied with it, because in 1907 he started to expand it. Campbell died at the beginning of World War I, and his sister, Helen, tried to complete the building. She died in 1927, but the trustees carried on the good work. The church was finally finished in the 1930s. The guide (buy one and put the money in the box for the upkeep of this exquisite little monument) from which we pilfered this information remarks that none of the stones used in the building was quarried: they were all boulders found at random in the vicinity.

The folly of the thing is that Campbell used every known Scottish ecclesiastical style, even down to Druidical standing stones. The overall result is astounding in a small church: Arts and Crafts and good Victoriana, changing from Saxon and

St Conan's Church, Lochawe

Norman to Gothic and back again. Apse and ambulatory produce a satisfying effect, and when you have finished the rounds of the church (the Bruce Chapel contains a beautiful wood and alabaster figure of the old warrior), it would seem that calling this picturesque amalgam a folly amounts to libel. But in true folly fashion, bits and pieces of this building came from other sources: screens from Eton College Chapel, a window from a medieval church, a bell from Skerryvore Lighthouse, wood from two old ships and so on.

There is also a story that a friend of Campbell's deemed the design of the

proposed apse dangerous. Campbell built a scale model and drove a steam roller over it. Not a scratch on the model.

New Selma

Lady Margaret's Tower (1754)
NM 907 384

North of Oban, near New Selma and overlooking Ardmucknish Bay, is Lady Margaret's Tower, erected by Lady Campbell 'anno 1754'. She was the second wife of Sir Duncan Campbell, who built the house on the estate. The tower is square, with a tall, blind arch in which is set a door with a classical pediment. At the top of the tower is a battlemented parapet with bartizan turrets and a domed elevation.

Oban

McCaig's Folly (1897–1900)
NM 855 292

John Stewart McCaig adhered to the Victorian philosophy that wealth obliged the holder to use it to better the education of the less fortunate. As a banker, philosophical essayist and art critic (self-styled), McCaig strove to improve the fishermen of Oban. In order to share the experiences of his tours in Italy, he lectured on several occasions to the Oban Young Men's Free Church Mutual Improvement Society (OYMFCMIS), and to accustom the Obanians to a free and casual communion with Great Art, in 1897–1900 McCaig built a poorly remembered copy of the Colosseum (his building is circular and the arches are pointed), giving work to the unemployed masons of the area into the bargain. The enormous blackened cylinder, with its two courses of open arches, dominates the town and harbour. It is known as McCaig's Folly or McCaig's Tower, after the 100ft (30m) tower he intended to build in the centre. The original scheme was that the building should serve as museum, art gallery and family memorial, but none of this came about. McCaig planned to sponsor Scottish artists, particularly sculptors, to produce a series of bronze statues of Scottish notables to place as acroteria around the parapet of the building, at a cost of a staggering £1000 each (the whole building cost £5000), but before this one-man Arts Council turned every aspiring young Scot into a sculptor overnight he was gently dissuaded, after just one statue had been completed—a bust of Major Duncan McCaig, now displayed outside the McCaig Museum.

McCaig's Folly, Oban

The huge hollow shell now encloses a prettily landscaped public garden. McCaig took the decision, whether deliberate or financial we do not know, not to flatten the land enclosed by the folly but to leave it as a natural rocky hilltop. This means that the crag is encircled by the building, and it allows the visitor to scramble over different levels within the structure to see different viewpoints through every arch, a strangely pleasing effect, combining the real and the artificial.

In the mid-1990s the local council closed the access road to the folly to prevent vandalism and general depredations to the structure. The downside of this admirable sentiment is that it prevents access to anyone who has difficulty with steep steps—not usually a problem for vandals.

As a philosophical essayist and art critic McCaig may not have achieved national prominence, but as a folly builder he ranks among the finest. His magnificent mad folly, unique in Britain, is unforgettable.

Hydropathic Establishment (1880)

Ruins, abandoned when the money ran out.

Rest and Be Thankful

Stone (18th century)
NN 230 077

Between Loch Fynne and Loch Long, on the side of the old road, stands an inscribed stone as a memorial to General Wade's soldiers, who built the military road here after the 1745 Jacobite rising. The name of the spot is taken from the inscription on the stone: 'Rest and Be Thankful.'

Torosay Castle

Pavilion (1988)
Gazebos (19th century)
NM 729 353

A new pavilion, in what can only be described as the Chinese-Gothick taste, is set in the equally new Japanese garden of Torosay Castle on the Isle of Mull, overlooking Duart Bay. There are some very good Italian statues in the older garden, together with fine castellated gazebos.

AYRSHIRE

Alloway

Burns Monument (1820)
NS 340 184

Opposite the church in Alloway (now a suburb of Kilmarnock) and overlooking the River Doon and its 'Auld Brig', is the tall Burns Monument, the result of a competition won by Thomas Hamilton in 1818. This version of the Choragic Monument of Lysicrates, this time mounted on an Egyptian base, was built in 1820–23. Some years later Hamilton built another Burns Monument, on Edinburgh's Calton Hill. Although Hamilton used a different design, his colleague William Playfair came up with yet another Lysicratic Monument for the Calton Hill site a year later.

The Camellia House at Culzean

Ayr

Miller's Folly (19th century)
NS 340 220

Easily found, easily forgotten is this tiny tower in South Harbour Street. It formed part of Ayr's citadel and was converted into an observation post in the 19th century by a Mr Miller. Nothing much to attract our notice, except for the established name.

Wallace Tower (1831)
NS 340 220

Standing 113ft (34.4m) high, the Gothic tower was built to a design by the Edinburgh architect Thomas Hamilton in 1831–4. The statue was made by local boy James Thom, who also did the hugely successful sculptures of Tam O'Shanter and other Burns characters for the town's Burns Monument.

Culzean Castle

Ruinous Viaduct (1775)
Sham Ruined Arch (1775)
Camellia House (1818)
Aviary or Pagoda (1811–25)
Swan Cottage (1825)
Pheasantry
Rockery Grotto (1870)
Rustic Hut
NS 233 103

Culzean (Cullane to the Sassenachs), a property in the hands of the National Trust for Scotland, is spectacularly sited on the Ayrshire coast. Its conversion by Robert Adam into a sham medieval castle for the 10th Earl of Cassilis during the last quarter of the 18th century is, in hindsight, inevitable, a course dictated by the *genius loci*. As at Alnwick Castle, Adam took great care in shaping the castle's surroundings. For the approach from Morriston he devised a striking design: a Romano-Gothick viaduct spanning the glen in front of the castle. In the end Adam had to tone down his plans, but the effect as realized is still remarkable. The entrance archway has been erected as a sham ruin with crumbling side towers. The fabric of the viaduct has also been given a ruinous appearance. The visitor finally enters the castle's forecourt through a castellated classical archway. The forecourt and some of the gardens are enclosed by cardboardy embattled walls, towers and turrets. Adam took the idea for the viaduct from the approach to Hadrian's Villa near Rome, which he sketched on an Italian journey.

In the gardens stands James Donaldson's spidery Camellia House of 1818, with ogee windows, battlements and corner pinnacles, and on the edge of Swan Pond stand the presently unrestored Gothick aviary known as The Pagoda—although blind ogee arched windows make it hard to draw a Chinese connection—and the recently restored octagonal Swan Cottage, both designed by Robert Lugar about half a century after Adam. A design for the Pheasantry at Culzean appeared in Lugar's *Plans and Views of*

Buildings Executed in England and Scotland in the Castellated and Other Styles (1823).

Further along the coast the Home Farm, the most elegant steading in Scotland, was built to Adam's designs in 1775–7. The buildings are on a canted square plan, with four archways connecting the four rectangular stables that make up the square. Four churchlike buildings, with crosses and embattled gables, stand at 90 degrees to the stables. The Home Farm has been extensively restored and was converted into a Park Centre in 1973.

Failford

Burns Pillar (mid-19th century)
NS 460 263

At Failford a globe on top of a square pillar marks the spot where Robert Burns took leave of Highland Mary—Mary Campbell, the recipient of his 'Will ye go to the Indies, my Mary?' The reason for the parting was Burns's intended emigration to Jamaica, but the financial success of his first collection of poems, printed at Kilmarnock, made the journey unnecessary, and Burns stayed in his native land. There are many, many monuments to Burns in Scotland; more, it would appear, than to Goethe, Dante, Shakespeare and Molière combined in the rest of Europe.

Girvan

Obelisk (18th century)
NX 180 980

This is a good obelisk, which looks out towards the spectacular Ailsa Craig, an island resembling a huge Christmas pudding dropped from a plane and floating, lost at sea.

Irvine

Eglinton Belvedere (1991)
NS 324 422

The highest point in Eglinton Country Park, Belvedere Hill, had a pleasant view, but something was missing. Luckily for us, in 1991 the enlightened and sensitive officers of the Irvine Development Corporation invested £10,000 in the construction of a small Doric rotunda to cap the hill.

Kilmarnock

Burns Monument (mid-19th century)
NS 431 383

As Kilmarnock played such a crucial role in the poet's life, the town has its own 80ft (24m) Burns Monument, standing in Kay Park. It is a splendid confection of more architecture than space, with external staircases, balustraded balconies and a central octagonal tower with bartizan pinnacle. It would have made a wonderful

The Burns erection at Kilmarnock

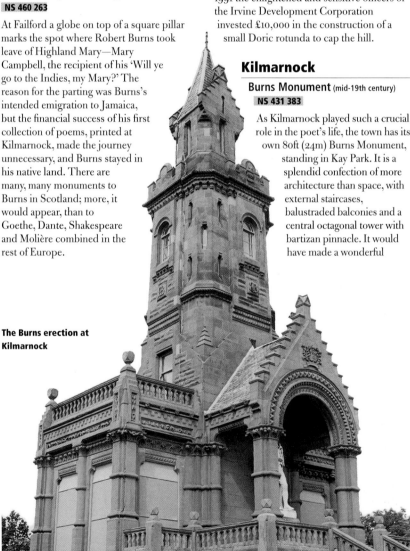

belvedere, but the monument is now protected from the citizens of the town by a high arrow-topped steel fence, gift-aided from the European Community. All the windows in the tower are boarded up, except for the one the catapults can't reach at the very top.

Largs

Tower (19th century)
NS 210 578

On the coast south of the seaside resort of Largs stands a tall, slim tower, rather like an Irish round tower. It commemorates the Battle of Largs (1263) when the Norwegian King Haakon was beaten, paving the way for the Hebrides finally to be brought under Scottish rule.

Mauchline

Burns Tower (mid-19th century)
NS 500 275

The Burns Tower at Mauchline is another top-heavy little tower in the favoured Scots Baronial style, with crow-stepped gables, tiny first-floor balconies and the customary bartizan turrets. To a southern eye the traditional Scottish Baronial architecture (traditional since the 19th century) is wildly romantic and exciting, and the Scots, well aware of the effect it has on susceptible visitors, have deployed it to great effect all over their country. It is a remarkable style, particularly when taken out of context, and it is surprising that it has failed to travel around the world. Some weak imitations can be found in North America, but they lack the harled verticality of the real thing. The Burns Tower is not harled, however.

Monkton

Monument (18th century)
NS 357 289

A classical monument stands at the crossroads of the A77–A78 Prestwick–Kilmarnock road. Surely not to Burns?

St Quivox

Auchincruive Tea House (1778)
NS 382 237

In 1778 Robert Adam added a tea house to Richard Oswald's estate at Auchincruive, near St Quivox, outside Ayr. The setting of this large and beautiful folly is almost as dramatic as that of Culzean and is disturbed only by the aeroplanes landing at Prestwick. It stands on a circular base, which has four turrets attached to it. The building's second storey is the actual tea house. It is circular with a course of blind arches and battlements hiding a low conical roof. The whole structure, also known as Oswald's Temple, is a concoction out of Theodoric's Mausoleum at Ravenna by the Tomb of Caecilia Metella in Rome.

Tarbolton

Barnweil Tower (1855)
NS 407 295

Burns, Scott, Wallace and Robert the Bruce would together have topped the Most Popular Scotsman Award shortlist in any 19th-century poll. In Ayrshire Wallace vies with Burns for first place, but at least at Tarbolton, which also has connections with Burns, the memorial to Wallace, the Gothick pinnacled and battlemented Barnweil Tower, actually commemorates something: his burning of the Barns of Ayr. It was in Ayr that the Hammer and Scourge of England began his fight for Scottish independence against those most hated of foreign invaders. It was as we arrived at the tower one summer afternoon that Jeremy Guscott, playing in a rugby team of men from Wales, Ireland, England and Scotland, dropped the goal that sealed the Lions' series victory over South Africa. The farmer may have thought it passing strange to discover a Welshman bouncing up and down in excitement in his farmyard, but the ecstasy was being repeated

Barnweil Tower, Tarbolton

across Scotland, England, Wales and the Emerald Isle. For one moment we were united, but that fleeting sense of national unity was quickly dispelled on reading the boiling resentment inscribed on the tower:

'AT WALLACE' NAME WHAT SCOTTISH BLOOD
BUT BOILS UP IN A SPRING-TIME FLOOD.'
EVER HONOURED BE THE MEMORY OF THE
MATCHLESS
SIR WILLIAM WALLACE, THE FIRST OF HIS
COUNTRYMEN,
WHO IN AN AGE OF DESPAIR AROSE AND
'DARED TO NOBLY STEM TYRANNIC PRIDE:'
THROW OFF THE YOKE OF FOREIGN OPPRESSION
AND MAINTAIN
THE INDEPENDENCE AND NATIONALITY OF
SCOTLAND, AND WHO
BY DEEDS OF SURPASSING VALOUR AND
STAINLESS PATRIOTISM,
HAS GLORIFIED THIS, HIS NATIVE LAND, AND
IMPERISHABLY
ASSOCIATED HIS NAME WITH THE DEFENCE OF
NATIONAL RIGHTS
AND THE LIBERTIES AND IMMUNITIES OF FREE
BORN MEN.
FROM GREECE, AROSE LEONIDAS, FROM
SCOTLAND
WALLACE, AND FROM AMERICA, WASHINGTON
NAMES WHICH SHALL REMAIN THROUGH ALL
TIME
THE WATCHWORDS AND BEACONS OF LIBERTY.

And then:

SIR WILLIAM WALLACE
REGENT OF SCOTLAND, MCCXCVII.
IN RESISTANCE OF TREACHEROUS INVASION AND
IN DEFENCE OF
THE LAWS AND LIBERTIES OF HIS COUNTRY, HE
FOUGHT AGAINST
FEARFUL ODDS THE DESPERATE BATTLES OF
BIGGAR, STIRLING
BLACK BARNSIDE AND FALKIRK, AND BETWEEN
THESE ACTIONS, IN
LITTLE MORE THAN A YEAR, HE STORMED AND
TOOK FROM THE INVADERS
EVERY FORTRESS, CASTLE AND TOWN WHICH
THEY HAD SEIZED IN
THE KINGDOM, THOUGH WORSTED AT FALKIRK
BY OVERWHELMING
NUMBERS, AIDED BY FATAL DISSENSIONS IN HIS
OWN ARMY HIS
UNDAUNTED SPIRIT WAS NOT SUBDUED, BUT
EVER ANIMATED BY
THE NOBLEST PATRIOTISM HE CONTINUED
WARRING WITH THE
OPPRESSORS OF HIS NATIVE LAND, UNTIL HIS
FOUL BETRAYAL
SEVEN YEARS AFTER THAT DISASTROUS BATTLE
BY THE
EXECRABLE MONTEITH

Turnberry

Turnberry Lodge (19th century)
NS 203 060

Of interest to golfers, perhaps, is the castellated eyecatcher façade to Turnberry Lodge. It is nothing fancy, but buildings like these are the mainstay of follydom.

BUTESHIRE

Brodick

Bavarian Summerhouse (1845)
NS 008 380

The Bavarian Summerhouse at Brodick Castle on the Isle of Arran boasts the most astonishing ceiling of rustic larchwork and pine cones, sweepingly arranged in geometrical patterns by genuine Bavarian craftsmen. Shored up by sham creepers, the building has an organic air, as if it had grown from seed.

DUNBARTONSHIRE

Helensburgh

Bell's Obelisk (1872)
NS 290 823

On the east side of Gare Loch the town of Helensburgh honours its adopted son,

Bell's Obelisk, Helensburgh

GOLDEN OLDIES

Ten Favourite Follies

(as chosen by members of the Folly Fellowship)

JACK THE TREACLE EATER *Somerset*	SCOTT'S GROTTO *Hertfordshire*
FORBIDDEN CORNER *North Yorkshire*	PORTMEIRION *Merioneth*
MAD JACK FULLER'S SUGARLOAF *Sussex*	RUSHTON TRIANGULAR LODGE *Northamptonshire*
MOW COP *Cheshire*	PETERSON'S FOLLY *Hampshire*
WIMPOLE SHAM RUIN *Cambridgeshire*	STOWE GOTHICK TEMPLE *Buckinghamshire*

Henry Bell (1766–1830), with a tall obelisk. During his lifetime men scorned his invention of *The Comet*, a steam-powered boat. 'Twill ne'er float,' was the considered opinion, and despite proving his detractors utterly wrong, Bell died a poor man.

ERECTED IN 1872
TO THE MEMORY OF HENRY BELL
THE FIRST IN GREAT BRITAIN WHO WAS
SUCCESSFUL IN PRACTICALLY APPLYING STEAM
POWER FOR THE PURPOSES OF NAVIGATION
BORN IN THE COUNTY OF LINLITHGOW IN 1766
DIED AT HELENSBURGH IN 1830

Nearby, in Hermitage Park, is the flywheel of *The Comet*, propped up over Bell's anvil.

Milngavie

The Folly (18th century)
NS 541 755

On the golf course on the outskirts of fashionable Milngavie stands a quiet little hexagonal tower, reminiscent, with its blind windows, of the Pepperpot in Wiltshire. It is known locally as The Folly, but it is much more likely to be yet another doocot.

Renton

Smollet's Column (late 18th century)
NS 384 780

There is a column to the memory of Tobias Smollett, author of *The Expedition of Humphry Clinker*, at Renton near his birthplace, complete with a Latin inscription by Dr Johnson. 'SISTE, VIATOR,' it begins, and rambles on for another 33 lines. The local viators meanwhile wobble unsteadily and uncomprehendingly past on their way to and from the pub.

Rosneath

Belvedere Steading (1802)
NS 265 810

On the other side of Gare Loch is Rosneath. Here the landscape painter Alexander Nasmyth designed a Gothick eyecatcher steading for the Duke of Argyll around 1802. The belvedere tower in the centre of the fabric is the most prominent feature, rising high above the farm roofs. Tall, blind pointed arches decorate the tower façade, together with a fancy balustrade and bartizans. Two octagonal towers with pyramid roofs echo the main tower, with the round towers that end the steading on both sides giving the impression that they belong to an earlier date.

LANARKSHIRE

Carluke

Milton Head Monument (19th century)
NS 825 495

A small monument commemorating someone without whom this book could never have existed. Major-General William Roy

(1726–90), the Father of the Ordnance Survey, who started his career in 1747 by mapping Scotland, is remembered by a triangulation stone.

Crawford

Obelisk (19th century)
NS 955 205

At Crawford a spire acts as a surrogate for a mausoleum that was never built. The mausoleum was to be erected for the Crawford family, but because of family squabbles it was never built, and the Crawfords have to make do with this obelisk.

Glasgow

Scott Column
Battle of Langside Memorial Column
Glasgow Green Obelisk (1806)
200 Nithsdale Road (1871–3)
Templeton's Carpet Factory (1889)
ICI Warehouse (1900)
NS 600 650

Like any large city, Glasgow is well endowed with monuments: there are the Scott Monument in George Square, the Battle of Langside Memorial in Queen's Park and the Nelson Obelisk on Glasgow Green, designed in 1806 by David Hamilton. But there are more exciting buildings in Glasgow than are

Templeton's Carpet Factory, Glasgow

dreamed of in a monumental philosophy— there are, for example, those by the native architect Alexander Thomson, better known as 'Greek' Thomson, although he would have had an equal right to the epithet 'Egyptian' on the strength of the persistent use of Egyptian motifs in his works. His churches, of which the best was the now-demolished Queen's Park Church, contained many examples, and in Union Street a warehouse of his design goes by the name of Egyptian Halls, although only the upper storeys show the characteristic bulging pillars.

Thomson struck a more Oriental chord in his design for a dwelling at 200 Nithsdale Road, where in 1871–3 he built a residence suitable for a minor official in the court of Ramses II. The portico pillars and the chimneypots on the flat roof are among the house's more conspicuous details, although today the well-grown front garden obscures much of the house from the eyes of the casual passer-by.

Much 19th-century Glaswegian commercial architecture favoured the exotic. One of its most explicit examples is Templeton's Carpet Factory in Templeton Street, Glasgow Green, which was built in 1889 by William Leiper, has been often threatened with demolition but is now finally saved, although subdivided into small offices and workshops. It is quite simply spectacular, with medieval Italian architecture carried far beyond anything the Guelphs or the Ghibellines could aspire to—the polychromatic façade beggars description. See it—and see too its rival, the ICI Warehouse in Tradeston Street, designed in 1900 by W.F. McGibbon, who was inspired by the Bargello in Florence. Pointed windows, crenellations and, on its corner a dominant tower give it, too, an unmistakable Italian aura.

Hamilton

Chatelherault (1732–43)
NS 737 539
Mausoleum (19th century)
NS 727 564

In industrial Hamilton a huge drum rises high above a colonnaded square base. This is the vast and impressive mausoleum of the Dukes of Hamilton. Perhaps its foremost claim to fame is the echo inside — a record-breaking 15 seconds.

But the great folly here is Chatelherault, an immensely long screen with four inset pavilions, built for the 10th Duke of Hamilton. Of what use is such a folly? The pavilions, rusticated and with vases on the roof, are connected to each other by a classical screen with a centre archway. The Dogg Kennill, as the original architect William Adam described it, was ostensibly built as kennels for hounds and as stabling but also allowed a degree of ducal leisure use. When we first saw the place in the early 1970s the absurdly small rooms in the pavilions still retained traces of fine plasterwork and grand fireplaces among the shattered windows and rotting floors. It would seem that the original banqueting rooms had been subdivided into much smaller spaces.

Building began in April 1732 and continued for 12 years. The East Pavilion was complete by the summer of 1733, the West Pavilion in November 1734, the screen wall connecting the two in 1735. The West

Hamilton Mausoleum

Pavilion has a sloping floor, dropping by nearly 18in (45cm) from one side to the other, a fact demonstrated enthusiastically by the guide, who happily placed a pound coin on the floor and watched it accelerate away from her.

Despite their palatial accommodation, the Doggs at the Kennill went mad in 1739. 'We are in continual fear here with mad dogs running up and down almost every day,' wrote Alexander Inglis, the duke's Master of Horse. The duke died in 1743 and interest in

the pack, and therefore the Kennill, gradually subsided. By 1979 the bowling green in front of the screen had been turned into a gravel pit, and the whole massive façade seemed inclined to follow it in, but its honey pink decay strengthened its romanticism and its role as a superb eyecatcher from Hamilton Park. Work was then beginning on a complete restoration by the architects Boys Jarvis. Now that it has been completed, Chatelherault has reclaimed its rightful place as one of the most spectacular buildings in Scotland. The alien name was inherited from the 2nd Earl of Arran, who was created Duc de Chatelherault by Henri II of France.

Cadzow Castle (15th century)
NS 734 538

Most arrivistes in the 18th century were impelled by fashion and snobbery to construct artificial ruins in their parks to give a glaze of antiquity to their parvenu background. The Dukes of Hamilton were more fortunate—they had the ruins of the 15th-century Cadzow Castle, which they cheerfully adapted into a romantic eyecatcher.

RENFREWSHIRE

Erskine Ferry

Blantyre Obelisk (mid-19th century)
NS 441 720

Erskine Ferry, the ferry itself now made redundant by the last bridge across the Clyde, has a tall, slender obelisk to the memory of the 11th Lord Blantyre, who had the misfortune to be killed in a riot in Brussels in 1830.

Lochwinnoch

Castle Semple Prospect Tower
(late 18th century)
NS 369 594

On Kenmuir Hill Captain William McDowell built an octagonal pavilion with tall, semicircular stilted windows, now hollow arches in an empty, roofless ruin.

Newton Mearns

Pollock Monument (19th century)
NS 516 526

A Gothick monument in Newton Mearns commemorates Robert Pollock, who wrote the mighty, flawed and now almost forgotten minor masterpiece *The Course of Time*.

TAYSIDE

ANGUS

Brechin

Kinnaird Castle Rustic Summerhouse (1800)
NO 635 569

Built *c.*1800 by Lady Carnegie.

Dundee

Triumphal Arch (1844)
Demolished

Built to commemorate Queen Victoria's visit to the docks in 1844, this was easily the most glamorous building in Dundee, a fantastic turreted triple arch, its turrets gift-wrapped with Gothic blind arcading. All was cleared away in the 1960s to make room for the Tay Road Bridge. A sad loss.

Montrose

Langley Park Steading (1874)
NO 681 602

The castellated steading at Langley Park, buried deep in the countryside near the Montrose Basin, is square, with a screen front consisting of a crenellated entrance arch and corner towers (or, rather, screens pretending to be towers), and decorated all over with cruciform arrowslits and pointed windows. It is probably late Georgian. When we visited, it was hovering between dilapidation and ruination, clearly abandoned and waiting for what? rescue and conversion? or decay and oblivion?

FORFARSHIRE

Arbroath

Hospitalfield Mortuary (1880)
NO 516 377

This is an extraordinary building. It is hard to believe in eternal peace while contemplating such architecture. For those of you who have difficulty in coming to terms with the notion of a chapel in a cemetery being classed as a folly, all we can say is, 'Go and see it'. It is as undisciplined and sprawling as a Stephen King novel.

Around 1850 Patrick Allen Fraser considerably enlarged Hospitalfield House, just outside Arbroath. The house, which is still owned by the Fraser family in the guise of a charitable trust, is now used for

Arbroath. Hospitalfield Mortuary

Comrie

Melville Monument (1812)
NN 766 238

Comrie, east of St Fillans on the end of Loch
Earn, has, on Dunmore Hill in Glen Lednock,
an 1812 obelisk to Viscount Melville. It is not
as fascinating as the surrounding countryside,
but it makes an excellent excuse to include in
your travels a beautiful part of Perthshire that
is otherwise bare of follies.

Dalnacardoch

Wade Stone (mid-18th century)
NN 730 708

Eight miles from Blair Atholl the A9 will
bring you, if you wish, to Dalnacardoch,
where General George Wade erected a pillar
to mark the completion of another section of
his Highland roads. The story has it that he
placed a penny on the flat top of the finished
pillar. When he returned a year later it was
still there, proving that the local inhabitants
were either short or honest.

Dunkeld

Dunkeld House Hermitage (1757)
NO 006 418
Ossian's Cave
NO 000 417
Murthly Castle Banqueting House (1669)
NO 072 399

One fine day in 1757 John Murray took his
uncle James, 2nd Duke of Atholl, for a stroll
through the woods near Dunkeld House.
The duke's reaction when he reached the
banks of the peaty brown River Braan is not
known, but what he saw was a brand new
building, the Hermitage, overlooking Black
Lynn Fall. It was his nephew and heir's
surprise gift to his favourite uncle, adding to
the already existing corpus of follies at
Dunkeld, among them a Chinese Temple
(1753) and a Temple of Fame, both now
destroyed. A similar fate lay in store for the
Hermitage but, rising like a phoenix from the
fire that devoured it, it still survives, although
in a somewhat simplified version. The outer
room is circular; the inner room used to be
lined with mirrors so that wherever one
stood one could enjoy a view of the falls. The
curved end walls cleverly amplify the sound
of the falls, and the effect is redoubled as you
pass through the round room to the viewing
platform—an excellent effect for blind
visitors. The Douglas Fir on the south side of
the bridge by the Hermitage is, at 212ft

(64.6m), the tallest tree in Britain.

Caught up in the fashionable enthusiasm
for the 2nd-century Gaelic bard Ossian,
perpetrated by James Macpherson's spurious
translation of *Fingal*, the 4th Duke decided
to reshape the Hermitage in 1785. He
employed the young architect James Playfair
to do the work, copying designs by the
duke's court painter, Charles Steuart. The
decorations included scenes from the life of

Inside the Hermitage at Dunkeld

Ossian, and the Hermitage was renamed
Ossian's Hall.

The Dukes of Atholl do not seem to have
been popular with their tenantry in the 19th
century. Ossian's Hall was fired in 1821, with
only minor damage, but the vandals were
more successful in 1869, this time resorting
to dynamite. Eventually it was rebuilt, and it
is now in the care of the National Trust for
Scotland. The folly is but a shadow of its
former self, but the scenery alone merits a
detour.

Ossian's Cave, about half a mile away,
probably also dates from the 4th Duke's
reign. There used to be an inscription from
Fingal above the entrance, but whether it was
removed in embarrassment when it was
discovered that the author was Macpherson
rather than Ossian, or whether it has simply
disappeared, we cannot tell.

The car park on the main A9 has a gate
allowing disabled visitors to drive right up to
the folly.

Errol

Round Square Tower (1811)
NO 246 229

In order to maintain large houses there had
to be substantial service sections for storage,
transport, heating, staff, stabling and so on.
As the wealth and importance of the main

house and its occupants increased, so did the size of the service area. By the end of the 16th century the noise, smell and bustle of the service parts resulted in their being housed in a separate section, usually a square yard like a stable block. The hand of improvement could not be restrained, however, and by the late 17th century the first 'square', as these service areas were called, had been beautified by building it in a circle, and the oxymoronic name 'round square' came into vogue.

The pleasant circular shape did not, of course, make the round square a folly, but at Errol Park there seems to have been little point in adding the huge blind-windowed clock tower, which erupts out of the stable block, square blending to octagonal and topped not with castellations but with an elegant and peaceful balustrade. Reminiscent of the much later Charborough Park Tower in Dorset, it was the work of John Paterson, Robert Adam's manager, for John Lee Adam (no relation).

Gartincaber

Murdoch's Folly (1800s)
NN 697 008

'It's like looking at a ghost,' marvelled the current owner, Farmer Brown, as he studied a postcard of the Tower of Gartincaber as it was in an earlier life: a hexagonal, castellated belvedere tower with an excellent external staircase coiling round to the top storey.

Unfortunately, the staircase no longer reaches to the first storey, so an indifference to imminent death is required in those wishing to ascend. The tower is now so ruined that it totters rather than stands on a low, sheep-dotted hill, which commands the most astonishing panoramic views. Indeed, the views—the 'wide and beautiful view it commands on both sides'—were the reason William Murdoch built the tower in the first place. Stirling Castle and the Wallace Monument are clearly visible.

The tower is now in a very advanced state of collapse, and despite the obvious affection the farmer holds for it, there is no money available for restoration or even consolidation. Another minor part of our heritage is slipping quietly away.

Kenmore

Rustic Lodges (1840)
Hermitage (early 19th century)
Taymouth Castle Dairy (1830)
NN 774 454
Taym outh Fort (1760)
NN 791 456

The keyword to Taymouth Castle is 'rustic', although there is a considerable amount of work from earlier than the 19th century, the period when rusticity was all the rage. The later buildings at Taymouth would seem to date from around 1806, when Alexander Nasmyth was called in, or from the late

The teetering remnants of Murdoch's Folly

1830s, when James Gillespie Graham worked at the castle.

The rustic lodges fall into two categories. There are those with irregular eaves, slate roofs and entire trees as supports, such as Rustic Lodge and Fort Lodge; and there are those counterfeiting miniature castles, such as Delarbe Lodge and Rock Lodge, that are rubble-built towers with additional wings, embattled and whitewashed. Taymouth Fort, or the White Tower, in separate ownership, used to be the gamekeeper's house, but it is now let out as a high, remote holiday cottage. The latter buildings possibly belong to the early 19th century, as does the Hermitage by Loch Tay, near the Falls of Acharn, now a dilapidated octagonal ruin with a grotto-tunnel, much like the Octagon Tower and tunnel at Studley Royal in Yorkshire. Down by the pretty red rusticated Fort Lodge a glimpse of another sham fort can be seen, engulfed in rhododendrons, over the castle wall.

The large and highly visible dairy at Taymouth is set on a mound in the park, and probably dates from the 1830s. It is in a mixed Swiss-Balkan style and is square with tree trunks all around, offset by the white quartz walls. There is a second storey with a balustrade, and inside there used to be some rustic furniture, the best pieces reminiscent of Edwards's and Darly's *A New Book of Chinese Designs* (1754). It is now a private house.

Near the castle, across the river, is an earlier tower, three storeys high, Gothick, with a battlemented wall running off from it. The castle itself hosts a golf club and needs some care and attention. To the east is the Star Battery, a small bastion, and the motif is repeated by The Fort, which is to the west, near Kenmore. It was built in 1774 by John Baxter to replace an earlier fort (1764) by John Paterson, although a map from 1754 shows the site already marked as The Fort.

Again near the castle is The Cross, also known as Maxwell's Temple after the 18th-century agricultural improver Robert Maxwell. This elaborate Gothick cross was built in 1831 by William Atkinson. The rustication extends to the estate village of Kenmore, with tree-root fencing painted a cheerful red.

A murder was committed at the Taymouth Fort. During World War II the castle was used as a hospice for Polish soldiers, one of whom struck up a liaison with the gamekeeper's wife. He quarrelled with her, killed her and left her body in the Tower. The alarm was raised. He was captured near Peterhead and hanged.

A spiky gateway at Taymouth—surely an influence for the Folly Fellowship logo?

Lanrick Castle

MacGregor Oak (early 19th century)
NN 683 029

Up the River Teith is Lanrick Castle, where in the woods Lieutenant-General Sir Evan John Murray MacGregor erected a stone tree as a memorial. The tree is huge and almost invisible—a case of not being able to see the tree for the woods. Although it is over 60ft (18m) high and 20ft (6m) in diameter at the base, the bottom half of it merges into the woods with all the other trees. It mossy and lichen-covered on the north side and complete with stumpy branches and

The MacGregor Oak

pollarded limbs. One could almost pass it without noticing. Then, 30ft (9m) up, everything goes awry, naturalism vanishes and the stone tree is truncated and bears a crown (of all the trees that are in the wood?). From here, a bizarre structure rises. Slender columns support a circular base, on which is another column and a couple of flambeaux and palmettes on square supports.

The reason for the construction of this disturbing building may lie in the history of the MacGregor family. The *Dictionary of National Biography* tells how, in the 17th and 18th centuries, the clan was under a ban that, among other things, prohibited them from bearing the name MacGregor—hence the General was given the name of Murray. In 1774 the ban was lifted and the General was called out to be the chief of the MacGregors. He did not, however, assume the name until the year of his death in 1822. So the tree may well have been intended to commemorate his resumption of his true name. The stone scars, boles and cicatrices in the stout stone trunk all held individual meanings, now forgotten—much like this phenomenal folly.

The site is private and should not be visited without a guide, as open mineshafts concealed in the undergrowth on the hill constitute a potentially fatal hazard. The hill is also home to a thriving bed of breeding adders, Scotland's only poisonous snake.

Megginch

Megginch Doocot (1809)
NO 241 246

For some reason, admirals, captains and other naval gentlemen often seem happier in a house accoutred with such items as portholes, masts or even a façade in the shape of a galleon's stern—think about the New York Yacht Club on 44th Street or the Admiral's House in Holly Bush Hill, Hampstead, London. Why sailors should feel this need to assert themselves while stockbrokers, publishers and dentists do not is a matter best left to sociologists.

Admiral Sir Adam Drummond went about the whole business of being a retired sailor rather unobtrusively. His ship-on-

The doocot and mains at Megginch

shore, Megginch Castle on the Carse of Gowrie, is a good 3 miles inland, and the only reference to his career is a weathervane in the form of a ship on top of a doocot. In other respects it is a standard 1809 Gothic doocot: octagonal with pointed windows and doorway, and a pyramid roof. What our dry description fails to convey is the dreamy Gothic of the ensemble. The farm buildings with the doocot in the middle of the yard are all of a piece in a glorious late-flowering, ogee Gothic style. Surely this is the most romantic farmyard in the country.

Meikleour

Meikleour Hedge (1746)
NO 164 387

Living follies generally exclude themselves from an innocuous guide such as this, being possibly too contentious. An exception has to be made for the Meikleour Hedge, a remarkable affair planted in 1746 and the tallest hedge in the world. It spans 586 yards (539m) and in places tops 100ft (30m). Unlike some well-known tourist disappointments, such as the Hampton Court Maze, this really is something to see, a hedge to gawp at. Trimming is a major operation—the A984 has to be closed to traffic—and because it is of beech, the best time to see the hedge is in high summer. It was raining when we saw it

one August, and only the bottom 12ft (3.6m) had been trimmed while the rest loured shaggily over the wet road.

New Scone

Obelisk (18th century)
NO 165 254
Monument (18th century)
NO 158 252

Another conspicuous landmark in the Perth region is an obelisk on a 918ft (280m) high hill near New Scone. Deadlines forbade a closer investigation—perhaps it is a memorial to a laird, a battle or a horse, or perhaps it is a monument to a laird's horse killed in battle. No doubt we will be told—perhaps it was built by Kinnoul's friend Gray?

Perth

Kinnoull Hill Tower (early 19th century)
NO 141 226

Most European countries have a few spots called Little Switzerland, but topographical names inspired by German scenery are quite rare. Britain does, however, provide instances of the latter—the area round Alton Towers is known as the Staffordshire Rhineland, and the 729ft (222m) Kinnoull Hill at Bridgend in Perth is surmounted by a sham ruin said to have been built in conscious emulation of the

Kinnoull Tower, superbly sited overlooking the Tay and the A96

many romantic ruins that stud the steep banks of the Rhine between Cologne and Coblenz. Prince Albert ceaselessly remarked on the similarities between parts of Scotland and parts of Germany.

This sequel to Lorelei-land consists of a round tower set between bits and pieces of wall, battlements and pointed arches. Overlooking the Tay, the tower was built by Robert Auriol Hay, 9th Earl of Kinnoull. The situation reminded him of the panorama of the Rhine he had enjoyed on his grand tour with his neighbour, Earl Gray of Kinfauns. Picnics were held by the tower, bringing back fond memories of 'Vater Rhein'.

In 1923 Lord Dewar of Holmestall gave Kinnoul Hill to Perth. The city handed it over to the Forestry Commission, which immediately planted the dullest and most prolific evergreens. Slowly awakening to their heritage responsibilities, they are now replanting some broad-leaved woodland. The hilltop has been repackaged as a country park, owned and managed by Perth and Kinross District Council, and there are nature trails through the woods. There are two good topographs.

Triumphal Arch (1848)
NO 119 237

Queen Victoria's discovery of Scotland left a spoor of memorials, usually arches and many temporary, in the Highlands. The finest of them all was Queen Victoria's Arch in Dundee, which was lost in the 1960s when it was demolished to make way for the Tay Road Bridge. A pinnacled riot of Norman Gothicism, rising twin-turreted to a height of 88ft (26.8m), it was built by J.T. Rochead in 1848. Excited contemporary observers noted that on first seeing it, the Prince Consort remarked 'Good morning, gentlemen', while the Queen wrote in her diary merely that 'a staircase, covered with red cloth, was arranged for us to land upon'. She did notice the arch at Camperdown House, probably a temporary structure, and commented on the number of triumphal arches in Perth (which reminded Albert of Basle). One by William Mackenzie remains from 1842.

Binn Hill Tower (1818)
NO 139 227

A mile or so to the east of the far more famous folly on Kinnoull Hill, in the fair land of Gowrie, is a tall, grey, pencil-thin tower, hidden in woodland on the edge of the bluff of Kinfauns Hill. Remote, isolated, forgotten, the century yet intrudes with the hum of

Binn Hill Tower

traffic from the A96 550ft (167.6m) below. Binn Hill Tower was built in 1818 by Lord Gray as an observatory. The views over the Carse and the river are as magnificent as from Kinnoull Tower. It was sold as a derelict shell in 1995 by Pavilions of Splendour, but at the time of writing had yet to be restored.

Pitlochry

Clunie Memorial Arch (1952)
NN 913 597

En route to another of the Duke of Atholl's estates, Blair Atholl, we pass through Pitlochry, where stands a younger brother of Yorkshire's Bramhope Tunnel Monument. The horseshoe-shaped Clunie Arch was erected partly to the memory of the men killed driving the Clunie Tunnel for the Tummel hydroelectric scheme, which also created the new reservoir of Loch Faskally, and partly to the greater glory of the directors, contractors and architects of the scheme. The horseshoe shape is a replica of the cross-section of the tunnel.

WESTERN ISLES

WESTERN ISLES

Buailedubh

Shell Bus (mid-20th century)
demolished

Although the Western Isles are increasingly popular, the subsistence-level communities predictably supported no real follies to speak of. However, to pass away the time of day on South Uist, Mrs Flora Johnson covered a bus standing in her garden in Buailedubh (pronounced Booale-adoo) with shells. Through the years she managed to cover almost every inch of metal with beautiful patterns formed from thousands of different shells found in abundance on the nearby

beaches. From a distance, the bus looked as if it might have risen from the sea encrusted with shells after an eternity as Neptune's coach.

Mrs Johnson, one of the few female folly-makers, died in the 1970s, and her shell bus, like Mr Bisset's at Leven, was ignored, fell into dereliction and finally disappeared a few years ago, shortly before Lord Snowdon arrived especially to photograph it, having read about it in an earlier edition of this book. Sorry!

Griminish Point

Scolpaig Tower (19th century)
NF 730 760

A distant mystery: a tiny, two-storey, castellated, hexagonal tower on a low round islet in Loch Scolpaig, almost nowhere.

Scolpaig Tower

Captain Fraser's Folly, Uig

Leverburgh

Folly Village (1920–25)
`NG 020 873`

Leverburgh, on South Harris, was built as a model village by Lord Leverhulme, who also features in Lancashire with his superb replica of Liverpool Castle at Rivington. As the owner of vast tracts of Harris and Lewis, Leverhulme had great plans to better the lot of the islanders by building a fishing port and kipper factory. He spent the prodigious sum of £250,000 on the project from 1920, but the islanders showed little interest in having their lots bettered by a foreigner, and this attempt to build a port to rival Stornaway to the north met with mind-numbing apathy. The usually indomitable soap baron as good as conceded defeat, and the project was abandoned on his death. A demolition company picked up the remains for £5000. Fragments survive of the glory that might have been.

North Uist

Callernish House (1961)
`NF 833 798`

On the northernmost tip of North Uist the wind howling in from the Atlantic is so strong that it is often impossible for a man to stand up. In 1961 the 5th Earl Granville crawled to within 50 metres of the raging sea with his architect, Sir Martyn Beckett, and shrieked: 'Build me a fourteen-bedroom, eight-bathroom house HERE!' It was agreed that the house had to be on one floor—anything higher would have blown down in a remarkably short space of time—and so Sir Martyn devised a ring-shaped house like the Hertfordshire model dairies at Drivers End and the 18th-century Scottish stable blocks known as round squares. The result isn't, technically, a folly, because shooting parties are probably the biggest growth industry in the Hebrides, but it's undeniably eccentric.

Uig (Isle Of Skye)

Captain Fraser's Folly (1870)
`NG 395 640`

Captain Fraser was the inevitably unpopular factor of the Snizort Estate, and two stories are linked to the construction of this squat little tower, with its arched windows and arrowslits. One was that he wanted to relieve local unemployment and the other was that he wanted to leave his mark on the community. As the factor was the only source of employment on these huge estates, which explanation is nearer the truth? It is now owned by the Uig Hotel.

Wales

CLWYD
GWYNEDD

POWYS

DYFED

MONMOUTH

GLAMORGAN

CLWYD

The first impression of Clwyd is that it is the least attractive of the Welsh counties. Escape from the coast and the flat industrial estate landscape of Flintshire, however, and a different land hesitantly reveals itself: as beautiful in its own way as the more famous tourist centres and with the benefit of many fewer people. Compared with English counties there are few follies here; compared with Powys there are plenty.

Every other large house in Clwyd seems to be called Plas Newydd (New Place), and if not this, it will be called Hafod. The only interesting Hafod we know of was in Dyfed, however, but Plas Newydd in Llangollen is still firmly in Clwyd. For some reason, Clwyd also has a fair few full-blown 19th-century castles that cannot be described as anything but follies, and a marvellous recent one to boot.

DENBIGH

Abergele

Gwrych Castle (19th century)
`SH 930 780`

Easily the biggest and most impressive of all the castles is the gigantic Gwrych Castle outside Abergele. This is a folly designed to impress by sheer bulk—it was built as a private house for Lloyd Bamford Hesketh, who designed it himself. Work started in 1814, but the foundation stone was not actually laid until 1819, and thereafter it is fair to say that work only meandered along. A massive marble staircase, leading—in best folly tradition—nowhere, was installed in the 1870s, and it is still unclear whether the house has actually been finished. At any rate, building has stopped and it is presently between jobs.

Hesketh called upon many architects to assist him in his grand design, including Charles Busby, Thomas Rickman and Edward Welch. The core of the house is built in the unremarkable, over-castellated Gothic popular at the time, but what makes it a cast-in-bronze folly is that from the road one can scarcely pick the actual house out from the immense curtain walls running for hundreds of yards along the steep hillside, containing a

Gwrych Castle

total of 18 towers. All this is sham; the walls
are blind façades fronting nothing, more or
less like Hesketh's library, which consisted
mainly of false bookbacks.

Bodnant

Pin Mill (1730)
SH 800 725

A removal folly, although done with a good
eye for garden ornaments. The 2nd Lord
Aberconway not only created most of the
glorious gardens at Bodnant but also had this
rather nifty little pavilion moved in 1938–9
from Woodchester in Gloucestershire, where
it already served as a garden building, having
started life as a workshop in which iron pins
were made. The central section, which is two
storeys high, has an elegant Venetian window
and is flanked by two side pavilions. For
some reason, pin mills were considered
worthy of ornamental architecture—the same
phenomenon can be observed on the
continent of Europe.

Brynkinalt

Rustic Cottage (1813–14)
SJ 320 380

This is Charlotte, Lady Dungannon's
territory near Chirk. One of the few lady
architects, if only an amateur, she amused
herself in the early 19th century with
redesigning the house and embellishing the
park. All appears to have been part of the
same building campaign, which started in
1808. Just across in Shropshire, near
Glynmorlas, is the castellated bridge over the
Ceiriog and its adjoining rustic cottage, which
is very pleasant and rough. In Chirk itself is
one of the lodges to Brynkinalt, also designed
by Lady Dungannon. It is just a little wrong,
so the right folly stuff, and its castellated walls
proclaim in Latin, among other languages,
that it is all for King and Law and gives the
dates as 1813 ('inchoatum') and 1814
('perfectum'). Apparently a 'china room and
dairy' were built in the park at exactly these
dates, but these have been destroyed—a pity,
when one sees the other buildings.

Clocaenog

Obelisk (1830)
SJ 065 552

> 'As a memorial of his having completed
> the large range of mountain plantations
> which in part skirt the base of this hill,
> William, 2nd Lord Bagot, erected this

> *pile of stones in the year 1830.'*

This rough and ready 'obelisk' was reused by
Eric Gill, who designed a second plaque,
stating that the Forestry Commission
replanted Clocaenog Forest after deforest-
ation in World War I.

Denbigh

Façade (19th century)
SJ 060 680

Near the Brigidine Convent on the A543
leaving Denbigh is a castellated wall
concealing a farm from the road. After
Gwrych, though, façade walls have to be
rather special.

Henllan

New Foxhall (1592–1608)
SJ 020 670

Inland near Denbigh is the site of one of the
most famous folly stories in Wales, although
the building that inspired it has as little of the
folly about it as Lyveden New Bield. A Mr
Lloyd had an estate at Foxhall, by Henllan,
when in 1592 Mr Panton, the local MP,
decided that he was going to build a grander,
newer mansion close by—much too close for
the liking of Mr Lloyd—and call it Foxhall
Newydd (New Foxhall). Lloyd predicted
financial disaster for Mr Panton; this duly
happened. Lloyd bought the nearly finished
mansion (a fireplace is dated 1608) and in the
orgasmic *schadenfreude* of which all true
Welshmen are secretly capable, he stripped
the roofs and the furnishings and left the
walls to stand in testimony to Panton's folly.
The ruin is remarkably beautiful, standing in
a cherry orchard behind the prosperous
working farm of Foxhall.

Llanbedr Dyffryn Clwyd

Castell Gyrn (1977)
SJ 150 590

Castell Gyrn at Llanbedr Dyffryn Clwyd has
another remarkable story, this time of
coöperation between two parties normally
seen at loggerheads: the county planning
officer and the householder. The architect,
the late John Taylor of Chapman Taylor,
wanted to build a house with a beautiful view
of the Clwydian range and Snowdonia, but
the planning authorities felt that a
conventional building would be scenically
detrimental. To general astonishment they
proposed that only a building 'which
punctuated the landscape in the manner of

Castell Gyrn

an 18th-century folly' would be permissible, and Mr Taylor joyously responded by building a four-storey castellated tower. Unlike most follies, it has solar heating and double glazing fitted as standard—after all, it was built in 1977. He didn't stop there, adding in the 1980s and 1990s a little gatehouse with an Alice-in-Wonderland window, a sacred grove, a classical sheep shelter and other assorted bits and pieces.

Llanelidan

Nantclwyd Hall Garden Temples and Tower (1950s–70s)
SJ 110 510

Sir Clough Williams-Ellis was, of course, also a working architect, mainly restoring, improving or adding to older structures. At Nantclwyd he was allowed to run wild, providing many garden structures from the 1950s onwards right up until his death. The landscaped garden has a Gothic tower, a rotunda temple and other odds and ends, and the formal gardens have been embellished by two gazebos. The whole would be most exciting if we didn't have Portmeirion itself. Further on, at Cwm, there is also a Swiss cottage by Williams-Ellis of around 1964.

Llangollen

Plas Newydd (1780 onwards)
SJ 220 420

History's most famous pair of lesbians, the Ladies of Llangollen, eloped twice in 1778 when they were aged 39 (Eleanor Butler) and 23 (Sarah Ponsonby). Second time lucky, they eventually resettled in Llangollen from Ireland and rented Pen-y-maes, which became Plas Newydd. Anyone who was anybody

(including several who were nobodies) came and visited when they were engaged on the then so fashionable picturesque North Wales Tour. The Ladies received their never-ending stream of visitors with hospitality, in the meantime keeping up their correspondence with a vast circle of blue-stocking ladies, reading, gardening, embroidering and assembling the unrivalled collection of carved wooden panels that adorns the outside and inside of Plas Newydd. The cottage changed into a black-and-white rural fantasy, Xanadu in blackened oak, to which a later owner, General John Yorke, added significantly in the later 19th century (although the house extension was demolished in 1963). The house, now a museum, includes some very exciting items, among them a rare survival: the Ladies' Aeolian harp. Their story is told in Elizabeth Mavor's essential book *The Ladies of Llangollen* (1971).

The 'real' follies have almost all disappeared, but Plas Newydd itself is the best folly. In the gardens were a rustic hut, a Gothick birdcage, a cowhouse, a Gothick gateway and other such ornaments. Lady Eleanor's Bower, near the house, and the dairy have survived, as has the grotto or Gothick niche across the brook that flows behind the house. This contains a font from the ruins of Valle Crucis Abbey and has a grotesque head over the pointed arched entrance with rough rockwork and benches at the sides.

Llanrwst

Maenan Tower (late 18th century)
SH 790 610

South of Llanrwst, in a garden in the beautiful Conwy valley, is the Maenan Tower. It commands the most amazing position, overlooking the whole of the valley and the mountains beyond. A lady at the house said it was at least 15th century if not before, but it looked a little more modern to us, perhaps Georgian. It was rebuilt and restored by Lady Aberconway in the 1960s. It has red brick in it—unusual for this part of the country, it has a modern flat roof, and it has modern stairs. On the first floor is a circular room with elaborate cane furniture and a carpet, a round window and four tall, arched windows. A spiral staircase climbs up on the outside, while on the ground floor is a circular paved area up five steps with a large, white statue of Bacchus in the middle. Inside the circular base area are two carved wooden goats' heads with little plinths on the top and also an elaborate stag's head coat-rack.

'We call it the Tower,' said the lady of the house, but nobody knew who built it.

Old Colwyn

Woodall's Folly (19th century)
SH 876 780

Woodall's Folly, a sturdy little toy castle in Tan-y-Coed Gardens, Cliff Road, was going to be demolished, as it was dangerously in need of repair. Clwyd Historical Buildings Trust stepped in and did just that—repaired it. The Trust also turned it into a small

Woodall's Folly in the 1950s

house. Good! Woodall's Folly was (and is) one of the most satisfying buildings around. Despite its castellations and rough stone, its stature or rather lack of it announces from afar 'Look at me, I'm a joke!' And so it is.

Woodall's Folly was apparently built as a smoking den on the Myn-y-Don Estate. There is a central towerlet, all covered in cross-shaped as well as rectangular arrowslits, with the miniature mass of only one room or so behind it, complete with very small, decorative side-turrets.

Ruthin

Ruthin Castle Ruins and Gatehouse
(19th century)
Peers Monument (1883)
SJ 120 580

The ruins of 13th-century Ruthin Castle received the picturesque treatment in the 19th century. Parts were added and a mock castle was built here in several stages, while the ruins were regarded as just another adornment for the gardens. To improve upon it, a little gatehouse was added.

In St Peter's Square is also the Peers

Monument of 1883, which was done by the very able Chester architect John Douglas. It is one of those multifunctional edifices the Victorians liked so much: a clock tower. It combines drinking facilities for both horses and people, and the latter are able to tell the time as well. To top all this, the clock tower purports also to be a monument to Mr Peers, who had the perhaps embarrassing experience of seeing the monument erected in his lifetime.

Trevor

King William's Tower (1827)
SJ 255 434

The village is also called Garth or Garth Trevor, and Trevor Hall is sometimes known as Garth Hall. Why the tower, about two-thirds of a mile north of the village on top of a hill, is called thus, we do not know. It is supposed to date from 1827, so predating King William IV by three years and it is round and castellated, with a slender side-turret.

Wrexham

Acton Park Screen (late 18th–early 19th century)
SJ 340 520

James Wyatt designed Acton Park (in the northern outskirts of Wrexham) for Sir Foster Cunliffe in 1786–7, but it has now been demolished. The great Doric screen put up as the entrance to the park, attributed to Moel Famau's Thomas Harrison, remains to overwhelm the pedestrian housing estate surrounding it.

Wynnstay

Sir Watkin's Tower (19th century)
SJ 213 497
Waterloo Tower (c.1815–20)
SJ 305 431
Nant-y-Belan Tower (1806)
SJ 304 401

If we counted aright, they were rather keen on towers at Wynnstay—there are three in all, excluding the rather grand column. The first and most enigmatic is Sir Watkin's Tower, 1843ft (562m) up on the top of Cyrn-y-brain above Pen-y-stryt, but this is merely laziness on our part, because the undoubtedly splendid walk necessary to see it would have taken us about three hours, which we didn't have. It is marked on the 1981 Ordnance Survey map as a ruin, so traces almost certainly remain. Sir Watkin was, of course, a Williams-Wynn, the great family who owned

Acton Park Screen

much of North Wales, and the family seat was Wynnstay, at Ruabon, now a school.

The house at Wynnstay is well documented architecturally, but there is no attribution or date for Sir Watkin's Tower, nor even mention of it in the more regular sources. The succession of Sir Watkins were all enthusiastic builders and consulted, among others, Francis Smith, Lancelot Brown, James Gandon and Benjamin Gummow. There are several interesting buildings left in the park, including a dairy by Brown, a large fluted Doric column tower, Waterloo, and Nant-y-Belan Tower. The column, about 75ft (23m) high, was built in 1790 by James Wyatt in memory of the fourth Sir Watkin Williams-Wynn. It is topped by an urn with ram's heads at each compass point above a viewing platform, and there are seven little windows for the spiral stairway. Yobs have been up it because there are sprayed graffiti at the top, but the entrance is now blocked up. There was no question of relieving unemployment at Wynnstay Park—the labour force consisted of French prisoners of war.

Waterloo Tower is often confused with Sir Watkin's Tower, but it is, in fact, a gate lodge, in all probability designed by Benjamin Gummow, who gave us so many good Gothic buildings. It is impossible to decide whether to name the main two-storey, square body of the lodge as the tower—it is rather too blunt—or whether to give that name to the so-called turret, which has, in fact, grown into a full-scale tower, tapering, polygonal and pierced with cruciform arrowslits. Of course, all and everything is castellated and machicolated, with an embattled screen wall next to it. It may

date from *c*.1815 to the 1820s.

Nant-y-Belan Tower still exists—just. One man we spoke to said it was demolished and all you could see were its foundations. If you walk along the track to it south of the house, past Penynant, you come across the foundations of something just before running out of parkland. Don't give up. Cross the field and go into the woods beyond, even further along the ridge, and you'll find the remnants of the tower, teetering on the edge of a precipice, marked very correctly on the map as a ruin. Half at least has already collapsed down the ravine, and now there is hardly anything left; it is very derelict and certainly beyond salvation. One part of the back wall still reaches its original height of 35–40ft (10.7–12.2m). In 1981 a man working on the estate reminisced:

'When I was a kid, it used to have plaques all the way round the walls recording the names of the people in the Charge of the Light Brigade. You could get inside and there were two huge oak doors and in the middle of the floor there was a huge eagle crouched over with a cup on its back and my friends and I—we were kids, mind— my friends and I went underneath and we found a room underneath and there was a big fireplace in the room and when you lit a fire in the fireplace the smoke came out of the ram's heads round the top of the tower. You should have seen it 30 years ago, it was wonderful then. The other monument in the park [the column] is a monument to something, the Wynns or something, they were all eagles or rams you know, but now they've blocked it up because the stairs were falling down inside.'

The eagle remained on site until fairly recently when the children of our generation threw it down the ravine and shattered it. The tower was designed by Sir Jeffry Wyatville in 1806 to commemorate the brother officers of the 5th Baronet who were killed in the Irish rising of 1798—not in the Charge of the Light Brigade. The Light Brigade referred to here is better known as the Ancient Britons Fencible Regiment. The destruction of this most important of Wynnstay's three towers is the more regrettable because Nant-y-Belan was based on the Tomb of Caecilia Metella in Rome, a monument that inspired several follies.

FLINT

Bodelwyddan

Bodelwyddan Castle (c.1830–42)
`SJ 000 750`

Locals call it a folly; the *Buildings of Wales* calls it a folly; we don't. But here it is: castellations were put along the house only some 20 years after the neo-classification of the old house had been completed. This was done by the partnership of Joseph Aloysius Hansom and Edward Welch, who liked their Gothic (see also Middleham and Leyburn), around 1830–42. In our time the county

Bodelwyddan Castle

council spent millions on it as a conference and exhibition centre, and by 1990 it cost £1.3 million a year to run it. So folly it is.

Bodfari

Pontruffydd Arch (early 19th century)
Eyecatcher
`SJ 008 705`

The *Buildings of Wales* reports a 'Gothic archway of grotto-like character' as well as a castellated farm near the site of a demolished house. The hamlet of Sodom is nearby.

Caerwys

Piccadilly Inn (19th century)
`SJ 120 720`

Piccadilly was a horse that ran at the Holywell races and won, and the money made on the bet was used to build the Piccadilly Inn.

Halkyn

Halkyn Castle (1824)
Screen Wall (19th century)
`SJ 210 720`

Halkyn Castle is a spite castle. It was built in 1824 to the designs of John C. Buckler, the painter, for the 2nd Earl Grosvenor, supposedly when he was refused a stay at the local inn. There are some nice matching lodges, also by Buckler. Benjamin Gummow oversaw the building work, but early on, in 1804, he designed what was probably a folly tower on Halkyn Mountain, long since gone (the building that is, the hill still remains). The folly façade behind Halkyn Old Hall may also be connected with the Earl's building campaign.

Hawarden

Hawarden Castle (19th century)
`SJ 320 650`

Hawarden has a genuine castle, improved in 1866, but otherwise real. It was a 13th-century English border castle in the park of an 18th-century country house and, following a precedent nobly set by Charles Grey of Colchester, the antiquary Sir Stephen Glynne restored the castle sufficiently for it to make an excellent garden ornament. Sadly, the cost of restoration proved too much, and he had to sell the estate to his brother-in-law, William Ewart Gladstone. In the grounds of the fake castle, which is the real house, is a Gothicky pavilion by H.S. Goodhart-Rendel, dating from before World War II.

The remains of the Moel Famau Jubilee Tower

Marford

Ornamental Cottages (c. 1803–15)
SJ 360 560

The remarkable village of Marford is enchanting. About 14 or 15 houses, right in the middle of the A483 with traffic thundering through, have been built in an uncompromisingly picturesque Gothic, with ogee windows everywhere. Everything is black and white—even the pub. Several were probably built to the designs of John Boydell, estate manager for George Boscawen of Trevalyn Hall. Turner painted Marford Mill but ignored the village, which must have been even more picturesque then, when all the roofs were thatched and there was no traffic. We also know of one builder, Julius Flower from Hungerford, who came in 1814 to Marford to help out with a least one cottage. Similar cottages are situated at or near the neighbouring villages of Gresford and Rossett and at Trevalyn itself.

Moel Famau

Jubilee Tower (1810)
SJ 161 627

The tallest mountain in the Clwydian range is Moel Famau, 'Mother of Bare Hills'. A superb, exhilarating long walk brought us in sight of a cairn, marked on the map as Jubilee Tower; seen closer, the cairn became an immense pile of rubble, all that remained of a gigantic obelisk that was erected in 1810 to commemorate George III's jubilee. The architect was Thomas Harrison, who also designed Lord Hill's Column in Shrewsbury and the Marquess of Anglesey's Column at Llanfair P.G., both of which are still standing, while the Jubilee Tower isn't. It was blown down in 1862; in 1970 the rubble was cleared up and four concrete staircases were built up to the 30ft (9m) plinth, which had remained relatively intact, to provide a viewing platform comparable with Castell Gyrn.

Waterloo Tower (19th century)
SJ 190 640

We were told of a castelled tower above Cefn Bychan celebrating the victory at Waterloo. We failed to find it, but it is quite probable that this is a mistaken site for Waterloo Tower at Wynnstay Park, or for the Moel Famau Jubilee Tower.

Mold

Sham Castle (1797 or c. 1813–20)
SJ 240 601

Nercwys Hall, south of Mold, was heavily Gothicized between 1813 and 1820 by Benjamin Gummow for Miss Gifford; he added an orangery and a porch (now removed to Portmeirion). The best here is the sham castle, which may either date from around 1797 (when the now demolished wings to the house were added), or from Gummow's later campaign. It stands in a high field, with a central round and embattled towerlet with blind arrowslits, a quatrefoil window and blocked-up door, flanked by two even smaller turrets, connected by narrow walls. The right turret is ruinated, apparently unintentionally. There are also castellated stables.

Alleluia Monument (1736)
SJ 210 630

Small but perfect: a vandalized obelisk in a field or, in fact, at Maes Garmon (Garmon's Field), just a mile west of Mold, near the River Alun of Alyn. This is the site, some believe, of the 5th-century battle between Britons and the amalgamated armies of Picts and Scots. The Britons were led by the bishop of Auxerre, Germanus (a German from France obviously), later also known as St Garmon. As the Picts and Scots thundered down from the hills, the army of Christian Britons suddenly shouted: 'Alleluia!' Picts & Scots 0, Britons 1. To record this, Nehemiah Griffith, the local landowner, erected this obelisk in 1736, round about the 1300th anniversary of the battle.

Gwysaney Windows (1820s)
SJ 220 670

In the garden of Gwysaney House are a couple of authentic church windows that came from the demolished chapel at Gwysaney.

Mostyn

Dry Bridge (1849)
SJ 260 800

The Dry Bridge Lodge at Mostyn is a fascinating building, which serves as a bridge, an archway, a house, a tunnel and an eyecatcher—it is one of the most economical buildings we have come across. It is a two-storey, castellated house with an archway through the middle, straddling the drive to Mostyn Hall. The drive to Mostyn Hall from Whitford itself crosses the minor road from Mostyn to Tre-Mostyn, and the wide arch is built on this bridge, making it more of a tunnel. It is very pretty and quite unexpected—a most enjoyable surprise. Another surprise is its date, 1849, by Ambrose Poynter, a most learned London architect and one of the founders of the

Institute of British Architects. We had rather expected it to be some 20–30 years earlier.

Talacre

Summerhouse (1750s)
SJ 120 850

A two-storey summerhouse, possibly designed by Lancelot Brown, of a classical design and in a sorry state. Talacre now houses Benedictine nuns, but it used to belong to the Catholic Mostyn family. The pavilion is certainly not a folly, but it would be a pity to see it go. At the last minute we have heard of more, even 'splendid', follies and garden buildings coming to light at Talacre.

Whitford

Tower (1810)
SJ 150 290

Thomas Pennant, the celebrated traveller, lived in Whitford, at Downing. The house has long since gone, but a folly tower in the park survives. It is too late to have been commissioned by Pennant (who died in 1798), but was probably built for his son, who enlarged the house. The embattled square tower in the park has a side turret and extensions. On Garreg Hill, to the west of Whitford, stands a round, ruined tower, which was considered by Pennant to be a Roman pharos. Not so. It is a beacon tower, which warned when pirates were believed to be in the vicinity. It was restored in 1897, in 'commemoration of the sixtieth year of the glorious reign of Victoria, Queen and Empress'.

Ornamental Cottages at Marford

DYFED

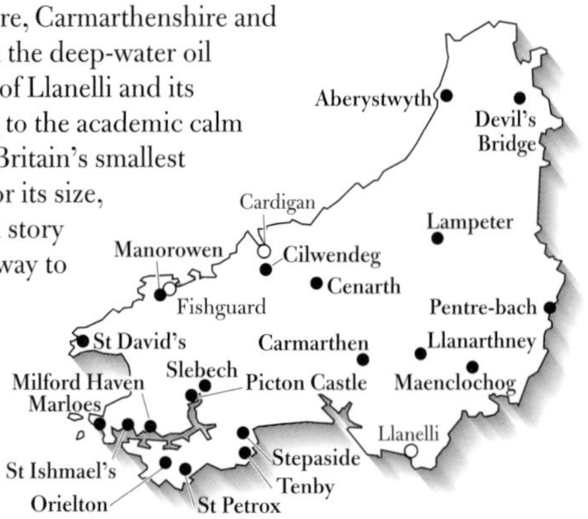

Dyfed consists of the counties of Cardiganshire, Carmarthenshire and Pembrokeshire. The variety is immense, from the deep-water oil terminal at Milford Haven, the rugby fervour of Llanelli and its massive tinplate works (hence Sospan Fach!), to the academic calm of Lampeter and Aberystwyth. There is also Britain's smallest city, St David's, with a population of 1,638. For its size, there are few follies in Dyfed, but the size and story of Paxton's Tower at Llanarthney goes some way to compensate for the rest.

The researches of Thomas Lloyd have helped us considerably in extending this section with previously unknown follies, large, smaller and smallest. He also informs us that in 1696 a Mr Hancock designed what was called 'a waterfollye' at Landshipping House, Landshipping Ferry, just across from Picton Castle.

Map labels: Aberystwyth, Devil's Bridge, Cardigan, Lampeter, Manorowen, Cilwendeg, Cenarth, Pentre-bach, Fishguard, St David's, Carmarthen, Llanarthney, Milford Haven, Slebech, Picton Castle, Maenclochog, Marloes, Llanelli, St Ishmael's, Stepaside, Orielton, Tenby, St Petrox

CARDIGANSHIRE

Aberystwyth

Wellington Monument (19th century)
SN 580 800

An Edwardian guidebook to Wales calls this a 'chimney-like monument', but it is not—at least, that is not its intention. The Duke of Wellington was supposed to be remembered and fêted here by a column in the shape of an upended cannon, but it was never properly finished. It was built on the top of Pen Dinas, the 413ft (126m) hill south of the town, by Major Richards of Bryn-Eithen Hall in nearby Llanfarian, which is now a folk museum.

A John Nash folly, a triangular Gothic castellated tower, built here for Sir Uvedale Price, was demolished in 1895.

Devil's Bridge

Obelisk (1803)
Jubilee Arch (1810)
SN 770 750

Tourists usually manage a quick scurry up the picturesque Vale of Rheidol on one of the country's last remaining steam train services, travelling as far as the remarkable Devil's Bridge; otherwise, Aberystwyth's hinterland is empty.

The Devil's Bridge itself still retains an air of mystery, despite its popularity and fame. One of the curiosities of Britain, it consists of three bridges riding piggyback over the River

Mynach. Pedantic historians may say that the bottom bridge was built by monks in the 11th century, but everybody else knows that Pont-y-gwr-drwg (literally the Bridge of the Bad Man) was built by the Devil himself. Above that is an 18th-century stone bridge, and above that is an iron bridge, dating from 1901.

To the south is the Ystwyth valley, and it was here in 1783 that Thomas Johnes conceived the finest flowering of the Gothick revival in Wales. Hafod Uchtryd was a bleak, untended estate, which Johnes inherited from his father. He had been brought up in comparative luxury in Croft Castle in Herefordshire and was expected to be yet another absentee landlord. But Johnes was a romantic. He secretly married a girl from Dolaucothi, by the Ogofau gold mines, and they decided to turn Hafod into their ideal home. Their ideals were in the school of the picturesque, influenced by, and influencing, their friends John Nash, Richard Payne Knight and Sir Uvedale Price. Together with the architect Thomas Baldwin, they created the finest Gothic mansion in the country. Built in 1786–8, it was destroyed by fire on 13 March 1807, rebuilt and then sat in almost forgotten splendour for 133 years until the artist John Piper rediscovered it in an article for the *Architectural Review* in June 1940. A spate of appreciations followed, culminating in a book, *Peacocks in Paradise*, by Elisabeth Inglis-Jones. In the wake of this acclaim, the house was blown up in 1958 to make way for a caravan site.

All that remains of Johnes's Xanadu in

Wales is an obelisk to the memory of the 5th Duke of Bedford, which was built in 1803 and designed by W.F. Pocock, and Johnes's Arch, a very Welsh-looking arch over the B4574, 2 miles southeast of Devil's Bridge. Two massive drystone-style piers support a spindly structure, built in 1810 to commemorate George III's Golden Jubilee. Once there were three such arches; this is the only survivor.

Lampeter

Derry Ormond Tower (1820s)
SN 590 520

The column tower on the A485 north of Lampeter, Derry Ormond Tower, is an excellent example of its type. A tall, crumbling column, erected to commemorate the battle of Waterloo, it takes its name from the Derry Ormond Estate on which it was built. There are said to be 365 steps inside to the top, but it has been blocked up since before living memory. The tower was probably designed by Samuel Cockerell's more famous son, C.R. Cockerell, who built Derry Ormond mansion for John Jones in 1824 as well as St David's College in Lampeter. Built of slate-coloured stone, it stands high and exposed and is now eroding badly. The railings around the top have fallen, and even the plinth is sagging. Urgent work needs to be done quickly to rescue this Lampeter landmark.

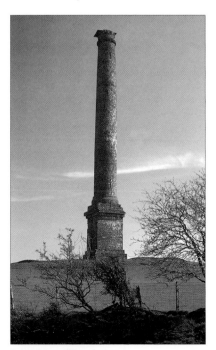

Derry Ormond Tower

CARMARTHENSHIRE

Carmarthen

Picton Obelisk (1847)
SN 410 200

In 1847 a 78ft (24m) obelisk was erected in Carmarthen to the memory of General Sir Thomas Picton, a local man who was a hero of the Peninsular Wars and who was killed leading his division to victory at Waterloo. In 1984 the district council decided it was unsafe, found it would cost £90,000 to repair and ordered it to be taken down. The protest from General Picton's regiment was such that they eventually decided to dismantle the top half only, to number the stones and to store them until such time when there would be enough money to reconstruct it.

Cenarth

Tower (19th century)
SN 260 370

We were told of a small, castellated, round tower on a hill on the River Cych at Lancych, about 2 miles southwest of Cenarth. It belonged to the house, which was possibly built in the 1830s by Peter Frederick Robinson (author of *Rural Architecture*, a book on ornamental cottages, published in 1823) for the Lloyd Jones family. Thomas Lloyd told us it was now overgrown, and one was unlikely to find it without knowing where to look. But then we couldn't even find Lancych.

Llanarthney

Paxton's Tower (1811)
SN 540 180

Sir William Paxton was a Londoner who made his fortune in India. He was evidently the sort of man who needed to be a big fish, so he set about looking for a small pond and found it in Carmarthenshire. The next step was to get elected to Parliament as member for the county, and here he made a miscalculation. He made the assumption that the voters of Carmarthenshire could be bought. The men of the county were delighted to sell themselves to Paxton's cause and accepted his prodigious hospitality with enthusiasm. They then went out and voted for his rival, as they had intended to do all along.

The story of the Great Election of 1802—Y Lecsiwn Fawr—has passed into folk history, along with an uncannily precise account of Paxton's expenditure. He spent

Paxton's Tower

£15,690 4s 2d on 11,070 breakfasts, 36,901 dinners, 684 suppers, 25,275 gallons of ale, 11,068 bottles of whisky, 8879 bottles of porter, 460 bottles of sherry, 509 bottles of cider, 18 guineas for 'Milk Punch' and £786 for campaign favours and bunting, the equivalent today of about £624,000. The Tory, Sir James Hamlyn Williams, was the victor, winning 1217 votes to Paxton's 1100, and the announcement was greeted by vicious fighting between the rival factions, the Reds for the Tories and the Blues for the Whigs (yes, that way round).

Once the initial emotions had calmed down, it is said that the Reds took to jeering that Paxton had overspent himself, and in order to disprove them he tried to build a bridge over the River Tywi (only to be prevented by the magistrates) and, some years later, a mighty folly tower on the hills above Llanarthney on the Tywi valley.

Paxton's Tower is now owned by the National Trust, which has restored it from its ramshackle state. It is a wonderful, grumbling, massive, proto-folly: triangular with round corner turrets springing from hexagonal bases. On top is a hexagonal turret, and the whole affair is lightly castellated. The entrance arches at ground level are big enough to drive a carriage through, and there was once a dining room on the first floor. Plaques above the first floor windows in Welsh, English and Latin commemorate the ostensible reason for the tower's construction:

'To the invincible commander Viscount Nelson, in commemoration of deeds before the walls of Copenhagen, and on the shores of Spain; of the Empire everywhere maintained by him over the seas; and of the death which in the fulness of his own glory, though ultimately for his own country and for Europe, conquering, he died. This tower was erected by William Paxton.

It was designed by Samuel Pepys Cockerell and built in 1811. And this is where the story begins to wobble, because that is rather a long time after the 1802 election, and (the story now breaks into violent shakes) Paxton won the election four years later, so there was no need to build himself a tower, unless, of course, he intended it as three fingers to his former detractors.

Paxton resided at Middleton Hall, long since gone, but bits and pieces of his ornamental grounds survive, including artificial cascades and waterfalls, the Holy Well and other wells, the foundations of bath houses and an ice-house with good brickwork, all the sad remnants of a failed project of Paxton's, Middleton Spa.

Paxton later turned his attentions to the town of Tenby and succeeded in making it a fashionable watering place. It appears that he always had to try twice, as his first project would always go wrong, be it elections, buildings or spas.

Pentre-bach

Mail Coach Pillar (1841)
SN 820 340

If we leave Dyfed on the A40 we pass a tiny curiosity, the Mail Coach Pillar, between Llandovery and Pentre-bach, almost on the Powys border. The road here skirts a wooded precipice above the River Gwydderig, and in a lay-by on the west side of the road is an awful warning of the perils of drunken driving. It is a small obelisk on a plinth with a cautionary inscription:

THIS PILLAR IS CALLED
MAIL COACH PILLAR AND ERECTED
AS A CAUTION TO MAIL COACH
DRIVERS TO KEEP FROM INTOXICATION
AND IN MEMORY OF THE GLOUCESTER
AND CARMARTHEN MAIL COACH
WHICH WAS DRIVEN BY
EDWARD JENKINS ON THE 19 DAY OF
DECEMBER IN THE YEAR 1835 WHO
WAS INTOXICATED AT THE TIME
AND DROVE THE MAIL ON THE WRONG
SIDE OF THE ROAD AND GOING AT
A FULL SPEED OR GALLOP MET A
CART AND PERMITTED THE LEADER
TO TURN SHORT ROUND TO THE RIGHT
HAND & WENT DOWN OVER THE
PRECIPICE 121 FEET WHERE AT THE
BOTTOM NEAR THE RIVER CAME
AGAINST AN ASH TREE WHEN THE
COACH WAS DASHED INTO
SEVERAL PIECES

And then on the next side of the pillar is a rather prim and self-satisfied comment:

I HAVE HEARD SAY WHERE THERE IS
A WILL THERE IS A WAY ONE PERSON
CANNOT ASSIST MANY, BUT MANY CAN
ASSIST A FEW AS THIS PILLAR WILL
SHEW WHICH WAS SUGGESTED
DESIGNED AND ERECTED BY J. BULL
INSPECTOR OF MAILCOACHES, WITH
THE AID OF THIRTEEN POUNDS
SIXTEEN SHILLINGS AND SIXPENCE
RECEIVED BY HIM FROM FORTY ONE
SUBSCRIBERS IN THE YEAR 1841.
The work of this Pillar was
Executed by JOHN JONES
Marble & Stone Mason Llanddarog
near Carmarthen.
REPAINTED AND RESTORED
BY POSTAL OFFICIALS 1930

PEMBROKESHIRE

Cilwendeg

Shell House (1770s–80s?)
Pigeon House (1835)
SN 225 385

Cilwendeg is just outside Boncath on the B4332. In the park is a pretty but dilapidated shell house, which is supposed to have been built by John Jones in the late 18th century. It used to have a domed roof, but that collapsed and was replaced by a flat one. Most of the decoration has now disappeared, but a knucklebone floor remains. It is interesting to see that in contrast to the Grotto in Pontypool, for example, the Cilwendig grotto has few if any exotic shells, but sticks instead to what could be found on the nearby coast. The bones and teeth used in the patterning add a rustic if somewhat grisly effect. Its rustic front provides one of the most pleasing follies in Wales. But there is more: John Jones's son, Morgan, became even richer than his father and started a model farm at Cilwendig. The counting house was inscribed 'Builded for Morgan Jones 1825', and the pigeon house, 'AD 1835'. This is an elaborate affair, taking its cue in the banding of the façade of the Shell House. It has a broad front, with a central tower and two wings connecting to side pavilions. Most typical is the pronounced banding, and there

Pigeon House, Cilwendeg

are round arched windows and doors everywhere. The tower held the doves; the turkeys and hens, geese and ducks were located in the other parts. The eyecatcher is screened at the front by an extraordinary display of 6ft (1.8m) tall railing, carved from slate. Everything is much decayed.

Maenclochog

Temple Druid (c.1795)
SN 650 170

John Nash, whose practice at Carmarthen helped him to become one of the most fashionable architects in the late 18th and early 19th centuries, was very active in Wales. Mention has already been made of the now demolished Aberystwyth tower and Clytha Castle in Gwent, and c.1795 he built a fanciful hunting lodge (now ruined) called Temple Druid at Maenclochog , for Henry Bulkeley.

Manorowen

Gazebo (18th century)
SM 940 360

In 1797 the area around Fishguard was in turmoil: the French had landed. Their plan had been to take Bristol, but they had to make do with Fishguard, or at least they tried to. Two ships full of pardoned thieves and murderers were landed at Strumble Head, but instead of pressing on, the French had an improvised drinking session from what they had looted on the farms. They eventually made their disorderly way to Fishguard, but their advance was checked by several misconceptions. The sight of the red-robed Welsh womenfolk made them think these must be British soldiers, and one woman even captured several French soldiers by threatening them with a pitchfork.

Another ruse was the garden gazebo at Manorowen, southwest of Fishguard. Some of the French mistook the little kiosk on top of a garden wall for the tower of a stronghold, and they took flight. Eventually the whole charade came to an end at Goodwick, were the yeomanry appeared, and the 1400-strong French invasion force capitulated. Once again, Wales saved England from the menace of the French.

Marloes

Clock Tower (1896)
SM 790 080

There is a good clock tower at Marloes, which is the laver bread (puréed boiled, then fried, seaweed—delicious with bacon) capital of the world. The inscription reads:

IN MEMORY OF WILLIAM
FOURTH BARON OF KENSINGTON
WHO DIED OCTOBER 1896
THIS CLOCK TOWER
WAS ERECTED BY MEMBERS
OF THE PEMBROKESHIRE
LIBERAL ASSOCIATION

He should have eaten more laver bread.

Milford Haven

Castle Hall Grotto (c.1800)
SM 910 050

Castle Hall, which was demolished in 1938, is supposed to have been the earliest house in the Hindu or Indian style in Britain. It had been acquired by the Admiralty in 1924 and was used as a depot until 1990. Some of the original layout remains, however, of which the most enigmatic is a longish crypt of

Castle Hall Grotto

whitewashed stone, at the end of an ornamental lake. It may have been the grotto, but there is nothing there—no shells, no bones, only gloom and dampness.

Orielton

Banqueting Tower (18th century)
SR 950 980

The brick, three-storey-high, classical banqueting tower at Orielton, south of Pembroke, is an empty shell. Despite its ivy-cladding, it stands quivering on the edge of a field and appears to do a Pisa on us. This building will not be long with us. No architect. No date.

The Banqueting Tower at Orielton

Picton Castle

Grotto (late 18th century)
SN 020 135

Mrs Morgan liked Picton Castle and its grounds. She said so in her *A Tour to Milford Haven* (1795). She was particularly pleased that Picton Castle was 'on the banks of a river' but noted that it was on the other hand: 'too far removed from it to be incommoded with damps, or the incroachments or rudenefs of mariners.' So she had already been to Milford Haven then. She was also much pleased by Picton's folly:

'In a part of the grounds there is an elegant fummer-house, called The Belvedere. From the top of this you see every thing in perspective that I have described. Under it is an arched way, through which you pafs to other parts of the grounds. From the roof of thefe arches hang long incruftations of the wall, which are exactly like large icicles, except that they are not tranfparent. This, I fuppofe, is an accidental circumftance; but it adds greatly to the beauty of the place. There are nitches in it, defigned for ftatues, but there are none in them, for what reafon I know not.'

This arched way, or grotto, was to be the downfall of the belvedere. The tower was built on the foundations of the original medieval Picton Castle. The grotto was right underneath it and so undermined the belvedere that it fell through the tunnel, half of which one can still see. To the east are also the ruins of a brick gazebo, pedimented, with a round window, but much dilapidated.

Slebech

Envies Despite Belvedere (late 18th century)
Church (1840s)
SN 030 150

Slebech Park is Picton Castle's immediate neighbour. In the wilds of the park is a ruined belvedere, classical and square, of which it was already noted in the early 19th century that it had seen better times and that only an intriguing snippet of an inscription was to be seen: '…Envies Despite…' One wonders—John Calvert of Swansea had a dispute in 1779 over his invoices for building Slebech Hall. Its owner was a John Symmons. A troublesome man perhaps given to writing weird inscriptions.

The Russian Baron de Rutzen had no such troubles. Somehow he came into possession of Slebech, and in the 1840s he

had himself a brand-new church built by Joseph Henry Good, who was the then Surveyor to the Commissioners for Building New Churches. There was an old, ruined church near the house (and it is still there), but de Rutzen had to have his edifice, complete with an enormous spire, right beside the road from Carmarthen to Haverfordwest. It was all 'to the glory of the De Rutzens and in memory of God'. The medieval ruins are doing great, the new church is subsiding.

Stepaside

Summerhouse (1730)
SN 120 060

To each his own: Marloes may be the pivot of laver bread production, but Kilgetty village, near Stepaside, brought most of the anthracite Wales had to offer to light. Kilgetty Park is just on the A477, and so is its ruined summerhouse, once part of a formal garden.

The summerhouse is of an interesting design. It is semicircular and built of rough stone, but it has a lily-white front consisting of three arches. At the back is a square stair turret, which must have led to the missing second elevation. That is not the only thing that is missing: the arcade has been broken away and was carted off a few years ago, the very same arcade probably that Thomas Lloyd found mentioned in the accounts of 1730 and on whom a mason called Aubrey was employed 'carving capitals for a summerhouse'.

St David's

Tower (19th century)
SM 751 248

A Victorian tower in the ground of the Warpool Court Hotel offers not much more than the usual castellations. Built into a wall, it is just an overzealous gazebo.

St Ishmael's

Malakof Tower (c. 1855–60)
Butler's House
Spray Wall
SM 834 073

Malakof, Malakoff, Malakov or Malakow—it's all the same. We had always wondered why Britain had no Malakof towers, when there are at least three in Belgium: La Tour Malakof (1855) in La Rochette, Liège; Malakofftoren (c.1855) at Lembeek, Brabant; and the former military prison at Kamp

Beverlo (1856), Limburg, which was taken down in 1950. In addition, the cooling towers for the coal mines in Dutch Limburg were nicknamed Malakof towers. Malakof, in case you were wondering why every European country should have one, is the name of a fortress at Sebastopol, where there was a hard, long and bloody battle. We have Sebastopol Terraces instead. There doesn't seem to be a prototype Malakof—the ones at Beverlo and La Rochette were round, and the St Ishmael's example more resembles the square tower at Lembeek.

The Welsh Malakof is perched on the cliffs and presents a stunning sea view. It is Gothick in so far that it has pointed windows and rough-and-ready castellations, and an outside stone stair leads to the second storey. The tower, which is on the Trewarren Estate at Monk Haven, is owned by the Warren-Davies family, which started embellishing the grounds in the 1830s. An embattled estate cottage, in the same stones-but-no-sticks style can, although ruined, still be seen. It is called the Butler's House.

On the beach is a tall wall, again castellated and of rubble, built not to hold off pirates but to keep the seaspray from invading Trewarren.

Butter Hill Shell House (19th century)
SM 830 075

Butter Hill, just north of St Ishmael's, has long since been left to its own devices and is going fast, although there is talk of it being restored. The part to restore first is the small shell house or, better, shell seat in the grounds. The semicircular structure is open at the front, but covered by a small dome, the ceiling of which has been decorated with bands of coloured shellwork radiating from its centre. *Pavilions in Peril* in 1987 anticipated the imminent collapse of this little bijou, but a later inspection in the mid-1990s found that it was still standing, although its condition had worsened considerably.

Butter Hill Shell House

St Petrox

Garden Seat (c.1832)
Grotto (18th century)
SR 970 970

The grotto may just, only just, be by William Thomas, but the garden seat, we're afraid, we have to give to Jeffry Wyatville.

Last things first. Wyatville made some improvements (rebuilding the house, a new and large bridge) for the 1st Earl of Cawdor at St Petrox's Stackpole Court. The three-arched Garden Seat is classical enough to have been designed by Wyatville as well. Good. But in another part of the park (the house has gone) is a little grotto next to a rough arch, and both are made of volcanic stone. Now, we would like to have this building designed by William Thomas, a Pembroke architect who died in 1800. In 1782 he designed part of Stackpole Court, which is nothing spectacular, but he was just the man to have made the grotto as well. Thomas designed a Gothick temple for Lord Shelburne, made a design for a column at Runnymede as a monument to William III, presented a drawing for a temple in Staffordshire, and in 1783 published a book of architectural designs, with a grotto among them. It must be his.

Tenby

Temple of the Winds (1922)
SS 130 000

Something seems amiss in this part of Wales. As we go south towards Tenby, the village names begin to change, and instead of the familiar Pontrhydygroes and Llanfihangel-y-pennant we get alien names, such as Yerbeston, Saundersfoot, Lydstep and Sunny Hill. This is Little-England-beyond-Wales. Like Gower, it was settled centuries ago by English speakers coming in from the sea. Little Welsh is spoken here, but some names retain their pre-invasion origins.

On Bowman's Point, Tenby, is Clovers, a house that replaced the bungalow of the dancer Jessie Allen. There is an amphitheatre here, where Jessie Allen had plays and music performed, and next to it stands the Temple of the Winds, a cupola on eight columns and topped by a brass bell. There used to be glass wind chimes hanging from the roof, tinkling away in the sea breeze. Both temple and amphitheatre were designed by Alan Strawbridge RA in 1922.

At Fern House in nearby Penally is a 19th-century gazebo.

GLAMORGAN

Glamorgan remains easily the most densely populated area of Wales, the bedrock of Welsh prosperity, the most savagely hit in times of recession and the archetypal image Wales offers of rainwashed, grey slate terraced houses, scarring once-beautiful valleys populated by a short dark race whose concept of heaven is a singing rugby team. Like all assumptions, it has scant basis in fact, being an amalgam of centuries-old English prejudices and fear. What is undeniable is that Glamorgan's mineral wealth is not matched by its architectural glory. The 18th- and 19th-century coal- and steel-masters were far more intent on stripping the country than on constructing fancies and conceits. It is not surprising, therefore, that these three counties provide only a dozen or so follies between them and that most of them should be found in the rural (and Anglicized) Gower, west of Swansea.

Aberdulais

Aqueduct (19th century)
SS 760 990

An old tinplate works at Aberdulais has one of the most baffling edifices in this area. The National Trust came across an ornamental and utterly useless Victorian aqueduct while restoring the works, the cradle of industry in South Wales. The site archaeologist could only class it as a folly because it seemed to be purposeless; a folly on an industrial site is a very rare creature.

Black Pill

Clyne Castle Follies (19th century)
SS 615 905

Behind the bay from the strangely named village of Mumbles (the whole area is now officially known as The Mumbles) is Swansea's playground, the lovely Gower peninsula, which offers the city dweller secluded coves and beaches, quiet country lanes, wild walks and follies. For the benefit of any locals who may read this, we would advise visitors that the quiet secluded beaches can be found only in mid-week January and February—for the rest of the year the Gower is one big traffic jam.

The bay road turns off towards the Gower at Black Pill, before one gets to Mumbles, and just by the turn-off is a small, low cottage with castellated ends, looking for all the world like an eyecatcher lodge. Surrounded by bungalows and garages, it looks more out of place in its modern setting than it must have done when it was an estate cottage for Clyne Castle, the home of the coal-mining Vivians/Vyvyans.

The house itself, built in the late 18th century for W.G. Vivian by William Jernegan (see Kittle), is now a college, but the park—a landscaped ravine, stunningly beautiful in early May when the rhododendrons are out—is now public and conceals an extraordinary little structure that still has us totally bewildered. It is a stone spiral staircase with an iron railing, wrapped around a thin column little more than a newel post, huddled among some trees at the bottom of the valley. It can hardly be a look-out—the site is totally wrong, because even if there were no trees surrounding it there would be no view. In addition, it is only some 15ft (4.6m) high. It is inexplicable but pleasing.

A thin, rubbly, castellated clock tower up by the house completes this little trio of Clyne Park follies, small, undistinguished but oddly memorable.

Cardiff

Cardiff Castle (1865 onwards)
ST 180 7661
Castell Coch (1875 onwards)
ST 133 827

Cardiff is a brash, ugly, exciting city, confident in its status to such an extent that it doesn't feel like a British provincial city. It has all the manners and charm of an American state capital, which, in a way, it resembles. Two hundred years ago Cardiff barely existed. The population in 1804 was under 2000; in 1871 it was 50,000, and it doubled in size in the next ten years. Now well over a quarter of a million people live in Cardiff, and the city's growth was due in the most part to the efforts of one man, the 2nd Marquess of Bute. Bute it was who built the docks that turned Cardiff into the largest coal port in the world; his son, the 3rd Marquess, built follies.

This is not to diminish the achievements of John Crichton-Stuart, 3rd Marquess of Bute; he was a remarkable man. Tall, dark, handsome, uncontrollably rich and gifted with a formidable intellect, he had a passion for language and literature, for building and the Scriptures, and of these several interests Cardiff benefited from his buildings. Cardiff Castle had been built in 1080, but its only claim to fame was that it was the prison where William the Conqueror's eldest son spent the last 30 years of his life. Henry Holland and Lancelot Brown had been employed in 1777 by Lord Mount Stuart to

scholarship was no less, and at this time he converted from Presbyterianism to Roman Catholicism. The sensuous, sumptuous grandeur of the castle design is likely to have been the product of the enthusiasms of both men; the distinguished architect and the fabulously wealthy client, half his age.

In 1871 Bute and Burges embarked on a new project, the 'restoration' of Castell Coch, a 13th-century ruin on a hillside at Tongwynlais, 5 miles north of Cardiff. Little remained of the original castle, but this did not deter Burges. In the following year he produced plans showing a sort of miniature Azay-le-Rideau, complete with conical roofs on the three towers. Despite his acknowledged scholarship, there was little doubt that the original Castell Coch did not

Castell Coch, Tongwynlais

rebuild it in the fashionable Gothic style, but Bute decided to turn it into a palace. When he was 18 years old he employed William Burges, one of the greatest—certainly the most individualistic—of all Victorian architects, to rebuild it. Over the next 16 years Burges added a mighty tower, state apartments and a succession of galleries and rooms running along the west side of the castle walls. The original keep itself was relegated to little more than a picturesque garden feature, a genuine sham castle on a mound in the garden. Lavishly decorated both inside and out, even the statues and shields in niches on the tower walls are gaily painted; the whole ensemble is more French than Welsh. Although Burges was renowned for his knowledge of French Gothic, Bute's

remotely resemble the proposed plans drawn up by Burges. Bute, however, was delighted, and work started in 1875.

The end result is magnificent by any standards. The building is now looked after by Cadw, and it is kept, as one would expect, in superb condition. It is a compact, tight, neat little castlet, and more than any other reason—more than the fanciful reconstruction, more than the enormous expense, more than the extravagant decoration—that's what made it a folly. The banqueting hall and the large drawing room are designed to cater for a large number of guests, but the only sleeping accommodation is the lord's bedroom and the lady's bedroom. The castle was obviously unusable, and Bute very seldom visited it. In a country where picturesqueness is the rule rather than the exception, this is Wales's most picturesque folly.

Lighthouse-cum-Clock Tower
(early 20th century)
ST 200 770

That the Roath Park clock tower is the best in Wales is due to its curiously isolated position, in the outskirts of the city, yet on an island in a lake. It serves as a memorial to R.F Scott, the Arctic explorer. By its shape it is a lighthouse, but there is no light—never has been—and by its function it is a clock tower, although it is, of course, mainly an ornament topped by a sailing boat as a weathervane. Of whitewashed stone, this is a delightful eyecatcher, but maintenance of clock and tower has to be taken seriously, as does the twice-yearly switching to summer- and wintertime: a park attendant has to row over in a boat to perform his duties.

Glyntaff

Towers (1838)
ST 080 880

Four miles up the road from Castell Coch brings us to Glyntaff, just outside Pontypridd, and to perhaps the most eccentric figure in Welsh history. In 1838 Dr William Price of Llantrisant, druid, Chartist, pioneer of cremation, who fathered three children in his eighties (no need for Viagra in Wales), who called his first-born Iesu Grist and cremated him in a barrel of petroleum jelly when he died of convulsions, who wore a fox-skin cap and a green tunic edged in scarlet and embroidered with druidical symbols when treating his patients, who went barefoot by preference—in 1838 this Dr Price decided to build a Druidical Temple of Harmony at Glyntaff, the site, so he thought, of an ancient burial ground of the druids. He collected £137 17s 11d from his fervent supporters and started his temple by building two squat, white-stuccoed towers to flank the gateway, which was aligned directly with the Rocking Stone on Pontypridd Common. Unfortunately, Lady Llanover got to hear about this ambitious project, and as she owned the land on which Dr Price was busy building, she not unnaturally made strenuous objections. He had

Dr. Price's Towers at Glyntaff

managed to finish the towers and the money before he was stopped and sent back to Llantrisant, where he became a Chartist. The towers remain, now part of a safe, non-druidical housing estate, which accepts cremation as a matter of course.

At Pontypridd, beside the River Taff, is an 8ft (2.4m) obelisk, claimed to be a copy of an obelisk in Cairo that has something to do with one of the pharaohs. We couldn't find our Egyptian Colvin, but the monument was paid for by latterday pharaohs, the Crawshays, the iron kings of Wales. Despite numerous expensive expeditions to Egypt in order to research this on our readers' behalf, we have failed to verify the reference. It would be tempting to link this to the more interesting of the Crawshays, Robert Thompson. But see under Vaynor.

Jersey Marine

Tower (1860s)
SS 730 940

At Jersey Marine along the B4290, the pitiful remnants of a 19th-century pleasure park huddle hopelessly around a pub. There's a plain but oddly attractive little hexagonal, four-storey tower with elongated castellations around the parapet which apparently started life as a camera obscura and is now roofless and floorless. Next to the pub is a pretty little (private) flower and kitchen garden, at one end of which is the crested back wall of an 1878 racquets court. The sound of vanished laughter haunts these light-hearted confections long after the

Racquets Court at Jersey Marine

heart has left them.

Kittle

Tower (1770s–80s)
SS 560 890

Near Kittle, the A4118, which is the backbone road of the Gower, passes the elegant Kilvrough Manor, and on the opposite hill to the house is a drystone walled enclosure with a tiny, embattled, round tower tacked on one corner. Rubble-built with faint Gothicisms, it may be by the Swansea architect William Jernegan, who built Kilvrough itself in the 1770s. Gymkhanas are sometimes held in the field, muffled tannoys announcing: 'Miss Tracy Thomas took a tumble at Tower Turn.'

The Mumbles

Grottoloo (1899–1913)
SS 623 877

The Grottoloo is near Mumbles Pier, which was started in 1898 and is, of course, complete with winter garden, new railway and other necessities for a good day out. Between 1899 and 1913 the public conveniences were built, a broad, two-storey, castellated façade with a central pavilion. Windows all along the lower storey give it a lighter appearance than its rough, grotto-like exterior would suggest. The entrances are at the ends of the façade.

The Grottoloo is a mongrel: the Gothick, rustic and classical styles are welded together into an awkward but strangely pleasing building, which could have been easily adapted to other uses. One source said it was originally built as the stationmaster's house for the Mumbles to Swansea railway—the world's first passenger-carrying railroad, which was operating by 1808 (horsedrawn, not steam). Whatever its original function, it is now the most glorious public convenience in Britain.

Neath

Gnoll Follies (18th century)
Ivy Tower (1795)
SS 780 980

At Neath turn right for Tonna, then right again up a small road on the outskirts of the town. About a mile along the road on the left you will glimpse the Ivy Tower, which is superbly sited, overlooking industrial Neath. Little ivy remains (obviously someone is prepared to look after it), but the building remains enigmatic. Some say it is a belvedere, some say a dance hall with stained-glass windows, but the big fireplace in the basement suggests another dining-room-with-

a-view, Kymin style. It is circular, castellated, rubbly, only one storey plus basement, with inordinately large Gothic pointed windows surmounted by blind quatrefoils. Perhaps the story of the stained glass is true, and the view would have been enjoyed from a flat wooden roof behind the castellations.

Since this was written not only has new light been shed on the Ivy Tower, but a whole series of buildings and ornaments has almost literally come above ground at what is now known as the Gnoll Estate, mainly near the hillside southwest of the Ivy Tower. Neath Council is to be commended for its splendid work, which was started by Steven O'Donovan around 1992.

Gnoll had its first days of glory in the late 17th century when Sir Humphrey Mackworth, recently knighted but relatively penniless, married the daughter of Sir Herbert Evans of Gnoll. Mary Evans had four sisters, but they

Ivy Tower, Neath

all died before her, leaving Mary (and Mackworth) with a fortune based on the copper smelting works at Neath. Mackworth decorated his estate with many ponds, which were both ornamental and functional as they supplied water needed for his industries. When he died in 1728, his son Herbert took over and proceeded to carry out more schemes for embellishing the estate, among them the Mosshouse Wood Cascades of 1740, which are believed to be the longest in Britain. They are astounding—sheet after sheet of water tumbling all the way down the hill, flowing to eternity. The cascade starts near a gazebo above a carefully constructed rough cave. At the bottom a path leads towards the site of the house (which was demolished in the 1950s), and here there is something called Half-house Folly or The Temple, rough-and-ready again and castellated.

A little further on is the Grand Cascade, formal this time, which rises up from a lake

The Mosshouse Wood Cascades, Gnoll Park

about 600ft (183m) in length and is undergoing restoration. Excavated under the direction of Steven O'Donovan, the water courses are designed so that water flowing over each level plays a different note; a harmonious concept.

Researches have also unveiled the Ivy Tower's date—1795. It was built for Molly, widow of the last Mackworth, but apparently to the designs of the architect John Johnson, who also built the new Gnoll Castle in the 1770s in the medieval style. The Ivy Tower is separate from the rest of the park, which is now open to the public.

Penrice

Penrice Wall (1780)
SS 500 870

The Penrice Wall is remarkable: over 200ft (60m) of sham ruin, with towers and battlements and a gate—not to scale—and gymkhanas behind, and even an occupied house incorporated in the façade. It looks real and it looks as if Cromwell slighted it, but the whole crazy structure was built by Anthony Keck in 1780 for Thomas Talbot of Penrice Castle (which is a real 13th-century castle at the bottom of the valley).

Reynoldston

Druid's Circle (mid-19th century)
SS 480 890

At the far end of the Gower a disappointing fake stone circle of 12 stones stood in the old grounds behind Stouthall Park at Reynoldston, right by the road going up to the village. It was small, boring and hidden behind a hedge. The stones were erected by John Lucas of Stouthall around the middle of the 19th century. On the other side of the road is a much more interesting object: a tomb in the middle of the field with a tree growing through it, apparently the grave of a favourite horse. There used to be a grotto as well.

The stones, or at least 11 out of the full dozen, have now disappeared, stolen in May 1996. They may have been small, but they weighed half a ton each and reached a full 4ft (1.2m) in height. Some say they were transported by mysterious force; others believe they were either stolen by would-be druids or jobbing gardeners doing up a rock garden.

Swansea

Sketty Chapter House (c.1806)
SS 630 940

West of Swansea City is Sketty Park; the house was pulled down in 1975. William Jernegan built Sketty Park around 1806, and, as at the tower at Kilvrough, Kittle, he may have been responsible for this belvedere. It is less rough-and-ready than most South Wales folly towers, wallowing in the luxury of having Gothick windows, with even some of the tracery left, and buttresses, but there is no evidence of any good castellations. The belvedere gives an ecclesiastical impression, not least because of its magnificent stone vault, which has rightly been likened to the one in the Chapter House of Salisbury Cathedral. Ten years ago one could still see the inscription 'Esto Perpetua', wishing the belvedere a long life. The most extraordinary thing about the folly is its present location: it is stranded in the middle of the most prosaic middle-class housing estate imaginable, an architectural jewel set off by drabness all around.

Sketty Chapter House

GWYNEDD

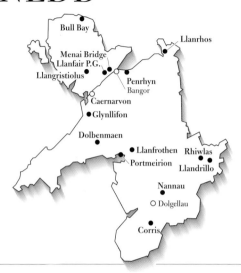

ANGLESEY

Bull Bay

Sham Roman Baths (early 20th century)
SH 430 940

At Bull Bay, north of Amlwch, a sea-bathing establishment in the Roman style was built by a Mr Fowler—or a Mr Evan Pritchard, accounts differ—at the turn of the century. It was still operating between the wars, but despite the attractions of changing rooms and a sweeping great entrance, Mr Fowler's potential customers found they could get just as wet without paying him a fee. All that remains is part of the enclosing wall and the circular, whitewashed, cone-topped turrets at either side of the old entrance, opposite a pub. Amazingly, the spot is still noted on maps as 'Roman Baths'.

Llanfair P.G.

Marquess of Anglesey's Column (1816)
SH 540 720

Outside Llanfair P.G. in Anglesey, beloved of car dealers for some reason and the town with the longest name in Britain (oh, all right then—Llanfairpwllgwyngyllgogerychwyrndrobwll-llantysiliogogogoch), is the Marquess of Anglesey's Column. The marquess was a brave soldier, whose claim to immortality reposes in the response made by Wellington to his strangled cry at Waterloo: 'By God Sir, I've lost me leg!' 'By God sir, so you have!'

Overlooking the Menai Strait, the fluted Tuscan column is 91ft (28m) high, and inside a spiral staircase of 115 steps climbs to the open parapet surrounding the pedestal on which stands the statue of the marquess. The sculptor was Mathew Noble, but the statue was not raised until Rear-Admiral Lord Clarence Paget, son of the marquess, supervised the operation on 24 November 1860. The column itself, which had been there since 1816, was designed by Thomas Harrison of Moel Famau fame. The inscription on the base of the column reads:
'The Inhabitants of the counties of Anglesey and Caernarvon have erected this column in grateful commemoration of the distinguished military achievements of their countryman Henry William Marquess of Anglesey the leader of the British cavalry in Spain throughout the arduous campaign of 1807 and the second-in-command of the armies confederated against France at the memorable Battle of Waterloo on the 16th June 1815.'
Waterloo was on the 18th, but never mind.

Nelson Monument (1816)
SH 540 710

From the top of the Marquess of Anglesey's Column one can see the Nelson Monument, just by the Britannia Bridge and almost in the water. Its slogan, facing out over the Menai Strait in the heart of Wales, reads:
ENGLAND (SIC) EXPECTS THAT EVERY MAN WILL DO HIS DUTY.

On the plinth is a large statue of Horatio Nelson, by the aforementioned Clarence Paget, Sculptor, 1873. Paget was not only an old salt but a trained sculptor as well. On the west side it says 'FELL AT TRAFALGAR 1805'; on the east it repeats this in Welsh 'ALADDWYN YN TRAFALGAR 1805'. The letters are incused in the slate and infilled with a strange yellow stone—mauve slate with bright yellow lettering gives a pleasingly odd effect.

There's a little entrance lobby and a metal ladder with 13 rungs leading up to a small viewing platform at the base of the statue, about 15ft (4.6m) high. Admiral Paget wanted to prove that a large monument or statue could be made out of local raw materials instead of marble, so Nelson was chosen as an apt subject on which to experiment.

Plas Newydd Gothick Boathouses
(early 19th century)
SH 510 700

James Wyatt provided the designs for Plas Newydd late in the 18th century. His assistant, Joseph Potter, was busy finishing what his master had planned for the next quarter of a century, so the two delightful boathouses (or rather landing stages) that are built into the bank might just be Potter's. Mimicking toy forts, they are very simple, with battlements, of course, and little pointed windows. The model farm, also in the Gothic mode, is quite a sight.

Llangristiolus
Round Lodge (19th century)
SH 430 740

A round, Gothic lodge along the B4422.

Menai Bridge
Glyngarth

The circular Victorian crenellated folly at Myn-y-Twr (House of the Tower), Glyngarth, Anglesey, overlooks the Menai Strait to Telford's suspension bridge.

CAERNARVON

Dolbenmaen
Bryncir Tower (1821/1859)
SH 523 434

There is a particularly beautiful battlemented folly tower at Dolbenmaen on the Bryncir Estate. It is square with chamfered corners, steps at the front and a driveway leading up to it in a curving sweep. There are six storeys, with a staircase climbing up between the outer and inner walls.

The date 1821 is on the keystone above the arched Gothic entrance doors.

The situation, like almost everywhere in this glorious county, is very fine. It was built by Joseph Huddart, who 'had great schemes for converting the Brynkir demesne into a paradise in the wilderness—a gentleman's country seat worthy of the name'. He had inherited a fortune from his

Nelson Monument

father, who had patented a new kind of rope for sailors, but by making an extraordinary proviso in his will he managed to lose the lot for his family. The will stipulated that whoever inherited Bryncir had to build new additions to the house, the purpose clearly being to fulfil Huddart's desire to found a mighty dynasty. Unfortunately, the income from the patent rope diminished as the years passed, but the codicil remained, so that new wings were perpetually being built as old ones crumbled away through lack of money to maintain them. The house snaked its way through Snowdonia, sloughing wings as it went. It is now in ruins and mich of the estate has been bought by the London Borough of Hillingdon, which uses the still extant stable block as a base for outward bound courses. Sir Clough Williams-Ellis appears on the scene: in the mid-1930s he offered Bryncir Tower as a home to Bertrand Russell, but got exceedingly short shrift!

In 1994 Bryncir Tower was subjected to a very fine restoration and conversion into a luxurious holiday home by the architects Adam and Frances Voelcker for Frances Williams. A stone with '1859' carved in it came to light during the restoration works, and this refers to the fact that three storeys had been added in that year, making what must have looked like a tall pavilion into a proper tower. This also explains why only the upper storeys had cast-iron window frames. It seems that Huddart originally intended his four-storey pavilion/tower as a place of study for his sons. Four storeys, four sons—or were they allowed in successively? The addition of the extra floors could also be an affirmation of the probate story, with the new building fulfilling the conditions of the will.

Glynllifon

Folly Group (18th—20th century)
SH 450 550

In the park of Glynllifon College, formerly the home of the Lords Newborough, is a standard octagonal battlemented folly tower, the sides sloping in for the first storey and vertical for the second storey, with an external stair turret rising one level higher—but no stairs, when we first visited. The tower has now been restored and reroofed; the lower room has a little fireplace, slate seats, slate windowsills and a plaque above the door reading 'Williamsbourg Fort'. There is a little circular viewing point in front with a slate floor, rather nicely made, and a little

chamber under the viewpoint has 'Magazine' inscribed above the door. A short tunnel leads from the little fort to a ballroom in a farmyard.

All this sounds like a pleasant, if rather unexceptional, folly tower, but few people realize that this was our first line of defence against an anticipated French invasion in the 1770s. Sir Thomas Wynn's predilection for toy forts and private armies soon grew to unmanageable proportions. Between 1773 and 1776 he created Fort Belan and extended Fort Williamsbourg into the real thing: Belan guarded the western approaches to the Menai Strait and was even provided with a dock and all the necessary equipment for maintaining a man o'war, while the area behind the first folly was extended to make a formidable redoubt. Fort Belan cost him over £30,000 to build, and at the same time he had more than 400 paid volunteers in his private regiment, the Royal Carnarvon Grenadiers.

Follies at Glynllifon have accumulated over the years, right up to the present day. The park, now owned by Gwynedd Council,

Williamsbourg Fort, Glynllifon

has acquired a recent grotto mound, built out of slate and named Mynydd y Plant (the Children's Mountain). Slim people can squeeze inside a narrow passageway, which doglegs to a small, central circle, open to the sky above, where toys were embedded in the slate walls. Most of them have now been prised out, and the skylight is used as a convenient receptacle for rubbish.

Beyond the great house, built by the

Shropshire architect Edward Haycock in 1836–49 (and offered for sale in 1998 for an absurdly low £500,000), is a formal lawn with fountains, apparently still in working order though seldom used. On the east side is the locked entrance to the grotto, a damp and repellent traipse into the side of a hill to a large, plain, circular cavern, completely undecorated.

To the west is a most baffling structure, called Melin y Plant (the Children's Mill) by the council but exhibiting the characteristcs of a nymphaeum. A raised walkway crosses the ruins of this enigmatic erection, clearly intended to have water flowing through its arches and gullies. Child-sized rooms are dotted here and there, and a covered path leads through the building to what would, in Catholic countries, have been a shrine room, but here leads simply to further bafflement. Further research needs to be carried out on this strange building, unique in Britain.

Further from the house the park becomes a wooded, hilly wilderness, and here among the cascades is the modern amphitheatre, slate built from the Greek model and delightfully peppered with inscriptions, some in English. Above the tumbling river in the most sublime setting is the rustic hermitage, or Eglwys y Cwn (the Dogs' Church), an octagonal, bark-covered temple by a now-vanished pet cemetery. Deep in the woods behind the hermitage is a mysterious system of narrow canals and waterways of unknown purpose.

A mile away across the farmland is the circular Newborough Mausoleum, a structure so huge and embedded into the landscape that it looks more Chaldean than Celtic. Work was abandoned in the 1830s, and it never served as a tomb. We climbed its echoing staircase up through vast, hollow, empty chambers to the top of the building (more like a meadow than a roof), with a small grove in the northeast quadrant and views to heaven.

The estate village of Llandwrog has the Harp Hotel, a splendid pub with two octagonal towers and a praiseworthy inscription in English and Welsh carved on a huge slate tablet:

ON LEVEL LAND, THE FINEST INN,
WITH PLENTY OF FOOD AND BEER WITHIN,
AND EVERY HOUR OF THE DAY
THE SONG OF BIRDS, TO MAKE ONE GAY.
ON HOLIDAYS AND SUNDAYS TOO
BEWARE OF DRUNKENNESS, BE TRUE.
ENJOY YOUR LIFE, BUT DON'T BETRAY
THE GOOD OLD BEER, COME WHAT MAY.

Eglwys y Cwn

One day in 1969 Lord Snowdon took a day off from stage-managing the Investiture of the Prince of Wales at Caernarfon Castle to sail his yacht up and down the Menai Strait. He was a greatly perturbed when a large cannonball shaved his bow. Enraged, he changed tack and headed for shore to confront the perpetrator, to discover a faintly embarrassed 7th Baron Newborough. 'You nearly killed us out there,' shouted Snowdon. 'Well, I didn't know it was you,' Newborough responded petulantly. In memory of his exploits at Fort Belan (obviously he didn't learn from his brush with Snowdon, because in 1976 he was fined £25 for bringing down the sails of another yacht in the Menai with a cannonball), his funeral in 1998 consisted of his ashes being fired from a cannon on his estate at Rhug. His son Robert Wynn recalled another happy habit reserved particularly for folly-hunters. 'There's a folly in the park, where father would direct guests to go and see a mythical couple, Mr and Mrs Jones. Ringing the doorbell would activate a bucket of water, dousing the poor visitor.'

In recognition of Sir Thomas Wynn's patriotism, King George III, himself none too stable in matters of the mind, gratefully created him Baron Newborough. This achieved, and having mortgaged himself irretrievably to fund his mighty military projects, Lord Newborough became deranged and decamped to Italy, where he married the 13-year-old daughter of a village constable. Architecturally, the Glynllifon story ends here, but who can fail to be stimulated by the revelation that the policeman's daughter turned out to be the heiress to the throne of France? But that's another story, another book…

Llanrhos

Bodysgallen Obelisk (1993)
SH 500 800

On top of Bryn Pydew stands an agreeable little obelisk, 64ft (19.5m) high, erected by the grand hotelier Richard Broyd of Bodysgallen Hall and Hartwell House Hotel (see Buckinghamshire). It nearly didn't make it. Although planning permission had been granted, locals started complaining that the obelisk could be seen for miles. The question why no one objected to the hideous and much taller Vodaphone aerial on another nearby hill brought a sound and logical answer: 'But that's a useful structure!' Quite. Mr Broyd also seems to have permission for a tower. We can't wait.

Penrhyn

Penrhyn Castle (1824–44) Eyecatcher
SH 602 719

Penrhyn Castle is also known as Hopper's Folly and rightly so. This time it isn't the patron, G.H. Dawkins Pennant, 2nd Lord Penrhyn, who is accused of going over the top or getting it totally wrong, but the architect Thomas Hopper. Lord Penrhyn had his mansion, originally designed by Samuel Wyatt, totally renewed in the Norman style, a job that took from the 1820s into the 1840s and cost him over half a million pounds. He had the money: he owned the slate quarries that provided Britain with much of what it needed of this building material.

Egged on by Lord Penrhyn, Hopper, 'who never drank anything stronger than water', produced a startling castle in the Norman-a-go-go style, a celebration of all that could be overdesigned, overpaid and overproduced. But it is Hopper's Llandegai Gate that is perhaps the most pleasing building here: a delightful essay in Norman architecture that almost wilfully seems to miss the point. The detailing is good, the historicity of it just slightly out of tune, or so we are informed by Mowl and Earnshaw.

Benjamin Wyatt had earlier been responsible for many other buildings around Penrhyn, largely because he was Lord Penrhyn's agent. His Penisarnant dairy farm in the Gothic style is supposed to exist south of

Penrhyn Castle Sham Church Eyecatcher

Bethesda, but we have not seen it (and another source insists on it being soundly neo-classical). The large slate quarries are here as well, the bedrock of Penrhyn's fortune.

Slate produced some local wonders too. In St Llandegai churchyard is a very pretty little pyramid, which serves as a memorial to Benjamin Wyatt, his wife and his son Arthur. It is, of course, made of slate. Queen Victoria, when offered one of Lord Penrhyn's showpieces, a slate bed at Penrhyn Castle, remarked 'interesting, but uninviting'.

The little eyecatcher at Penrhyn is a small wall with a large church window, slightly up a slope to the northwest of the castle itself. Five racehorses have been buried in front of it.

MERIONETH

Corris

Little Italy (1978 onwards)
SJ 751 083

'A master plan would have been fatal,' decided Mark Bourne, contemplating his 20-year recreation of the architectural glories of Italy on a third of an acre of Welsh mountainside. Bramante's Tempietto, Palladio's Villa Capra, the Torre Mangia at Siena, the Rialto, the Leaning Tower of Pisa—all are painstakingly recreated and piled on terrace upon terrace surrounding

Bourne's ancient cottage, Carreg Llwyd. For over 20 years Bourne, a retired caravan park owner, has been mixing and pouring concrete to build his three-dimensional holiday postcards, with annual visits to Italy providing the inspiration. 'Mind you, I couldn't live there,' he added, 'there's too much sun. Makes you depressed.'

The garden is a cascade of captions and inscriptions, each building identified and interspersed with quotations from his favourite poets, such as A.E. Housman and Wilfred Owen, carved carefully and deliberately. This is perhaps the most sophisticated *jardin imaginaire* we have encountered; the majority of our concrete revellers would scarcely have heard of Italy, let alone Dante or Borromini. Bourne's work is methodically accurate, given the limitations of his chosen material, and, for a change of pace, parts of the garden have been enhanced with street furniture, road and advertising signs. There is also a small demonstration of various bonds and courses of bricklaying, as well as a selection of bricks laid on their sides so that the various manufacturers' names can be clearly read.

Italy is by no means an obsession. There is an astonishingly good replica pillar from Gaudí's Parc Güell in Barcelona, sparkling with broken glass and ceramics as if by the hand of the master himself. The garden is a homage, not an infatuation. The only mistake Bourne seems to have made is to construct it in a curiously inaccessible location for the hordes of folly enthusiasts who will want to visit it—the nearest place to park more than one car is a couple of miles away, and coaches are out of the question. On second thoughts, what mistake?

Llandrillo

Eyecatcher (c.1870)
SJ 030 360

Barbara Jones was told of an eyecatcher 'built to look like a chapel'. We've been to Llandrillo. Beautiful place. Good pub. Must have been that chapel we saw.

Llanfrothen

Watch Tower (early 20th century)
SH 615 420

Plas Brondanw in the parish of Llanfrothen is the family home of the Williams-Ellises. It is over 500 years old, and the proud boast of the family is that the house has never been bought or sold. To Brondanw the young

Lieutenant Clough Williams-Ellis brought his bride, Amabel Strachey, whose reaction to the wedding present given by his fellow officers is not recorded. In his autobiography Sir Clough recounts the incident with glee:

COMMANDING OFFICER: *Ah! I have been asked by your brother officers of the Welsh Guards to present you with this cheque on their behalf and my own as our wedding present. I don't want you just to blue it on night-clubs or any such nonsense, but to have some lasting memento of our regard. I suggest it should take the form of a silver salver, engraved with our signatures, which would be the usual thing and in order.*

LT. WILLIAMS-ELLIS: *Thank you very much, Sir. That would indeed be delightful. But it so happens that we already have a certain amount of family silver that just lies at the bank or stored away as we have small hope of using it. So might we perhaps choose something else?*

C.O.: *Why, yes, of course, but what—because I should like to know.*

LT. W-E.: *Well, Sir, what I should really like would be a ruin.*

The authors on top of Clough Williams-Ellis's wedding present at Llanfrothen

C.O.: *A ... WHAT?*

LT. W-E.: *A ruin—as an outlook tower. You see, Sir, there happens to be a rocky eminence close above my home on which I have always felt there should be a tower of some sort as a fitting crown and as a superb viewpoint commanding wonderful panoramas from the summit of Snowdon to the sea.*

C.O.: *Well, if you want a ruin, I suppose you had better have a ruin—though it's an odd sort of wedding present, I must say.*

And that is how the watchtower at Plas Brondanw came to be built, although, of course, there are now locals who swear it was put up by Owain Glyndwr. To counteract such silly notions, a plaque has now been put up, giving the history of the folly and adding: 'In the Second World War it was prepared as a local military strongpoint to repel the expected German invasion.'

As is to be expected, Plas Brondanw has received something of the full Williams-Ellis treatment—little bridges, tinplate kiosks, all the frilly bits one can see at Portmeirion as well, including a wonderful two-dimensional tin obelisk to close an allée. It brings the sudden realization that there is really no need for a three-dimensional obelisk if it is seen from only one viewpoint.

Nannau

Arches (1820)
SH 738 200; SH 742 208

Nannau is famous for its Precipice Walk, a 19th-century beauty spot. For us, however, the main attractions are the arches and gateways at Nannau, the ancient seat of the Vaughan family in Llanfachreth, above Dolgellau. At the entrance to Maes-y-Bryner, a farm on the Nannau Estate, a small arch, which joins piers pierced either side with window slits, carries a crudely carved plaque reading:

THIS Arch was finished

The Day

Good KING GEORGE IIIrd

Died

There is also a very good entrance gate to Nannau on the road from Dolgellau to Llanfachreth. Now heavily overgrown, the drive to the house used to go through it to Maes-y-Bryner, through the folly arch and thence to the main house, now a restaurant. Sir Robert Williams Vaughan (1768–1843), who ruled the surrounding countryside with benevolent autocracy for over 50 years, was a progressive estate manager who carried out

An arch at Nannau

many improvements to roads, buildings and farming methods. He built five carriageways radiating from Nannau like the spokes of a wheel and another arch at the entrance to one of these, known locally as 'Y Garreg Fawr' (The Great Rock) because of the huge flat stone that spans the road. It is said to have been brought from Harlech, 20 miles away, and, of course, it was built to provide employment after the Napoleonic wars.

Portmeirion

Folly Village (20th century)
SH 590 372

From this stunningly beautiful corner of the country comes the finest, most elaborate, imaginative and sustained piece of folly work in Great Britain—the village of Portmeirion. The genius of one man built it; its worldwide fame will preserve it.

Sir Clough Williams-Ellis was the architect errant, as he described himself in his autobiography, and it was his dream and his vision that created this extraordinary fantasy town on the little peninsula between the estuaries of the Glaslyn and the Dwyryd. The dream had been with Sir Clough all his life, for initially he had wanted to buy an island on which he could express his architectural thoughts concretely. Unusually for a folly builder, common sense prevailed, and when an uncle offered to sell him the Aberia peninsula he realized at once that this was the ideal site to build his ideas. This part of North Wales has its own micro-climate— we ourselves have sunbathed in Portmeirion in January with the temperature over the 20s—and as a result the estate was already covered with exotic plants when he bought it. With pure Welsh practicality, the first thing Sir Clough did was to open the existing house as an hotel and invite influential

Portmeirion

friends to come and stay. The food, as he admitted, was terrible (and has remained so for long periods), but the natural beauty of the renamed Portmeirion peninsula captivated the guests so much that word quickly spread and the hotel became a fashionable success.

Sir Clough was able to embark seriously on an unprogrammed expansion, building the major features of the village, such as the campanile and the dome, quickly, like an artist delineating a scene with a few bold brush strokes before filling in the detail. From 1926 to the end of his long and fruitful life he added continuously to the village, his 'home for fallen buildings', as he called it. There are columns, a shell grotto (with a very low roof, the top of which doubles as the Belvedere Outlook), arches, fountains, statues, paths, the Gloriette, steps, cottages, balconies, cobbles, gateways and every other imaginable form of explorable architecture. There is colour, too. Not content with the grey-washed Merioneth stone and slate, Sir Clough picked a Mediterranean paint pot and poured its rainbow colours over the village. It is a jewel in a magnificent setting, a gem, inspired partly by medieval Tuscan hill towns and partly by Portofino, as Sir Clough wrote:

How should I not have fallen for Portofino? Indeed its image remained with me as an almost perfect example of the man-made adornment and use of an exquisite site …

Portmeirion today is so much more than Portofino today. The very random variety of the village has its own cohesiveness, whereas Portofino's undisputed beauty has been masked by its obtrusive commercialism, the overpainted face of a beauty long past her prime.

Rhiwlas

Mausoleum (19th century)
SH 930 360

At Rhiwlas, just north of Bala, is a mausoleum built by a horse. An unlikely story, but one that has given pleasure to generations of Bala schoolchildren, because the inscription clearly states:

I bless the good horse Bendigo
Who built this tomb for me.

Bendigo, of course, was a famous racehorse owned by the Thelwall Prices; his winnings paid for the mausoleum.

Rhiwlas Mausoleum

MONMOUTH

Monmouthshire was a county administered jointly by Wales and England until the county changes of 1972, when its name was changed to Gwent and it became firmly Welsh. Now it's Monmouth again; still Welsh.

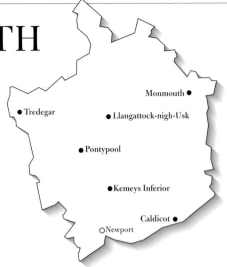

Caldicot

Dewstow Tunnels and Ferneries (c.1900–10)
ST 480 890

Our grotto expert Vernon Gibberd came back with a glowing report on Dewstow House near Caldicot. Some aficionado had gone the whole hog and dug a tunnel system under the lawn, or rather, as Mr Gibberd suggests, they must have dug out the field, laid the plan, and then covered it up with concrete roofing and put the original field back on top of that. The underground corridors eventually emerge into a small rocky retreat, built much like the tunnels itself, but open, and with a small pond. Everything is made from artificial stone, ruled not to be Pulhamite—but one is allowed to say 'in the Pulhamite manner'.

Near to the house itself are two ferneries, both damaged, but still (or rather because of it) picturesque.

Kemeys Inferior

Sham Castle (1807)
ST 384 922

Off the A449, at Kemeys Inferior, stands a bog-standard folly tower, which was built in 1807 (altered in 1914) with the traditional view of seven counties. It is now a private house, and sightseers are actively discouraged. The standardization of tower design among folly builders is a surprise with which one never quite comes to terms. Towers are either wildly eccentric or stultifyingly predictable, and Kemeys falls into the latter category. Imagine a plain Perpendicular church tower, stripped of ornament and delicacy, rectangular, with an octagonal stair turret at one corner, higher than the main tower. This is the unenterprising model for so many of our less distinguished follies, a fashion that seems to have been started by Sanderson Miller of all people, with his Edgehill Tower, now the Castle Inn at Radway.

Llangattock-nigh-Usk

Clytha Castle (1790–92)
SO 350 090

On the road to Abergavenny stands Clytha Castle. Like its contemporary, the Naval Temple at the Kymin, Clytha is a memorial but in a very different mood. The memory here is so touching, so pathetic, so genuine, and the building itself so ghostly and remote that it goes straight for the emotional jugular. It is impossible to stand in front of Clytha and read the inscription without feeling that this, in spirit, is the Taj Mahal of Wales:

This Building was erected in the year 1790 by WILLIAM JONES of Clytha Houſe Eſq Fourth Son of JOHN JONES of Lanarth Court Monmouthſhire Eſq and Huſband of ELIZABETH the laſt ſurviving Child of Sir WILLIAM MORGAN of Tredegar KB and Grand-Daughter of the moſt Noble WILLIAM Second Duke of Devonſhire It was undertaken for the purpose of relieving a mind ſincerely afflicted by the loſs of a moſt excellent Wife whoſe Remains were depoſited in Lanarth Church Yard A.D: 1787

Clytha Castle

and to the Memory of whose virtues
this Tablet is dedicated.
William Jones, like Shah Jahan, needs no
more eloquent testimony of his loss and grief.
As a lesser soul might find solace in spirits,
so Jones found solace in stone. The building
he left us is pure magic. Derivative yet wildly
original, it is a late fling of Strawberry Hill
Gothick, to a pattern that is its own master.
Built in an L-shape, it consists of three towers
joined by two curtain walls. The first tower is
oval and hollow; joined by the north-facing
curtain wall to the square, centre block tower.
This in turn is joined to the south, round,
two-storey tower, but with only the ground
floor habitable. The most remarkable feature
of the building is the aptly named north
curtain wall, which sweeps like a
battlemented theatre curtain up to a
coronated pinnacle; there is nothing else like
it in folly architecture—or, for that matter, in
the real world.

Clytha has been ascribed to John Nash,
and there certainly is record of a payment
from Jones to Nash for Clytha Castle,
perhaps for some additional work or for
checking the details of the design, but it
would seem that William Jones was his own
architect, assisted by the Shropshire
landscape architect John Davenport, who
had earlier designed a Gothick orangery for
Warren Hastings at Daylesford House. J.C.
Loudon dismissed Clytha as 'gaudy and
affectedly uncommon', but time has
weathered its initial assault on the landscape,
and now the Landmark Trust has bought the

castle, refurbished it and lets it out for villa
holidays with a difference—not everyone can
boast of spending a holiday in a memorial.

Monmouth

The Roundhouse (1794)
Naval Temple (1800)
SO 520 120

If you should happen to be in Monmouth,
the old county town, on one of those rare
days that always appear in tourist brochures
but so seldom in real life when the air is so
clear it sparkles and the sky is as blue as a
sapphire, then cancel all other plans and take
the Forest of Dean road out of town,
following the National Trust signs to the
Kymin.

At the top of the steep little hill, less than
1000ft (305m) high, one of the most
sensational views in the British Isles unrolls
over the undulating hills of Gwent. It looks
like nothing so much as a map of Tolkein's
Shire, with patchwork fields and copses lying
contentedly under the sun for as far as the eye
can see. Right on top of the hill is a building
Bilbo Baggins would have been proud to call
home: a round, castellated, whitewashed, two-
storey tower with a little mast, with the Welsh
flag and the National Trust flag fluttering in
the breeze. 'It's not a folly,' said the occupant
indignantly. 'Don't make the mistake of calling
it a folly. How can it be a folly when it was
built for a purpose?' This is true, but when
one learns that its purpose was to serve as a
dining room for a group of gentlemen to dine

in once a week, it can hardly be regarded as an essential structure. The Roundhouse was built in 1794 by the Monmouth dining club, headed by Philip Hardwick, but in proper Welsh tradition the area of the Kymin, which they had landscaped the year before, it was open to the public, not jealously guarded as private property.

Its popularity was immediate, and other buildings and works turned the Kymin into the smartest recreation area in Monmouthshire. A bowling green and racquets court was built, stables, another dining room (given by the Duke of Beaufort), a summerhouse, the Naval Temple and Mr Swinnerton's Beaulieu Walk, which ran north

The Round House on the Kymin

of the Roundhouse as a high-hedged promenade with 'windows' cut into the hedge at intervals to show different aspects of the view.

The Kymin's finest hour came in 1802 when Lord Nelson visited Monmouth with Lady Hamilton. It is said that his boat was spotted sailing down the Wye and he was recognized through the telescope that was mounted on top of the Roundhouse. A warning gun was fired from the Naval Temple, and by the time Nelson's party moored at the quay, the Mayor and Corporation were there to greet him. So impressed was the Admiral at being recognized that he returned three weeks later on 19 August and had breakfast at the Roundhouse, where he thought the view was one of the finest he had ever seen. The glory

faded; even during Philip Hardwick's lifetime the pleasure gardens were overgrown, and by the mid-19th century the site was derelict. Eventually, it was bought by the people of Monmouth, and in 1902 it was presented to the National Trust as one of its earliest properties. The Roundhouse and the Naval Temple, restored and refurbished, still remain to grace this beautiful hill.

The Naval Temple, a curious structure rather like a rustic summerhouse, is topped with a stepped roof, an arch and a figure of Britannia, commissioned by the National Trust and installed in 1979. A plaque on the wall commemorates that:

THIS NAVAL TEMPLE
WAS ERECTED AUGUST 1st. 1800
TO PERPETUATE THE NAMES OF THOSE
NOBLE ADMIRALS
WHO DISTINGUISHED THEMSELVES BY THEIR
GLORIOUS VICTORIES FOR ENGLAND
IN THE LAST AND PRESENT WARS
AND IS RESPECTFULLY DEDICATED TO
HER GRACE THE DUTCHESS OF BEAUFORT
DAUGHTER OF
ADMIRAL BOSCAWEN

Around the frieze are the names of British admirals and the dates of their famous victories. It was opened to the public on 20 June 1801. The architect's name is not known for sure, but the National Library of Wales holds two unexecuted designs for the Naval Temple by T. Fidler, dated 1798. Fidler may

The Naval Temple, Monmouth

have been successful in his third attempt. Nearby Fiddler's Elbow doesn't appear to have anything to do with him.

Pontypool

Grotto (1830s–40s)
Folly Tower (1994)
SO 300 000

At first glance, Pontypool may not have much to recommend it, except the former international fame of its rugby club. A pilgrimage to the hallowed turf will come as a surprise to the stranger, for Pontypool Park, where terrible deeds used to be wrought on hapless visiting teams by the fearsome Pontypool Front Row, is one of the most beautiful sports grounds in Britain. It is sylvan, arcadian even, and the reason for this is that the ground was laid out in the park of the Hanbury family, which has now become a municipal garden. Yet within the ordered regimentation of a council park there exists a fantastic survival—one of the best grottoes in the country. It was built by the Hanburys in or around 1836.

The interior of the grotto was dilapidated

The Pontypool Folly Tower

The interior of the Pontypool Grotto before the Second World War

by the 1980s, and seemed set for a slow slide down the hill of neglect and vandalism, ending in inevitable oblivion, rather like Pontypool RFC. However, as a result of a local campaign to re-erect the folly tower nearby (it was taken down in 1940 for fear it would serve as a reference point for German bombers), a restoration was planned and duly carried out in the mid-1990s by St Blaise, a company that has undertaken many superb folly restorations these last years.

The interior of the grotto is a riot of animal bones, pebbles, shells (both common and exotic), minerals, all in the most intricate of

patterns, the most peculiar aspect being the shell-covered, palm tree-like columns. Five rustick chairs go with it. The grotto was built by Capel Hanbury Leigh and finished by 1844. There was an architect, a Mr S. Gunston Tit from Bath (strange name that, Gunston), although it is alleged that a hermit lived in the grotto and spent his seven years' tenure there by doing it up in shells and bones.

The group that renewed interest in the Hanbury follies is CROFT (the Campaign for the Rebuilding of the Old Folly Tower), and in 1995 it was awarded the Prince of Wales's Award for improving the Welsh environment. Sadly, one of CROFT's leading committee members, Don Evans, died of a heart attack on the morning of the ceremony, but both tower and grotto are fitting memorials to his and CROFT's stamina and perseverance.

The tower itself, an octagonal, battlemented edifice with round arched windows, was finished in 1994.

Tredegar

Bedwellty Park Rock Garden (19th century)
SO 140 090

At Bedwellty Park a rock garden has been reported, together with a small temple.

POWYS

Powys is almost completely rural, the largest town being Brecon, which has a population of fewer than 8000—but in length it stretches the equivalent of the distance from Oxford to Derby. With over a million and a quarter acres and a population less than that of Newport in neighbouring Monmouth, the average density is 10 acres (4ha) per person, and as may be expected this sparse population has produced virtually no follies. A few monuments are worthy of note, however, among them the apparently ubiquitous Mid-Wales Victorian clock towers that are found in almost every market town commemorat-ing every imaginable royal or patriotic event.

Sometimes the follies that have long since disappeared are among the most intriguing, and there are also some wild geese: at Guilsfield is a house called The Folly, but it turns out to be a 17th-century house, with no story attached. One of the more eminent losses to follydom was also at Guilsfield: the splendidly incongruous Morisco-Iberian-Gothick Garth House (probably by Loudon, who later published a toned-down version for a similar house), which was built in 1809 for £100,000 for the East India nabob, the Rev. Richard Mytton (so the effect aimed at may just have been Indian), and demolished just after World War II. A loss.

The other folly loss in Powys is the exact reason for its being a folly. Hubert's Folly stood just south of Sarn and is now known as Old Hall Camp—here he started on a castle in 1228 to subdue the unruly locals, but after only a few weeks it turned out to be contrary to the stipulations of a border treaty by the Welsh and the English, and work had to be stopped and the fabric razed to the ground. It was at the time described as Stultitiam Hubertam, Hubert's Folly. The earthwork ring of the castle is said to be still visible.

Map locations: Llanrhaeadr-ym-Mochnant, Lake Vyrnwy, Criggion, Welshpool, Leighton, Machynlleth, Knucklas, Norton, Elan Village, Fron, New Radnor, Llandrindod Wells, Builth Wells, Knighton, Vaynor, Hay-on-Wye, Brecon, Cwmdu, Crickhowell

BRECKNOCK

Crickhowell

Gazebos (early 19th century; late 17th century)
SO 210 180

The River Usk flows through Crickhowell, and gazebos always go well with rivers. There are two here. One, behind the Malt House in Standard Street, is in the Gothic style. The other, reported to be on Pen-y-Dre farm, is more ordinary.

Cwmdu

Menhir and Cromlech (c.1840)
SO 180 240

Thomas Price had a menhir and a cromlech installed here as fake prehistoric monuments in the 1840s.

Hay-on-Wye

Arch and Obelisk (1827)
SO 230 420

A Gothic arch and obelisk were erected by Miss Anna Stallard-Penoyre to the memory of her father.

Vaynor

Hy-Brasail Tower (1912)
Crawshay Tomb (1879)
SO 050 110

Richard Haslam in *The Buildings of Wales* speaks of 'a ponderous Italian folly', a three-storey tower attached to a cottage, everything in the Italian style, and built in 1912, presumably in order to entice an Italian contessa to her Welsh lover. The reality is at once more exciting and more ordinary. This is, indeed, an Italian villa, plucked intact from the southern sea coast of Leghorn, with its Tuscan belvedere for gazing over the sheep-sodden countryside, but the tower is an integral part of the design of the house, and its only folly is its rarity in the locality. A friendly horse lives in the drive, along with a collection of vintage Ladas, Skodas and Moskviches, which all need a little attention. The house also needs some attention.

There is more at Vaynor. The church is the product of a Cardiff architect called Robinson, probably at the behest of his employer Robert Thompson Crawshay (see Glyntaff). It is a curious neo-Gothic building, dating from 1870, but it is Crawshay's enormous tomb in the churchyard that astonishes. It reads 'God Forgive Me', and there's a story to it. R.T. Crawshay (1817–79) lived at the Gothic Cyfartha Castle, southwest of Vaynor. This had been built in 1823 by Robert Lugar for R.T.'s father, William Crawshay. Lugar dedicated his *Villa Architecture* (1828) to him. Robert Crawshay was not only the last of the Welsh iron kings, he was, despite his wealthy upbringing, something of a self-made man, insisting on eating the same food as his workers. But once the strikes of the 1870s erupted, he showed his teeth and forbade trade unions. He is reputed to have been a great photographer and to have entertained lavishly at his castle near the iron works, but he also possessed some typical Victorian idiosyncrasies, including the habit of summoning his daughters by means of a whistle. He turned deaf during the last two years of his life, and after death left over

£1,200,000. Crawshay was an infamous philanderer, and that, or the treatment of his workers, may have inspired that singular text on his tomb.

MONTGOMERY

Criggion

Admiral Rodney's Pillar (1781)
SJ 290 140

Admiral Rodney's Pillar at Criggion in the far north of the county is a Doric column, superbly sited 1186ft (361m) up on Briedden Hill, to commemorate Admiral Rodney's victory at Domenica in 1781.

Lake Vyrnwy

Valve Tower (late 19th century)
SJ 010 210

Disguising pump houses and water towers as follies is part of a long tradition, practised all over Europe. Like the Elan valley (see Elan Village), the valley of the Vyrnwy was flooded, in 1881–8, to provide an enormous reservoir. The old village was rehoused at present-day Llanwyddyn (old Llanwyddyn can be visited only by scuba divers), and the architect George Frederick Deacon designed the enormous valve tower—or straining tower—along the 'Rumpelstilskin-goes-to-war' theme. It is a hysterically Teutonic round tower, which would be considered over the top even in the German heartlands.

Hy-Brasail Tower, Vaynor

Leighton

Leighton Hall Tower (1850–56)
SJ 240 060

Southeast of Welshpool is Leighton, which
exists, church and all, only because of the
house. It was built for John Naylor, a
Liverpool banker, by W.H. Gee. It doubles as
a model farm and includes a highly ornate
Poultry Palace. Naylor was greatly interested
in the newest methods of industrial farming,
and in the grounds are the remains of a
funicular railway, which was built to transport
slurry from the piggeries and cow-houses.
Like several other experiments in agriculture
on a large scale, things started going wrong at
an early stage, but Naylor adapted his railway,
and instead of farm waste it transported house
guests. One of the associated buildings was
converted into a summerhouse, while at the
top of the railway is a little belvedere. Other
structures included the High Bridge of 1858, a
dry bridge carved with elephants, and a statue
of Icarus falling into one of Leighton Hall's
ponds. In 1994, however, despite the
'protection' of listing, much of the above was
torn down or removed. The Hall's most
remarkable folly (or half-folly) still stands—
the octagonal tower is Powys's answer to
May's Folly at Hadlow, but here it is still
attached to the main building.

Llanrhaeadr-ym-Mochnant

Rustic Cottage (early 19th century)
SJ 070 290

Some 4 miles west of the village of
Llanrhaeadr-ym-Mochnant (not to be be
confused with Llanrhaiadr-ym-Mochnant),
the road ends at Wales's most famous
waterfall, Pistyll Rhaeadr (a tautology,
because it means the Spout of the Waterfall
River). There is a rustic cottage, partly
covered by bark, with a portico on primitive
tree trunks. This was built by Sir Watkin
Williams-Wynn, the 5th Baronet (see also
Wynnstay). It probably surplaced an earlier,
18th-century rustic cottage that had been
built by Dr William Worthington, vicar of the
village and apparently an avid antiquary,
although he wrote only religious tracts. He is
supposed also to have built several sham
ruins near Llanrhaeadr. These appear to have
gone, but south of the village is a standing
stone or menhir, moved (and inscribed) in
1770 by William Worthington from another
site. In this century it was moved again to the
side of the road where, until 1925, it was used
as a lamp post.

Machynlleth

Clock Tower (1873)
Forge (c.1900)
SH 750 010

The clock tower of 1873, one of many such
monuments in Mid-Wales, celebrates Lord
Castlereagh's 21st birthday. The
Londonderries had become the owners of
Plas Machynlleth (and later they went on to
build the Smithy; see below). The old market
cross had to be taken down for this grand
design, which is by Henry Kennedy, and it is
certainly one of the largest clock towers in the
country. In addition to telling the time, it
provides enough turrets, weathervanes and
Gothic paraphernalia from which to build a
decent sized church.

The Forge on Pentrerhedyn Street, the
main A487, has an appropriate horseshoe-
shaped entrance arch, a concept taken up with
enthusiasm in America in the early years of the

The clock tower at Machynlleth

motor age, when every filling station seemed to be designed in the shape of an oil drum, petrol pump, doughnut or whatever—a form of architecture by association. Barbara Jones noted that the nails depicted are the wrong number. No doubt someone else will tell us what the right number is supposed to be.

RADNOR

Elan Village

Valve Tower (c.1904)
SN 920 670

Like the Vyrnwy (see Lake Vyrnwy), the River Elan was dammed in the late 19th century and opened in 1904 (although construction went on until 1907). Unlike the massive valve tower at Vyrnwy, however, the choice here fell on a more elegant design: a Renaissance cupola with a copper dome, somewhat like an overblown fishing temple.

Fron

Grotto (late 1990s)
SO 080 660

Near Fron is Coed Gwgan Hall, where the architect and Folly Fellowship grot secretary Vernon Gibberd (also known for his grotto at Leeds Castle, Kent, and his astounding designs in postmodern furniture) is slowly making his very own grot, the design of which seems to change according to the availability of the material and any new ideas he comes up with. It is well sited, with a view across a small pond into the Radnorshire countryside. There is also something called the Singing Door, a stainless steel and coloured glass fantasy from the 1930s that, when opened, plays 'There'll be Bluebirds over the White Cliffs of Dover', which may or may not end up in the grotto. A door in the village further on in the valley holds what once was Churchill's letterbox; not a lot of people know that.

Knighton

Clock Tower (1872)
SO 290 720

This clock tower was built by the Haddon brothers in the usual Gothic clock tower style, but it has a story attached to it that was presumed to be exciting enough to be passed on from generation to generation. When he was finishing the last stage of this pretty little tower, the mason was so clumsy as to lose his glasses. Once recovered from the ground, they turned out to be completely undamaged. That's it.

Knucklas

Arboreal Graffiti (20th century)
SO 240 750

On a slope between Llainey and Knucklas is a tree plantation, in the centre of which a different shade of green (it's no use asking us to distinguish types of trees—they're all oak to us) depicts the initials RP or PP. Exciting stuff. Are there more such pieces of arboreal graffiti in the country?

Llandrindod Wells

Winter Garden (c.1899)
SO 060 620

The Hotel Metropole dates from around the turn of the century, so the Pulhamite rockery or winter garden must date from about the same period. It is a jolly affair and in a very good state, a must for Pulhamite connoisseurs.

New Radnor

Lewis Monument (1864)
SO 210 610

The best monument in the county is at New Radnor, which was once a county borough but is now little more than a village. The monument is a 77ft (23m) high, Victorian fantasy—the Albert Memorial of Wales. It is a gabled, Gothic chess piece, designed by John Gibbs, who built the equally overblown Tatton Sykes monument in Humberside. It was built in 1864 to commemorate Sir George Cornewall Lewis, a gifted classical scholar who became Palmerston's first Chancellor of the Exchequer—'cold as a fish but good humoured,' as a contemporary described him.

Norton

Obelisk (19th century)
SO 280 680

On Offa's Dyke near Norton and Rhos-y-meirch, is a plain obelisk to the memory of Sir Richard Green Price MP, a local 19th-century worthy who preserved both nature and Offa's Dyke. This part of the world is high and windy, and it is perhaps surprising that the monument lasted until January 1976 before being blown down.

England

NORTHUMBRIA

DURHAM

CUMBRIA

YORKSHIRE

ISLE OF
MAN

LANCS

CHESHIRE DERBY LINCS

NOTTS

STAFFS

SHROPS LEICS NORFOLK

WARWICKS CAMBS

NORTHANTS SUFFOLK

WORCS BEDS

BUCKS ESSEX

HERTS

GLOUCS OXON

LONDON

BERKS

WILTS SURREY KENT

HANTS

SOMERSET SUSSEX

DEVON DORSET

CORNWALL ISLE OF
WIGHT

BEDFORDSHIRE

Unsung, unfashionable Bedfordshire! A small, crowded county, nervously squeezed away from London by its more confident and urbane neighbours, it is difficult to assign it an identity. It is a county without castles, and its largest town is undeniably frightful and lacks a river, which all towns need for their souls. It is hard to think of anything other than trucks, bricks and Bunyan to go with Bedfordshire. Yet it is not at all a bad place to be. Once away from unlovely Luton, the brickworks and the M1, rural Bedfordshire takes on a quiet attractiveness, which is all the more enhanced by being unexpected, rather like a 1950s movie starlet taking off her glasses so our lantern-jawed hero can gasp: 'But Miss Bedford – you're beautiful!'

Pertenhall
Bushmead Priory
Rexton
Great Barford
Turvey
Chicksands
Priory
Apsley
Guise
Old Warden
Southill
Ampthill
Woburn
Abbey
Flitwick
Toddington
Wrest Park
Heath and
Reach
Leighton
Linslade
Luton

Ampthill

Obelisk (1785)
`TL 034 381`
Catherine's Cross (1773)
`TL 024 383`
Gazebo (18th century)
`TL 034 379`

Ampthill is a small, not particularly distinguished town without any obvious attractions or notable sights.

But the visitor feels a sense of satisfaction, of completeness, about a town that so obviously works and works well. Everything has been put together sensibly, and the few buildings of architectural merit are placed at intervals rather than crowded together in one quarter; the ensemble is pleasing. The town grew up around a crossroads, Bedford–Dunstable and London–Woburn, and in 1785 the 2nd Earl of Upper Ossory (an Irish title—his seat was Ampthill Park) erected an extremely useful multi-functional object here, of the sort that seems to have been popular in this part of Bedfordshire. It was designed by Sir William Chambers and has recently been restored. There is no one word to describe it—it is unique, a combination of mile post, street lamp and town pump in one short obelisk.

To the west of the town stands an earlier work by the earl, an all but forgotten cross, which achieved sudden fame in 1982 as the climax to a treasure hunt. Catherine's Cross was erected in 1773 by James Essex on the site of the long-vanished Ampthill Castle (one of Bedford's missing castles), where Catherine of Aragon stayed while the fate of her marriage to Henry VIII was being decided. Horace Walpole, that indefatigable traveller, composed an ode for the base of the cross, and it is still just legible:

> In days of old, here Ampthill's towers
> were seen
> The mournful refuge of an injured
> queen;

Ampthill's Gazebo

Here flowed her pure but unavailing tears
Here blinding zeal sustained her sinking
years.
Yet Freedom hence her radiant banner
waved
And love avenged a realm by priests
enslaved;
From Catherine's wrongs a Nation's
bliss was spread
And Luther's light from Henry's lawless
bed.

In Walpole's and Ossory's eyes at least, good came out of injustice. The progress of the design and subsequent erection of the cross is traced in Walpole's correspondence with the Rev. Mr Cole:

22 June 1771—I promised to Lord Ossory
to erect a Cross to [Catherine's]
memory… ;
12 October—Lord Ossory is charmed
with Mr Essex's Cross [and Walpole
sent Mr Cole the poem for the
inscription];
12 July 1774—I have lately been at
Ampthill, and saw Queen Catherine's
Cross… Lord Ossory is quite
satisfied… and designs Mr Essex a
present of some guineas.

A hundred yards away, over the flat top of Ampthill's castle mound, stands another cross, at first glance identical—same size, same shape—but the two crosses differ in almost every detail. This second cross was put up as a war memorial in 1920 by the Duke of Bedford, to commemorate the 707 men trained at Ampthill camp who died in World War I. It is not easy to understand why the Duke chose to make his cross so similar yet so different.

In Dunstable Street, back in the town, stands a strange little triangular two-storey building just in front of a new supermarket. Here, says local legend, Catherine of Aragon used to teach pillow lace-making to the women of Ampthill, but as she died 200 years before the Gazebo was built, another legend falters. The house it served is now demolished, and the quaint little building's survival as the Gazebo Flower Kiosk has to be applauded.

Apsley Guise

Henry VII Lodge (1811)
SP 931 352

Outside the northwest corner of Woburn Park, in the prettily named village of Apsley Guise, a quaint and ancient house, known as the Henry VII Lodge, turns out to be another

commission for Humphrey Repton from the Duke of Bedford. Not built, as a student of architecture might guess, towards the end of the 15th century and perfectly preserved, it was actually built in 1811 by Humphrey and his son, John Adey Repton, as a deliberate attempt to recreate a 15th-century house from known details. It is a true mongrel of a building. Repton wrote:

The hint of the lower storey was taken
from Eltham Palace, the hints for the
brick-nogging from a house at King's
Lynn, for the arches at the top of the
narrow panels from a house near
Kelvedon, for the barge-boarding from a
house near Bury St Edmunds, for the
pinnacles from a house near
Shrewsbury, for the oriel from Norwich,
and for the chimneys from Wolterton
Manor House, Barsham, Norfolk.

Bushmead Priory

Tower Grotto (18th century)
TL 820 600

At the corner of a wood south of Bushmead Priory stands a minute tower, with three storeys, a pyramidal roof, battlemented corner turrets and one room per floor. At one time it was supposed to be an observatory, then a gamekeeper's lodge; now it is a small house called The Grotto, which refers to the remnants of a shell grotto stuck to its northern side. It was built by the Gery family when the Priory was rebuilt as a private house in the 18th century.

Chicksands Priory

Three Obelisks (c.1816; 1771; 1889)
TL 130 390; TL 097 395; TL 104 407

The Ordnance Survey map marks a Monument and an Obelisk. The monument, also an obelisk in fact, was for General Sir George Danvers to commemorate the peace of 1815, but it was moved in 1975 to a position near the house and a new inscription added.

The second obelisk, or rather the first, remains on its original site near Appley Corner, where it was erected in or after 1771 on the death of the Duke of Halifax, brother-in-law of the then-owner of Chicksands. The object is that rare thing: a Gothick obelisk, more of a large pinnacle with slender corner buttresses and probably designed by James Wyatt (compare it with his work at the Priory). There's another obelisk, a mile along the way, in memory of Henry John Robert Osborn 'who perished in a collision in the

English Channel 29 March 1889'.
Obelisks galore!

Flitwick

Dry Bridge (late 18th century)
`TL 030 350`

The little bridge in the grounds of Flitwick
Manor is a charming little conceit: a grassy
bridge spanning grass, one side classical, one
side Gothick, with a pebble grotto area
underneath. Nothing is known of its history;
we can date it to the end of the 18th century,
but no nearer.

Flitwick Dry Bridge

Great Barford

Eyecatcher Gateway (18th century)
`TL 140 520`

Just outside Great Barford, on the road from
Bedford to the A1 and on the right hand side,
is a gateway, now unusable because the level
of the road has been raised. It is
unremarkable in itself, but 10 yards (9m)
further on, an almost identical gateway has
been recreated in brick relief on an otherwise
blank wall. It was never used, never filled in.
Why was it constructed? The only
reasonable explanation was that it was built
as a simple eyecatcher to be seen from
Barford House on the other side of the road.
Trees and traffic now conspire to keep this
little oddity from fulfilling its original if
mysterious purpose.

Heath and Reach

Clock Tower (1873)
`SP 925 280`

Just north of Leighton Buzzard, in the village
of Heath and Reach, is one of Bedfordshire's
multi-purpose buildings. It sits on the village
green looking like a concertinaed church, but
it is in fact a combined well-house and clock
tower, allegedly erected by public
subscription, but, as Baroness Angela
Burdett-Coutts turns out to have been
involved, the extent of the public's
contribution would appear to have been
minimal. Her philanthropic efforts may be
seen in London's Victoria Park and Holly
Village, and this extraordinary little
structure, while not as ostentatiously
expensive as her London offerings, clearly
bears the stamp of her determined charity.
Plaques on the building admit only to
Baroness Burdett-Coutts having shared the
cost of the clock with Baroness de
Rothschild, while a Mr Branton presented
the pumping equipment in memory of a Mr
William Abraham, but somehow everything
points to the baroness as the onlie begetter.

Leighton Linslade

Railway Tunnel (c.1838)
`SP 918 261`
Gazebo (late 19th century)
`SP 910 250`

In the 1960s an attempt was made to join the
towns of Leighton Buzzard and Linslade
under the name of Leighton Linslade. It failed
as far as the public was concerned; Leighton
Buzzard is a deeply pleasing name, one that is
satisfying to repeat quietly to oneself. But
there are follies in Linslade. One is an early
example of the popular Victorian hobby of
castellating railway tunnels, and the north
entrance of Linslade Tunnel has two towers,
arrowslits, battlements—everything a good
railway tunnel could desire. Although it is not
as elaborate nor as famous as Clayton Tunnel
at Hassocks in Sussex, it is particularly
interesting because it must be the first
example of its kind, having been built c.1838.

The other is a late example of its kind, a
gazebo built at the end of the 19th century.
Gazebos had been in declining popularity a
hundred years previously and few were
subsequently built, but at The Lodge in
Bossington Lane this pleasing sample can be
found. It is a plain, two-storey, castellated
building with an external staircase, but its
particular attraction is a finely carved stone

fountain on the west side, with bullrushes and a spouting fish.

Luton

Water Towers (1900; 1901)
`TL 100 220`

Luton is the cuckoo in the Bedfordshire nest. It is easily the largest town, bursting through the bottom of the county like an overweight fledgling. It also has the rare merit of being wholly undistinguished. As Pevsner, always the first with a kind word, writes: 'it is a town of very little architectural interest ... it is no good pretending that a perambulation is possible.' In only two instances has Luton's imagination been untethered—in 1900 and 1901, when the Luton Water Company built two massive water towers, one on Hart Hill and the other on West Hill. We know water towers should not be admitted as follies, but these two are so joyfully bizarre that even the most pedantic would unbend to include them.

The West Hill tower, designed by Henry Hare in 1901, was described by Pevsner as:

HEADLEY IN THE CLOUDS

Some Tall Follies

COLLCUT TOWER
London

———

PETERSON'S FOLLY
Hampshire

———

MAY'S FOLLY
Kent

———

WAINHOUSE'S TOWER
West Yorkshire

———

BECKFORD'S TOWER
Somerset

———

CABOT'S TOWER
Bristol

———

BLACKPOOL TOWER
Lancashire

———

HOOBER STAND
South Yorkshire

———

WAINHOUSE TOWER
West Yorkshire

'One of the most enjoyable buildings of Luton. Decidedly Arts and Crafts and resourcefully handled.' Over on Hart Hill the tower is decidedly eclectic; as Alan Cox of the County Planning Department put it: 'It is difficult to say whether its style owes more to a French Gothic chateau or a Chinese pagoda.'

Old Warden

Swiss Garden (19th century)
`TL 149 446`

Between Southill and Northill is Old Warden, famous as the home of the Shuttleworth Collection of vintage aeroplanes. Right behind the aerodrome is another extraordinary survival—an enchanting, complex and hidden garden of less than 8 acres (3.2ha). Known as the Swiss Garden, it is now administered by Bedfordshire County Council. The Swiss Garden was first laid out in the early 19th century by Lord Ongley as a romantic adjunct to his Old Warden Park Estate. With ponds, winding paths, bridges, terraces and islands, it had all the right qualifications for the role, and to this foundation the Ongleys added a Swiss cottage, a grotto, a thatched tree shelter, a fernery, a wellhead, a sham chapel, an Indian kiosk and several other small conceits.

The cottage itself is an elegant thatched room with extensive fretworked balconies, set high on a mound above the garden. It is said that the name of the garden derives not from a general Swiss style but that one of the Lords Ongley had a Swiss mistress for whom the garden was originally built. The grotto and fernery were built c.1830, and while the grotto is fairly unexceptional, the cross-shaped fernery is an interesting example of an early cast-iron glasshouse in the style of Paxton and the Crystal Palace. It predated Paxton by several years, being built by Barwell & Hagger at the Eagle Foundry, Northampton, in 1830–33.

Joseph Shuttleworth bought the estate from Lord Ongley in 1872 and continued to improve the garden. He still found time to build the Queen Anne's Summerhouse in 1875, a square brick building with corner turrets and balustrades, which is attributed to Henry Clutton, who designed Old Warden Park for the Shuttleworths.

After World War II the Swiss Garden fell into decay, and only in 1976 was the decline halted, when the council took over the lease with the aid of the Historic Buildings Council. The garden is beautiful, unspoilt

Roxton's Church Orné

and as yet relatively unknown—another plus point for Bedfordshire.

The estate village is in a very sympathetic style, with a delicious arbour or two, Tudor and rustic details on the houses, and near the church stands a mysterious mausoleum. In the church itself the old squire has gone berserk, filling it with wooden spoils both old English and continental.

Pertenhall

Garden House (1850s)
TL 080 660

There is a frippery worth mentioning right on the Cambridgeshire border: between Pertenhall and Kimbolton is a small garden house, hexagonal with a hexagonal lantern, in the grounds of Woodend House.

Roxton

Church Orné (1808)
TL 160 540

Congregational churches are usually somewhat severe architecturally; if any style in particular is favoured, classical Greek is the choice. What a surprise, therefore, to find at Roxton a congregational church—any church for that matter—built in the style of a thatched Gothick rustic cottage *orné*. The only other thatched church we have come across is at Little Stretton in Shropshire.

Roxton church was built by Charles Metcalf, the local squire, because he was bored with travelling 6 miles to his nearest congregational chapel. It is T-shaped, with massive overhanging eaves forming a veranda right around the building and supported, visually at least, by gnarled and weathered tree trunks. The main body of the T is the

delightful little church, while the cross-bar houses a utility room on the north side and a Sunday School on the south. The Metcalf family used to use this part as a summerhouse, hence the fantastic and somewhat too secular entrance.

Southill

Obelisk (1864)
Fishing Temple (1807)
TL 132 419

On the road from Ireland to Old Warden, in a wood called Keeper's Warren, on the Whitbread Estate at Southill, stands a small, negligible obelisk, cowed by conifers, dedicated

TO

WILLIAM HENRY

WHITBREAD

ESQUIRE

FOR HIS ZEAL AND ENERGY

IN PROMOTING RAILWAYS

THROUGH THE

COUNTY OF BEDFORD

1864

ERECTED BY

PUBLIC SUBSCRIPTION

It lurks by the side of the old Bedford–Hitchen railway line, unemotionally torn up by Dr Beeching.

If the Beerage's railway has gone, an earlier work remains. In the park at Southill itself stands an exquisite white brick fishing pavilion, modestly set back a little way from the lake. It is small—one room—with tetrastyle pedimented Tuscan porticoes at the front and back. On either side red brick arcades run away from the pavilion and lead to large arches standing on the east and west. There is a cottage on the east side as well. It was probably designed by Henry Holland and built posthumously in 1807; it was carefully restored in 1983. Originally, it was built on a spur of land between two lakes. Now, across the greensward, across the lake, it stares intently at the big house, so directly that one is driven to the map to see if it is part of a greater plan. And, yes, satisfyingly, an avenue runs south of the house, lining up the Fishing Temple with the church at Meppershall, 4½ miles away, and 2 miles due north, on the identical orientation, is the parish church of Northill. There is a contentment in working out ley lines on a map; there is a quite different and sometimes alarming gratification in pacing one out on the ground. There does seem to be something other-worldly about these old straight tracks.

Toddington

Grotto (19th century)

`TL 010 280`

A little summerhouse at Toddington Manor contains a wet grotto (more of a fernery), made of rough stone and clinker, and small stalactites drip from the roughed-up ceiling into a mossy basin. It is hard to date. It looks 19th century but with much recent restoration work. Start reading your usual volume of hermit's verses here and the book will be soggy within the hour.

Turvey

Jonah and his Wife (1844–1953)

`SP 938 523`

Gazebo (1829)

`SP 947 522`

On the Buckinghamshire border an odd couple live on an island in the Great Ouse. 'Jonah and his Wife' the locals have dubbed them, despite the fact that the 'wife' sports an all too obvious beard. Jonah originally came from Ashridge House in Hertfordshire, which was demolished in 1802. The squire of Turvey found him in a stonemason's yard and installed him on the island in 1844, where he waited patiently for 109 years until his wife joined him in 1953. The wife was found as a headless female torso built into the side of a barn along with several assorted

heads. Despite the female body, a bearded head was felt to be the most suitable, so s/he went to join Jonah on the island. The people of Bedfordshire may not be as conformist as they would have you believe.

Turvey Abbey is at the other end of the village. A short trip through the fields backing the house and its large walled garden reveals a Gothick gazebo, a pretty little thing, square, battlemented, pointed windows all round, made of local sandstone, and underneath the first storey is what looks like a cattle shed. From the garden side a flight of stone stairs leads directly to the viewing room. Most striking are the two gargoyles: grotesque faces. We dated this *c.*1850, but Pevsner is adamant: 1829.

Woburn Abbey

Garden Buildings (17th–19th century)

`SP 970 350`

Woburn Abbey is arguably the most famous stately home in Britain. It is magnificent, the abbey and the park together providing the best that Bedfordshire has to offer. It now seems to be entirely dedicated to catering for visitors, which at least ensures its preservation. The trippers assuredly do not visit Woburn to see its follies, the finest group in Bedfordshire, but their money pays for their survival. Woburn's follies are enjoyable and accessible, if not follies in the grand

A seat at Woburn

manner. They are follies of style and fashion rather than mania, and they were largely the work of two brothers, the 5th and 6th Dukes of Bedford. There are at least ten buildings that could be mentioned; some are marginal, but taken as a group their inclusion is demanded. Descriptions abound in guide books and all are easily visited, unlike the majority of follies, so we will content ourselves here by listing what we have recorded and describing the major follies.

At Woburn there can be found a Chinese dairy, a Chinese temple, a pavilion, a Temple of the Graces by Wyatville, a very early grotto (1630, by the French architect Isaac de Caus), the Thornery, a log cabin, columns from a ruined gateway in a wood, a sample mock prefabricated Tudor house from the 1878 Paris Exhibition (now a posh restaurant called Paris House), and a round ice-house with dome and battlements, built in 1788 by Henry Holland.

The most important buildings are the Chinese dairy and the Thornery. The former was built by Holland again, probably around 1794, and with its covered gallery running alongside the lake it recalls Le Hameau at Versailles. Built entirely of scarlet-painted wood, it is exquisite in its picturesqueness,

and the care and attention in its detailing are equally pleasurable. There are decorations, etched and painted glass with flowers, birds and butterflies all around. No Chinese milkmaids; no room for cows even, but the building is fun and immensely cheerful.

Not that the Thornery is depressing. It seems to have been built as a thatched luncheon box by Humphrey Repton in 1808, and again the flowers and the birds motifs reappear, this time around the dome and as murals, painted by Augustine Agilo. If the idea of a thatched dome strikes one as bizarre, the execution is even stranger; inside, the building has two rooms, one up, one down, and the upper, painted room is octagonal with a domed ceiling. The lower, white-tiled room is tunnel vaulted. Outside, nothing could be more different; the building is square, with four steeply pitched gables and a veranda similar to the church at Roxton, also built in 1808. The least peculiarity of this Hansel and Gretel house is its name; it is surrounded by hawthorns.

For students of building materials, the buttresses on the renewed brick wall surrounding the estate between Ridgmond and Husborne Crawley are of great interest. Alan Cox has noted that the fake brick buttresses are of iron, bought by the 11th Duke of Bedford *c.*1900 'to save a friend who owned an ironworks from bankruptcy'.

Wrest Park

Archer Pavilion (1709–11)
Garden Buildings (18th century)
`TL 090 350`

Before the Russells, the family name of the Dukes of Bedford, came to pre-eminence in the mid 1700s, the leading family in Bedfordshire was the Greys of Wrest Park near Silsoe. As early as 1295, Reginald de Grey was lord of the manor of Flitton-cum-Silsoe, and the Greys were in possession for the next 622 years. Henry Grey, 12th Earl of Kent, was created Duke of Kent in 1710, at the time that Thomas Archer was building for him the magnificent pavilion in the grounds of Wrest Park.

It was an early work by Archer, who trained under Vanbrugh, and it is such an arresting building that it has been accepted by the architectural establishment in its own right, conveniently ignoring its pre-eminent claim to be a folly, being huge, useless, ostentatious and wildly expensive. It is undeniably magnificent, the finest individual building in Bedfordshire, built to a complicated plan that is based on Borromini's Sant'Ivo della Sapienza in Rome. In 1773 Walpole, having no taste for the 'old fashioned manner', had only one word for Archer's temple—'frightful'.

Wrest Park is a rarity among English gardens in that it has remained formal, despite the attentions of Lancelot Brown, who worked here for three years. Archer's Pavilion stands at the end of a formal canal called the Long Water, ½ mile from the house. The house incidentally was designed and built by Earl de Grey himself, first president of the Institute of British Architects. The garden is packed with buildings, all verging on the folly without, as at Woburn, sufficient individuality to stand alone. There is a very well-sited rustic-Gothick bath house or cold bath, designed in 1770 by Edward Stevens (but possibly inspired by Thomas Wright), together with a cascade-bridge, the Bowling Green House, designed for the duke by Batty Langley in 1735, two half houses (encouragingly called the West Half House and the East Half House) and a bizarre Tuscan column, which commemorates the work done on the gardens:

These Gardens were begun in the year 1706 by the Duke of Kent, who continued to beautify them until the year 1740;

the work was again carried on by Philip Earl of Hardwicke and Jemima, Marchioness de Grey, with the professional assistance of Lancelot Brown Esq. 1758–60.

No trace remains of the hermitage that Brown is supposed to have built, but another column on Cain Hill commemorates Jemima again—she inherited Wrest in 1740 from her grandfather, the duke. It was erected in 1831 by Earl de Grey. The final touch to the gardens is the Chinese bridge of 1874, which was supposed to give to the landscape a willow-pattern atmosphere. Nowadays an energetically inventive mind is required to make the connection, but the Chinese temple of 1761 helps, and there used to be a weeping willow as well, while a junk sailed the waters.

If Archer's pavilion is Wrest's best building, its most mysterious ornament is the Mithraic Altar of 1740, which was erected by Jemima and husband to celebrate their wedding. It purports to display 'strange Persic characters', but in fact they tell us something else—suffice to say we didn't get it.

Wrest Park is now the National College of Agricultural Engineering, but the gardens are managed by English Heritage; the curiosities will surely be preserved. The most surprising thing is that Archer's Pavilion is not listed Grade I.

Thomas Archer's egregious pavilion at Wrest Park

BERKSHIRE

Until Oxfordshire swallowed nearly a third of the county in 1974, Berkshire, or the Royal County of Berkshire to give it its full and unique title, looked like a mirror image of the map of Austria. Nothing remotely resembles Austria on the ground; the nearest Berkshire gets to an alp is Walbury Hill on the Wiltshire-Hampshire border at a trifling 974ft (297m). But as Austria is divided into alpine and lowlands, so Berkshire is divided into Commuterland and Otherland. Reading, the county town, is the pivot and the border dividing the two Berkshires, half an hour from London by train and straddling the wild west and the stockbroker's splendour of the less than mysterious east. Strangely, Berkshire is the only shire county that did not derive its name from the quondam county town.

For our purposes, the biggest surprise about the county is the scarcity of follies. Follies are the playthings of the rich or eccentric, and Berkshire is undeniably rich, although one gets the impression that eccentricity is not an admired trait here. The nurturing of a good crop of follies requires a generous sprinkling of large estates, and these Berkshire lacks. Perhaps the old lords were made nervous by the proximity of the monarch. The Royal County is so honoured because of urbane Windsor, frowning across the river at squat and urban Slough, indisputably unfit for humans but the second largest town in the county since it was acquired from Buckinghamshire in the reorganization. What were the planners thinking of when they swapped all those towns around?

The people of the county guard their privacy carefully. The commonest signs to be seen read PRIVATE—KEEP OUT—NO ENTRY. Even a police station we passed had a sign reading POLICE NOTICE—NO TURNING on its forecourt. It's the sort of county that given half a chance would impose a toll to keep out the riffraff and, as such, it attracts the sort of riffraff who have acquired sufficient money to be allowed in.

Ascot

Grotto (18th century)
Garden Buildings
SU 910 720

Berkshire's grandest folly is unquestionably the grotto at Ascot Place, northwest of Ascot. Indeed, it is difficult to think of a finer grotto in Britain. This has been recognized by the Department of the Environment, which has listed it Grade I along with Kent's Margate Grotto. It is intact, beautiful and unvandalized, and for once the county's PRIVATE—KEEP OUT—NO ENTRY greeting to all visitors is here justified, for this is protecting something more fragile and more valuable than privacy. The grotto has

not been restored recently, which in most situations means you can fall in through a gaping hole in the roof, but here what astonishes the visitor most is the preservation of the grotto—here is the real thing, the living incarnation of all those pitiful shards of shells and glass and rockeries seen as remnants in old forgotten gardens. It has been made solely with stones and minerals, mica and feldspar, and we have no hesitation in saying that this is the finest non-shell grotto in Great Britain. Here everything is pristine and elegant, yet not institutionally precise. It is still a private, homely—albeit a very grand home—garden. It remains in excellent condition, well preserved and well maintained.

There are three other pieces in the grounds of Ascot Place so immaculately preserved that in any other context they would deserve a couple of pages each. Very closely packed together, in an autumnal garden to the northwest of the house, are a Gothick seat, a rotunda temple and a dry bridge, all in a remarkable state of preservation—even the stonework shows no signs of crumbling. It's as if they were built 20 years ago rather than 200.

The Gothick seat has four clustered columns separating three four-centred arches, topped with crocketed pinnacles and delicate frieze tracery. Facing the seat at the end of a short avenue is a giant urn with snake handles. The rotunda, with its Corinthian columns, is no more than 30 yards (27.4m) away, an echo of how Halswell in Somerset must have looked.

Facing it is the dry bridge, a tunnel joining two gardens, with the bas-relief head of a woman over the entrance on the west and two monkeys over the east entrance. A serene and peaceful garden—at the time of writing. There is a proposal to run a public footpath and long-distance cycle track 100 yards (91m) south of the grotto. Now, we are great supporters of Sustrans and their long-distance cycle routes, which are desperately needed in Britain, but all it takes is one deranged cyclist or walker to discover this incredible, unique, vulnerable grotto and it could be destroyed forever. The path must be re-routed further away.

Inside the Grotto at Ascot Place

Ashampstead

Tower (c.1830)
SU 560 760

Ashampstead is Berkshire before the commuters and weekenders and fat cats discovered it. It is a peaceful, pretty, remote village on a low hill, built around a crossroads. Two miles south of Abergavenny in Gwent is a mountain with the peculiar name of Blorenge, and here in Ashampstead, 80 miles away, is Blorenge House. (Blorenge is also the only known rhyme for orange.)

In the garden is a small, brick, two-storey, castellated tower, with a substantial flight of steps leading up to the first floor. In fact, there seem to be more steps than tower, explained by the fact that it was built by Isaac Septimus Nullis, a local preacher, as somewhere to practise his sermons. From his personal and private brick pulpit he could harangue and rant at the cows incuriously grazing in the meadow below.

Blorenge House also has a rather wonderful coach house, with stepped gable roof and ornamentation added by the present owners—panels depicting the four seasons and a Madonna-style figure, which appears to have been made out of the brown leathery stuff they sell in supermarkets for dogs to chew in place of slippers.

Basildon

Peacock Pavilion (1956)
Eyecatcher (early 19th century)
SU 610 780

At Basildon we can see one of the magnificent fountains that once graced Whitaker Wright's Witley Park in Surrey (there is another at York House in Twickenham); now it spouts in the company of others in the grounds of the Child-Beale Wildlife Trust, a sort of open farm with rare breeds of cattle, llamas and little bits of sculpture dotted throughout the grounds. In addition, a pavilion, most of which came from Bowood in Wiltshire, was erected in 1956 by the owner, Gilbert Child-Beale, in memory of his parents. Nearby there is a monkey orchestra in stone, echoing de Clermont's work at Monkey Island. But are these follies? The real folly at Basildon was the famous grotto at Basildon Park, long gone, but Lady Fane's fine house is still known as The Grotto.

At the end of the west drive from the house stands the perfect eyecatcher, a curvaceous gabled house squarely facing the drive gates, perhaps by John Buonarotti Papworth. But the drive dips down into a wooded valley and nothing can be seen from either house or eyecatcher.

Bray

Monkey Island (mid-18th century)
`SU 930 770`

Berkshire's few follies seem to have a preference for water—most are on or by the Thames. Travelling upstream from Slough–Windsor, the river is studded with a remarkable number of tiny islands, known to Tamesians as eyots. Monkey Island by Bray is now a hotel, its past tranquillity lost for ever to the M4 thundering over the river 400 yards away. In the 18th century it must have been idyllic. Charles Spencer, Duke of Marlborough, thought so when he bought the island. There was an octagonal fishing lodge built from the most massive blocks of cut stone—at least it looked like stone until the young duke tapped it and discovered to his delight that they were blocks of wood carved to look like stone. The lodge has spawned, and now it is crushed in the middle of the hotel, which has at least made an attempt along one wall of the bar to reproduce the massive woodstone blocks. The domed ceiling of the lodge was decorated by Andien de Clermont, who specialized in 'singerie', with paintings of monkeys indulging in river sports. It has been speculated that the island derived its name from these paintings, but the probability is that it is a tautologous corruption of 'monk's eyot'.

The Duke built a pavilion to go with the lodge. Originally it was one room standing on an arcade, a pleasant belvedere, but the hotel bedrooms are linked to it, the arcading has been filled in and it now forms the conference room of the hotel.

Farley Hill

Farley Castle (1808–10)
`SU 750 650`

Farley Castle has always been called a folly. Only thing is—we don't get it. It certainly is a brick mock castle, petite crenellations, little half-towers, small windows and all. It was designed by the little-known architect W. Fellows for E. Stephenson. For a while it was run as the butch-named Hephaistos School, and in 1990 it was allegedly torched by people who had been removed from the site. Although the demolishers were called in, Farley Castle was saved and turned into three houses, with four more added 'in the same style'.

Purley

Culloden Pavilion (1746)
`SU 640 750`

Purley Hall is said by locals to have been the residence of Warren Hastings, the impeached Governor-General of India—except that he lived in Gloucestershire—but the sight of the house confirms what Macaulay described as his honourable poverty. Facing the house on the shores of a lake (PRIVATE—KEEP OUT—GUARD DOGS), is a little flint and brick pavilion painted, on the inside, in a virulent Datsun ochre.

One of the monkey musicians at the Childe-Beale Gardens, Basidon

ERECTED, ACCORDING TO TRADITION,
TO COMMEMORATE
THE BATTLE OF CULLODEN
1746
RESTORED 1913.
H.C.W.

On the pediment is a magnificent grotesque face, with blackstone pebbles for eyes and an expression of such salacious malignity that one feels quite benevolently disposed towards it.

Reading

Grotto (19th century)
SU 730 720

Part of the famous arboretum and exotic plant collection of the Marquess of Blandford has survived; the house has not. The grounds of Whiteknights Park now house Reading University, in the usual white buildings. It has a grotto though, which has even been restored. In Reading itself, in Forbury Gardens, is a wonderful war memorial (Afghan Wars of 1844) in the shape of a lion (1886).

Remenham

Fawley Temple (Temple Island) (1769–71)
Spire (1837)
Druid's Circle (1785)
SU 770 840

Further upstream from Monkey Island, near Remenham, is an even more peaceful fishing lodge, built this time in classical Grecian style by James Wyatt in 1769–71. A little cottage on Temple Island has a three-light bay crowned with a rotunda of Tuscan columns all painted white, supporting a shallow dome. It is surrounded by a small arboretum, spectacular in its autumn foliage. It was built as an eyecatcher to Fawley Court, over on the other side of the river in Buckinghamshire (in fact on the borders of Buckinghamshire, Berkshire and Oxfordshire), and its serenity is disturbed only by the stertorous breathing of scullers powering their way up and down from Henley.

At Remenham itself, down a bumpy track off the Marlow–Henley road we see the top of a church spire sitting on a plinth in a meadow. About 30ft (9m) high, it does nothing, says nothing, but Fuller Maitland, who erected it here in 1837, has done us a good turn by preserving it. The spire is elegantly fluted and has a small carved figure on the tilting top—Job? A monkey? It turns out to have been the spire of St Bride's Church in the City.

A little further along, the track leads into the rear entrance of Park Place School (PRIVATE) once the residence of Field Marshal Henry Seymour Conway. In the tangled wood on the right lies a small ruined edifice—a tower say some, an ice-house say others. It proves to be an ice-house. The entrance to the cellar has been opened up and a beautifully made circular brick room can be seen, with a domed brick roof and matching floor, now silted up; like a large

Wyatt's Temple in Temple Island

squashed sleeping-pill. It's worth seeing if you are looking for the spire, but be careful, for the cellar roof—hidden under the mound—is none too safe.

Conway was soldier, statesman, cousin and closest friend of Horace Walpole, the man who epitomized the 18th century. The Field Marshal was the epitome of the English fighting man: brave, upright, honourable, courteous, dashingly handsome, beautifully spoken, but as William Hunt pointed out: 'he was a better soldier than he was a general, a better general than he was a statesman.' With his tremendous presence, genuine popularity and Walpole's sustained assistance, success and great office were inevitable. It is unlikely, however, that a simple manly soldier would have been greatly concerned about the amelioration of his estate with architectural conceits and fripperies, and we suspect that the 'improvement' of Park Place, a mile or so south of Remenham, and the surrounding area owed not a little to Cousin Horace.

At Temple Combe, just down the road (PRIVATE—KEEP OUT) stands a druid's circle, complete with burial chamber. This is not a folly as Ilton Stonehenge is; this small stone circle is as real as Hetty Pegler's Tump. Its inclusion here is because of its situation; discovered in Jersey in 1785, it was given to General Conway (as he then was) by the people of the island of which he was governor. The inscription shows that Conway inspired a very real respect among his people:

CET ANCIEN TEMPLE DES DRUIDES
DECOUVERT LE 12ME AOUT 1785 SUR LE
MONTAGNE DE ST. HELIER DANS L'ISLE DE
JERSEY: A ETE PRESENTE PAR LES
HABITANS A SON EXCELLENCE LE
GENERAL CONWAY LEUR GOUVERNEUR.
POUR DES SIECLES CACHES, AUX
REGARDS DES MORTELS CET ANCIEN
MONUMENT, CES PIERRES, CES AUTELS,
OU LE SANG DES HUMAINS OFFERT EN
SACRIFICE, RUISSELA, POUR DES DIEUX,
QU'ENFANTIOT LE CAPRICE. CE
MONUMENT, SANS PRIX PAR SON
ANTIQUITE, TEMOIGNERA POUR NOUS A
LA POSTERITE, QUE DANS TOUS LES
DANGERS CESAREE EUT UN PERE
ATTENTIF, ET VAILLANT, GENEREUX, ET
PROSPERE; ET REDIRA, CONWAY, AUX
SIECLES A VENIR, QU'EN VERTU DU
RESPECT DU A CE SOUVENIR, ELLE TE FIT
CE DON, ACQUIS LA A LA VAILLANCE, COMME
UN JUSTE TRIBUTE DE SA
RECONNAISSANCE.

The old house at Temple Combe has long gone and with it, one assumes, much of the atmosphere. Empty for 30 years, it must have been truly exciting to come across this Stonehenge in the wilderness. Now the lawns are carefully tended, clumps of daffodils grow among the monoliths and a modern, circular, yellowstone and glass house sits blindly by.

More Conwayana—an obelisk, a large but uninteresting grotto at the head of Happy Valley and at the bottom of the valley, bearing the A321, Conway's Cyclopic Bridge, a remarkable piece of work, which used stones from fourteen different counties. It resembles, and is probably contemporary with, the Rock Arch at Encombe in Dorset, and coincidentally both were probably designed by Pitts. Thomas Pitt, Lord Camelford, built it for Conway in 1763, and work was well in progress when Walpole wrote to George Montague on 7 October that year, after a visit to Park Place:

> The works of Park-place go on bravely; the cottage will be very pretty and the bridge sublime, composed of loose rocks, that will appear to have been tumbled together there; the very wreck of the deluge. One stone is of fourteen hundredweight. It will be worth a hundred of Palladio's bridges, that are only fit to be used in an opera.

Sulham

Tower (19th century)
SU 650 730

Just before Junction 12 on the M4, the Theale exit, heading to London, on Nunhide Hill there is a small folly tower standing solitary in a field on the left. This is a plain, red brick, castellated, hollow round tower, with blind, pointed windows and ditto entrances (not blind). It now overlooks yet another golf course.

There's a story to the tower, in two variations. A young Victorian gentleman lived at Maidenhatch House and fell in love with a girl living at Sulhamstead House (no, Folly Farm at Sulhamstead is the famous Lutyens-designed house, built three-quarters of a century later), and he erected the tower to 'honour his forbidden love'. This version has the girl being of substantial means, so why the 'forbidden'? Version two has the same young man falling in love with the daughter of one of the estate workers. That's more like it! But this has the man just climbing, not building, the tower, in order to wave at the girl. People were more easily satisfied in the olden days. A subsequent

Sulham Tower

discovery that the tower once served as a dovecote does nothing to diminish our enjoyment of the stories.

By its very position, the tower must be one of the most frequently seen follies in Britain. Yet pedestrian though it is, it grows on one after a while and now every journey down the motorway is punctuated by yells of 'There it is!' when Sulham Tower heaves into view.

Sunninghill

Folly (late 20th century)
SU 950 670

Tittenhurst Park in Sunninghill, near Ascot, was the home of the former Beatle Ringo Starr, and in the grounds he had a folly (about which we couldn't find anything, nor were we on visiting terms), which he wanted to turn into a video studio—the local council first refused (rightly) to give him a grant but then refused to allow him permission for 'change of use'. One can scarcely imagine the planning meeting where it was decided that 'this building is used as a folly and no other usage can be permitted'. The estate is now owned by a Middle Eastern sheikh, who exhibits at the Chelsea Flower Show, so proud is he of his gardens. However, the detailed map he supplies to visitors omits the mysterious folly. Is this all Lucy in the sky?

Windsor

Grotto (18th century)
Sham Ruin
SU 980 760

The private gardens at the castle show that royalty were just as susceptible to the whims and the fashions of the day, for here is an 18th-century grotto and a Gothick sham ruin, as if living in the biggest inhabited castle in the world was not enough. The grotto is cut out of chalk and lined with flint and pebbles rather than the shells and crystals of flashier neighbours. One part, the central octagon, used to be covered in mirrors, but interests fade and money for upkeep ceases to become available even in the highest circles; the mirrors have fallen and broken and only the bare brick remains.

The Gothick Ruin at Frogmore

At Frogmore the Gothick Ruin is said to have been designed by James Wyatt for Queen Charlotte as an elaborate summerhouse. The window tracery is of a higher quality than in most sham ruins and in the right season it ranks among the prettiest anywhere, enveloped as it is in an ancient wisteria.

An Indian kiosk was added in 1858 and came straight from Lucknow. The Cumberland Obelisk is in Windsor Great Park, and commemorates Cumberland's services to his father at Culloden. For Fort Belvedere and the ruins at Virginia Water, see Surrey.

Sham Ruin Dairy (19th century)
SU 950 760

In the town of Windsor itself a folly has emerged that is more gratifying than all the grand designs at the castle. It stands at Bachelors Acre, behind the High Street. It served as a cooling house or dairy to the Bunting family, who had a dress shop at 7 High Street. Its use must have been an afterthought, for it is first of all a sham ruin, probably using spoils. The windows at the back look older than its Gothick front (which may, indeed, be Victorian) and have that very fine distressed appearance. Jutting from the side of the small semicircular building is an arch made from cinders or slag with a ditto window. The dairy is assembled from rough stone, spoils and cinders. On top is what looks like a ventilation shaft covered by a little spire. Unfortunately the ivy has very recently been removed. As there are windows all round, it can't have been much of a cooling house, unless there were shutters.

Winterbourne

Hop Castle (1760s–70s)
SU 460 740

In the parish of Winterbourne, bisected by the M4, is one of Berkshire's best follies, the Hop Castle, close to Chieveley. It is now derelict and vandalized, and as a result the owners are loath—no, refuse—to let anybody near it. This is the folly that has attracted virtually all the folly stories in the county. The stories are, as usual, without foundation—or are they? The Hop Castle is still remote and inaccessible, despite a busy motorway less than 600 yards (550m) away, and so it is a perfect breeding ground for legend. King John liked to hunt around Newbury way— therefore it's King John's Hunting Lodge. And Bad King John used to keep his wife Queen Isabella locked in the coal cellar.

The Hop Castle

There's a secret passage running from the castle to the Blue Bear Inn on North Heath.

Unfortunately for legend, King John was lurking in the area many, many years before the Hop Castle was built. There is no trace of it on a local map dated 1761, and the likelihood is that it was built by John Elwes of Marcham near Abingdon, MP for Berkshire from 1771 to 1784, who succeeded to his uncle's estate in 1763, changing his name (from Meggot, presumably not unwillingly) in order to do so. He was renowned for two things: his miserliness and for keeping the best pack of foxhounds in Berkshire, so it was almost certainly built as a hunting lodge. But why the tunnel? For here, as rarely among folly stories, the legend is the truth. There is (or rather was) a tunnel that ran from the Hop Castle to the nearby Penclose Farm. Within living memory there were people who remembered exploring it as children. Now it has caved in completely, but its course can still be traced as a shallow indentation running across the fields. And what about the tunnel to the Blue Boar? A few years ago a neighbouring farmer was ploughing the field up by the main road near the pub when his tractor fell into the field; the ground he was working on collapsed into a ditch. Did the covered ditch lead to the Hop Castle?

The building itself is rather substantial. It is made from brick and flint and bones, with an octagonal first-floor room with four smaller rooms leading off it. The ground floor contains what could have been a kitchen, a wine cellar (or coal cellar for Queen Isabella?) and three more rooms. The halls and staircase are covered with shells and pebbles. The central octagon has an ogival roof, while the side wings are terminated with hop finials, which give this attractive folly its name.

BUCKINGHAMSHIRE

The best follies in the Home Counties are to be found in Buckinghamshire. From the gardens at Stowe, which have more follies than most counties, to the dubious delights of West Wycombe, Buckinghamshire's follies are rich in style, variety and quantity. Buckinghamshire itself is otherwise a county without an assertive character, probably because of its lack of a clearly defined centre. The town of Buckingham has a population of just over 5000, while ugly Aylesbury, the county town, is still small with 40,000. Slough was the largest and least typical of Buckinghamshire's towns, but in the 1974 county reorganization it sidled over to Berkshire; Milton Keynes in the north, with its projected population of 250,000, looks like being more than its replacement. The only other town of any size is now High Wycombe, which means that the county is endowed with more than its normal share of parks, and a plentiful supply of follies. South Buckinghamshire is stockbroker land, the Chalfonts, Gerrards Cross, Beaconsfield, solidly Tory, London commuters, the greenback belt. Yet there are 18 follies south of Amersham, and that's on the London Underground line.

Fashion, style and appearance have always been important to the Buckinghamshire mind, more so than in neighbouring Berkshire where money is the criterion. In the 16th century the county was swept by a mania for building moats, so that now there are more moated houses in Buckinghamshire than in any other county in England. For our purposes, it is interesting to see that the classic folly story of a man building himself a house so grandiose that he bankrupts himself in the process occurs six times in Great Britain, and no fewer than three of those instances are in Buckinghamshire.

Aylesbury

Eyecatcher (1975)
SP 820 140

The county town can't boast anything as grand as little Buckingham's castle gaol, but at Green End House in Rickfords Hill a printer, Elliott Viney of Hazell Watson & Viney, took a fancy to the 15th-century rose window from the parish church and had it erected in his garden. For more than a century it stood at Ardenham House, which became a hospital, hence the second removal of the screen. Originally it had become available during the restorations (rebuilding more like) of St Mary's church by G.G. Scott in the 1850s and 1860s.

The fortress-like county offices, which dominate the centre of the town, are locally known as Fred's Folly, after the county architect F.B. Pooley, who built them in 1966.

Buckingham

Buckingham Gaol (1748)
SP 690 340

Lord Cobham was probably the most prolific folly builder of all time. A list of the architects and designers he employed sounds like a roll-call of the country's greatest 18th-century artists—Bridgeman, Brown, Gibbs, Kent, Leoni, Vanbrugh—but the architect he employed to build his gaol in Buckingham is unknown. The most likely attribution is James Gibbs, who was working at Stowe in 1748 when the gaol was built.

How can a gaol be a folly? Well, Lord Cobham built it as a speculative venture, Buckingham having lost the County Assizes to Aylesbury before the mid-18th century. There was no point having a courthouse if there wasn't a gaol to put people in afterwards (or before), argued the Tories, so

Cobham, a staunch Whig, built one, complete with medieval towers, crenellations and battlements. A hundred years later George Gilbert Scott, the controversial Buckinghamshire-born Victorian church architect, added a semicircular gaoler's house to the front, in the same design. Alas, despite all this pomp and show, Aylesbury still retained the County Assizes.

Burnham

Dairy (19th century)
SU 940 830

There is a thatched dairy—square, with pyramidal roof and overhanging eaves, once presumably supported by rustic wooden columns—at Brookend Farm in Burnham, where the carved oak lodge prepares us for greater things at Hall Barn.

Chalfont St Giles

Cook Memorial (late 18th century)
SU 980 940

At Chalfont St Giles a castellated arch shelters a column on top of which sits a globe. It was built by Sir Hugh Palliser in the late 18th century to commemorate Captain Cook, which is done at inordinate length by the inscription. It is behind a house called The Vache, which makes us think of dairies again.

Chalfont St Peter

Obelisk (1785)
TQ 020 890

The lack of obelisks also says a lot for the originality at least of the Buckinghamshire mentality. In Chalfont St Peter, in Monument Lane outside the Passmore Edwards Colony, is a rubbly flint obelisk along the lines of the one at Barwick Park in Somerset but smaller (it used to be a lot taller), built as a beacon, a milestone and to mark the spot where George III killed a stag. The other story about the obelisk is better, but less probable. A German servant of the king used to hunt here, which was believed to be only a ploy for carrying on an affair with one of the local girls. George was annoyed by the servant's frequent excuses for losing his way in the wilds of Buckinghamshire, and had the obelisk erected as a milestone. The inscription on the stone reads: 'Built by Sir M.T. Cott/Restored by W. Brown in 1879.'

Cliveden

Pagoda (1867)
SU 920 850

The pretty cast-iron pagoda at Cliveden was made for the Paris exhibition of 1867. It was bought and removed to Bagatelle, but by the 1890s Lord Astor acquired the bauble and put it in his Cliveden garden.

Dinton Castle

Mock Castle (1769)
SP 770 120

The mock Dinton Castle crumbles halfway between Aylesbury and Thame on the A418. It was built by Sir John Vanhatten in 1769 to house his collection of fossils, but it is not certain whether he intended his collection to be in or part of the building—ruined, roofless and floorless, this brave little building appears to be largely built with ammonites, trilobites, pterosaurs for all we know and other fossils. Some time ago the *Wycombe Star* went bananas over some candle wax found in the building: witches! ritual magic! occultists! ley lines! UFOs!—yes, Dinton is supposed to be on the so-called St Mary ley line, and various UFOs have been spotted hovering over Dinton Castle. Teenagers having an impromptu drinks party are ruled out as absurd by commentators.

Part of Dinton Castle

Dorney

The Hermitage (late 18th century)
SU 930 780

Dorney, cut off from the rest of the county by the M4, has a hermitage that may once have served as a lodge to Dorney Court. Flint and stone, like many buildings in the area, with a small octagonal central tower, it is not wildly exciting but has splendid rubble pillars on the garden side and the bottle bottoms Buckinghamshire builders seemed to enjoy using to delineate floor levels.

Dropmore

Aviary (c.1806)
SU 940 860

The astonishing aviary at Dropmore was perhaps built for Lady Grenville *c.*1806 by C.H. Tatham. Tatham had a taste for designing ornamental metalwork and was paid £10,000 for working at Dropmore over three years, so this fantastic parrot-coloured edifice may well be attributed to him. It is built of red-painted iron with green chinoiserie tiles, surmounted with domes, enhanced with wings and blue bays—an aviary fit for an eagle.

Ellesborough

Grotto (19th century)
Obelisk (1902)
SP 840 060

There is said to be a grotto at Chequers, near Ellesborough, but not surprisingly we haven't been able to see it. On Coombe Hill, north of Chequers, on National Trust land, stands one of the county's few obelisks, a Boer War memorial of 1902.

Fawley Court

Gothic Sham Ruin (1731)
Dairy (18th century)
Mausoleum (1750)
SU 750 860

Fawley Court outside Henley-on-Thames, now the Divine Mercy College for the Marian Fathers, has a vista over to Temple Island (see Berkshire); but in the grounds there is a sham ruin with a genuine church window. The ruin is big. It is flint, with brick highlights and surrounds again, but here some real enterprise has been shown—a circular room has been built with a flint and knucklebone dome, tiled on the outside, and with a spike on the top. The floor is tiled

with a swastika pattern from the time when swastikas meant good luck, and the whole eclectic structure confidently melds its differing styles.

The dairy is a delight, flint again, but classical yet with Gothicky fringes (buttresses) and a genuine Norman doorway. The watergate, near the sham ruin, is of the same style.

Fawley's mausoleum (in the churchyard) is yet another major folly building, a near-enough copy of the famous Tomb of Caecilia Metella on Rome's Via Appia.

And perhaps most interesting of all are the dates and the builder. Until now the follies were mostly ascribed to Wyatt and Lancelot Brown, but we have been put out of our misery by the researches of Geoffrey Tyack,

Fawley Court Sham Ruin

who in 1989 published his findings: John Freeman, the owner of Fawley, most probably designed the follies himself. The sham ruin was built around 1731 (in 1732 it was described as 'a Ruin of Flints erected but a year since, with a very good effect') and housed some of the Arundel Marbles Freeman had just acquired. It also explains the domed room behind the Gothick façade. So the Fawley ruin predated Alfred's Hall in Cirencester by at least a year. 1731 was also the year when Freeman perpetrated his famous antiquarian joke when he constructed a sham long barrow at Henley. Two centuries later the site was excavated, and surprised (and no doubt miffed) archaeologists managed to secure its contents: an urn containing an inscription on glass that confessed the mound was built by John Freeman of Fawley Court in 1731.

The mausoleum was built in 1750, and a drawing was made of the prototype in 1746 by Freeman's son, Sambrooke, on his Grand Tour, but the original source appears to have been a 17th-century engraving in his library.

Filgrave

Clock Tower (1936)
SP 870 480

In Filgrave the Coronation Clock Tower, by Sir Edwin Lutyens, dominates the little village.

THIS

CLOCK TOWER

COMMEMORATES

THE CORONATION OF

KING GEORGE VI

AND

QUEEN ELIZABETH

AND WAS ERECTED

BY FREDERICK KONIG

GERDA HIS WIFE

AND HENRY HIS

BROTHER

The tower is now used as a bus shelter. It is obviously much too big for Filgrave, and Lutyens used motifs he had tried and enjoyed in the past—the tower top with its diminishing stages has bisecting arches in half-hearted echo of his great war memorial at Thièpval.

Gayhurst

Hell Khazi (1850s)
Lutyens Pavilions (1926)
SP 840 460

The extraordinary Victorian architect William Burges was at work in the county, at Gayhurst to the north of Milton Keynes, where he constructed a circular outdoor lavatory for the menservants of Lord Carrington. It was used as a hen house by Wrens during World War II, and is now a private house, known as the Round House or the Dog House. Topping the lot is Cerberus, the three-headed dog from Hell, with red glass eyes: why Cerberus?—we do not want to know.

Elsewhere at Gayhurst is a tunnel running under the main road from one abandoned Repton garden to another, with a splendid pointed arch entrance surmounted by the Carrington crest. The walk eventually leads to the Great Ouse and to an urn marking a chalybeate spring and a converted Gothic bath.

Such an eminent 20th-century architect as Sir Edwin Lutyens could scarcely be accused of perpetrating follies, yet at Tyringham House near Gayhurst the two pavilions his clients the Konigs ordered him to inflict upon Sir John Soane's grand design come perilously close. Identified as a bathing pavilion and a music-room-cum-chapel, the two domed temples—for that is what they are—stand awkwardly and ill-at-ease in their environment, even 70 years after they were built.

Gerrards Cross

The Keep (late 18th century)
SU 980 880

The only true folly tower in the whole county is the 'Tudor' gatehouse called The Keep, which was probably built at the turn of the 18th century by Humphry Repton, at Bulstrode Park.

The Keep at Bulstrode Park

Great Missenden

Summerhouse (c.1787)
SP 900 010

Great Missenden has a Gothic summerhouse at the abbey that was probably built by a millionaire Holborn ironmonger, James Oldham. The area must have been popular with these people or their descendants, because only 5 miles away at Great Hampden a Thomas Iremonger in 1751–4 converted his hall into a Gothick extravaganza in the best possible taste—i.e., add a few castellations, insert ogee arches about the place, throw the stucco on and that's it. The sort of thing we truly love to see.

Haddenham

Bone House (1807)
SP 740 090

Folly Farm outside Haddenham is yet another misleading name—there is no folly to be found—but in Haddenham itself is a weirdly decorated cottage, the Bone House in the High Street, dated 1807. This is vernacular architecture at its most vernacular: not for this villager the marble columns and dressed stone of the squires. The cottage was built with whatever came readily to hand, and the most plentiful commodity in 1807 would appear to have been dead sheep. Knuckle bones were formed into patterns to make faces, animals, tools, hearts, diamonds and the proud date, but the artist, with rare modesty, forebore to write his name in bones.

Hall Barn

Garden Buildings (18th century)
Oak Lodge (19th century)
SU 950 890

The Hall Barn Estate is just outside Beaconsfield, neatly sliced off by the M40. The house is small and tall for a country house (part of it was demolished). Colen Campbell worked here, and in the grounds are an obelisk with ball finial and a finely detailed carving of agricultural implements (on the iron gates are little elephants), as well as a large and elegant three-bay Doric covered seat, the remains of a grotto called Milton's Cave (well sited but eminently uninteresting) and a Temple to Venus. One of the 18th-century busts in the grove looks

suspiciously like Virginia Woolf.

But the Oak Lodge north of the M40 is the prize: a remarkable house, completely covered on two sides with elaborately carved black oak. From ground to roof it is decorated with patterns, portraits, mottoes, scenes, crests, fruit until it seems that the fabric would collapse through over-ornamentation but for the support given at the front by the carved Borromini-style coiled pillars. Among the bas-relief portraits is one of Edmund Waller, poet and quondam owner of Hall Barn, and above the ram's head crest of Lord Burnham, the present owner, is his motto OF OLD I HOLD. As the carvings on this astonishing, unique building (the one at Brookend Farm Burnham pales to insignificance) decay, they are replaced by superb modern carvings from Colin Mantrip, who was working on the building in the 1980s.

Hedsor

Lord Boston's Folly (1793)
SU 910 860

The only real eyecatcher in Buckinghamshire far outstrips the others. So big is it and so complicated a structure, that its role as an eyecatcher must have been sublimated in the mania for building. On top of a small hill above the Thames valley sits Hedsor Priory, a large, well-chimneyed house with the parish church huddled slightly below it.

In 1970 another small hill to the north was seen to have strangely regular vegetation on its crown, which on closer inspection turned out to be Lord Boston's Folly. When we visited it ten years later the submerging ivy

Lord Boston's Folly, now a modern house

and creepers had been cut away, and the true extent of the building was revealed. It is surprisingly large—not in height, for the tallest tower is only about 40ft (12.2m), but in area. It seems to wander all over the summit of the hill and continually reveals new aspects as one walks around it. There are three asymmetrically placed towers, one square, one circular and one hexagonal. There's the front half of another hexagonal tower, a piece of wall standing buttressed in cramped isolation between the round tower and the hexagon. Somehow it looks as if once it could all have had a purpose—but no, the romanticism of the setting and the absurd little castellations on all the towers, the careful flint and brick construction—this was for contemplation and enjoyment.

Lord Boston did a fine job, but despite its size, his folly remains a mystery, apart from an alleged dedication to George III and a suspicion that Sir William Chambers, who worked for Boston, may have helped in the design. No stories appear to have grown up around it—people living half a mile away were unaware of its existence—and little is known of Lord Boston himself. This is a blue-chip folly, which has recently been converted into a most luxurious home with yet another wing added to it.

High Wycombe

Castle Folly (19th century)
Witches' Grotto (19th century)
SU 874 919

Pevsner mentions Castle Hill House in Priory Avenue and says there is 'a castellated Folly' on the castle mount in its grounds. The Witches' Grotto in The Rye, John Hearn informs us, has gone. It was simple, more of an alcove, and made of flint, but the unspectacular cascade to which it was the companion still survives.

Hughenden

Pillar (1863)
SU 850 950

Benjamin Disraeli erected a pillar at Hughenden, his country house, in memory of his father Isaac d'Israeli, the compiler of the magnificently unreadable *Curiosities of Literature* (1791–1834). It is 50ft (15.2m) of pink granite, and was designed by E.B. Lamb, a High Victorian architect who rivalled S.S. Teulon in Sir Nikolaus Pevsner's estimation.

Ibstone

Wormsley Follies (1990s)
SU 739 945

Even if John Paul Getty II were not known for being reclusive, we would probably not have succeeded in seeing this collection of follies. But thanks to aerial photography and planning permissions we do know a little about what we should expect here. There are, however, some definites and some don't knows. Those that are finished or under way have, of course, the crass newness of any building, but they will mellow (unless they are demolished before their time— millionaires are a fickle breed). It started out with the rather unimaginative revamped mansion—as dull as calling your son John Paul Getty III—but soon the sham castle behind the mansion was planned—as quirky as calling your second son Tara Gabriel Galaxy Gramophone Getty—as well as a tunnel. Here's a list of the projects:
Definite:
- A fake classical house (with a supposed Elizabethan core), and a ditto Norman castle at the back, a little larger than the house itself, the whole serving as a library (much like our own modest homes).
- Badminton-style gateway (you know, those pointy bits on top that Thomas Wright liked so much).
- A tremendously long, winding grotto tunnel, the entrance rusticated, with a grotto at the end.

Don't know (planned and permission granted):
- A hermitage (to be made from wood, bark

I COULD DO WITH A DRINK

Some Follies as Pubs

CASTLE, EDGHILL
Warwickshire

———

SHIP ON SHORE, SHEERNESS
Kent

———

BLACK CASTLE, BRISLINGTON
Bristol

———

THE GROTTO
South Shields, Durham

———

CROCKER'S FOLLY
St. John's Wood, London

and so on).
- A reading hovel (a stone hut).
- A sham ruin on a sham island.
- A satellite tower disguised as yet another sham ruin (the design a fusion between Sturt's Folly and Racton Tower, but smaller).

Move over Mr Getty, we're coming to stay. Mine's the hermitage!

Iver

Oddments (late 18th–early 19th century)
TQ 040 810

Iver, now in imminent danger of being engulfed by the Great Wen, used to boast a pretty house called Richings Park, which had in its grounds cascades, an ice-house and a bridge. Traces remain of these, as they remain of the house, but only the real enthusiast will be able to make much sense of them.

Lower Hartwell

Egyptian Spring (1851)
Garden Buildings (19th century)
SP 800 120

Lower Hartwell (there is no Upper Hartwell) has Hartwell House, a discreetly smart hotel. There is an obelisk (1757) and a column of George II (statue 1757, column itself 1735, originally holding up a statue of King William), but the unjustifiably well-known folly here is the Egyptian Spring, a wellhead designed by Joseph Bonomi Jr in 1851, a severely plain little structure, distinguished only by a line of hieroglyphs running along the lintel. Do they mean anything? Our hieroglyphics are a little rusty.

A castellated and domed round tower with quatrefoil windows (mentioned by Pococke in 1751) stands near the ruined Gothick church—real not sham—by Henry

Keene, 1753–5, and there are scattered bits and pieces throughout the grounds, pieces of older houses and churches incorporated into the park walls and a façaded dry bridge under the drive, it replaces another bridge and is a removal: the central span of James Paine's Kew Bridge.

Marlow

Quarry Wood Hall (early 20th century)
SU 850 860

This is one of those instances where everyone is shouting 'Folly!' and we don't have a clue why. The house, originally a hunting lodge, is a straggling castellated affair along the river, with pointed windows, arrowslits—all the usual. The only curiosity about it is its late date: Edwardian. In 1990 the stair tower was rebuilt.

Medmenham

Medmenham Abbey (c.1755)
SU 810 840

Before moving to West Wycombe the egregious Sir Francis Dashwood lived at Medmenham Abbey on the banks of the Thames. He leased the place from 1752 and founded the notorious Hell Fire Club here, originally called the Order of St Francis of Medmenham. The stories are too widely circulated to bear repetition here—there are no end of books, articles and stories about the Hell Fire Club, some more imaginative than others. There is little indication that there were many follies built at Medmenham, and the pleasantly sited, ruined abbey tower adjoining the house looks genuine enough, although it is credited to Dashwood and dated *c.*1755.

Long after Dashwood's time, Medmenham came again into the public eye. A minor event was commemorated by a minor but pretty monument, a plinth with a tiny sloping tiled roof and a plaque:

THIS MONUMENT
WAS ERECTED TO COMMEMORATE
THE SUCCESSFUL ACTION
FOUGHT BY
HUDSON EWEBANK KEARLEY
FIRST VISCOUNT DEVONPORT PC
WHICH RESULTED IN THE
COURT OF APPEAL DECIDING
ON THE 28TH MARCH 1899
THAT MEDMENHAM FERRY
IS PUBLIC

There is no longer a ferry.

The Egyptian Spring

Milton Keynes

Cows (1978)
Clock Tower (mid-1970s)
Peace Pagoda (1978–80)
SP 880 380

Despite its newness Milton Keynes has already provided us with eccentricities—at Bradwell, circumscribed by roundabouts and dual carriageways, is a scene of rural felicity with four Friesian cows and two calves gambolling around them. They gambol in permanence, for they are made of ferro-concrete and placed in a field among housing estates in order to de-urbanize the area. They were made by Liz Leyh, artist in residence, in 1978 and presented as a gift to the town.

Neath Hill in Milton Keynes has a surprising touch of chinoiserie in a clock tower built in the mid-1970s, and japanoiserie at Willen, where Japanese Buddhists and the architect Tom Hancock erected a Peace Pagoda in 1978–80, all exterior, solid inside, and made of concrete. A similar one has been built in London's Battersea Park.

North Crawley

Eyecatcher (1719)
SP 930 450

Eyecatchers are uncommon in Buckinghamshire, but an early example was built in 1719 at Grange Farm in North Crawley, near Newport Pagnell, to answer the view from the newly built Chicheley Hall. It has now been restored, but lacks all fancy, being only a two-storey, five-bay blank frontage. The Hall also has a dovecote with an ogee roof, and at Astwood, just down the road towards Bedford, a tall octagonal dovecote has been converted into a smart house.

Penn Street

Grotto (19th century)
SU 930 960

Flint and brick were the predominant building materials in the southern part of the county, not just for the follies. Tufa, limestone and shells were rare materials in landlocked Buckinghamshire, which may explain the paucity of grottoes. Even the larger estates seem to have eschewed the form, which is peculiar, when neighbouring counties can boast fine examples. Woodrow High House at Penn Street has an octagonal domed grotto built of black and white pebbles.

Slough

Grotto Wall (19th century)
TQ 020 820

Langley Park, north of Langley Marish, which now forms part of Slough, has a grotto wall in a conservatory, possibly one of those pleasing Pulhamite artefacts. After World War II the 1805 column to Robert Harvey was demolished, which is a pity as Pevsner described it as 'very oddly shaped and decorated … with a kind of iron cage or pavilion on the top'.

Stoke Goldington

Arthur Mead's Follies (1988 onwards)
SP 840 490

Arthur Mead was well known in Stoke Goldington for his prize-winning vegetables and for the impromptu arboretum near his bungalow. But a load of limestone from a demolished cottage in Ram Alley led him to construct a sham ruin, or rather a sham ruined wall. He started building it in 1988 but was, as is any folly builder worth his salt, not content with only one folly and progressed to stage two. It included the building of a hermit's cell, now inhabited by a manikin called Jerome. Mr Mead willed his follies and his plot of land to the Folly Fellowship and even went as far as to inscribe a stone with the Folly Fellowship logo and the initials of the three Founding Fathers (or FFFF). We blush.

Arthur Mead and his folly wall

Stoke Poges

Column (1800)
Alcove (late 18th century)
`SU 990 840`

A 68ft (21m) Doric column surmounted with a statue by J.F.C. Rossi to the memory of

SIR EDWARD COKE

1552–1634

FIRST LORD CHIEF JUSTICE OF ENGLAND

was built by James Wyatt in 1800, and is now on the golf course at the white wedding cake house of Stoke Park in Stoke Poges.

At Stoke Court is a Gothic arch with a niche for a seat, built out of a rubbly conglomerate, for Thomas Gray. Gray himself is commemorated by a massive Wyatt-designed sarcophagus placed, not in the churchyard as tradition dictates, but in a field nearby where it could the more easily be seen from Stoke Park.

HARD BY YON WOOD NOW SMILING AS IN SCORN

MUTTERING HIS WAYWARD FANCIES HE WOULD ROVE

NOW DROOPING, WOFUL-WAN LIKE ONE FORLORN

OR CRAZED WITH CARE, OR CROSSED IN HOPELESS LOVE.

Humphrey Repton is said to have organized the siting. It is now owned by the National Trust.

Stowe

Follies (18th century)
`SP 670 360`

And so to Stowe. There are more follies in a smaller area at Stowe than there are anywhere else in the world (except perhaps at Wörlitz, Germany), and anyone with any interest in the subject should make a pilgrimage there. The mansion now houses the eponymous public school, but the grounds are often open to the public during school holidays. Some 221 acres (90ha) of the grounds were covenanted to the National Trust by the school in 1968, and work is continually going on to maintain the follies in reasonable condition. It is a long and expensive task, which deserves support from the widest possible quarters, and partly for that reason and partly from sheer fear at the enormity of the subject we will not discuss the buildings at Stowe in depth here. The basic book is *Stowe: A Guide to the Gardens*, written by Laurence Whistler, Michael Gibbon and George Clarke, first published in 1956, with revised editions every decade. In the late 1980s a series of booklets was started by Michael Bevington, describing each of the many, many garden features in tremendous and exhaustive detail, in effect providing each folly at Stowe with its own monograph.

So we will list the still extant buildings, single out a few favourites and summarize the chronology.

Arches:
• The Corinthian Arch designed by Thomas Pitt (1765)
• The Doric Arch (erected 1768)

Pavilions:
• Oxford Lodge by William Kent (re-erected 1760)
• Boycott Pavilions by James Gibbs (1728)
• Lake Pavilions by Sir John Vanbrugh (1717)

Bridges:
• Oxford Bridge
• Shell Bridge by Kent (c.1742)
• Palladian Bridge by Lord Pembroke (c.1740)

Obelisks, towers, columns:
• Wolfe Obelisk (1760)
• Grenville Column (1747)
• Cobham Monument by Gibbs (1747)
• Bourbon Tower by Gibbs (c.1740)

Temples:
• Ancient Virtue by Kent (1734)
• Friendship by Gibbs (1739)
• Rotondo by Vanbrugh (1721)
• Venus by Kent (1732)
• Concord and Victory by Lord Temple (1747; recently a series of caverns were discovered underneath the temple)
• Queen's by Gibbs (1744; a substantial undercroft, which may once have held a waterwheel, was discovered by two students researching for the Folly Fellowship Measured Drawing Award in 1992).

Monuments:
• Captain Cook (1778)
• William Congreve by Kent (1736)
• Queen Caroline (1732)

Others:
• Season's Fountain (19th century)
• Fane of Pastoral Poetry by Gibbs
• Gothic Umbrello near the obelisk
• Pebble Alcove by Kent
• Cascade
• Menagerie (1780; now the school shop)
• Hermitage by Kent
• Grotto (1741)
• Dido's Cave
• Stowe Castle by Gibbs (1740; outside the grounds)
• Chinese House (c.1738; this was in exile in Co. Kildare, but has recently been returned to Stowe)
• Gothic Cascade

Gibbs's Gothic Temple is doubtless the most striking building at Stowe. It is ugly (even to aficionados), a hideous rusty brown colour, big, intrusive and wonderful. It is triangular and has nothing to recommend it apart from its solidity and its leering self-confidence. It predates Flitcroft's triangular follies, but Gibbs may have been influenced by Thomas Archer's now demolished triangular rectory at Deptford, built in 1724.

The bulging Bourbon Tower is some way from the main gardens, but its dumpiness and its decrepitude are immensely appealing. Originally a keeper's lodge, it was renamed after a visit by exiled French royalty in 1808. The Cobham Monument is a tall column with a domed cupola; once there were stairs to the top, but the doorway is now sealed. The Grenville Column is an extremely rare example in Britain of the free-standing *columna rostrata*, a column decorated with the prows of ships jutting like beaks out of its shaft, looking more like a totem pole than a classical architectural motif. William Kent's buildings are grandiose garden ornaments rather than follies, nevertheless the Temple of British Worthies rewards a close study. Perhaps the finest of Kent's buildings is the Temple of Ancient Virtue, an elegant domed rotunda with an Ionic colonnade, a reinterpretation of the Temple of the Sibyl at Tivoli.

Stowe was the seat of Sir Richard Temple, Viscount Cobham, a general and the leader of Whig society in Buckinghamshire. His garden was more than a pleasance, it was also a political statement—for example, the Temple of Ancient Virtue was adjoined by the now vanished Temple of Modern Virtue, deliberately built as a ruin in a sharp

The Temple of Ancient Virtue, Stowe

comment on the policies of Walpole.

The remarkable works at Stowe began when Cobham appointed the unknown Charles Bridgeman to design the grounds. Bridgeman was the catalyst for the revolution in landscape design, the father of the natural line of succession of William Kent, Lancelot Brown, Humphrey Repton and J.C. Loudon. The ha-ha was his innovation, and he was the first to abandon rigid formality in garden design. Cobham played safer but no less brilliantly with his architect, choosing Vanbrugh, like himself also an old soldier but then at the height of his architectural fame. On Vanbrugh's death he was succeeded by James Gibbs, Giacomo Leoni and William Kent. Kent followed Bridgeman as garden designer, as he did at Rousham in Oxfordshire, on a much smaller scale, and in 1741 the 24-year-old Lancelot Brown, later to be nicknamed 'Capability' Brown and the only landscape architect ever to achieve international fame, was appointed head gardener. With such a galaxy of stars, it is not surprising that Stowe has probably the most important position in English garden history.

We have said elsewhere that builders of follies were not necessarily a pleasant breed—here is an instance. In 1748 two men were caught poaching on the Cobham Estate and were held captive. Their wives came before Cobham to plead for their release, and the viscount received them with every kindness, was charm personified. Concern, benevolence and good humour radiated from him; of course, the men were to be released—in fact, he promised they were to be returned home the very next Tuesday. Puzzled but mollified by his lenience, the women went home. On Tuesday the carter arrived with two coffins. 'Here are your husbands,' he said. 'Lord Cobham says to remind you that he kept his word.'

Thornton

Grotto (late 18th century)
Eyecatcher (late 18th century)
SP 750 350

Thanks to Tom Sargant a grotto has come to light at Thornton Hall, now a convent, adding to the county's low stock of such buildings. It is made of rough stone, with a central pointed entrance and two ditto niches at the sides. The grotto has a crow-stepped gable, and behind it the roof has collapsed and pieces of the stained glass windows are still preserved. At the back it had a cave, which is now almost totally destroyed. The

Thornton Grotto

grotto held left-overs from a church restoration, and sadly most of these have now gone.

An eyecatcher arch, resembling the design of the grotto, is in the wall of the kitchen garden.

Waddesdon

Grotto (late 19th century)
Aviary (late 19th century)
SP 750 160

In the mid-19th century Buckinghamshire was discovered by the Rothschilds. Mayer Rothschild bought Mentmore in 1850, and he was closely followed by brother Lionel (Halton, 1851), brother Anthony (Aston Clinton, 1851) and, a generation later, Nathan (Ascott, 1874) and Ferdinand (Waddesdon, 1874). The Rothschilds, being in the main a pragmatic banking family, tended not to go in for fripperies in the park, preferring to lavish vast sums of money on their actual houses. But in all families there are exceptions, as Sir Anthony Rothschild discovered when he was bitten in his park by a large cassowary, a friend of his son Alfred. Poor Alfred was banished to build Halton, which he finished in 1888, and where he took great delight in driving around his park in a carriage pulled by two zebras. Yet the only Rothschild building that approaches follyship, if one discounts the sheer opulence of the chateau-cum-railway-station baronial magnificence of Waddesdon, is the Swiss Chalet at Aston Clinton, the only relic from Sir Anthony's time now that the great house has been demolished.

At Waddesdon, now a National Trust property, the famous French landscape gardener Lainé was employed to design the park, and among the incidentals he produced a little rock grotto and a delightful aviary. The trinkets in the park are eclipsed by the sheer audacity of decoration shown in the estate village: the lodges, pubs, houses are at the same time uniform and totally different from each other, avoiding the strangled similarities of the average estate village.

West Wycombe

Follies (mid-18th century)
`SU 840 930`

When Sir Francis Dashwood moved to West Wycombe from Medmenham, his previously sublimated urge to build broke out. The National Trust now owns West Wycombe, and a Sir Francis Dashwood still lives in the house, which is surrounded by a number and variety of follies that would be unequalled in any county that did not also contain Stowe. Visible from miles around is the golden ball on the church tower, which Sir Francis added to the existing 14th-century church in 1761–3. It is reached by ladder from the roof of the tower, and is big enough to hold six people inside. Stories of black magic rites abounded and were never really convincingly denied.

St Crispins Cottage, West Wycombe

Below the church is the mausoleum, a mighty, hexagonal, roofless monument built by John Bastard for Sir Francis in 1763–5 with £500 provided from the will of Lord Melcombe, the George Bubb Dodington whose column in memory of his wife was re-erected in Savernake Forest after he died, to commemorate George III's recovery from madness. The design was inspired by Constantine's Arch in Rome.

Not so the entrance to the Hell Fire Caves. This is real folly stuff, gloomy, sinister, amateur and threatening, despite the large numbers of visitors going in to see the waxworks and recorded commentaries that sanitize the caves themselves. The façade is knapped flint, with pointed and broken arches rising on top of each other like shark's teeth, a jaw open for swallowing or biting. Inside is a salute to our American cousins: most of the exhibits inside concern Benjamin Franklin, who once stayed at West Wycombe, and there is virtually nothing about the

A crowstepped garden wall at West Wycombe

lascivious and immeasurably more interesting John Wilkes, a much more frequent visitor—but our American cousins know nothing of Wilkes and care less, and they provide much of the income.

At the bottom of the hill is the Pedestal, a plain column with a ball on top built to mark distances and the completion of Sir Francis' new road:

FROM THE UNIVERSITY MILES XXII

FROM THE CITY MILES XXX

FROM THE COUNTY TOWN MILES XV

SIR F. DASHWOOD DERAE CHRISTIANAE MDCCLII

The park is on the south side of the road. It is said that the trees were originally planted in patterns of great vulgarity (how?) but that Repton scrubbed it all up when he worked here. What remains are the temples, several of which were designed by Nicholas Revett. The Temple of Venus, an Ionic rotunda with dome and ball finial set on a mound above a flint tunnel archway flanked by pyramids, was painstakingly restored in 1984. The other temples are the Temple of the Four Winds, Daphne's Temple, Flora's Temple, the Temple of Bacchus, a Music Temple on the island and another small temple. There is also an exedra, a cascade and a triumphal arch. Wilkes mentions a 'lewd temple', probably demolished by Repton, although he may have meant the Temple of Venus, the entrance of which is indeed extremely naughty if one's mind is set to such things.

Many of the estate cottages are built in brick and flint, the commonest local building materials, and flint is for some reason irresistible to folly builders. The cottages visible from the house usually have some monstrous flint excrescence grafted on, but in the case of St Crispin's Cottage the addition is a beautifully proportioned and well-worked church tower with quatrefoil windows and fretted belfry window, the equal as a sham church eyecatcher of Suffolk's Tattingstone Wonder.

The affairs at Medmenham and West Wycombe were written up by Charles Johnston in his *Chrysal: or, The Adventures of a Guinea* (1768, we have used the 1797 'Cooke's edition'), and Medmenham and its 'gross lewdness and daring impiety' is indeed mentioned, with Wycombe's church described as:

a church, on an eminence near his house, that answered the double purpose of convincing the populace of his regard to religion, and of making a beautiful termination to a vista which he had just cut through a wood in his park.

What it does not mention is how Dashwood and his cronies could have enjoyed the lavish entertainments of the erotic layout of part of the gardens: from the golden ball on top of the church one would have had a splendid overview!

Weston Underwood

Cowper's Alcove (1753)
SP 870 510

At Western Underwood in the far north of the county is a garden that used to belong to the Throckmortons of long-demolished Weston Manor. Still called The Wilderness, it has a Gothic temple, a Gothic alcove and other bits and pieces where poor mad William Cowper found solace. The pedestals that once held busts and urns remained; then the garden became part of the Flamingo

---

DAMP, DARK AND WONDERFUL

Some Sublime Folly Gardens

HAWKSTONE
Shropshire

STOWE
Buckinghamshire

FORBIDDEN CORNER
North Yorkshire

HACKFALL
North Yorkshire

PAINSHILL
Surrey

STOURHEAD
Wiltshire

STANCOMBE PARK
Gloucestershire

HELIGAN
Cornwall

MOUNT EDGCUMBE
Cornwall

BIDDULPH
Staffordshire

Tropical Bird Gardens and Zoo; now it is derelict again.

Cowper's Alcove is set a little way up the slight hill, hexagonal and surprisingly tall, with a splendid panorama of the English countryside, which here has scarcely changed since Cowper's day. His poem 'The Task', a diatribe against graffiti, completes the scene:

> The summit gain'd, behold the proud
>   alcove
> That crowns it! yet not all its pride
>   secures
> The grand retreat from injuries
>   impress'd
> By rural carvers, who with knives deface
> The panels, leaving an obscure, rude
>   name,
> In characters uncouth, and spelt amiss.
> So strong the zeal t'immortalize himself
> Few transient years, won from th'abyss
>   abhorr'd
> Of blank oblivion, seem a glorious prize,
> And even to a clown. Now roves the eye
> And, posted on this speculative height,
>   Exults in its command.

Wotton Underwood

Tartar Temple (18th century)
Garden Buildings (18th century)
Chinese Bridge (1995)
`SP 680 160`

Wotton Underwood's most unusual

Tartar Temple

possession is a Turkish Temple (or rather Tartar Temple Tent), of which almost all examples in Britain have gone, so this is a most important building. For a long time it was seriously at risk, but it was restored to a pristine state by Elaine Brunner, as have been the Rotunda and the Octagon Temple. Mrs Brunner bought the estate for £6000 in the late 1950s and devoted her life to the rescue of the house and grounds. She would have been appalled to discover that her contractors for the restoration of the Tartar Temple used cheap unseasoned timber, and already it is rotting badly. It will all need to be replaced within a couple of years. In today's unstoppable rush for short-term, quick profits, time spent leaving timber to season is money thrown away, so instead it is quickly dried in a kiln, then shoved onto the market. This allows it to decay and rot in as little as seven years instead of the old-fashioned seventy. It's not surprising poor people are turning to plastic windows instead of wooden ones. Of course, if some old-fashioned fogey does insist on using wood, the chippies will be able to come back and do the job again within the decade. Everybody benefits: lumberjacks, the timber merchants, the carpenters; only the punter and the buildings suffer. Eventually we'll all be forced to buy plastic replacements, and then there'll be no more lumberjacks, timber merchants or carpenters.

Back to Wotton after that little rant. It also has a bridge-cum-dam of 1758 designed by Sanderson Miller. It once had a Chinese house, but that was removed to Harristown, Co. Kildare, and has recently been returned in triumph to Stowe from whence it originally came.

Wotton abounds with garden buildings, never overstepping the brink towards follydom: a rustic temple that looks Indonesian; a round Tuscan temple with a grotto underneath; there's a rebuilt Octagon; a new 'sentry box' on an island with a small rustic bridge; a covered bridge owing a little to Palladio; a pair of classical temples as well as lots of statues, urns, vases—building never ended at Wotton while Mrs Brunner was the chatelaine.

One of her last landscape enhancements was a surprisingly big and very solid Chinese bridge, built in 1995 and so steeply pitched that it is possible to cross it only by hauling oneself over, using the balustrade as a climbing frame. Apparently this is not necessarily a design fault; the bridge awaits the steps which will make the crossing a breeze. We wonder.

CAMBRIDGESHIRE AND HUNTINGDONSHIRE

There is only one folly of national importance in the whole of Cambridgeshire, even after Huntingdonshire and Peterborough were added in the county shuffle. This makes it the most barren ground in Britain for the folly-hunter in follies per capita, but no picture can be seen in full at a glance: the architect Peter Foster lived in the county, the bellwether, with Quinlan Terry, of the 20th-century folly revival.

CAMBRIDGESHIRE

Cambridge

Hobson's Conduit (1614)
`TL 450 580`

One of the county's few follies has been demolished since 1967: the little sham ruin at Laundry Farm, Barton Road. That leaves Cambridge with only one folly, Hobson's Conduit. Like the far grander Carfax Conduit in Oxford, it was built for a specific purpose, but when it became redundant it was moved: not, like Carfax, to grace an exquisite rural landscape, but from Market Hill to a humbler site on the corner of Lensfield Road and Trumpington Road.

Hexagonal, with niches and topped with a cupola, it was endowed in perpetuity by the will of Thomas Hobson, who achieved a kind of immortality by allegedly being the first person to rent out horses, a sort of 17th-century Hertz. Unlike that worthy organization, Hobson's clients had to take the first mount they were offered—hence Hobson's Choice.

Gamlingay Cinques

Full Moon Gate (1712)
`TL 230 530`

On the Bedfordshire border is the hamlet of Gamlingay Cinques with a charmingly named folly, the Full Moon Gate. The name is the most attractive thing about the folly, which stands rather forlornly in a hedge at the side of a public footpath dividing two large fields in the village. No road leads up to or from it, and it is getting more and more difficult to tell that it once was a gate. It was built in 1712 by Sir George Downing, and originally there were two large rusticated brick piers flanking a large lunette, which gave rise to the name. Now it is ruinous, rubbly and overgrown, standing about 20ft (6m) high. The magic has all but disappeared.

Grantchester

Sham Ruin (1857)
`TL 430 550`

In the garden of Mary and Jeffrey Archer's home, the Old Vicarage, is a small sham castle, or 'Castle Ruin' as its builder Samuel Page Widnall would have it: a Tudorish, polygonal, embattled tower with a new conservatory, which was added by the Archers. Widnall was a florist and market gardener who must have made a fair amount

Grantchester Sham Ruin

of money because he also built himself a Swiss cottage, a bath house and a dovecote, but sadly these buildings were destroyed by floods in the late 19th century. Widnall not only designed his own buildings, but he used the folly as a photographic studio and had his own private printing press. Rupert Brooke lived here in 1911 and the folly is supposed to be 'the falling house that never falls' in his poem about the Old Vicarage.

Harston

Wale Obelisk (1739)
TL 440 510

Just south of Cambridge at Harston, clearly visible from the M11, is the only obelisk of note in the county. It commemorates Gregory Wale and was made by the Cambridge mason and sculptor Charles Bottomley.

Madingley

Sham Bridge (c.1756)
TL 390 600

Lancelot Brown worked at Madingley Hall, now part of Cambridge University, where all that remains of his landscaping is a small serpentine lake with a sham bridge at the end.

Six Mile Bottom

Windmill Folly (mid-19th century)
TL 570 570

On Bungalow Hill, near an old windmill, is a remarkable Sino-Gothic house. It has flint walls with brick detailing and pointed windows and a sweeping pagoda roof, the theme repeated in its two side wings. It was apparently built by the owner of the windmill in the middle of the 19th century.

Wimpole

Sham Castle (1749–72)
TL 330 510

Cambridgeshire's best folly is the sham ruin at the National Trust's Wimpole Hall. It was commissioned in 1749 by the then Lord Chancellor, Philip Yorke, 1st Earl of Hardwicke, from Sanderson Miller, one of his early ventures outside the Midlands, although it appears not to have been built until 1772. Again, Lancelot Brown seems to have been involved, and either he or James Essex was actually responsible for overseeing the construction, which may well have taken place during one of Miller's periodic bouts of insanity. The Lord Chancellor dealt with Miller through an intermediary, Sir George Lyttelton, and his purpose was clearly spelt out in one of the few precise instructions— well, commands—to build a folly that has come down to us:

> As the back view will be immediately closed by the wood there is no regard to be had to it, nor to the left side, but only to the front and right side as you look from the house. As my Lord desired it merely as an object he would have no staircase or leads in any of the towers, but merely the walls so built as to have the appearance of a ruined castle.

The tower was, in fact, built with floors, stairs

The Sino-Gothic Mill House folly at Six Mile Bottom

Wimpole Sham Castle

and roof, but the overall plan was followed. The structure is huge, and the eye is, of course, immediately caught by the massive four-storey tower, but joining it are some 200ft (61m) of curtain wall, pierced with doorways and arches (including one with a Gothick window above) and terminated at either end with two more towers.

Many years ago, long before Wimpole became a National Trust property, it was into one of these towers, pitch black inside, that we pushed through the brambles and bracken and choking undergrowth that effectively concealed the enormous size of the folly. Nervous, because of the plethora of NO TRESPASSING signs (we couldn't find anyone to ask permission), we entered cautiously, hoping not to be caught. As Gwyn walked into the room, a white, staring face silently and suddenly rose up at him, draining the intruder of strength, confidence and the ability to think logically. The sound of a man screaming on a hot summer's afternoon in the country could have been unnerving to his partner, sunning herself on the edge of the field, having seen as much of the folly as she needed to. But no. 'Frightened of a barn owl,' she observed dispassionately, as she watched the equally terrified bird shoot silently past. The undergrowth (and, one assumes, the owl) has now all been cleared away; its preservation as a ruin is now assured.

Wisbech

Flint House (19th century)
Grotto (19th century)
TF 470 090

In King's Lynn Road stands a Gothicized flint house in King's Lynn Road in Wisbech. It is now used as an office. There is a little grotto in the gardens of Peckover House in the same town.

Wisbech Flint House

HUNTINGDONSHIRE

Abbot's Ripton

Garden Buildings (20th century)
TL 230 780

Peter Foster's works in the county were confined to his own garden at Hemingford Grey and Lord de Ramsey's garden at Abbot's Ripton. The majority cannot be classified as follies in the truest sense of the word, being elaborate garden structures and ornaments, but one or two take a delicately trellised step across the border.

Take, for example, a wooden Gothic temple built entirely of trelliswork in the centre of Lord de Ramsey's herbaceous borders. Traditional British gardening would dictate that trellis should be used only as a framework for climbing plants, but this one is innocent of creepers, its skeletal quality being used to stir the mind to provide the infill. Deliberately unpainted, the wood from which it was built was chosen by Foster for its quality when weathered, but the crockets on the gables have weathered differently—they turn out to be fibreglass. Also fibreglass are the massive urns that surmount the gate piers at the end of the path: one would have to touch them to discover their provenance, so real do they look. Fibreglass mouldings are as much a feature of the 20th-century folly as Coade stone was of the late 18th and early 19th centuries.

On the wall of the house are three trellised alcoves, but here again the eye deceives, for the trellis is flat, and only the ingenious curvature of the slats gives the impression of depth.

There is a Chinese bridge (looking not at all Chinese, but the original design was too expensive to build), with a white-painted latticed aviary nearby and a small grotto fountain on the wall at the end of the stream, a tributary of the Nene. Through the colonnaded indoor swimming pool, the conservatory has a Moorish temple looming at one end—but again it is all sham, painted and jigsawed plywood fixed to the road wall.

A number of structures were designed but remain unbuilt, including a medieval jousting tent complete with struts and stays, again built of fibreglass. The most substantial building is the Fishing Temple, a few hundred yards out of the garden on the shores of the lake. The flat fenland would not be an inspiration to most of us, but with the help of his faithful gardener of more than 20 years and Peter Foster's follies, Lord de Ramsey has created a remarkable garden. 'I can't paint,' he is quoted as saying. 'I can't compose music, I'm not sure that I can write—but I can garden.'

Hemingford Grey

Garden Buildings (1960s–80s)
TL 290 710

Having a smaller area in which to operate, Peter Foster's own follies at Hemingford Grey were more modest than his work at Abbot's Ripton, but there is a delightful temple built with his own hands over 30 years ago, a Pompeiian Grotto, which sounds and is marvellous, even if it is only 3ft big, and columns and urns everywhere. Some years ago he designed a three-piece column mould, elegant, fluted and with the correct degree of entasis, and discovered that making columns was an immensely enjoyable occupation. They sprang up all over his garden until friends also discovered the delights of column making, borrowed the moulds and passed them around the country. There must be columns of the Foster order in every English county.

Norman Cross

Column (1914)
TL 160 910

On the A1 at Norman Cross stood a plain column, about 20ft (6m) high, built in 1914 to commemorate:

ONE THOUSAND SEVEN HUNDRED & SEVENTY
SOLDIERS AND SAILORS
NATIVES OR ALLIES OF FRANCE
TAKEN PRISONERS OF WAR DURING THE
REPUBLICAN AND NAPOLEONIC WARS
WITH GREAT BRITAIN A.D. 1793–1814
WHO DIED IN THE MILITARY DEPOT
AT NORMAN CROSS, WHICH FORMERLY
STOOD NEAR THIS SPOT, 1797–1814
DVLCE • ET • DECORVM • EST • PRO • PATRIA •
MORI

It vanished during an A1 road widening scheme carried out since the second edition of this book appeared, and it may well enhance a contractor's garden.

CHANNEL ISLANDS

GUERNSEY

SARK

St Peter Port

St Andrews

JERSEY

Quotation House

GUERNSEY

St Andrews

Les Vauxbelets Little Chapel (1923)

Picassiette of Chartres would have loved this, and he could well have built it, but we do know the builder: a Brother Deodat. Apparently from 1914 onwards he tried twice to build this reverential little chapel, before getting it right at last in 1923. This is not a chapel first and foremost, but an imitation Lourdes grotto, constructed in the old, approved manner, but the chapel on top has rather taken over and it is promoted as the Little Chapel, not the Lourdes Grotto. Brother Deodat worked on both chapel and

The Little Chapel and its builder

grotto until his death in 1951. Like the great plate-breaker's work at Chartres, the chapel is decorated with thousands of pieces of broken crockery, intact souvenir-ashtrays, pebbles and even a few shells, and the grotto itself mainly consists of slag. The whole ensemble would not have looked out of place in northern France.

St Peter Port

Victoria Tower (1848)

The inhabitants of the Isle of Man seems to have been especially fond of Victoria and Albert, and so the royal couple chose to holiday on the Isle of Wight; but Guernsey was early in the race for the Queen's insular affections—after she visited in 1846, they erected a Gothic tower with a very decorative top (where the battle of the styles appears not yet to have been resolved), and with a surprisingly airy turret.

JERSEY

Quotation House (1970s)

Somewhere on the island (we visited only 25 years ago), there must be, there should still be, the bizarre house, which was covered with *mene tekels*: all over the house itself, in the garden, on the gate posts and on the garden wall, everything covered with biblical quotations. Why do disturbed people so often rely on the Bible to broadcast their insanity? A small sample reads: 'Murderers'; 'If a man B found lying with a woman married 2 an husband, then they shal [sic] both of them die'; 'It is an honour for a man to cease from strife: but every fool will B meddling'.

We would really like to know if Quotation House still survives—drop us a line on your next visit for tax reasons.

CHESHIRE

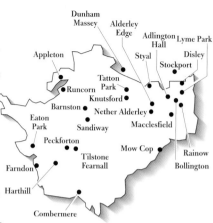

Cheshire has a fair number of follies, although many of them turn out to be the result of Tutankhamen's curse: obelisks. Usually where one finds obelisks, one also finds columns, a phenomenon Cheshire has ignored. Antiquity here is represented by one or two fake stone circles and a good number of sham ruins. There is no full-blown folly estate, however, no folly garden or squire's collection of stone eccentricities, other than the metaphysical Pilgrim's Progress garden at Rainow, which is more in the mind than in the stone. The group in and around Knutsford makes for a late but charming urban exception.

Adlington Hall

Temple of Diana (1760)
SJ 905 805

The Legh family's Adlington Hall, an ancient half-timbered hall with a brash new brick extension with a mighty portico (new, that is, in the 18th century), has a deer park. The Hall stands on the site of a former hunting lodge, and in the old deer park is a sham castle dating from about 1760. There is also a prettily decorated shell room and a rotunda.

Alderley Edge

Stone Circle (19th century)
SJ 860 780

Preferring sham British artefacts to sham Egyptian artefacts, Cheshire has two stone circles, both in the care of the National Trust: a 19th-century one on a Neolithic site on Alderley Edge, while at Styal...

Appleton

Obelisk (19th century)
SJ 614 843

Four-lion obelisks can be found at High Warren near Appleton, and at Farndon.

Barnston

Barnston Tower (19th century)
SJ 282 835

A small, anonymous but pleasantly built round brick tower, four-banded with diapering and castellations, happily settled among housing but with no story to tell.

Bollington

White Nancy (1817)
SJ 939 771

We have reached an age in our lives when we can justifiably stop to admire the view when

White Nancy

ascending a particularly steep hill. Kerridge Hill affords many such opportunities. On the top is White Nancy, which is visible from miles around and vies with Mow Cop as the most famous folly in these parts. It is in the shape of a small, domed, sugar loaf, topped with a small ball finial, infrequently whitewashed, inevitably scarred with graffiti, always an eyecatcher. Probably solid, it is said to have been built in 1817 by Colonel Gaskell of North End Farm as a Waterloo monument. Being small, white and noticeable, Nancy has had to suffer various indignities over the years at the hands of the affectionate locals, who one Christmastide painted her as a plum pudding.

Clayton's Chimney (1840)
SJ 938 766

Bollington has a medieval European equivalent to Knutsford's minaret: a short but attractive rubble stone chimney, built in 1840 for William Clayton and decked out like

Clayton's Chimney, Bollington

some robber baron's tower. It is round, with arrowslits, and castellated, standing on an octagonal plinth. Locals claim that by virtue of its location at the top of a high, steep cliff it could never have formed part of the local industrial scheme and should, therefore, be counted as a folly. The story has it that Clayton built the ornamental chimney in such a prominent location in an unsuccessful attempt to attract investors; we reserve judgement. Perhaps the unclassified road beside which he built it was then more important than it is now. There is certainly little enough space in the wooded hillside to erect any form of factory—there is only just enough room for the chimney.

Combermere

Brankelow Folly (1828)
Obelisk (1865)
SJ 581 443

Heavily Gothicized Combermere Abbey, in the south of the county, has a distant eyecatcher, also Gothic, in the shape of Brankelow Folly. A track leads to it around a huge private lake and over a bridge of rotting timbers. It would be unwise to attempt to cross this in a vehicle. The meaning of Brankelow is not known, but the folly appears to have served as a keeper's cottage with attached kennels and the essential pinnacles and battlements required by all good keepers. Thanks to its fearsome access bridge, it is now one of the most isolated private houses in Cheshire. It was built before 1828, probably by two Irish architects called Morrison. The owner of the estate, Stapleton Cotton, Viscount Combermere, was Commander-in-Chief in Ireland between 1822 and 1825, and he may well have brought the Morrisons back with him when his tour of duty ended. A pierced obelisk commemorating the Field-Marshal's death in 1865 stands a little way behind the eyecatcher.

The drive leading to the Abbey passes what is either a brand-new Gothick house or the most complete rebuilding of an existing Gothick structure we have seen in the past decade. Either way, it is to be welcomed.

Disley

Wybersley Hall Eyecatcher (19th century)
Woodbank Garden Tower (19th century)
SJ 964 854

Disley is bisected by the county border, and strictly speaking the eyecatcher to Wybersley Hall is in Greater Manchester. The eyecatcher is a farm near Windlehurst, which has been made more agreeable with the help of a castellated façade with tall, arched windows. Woodbank Garden, which has a 19th-century brick belvedere tower, four storeys high, with an iron-railed top balcony, is definitely in Cheshire.

Dunham Massey
(Greater Manchester)

Obelisk (1714)
SJ 735 870

The National Trust's Dunham Massey Hall, acquired in 1976 and including 3000 acres of Greater Manchester on the Cheshire border near Altrincham, has a 1714 obelisk.

A rustic seat at Dunham Massey

A visitor to the park in September 1994, clutching an earlier edition of this volume, would have shaken his head in pleasurable disbelief on discovering an undocumented and spectacularly imaginative group of follies—Castle Melancholic, Duckhouse Indomitable, the Horn of Morpheus, Watchtower of the Winds and the Arch of the Harpies. These bizarre creations were dreamed up by a group of northern sculptors and artists co-ordinated by Tony Lewery, but sadly they were extremely temporary, being demolished after only two days. We hope the group will be able to provide us with some more permanent memory of their talent for building follies.

Eaton Park

Obelisk (1890)
SJ 409 608

William Porden's Eaton Hall, once Cheshire's Gothic showpiece, has been demolished to make way for the Duke of Westminster's new Eaton Hall, as modern as a 1970s airline terminal. There remain lots of neo-Gothic lodges, a magnificent, enormous clock tower and an obelisk in the park, built for Hugh Lupus Grosvenor, 1st Duke of Westminster, in 1890. The duke was born in 1825, too late to become a folly builder by fashion, so instead he devoted his time to such good causes as the Presidency of the Metropolitan Drinking Fountain and Cattle Trough Association—the fruits of his works can still be seen all over London today—and the United Committee for the Prevention of Demoralization of Native Races by the Liquor Traffic,

UCPREDEMNATRALIQTRA for short, a somewhat less successful organization.

Farndon

Obelisk (1858)
SJ 413 552

Another four-lion Victorian obelisk is at Farndon, on the Welsh border south of Eaton. Designed by E.A. Heffer, it commemorates a Major Barnston.

Harthill

Mickerdale Cottage (mid-19th century)
SJ 511 552

We were told that Mickerdale Cottage at Harthill was built in the mid-19th century for Robert Barbour and that the actual cottage is connected to a cowshed by a Gothic arcade, the whole being typical, although late, medievalizing. Harthill is little more than a hamlet, and we passed Mickerloo and Mickerra, but no Mickerdale. 'Lots of people get lost round here,' smiled a tiny woman, who had never heard of Mickerdale. There's a challenge for you.

Knutsford

Watt's Follies (early 20th century)
SJ 748 780

To Americans, Knutsford could be seen as a quaint old town; its comfortably prosperous inhabitants, on the other hand, look on it as a convenient place from which to commute to Manchester. A few years ago an Arab's eye would have been caught by a rare sight in middle-class commuterland—the Drury Lane Minaret. No loudspeakers were visible on the parapet, so one surmises that followers of the True Faith in suburban Cheshire were called to their morning devotions by a real live muezzin. Alas, it was recently demolished to make way for a new housing estate, designed in homage to the man who decided on a minaret as a suitable adornment for Knutsford: Richard Harding Watt, a wealthy and eccentric glove-maker.

Watt used professional architects like W. Longforth for the practical side of building, but he otherwise kept a tight rein over his scenic and architectural improvements. The minaret, built at the turn of the century, served as a water tower to a laundry and was modelled on an actual example from Damascus. A row of galleried cottages alongside culminates in the Ruskin Rooms, a bizarre recreation hall in assertive but unadopted Art Nouveau style, with extraordinary towerlets capped with realistic, oversized, upside-down acorn cups. The total ensemble would be more at home in Muscat than Cheshire.

Mr Watt also built several unorthodox houses in Legh Road, his own Old Croft (1907) among them, and one with a gazebo at the gate.

Gaskell Memorial Tower (1907)
SJ 754 784

Knutsford's other high spot is King Street, where Watt's King's Coffee House (galleried again) jars magnificently against the soaring white stone pile of the Gaskell Memorial Tower, joyously out of keeping with everything else in the town. Taken by itself, it is a well-handled if whimsical example of Glaswegian Art Nouveau, started in 1907 with stones from Manchester's demolished St Peter's Church and Royal Infirmary. Mrs Gaskell, one of the few Victorian novelists still read today, is commemorated by a bust, a plaque and a list of her works. The original inscriptions, carved deep into the soft white stone, have weathered so badly that the plaque repeats them.

Obelisk (1750)
SJ 750 780

In the grounds of Norbury Booths Hall on the edge of town is yet another Cheshire obelisk; this time dating from 1750 and honouring that old county family, the Leghs.

Lyme Park

Lyme Cage (1580)
The Lantern (16th century)
SJ 966 830

Lyme Park is now owned by the National Trust; formerly it was home to the Legh family for 600 years. The original Hall was Elizabethan and so was the Cage, originally built in 1580 as an immense hunting box with four rusticated towers and a central square block with balustrading on top, giving a prospect over the extensive deer park. It is a terrifying building, solitary, bleak, huge and grim in the extreme—even in sunshine there is something of the night about it. The aspect was not enhanced by blocking up all 26 windows. In 1726 Giacomo Leoni palladianized the exterior, adding the towers, then the records appear to say that it was demolished eight years later and rebuilt in 1737. The reasons for this are unclear. At one stage in its history it appears to have been used as a lock-up, hence its name, and in the late 19th century it found new employment as a shepherd's house. This is a building which was presumably built for pleasure, but what is pleasure to some is torture to others.

There are three sundials on the walls with inscriptions; on the south—
Remember now thy Creator
in the days of thy Youth
on the west—
Cras minus aptus eris [tomorrow is not attached?]

The grim Lyme Cage

and east—

Vive Hodie [Live today?]

East of the Cage, and partly visible from it, is the Lantern in Lantern Wood (the Leghs liked to keep nomenclature simple), which was originally a part of the 16th-century Hall. It was taken down by Samuel Wyatt in the last quarter of the 18th century, refurbished and re-erected in the wood. Its design is rather plain: three storeys with a pyramid roof and an archway running through the base.

Macclesfield

Capesthorne Hall Obelisk (1719)
SJ 843 726

On the left side of the main drive stands a small brick pillar topped with a stone ball finial, which marks the site of the old hall and chapel, demolished to make way for the new house in 1719.

Mow Cop

Mow Cop (1754)
SJ 858 575

White Nancy's rival as the most famous folly in Cheshire is on the Staffordshire border near Biddulph. Mow Cop, or Mole Cop as it used to be known, has on its summit a small, round, machicolated tower with attached arch, running off into a rubbly wall. It is the prototype sham ruin, copied nearly everywhere, and, of course, it was one of the first, built in 1754 for Randle Baker Wilbraham as an eyecatcher to nearby Rode Hall. In 1807 the site became a place of pilgrimage for Methodists when the first open-air camp meeting was held here, followed by a larger meeting in 1812 when Primitive Methodism was founded. On the centenary of the first assembly more than 70,000 people climbed the hill; many more have since followed the same path, some out of religious fervour, others simply to enjoy the spectacular view. Now in the ownership of the National Trust—and rather zealously policed, according to several visitors—it was originally built as a two-storey summerhouse, with a strange roof in the shape of an inverted cone, which could have been used as a beacon.

Nether Alderley

Stanley Obelisk (1750)
SJ 859 743

The Stanley Obelisk at the Old Hall in Nether Alderley was erected by Sir Edward Stanley.

Peckforton

Elephant and Castle (1840)
SJ 538 609

Mr Watson used to walk to work every day. He was a stonemason, working on the Grosvenor Bridge in Chester. However, he lived in Peckforton, 10 miles and a substantial hill away as the crow flies. Each morning he would set off with his tools; each evening he would walk home, take his tea, then set off again with his tools up the steep hill to take his ease. He had discovered a quarry of the most delicious pink sandstone, and his relaxation was to carve and carve. His young son held candles for him so that he could carve as darkness deepened.

This is why, today, in the hedge of a Peckforton cottage, stands an 8ft (2.4m) high stone elephant with a castle as its howdah. The tiny windows of the castle are glazed, like the much smaller castle at Yarm. Why an

Peckforton's Elephant & Castle

elephant and castle? We will never know. Mr Watson's legacy was written on stone, not on paper.

Rainow

Pilgrim's Progress Garden (1844)
`SJ 944 765`

MY SWORD I GIVE TO HIM THAT SHALL SUCCEED ME IN MY PILGRIMAGE, AND MY COURAGE AND SKILL TO HIM THAT CAN GET IT † SO HE PASSED OVER, AND ALL THE TRUMPETS SOUNDED FOR HIM ON THE OTHER SIDE

Because these beautiful, passionate words were inscribed around the dome of the hated school dining room, we were very nearly prevented from attempting John Bunyan's *Pilgrim's Progress* at all, but at least a passing acquaintance with his difficult but influential allegory is needed to interpret—indeed to decipher—this initially unexceptional, though attractive garden. For as one progresses around the grounds, which are open through the National Gardens Scheme on summer bank holidays, the stages in Christian's journey to salvation unfold and reveal themselves.

James Mellor of Hough Hole House spent much of the middle of the 19th century in constructing this garden, physically depicting Christian's travels, in order to publicize the works of the Swedish mystic Emanuel Swedenborg. This rather convoluted mission resulted in a curious and wonderful garden, still largely intact after a century. Here is Doubting Castle and the Slough of Despond, Mounts Gerizim and Sinai, the Valley of the Shadow of Death and Vanity Fair, all packed together in little more than an acre, rather like walking through a virtual Victorian aquatint.

The journey begins at the Slough of Despond, now the driveway in front of the house. The house itself is Vanity Fair; then the tour circles the lake, dammed at the house's first-floor level, passing inscription after inscription, all urgently carved by Mellor himself, past the monster Apollyon (a small carved figure of a dolphin), the Mouth of Hell, a grassy bank symbolizing the mounts, and towards the Celestial City. It passes the Howling House, a small summerhouse with a fireplace on which Mellor threw sulphur to conjure up the burning pits of hell, where in the back wall is a curious long rectangular slit, covered by a sliding panel. The panel can be removed, and in its place slides an Aeolian harp which, when the wind blows, simulates the howls of souls in torment. The box harp is still kept in

Apollyon in the Pilgrim's Progress garden

the summerhouse, but the mechanism no longer works.

Finally, passing Mellor's own tomb, we arrive at the Celestial City:

With all
thy getting
get
understanding
1844

reads the inscription on a plaque above the doorway. The Celestial City is a luminous and peaceful first-floor chapel room reached by a tiny spiral staircase at the end of the garden. In front is a sundial, inscribed

MIND YOUR OWN PEACE JEMMY JEMMY

Jemmy was Mellor's father, who evidently did not share his son's Swedenborgian enthusiasms.

When Terry Waite was being shown around the garden by the present owner's young daughter, he commented that the pit into which Christian cast his sins seemed a trifle small (it contains the stop-cock for the lake). 'Ah yes,' retorted the girl, 'but Christian was burdened with very few sins.'

Tower (1837)
`SJ 948 758`

A squat, castellated stone structure, unusually marked on the Ordnance Survey map as 'Folly', was erected on the bend of

Tower Hill from the remains of ruined mill-workers' cottages. It now heralds a B&B. We are not told whether the cottages or the workers were ruined; we suspect the latter.

Runcorn

Halton Castle (late 18th century)
SJ 538 821

The eyecatching qualities of the genuine ruins of Halton Castle near Runcorn were assisted and improved by James Wyatt in the 1770s. In order to enhance the skyline towards Norton Priory, modern bits and pieces were added in a number of strategic sites, thereby creating yet another sham ruin for Cheshire. It must be the only county with as many sham ruins as obelisks—something to boast about.

Sandiway

Tollbooth Tower (19th century)
SJ 611 709

Another difficult-to-assign building is the heavily battlemented toll tower at Sandiway on the A54. Lacking the porcelain prettiness of the four-square, castellated tollbooth at Halfway in Berkshire, it still seems unnecessary to fortify such an inoffensive 19th-century working building so aggressively. It is hard to miss this folly, standing as it does on the central reservation of the A54, and indeed it bears the scars of

multiple encounters with motorists who didn't.

Stockport

Godley Castellated Pigsties (1767)
SJ 910 900

Buried in the large back garden of a substantial listed terraced house in the once prosperous district of Godley, is an extraordinary edifice, which at first sight resembles a miniature castle, a huge toy fort for a very spoilt child. The spoilt children here appear to be pigs, because this was constructed as a palatial pigsty. Pigs are capable of exciting the most remarkable devotion in their owners, more so than dogs—look at the pigsty at Fyling Hall in Yorkshire—and this crazy castle bears powerful testimony to this curious fact. There are no temples to Man's Best Friend; an obelisk or two is scant recompense. Even Ringwood, 'an otter-hound of extraordinary sagacity,' merits merely an inscription at the bottom of a cascade, while all around the Dormers were adorning Rousham with unattributed arches and arcades.

The Godley pigsty came to public attention when the owner applied for planning permission to demolish it and build a housing estate. A neighbouring Folly Fellowship member managed to get it spot-listed because she had its twin at the bottom of her garden. The builder really adored his pigs.

TAKE A LOOK AT THIS
Some Exceptional Eyecatchers

ROUSHAM *Oxfordshire*	HUNDY MUNDY *Berwickshire*
SHOBDON *Herefordshire*	HEAVEN'S GATE *Hampshire*
CREECH GRANGE *Dorset*	THE WHIM *Perthshire*
MOW COP *Cheshire*	RALPH ALLEN'S SHAM CASTLE *Somerset*
OLD JOHN *Leicestershire*	GATES OF NEGAPATAM *Ross & Cromarty*
WHITE NANCY *Cheshire*	WROXTON (OR THE SPECTACLES) *Oxfordshire* (or *Northamptonshire*)

Styal

Stone Circle (19th century)
`SJ 829 835`

… the other stone circle is virtually underneath the main runway of Manchester Airport at Norcliffe Hall, near the village of Styal. This one owes its existence to the antiquarian pursuits of Robert Hyde Greg. The Gregs owned the cotton mills in the village, and young Robert took to accompanying his father on commercial trips that covered Europe and a fair part of the Middle East. All this travel affected Robert so much that he wrote monographs on *Cyclopean, Pelagic and Etruscan Remains* and *Remarks on the Site of Ancient Troy*; when his studies reached prehistory he went for the real thing and built himself a Stonehenge at home.

Tatton Park

Sheep-stealers' Tower (late 17th century)
Choragic Monument (1820)
Shinto Temple (1910)
`SJ 743 813`

Tatton Park, the seat of the Egertons, is now a National Trust property just outside Knutsford. Tatton Hall's formal garden is the site of a mysterious two-storey towerette, the Sheep-stealers' Tower or Shepherds' Watch Tower. It is thought to predate the formal gardens and to have served as an outpost for shepherds to keep watch over their sheep—rustling was as prevalent then as it is now. A rotunda at a *rond-point* further along the walk is one of the many British copies of the Choragic Monument of Lysicrates. This one was built by William Cole III of Chester and appears to be his first building, as it was erected in 1820 when he was only 20 years old.

A more recent addition is the Japanese Garden, where on a small island in Golden Brook stands a Shinto Temple, which was imported, along with several workmen, in 1910. This particular period appears to have been quite rich in Japanese architectural imports: the Japanese Gateway in Kew Gardens was brought over to England in 1912, and a garden in The Hague, Holland, was designed in 1895–6 with professional advice from the Japanese Embassy and consecrated by a Buddhist monk. Japan in Cheshire is not as remarkable as it sounds, when one takes into account the various exploits of the then owner of Tatton Hall, Maurice, 4th Lord Egerton. He was an

The Sheep-stealers' tower

adventurer who prospected for gold in the Yukon (one would have thought he already had enough), lived in the Gobi Desert for a while and took his aviator's certificate the same year the Shinto Temple was erected.

Egerton's astounding collection of big game trophies (of course he was a Great White Hunter as well) is permanently exhibited in the specially built Tenant's Hall. The Lewis Wyatt-designed Orangery and Paxton's Fernery were restored in 1996 at a cost of £300,000.

Tilstone Fearnall

Tilstone Hall Folly (16th century)
`SJ 572 609`

This is an enigma: is it a folly or is it the genuine ruin of a Jacobean gatehouse? The central arch is much too small to allow a mounted horse to pass through, and its very top heaviness makes it likely that this is the upper half of a discarded gateway to the Hall. It no longer stands on a drive, or even in the path of a former drive, nor has it been resited as an objet. Certainly it seems to have been left to decay picturesquely, and it now serves as a glorious garden shed for a village cottage.

CORNWALL

They are called emmets in Cornwall, and grockles in Devon. They are at once the bane and the salvation of this section of Britain; they are tourists. Once Cornwall's prosperity lay underground in tin and copper, but the ruins of the wheal engine houses (wheal is the Cornish word for a mine) stand in mute testimony to the passing of the industry, and now the tripper rules. Only ugly inland towns like Camborne and Redruth remain unscarred by the ubiquitous traveller; more attractive seaside resorts like St Ives even have to go so far as to ban visitors' cars from the town during the season. The real Cornish are difficult to find, having either emigrated or remaining distrustful of the English, a people they hold in scarcely higher regard than they do Devonians. The country looks and sounds Celtic:

> *By Tre, Pol and Pen*
> *Shall ye know the Cornish men*

and indeed, it has much more in common with Wales and Brittany than it does with the rest of England. Its beauty and its romance attract visitors in herds, and it is second only to Ireland as a romantic novelist's choice for a setting, fuelled by tales of insanely brave and arrogant men like Sir Richard Edgcumbe of Cotehele, Sir Richard Grenville of the *Revenge* or unyielding priests like Bishop Sir Jonathan Trelawny, who, accused by James II of seditious libel, finally achieved immortality through R.S. Hawker's 'Song of the Western Men', which has become the unofficial Cornish national anthem. (Some doubt has been cast on the relevance of Hawker's verse to Sir Jonathan, as the last three lines are thought to have been a popular rallying cry as early as the 17th century, referring to an entirely different Trelawny.)

Boconnoc

Obelisk (1771)
SX 140 620

At Boconnoc is a tall obelisk erected by Thomas Pitt, 1st Lord Camelford:

> *IN*
> *GRATITUDE AND AFFECTION*
> *TO THE MEMORY OF*
> *SIR RICHARD LYTTELTON*
> *AND TO PERPETUATE*
> *THAT PECULIAR CHARACTER*
> *OF BENEVOLENCE*
> *WHICH RENDERED HIM THE*
> *DELIGHT OF HIS OWN AGE*
> *AND WORTHY THE VENERATION*
> *OF POSTERITY*
> *MDCCLXXI*

This inscription is, unusually, carved in a rather elegant capital italic script, and the obelisk stands at the end of a long drive, which is bordered by ornamental trees. Also at Boconnoc is a stump in a clump, a tiny pillar in the middle of a ring of trees called the Wellington Plantation, to mark the battle of Waterloo. Pieces from the original Boconoc have been eased into estate buildings and garden walls.

Bodmin

Obelisk (1856–7)
SX 080 670

Cornish obelisks are generally big. The biggest is the Gilbert memorial in Bodmin, 144ft (44m) tall on the highest point in town and visible for miles. It was built in 1856–7 for Walter Raleigh Gilbert, Lieutenant-General in the Bengal Army, 'at the earnest request of his fellow town's men of BODMIN'.

The centre of Bodmin also boasts something called Mount Folly, possibly referring to a tree-covered hill. (There is another Mount Folly, in Devon, near Bigbury-on-Sea, and reaching 378ft/115m.)

Botus Fleming

Obelisk (1762)
SX 410 620

The smallest obelisk in the county is scarcely an obelisk at all, merely a tiny marker on a tomb. This stands solitary in a field called the Burial Field near Botus Fleming, in the far east of the county, and the whole story of this lonely grave is recorded by the fascinating but rapidly weathering inscription:

> *Here lies the body of WILLIAM MARTYN of the Borough of Plymouth County of Devon; Doctor of Physick, who died the 22d day of November in the year of our LORD IESUS CHRIST 1762 Aged 62 Years. He was an honeft good natured Man willing to do all the Good in his Power to all Mankind and not willing to hurt any Perfon, He lived and died a Catholic Chriftian, in the true not depraved Popifh senfe of the word, had no fuperftitious Veneration for Church or Churchyard Ground, and willing by his Example, if that might have influence to leffen the unreafonable Efteem which fome poor Men and Women, through Prejudice of Education Often fhew for it in frequently parting with the Earnings of many a hard Days Labour, which might be better beftowed in Suftenance for themfelves and families to pay for Holy Beds for their Kins-folks Corpfes through a Ridiculous Fear left their Kins-folks at the Day of Judgement fhould fome way or other fuffer becaufe, their corpfes were wrongly fituated or not where Worldly Advantage of their Spiritual Guides loudly called for them.*

The grave is difficult to find; we asked directions in the Rising Sun, the most authentic village pub we have ever discovered, and were told a story that they said had been passed down in the village for over 200 years: every day Dr Martyn used to walk out to the spot where his tomb now stands and walk around and around the site.

Moditonham Dovecote (late 18th century)
SX 410 620

At Moditonham, near Botus Fleming, a ruined eyecatcher-dovecote stands near Moditonham House. Octagonal and built of rough stone, it is a real beauty: it runs the whole gamut of simple decoration, a round arched entrance, cruciform arrowslits, pointed windows and an *oeil-de-boeuf*. Someone later (perhaps even in this century) tacked a rubble wall to it, complete with a hastily built pointed window.

Bude

Tower of the Winds (1830s)
SS 200 065

Tower of the Winds it certainly is, this storm tower at Compass Point on the cliffs west of Bude. It is octagonal and was built in the 1830s by Sir Thomas Dyke Acland, following the model of the Athens tower. But the cliffs on which it was originally built started to crumble, and in the 1880s it was moved to its present position, which explains why, when it was supposed to give the points of the compass with its eight sides, it is now about 90 degrees out.

Castle Gate

Roger's Tower (c.1800)
SW 480 340

The road to Penzance from St Ives passes Castle-an-Dinas (of which there are several in Cornwall) on the left, and on the top of the hill is a tiny folly called Roger's Tower. Perched above an escarpment, it looks like a cover for a cheese dish: square with four tiny round corner turrets, pointed entrance and a blind quatrefoil above it. It was built as a prospect belvedere; the views across to St Michael's Mount are superb.

Cotehele

Tower (1789)
SX 430 680

Cotehele is some miles north of Botus Fleming. The warm wet banks of the Tamar valley provide an enchanting setting for lovely houses and narrow Devonian lanes, but this is still Cornwall, where the wild romantic heroes of yesteryear linger on in the memory. None more so than Sir Richard Edgcumbe of Cotehele, whose literally cliff-hanging lifestyle can only be hinted at in a book like this. He was MP for Tavistock, rebelled against Richard III and consequently was pursued by Sir Henry Trenowth, Richard's feared and loathed Cornish agent. Trenowth drew Edgcumbe's cover at Cotehele and chased him to the cliff's edge, where Edgcumbe threw his hat into the river twenty metres below, while he clung to a branch on the overhang. Trenowth looked down to see his adversary's hat floating down the Tamar and assumed Edgcumbe was still underneath it; an assumption he was to regret years later when Edgcumbe became a favourite of Henry VII and had the gory satisfaction of chasing

Trenowth off the edge of a cliff into the sea at Bodrugan's Leap. Sir Richard built the Chapel of SS George and Thomas à Becket on the cliff edge at Cotehele to commemorate his escape, and after restoration in 1620 and 1769, it is still open. It is now owned by the National Trust, but there is a genuine folly at Cotehele which has everything in its favour except for a wonderful story like Sir Richard's.

The Prospect Tower, like most follies, has an uncertain history. The local story is that it was built so that the Edgcumbe's servants could signal to Maker Church, 11 miles away near Mount Edgcumbe, when the family was in transit from one house to another. A more likely explanation is that it was built to celebrate the visit of King George III and Queen Charlotte to Cotehele in August 1789; Fanny Burney noted in her diary that the Edgcumbes were 'vastly Excited' by the visit of the Royals and 'were full of the honours done them and told me of the obelisks and arches they meant to construct in commemoration'—there are no arches or obelisks at Cotehele, so perhaps the Prospect Tower is the sole result. It is a very satisfying tower, about 60ft (18m) high, built of slaty stone with dummy church windows. Architecturally it is similar to a straightforward Perpendicular church tower from a distance; the ingenuity and *trompe l'oeil* effect only reveals itself as you approach. For the building is triangular, and each wall is distinctly concave. A sturdy wooden staircase was installed in 1980 and three visitors at a time can now climb to the top to admire the view—and yes, Maker Church can be seen.

Falmouth

Obelisk (1737)
SW 800 330

The obelisk in Grove Place, Falmouth, was put up in 1737 in memory of the Killigrew family. Sir Peter Killigrew obtained a licence to establish the village of Smithwick as a market town and optimistically changed its name to Pennycomequick. Charles II felt this to be overly commercial and had the town's name changed yet again, this time to Falmouth.

Round House (19th century)
SW 800 330

On a road leading to the new industrial estates stands that little darling of all folly-hunters, a round house. This one looks as romantic as a gasometer, and we haven't been able to find out anything about it. There are tiny castellations with wide spaces in between and curiously low and broad windows.

Fowey

Menabilly Grotto (1780s)
SX 090 520

Surprisingly for such a coastal county, grottoes and shell houses are largely ignored except for the stretch of coast between Gribbin Head and Rame Head. Menabilly, outside Fowey, was built for the Rashleigh family, and in the landscaped grounds looking out to sea is a tiny dilapidated grotto made entirely from Cornish granite and shells. It was built in the 1780s by Philip

Cotehele's triangular Prospect Tower

Rashleigh (1729–1811) from the overstocks of his enormous collection of minerals (his two-volume book *Specimens of British Minerals* was published in 1797 and 1802, and he also contributed to a book on curious hailstones, models of which he had made in glass). Whale bones (an underrated folly-material) were also used in the grotto, as well as pieces from the chain that prevented unwanted boats from entering Fowey Harbour.

The Rashleigh Mausoleum of 1871 at Fowey is also worth seeing: a great bell-shaped structure overlooking the ruined fort. In 1992 the gardens and grotto at Menabilly were restored to their former glories.

Obelisk (1846)
SX 120 520

An obelisk marks the spot where Victoria and Albert landed on their visit to the town.

Germoe

St Germoe's Chair (15th century)
SW 580 290

In the peaceful churchyard of Germoe, just north of the A394, is an enigmatic alcove named St Germoe's Chair, which several writers, including Betjeman, have felt has more in common with an 18th-century rustic covered garden seat than with the 15th century, when it was supposed to have been built. Its 15th-century purpose is unclear; its 18th-century purpose is obvious to anyone with an eye for a view. It looks genuinely medieval, but many follies were built using medieval stones and materials. What convinces us of the medieval dating is its size: the opening arches are of a size to accommodate medieval man; they are too small for the 18th century. Perhaps it was built as a seat for the view, in which case it was built 300 years before its time.

Helston

Gateway (1834)
SW 660 270

In Helston, one of the four coinage towns of old stannary Cornwall, the main street is called Coinagehall Street. At the bottom end is an elaborate Gothic gateway, opening onto a bowling green, erected in 1834 by public subscription to the memory of Humphrey Millet Grylls. The architect was George Wightwick, a Londoner who failed to find sufficient work, so he moved to Plymouth, where he was inundated with commissions.

Liskeard

Treworgey Clock Tower (1730)
SX 250 670

Just north of Liskeard is the ancient dwelling of Treworgey, where John Connock built a clock tower in 1730. It has three stepped storeys, rather like a pagoda, and the top two storeys are clapboarded—it looks more Kentish than Cornish. The clock-face has only an hour hand and was made by John Belling of 'Bodmyn' in 1733. A huge pointed arch window takes up almost the whole of the west wall of the ground floor of the tower, which the present owner finds handy as an exotic garden shed. The clock is in perfect working order and is wound daily; the bell is inscribed 'John Connock His Bell A. D. 1620', presumably an ancestor of the builder.

Morwenstow

Vicarage Chimneys (1837)
Hawker's Hut (c.1843)
SS 210 150

The Rev. Robert Stephen Hawker (1803–75) seems to be well qualified as an eccentric. At the age of 19 he married a lady aged 41, and the marriage lasted happily for 40 years. When his wife died, he remarried the following year and quickly fathered three daughters. His folly, if such it can be called for

Grylls' Gate in Helston

it is more of a caprice, is famous; the chimneys of his 1837 vicarage at Morwenstow, a secluded hamlet north of Bude, are models of church towers, which he liked, apart from the kitchen chimney, which is a copy of his mother's tomb. The design for the rest of the vicarage was taken straight from Thomas Frederick Hunt's *Designs for Parsonage Houses*, published in 1827. The model used was 'a Clergyman's house, on a modest scale'. Modern estate agents would describe it as a substantial detached residence.

Hawkeriana are nearby: in the churchyard stands the solemn white figurehead of the *Caledonia*, a ship that went down in 1842 (shipwrecks were a common occurrence on this stretch of the Cornish coast), and the wooden statue marks the grave of the *Caledonia*'s captain. Eventually it gave rise to a rather cruel joke: 'The figure of *Caledonia* is Morwenstow's one and only virgin.'

Under the top of the cliff near the village, Hawker built himself (in or around 1843) a small hut, made from the debris of the all too many shipwrecks along the coast, and here he wrote and read and became his own ornamental hermit. He was adamant that from this hut he could watch the mermaids frolicking in the sea beneath, but they seem to have disappeared because of oil spillages.

Mount Edgcumbe

Sham Ruin (c.1750)
Shell Seat (18th century)
Garden Buildings (18th century)
SX 460 530

Mount Edgcumbe, another seat of the Edgcumbe family, overlooks Plymouth Sound and is now a Plymouth park, although administratively still in Cornwall. The view was, and is, famous. Loudon noted in 1842:

> High as were our expectations from the published descriptions and the long celebrity of the place, we were not disappointed. We never looked down on the sea, on shipping, and on a large town, all at our feet, from such a stupendous height. The effect on the mind is sublime in the highest degree.

And it still is. The folly here, known as the Ruin, was built in Devon—Cornwall took over Mount Edgcumbe in 1844. The Ruin was probably built *c.*1750 by Timothy Brett, and it is a superb example of what a good sham ruin should be. The position overlooking Plymouth and the Sound is spectacular; the ruination is extensive; yet the large traceried window offering the view is high enough from the ground to give a noticeably different perspective. Also in the park is a 14ft (4.3m) triangular Coade stone monument to Timothy Brett (1791), with tortoises, and a little Tuscan temple called Thomson's Seat. The beautiful shell seat was restored by Diana Reynell in 1990.

At Maker, south of Mount Edgcumbe, is a strange coach house with battlements, which obviously has something to do with the estate. And even further south, still belonging to Edgcumbe, is Queen Adelaide's Chapel on Penlee Point, a grotto/seat in honour of her visit to Edgcumbe. It was later used as a belvedere, and its platform was found handy for signalling when incoming boats were spotted.

Newquay

Huer's House (1835)
SW 800 630

The Huer's House at Newquay was built for a specific if unusual purpose, so it is not a folly—but it is undeniably an eccentric structure. Built of whitewashed rubble, it would not look out of place on a Greek island, with its outside stair climbing one floor at the side of a squat tower. It has diamond-shaped windows and rudimentary castellations, and its function was to serve as a look-out post from which the Huer could spot shoals of pilchard and direct the fishing boats accordingly. Their shout was 'Heva! Heva!'—and why not?

Padstow

Temple (1738–9)
Grotto
SW 920 750

In the grounds of Prideaux Place are not only a temple of 1738–39 but, more importantly, a grotto of rough stone, which is pedimented, with two arches, one for a door, the other for a window next to it, and a circular window in between them—it looks architect-designed or at least by someone pretending to know what they were doing. Extremely pleasing. Inside, shells and shellettes are formed into snails, thistles and butterflies, and there is also a motto (the Prideaux family's?): 'Toujours Pret.'

Obelisk (1889)
SW 920 760

The obelisk on Dennis Hill, above Padstow, was built to celebrate Queen Victoria's jubilee.

Pentillie Castle

Tower Mausoleum (1712)
SX 400 650

The excellently decayed and really creepy tower on Mount Ararat, a couple of miles to the south of Cothele, is in poor condition. This was built as a mausoleum by Sir James Tillie in 1712, where he intended to be put to rest seated in an upstairs room with his roast and his port, awaiting the Day of Judgement. There is no longer an upstairs room, and the tower is neglected and overgrown, but few things can surpass the delicious thrill of terror we felt when we peered through a stone grille in the tower's wall to see the body of a man sitting on a chair inside.

A fairly long pause to recover our breath, then a second look. Covered in ferns and brambles he may be, but inside is the petrified image of Sir James, sitting on his seat, hands firmly placed on his thighs, awaiting the Resurrection. The square, three-storey tower is surrounded by a wall, and ten

Can you make out Sir James's knees?

steps lead up to the blocked entrance porch. There was probably once a plaque above the doorway, in which is now set the stone grille.

Penzance

Legrice's Folly (19th century)
SW 470 300

Legrice's Folly at Penzance is another minute coastal 'tower', although how a one-storey building gets labelled as a tower puzzles us. It was probably built as another Huer's House, the heavy castellations of solid stone giving it a toy fort feeling.

I DO LIKE TO BE BESIDE THE SEASIDE

Some Seaside Follies

CLAVELL'S TOWER
Dorset

BURT'S FOLLIES
Dorset

SHEERNESS
Kent

LUTTRELL'S TOWER
Hampshire

PORTMEIRION
Merioneth

BLACKPOOL TOWER
Lancashire

MARSDEN BAY GROTTO
Durham

Egyptian House (1830)
SW 470 300

The finest thing to see in Penzance is John Foulston's Egyptian House of 1830 in Chapel Street, a style so exotic and fantastic to our eyes nowadays that most people would unhesitatingly regard it as a folly. It was built for George Lavin, to house his collection of minerals. Foulston worked earlier at Devonport, where he came up with another Egyptian jewel.

Polperro

Shell House (1937)
SX 210 510

Picturesque Polperro has a house in the Warren with its façade decorated with shells, all done by a Mr Sam Puckey just before World War II.

Port Isaac

The Birdcage (18th century)
SW 990 810

The Birdcage is always mentioned as a folly, but in reality it is merely an asymmetrical fisherman's cottage just above the harbour. It belongs to the National Trust, but is let privately.

Dryden Point Tower, Portquin

Portquin

Dryden Point Tower (19th century)
SW 970 820

The real folly is on National Trust land at Doyden Point by Portquin, a village that probably looks like Port Isaac looked before the tourists discovered it. The folly is a boxy little two-storey tower, hesitantly castellated, with one Gothic window in each wall and a shallow, one-storey extension, also castellated, on the east side. The legend about it is that it was built by someone who wished to drink himself to death. The true story is even sadder: it was erected to commemorate the loss of the Portquin boat, which went down with every man in the village on board—all were drowned, none saved.

Redruth

Tower (1836)
SW 680 420

The towns of Camborne and Redruth are separated by the 816ft (249m) of Carn Brea, not a particularly high hill but one that dominates the surrounding landscape. The summit is topped with an extraordinary monument to the memory of Francis, Lord de Dunstanville and Bassett, erected by the county in 1836. It can be seen for miles around, virtually from all over north Cornwall, although it seems surprisingly small when approached. Again, this is

deceptive; the tower is big, but it is the design that deceives the visual scale. Built by Joseph Prior of Gwennap, it is strikingly futuristic and a remarkable work for its date, a tapering hexagonal column rising to the stumpiest cross ever seen, surrounding a diamond lozenge. There is a doorway in the plinth where one can enter right into the column, which is circular and hollow, rising up 90ft (27m). A niche off the entrance passage leads to the staircase, which climbs up inside the wall of the monument to a viewing platform at the top, according to two boys who were sheltering inside from the pelting rain, but as the bottom 8ft (2.4m) or so of the stairs had been destroyed, we forbore from making the climb.

Carn Brea Castle (18th century)
SW 680 420

Carn Brea Castle, just along the ridge, is a beautifully preserved 18th-century sham castle, perched on a crazy jumble of rocks like the chapel at Roche. From underneath it gives the bizarre impression that it was once a straightforward building with aspirations to normality—then some frightful disease attacked the stone, warping it, moulding it and disfiguring it beyond imagination so, like the architectural equivalent of the Elephant Man, this abominable excrescence seemed gradually to be devouring the rest of the building. It was originally built as a hunting lodge for the Bassetts, and now it is one of Britain's remoter restaurants. A Land Rover would seem to be the most suitable means of getting to it, but once there, the diners could feast their eyes on what is probably the finest view in Cornwall. We say probably, because we bumped along there one day in August in driving rain, scraping the bottom of the car on the rocky road not once but a dozen times, only to find it was closed on Mondays—and we couldn't even admire the view because we were standing in a cloud!

St Austell

Grotto (c.1800)
SX 030 520

About a mile or so southeast of the town is Duporth Holiday Camp, taking its name from Duporth House, which was demolished in the late 1970s to make way for the campers. There is supposed to be a grotto of around 1800 there, but in 1993 it was threatened by further developments at the camp. We do not know whether it managed to escape or was rounded up.

St Ewe

Gothick Temple (18th century)
Grotto
SW 990 460

Restoration work is being carried out on the gardens of Heligan, a mile or so east of St Ewe. An eyecatcher temple has stuck its ruined head out of the undergrowth, a grotto has come to light, rockeries, old pavilions— all is in the process of being sorted.

St Ives

Knill Monument (1782)
SW 520 390

Near Halsetown, above St Ives and Carbis Bay on top of the hill, is the Knill Monument, a strange, triangular pyramid with even stranger stories surrounding it. The inscription on each side are incused: 'RESURGAM' above a freshly painted coat of arms with the punning motto 'NIL DESPERANDUM JOHANNES KNILL 1782'; and on the third side 'I KNOW THAT MY REDEEMER LIVETH'.

John Knill, a bachelor, was Mayor of St Ives and had excavated a hole in the rock at Mount's Bay, which he intended to serve as his mausoleum. Sadly, he died in London and in the excitement the original plan was quite forgotten and he ended up buried in Holborn. Knill had a number of little weaknesses, which seem to have afforded him great pleasure and offended no one; his predilection for pubs while in London led him to sample four or five every day before inevitably dining at Dolly's Chop House. He made provision in his will for a peculiar ceremony to be performed at the monument, which still continues after 200 years. Every five years on 25 July ten girls, each ten years old and dressed in white, climb up to the monument accompanied by two widows, a clergyman, a fiddler, the Mayor of St Ives and the local Customs and Excise man. There they sing the 100th Psalm, after

The Knill Monument

which the girls dance around the monument for a quarter of an hour to the tune of the fiddler, singing an old song which begins 'Shun the barter of the bay Hasten upward, come away…' For performing this inexplicable ceremony the young girls, the fiddler and the two widows receive ten shillings each, while the parson, the mayor and the VAT man get £10 each, which they must use to give a dinner party to which they can invite two friends. The next performance is scheduled for 2001. The unwavering charms of Dolly's Chop House led Knill to refuse every invitation to dine privately during his lifetime. The presence of the customs man leads one to speculate that he might have been a smuggler, but the reasons for the ritual lie buried with him.

Joseph Hocking (1860–1937), Cornwall's truly great bad novelist, set *The Eye of the Triangle*, one of his more atrocious efforts, at the Knill Monument; he was as fascinated by the rite as we are, so draw your own conclusions. 'Resurgam' on the side of the monument means 'I shall rise again'; whether Knill shared the same interpretation of life after death as Mad Jack Fuller, Major Peter Labelliere and Sir John Pentillie or not, he at any rate caused something to be done about it. It is merely unfortunate that he isn't inside the monument, with the expected bottle of port, waiting for the Day of Judgement and enjoying the virgins' dance.

St Merryn

Prynn's World (1982 onwards)
SW 880 740

Mostly folly builders are eminently unsuitable to their task: usually a little gauche, mystics and dreamers and in the proud possession of two left hands (if that is not a right-handist remark). Edward Prynn, of Tresallyn Cross, St Merryn, likes to move big slabs of stone about, each several tons in weight. Edward Prynn is in luck—he is, or rather was, a shovel driver in a quarry. He is also an archdruid, who builds his own henges around his bungalow. He says of himself

I am known as a Cornish Eccentric. I have just completed ten years of building my own Stone Temple in my front and back garden… I have completed a Cornish Hall of Fame… the next project is to clad the outside of my home with nameplates, and these will be the names of famous eccentrics around the world.

There is also an Angel's Runway, and an underground chamber, and a marriage stone, and the Dreckly Stone, which involves people taking their clothes off 'directly'. It is all on and underneath his prim lawns and next to the equally prim white bungalow, and it looks great. Prynn asked us for our names to put on his slate plates. We, not being eccentrics, refused.

Stratton

Monument (17th century)
SS 230 060

Just outside Bude is Stamford Hill in Stratton, where the Civil War battle was fought in 1643. A little oddity marks the spot: a tiny arch one has to stoop to walk through,

Stratton Arch

crowned with a crocketed pinnacle taken from the tower of nearby Poughill Church. Ye inscription quaintly records the valour of another romantic Cornishman, Sir Bevill Granville, who defeated the Earl of Stamford's army here. It is strange how the word Stamford often seems to involve fighting.

Trelissick

Tower (c. 1860)
SW 840 890

By the popular and therefore very crowded King Harry Ferry is the National Trust estate of Trelissick. Described by Pevsner as 'the

Veryan Round Houses

severest neo-Greek mansion in Cornwall', it nonetheless boasts a delightful piece of whimsy in a substantial round tower in the garden by the side of the road. It is circular, with a conical roof with lucarnes and a circular stair turret, also with a conical roof. Peter Robinson was the architect of the house, but this is much later and reminiscent of Burges's Castell Coch outside Cardiff.

Truro

Lander Column (1835)
SW 823 448

The Lander Column in Truro is a welcome change from the omnipresent commemorative obelisk. It was built in 1835 by Philip Sambell, a deaf and dumb architect, and takes the form of a fine Doric fluted column in granite, crowned with a statue, finished only in 1852, of Richard Lander by Nevil Northey Burnard, a Cornish sculptor, who in his later years took to drink and tramping about Cornwall, ending his life in Redruth workhouse.

> TO HONOUR THE
> ENTERPRISE AND SUFFERINGS
> OF THE BROTHERS
> RICHARD AND JOHN LANDER
> NATIVES OF THIS TOWN
> AND ESPECIALLY TO
> COMMEMORATE THE EARLY
> FATE OF RICHARD, EXPLORER
> OF THE RIVER NIGER,
> BORN 1804 DIED FERNANDO PO 1834

Veryan

Round Houses (c.1811)
SW 920 390

If you have the patience to queue for the ferry, you can reach Veryan in a matter of minutes. Veryan's claim to fame is its round houses, built at the ends of the village so, the story goes, that if the Devil decided to come prowling around the village he would first be confronted with the round houses, which he would circle all night, like the messenger boy with Dunston Pillar in Lincolnshire. The houses are completely circular, with conical thatched roofs surmounted by crosses, and they do stand in pairs like sentries at the entrance to the village. They are said to have been built in the early 19th century for £50 each by Hugh Rowe of Lostwithiel on the orders of Parson Trist, who had a poor regard for Satan's intelligence. Designs published in Worgan's *Agricultural Survey* (1811) are almost identical and were intended for labourer's cottages.

Werrington Park

Sugar Loaves (late 18th–early 19th century)
SX 340 880

We couldn't find these. The folly is in Werrington Park, a beautiful private estate just north of Launceston, and there is a good picture of it in Barbara Jones's book: a rough stone plinth with a round-arched seat set into it, with three Barwick Park-type cones placed above, rising up to a height of about 25ft (7.6m). In the photograph it sits on a bare, open hillside, presumably staring across at the house and serving as an eyecatcher. The owner gave us detailed instructions, warning us that trees had grown up around it and that it was now in the middle of a wood, but that we couldn't miss it. After an hour and a half stumbling around in the stifling little wood we emerged to admit defeat. 'Funny that,' ruminated the owner, 'my wife couldn't find it when she looked last week.'

Luckily, the Sugar Loaves are confirmed as still standing. It has been argued, on serious grounds in both cases, that it may either be based on the famous tomb of the Horatii and Curiatii in Rome or on one of Thomas Daniell's plates of similar monuments in India. The monument is supposed to have been built by Sir William Norrice, and another monument of his, a triumphal arch, which was sited south of the house, was blown up in the late 19th century.

Whitesand Bay

Lugger's Cave (1784)
SX 390 520

The National Trust has a popular and recently restored grotto at Sharrow Point in Whitesand Bay called Lugger's Cave or Sharrow Grot, which was excavated in 1784

by James Lugger, an ex-Navy purser who suffered from gout. The cave is 15ft (4.6m) deep and 7ft (2.1m) high, with a semicircular seat at the end, also carved out of the solid rock. When Lugger finished the work after a year, he started to inscribe welcoming verses on the walls, such as

But, as thou walk'st, should sudden storms arise
Red lightning flash, or thunder shake the skies
To Sharrow's friendly grot in haste retreat
And find safe shelter and a rocky seat.

Unlike many holiday-makers, Lugger evidently had no illusions about the Cornish climate, but certainly it proved to be beneficial:

By this, and exercise, here oft endured
The gout itself for many years was cured.

Zela

Tinker's Castle (18th century)
ST 820 520

The name is a mystery. Tinker's Castle is now a modernized house, built around its centrepiece, a polygonal belvedere to which wings were added later. Made of local rough stone, it is totally charmless, although the windows have a slight Tudory-Gothicky touch.

SHELL SHOCKED
Some Great Grottoes

ASCOT PLACE *Berkshire*	ST. AUDRIES GROTTO *Somerset*
LEEDS CASTLE *Kent*	GOLDNEY'S GROTTO *Bristol*
HAMPTON COURT HOUSE *Middlesex*	MARGATE GROTTO, *Kent*
SCOTT'S GROTTO *Hertfordshire*	WEST WYCOMBE *Buckinghamshire*
HIGH BEECH CATACOMBS *Essex*	HAWKSTONE *Shropshire*
PAINSHILL PARK GROTTO *Surrey*	STOURHEAD *Wiltshire*

CUMBRIA

For most of us, Cumbria means the Lake District and little else. There are a fair few follies in this area of Britain, although there are also concentrations round Carlisle and Furness, originally in Lancashire and therefore ceremonially covered in the chapter on that county. In the Lake District William Wordsworth has become a major cottage industry, and consequently we find his name linked with a number of follies of which, in all probability, he was totally innocent. The crush at Dove Cottage has now become so severe in the summer that there is talk of moving the contents to London to ease the pressure on the house and its surroundings. One wonders if contemporary icons such as Damien Hirst or Oasis will be remembered as enthusiastically in 200 years. Here, as in Northumberland the folly tends to blend with its surroundings, so the favoured style is Gothick.

Kirklinton
Aglionby
Stanwix
Sandsfield
Carlisle
Little Orton
Wigton
West
Woodside
Netherby
Newby East
Brampton
Corby Castle
Castle Carrock
Wreay
Brisco
Greystoke
Sebergham
Derwent
Island
Penrith
Brougham
Appleby
Thirlmere
Ullswater
Brough
Striding Edge
Shap
Wells
Ambleside
Muncaster
Coniston
Lake
Wray
Ravenstonedale
Storr's
Point
Kendal
Milnthorpe
Kirkby Lonsdale
Beetham

CUMBERLAND

Aglionby

Whoof House Folly (1868)
`NY 445 565`

The small town of Wetheral had a wonderful folly house built by the Misses Waugh in 1790, but it has now been demolished.

Northwest on the A69, about 1½ miles away, is Whoof House Folly, a large church window encased in brickwork. It is round headed with an oval in the tracery. The window comes from Arthureth Church in Aglionby near Longtown, and it is, in fact, Gothic Survival as the church was built in the 17th century. The window was re-erected in the garden of Whoof House in 1868.

Brampton

Howard Memorial Shelter (1922)
`NY 527 612`

The Howard Memorial Shelter in the centre of the attractive town of Brampton is an octagonal open building, which commemorates George James Howard, 9th Earl of Carlisle, of Naworth Park, who died in 1911, and his wife Rosalind Frances, who died ten years later. Few local publicans would have subscribed to the erection of the building, for as soon as Howard inherited the earldom he closed all the pubs on his extensive Yorkshire and Cumberland estates. On this matter he was wholeheartedly supported by his wife, who had Radical as well as Temperance leanings.

Brisco

Langarth (mid-19th century)
St Ninian's Well
`NY 423 520`

The styles employed by Sarah Losh (see Wreay) varied. At Langarth, Brisco, she built a Tudor-style house, long before Messrs Barrett, Bovis and Wates rediscovered the genre, and she also designed and decorated the tiny and well-hidden sandstone wellhead at St Ninian's Well in the same village. The inscription is no longer legible.

St Ninian's Well

Carlisle

Bunkershill Windows (1856)
NY 400 560

Carlisle Cathedral was radically restored in 1856. Most of the windows were renewed, and four of the old windows found their way into mansion gardens, a fashion that lasted for about 20 years in England. If there is a re-erected church window in your garden, you can be reasonably certain it was put up between 1850 and 1870. Two were incorporated in a small building in Nelson Road, demolished in 1967, but two others survive in the grounds of Bunkershill House (there is strong pro-American sentiment hereabouts) on the Orton road, going west from the town. Nothing much has been done with them except for their re-erection.

Castle Carrock

Tarn Lodge Belvedere (1807)
NY 530 548

In between the hamlet of Faugh and Castle Carrock, south of Brampton, is Tarn Lodge, and on a hill overlooking the house is a small, square, embattled two-storey tower. The architect is unknown; the provenance is unknown; the reason is unknown.

Corby Castle

Folly Group (mid-18th century)
NY 473 542

A sufficient number of follies has matured in the area immediately to the east of Carlisle to make an enjoyable if busy day trip. At Corby Castle, along the River Eden, the earlier garden buildings, many of them listed Grade I, appear to be the result of a Grand Tour their builder Thomas Howard must have taken, for the Italian influence pervades the garden. First, there is the cascade, looking like the waterworks in a minor Tuscan villa. The head of the cascade is crowned by a temple with carvings of Neptune, a lion and mermaids. The cascade itself spouts from a grotesque monster head, assisted at the flanks by two hounds of Hades, each of which has the traditional three heads. Perhaps Howard interpreted the Eden as the Styx. A 10ft (3m) high amateur statue of Polyphemus the Cyclops near the cascade leads us to expect a Cyclopean Grotto. Thomas Howard wrote plays to be enacted in this area; the suggested date is the early 18th century, as Buck engraved the cascade in 1739 and Sir John Clerk of Penicuik noticed the statue in 1734.

The cascade now ends in a pond with a statue of Lord Nelson, put there by Philip or Henry Howard.

From here the River Walk starts. Two square grotto rooms give views of the river and the village of Wetheral, and in one of the rooms there used to be a tablet bearing lines from *Paradise Lost*. Along the walk stood a

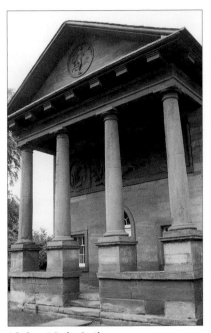

A lodge at Corby Castle

Roman altar as well as a tablet bearing quotations from Horace and Shakespeare, but as early as 1794 they were reported as having been 'much damaged by mischievous people'. The walk is terminated by a classical tempietto with a carved pediment, which was built for Thomas Howard. Inside are Alpine scenes painted by Matthew Nutter in 1832.

Southeast of the castle is an 1813 dovecote, which is disguised as a classical temple, or at least the front is. An Ionic portico carries a balustrade and pediment. On the frieze is an inscription in Italian: A QUELLA CHE MERITA ('To she who merits'). Philip Howard is credited with arranging the conversion of the dovecote, but the best motive must surely have been had by his son Henry, whose wife, Maria, died in 1789 aged 23, a year after they were married.

Like grandfather Thomas, father and son were inveterate travellers, and accounts of their journeys would shed more light on the Corby garden. In 1833 Henry Howard placed a statue of St Constantine on the river bank opposite

St Constantine's Cells, medieval caves that served as hermitages. The estate, now owned by a Dr Haughey, a reclusive Irishman, is zealously guarded—even stopping to peer through a gate triggered a frenzy of inquisitive Land-Rovers and an in-depth interrogation, sadly without success on our side.

Vulcan's Forge (1833)
NY 472 544

The smithy in the village of Great Corby was built as an imaginative reconstruction of Vulcan's Forge. Horses were shod under the classical porch at the front; at the back is an arched doorway with medieval fragments.

Derwent Island

Pocklington's Follies (c.1780)
NY 261 224

Derwent Water cradles several islands: Derwent, St Herbert's, Lord's and Rampsholme. A disputed fifth, the Floating Island, appears now and then and consists of weeds floating on the lake's gases. On Derwent Island are the ruins of the remarkable buildings Joseph Pocklington sprinkled about his territory. Like the other islands and most of the lake, it is now the property of the National Trust, which wrote to us in 1984 to say that:

> the features ... cannot really be described as follies. Their present condition is in any case so poor that you would need to be an archaeologist to be able to locate them. They are definitely not worthy of mention in your book—particularly as the Island is not open to the public.

Pocklington was connected with Peter Crosthwaite, an early exploiter of Lakeland tourism. He bought the island in 1781, renamed it Pocklington Island and proclaimed himself Governor. He built a boathouse in the guise of a picturesque chapel, a Druid's circle, a proper chapel and, in order to defend the island's sovereignty, a fort and battery. Pocklington's crony Crosthwaite, who had just settled at Keswick after a considerable time spent on the high seas, was not slow to capitalize on the venture. He installed himself as publisher of guides, curator of the Keswick Museum and general tourism officer, billing himself as 'Admiral at Keswick Regatta; who keeps the Museum at Keswick, & is Guide, Pilot, Geographer and Hydrographer to the Nobility and Gentry, who make the Tour of the Lakes'. In connivance with Pocklington, who had published his own map with views of the follies under Crosthwaite's imprint, he organized a mock naval battle in 1781: 'The Storming of Pocklington's Island.'

Greystoke

Bunker's Hill (1789)
NY 459 308
Fort Putnam (1789)
NY 452 310
Spire House (1789)
NY 463 312

The entry for Greystoke in Hutchinson's *History of Cumberland* (1794) partly reads:

> The farmholds near the castle have some ornamental buildings, and extensive plantations, made by his Grace the Duke of Norfolk, as objects from the road leading to the castle ...

Hutchinson underrated the three first-grade follies at Greystoke. Like several other buildings of their type, these rural conceits referred in name to the American War of Independence. Their more specific purpose is said to have been to irritate the Duke's Tory neighbour, the Earl of Lonsdale. They are heralded from the south by an octagonal

Fort Putnam

obelisk on the B5288, called the Greystoke Pillar.

Mount Putnam (now Fort Putnam), which was named after General Israel 'Puffing' Putnam. Fort Putnam is a screened farm with sturdy castellations, a turret, pointed arches and a tall Gothic window. The wall screening the byre is executed in a baffling manner. Pointed arches along the whole length are interspersed with pillars used as buttresses. The tops of the pillars are banded with stone leavage. On some pillars the top is extended with a round shaft with ball finial, like the minarets on the stable block at Hope End in Hereford.

Bunker's Hill is less well screened, for only the centre part of the farm, in which pointed windows are set, is castellated on three sides. Another farm does without any decorations but is granted the name Jefferson.

Spire House is a farm made into an eyecatcher in a rather off-hand but effective manner. Only part of the façade has a range of castellations, with two double-pointed and two round blind arches below. In between these are a rectangular and a pointed window. The resemblance to a church spire is intentional. A local farmer had told the duke that, according to his creed, worship did not necessitate church attendance and that his own house would suffice. The duke took this dictum to its logical conclusion and built the farmer a house that looked like a church. A third and much smaller polygonal storey supports the lead spire.

The architect for these delightful follies is unknown, but in 1787 Francis Hiorne was

staying at Greystoke to discuss with the Duke of Norfolk the projected repairs and alterations to Arundel Castle in Sussex that culminated in the triangular folly tower known as Hiorne's Tower. The party made an expedition to Alnwick in Northumberland 'for Mr Hiorne's information', where they must have seen Robert Adam's Brizlee Tower, then only six years old. The 11th Duke's enthusiasm for building (and for an independent America) could well mean that he was the responsible architect, with Hiorne working in an advisory capacity. Whoever was responsible knew what he was doing; these follies wear their 200 years well.

Kirklinton

Eyecatcher Columns (1845)
Privy Dovecote (18th century)
NY 435 670

Near the village of Kirklinton, off the A6071 northwest of Brampton, the Rev. G.E. Bell erected a couple of columns as an eyecatcher. They were taken from the medieval church of St Cuthbert when it was rebuilt in 1845.

East of the village, towards Hethersgill, is the best surprise of the region: a beautiful 18th-century dovecote, incorporating a coat of arms dated 1599, is found to contain a two-seater privy.

Little Orton

Tempest Tower (1875)
NY 351 552
Drumburgh House Tower
NY 265 600

Little Orton, west of Carlisle, has a tower farm, the well-named Tempest Tower of 1875, while Drumburgh House, overlooking the Solway Firth, has a plain and tiny Georgian folly tower.

Muncaster

Henry VI Monument (c. 1800)
Summerhouse
SD 111 975

Some follies have all the right ingredients: size, location, style and mystery. The Henry VI Monument scores highly on most counts, although we do know a reason for its erection, however spurious.

Sir John Pennington, 1st Baron Muncaster, erected around 1800 a tall Gothick tower north of Muncaster Castle, near Ravenglass on the River Esk, to mark the spot where Henry VI, in flight from

Spire House

someone during the Wars of the Roses, encountered a shepherd who led him safely to the castle of his master, Sir John Pennington. The octagonal tower is on a promontory overlooking the Esk valley. It is three storeys high, with a broad door, cross arrowslits and lancet windows all around the third storey and a pyramidal roof. A wash drawing (*c*.1810) by Thomas Sunderland shows the tower topped by a slender needle. The stables at the castle are screened by a

Muncaster Tower

highly decorated Gothick wall, castellated and flanked by a turret.

In the wilderness of the gardens there is also a decaying rustic wooden belvedere summerhouse with a view over the valley. Inside is a domed room, with four niches starting about 5ft (1.5m) from floor level and two higher niches facing the entrance.

Netherby

Fortified Salmon Coop (*c*.1800)
NY 396 716

Netherby is virtually on the Scottish border, and many of the estate buildings have been screened with embattled walls. One solitary screen, consisting of a wall between two towers decorated with cross arrowslits, guards a salmon coop. Netherby lost a bride to Young Lochinvar; it certainly didn't want to lose its fish as well. According to Hutchinson, the house at Netherby was built by Sir Robert Graham, and it was he who laid out the pleasure walks. Around 1820 Sir James Graham rebuilt many of the farms on the estate and did much to improve the land.

So either of these owners may have put up the screens, although they do have an 18th-century air. The difficulty here is to decide whether or not they were purely ornamental; border lords did not remain border lords through their love of frivolity, and it was not long since castellations and machicolations really meant something.

Newby East

Gazebos (mid-19th century)
NY 476 584

At Newby East, near Newby Demesne farmhouse, two circular gazebos terminate a wall. The gazebos, one roofless, and the adjoining Scottish Baronial farmhouse probably belonged to Thomas Henry Graham of Edmond Castle, which was Tudorized by Smirke in 1824 and 1844, and the gazebos probably date from the 1840s.

Penrith

Penrith Beacon (1715–80)
Clock Tower (late 19th century)
Stott Gatehouse (1994)
NY 511 400

The Penrith Beacon, just outside the town on a high hill, doesn't really count as a folly because it was genuinely built as a warning tower, replacing an earlier beacon on the same spot. It was built because of the threat to the town by Scottish troops in 1715. It was restored for the second time in 1780, by which time the threat of a Scottish invasion must surely have receded, and the work purely cosmetic. The tower, a plain square building with a pyramid roof and round arched windows, merits a Grade I listing. The beacon proved to be of unexpected use in 1805 when it flashed the warning of a Napoleonic invasion. This event caused Scott to curtail his tour of the Lakes and hurry back to Scotland, where he joined the volunteers, but it proved to be a false alarm.

In Penrith itself is a small Victorian clock tower commemorating Philip Musgrave of Eden Hall.

There was a planning fuss in 1994 when nursery garden owners Peter and Briony Stott built a mock medieval oak gatehouse without first getting planning permission. They defended themselves by claiming it was erected as a folly. At the resulting public hearing an expert on historic buildings said it could not be described as an authentic folly, because, as a gatehouse, it was built for a specific purpose. They never asked us—how little people know about the true meaning of follies. Except you, of course, dear reader, if you've managed to plough this far.

Sandsfield

Edward Memorial (1803)
NY 357 608

Near the mouth of the Eden in Sandsfield, north of Burgh by Sands, is a memorial column to Edward I, who died here on 7 July 1307 on his way to fight the Scots. A flood demolished the monument in 1795, but eight years later it was re-erected on the same site and in exactly the same manner as the original had been built by Thomas Langstaffe in 1685. The square pillar is about 20ft (6m) high and has four arched openings on the top, from which a cone and a stone cross rise.

Sebergham

Fletcher Eyecatcher (late 18th century)
NY 355 418

At Sebergham Sir Henry Fletcher, a Whig like the Duke of Norfolk, converted a farmhouse into a castellated eyecatcher; the resemblance to the Greystoke follies is perhaps not accidental. The screened house was duly noted in Hutchinson's county history of 1794, some years after it was built.

Stanwix

Towers (early 19th century)
NY 390 570

The agreeably named Mr George Head Head of Rickerby House (now Eden School) in Stanwix, Carlisle, is supposed to have had a fondness for folly towers. Near the old house is one that looks like a dovecote—it has three storeys and is octagonal and has lancet windows. It was built about 1835, when not only had dovecotes gone out of fashion but culinary habits had changed as well. The solution offered is that the dovecote was moved here from another site to serve as an ornament. One of Head's cottages was converted into a girls' school, and about this time he raised a classical lodge to Rickerby House and had his arms carved in the tympanum, accompanied by the motto STUDY QUIET. An exhortation to the girls?

George Head Head's predecessor at Rickerby House was 'Nabob' William Richardson, who towards the end of the 18th century built himself a belvedere tower on a tumulus next to Hadrian's Wall near Oldwall, north of Carlisle Airport.

Toppin Castle (early 19th century)
NY 498 571

Another of Head's follies is Toppin Castle, a mile southwest of Hayton. It is a farm converted into a tower house. The battlemented, four-storey tower has Gothic windows, Head's coat of arms and a smaller side turret.

Thirlmere

Brothers Parting (1806)
NY 320 288

The slopes of Helvellyn shoulder several monuments to dramatic events. At Grisdale Tarn above Thirlmere a rock is known as 'Brothers Parting'. Some lines by Wordsworth were inscribed on the rock at the suggestion of Canon H.D. Rawnsley, one of the founders of the National Trust. Most of the carving has weathered away, so a new inscription has taken its place. 'Brothers Parting' was originally placed on the spot where, in 1805, the brothers John and William Wordsworth took leave of each other, as John was on his way to join the East Indiaman the *Earl of Abergavenny*. The ship struck a rock on the Dorset coast and foundered with the loss of 200 men, John among them. Canon Rawnsley rescued the memorial, which had been dynamited to make way for a reservoir, and had it reassembled near the Straining Well above Legburthwaite.

Ullswater

Lyulph's Tower (1780)
NY 435 215

The last of the follies associated with Wordsworth is Lyulph's Tower in the National Trust's Gowbarrow Park on the shores of Ullswater. Ullswater was the lake that found most favour with 18th-century amateurs of the picturesque, not least because of its sextuple echo—the Duke of Portland, who owned property locally, kept a vessel on the lake 'with brass guns, for the purpose of exciting echoes', wrote Gilpin in 1772. The opening line of the Lake poet's 'The Somnambulist' is 'List, ye who pass by Lyulph's Tower', while the Gowbarrow daffodils inspired a more famous poem.

The tower, a hunting box once lived in by the Duke of Norfolk's gamekeeper, is castellated with octagonal turrets on each corner and a trapezoidal ground plan; it dates from 1780. It stands on the site of the medieval tower of Baron de l'Ulf of Greystoke, 1st Baron of Ullswater, who gave his name both to the lake and the present building.

West Woodside

Fiddleback Farm (1709)
NY 308 492

South of Thursby near Carlisle stands this peculiar house, with the date 1709 carved in a door lintel. The round house and round barn at the back merge into each other in such a way that what seems to be the premeditated shape of a fiddle, or a figure-of-eight, is achieved; an ambitious owner in the 19th century dubbed it Fiddlecase Hall. Black-bordered windows and an ogee-arched front door speak of later Gothicization—unless this is the first Gothick building in the country. Bordered by the railway to the north, the once tranquil setting of this strange, unique house is further diminished by the A595 embankment lowering to the east and south.

Wigton

Highmoor House Tower (1887)
NY 265 477

Wigton is a good place to get your head kicked in on a Saturday night after a curry and a few lagers, but it's all good-natured stuff and they wouldn't dream of pulling a knife on you—it is Melvyn Bragg's home town, after all. It's just that there's little else to do, except gawp at the tallest folly tower in Cumberland, 136ft (41.5m) of neo-renaissance fantasy with a lovely ogee roof, attached to an otherwise undistinguished house.

The tower was built by the sons of William Banks, who had made his fortune in the clothing business. Henry and Edwin had no interest in the clothing or any other business, feeling they had little need to do so as father had left them very well provided for. Having inherited the house with a small clock tower (dating from 1870), they decided that what they really wanted was a carillon. Edwin appears to have been the driving force here; a full carillon programmed to play any one of 36 tunes at 9 a.m., 12 noon, 3 p.m. and 6 p.m. was installed, together with Big Joe, a tenor bell with a range of 12 miles, and a keyboard for practising at night-time, much to the delight of the neighbours. The bells were installed in the huge new tower in 1887, just too late for Queen Victoria's jubilee, and by 1891 Henry had gone away to die in London, perhaps to get away from the incessant ringing of bells. Edwin consoled himself with a small menagerie of flamingos, wallabies and a llama and carried on building, mainly laudable public works in Wigton but also a pair of Swiss cottages named Alpha and Omega. It was not surprising to learn that neither brother married. Unfortunately, inherited money has a habit of running out, and Edwin was finally bankrupted in 1908. The house was converted into flats as early as 1934, and the tower with its stopped clock survives as the most prominent landmark from the town and as a monument to Banks's folly.

Fiddleback Farm

Wreay

Sarah Losh's Follies (1830–50)

NY 435 4890

'Ray?' asked the dog-walker, scratching his head, stretching out the vowels to near breaking point—'Raaay?' Sudden enlightenment. 'Y'mean Reeah!' St Mary's Church in Wreay, peaceful despite being trapped between the M6 and the A6, is a freak in architectural chronology. Visually, both the exterior and the interior differ widely from their actual date, 1840–42. What is even more surprising for the time is that the architect was a woman, Miss Sarah Losh. Sarah's grandfather was John Losh, 'The Big Black Squire' from Woodside near Carlisle. Of his seven sons, John, the father of Sarah and her sister Katherine, inherited the house, while a younger son, William, went to Sweden, became consul for Sweden and Prussia in Newcastle, and managed John's ironworks. Sarah was known for her beauty and intelligence, and in 1817 the two sisters and their uncle William went on the Grand Tour, travelling at least as far south as Naples.

In the early 19th century a woman's involvement with architecture would consist at the most of doodling plans for a model farm cottage. Sarah Losh, however, started practising architecture in earnest about 1830. Of course, no one would ever dream of employing a female architect, but as the squire's daughter she had the advantage of having an entire village at her disposal. In Wreay and along the road to Brisco are several houses built by Miss Losh. Around 1830 she built the village school and provided the master with his own two-storey house, very simple and none too beautiful, yet it has the distinction of being based on the measurements of an 1800-year-old house Sarah had drawn and measured when in Pompeii in 1817. The Pompeiian Cottage is not the only result of her travels; the Sexton's cottage next to the churchyard appears to have the same provenance, although there are modern additions.

The church is Miss Losh's masterpiece; although not a folly it is too unusual to omit. It seems to have been largely based on the basilicas she had seen in Italy, but the details and the carvings are indisputably Arts and Crafts—50 years ahead of the movement. Much of it was done by Miss Losh and the local sculptor, William Hindson. Her cousin William S. Losh also assisted in sculpting as well as supplying the stained glass from France. The death of her sister Katherine in 1835 prompted Sarah to build St Mary's, and in the churchyard is her sister's mausoleum, dating from *c.*1850 and built of huge stones assembled in the Cyclopean manner. Inside, a white marble statue of Katherine by the professional sculptor David Dunbar the Younger startles the unwary visitor who peers through the tiny window—but not you, forewarned as you are. On the walls are medallions of Sarah's parents, John and Isabella Losh. The churchyard also houses a sundial, a memorial cross and a mortuary chapel, now used as a shed. This is a replica of St Perran's Oratory, excavated near Perranport, Cornwall, in 1835. Sarah had accurate measured drawings made for her and immediately built this copy. (See also Brisco.)

Designed c. 70 AD built c. 1830 AD

WESTMORLAND

Ambleside

Bridge Cottage (18th century)
NY 377 043

Ambleside, at the northern end of Lake Windermere, has a vernacular cottage built on a bridge across a little beck. Bridge House is owned by the National Trust. Its striking site ensured that a story that it was built by a Scottish family in order to avoid paying ground rent quickly sprang up—but it has no foundation. In fact, it was a summerhouse to Ambleside Hall, although in Victorian times a family was crammed into the tiny house, said to be the smallest in England.

Appleby

Brampton Tower (mid-19th century)
SD 680 223

A mile or two north of Appleby is Brampton Tower, a Victorian castellated tower house, worth seeing if one is in the area.

Beetham

Ashton House Gazebo (1791)
SD 496 796

A battlemented summerhouse is almost oxymoronic; a blend of peace and aggression.

Brough

Fox Tower (1775)
NY 787 163

On a rocky outcrop high over the Eden valley in Helbeck Wood stand the remains of a hunting tower built by John Metcalf Carleton. There are two round towers, one tall and thin and one short and fat, like Laurel and Hardy. The spiral staircase in the taller tower was still intact in 1961.

Brougham

Countess Pillar (1656)
NY 548 280

There are few women folly builders; whether that was out of choice or out of economic deprivation only the next millennium will tell. Lady Anne Clifford, Countess of Pembroke, Dorset and Montgomery was rich enough to indulge all her architectural fantasies. Born in 1590, she was married twice, which accounts for her string of titles. After her last husband died in 1650, she set to

work in earnest. She was 59, her face mutilated by smallpox since she was 34, and had no further interest in the marriage game. So this formidable woman rolled up her sleeves, put on a pair of stout boots, assembled a band of dedicated labourers and set to rebuilding, restoring and repairing the castles that belonged to her northern estates: Appleby, Barden Tower, Brough, Brougham, Pendragon and Skipton. Churches and chapels followed: Appleby, Barden, Bongate, Brougham, Mallerstang, Ninekirks and Skipton, as well as almshouses at Appleby and Bethmesley, now Beamsley. Throwing in a few oddments, Anne Clifford erected the statues to Spenser in Westminster Abbey and that to her old tutor, the poet Samuel Daniel, in Beckington Church, Somerset.

Among these trifles was also the Countess Pillar on the A66, east of Brougham Castle. It is octagonal with a cube on top, decorated with a sundial and an inscription. The pillar was erected in 1656 to commemorate the death of her mother Margaret in 1616. She describes her as a woman of:

> *greate naturall wit and judgment, of a swete disposition, truly religious and virtuous, and endowed with a large share of those four moral virtues, prudence, justice, fortitude and temperance.*

At Appleby Castle, sold for £1.5 million in 1994, is the plain Bee House and at Mallerstang, some way from Pendragon Castle, are the rudiments of Lady's Pillar of 1664, the purpose of which is unrecorded. Lady Anne inexorably went on building until her death at the remarkable age for that time of 86.

Coniston Lake

SD 302 977
The Labyrinth

On the west shore of the lake is a strange series of spiral mounds overgrown with ornamental shrubs. Who, what and why?

Rowlandson Ground Summerhouse (1984)

Back in the 1980s the concept of building purely for pleasure was as alien to the national psyche as it was ever likely to get, so it was therefore with no surprise that we learned of the Lake District planning board's decision to reject an application by Viscount Ednam to build a domed octagonal summerhouse, on the grounds that it would be 'out of character' in the Lake District. An anonymous but enlightened Department of the Environment inspector overruled the decision, pointing out that 'the countryside would be the poorer if it lacked such occasional eccentricities'.

Ednam's Staircase (1983)

An earlier work by the noble lord—a triumphant rambler told us that he built an enormous stone staircase in a field and tried unsuccessfully to get a public footpath diverted on to it. This actually sounds rather thoughtful of the viscount, but seething passions are engendered by footpaths, and it is unwise to side with either landowner or rambler.

Kendal

Castle Howe Obelisk (1788)
SD CK12 924
Tolson Hall Obelisk (1816)
SD 497 951

East of Windermere are two obelisks; one, erected in 1788 on Castle Howe in the centre of Kendal, celebrates Liberty; the other, at Tolson Hall 2 miles northwest of Kendal, was erected by James Bateman immediately after Waterloo to extol the statesmanlike craft of William Pitt. Do not be distracted by mention of the Finkle Street Folly; it is

merely a modernist bus shelter, once denounced as a 'metal mystery' by a local councillor.

Kirkby Lonsdale

Gazebo (18th century)
SD 611 790

At first sight this plain little octagonal gazebo with cement block battlements could be taken for a watch tower guarding the cemetery against grave robbers, but it predated the graveyard by some years, being an authentic gazebo in the vicarage garden wall before part of the garden was taken over as a burial plot. It was used by Turner in 1822, while he was painting his *View of the River Lune*.

Milnthorpe

St Anthony's Tower (mid-19th century)
SD 498 820

The first town to welcome us to Cumbria as we arrive on the A6 from Lancashire is Milnthorpe. Here is a small, round folly tower, possibly first built in the park of Dallam Tower by architect George Webster as a summerhouse in the late 1830s when he

St Anthony's Tower

worked on Milnthorpe Church. It was moved to the summit of St Anthony's Hill in the late 19th century.

The park at Dallam Tower, west of the village, which is open to the public, also has a beautifully-sited rustic deer house.

Ravenstonedale

The Lanes Cottage (late 18th century)
NY 723 042

The Lanes Cottage is a chimeric collection of late Gothic elements. The idea of architecture as a joke is impressed upon it by the 'signature' the builders made, and inscription running 'T. Hewitson del. W. Hodgson sculp.' as on an 18th-century engraving. The name of Hodgson is well known around these parts, so the cottage must be of local manufacture.

Shap Wells

Britannia Pillar (1841)
NY 570 095

Shap Wells, some miles southwest of Shap, enjoyed a brief spell as a spa in the 19th century, but a covered wellhead is all that remains. William Lowther, Earl of Lonsdale, took an interest in developing the possibilities of the mineral wells, and it was he who paid for the monument celebrating Victoria's accession to the throne. According to *The Builder* of 1842, the sculpture of Britannia on top of the octagonal pillar and the symbolic bas-reliefs on three sides of the base were done by Thomas Bland, a self-taught sculptor. A Mr Mawson from Lowther village was the architect. Lonsdale was enthusiastic about giving local talent a chance; Bland hailed from Reagill, a hamlet 3 miles northeast of Shap. Here many of his efforts, those he wanted to keep to himself, can be seen in a large garden behind a farm building. They represent the expected output of a naïve but able craftsman: fairy figures, monarchs, animals and quaint vases.

Storr's Point

Storr's Temple (1804)
SD 391 941

In 1825 William Wordsworth, together with Robert Southey, John Wilson and George Canning made up a party to celebrate Sir Walter Scott's birthday by way of a regatta, a popular event on Windermere. It started from Storr's Point, south of Bowness. In all probability the Lakers were watching the show from Storr's Temple, an octagonal building with four arches and four tablets remembering four Admirals of the Fleet: Duncan, St Vincent, Howe and Nelson. The distracted architect Joseph Gandy built this monument on the lake's edge at Storr's Hall, now an hotel, for Sir John Legard in 1804.

Striding Edge

Gough Memorial (1890)
NY 345 150

East of Helvellyn is Striding Edge, where the Gough Memorial was erected in 1890. Gough was a Quaker who frequently visited the Lakes. In 1804, walking on Helvellyn with his dog, he fell to his death, and the following spring a shepherd found his body with the dog beside it, still guarding his master. Soon after the tragedy became known Wordsworth, Scott and Humphry Davy climbed to the spot, and the two authors wrote verses about the faithful dog. They are quoted on the simple stone monument.

Another, less emotional, monument records the coming of the Machine Age by commemorating the landing of an aeroplane on Helvellyn's summit in 1926.

Wray

John Longmire's Folly (1840)
NY 010 374

Although Wordsworth planted a tree in the grounds of Wray Castle, one senses his heart was not in it. As we have seen, he was never one for spoiling Nature by Art. Still, in the final years of his life he had to witness the wealthy Liverpudlian surgeon James Dawson come to the banks of Windermere and build himself a neo-Gothic pile, all arrowslits, corbels and battlements, to the designs of H.P. Horner. Adding insult to injury, after felling a few trees to make room for an adequate park, Dawson erected a string of sham ruins in the grounds of the castle. Most have now been demolished, but John Longmire's Folly is one of those remaining, a small, squat, embattled tower with arrowslits and quatrefoils. A fortress is beside it. Longmire himself, an original from Troutbeck, did not have much to do with it except that the building incorporates some of the stones he used for carving his mottoes and poetry on. One stone even carried an 'Ode to the National Debt'. H.P. Horner must have been the architect, for the tower echoes Wray Castle, and it must have been built around the same time, 1840–47.

DERBYSHIRE

Coming in to Derbyshire from the east one immediately senses the difference. Here are hills and moors ideal for striding over, craggy rocks of no great height but of fearsome aspect, ideal for carving and tunnelling. Most counties have a characteristic type of folly. Derbyshire's would be the Rock Hermitage, were it not for the fact that they are well-intentioned, honest to goodness real hermits' caves – although many of them were enhanced in the 18th century. Such beauty surrounded by so many conurbations means that at weekends and holidays Derbyshire gridlocks. The county is best appreciated on a winter Tuesday.

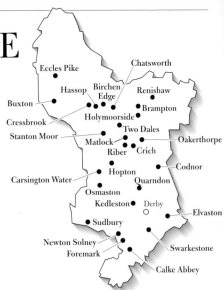

Eccles Pike • Chatsworth • Hassop • Birchen Edge • Renishaw • Buxton • Brampton • Cressbrook • Holymoorside • Two Dales • Stanton Moor • Matlock • Oakerthorpe • Riber • Crich • Hopton • Codnor • Carsington Water • Quarndon • Osmaston • Kedleston • Derby • Sudbury • Elvaston • Newton Solney • Foremark • Swarkestone • Calke Abbey

Birchen Edge

Nelson Monument (mid-19th century)
Wellington Monument (mid-19th century)
SK 278 731

On Birchen Edge is a memorial to Lord Nelson; close by is the Wellington Monument, a large stone cross on Baslow Edge. Both are visible from the A621, the Baslow–Sheffield road, near Ramsley Moor.

Brampton

Brampton Manor Gazebo (early 18th century)
SK 360 720

On the western outskirts of Chesterfield stands this charming ogee-roofed gazebo, in a sad condition. Having a Grade II* garden shed is evidently a problem for some people, for although consent for repair was granted some time ago it remains neglected.

Buxton

Solomon's Temple (1896)
SK 054 717

Spas and towers are made for each other. Here is Solomon's Temple or Grin Low Tower. A round tower, made of different hues of rough stone, its treatment is such that it has a very smooth appearance. It was built in 1896 on the site of a Bronze Age barrow by a publican, Solomon Mycock, who economically ran a public subscription to build the tower and relieve unemployment. On weekends a lady sold ginger beer to walkers who had climbed up to the 1440ft (440m) moor from the town. It was restored

by Derbyshire County Council as the focal point of Grin Low Park in 1987.

Calke Abbey

Grottoes (c.1746; 1809–10)
SK 367 227

Calke Abbey, transferred to the National Trust with much fanfare, has the remains of not one but two grottoes: the first built, along with a now-vanished Chinese House, c.1746 for Sir Henry and Lady Caroline Harpur-Crewe, and the second built in 1809–10 by the architect Samuel Browne.

Solomon's Temple

Carsington Water

Stone Island (1991)
SK 244 515

Here is a recently built stone circle, allegedly aligned with other mystical sites across Derbyshire, although to the outsider Derbyshire and mysticism may seem odd bedfellows. Odder still when we discover the identity of the builder—not some belled and bearded aristocrat but the sober-sided Severn Trent Water Company, which happily spent £50,000 of its shareholders' money on this sham Stonehenge. Of course, it's not a Stonehenge; nor is Stone Island an island. It's a peninsula jutting out from the new Visitor's Centre for the reservoir. The structure was designed by Lewis Knight as 'Severn Trent's contribution to the long-standing tradition of Derbyshire hilltop monuments'. Hello? The artist explained it better: the standing stones set on a snail shell mound work both ways—as an eyecatcher from a distance, and then at the site the pierced stones direct your attention back out to the surrounding countryside.

Chatsworth

Folly Group (1582 onwards)
SK 265 707

Chatsworth is large, beautiful and rewarding for all, but there are no follies from the heroic period of the 18th century except for the grotto. The other buildings date from the 16th and 19th centuries. There is, however, one remarkable building, which has been all but ignored by architectural historians. The Hunting Tower to the northeast of the house is a four square, four-storey tower with round corner turrets, each capped with a little dome (afterthoughts?), which make it look like an early observatory. It was built by Bess of Hardwick, and it was unquestionably intended to be a prospect tower—the fenestration alone proves that. Bess was fond of windows—remember 'Hardwick Hall, more glass than wall'—and this stand has 36, at the third count. They are large, attractive, mullioned and leaded Tudor windows, much admired. Barbara Jones, that most enthusiastic of writers, dismisses it as 'carefully preserved and dull'; Pevsner notes it but does not single it out for praise; other writers pass it by as an ordinary gazebo. But this tower is probably the most important folly in Derbyshire, for it is over 400 years old. Only Freston Tower in Suffolk is earlier, and there is a suspicion that Freston was

originally part of a long-demolished house, which would make the Hunting Tower the oldest free-standing, purpose-built folly tower in Britain. It is in remarkably good condition for a tower built in 1582, and it is beautifully sited.

Queen Mary's Bower is a structure looking like the foundations of a house, surrounded by a moat. It was in fact a walled-in garden in which Mary Queen of Scots is said to have walked during her five periods of captivity at Chatsworth. The bower was reconstructed by Wyatville in the early 19th century. In the southeast corner of the garden is a neat grotto overlooking a sheet of water. This was built under the direction of the Duchess Georgiana in the last quarter of the

The Hunting Tower at Chatsworth

18th century. It contained a collection of minerals found by White Watson, a Bakewell geologist. The round rustic hut on top of the grotto arch must date from the same period—at least it should, as hut and grot are in perfect balance to each other.

There is an earlier 'grotto' at Chatsworth: a dark room under the great stairs adorned with a fountain and created by the 1st Duke *c.*1692. As at Woburn and Osterley, these early indoor grotto rooms marked the first playful influences of Italian mannerism imported to the grey skies of England; where better than to place them out of weather's way?

The majority of follies at Chatsworth date from the time William Cavendish, 6th Duke of Devonshire, began to take an active interest in the gardens. (A piece of irrelevant but interesting trivia here: there is no such place as Devonshire—the county name is Devon—so how come there's a Duke of Devonshire? It was in fact a 17th-century clerical error: they were going to be created Dukes of Derbyshire, but a clerk made a slip in transcribing the name, so Devonshire they became.) It starts with the village of Edensor at the estate gates, built in 1839–45 by Joseph Paxton and John Robertson, who specialized in cottage and villa architecture. Robertson appears to have been inspired by the popular work of P.F. Robinson, *Rural Architecture; or a Series of Designs for Ornamental Cottages* (1823). The village was populated by the homeless inhabitants of the old Edensor, which was razed because it interfered with the view from Chatsworth. New Edensor was smaller, so the surplus villagers were billeted in nearby Beeley and Pilsley. The inhabitants of New Edensor were all directly connected with the running of the Chatsworth Estate. The result of this feudal autocracy is a most picturesque village with rather large houses in the rustic, Swiss and Gothic styles. Set apart, several of the buildings might count as follies: there are water tower-like outcrops and miniature castles, together creating a never-never-land of rural felicity, despite being built during the Chartist troubles.

The cottage style spread into the park. There is a Swiss cottage of 1839 and a beautifully decorated Russian cottage, now used as a gamekeeper's house. The Russian, or Muscovite, style is a rarity in Britain, but was used quite extensively in Germany, and the duke may have picked up the idea there. The cottage was probably built in anticipation of a visit by Czar Nicolas in 1843. The Duke of Devonshire had been on a mission to see the Czar of All the Russias in 1826, spending £50,000 of his own money on the journey. The two Emperor Lakes were made in honour of the expected visit but, although the czar met the duke in London, he never came to Chatsworth.

One folly came directly from Germany: the aqueduct of ruined arches serving as a cascade, built, like the Swiss cottage, in 1839. Cavendish had seen a similar aqueduct in the folly garden of the Schloss Wilhelmshöhe near Kassel. Ruined aqueducts are a staple ingredient of German folly pattern books, and this one looks remarkably like a design in Grohmann's *Ideen-magazin* of 1796–1810.

In the northeast corner of the garden is a Moorish summerhouse. It is small but elegant, with two plaques, one reading:

Won from the brow of yonder Headlong Hill,
Through grassy channels, see, the sparkling rill
O'er the chafed pebbles, in its murmuring flow
Sheds freshness on the thirsty valley below,
Quickening the ground till trees of every zone
In Chatsworth's soil, and clime, forget their own.
H.L. sept. MDCCCXXXIX

Chatsworth's Cascade House

A very rare and whimsical object stands in the middle of the garden, reminding one of the practical jokes to be encountered in Italian mannerist gardens. Set in an area dominated by huge boulders forming tunnel passages and artificial rocks is the Willow Fountain, a metal construction imitating a weeping willow to perfection, the drooping branches simulated by jets of water. A pipe made up to look like a gnarled old log provides the water supply. A 'heathen' pedestal is nearby. The fountain is supposed to be a replica of one standing in the gardens at the time of the 1st Duke of Devonshire, who had the famous cascade built.

Codnor

Jessop Memorial (1815)
SK 432 510

East of Ripley in Codnor Park stands a tall Doric column on a plinth. The Jessop Memorial is a monument to William Jessop, engineer and founder of the Butterley Iron Works. The column looks and is unsafe, and one can no longer climb the spiral staircase. It was built the year after Jessop died. This prepares us for the crescent loop of follies running south of Derby.

Cressbrook

The Gothic (1823)
SK 173 727

The road drops down from the high open moors, trampled and overrun by ramblers, through a mossy valley into Cressbrook. Here an otherwise unremarkable rural row of terraced houses is corked by a cascade of castellations. Although wonderful to see, it was common practice to disguise otherwise unsightly workmen's housing that may have been glimpsed from a great house—but where is the great house? In order for this to have worked as an eyecatcher it should have been set in a sheer cliff face on the other bank of the River Wye. What explanation is there for this intriguing edifice? Its bizarre aspect has been seized on by a local entrepreneur, who has opened it as the DS Brew Stop, providing tea and cakes for thirsty ramblers who can see it clearly from the other bank of the river. Its function as an eyecatcher has at last been put to good use.

Apprentice Terrace, now Dale Terrace, was originally built by William Newton in 1817 as an apprentices' house for his Wye or Big Mill, with boys downstairs and girls upstairs, and separate entrances so they never

'The Gothic' at Cressbrook

met. The Gothic, as the castellations are called locally, was added to enclose a staircase from the dining room to a music room. Newton must have been an enlightened man; certainly his now ruined Grade II* Big Mill of 1814 is an industrial Palladian palace, as stately as any stately home, with elegant late Georgian proportions and immense windows to allow in as much light as possible. Work has now begun on its restoration and eventual conversion into apartments, which should find a ready sale to people with muddy boots.

Crich

Crich Stand (1923)
SK 344 554

The most visible tower in these parts is a 63ft (19m) lighthouse called Crich (pronounced Cryche, to save you embarrassment) Stand, above the road to Ripley. Seventy miles from the nearest sea—which is as far away from the sea as one can get in England—it was built as a war memorial in 1923 to the now disbanded Sherwood Foresters, so it cannot be classed as a folly. But why build it as a lighthouse, and why so far from the sea? The thinking behind it was that it was placed on the highest ground overlooking the counties of Lincolnshire, Nottinghamshire and Derbyshire, from where the regiment was recruited, and designed as a lighthouse so that the light could shine over those counties as an eternal flame. Unfortunately, the local residents complained that the eternal flame kept them awake at night, so it was extinguished.

Further investigation proved that there was more than a touch of folly about the whole enterprise. A datestone on the tower read 'F. H. 1788'. How can this be, if the memorial was built in 1923? What happened was that there had been a folly 40 yards (37m) northwest of the site, built by Francis Hurt in 1788 as a prospect tower to take advantage of the spectacular views. By 1922 the tower was on the verge of toppling into the quarry to the north, so Hurt's descendant, also a Francis Hurt, offered the folly and the site to General Smith-Dorian, the CO of the Foresters. The tottering tower was taken down and the stones reused for the erection of the war memorial. And there are no neighbours close enough to the tower to complain about the light.

Derby Assembly Rooms (1986)
SK 346 549

Crich also boasts the National Tramway Museum, and the National Tramway Museum boasts the façade of the Derby Assembly Rooms. The story behind this modern removal is the same as for all removals, and it is encouraging to hear. The Assembly Rooms in Derby was an attractive but not particularly distinguished building dating from 1755. Unfortunately, its builders had not anticipated that 200 or so years later it would be dreadfully in the way of a new building development in the heart of Derby, and as the building meanwhile had gone and got itself listed as being of architectural importance, it couldn't be demolished. So regrettably there was a fire, and the Assembly Rooms was declared unsafe and was promptly demolished. But the blackened façade, like a bedraggled black phoenix, has been triumphantly re-erected at Crich, in the old quarry among the old trams, and it now acts as the frontispiece to the museum.

Eccles Pike

Ruined Arch (20th century)
SK 035 811

A small by-road west of Chapel-en-le-Frith leads to the National Trust property of Eccles Pike and a folly in the making. One of the lanes ascending the hill has a crenellated gateway, two turrets connected by two arches of which one has been knocked down by a lorry, unintentionally creating a picturesque sham ruin. Time and ivy will accord it its folly status.

Elvaston

Moorish Temple (1860)
SK 407 328

Just southeast of the county town is Elvaston Castle. The western lodge cautiously introduces the visitor to the ebullient Sino-Moorish-Gothick (yes, it's unique) style of Elvaston's famous Moorish Temple. As so often with Moorish Temples, Tents or Kiosks this can also mean a Chinese Temple. Its huge round windows and bulbous forms are roofed by a curved baldachin, the whole fascinating melange a fitting tribute to the confusion of styles of the mid-19th century and the mild eccentricity of its builder, the Earl of Harrington, who crested the doorways of these most curious buildings with a large gilt 'h'. As far as the French are concerned, this could be the defining moment of *le style anglo-chinois*.

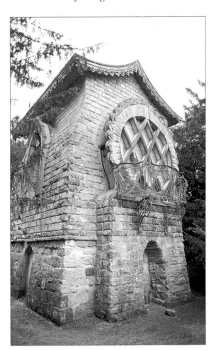

The Moorish Temple at Elvaston

The present condition of the Moorish Temple is disgraceful. Despite the claim that it is waiting for lottery funding to implement a restoration plan and while acknowledging that it is doing an excellent job of controlling the phenomenal topiary gardens at Elvaston, Derbyshire County Council must be censured for allowing this peerless building to deteriorate as much as it has. The council has owned it for nearly three decades, and apart from its sister lodge and water mill on the same site there is nothing else like it in Europe.

As Lord Petersham, Harrington invented the eponymous overcoat, owned 365 snuff boxes, refused to appear in daylight, employed 90 gardeners and devoted most of his life to litigation and temperance reform. William Barron of Edinburgh was employed to build the temple and the other conceits between 1830 and 1860, including some very extensive grot-work by the lake, and was under strict instructions from the earl not to let in hoi polloi: 'If the Queen comes, Barron, show her round, but admit no one else.' He would be apoplectic if he saw Elvaston today; the *grex venalium* have the run of the park and at the weekends it is as crowded as Oxford Street during the sales. Derbyshire County Council opened it to the public in the early 1970s. The big rock grotto on the north side of the lake is heavily used by acrobatic young mountain bikers, despite plenty of signs forbidding cycling. The grotto bears it all with quiet resignation.

Foremark

Anchorage Church (early 18th century)
SK 332 228

Derbyshire's geology has endowed it with some delightful natural rock formations, which proved irresistible to 18th-century lovers of the picturesque. There is a series of natural caves at Foremark, which includes the Anchorage Church, improved, enhanced and extended by the local squire as a hermitage, a refuge for a hired anchorite, an oxymoron if ever there was one. The medieval Hermitage at Dale was enlarged by Sir Robert Burdett, father of Francis Burdett the radical politician, and used as a meeting place for convivial evenings, rather like a damped-down Hell Fire Club.

Birchover has natural caves that were 'improved' by the vicar Thomas Eyre in 1717; he also built the local chapel. The Rowter Rocks at Birchover, with their rocking stone, have not unexpectedly been associated with the druids; hence the Druid's Inn at the foot of the hill.

Hassop

Hassop Hall Tunnels (19th century)
SK 221 722

As well as a Tudor revival gazebo here, there is the sunken delight of tunnels leading here and there to no discernible end.

Holymoorside

Belmont Tower (early 19th century)
SK 342 705

The Belmont Day Nursery is handsomely endowed with a monstrous erection on its north front, a tall, thin, castellated wall, which looks like a tower at first glance, but behind it there is nothing, just a conventional house at the base of a two-dimensional tower. The owners know nothing of its origins.

Belmont Tower

Hopton

Gell's Tower (1790)
SK 257 534

The pretty estate village of Hopton runs along a south-facing ridge, which formerly overlooked a valley but now finds itself spectacularly sited above the new reservoir of Carsington Water. For generations the Gell family has owned Hopton Hall, in the grounds of which stands a 30ft (9m) tower with two doors and no windows, linked to a fine crinkle-crankle wall. It was probably built by Sir Philip Gell, an active and enthusiastic builder. Barbara Jones tells an amusing story of how Gell's Tower came to have no windows: Sir Philip was impatient to get to London, so when the builders came to him for instructions, he replied with exasperation, 'Oh for God's sake go on building', which they did. When Sir Philip returned and saw the results of their handiwork he managed, with great equanimity, to accept the situation, muttering, 'Nothing to do now but put a roof on it.'

The Gell family was interesting and varied; Admiral John Gell died of apoplexy in 1806, probably on hearing that his cousin, William, had been knighted at the age of 26. Sir William, who loved bright colours and gay conversation, died a bachelor and left all his papers to his great friend Craven. He lived in Italy for a time, and thus may have dreamed up the name 'Via Gellia' (locally pronounced Vyer Jellier), rather grandly given to one of Sir Philip's road building projects, now more prosaically known as the A5012. The trade name 'Viyella', that comfortable combed cotton cloth they make expensive shirts out of, is a bastardization of Via Gellia, as it was first made in a mill on Sir Philip's road.

Kedleston

Gothick Temple (18th century)
SK 311 408

Nathaniel Curzon employed Matthew Brettingham to build the finest house of its time in the county. Later Robert Adam was involved, then Samuel Wyatt. The Curzons were at the cutting edge of 18th-century wealth, power and fashion—there had to be follies or, at the very least, a plethora of

garden buildings. Alas, there are very few. There is a three-bay, ogee-arched Gothick temple, now a house, which suffers in comparison to the Museum at Enville, Staffordshire (in fact, it does not begin to compare with it at all). There is a bath house, a boathouse, miscellaneous bits and pieces, but one gradually realizes that the Curzons were not inclined towards park conceits.

The family continued some desultory attempts to follow, or even steer fashion; Adam was commissioned to produce some designs for picturesque, asymmetrical estate cottages, which prefigured Marie-Antoinette's Hameau at Versailles by some ten years, but it appears they were not built.

Matlock

Grotto Façade (19th century)
SK 298 603

Derbyshire's follies are in two main groups; one running down Derwentdale from Chatsworth, the other in a crescent south of Derby itself. The heart of Derwentdale is Matlock, a damp delight with its Petrifying Well, Lover's Walk, Wishing Stone, Venetian Nights and Dioramas—the trappings of a spa that saw its great days when Victoria was queen but that still attracts tourists who can pay an entrance fee, fill up slot machines and enjoy soggy fish and chips. There are two follies here, plus a report of a three-arched

The alleged grotto façade in Matlock

grotto façade standing neglected in a car park behind a Matlock Bath hotel; we couldn't find it, although many members of the Folly Fellowship have since gleefully reported on its existence.

Victoria Tower (1844)
SK 295 587

The Heights of Abraham, above the town on the west bank, are so called because they reminded a visiting old soldier of the Quebecois battlefield, and after a walk to the Victoria Tower one begins to appreciate the stamina Wolfe's men must have had. Walking up this hill is bad enough; storming it must have been highly unpleasant, but here we are recompensed by a view that can even be improved by climbing the tower itself. There is no special feature to distinguish this tall, slim, round, rough stone tower; it was built to relieve unemployment among local miners and stonemasons. There is invariably a flag flying from the top of the tower. Perhaps Victoria's visit to Matlock in 1832 inspired the choice of name, but John Petchell, who then owned the Heights of Abraham, didn't build it until 12 years later. It is nicely echoed by the round turrets of two large houses on the south slope of the Heights.

Millennium Tower (1999)

In 1997 a proposal to build a 250ft (76m) tower on the Heights to mark the millennium was put forward. A revolving cabin at the top would allow 50 visitors at a time to savour 30 miles of panoramic views over the Dales. Presumably the revolving cabin would be for the benefit of visitors too exhausted by the climb up to the tower to stagger around the top. Planning consent had yet to be granted when this was written.

Newton Solney

Bladon Castle (1805)
SK 270 250

Bladon Castle is enormous. It looms over the village of Newton Solney like the cape of Dracula, devouring the length of the ridge between the village and Burton. Battlements, towers, unscaleable walls frown down at the cowed population—but it's all harmless really, because there's nothing behind it. Bladon is basically just a wall. It was designed and built by Sir Jeffry Wyatville for Abraham Hoskins (so it is sometimes known as Hoskins's Folly) and finished—as far as it could be called finished—in 1805. He really went over the top. This is the only example

in Britain that we have discovered of a double folly; two perfectly legitimate reasons for the place being a folly. First, it was built solely as an eyecatcher—a folly—by Hoskins, but it was so big, so egregious, that the builder found that he had local opinion to contend with as well. There was no way that the populace was going to stand such ostentation and let it pass as a mere whim. Wagging tongues forced Hoskins to move into his folly to justify its being built. Second, having moved in, he discovered a basic flaw in its conception as a house—there was no water. No well, no stream—not a problem for an uninhabited eyecatcher, but a major snag for a house and home. So having made his folly habitable, Hoskins endured two seasons of having his water yoked 1½ miles up the hill in buckets before he cracked and made his getaway. Part of Bladon is inhabited now by a farmer and his wife; a simple electric pump has solved the water problems.

We have been told of a folly boathouse to Bladon on the banks of the River Trent, castellated with a tree growing inside the roofless wreck; it may have disappeared.

Oakerthorpe

Horse Obelisk (19th century)
SK 389 550

Strangely Derbyshire is a county with very few obelisks. The first is a small monument to a dead horse, removed to a private garden in Oakerthorpe, north of Ripley. It originated from the Manor Park, where it had been erected by a member of the Strelling family.

Osmaston

Chimney (1849)
SK 200 438

Just outside Ashbourne on the Derby Road (until it closed in 1992) was Osmaston Garden Centre, built in the kitchen garden of Osmaston House, which was demolished in 1966. The house was built for the industrialist Francis Wright in 1849, and Mr Wright loved novelty. H.J. Stevens, the architect, provided him with a real wonder for the 19th century—a house with no chimneys. The idea was that the place should be heated by hot-air ducts, and the used air should be exhausted through a single chimney set in the kitchen garden above the house. Mr Wright was delighted. When preliminary calculations proved that in order to make the system halfway workable the exhaust chimney needed to be at least 150ft

(46m) high, he took the opportunity to make the chimney double up as a belvedere tower, and equipped it with a spiral staircase. Now the big square Italianate tower dominates the garden centre, having outlived the house as well as its usefulness long ago. A photograph of Osmaston taken at the turn of the century shows the rooftops packed with chimneys.

Quarndon

Well House (19th century)
SK 335 411

Just north of Derby is Quarndon, a village that once had hopes of becoming a spa. After a small Gothic building had been erected to protect the newly discovered spring with its wealth-giving properties, a rather insignificant earthquake opened up a cleft, which promptly swallowed the source again. The machicolated well house was undamaged and remains as a tiny, sad monument to frustrated ambition.

Renishaw

Gothic Arch (1808)
SK 441 785

Near Chesterfield with its crooked spire is Renishaw, home of the tumultuous Sitwells, and the most courteous No Trespassing sign we have ever encountered: 'Please Do Not Tread On Mr Sitwell's Snakes.' Osbert Sitwell tells us in his autobiography that it was the then owner, Sir Sitwell Sitwell himself, who

sketched out on a piece of paper the design for the Gothic archway in the park. Both its pinnacles and battlements, however, are in a similar style to the house, which was enlarged and Gothicized between 1793 and 1808 by Joseph Badger, a local man. Sir Sitwell may well have sketched the arch, one of the inspirations for the logotype of the Folly Fellowship, but it would appear that Badger put the professional touches to it to keep it in line with the overall style. The arch, with its great painted crest and the Sitwell motto, 'NE CEDE MALIS', is curiously placed at the bottom of a dip, just above the river, and evidently was never intended to serve any particular purpose unless there was formerly a bridge across the river at this point.

By the middle of the 19th century the castellated house itself was considered to be the folly. An owner of the time, Colonel Herbert Hely-Hutchinson, commented: 'By whom, or by how many, Renishaw was built, it is a folly.' Later, Sir George Sitwell was let loose on both house and garden, and he started well by stencilling all his white cattle with a blue willow pattern design. He brought 4000 unemployed men over from Scarborough to dig the lake and was forever planning follies on the estate, of which sadly only a few were built. The shell of an octagonal aviary lingers on, hopefully described as 'the Gothic Temple'. Today, Renishaw hosts corporate events, and the flags of Japanese car makers fly proudly from the parapets. There is an Arts Museum and

Renishaw Gothic Arch

Centre in the stable block, and instead of picturesque willow-patterned cattle dotted around the park, the house looks out over crowds of middle-aged white men wearing inappropriate clothing—not a gathering of the Folly Fellowship, but a golf course.

Riber

Riber Castle (1862)
SK 307 581

On a hazy day Riber Castle, between Matlock Bath and Matlock proper, offers a view that will find its equal only in Switzerland. From Matlock the view up to the castle is even more impressive—it dominates the town even more than McCaig's Folly dominates Oban. Nervous drivers should think hard before

Riber Castle

attempting the road up to the castle. A small castellated lodge of blackened stone prefigures the main building, then the castle itself, crouching on a crag, usurping the skyline for miles around, the guardian of centuries. In fact, it was built between 1862 and 1868 by John Smedley, a mill owner who made a considerable fortune. He took unusual care of his workers, providing them with rainproof capes and boots, sleeping places and a religious service at the start of each day, and dispensing Fearn's Family Pills to those taken ill. Although he placed his complete trust in this particular medicament, he even paid sickness benefit to those workers too ill to get to work.

After a long illness caused by catching typhoid while he was on honeymoon in Switzerland, Smedley was cured at a hydropathic establishment in Yorkshire. Convinced of its efficacy, he converted to Hydrotherapy and Free Methodism and brought his huge enthusiasm to both creeds, building six chapels and buying an already existing hydro in Matlock. He enlarged it considerably and made it an enormous

success, ensuring the town's prosperity. Riber Castle cost him £60,000, but he lived to enjoy it for only six years. Smedley's original plan was to build a 225ft (69m) tower on the hilltop, but he abandoned the idea when he discovered that the telescopes he intended to order wouldn't fit the tower.

Later, the castle became a small private school, then in 1936 it was sold to the local council for £1500, and by the 1960s it was derelict. The architectural critic Sir John Summerson, who was educated at the school, later remembered that:

> *Riber possesses the rare distinction of being not only ugly, but perfectly styleless; no building, surely, was ever so lacking in grace. Hard and hideous in profile, every formal relation a disharmony, every room and every corridor proclaiming that no critical mind had foreseen or determined its dimensions. I cannot recall one agreeable ornament, one pleasing arrangement in the entire building. Everything was big and comfortless.*

A splendid damnation. The shell now houses a small fauna reserve and wildlife park. In 1990 it was optimistically offered for sale at £1.5 million, having been bought from the council for £500 in 1963.

Stanton Moor

Reform Tower (1832)
SK 251 634

The B5057 swings round off the A6 to Stanton Moor, where a square, sturdy, rough stone tower commemorates the Reform Bill of 1832. It is exactly right for its setting: bleak, with only a few arrowslits for ornament. An inscription reads 'Earl Grey 1832'. The builder was probably Lieutenant Colonel Thornhill of Stanton Hall.

Sudbury

Deerfold (1723)
SK 161 325

Along the Staffordshire border, Sudbury, with its eyecatcher deerfold, is owned by the National Trust. The problems here are: Who was the architect and when was it built? It first appears on a map of 1751, but tradition says it was built for the Vernons in 1723, which stylistically is very early. The corner towers look a little like Thomas Wright's work, but the entrances and quatrefoil windows resemble the designs for a banqueting house at Wallingford,

Northumberland, attributed to Lancelot Brown, although Wright worked there as well. The deerfold, a good piece of Gothic, is as simple as it is effective. The four towers are connected by crenellated walls, while the façade to the house has been given a tall gateway, which may have been added later.

Swarkestone

Swarkestone Stand (1632)
SK 365 286

Swarkestone Stand has been called a summerhouse, balcony field, jousting tower, bull ring and banqueting house. As Swarkestone Hall, the house it served, was demolished by 1750, no one now remembers exactly what it is, but there is a record of a local mason, Richard Shepherd, being paid £111 12s 4d between 1630 and 1632 for the building of the 'Bowl-alley House', which argues reasonably convincingly that the Cuttle, the flat arena in front of the Stand, could well have been a bowling green, or a pall-mall alley—whatever it may have been, it was certainly built for recreation and entertainment. The Stand is two-towered, with a cardboardy silhouette of battlements, and it has ogee arches. The Landmark Trust, which has now restored it as a holiday home with its usual attention to detail, attributes the design of the Stand to John Smythson.

Two Dales

Sydnope Stand (1865)
SK 299 634

Beside a minor road returning to Matlock is Sydnope Stand, a castellated eyecatcher to Sydnope Hall, screening a little cottage and built of a lavishly dressed dark stone. In style and substance, although not in location or presence, it resembles a miniature Riber Castle. All is not quite as it seems, however. The eyecatcher façade faces away from the Hall, and despite an 1865 datestone on the tower, Sydnope Stand is clearly marked on an estate map of 1830. We would guess there was an earlier tower on the site, and that it was enlarged and converted into a cottage in 1865. These little cottages now suit modern life better than the grand halls, and Sydnope Stand with 11 acres (4.45ha) was sold for £63,000 in 1986. It looks as if it will stand for ever.

A romantic story goes with it. An architectural historian, researching for her thesis on the garden buildings and pleasure pavilions of Derbyshire, came to research the Stand, and ended up marrying the owner.

According to the owners of the Stand, buried deep in the woods across the road is a stone hermitage; we have not seen it.

Swarkestone Stand

DEVON

Devon has a fine variety of remote and mysterious follies. For such a big county—only Yorkshire and Lincolnshire are bigger—there are not as many as we could have hoped for, but most of them are well worth a visit and one or two are outstanding in any context. This is a county of ornamental cottages— there are dozens—but we have included only the best and most exciting. Chanter's Folly at Appledore was the original for the popular folly story of the merchant who built a tower so that he could watch for his ships coming into harbour, but then found that he'd built it on the wrong side of the hill and couldn't see the sea. It was built in 1812 and demolished in 1952.

Arlington

Obelisk (1887)
SS 610 410

At Arlington Court, the National Trust property near Barnstaple, the object known as the Obelisk is actually a rubble cone some 15ft (4.6m) high, erected to mark the spot where 'a bonfire was lit to commemorate the jubilee of Queen Victoria, June 21 1887'. Traditionally, this was also the site of one of the previous houses at Arlington.

Also on the estate but more folly-like are the two mighty bridge piers either side of the lake, which were built to support a suspension bridge planned by Sir John Chichester. It would have led nowhere but over the lake and back again, although it was intended to provide a more impressive western approach to the house. Unsurprisingly, it was never completed after Sir John's death in 1851.

Upcott House Arch

Ashford

Arch (19th century)
SS 540 340

A small arch, more a folly gatehouse, stands on a ridge in a field overlooking the River Taw between Ashford and Barnstaple as an eyecatcher to Upcott House. It is a single arch with castellated towers either side, one now loosing its castellations as an old man loses teeth.

Berrynarbor

Arch (early 19th century)
SS 560 480

There is a re-created arch at the Gothick Watermouth Castle near Berrynarbor. The castle is now a holiday centre, but the arch remains, castellated and pinnacled, opening into part of the famous gardens and notable because it was built with pieces—one dated 1525—from the 16th-century porch of Umberleigh House, which was demolished in the 19th century.

Bideford

Belvedere (1848)
SS 460 270

In Bideford in 1848 a folly in the old grounds of Wooda was built by a Mr G. Richards, who was the partner of Mr Abbott, an iron foundry master who lived at Wooda. It is a little, very Victorian Gothic, two-storey belvedere, with a good view over the town and the River Torridge. In 1981 the then owner applied for planning permission to

Bideford Belvedere

demolish it as it had become dangerous; permission was refused and it has now become an unusual and appealing home.

Blackawton

Shell House (18th century)
Grotto (18th century)
SX 810 520

The derelict estate of Oldstone, ½ mile northeast of Blackawton, has the perfect folly atmosphere. There is something ineffably weird and remote about the still visible remains, standing mutely among the activities of a bustling, modern farm, written over the old pleasure gardens like a palimpsest. The magnificently ruined house stands in a valley, protected from the barbarians by a fine fort, strategically placed by the old main drive, now a cowpath. The cattle graze unconcernedly round its ivy-covered ramparts; it was all a sham really, so it cannot be blamed for not protecting such a fine house.

Directly behind the sham fort is the shell house. This is a very large and elaborate affair, notwithstanding that the effect is somewhat reduced by a giant plastic sheet in front of the building, held down with old car tyres and covering a pile of manure. The shell house has a central rectangular room, still decorated with stones and bones and shells, entered through an archway. Two wings either side have archways into roofless rooms from which all the decoration has now disappeared.

Back between the old house and the farmhouse, the path leads under a dry bridge across a field into a wood. Here the path drops down to the three brackish, overgrown ornamental lakes, beside which there are a grotto, an arch and a hermitage. We found the grotto, now in a perilous condition, but the arch and the hermitage remained hidden. There is talk of subterranean passages. The now collapsed arch has a plaque reading:

> *Within a Wood unknown to Public View*
> *From Youth to Age a Reverend Hermit grew*
> *The Moss His Bed, the Cave His Humble Cell,*
> *His Food the Fruits, His Drink the Crystal Well*
> *Remote from Man with God he passed His days*
> *Pray'r all his Business, all his Pleasure Praise.*

Oldstone is in peak folly condition at the moment of writing; a vision perhaps of life in the future with mankind eking out a living amid the mouldering magnificence of a once glorious past.

Blackborough

Garnsey's Tower (19th century)
ST 101 095

Like Blackborough House itself (which was built for Lord Egremont in 1838), this circular tower is in sad condition. It has collapsed and only part of it now stands. It must have been a belvedere. Why the name Garnsey is attached to it we do not know.

Braunton

Mortimer's Folly (1846)
SS 492 367

We nearly missed the tower known as Mortimer's Folly in Braunton. It is clearly marked on the Ordnance Survey map, but it is possible to pass within feet of it without noticing, so covered with ivy has it become. It stands, its slaty stones probably held up only by the ivy, in a wood at the edge of a field, totally ruinous, but with the remnants of three storeys still visible from the inside. It was built by Thomas Mortimer in 1846 to celebrate the repeal of the Corn Laws, at a time when the views from the now undergrowth-choked hill would have been magnificent.

Buckland-in-the-Moor

Buckland Beacon (1928)
SX 750 740

Mr Whitley of Buckland wanted to engrave the Ten Commandments on two tablets on the tor of Buckland Beacon to commemorate the defeat in Parliament of the Revised Prayer Book. He employed Mr W.A. Clement, a stonemason from Exeter, to do the job, which took him from 23 July to 31 August 1928. An interesting sideline here is Mr Clement's conditions of employment: at night he slept in a cowshed, on wire netting covered in blankets that he had to bring himself, while as for his food, a loaf of bread was left on the roadside wall each Thursday—Mr Whitley appears to have treated him as a 20th-century hermit, even going so far as to nickname him Moses.

Chagford

Rushford Tower (19th century)
SX 700 880

Rushford Tower near Chagford became a familiar folly to many people throughout Britain in the early 1980s through its location use in the television adaptation of R.F. Delderfield's *Diana*, in which the lovers used it as a trysting-place. People who believe

Rushford Tower

what they see on the screen would be surprised by its actual size, because inside there isn't enough room to swing a television camera, let alone indulge in a close encounter in front of a production crew. Nevertheless, the BBC left the little folly with an imposing entrance: a wooden door gnarled with age (courtesy of the paint department) and metalwork held on with Pozidrive screws, a folly door for a real folly. All it is, is a square unroofed room with a circular stair turret attached (complete with solid and climbable stone spiral stair), from the top of which there is an excellent view of Castle Drogo. It was built for the Hayter Ames family of Chagford House.

Chudleigh

Tower (c.1845)
SX 850 780

Pitt House, between Chudleigh and Chudleigh Knighton, was built in 1845 by Sir George Gilbert Scott in the Jacobean style. It seems logical to assume that the folly tower in the field above the house was conceived at the same time, although it is far from Jacobean. It is a round, castellated, two-storey tower with a gentle batter, like a chess castle. Unusually, the staircase is on the outside; it is still solid, with a metal handrail, and leads up to a little room with a rotting floor, lit by three thin arched windows. From this room a staircase rose a quarter circle to the roof, but all that remains are the positioning holes in the walls. The room at the bottom is used as a cowshed. It is a small tower, an unimportant folly, yet strangely pleasing and memorable in its honest solidity.

Clovelly

The Cabin
Angels' Wings (c.1826)
Gallantry Bower
SS 310 260

The Hartland peninsula is largely unspoilt because of the tourist magnet that is Clovelly, the extraordinary picture postcard village that epitomizes the West Country. It is the estate village of the Hamlyn family, whose Clovelly Court stands in its park near the village. With magnificent coast and seascapes abounding, the Hamlyns took the advantage of erecting several fanciful summerhouses and ornamental seats, including Miss Woodall's Seat and the prettily named Angels' Wings. The walk starts with The Cabin, and then follows the cliffpath to Angels' Wings, a beautifully carved umbrello-seat, decorated, yes, with wings and angels, supposedly done by Sir James Hamlyn's butler in 1826.

Gallantry Bower is another seat, the last, with a summerhouse nearby. Gallantry Bower is also known as Miss Woodall's Seat and is in memory of her and her friend Kathleen Scott. Unconnected is the story that Gallantry Bower came by its name for being a lovers' leap.

The approach to all this, the Hobby Drive, a 3 mile coastal road often open to the public, is truly in the new wave of romantic landscaping—Sir James Hamlyn, who built it between 1811 and 1829 (giving employment to former soldiers), deliberately left it as wild as God intended, resisting the then virtually compulsory reshaping of nature—but it must be said the canvas had already been prepared and painted by a greater hand.

Colaton Raleigh

China Tower (1839)
SY 070 860

The Bicton Estate at Colaton Raleigh is famous for its gardens and has been so for 250 years. There is a shell cottage, a hermitage, one of the best proportioned obelisks in Britain (1734) and the China Tower. It is not remotely Chinese in appearance: from a distance it is the standard Perpendicular folly church tower shape, with

higher stair turret, but there are sufficient detail changes to please the jaded eye. The turret is square, not round or octagonal, and it is attached to the main tower, which is octagonal. The appellation comes from its *raison d'être*—the tower was a birthday present to Lord Rolle from his wife on 16 October 1839; and the next year, on the same date, Lady Rolle presented him (for his 88th year!) with another surprise: she fitted out a room with her porcelain collection. J.C. Loudon, who visited Bicton three years after the tower had been built, found it 'the best piece of architecture at Bicton' and subsequently gave its story in detail.

Combe Martin

Pack o' Cards (early 18th century)
SS 580 470

Easily the most bizarre building in the county is the Pack o' Cards pub in Combe Martin, a long, straggling village running down to the north coast. Photographs cannot prepare one for the shock of delight when it suddenly comes into view. It is much bigger than one anticipates, and at first glance the chimneys seem to be piled on top of each other without any semblance of order, giving an extraordinary overbalanced feel to the whole structure. In addition, the inn has recently been painted a glistering white, so it leaps at the eye. Ann Jellicoe, in her *Shell Guide to Devon*, describes it as 'a folly said by the literal-minded to have windows and chimneys relating to the number of cards in a pack,' but Mrs Philips, the present owner, swears this is true.

There were originally 52 windows, but many were blocked up to escape Pitt's window tax; there are indeed four main floors; and we certainly counted 13 doors on the basement floor. What is less easy to establish is when and why it was built, and for once the familiar old gambling story used as an apologia for several follies throughout Britain (but, for example, denied by the owners of Roebuck's Folly in Somerset) could have a ring of truth. There is no other good reason to explain why a vernacular building should be built in this anti-style.

The popular tale, written on parchment and framed in the pub so that curious drinkers can answer their own questions, says that the house was built by Squire George Ley, who died in 1716, to celebrate a very handsome gambling win. There seems little reason to doubt the story; it is a most singular building, which incontrovertibly

The Pack o'Cards, Combe Martin

uses units of 4, 13 and 52 in its construction. The actual date of the Pack o' Cards is uncertain; the landlady claims the 17th century, but nearly all pubs in Britain are claimed to be at least a century older than they actually are. The Venetian windows in the gable ends would suggest a date of around 1710, surprisingly early for such a motif to appear in vernacular architecture. Less authenticated, alas, is the name the Pack o' Cards: old photographs clearly show it as the King's Arms Hotel.

Devon seems keen on card suits as motifs—although not a heart or a club can be found at the Pack o' Cards, the International Stores at Ashburton has a clapboarded façade where the first and second floors are decorated with patterns of spades, diamonds, hearts and clubs, while near Sticklepath on the A30 a cottage has shutters with the suits boldly carved out.

Crediton

Seat (19th century)
SS 870 020

Shobrooke Park, near Crediton, was demolished after a fire in 1947, but high on an eastern hill remains a huge walled and covered seat for drinking in wonderful views over Dartmoor. It is semicircular, flanked by columns with ball finials and covered by a half-dome. The low surrounding wall had balls on each of its six piers, but every one of these has been knocked off by vandals.

Devonport

Foulston's Follies (1823–4)
SX 450 550

In his remarkable tome, *Devon*, W.G. Hoskins complains that the *Dictionary of National Biography* does not devote a single line to John Foulston, 'this most notable of Devon architects'. Yet his fellow countrymen have also done this individualistic architect down: his sterling work in designing from scratch a new civic centre for the newly created borough of Devonport has been left to decay to such an extent that it now merits inclusion in a book on follies. The grand approach to the Greek Revival Town Hall was along Ker Street, with Foulston's great monumental Doric column (1824) set off to the right on a massive plinth. At the right at the top of the street is one of Foulston's set pieces, the Egyptian Library of 1823, now the Odd Fellows Hall. More restrained than his Penzance Egyptian house, its juxtaposition to the classical Greek motifs in the Town Hall and the Doric monument make it, if anything, more startling in context. And one should remember that until *c.*1952 the Moorish ('Hindoo') Non-Conformist Mount Zion chapel stood almost next to the Egyptian House. Only a Gothick and a Chinese building were missing. The ruination of the street is in the building of municipal dwellings—there is no other word—of a style and quality one would associate more with an early 1950s suburb in Amiens. A real extravaganza is the clock tower at nearby HMS *Drake*. It is in Portland stone, with columns, pilasters, sprouting balconies, diminishing storeys, carved corbelling, bosses sporting anchors and 'VR'—a confectioner's grotesque fantasy. It is magnificent in its own tacky way, but is it Art?

Despite the *DNB* ignoring Foulston, Colvin offers us some delightful glimpses into the great architect's personal life, including his habit of driving round in a gig fitted out like a Roman chariot.

HMS Drake's Clock Tower

Dunchideock

Haldon Belvedere (1788)
SX 890 870

Devon's best known folly must be the superb Haldon Belvedere, also known as Lawrence Castle, high above Dunchideock. A proto-folly, it is triangular and has three big storeys, with round castellated turrets at each corner and Gothick detailing, even down to mighty Gothick Venetian windows on the first floor.

Years ago we were shown around the building by the Dale brothers, who lived there and who angrily refuted any suggestion that the building might be a folly, convincing us more and more with every word spoken that this could stand for all follies. A visit in August 1984 found it closed to the public. It was a private house, which remained occupied since shortly after it was built, probably by people who did not have enough spare money to carry out restorations or renovations. Consequently, the interior remained intact and original, if a little worn. It was remarkable: marble and mahogany and Wedgwood blue and white—faded glories of the past. The last Dale died in 1994, and three days before his death he signed over the belvedere. It has now been admirably restored, in 1994–5, by the Devon Historic Buildings Trust, although those who prefer to 'keep the ivy on' will experience an initial shock when they see the tower shining white in its new plaster coat.

Sir Robert Palk built it in 1788 in memory of his great friend Major-General Stringer Lawrence; they had known each other from service in India, and Palk named his only son after Lawrence. In 1775 Lawrence, who lived in retirement with the Palk family at Haldon, left all his property, valued at some £50,000, to the Palk children. No expense was spared in the castle's construction, nor need there have been with that size of inheritance.

Exeter

Grotto (mid-19th century?)
Tower (late 19th century)
SX 920 920

There is a grotto—at least we think it is a grotto, for we were not able to get inside to see it—in the grounds of the Bishop's Palace in Exeter, remarkably forgotten and unknown for a city centre folly; even the Bishop could not tell us anything about it. Possibly an old archway, its park entrance was decorated in the 19th century to make it more picturesque.

A two-storey brick tower or gazebo is in

A La Ronde

the grounds of a large house in Victoria Park Road, St Leonard's. It used to present a view of the Cathedral, but this is now blocked by modern buildings. Nearby, in the grounds of where an 1870 house called Larkbeare stood, is an earlier gazebo.

Exmouth

A La Ronde (1798)
Point In View (1811)
SY 010 830

Some strange houses season this beautiful county, and there are few stranger than the sibling houses in Exmouth, A La Ronde and Point in View. A La Ronde is famous throughout the country and is a magnet for tourists—justifiably, because it is astonishingly appealing. It was built in 1798 by the cousins Jane and Mary Parminter, and the exterior was allegedly inspired by the Church of San Vitale in Ravenna, Rome's St Peter and even Batalha in Portugal, the church so well-liked by William Beckford, although the similarities are difficult to detect. The name is, in fact, misleading, for the building has 16 sides rather than being round. Inside, the octagonal hall is 60ft (18m) high, surrounded at the top by the Shell Gallery, a grotto with a view, and the collections and handiwork of the Parminter cousins, which are remarkable in their leisured intricacy. Now it is owned by the National Trust, which has decreed that the Shell Gallery is too fragile to be visited by the lumpen tourist, so instead we are treated to a video walk-through. Fame has its handicaps. Here is an opportunity for a virtual heritage recreation.

A La Ronde has only once been owned by a man (the Misses Parminter were not interested in men); it is the most feminine house we know, and if that conjures up pictures of pink frills and chintz, you seriously misunderstand our meaning. We strongly recommend a visit; there is nothing like this anywhere in Europe… except, perhaps, a little way up the road, where the more inquisitive visitor will discover Point In View, which was built in 1811 by the Misses Parminter as a little chapel surrounded by four almshouses, strictly reserved for single women. Awkward little pointed windows rob it of the charm that typifies A La Ronde, but as a curiosity it should be seen when visiting the better known house. Its name is explained by the inscription above the chapel door: 'Some point in view we all pursue.' Indeed.

Hugh Meller has recently tried to demolish some of the stories about A La Ronde. He proposes that it may have been based on plans by John Lawder of Bath, an amateur architect, related to the Parminters. But the snag is that Mr Lowder was only 17 years old when A La Ronde was built, and the edifice that is so reminiscent of A La Ronde dates from 1816. We propose, therefore, in order to save the Misses Parminter's reputation as female amateur architects, that it is the other way round: A La Ronde influenced Lowder's District National School at Bath.

Temple of Theseus (1824)
SY 010 820

Exmouth's Imperial Hotel could have had two temples, but when the hotel was built in 1869 the existing Temple of the Winds was demolished. The other temple survives, however: a copy of the Temple of Theseus, Athens, built for William Temple in 1824. It has long been used by the hotel to house staff, and there is a precedent because the naval architect Westcott Abell had lived there earlier.

Filham

Sham Ruin (late 18th century)
SX 650 550

At Filham, an Ivybridge village bisected by the new A38, the Manor House appears to have an enchanting sham ruin on the smooth lawn right in front of the house. It proves to be a genuine 15th-century chapel, which preceded the Manor House and to which an owner added, in the late 18th century, an octagonal stair turret. The chapel finally collapsed in the 1960s, leaving the stair turret pointing up from the ruined chapel like an index finger from a clenched fist. It is possible to climb it if one has a head for heights; on seeing our faces after our abortive attempt, the then owner took pity on us and provided an enormous dish of wild mushrooms on toast—rare hospitality!

Filleigh

Castle Hill Follies (1730s; 1750s)
SS 670 280

Castle Hill used to be famous, and every self-respecting 18th-century tourist would visit it. Now it is almost completely forgotten, but the owners are restoring it, bit by bit. One of the follies has given its name to the house, a

Castle Hill Arch

rare occurrence: the sham castellated Vanbrughian building on the hill has recently been repaired. Castle Hill was built by the Fortescues, and Robert Morris and Lord Burlington were both involved. Even in its formal phase, Castle Hill was folly heaven, as revealed in two paintings of 1741, sadly destroyed by fire in 1934 (photographs remain): there was a copy of the Cestius pyramid, a ruin, temples, the arch, obelisks and something looking remarkably like the Sugar Loaves at Werrington Park, Cornwall.

Most interesting was a 'Sham Town', consisting of several cottages and a 'church', which was destroyed in the 1940s. This was a sublimely rare feature in British parks, although the idea caught on in Germany, for example in Hohenheim, in Schönbusch (a Dutch and a Swiss village, still existing) and Wilhelmshöhe (a Chinese village of which one pagoda temple survives), while the Prince de Ligne planned a Turkish village in Baudour, Belgium. And yes, there was a Chinese temple at Castle Hill as well.

What survives besides the 'Castle'? The Cave, Satyr's Temple and 'Ugly Bridge' form one site and were restored very well by the present Fortescues. The Ionic Temple, dating from 1782 and built in memory of Hugh, Earl Clinton, is still unrestored. And then there is the tripartite triumphal arch. It looks unusually clean and well cared for; the reason is that it is relatively new—it was blown down in a storm in the 1950s and rebuilt in 1961. Aligned directly with the arch and the house at Castle Hill is a sham castle on the top of the opposite hill.

Reinstate the 'Sham Town' and other follies, and we have another Painswick or Painshill on our hands. Castle Hill Revividus!

Gidleigh

Prinsep's Folly (1846)
SX 650 870

One Devon house became a folly because of its situation; another Devon folly became a house for similar reasons. Prinsep's Folly on Gidleigh Tor was a house built in 1846, but the builder, Thomas Levett Prinsep, died before he could move in. The house was demolished before 1850 for reasons that remain unclear. Prinsep's intention was to blend the house in with the rocks of the tor, and to that end he chose the most difficult site he could. Some portions of the wall can still be made out, as well as a small octagonal roofless tower just by the summit of the hill.

Great Torrington: the Waterloo Monument

Great Torrington

Waterloo Monument (1818)
SS 500 190

At Great Torrington is a fine example of that peculiarly English adaptation of Egyptian motifs in producing either a very fat obelisk or a very elongated pyramid—after all, why else should we dream of calling those monstrosities that stride across the countryside 'pylons'? Here it serves, beautifully sited above the ravine of the Torridge, as a Waterloo monument, a pike rather than a tower:

ERECTED JUNE 1818

TO COMMEMORATE

THE BATTLE OF

WATERLOO

JUNE 1815

PEACE TO THE

SOULS OF THE

HEROES ! ! !

Hartland

Highford Farm (1886–1902)
SS 260 250

Good doggerel can be found at Hartland around Highford Farm. In the farmyard is a semicircular, stilted arch set in a giant triangle made of three different types of coloured brick and surmounted by a buzzard. It leads nowhere, serves no purpose, but must have been immensely satisfying to build. A cautious early inscription is here: the adjacent building carries a plaque reading 'DAIRY JB 1886'. Ten years later and there's a little more confidence on the gate pillars:

OH HOW PEACEFUL THOU ART

O HIGHFORD

JB 1896

Six years later and all reticence disappears:

E 👑 R

JUNE 26TH 1902

KING EDWARD VII CROWNED. BOER WAR ENDED.

I BELIEVE IN CHURCH AND STATE AND ALL

OTHER

RELIGIONS THAT DO GOOD AND TO BE

PATRIOTIC

TO MY COUNTRY

JAMES BERRIMAN

THE ABOVE BRINGS CIVILISATION TO OUR

GREAT

This is inscribed on a gate pier a mile or so to the east of Highford. The piers, each about 10ft (3m) high, are capped with pyramids and set in a stuccoed semicircular wall, crudely decorated with plain block pargetting. An iron medallion with a bas-relief of Charles Martell is set into the other pier, above another inscription:

ALPHA THOU ART FIRST I'M SURE

AS OMEGA IS IN THE WEST

AND THOU'LT BE FIRST FOR EVERMORE

NOW SLUMBER ON AND REST.

THIS FIELD WAS ONCE A COMMON MOOR

WHERE GORSE AND RUSH GREW FREE

AND NOW IT GROWS GREEN GRASS ALL OE'R

AS ALL WHO PASS MAY SEE.

JS BERRIMAN NEW INN CLOVELLY JAN 10TH 1902

Omega in the west? A couple of miles due west we discovered an identical gate (but with the medallion torn out) and the inscription:

OMEGA THOU ART LAST I'M SURE
AS ALPHA IS IN THE EAST
AND THOU'LT BE LAST FOR EVERMORE
TILL ENDLESS AGES CEASE.
WHEN I AM DEAD AND GONE
THESE VERSES WILL REMAIN
TO SHOW WHO WROTE THEREON
BY WORKING OF THE BRAIN.

Js BERRIMAN NEW INN CLOVELLY JAN 10TH 1902 What can possess a man to immortalize words such as these?

Berriman aroused the curiosity and envy of his neighbours by transfiguring Highford from 1878 onwards into a model farm—his livestock had better living conditions than many of the local farm labourers.

Hartland also has the ruins of The Pleasure House at The Warren overlooking Hartland Quay, probably a belvedere erected by the Abbott family before 1738, when it first appears on a map.

Hatherleigh

Obelisk (1859)
Pearce Belvedere (1879)
SS 550 040

At Hatherleigh Down, in the middle of the county, is an ungainly obelisk, built in 1859 and redeemed by a finely executed bas-relief of Balaclava by Edward Bowring Stephens of London (although he was born in Exeter and most of his commissions came from Devon). Stephens is supposed to have got his ARA because he was confused with Alfred Stevens:

TO THE MEMORY OF
LIEUT COL.
WILLIAM MORRIS CB KLH
MAJOR 17TH LANCERS
BORN AT FISILLEIGH IN THIS COUNTY
DEC 18TH 1820
DIED AT POONA BOMBAY
JULY 11TH 1858

The builder of the new concrete plinth on which it stands also wanted to be remembered, and scratched 'W.R. BIRDSON 1981' in the wet cement—but where is Fisilleigh? It's not in our gazetteer.

A hundred yards along the ridge from the Morris obelisk is a much more interesting folly: a single-storey belvedere, which was built in 1879 to commemorate Colonel Pearce, a local landowner and marksman. It is castellated, with two arches opening to the

west, while on the south side a stairway leads up to the flat roof for the view. The arches and the entry to the stairway are highlighted in white brick, giving the little building a faintly lavatorial air. The bottom part is now used as a cowshed, which adds to the illusion.

Kenton

Hermitage (1790)
SY 960 830

In the garden of Spring Lodge at Oxton House near Kenton, just north of Mamhead, is an arch in a rock cliff. It opens into a tiny, bare, grotto room, now handily used as a garden shed. One window and a curious arrangement of latticed strips by the door let in light. This is the hermitage in which, according to the inscription in the cave, next to a cross, I. Bidgood was a hermit. Whether anyone really lived here is unknown. It was conceived by the cleric and antiquarian John Trip, who changed his name to Swete. The park gave rise to much contemporary admiration.

Killerton

Hermit's Hut or Bear's Hut (1808)
SS 970 010

The thatched Hermit's Hut in the gardens of the National Trust's Killerton House housed both a hermit and a bear, but neither of them got hurt: the hermit is supposed to have lived there in or around 1808, when Sir Thomas Acland surprised his lady wife with this rustic hut, its floor made of deer knuckles. Around the middle of the 19th century, the hermit long since gone, one of the Aclands returned from a stay in the wilds of Canada with a tame black bear. The creature was domiciled in the hut before being presented to London Zoo.

It has been well restored, but hopefully by this time the plants and shrubs that grew around it and provided the right atmosphere will have returned.

Kingswear

Daymark (1864)
SX 880 520

The most individualistic structure in this part of Devon is not a folly at all. It was built for a specific purpose, which it performs as well today as it did the day it was built. We must admit that seeing it for the first time, on the National Trust headland at Froward

Point near Kingswear, we had no idea of its function, nor did we even stop to consider that it might have had one. It is a tall, octagonal tower, 80ft (24m) high, completely hollow and open at the top. There is no trace of there ever having been floors or a staircase. The sides taper steeply and evenly from the bottom to the top, the bottom being pierced by eight pointed arches, each about 30ft (9m) high. This is what Isambard Kingdom Brunel would have built had he built a folly. It is, in fact, a Daymark, erected by the Dart Harbour Commissioners in 1864 as a sort of lightless lighthouse. A lightless lighthouse? Perhaps a folly after all.

Lewtrenchard

Lee Tower (late 19th century)
SX 444 841

On the Lee Downs stands a round, castellated tower, with yellow bricks around the door and windows. It belonged to Coryton Manor and was obviously a belvedere, doubling as a hunting stand.

Lydford

Arch-dovecote (19th century)
SX 511 848

An arch with a dovecote on top has been reported in the garden of a private house in the village of Lydford. Apparently, it also has an armorial relief.

Lympstone

Mrs Peter's Clock (1885)
SX 990 840

Right on the edge of the mudflats at Lympstone is Mrs Peter's Clock, an immense structure for a village, with a passing resemblance to St Stephen's Tower, a sort of Little Ben. It was built by Mr Peters in 1885 to show how good his wife was to the poor. It is about 70ft (21m) high and has four storeys, with the riverside fenestration increasing with each floor—one, two, three, then the clock. Topping it all is an elongated pyramid with lucarnes. The Landmark Trust has restored it for use as a holiday home.

Lynmouth

Rhenish Tower (1860)
SS 730 490

On the seafront at quaint, rebuilt Lynmouth is the little Rhenish Tower, built in 1860 by General Rawdon to store salt, a purpose for which massive fortifications and two heavily machicolated balconies on different levels were evidently felt to be necessary. A scratched inscription on the tower reminds us tersely of the Lynmouth flood disaster: 'Destroyed August 1952, Rebuilt April 1954.' For the many Gothicky hotels and B&Bs at Lynmouth, the happy term 'Honeymoon Gothick' has been invented.

Duty Point Tower

Lynton

Duty Point Tower (c.1850)
SS 700 495

Duty Point Tower at Lee Abbey outside Lynton perches pugnaciously on the clifftop, a squat, little, two-storey belvedere with large windows on the ground floor, a smaller, castellated upper storey and a slightly taller stair turret. It was built c.1850 for the mansion that has finally fulfilled its name: built as a private house, it is now the headquarters of a religious organization.

Maidencombe

Grotto
SS 930 680

A small grotto behind a Gothick house has been reported at Maidencombe in Babbacombe Bay, Torquay.

Mamhead

Obelisk (1742)
Sham Castle (1829)
SX 940 820

The 100ft (30m) tall, inscriptionless obelisk at Mamhead was built in 1742, supposedly as a navigational aid to sailors, but it is eclipsed by the magnificent sham castle stable block, built by the young architect Anthony Salvin in 1829 as a replica of Belsay Castle in Northumberland. The contrast between house and castle is heightened by the house being built of grey stone, while the castle is red. It is an extremely large folly, said to be built on the foundations of a genuine medieval castle, with bartizan turrets and a massive gatehouse with sham portcullis. A spiral staircase in one corner of the courtyard leads directly down into the main house, which is now used as a special school. Mamhead's setting is exquisite, with sweeping views along the Exe estuary. When last heard of, the sham castle was advertised as providing '8,514 sq.ft. of character office accommodation in the grounds of Mamhead and offering easy access to the M5'—Salvin wept.

Milton Abbot

Cottage (c. 1810–15)
Grotto (c. 1810–15)
Dairy (c. 1810–15)
SX 410 790

Endsleigh Cottage near Milton Abbot, now a private fishing hotel, was begun for the Duke of Bedford and his second wife in 1810 by Sir Jeffry Wyatville, and the grounds were landscaped by Repton. The 'cottage' took six years to build and cost the prodigious sum of £47,500. The shell grotto is of high quality, as might be expected. Its polygonal, virtually conical roof serves as the focal point of a broad yew walk, above the valley of the young Tamar. Wyatville's garden buildings at Endsleigh were restored in the 1980s by Paul Pearn, and include a thatched Swiss cottage and an octagonal dairy, now rented out by the Landmark Trust.

Monkleigh

Petticombe Manor Hermitage
(late 18th century)
SS 450 212

We have heard of an octagonal Gothick hermitage in the woods at Petticombe Manor, near Monkleigh.

Moretonhampstead

Sham Church (19th century)
SX 770 840

At some point the Tudor house of Wray Barton, some 3 miles southeast of Moretonhampstead, was Gothicized. A farm building followed and was turned into a mock church.

Offwell

Bishop Copleston's Tower (1830s)
ST 190 990

Bishop Copleston's Tower at Offwell on Honiton Hill is a familiar landmark to the south of the town. Again, the family vehemently insists that it was not a folly but a water tower, which was built to relieve unemployment, and indeed there is a small water tank at the top of the tower—but if that was its sole purpose, why should it have been necessary to put fireplaces in all the other rooms? In any case, it really is absurdly large for its alleged function; a tower that size could provide water for a whole village, and when it was built in the 1830s there was no house near by. The house it now dominates was built in 1847—perhaps to take advantage of the water supply? Stylistically the 8oft (24m) tower would be more at home in a Lucchesan side street, but a touch of old Italy on a Devon hilltop is indeed a pleasurable sight. The stories are there, of course, the best one being that Edward Copleston, being Bishop of Llandaff, felt a twinge of remorse about staying in the parish where he was born and

Petticombe Manor Hermitage

brought up, so he built a tower to keep an eye on his flock in South Wales, 50 miles away as the crow flies.

When we first visited, the tower staircase was too rickety to climb, but the owners had been on the roof through the ingenious (if ostentatious) method of climbing down from a helicopter.

At the bottom of the hill on the edge of Honiton is an ochre-coloured, Gothic, castellated cottage, shaped like a horseshoe with a single-storey porch bolted onto the front—perhaps a toll house.

Paignton

Little Oldway Tower (c.1900)
SX 880 610

Behind the Singer mansion of Oldway in Paignton, now the council offices and a public park, is Little Oldway Tower, a conventional red square castellated tower, which was built as a water tower for the mansion but is now part of a private house.

Plymouth

Fort Bovisand (18th–19th century)
SX 480 550

No other sham castle in Devon, and few in Britain, can approach this scale and grandeur, although a sham fort above Plymouth attempted to perpetrate a national illusion. From the sea, Fort Bovisand looked like a mighty fortress, which would strike terror into the hearts of foreign navies. In reality it was simply a 90ft (27m) high wall, 200–300ft (61–91m) long, decked out to mimic a fort as a low-budget deterrent.

Grotto Temple (1822)
SX 480 550

On King's Hill, at Her Majesty's Dockyards, is the Temple of Minerva, built above an older grotto. It had an 1816 poem by Devon poet N.F. Carrington. The temple was:

erected in the year 1822 to perpetuate recollection of the visit of King George III of blessed and glorious memory of his majesty's admiration of the Rock on which it stands and the scene around.

George had demanded the retention of the hill at his visit to the dockyards in 1780.

Leigham Tower (19th century)
SX 515 574

There are some elusive towers in and around Plymouth, but apparently none of them is a real headbanger: a three-storey Gothick

tower has been reported in the garden of a detached house at Derriford, Plymouth, formerly belonging to the Powisland Estate; and at Leigham is Leigham Tower, 'a plain octagonal shell with two tiers of windows', no date, no nothing. Radnor near Plymstock has a sham castle gatehouse.

Powderham

Powderham Belvedere (1773)
SX 970 840

Powderham Belvedere, in the grounds of Powderham Castle on the west bank of the Exe, is visible from virtually all along the east bank. At first glance, it appears to be a

Little Oldway Tower

copy of Haldon Belvedere (Lawrence Castle) at Dunchideock (see above), except for its hexagonal corner turrets, but it actually predates its more famous neighbour by some seven years, having been built in 1773 for the 2nd Viscount Courtenay. The Belvedere might owe something to Flitcroft's Shrubs Hill Tower at Virginia Water, Surrey, the Mother Of All Triangular Towers. It is now floorless and completely ruinous, but a curious relic remains in the eastern stair turret: a retractable flagpole. The flagpole was a mighty affair, as high again as the belvedere, so one assumes that having lost it once or twice in a high wind this system was devised for reasons of economy.

Roborough

Sham Ruin (early 19th century)
SX 470 640

Maristow, 3 miles northwest of Roborough, has a sham ruin erected from architectural elements salvaged from an old chapel on the estate, enhanced with two Ionic columns.

Saltram

The Castle (1772)
SX 520 560

Just east of Plymouth is Saltram House, which has a Gothic octagonal belvedere known as The Castle, which is little more than an elaborate summerhouse. It has been beautifully restored by the National Trust, with Wedgwood blue and white plasterwork inside. It was built in 1772 to the designs of Stockman, Saltram's head gardener, and an interesting feature is the tunnel opening out into the side of the hill at some distance from the castle, through which servants could enter to prepare food in the basement room.

Below the gardens, on the banks of the Plym, is the Amphitheatre, a mid-18th-century classical façade built across a quarry face. Grotesque faces are carved on the keystones of the arches.

Near Saltram, above the Plymouth suburb of Woodford, is a huge and splendid red brick arch with wings either side, one of which serves as a cottage and the other as a barn. The cottage is called Triumphal Arch Cottage, but it was unoccupied when we visited and we could find no additional information. Perhaps it was built as an eyecatcher for Saltram, as it is close to Boringdon, the old seat of the Parker family before they moved to Saltram.

The Castle, Saltram

St Germans

Tower (18th century)
SX 321 582

Off the road near Bake Farm in St Germans is a square tower, the remains of a landscaped park.

Shaldon

Sham Castle Kitchen (c.1920)
SX 940 720

According to Sharon McGinn, William Honeyard is locally famous. Honeyard, after inventing his claim to fame, Liqufruta cough mixture, came to live at Shaldon shortly after World War I. In his garden he built a sham castle, an arched wall with two flanking battlemented towers and steps leading up to it. Arrowslits in the walls and narrow round-arched windows. All in readiness for some serious fighting. The sham castle was built as a kitchen for Honeyard's wife so that, when she was in the garden, she could go and make her (and his?) tea. After her death the gardens were given to the public.

Sheepstor

Arches (1928; 1934)
SX 560 680

These arches are buried in a typical Devon sunken lane. The sunken lane used to run from Dousland to Sheepstor until 1895, when the Meavy valley was drowned under the waters of the Burrator reservoir. George Shillibeer, of the Plymouth County Water Works, rescued the door arch stones from the farmhouses in the catchment area and incorporated them into two arches, built in 1928 and 1934, spanning the narrow and disused old Sheepstor road. Two huge millstones are built into the wall either side of the first arch, and the keystone is dated 1668. Through the arch the road has been converted into a serpentine walk by building fern-covered cairns alternately either side against the old banks. The second arch, at the bottom, is built with stones dated 1637 and 1633, taken from Longstone Manor House, as was the arch itself, one of the old house's original doorways.

Sidmouth

The Old Chancel (1865–90)
SY 130 870

As at Lynmouth (see above), there is quite a lot of 'Honeymoon Gothick' here, but the star

Shaldon Kitchen

prize is the Old Chancel in Heydons Lane, off Coburg Terrace, an assemblage by Peter Orlando Hutchinson, a local eccentric. The main body of the house is the nave of Sidmouth's St Nicholas Church, which was going to be demolished and was subsequently acquired by Hutchinson and moved to the present site. Obviously, that would never be enough for any folly builder, so Hutchinson bought, begged or borrowed a window from old Awliscombe Church, acquired his wooden planks from a wrecked ship or two, installed an organ, which he attached to his bell-pull, and carved his own caricature along the stairs. And finally, he made sure that the many large and small windows in his house did not look out over the sea.

On several occasions Hutchinson would stalk Queen Victoria, of whom he was inordinately fond, once dressing up in the uniform of an officer in the Devon Artillery Volunteers (which may explain why he also kept a donkey that pulled a cannon along the seafront), and he was very fond of his cat and his pet raven. At last, in 1890, he had finished the house, or so he thought, although he was still adding to it. And all the time not spent on doing up the house was lavished on writing a five-volume history of Sidmouth. It was finished but never published.

Grotto (early 19th century)
SY 130 870

Knowle Grange Hotel in Station Road is now council offices, but before being a hotel it was Mr Fish's marine villa, and originally a 'cottage' for the use of Lord Despenser. It has a rather good, early 19th-century grotto in the grounds. Lots of pebbles.

Stowford

Grotto (18th century)
SX 430 860

Hayne or Haine at Stowford has been ascribed to Jeffry Wyatville and the grotto in its grounds, a sturdy stone building with a shellwork vault, to the influence of Horace Walpole.

Tapeley

Grotto (18th century)
SS 490 290

Grottoes were certainly popular in Devon, but they never reached the height of artistic decoration that was achieved in, for example, Cornwall. None is particularly memorable, with the possible exception of the grotto at Tapeley, on the A39 north of Bideford. The house and gardens are often open to the public, and the strange little grotto by the well-preserved ice-house is a curiosity well worth seeing. More a shell house than a grotto, it is a small, grey, circular building with two pointed arch entrances and four diamond windows picked out with a red brick surround. The roof is steeply sloping, single pitched, as if a child had sliced a diagonal through a Smartie tube. The entrances are barred by chicken wire, but one can peer inside to admire the well-preserved but uninspired decoration.

Tawstock

Tower (19th century)
SS 550 290

In the first edition of this book we wrote that Tawstock Tower, circular with a higher circular stair turret, was still standing in 1954 but 'no trace now remains'. This phrase came back to haunt us time after time, as photographs of cheery people holding up current newspapers in front of a palpably extant tower regularly flooded through the letterbox. It has now even been added to and over-restored and is clearly visible from the train running in to Barnstaple. We missed it—but even Homer nods. Tawstock Court was castellated by John Soane in 1786, but the tower must certainly be later than that.

The magically reinstated Tawstock Tower

Teigngrace

Stover House Grotto (late 18th century)
Temple (late 18th century)
SX 840 730

Teigngrace is really only Stover House and its church, all built by the Templer family in the last quarter of the 18th century. In the grounds are a classical temple and a grotto.

Teignmouth

Sham Lighthouse (1845)
SX 950 730

Teignmouth has a jocular little 25ft (7.6m) sham lighthouse, dating from 1845, at the south end of the promenade, Den Crescent, but why nobody knows. Years ago there was also a wooden castellated gazebo at the Yacht Club. We don't know if it survives.

Two Bridges

Cowsick Valley Inscriptions (early 19th century)
SX 573 777

The dogged reader will by now have noticed that we have a particular fondness for inscriptions, the more nonsensical or opaque the better. We share this with the Rev. Edward Atkyns Bray of Tavistock, who in the early 19th century felt impelled to improve the Cowsick (unhappy name!) valley by providing mental as well as visual stimulation to visitors. His intention was to inscribe a treasury of classic poetry on the rocks in the river, and he went so far as to make his selection before realizing that the boulders didn't provide a suitably flat surface for the carver and that Dartmoor granite was not the easiest material to work with. Relatively undeterred, he modified his plans:

> As the name alone of Theocritus or of Virgil could not fail to communicate to a poetical mind a train of pleasing associations, I did nothing more, at first, than inscribe upon a few rocks 'To Theocritus', 'To Virgil', etc. This of itself, in so wild and solitary a scene as Dartmoor, was not without its effect: it seemed to people the desert; at any rate one might exclaim, 'The hand of man has been here!'

Years of water and wild weather have worn away the works; when we were there we could only find 'TO MILTON' and 'TO SHAKESPEARE', although 'TO SPENSER' and 'TO HOMER' are said to remain legible.

Water

Tower (19th century)
SX 760 810

Moretonhampstead, on the edge of Dartmoor, is surrounded by some pleasant little towers. Near Freedlands Cottage in Water, a hamlet directly south of Manaton, is a mysterious tower shrouded in the tree, used as an observation post during World War II. It is three storeys, 30ft (9m) high, built of rough stone, round and tapering. No date.

Water, Tower

Widecombe-in-the-Moor

Scobitor Round House (19th century)
SX 730 770

Scobitor Round House, above Widecombe-in-the-Moor, is a circular, one-roomed building with a slightly domed roof and random fenestration, but the really fascinating part of its construction are the nine massive granite beams radiating from the top of the central pillar. They are far too heavy for the sole purpose of supporting the modest roof; another reason has to be sought. It has been speculated that it was intended as a beacon, but although the views across Dartmoor are spectacular, the only village it can be seen from is Widecombe. Perhaps the intention was to provide a firm base for another storey or two; certainly the random pattern of windows seems to have been chosen to frame particularly superlative views. A belvedere, then.

Winkleigh

Belvedere (19th century)
SS 640 070

Winkleigh had two castles, both ruined. On the mound of one of them is the Court Castle belvedere, crumbling, Gothic—what else?

Zeal Monachorum

Reeve Castle (1900)
SS 730 040

Reeve Castle has often been described as a folly, but simply looking unusual is not the sole qualification. But mouths start watering when its dominant but slender 'machicolated water turret' is described as 'resembling the superstructure of a Jellicoe battleship'. It does. In 1900 William Carter Peddler, landowner and amateur architect, presented his bride with her own home and castle: Reeve. It bewilders. Is it Gothic, is it Italian, is it Moorish? Some of the roofs are of glass and have been likened to Crystal Palace. The gardens are Japanese. They would be.

HUNH?

Some Enigmatic Follies

SHEPHERD'S MONUMENT
Staffordshire

RUSHTON TRIANGULAR LODGE
Northamptonshire

JACK THE TREACLE EATER
Somerset

HORTON TOWER
Dorset

CHEWTON OWL HOOT
Somerset

KNILL MONUMENT
Cornwall

VERYAN ROUND HOUSES
Cornwall

DR. PRICE'S FOLLIES
Glamorgan

DORSET

Dorset is a broad sweep of a county, a county of seascapes and landscapes, of prospects and sonorous village names—Ryme Intrinseca, Whitchurch Canonicorum, Cerne Abbas, Wooton Fitzpaine, Child Okeford, Gussage All Saints— leavened with villages of a lesser euphony—Gribb, Droop, Throop, Stony Knapps and Piddletrenthide. Wool and Beer make their appearance; the traveller in Dorset will be distracted more than by the profusion of follies.

Sherbourne Castle · Wimborne St Giles · Wimborne Minster · Melbury Sampford · Stalbridge · Horton · Durweston · Hinton Martell · Milton Abbas · Milborne St Andrews · Nottington · DorchesterO · Moreton · Creech Hill · Bournemouth · Portesham · Nottington · Swanage · Lulworth Castle · Encombe · Kimmeridge Bay

The scarcity of Dorset follies is no bad thing. It gives us time to appreciate fully the greatness of the few we have. In terms of quality to quantity, Dorset outranks every other county. In one small area we can find three of the best follies in the whole of England, and a folly group by one of the last insatiable builders, which, taken as a whole, is one of the most sustained and imaginative urban improvement schemes of the Victorian era.

But magnificent though these few are, there is a distinct lack of variety. Obelisks were particularly popular—there are six major ones, if the Moreton Pillar is included—and so were towers—five superb examples. Dorset is a county that enjoys its panoramas, and additional ornamentation does not seem to have been popular. One good eyecatcher and one little sham ruin complete the scene—it's as if the 18th century gracefully skirted the county.

The landscape garden, the *raison d'être* for so many follies, never achieved the level of importance in Dorset that it achieved in the rest of the country, perhaps because the natural beauty of the county needed little enhancement. As follies followed fashion, the lack of squire follies in 18th-century Dorset is noticeable. The majority of squire follies were built to be seen; in Dorset the fashion was to build follies to see from.

Creech Hill

Creech Grange Arch (1746)
SY 920 820

Denis Bond's folly, Creech Grange Arch, is massive, but not physically large; it crouches at the top of Creech Hill near Steeple—grey, lichen-covered stone in the sunshine. It is one of the earliest eyecatchers in the country, dated to 1746. The arch is simple and elegant, but to be seen in three dimensions it has to be viewed from the back: it presents itself

Creech Grange Arch

permanently in silhouette when seen from the house below. It is reminiscent of Vanbrugh's work, but there is no record of the architect. The Bond family, who developed London's fashionable Bond Street in 1684, gave the eyecatcher to the National Trust in 1942.

Durweston

Folly Farm
ST 842 083

On the Durweston–Turnworth road is Folly Farm or The Folly. We have not found out what the name refers to. It may have to do with a *feuillée*.

Encombe

Obelisk (early 19th century)
Rock Arch (c.1780–90)
SY 945 781

At 40ft (12m), this is a small but beautifully sited obelisk. It was erected by his brothers in honour of Sir William Scott, created Baron Stowell, and the first stone was laid by his niece, Lady Frances Bankes, younger daughter of the 1st Lord Eldon, who as John Scott had bought the Encombe Estate in 1808.

All this may seem peripheral, but it is the only background information we have to the puzzle of who built the unique Rock Arch at Encombe, the real folly of the piece. The Scott family, who still live at Encombe, refer to it as a grotto, which is not strictly accurate. Huge blocks of stone have been laid higgledy-piggledy at the end of the lake, and the road to the dairy passes over the top. The interior is devoid of any decoration at all, relying for its effect on the massiveness of the stone. Two passages, leading through it from north to south, are joined at the southern end by a lateral passage, which opens to the south halfway along its length. At that point a rough seat is hewn out of the rock, looking out over a marshy grove of saplings. It is said that once the sea could be seen from here, but this seems unlikely.

The puzzle is whether this remarkable structure, quite unlike a grotto, was by the gifted amateur architect John Pitt, who built Encombe House for himself in 1734, or by a member of the obelisk-building Scott family. Hutchins's *History of Dorset* dated it to the first half of the 19th century; Pevsner points out the existence of a painting of the Rock Arch with tricorn-hatted gentlemen, which would seem to place it some 60 years earlier. Pitt's work on Encombe House would appear to commit him to pure classicist architecture; the most likely begetter of the Rock Arch would be his son, William Morton Pitt, who sold to the Scotts.

Hinton Martell

Cottage Orné (c.1809)
SU 003 058

Hinton Martell's *cottage orné* is one of Britain's best. It is right on the Wimborne–Cranborne road and forms the lodge to what used to be Sir Richard Carr Glyn's villa of 1809 (now part of a much larger building). Possibly by the villa's architect William Evans (who built a picturesque cottage in Bournemouth a year later), it first appears like a cascade of thatch but is actually quite symmetrical. Like a giant umbrello, it spouts umbrellettes at the sides. A delight.

Horton

Sturt's Folly (early 18th century)
SU 030 070

There is nothing like a good folly to produce that inexplicable frisson of fear, and not many are as chilling as Horton Tower, known as Sturt's Folly. Even approached at noon on a hot summer's day, there is an air of menace around. Few unsupervised people expect buildings to talk to them, but this one positively exudes silence. It stands in an open field, easily accessible on foot from the road, solitary, massive and unusually ugly. Recently, Vodaphone have used the tower to put up six of their aerials, but that is a reversible change.

Horton is an elephantine tower, seven-storey, red brick, hexagonal, with three domed round towers reaching two-thirds of the way up its 140ft (43m). Regrettably, there is no horrific story to go with it; no one even knows when

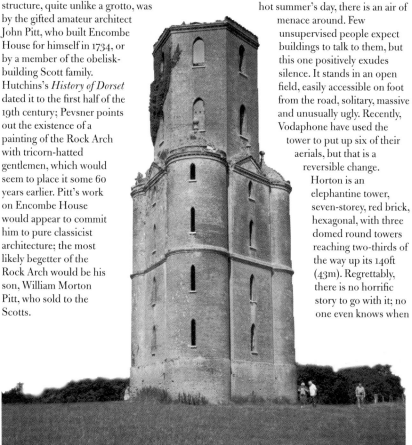

Sturt's Folly before its rescue by a mobile 'phone company

it was built. The difficulty in dating it is that everyone in the family seems to have been called Humphrey Sturt.

Horton Church was rebuilt around 1722 by a local mason called John Chapman. If this first Sturt employed Chapman to build the tower in the 1720s, then this virtually unknown man (using brick—an unaccustomed medium for a mason, surely) broke new architectural ground and was at least 30 years ahead of his time. Because of its three massive corner turrets, Horton gives the impression of being triangular; the only other triangular buildings in the county are the ruined North Lodges to the derelict Lulworth Castle, built in 1785 as eyecatchers by Thomas Weld. Thomas Archer has been suggested as the architect for the tower; he at least was conversant with triangular buildings and lived about 15 miles away.

The Humphrey who built it intended to use it as an observatory. However he is supposed to have tired of star-gazing, and used it instead to watch deer on Cranborne Chase. Originally there was supposed to have been a spire (on an observatory?) but that has long gone, as have the floors and roof. Traces of white plaster remain in one of the three smaller towers; no traces of the staircase can be found. Edward Gibbon visited Humphrey Sturt in May 1762 and saw:

> *an artificial piece of water of two hundred acres and an elegant turret 140 feet high; but such is the nature of the man that he keeps his place in no order, sells his fish, and makes a granary of his turret.*

Could this have been the same Sturt who built the tower? This one inherited Crichel House in 1765 and embarked on a massive building programme there. The Horton lake has long gone.

Kimmeridge Bay

Clavel Tower (1820)
SY 910 780

Clavel Tower, crumbling, forgotten and desolate on the headland above Kimmeridge Bay, was built in 1820 by the Rev. John Richards, who took the name Clavell when he inherited the Smedmore Estate in 1817. Why the tower has one 'l' and its builder two is not certain. Richards/Clavell was a reclusive man, but he evidently enjoyed his views in comfort; there was a fireplace on each floor of his derelict tower. It was built as solidly as could be expected, from stucco-covered stone, with brick surrounds on the

doors and windows, but years of neglect and the biting Dorset winter have taxed the presumption of building on such an exposed site. The cliff face is crumbling into the sea; every year the precipice inches closer to the petrified tower. English Heritage disapproves of moving buildings, muttering something about letting nature reclaim its own (a bizarre stand for a conservation body to take), but this would be the Belle Tout solution.

An interesting postscript: Rev. Clavell

Clavel Tower

enjoyed his tower for 13 years until he died intestate in 1833. A will was discovered that made the estate over to his steward and his housekeeper, but two years later it turned out that the will was a forgery, and the greedy servants paid their penalties.

Lulworth Castle

Clare Towers (1796)
SY 850 830

Lulworth Castle at East Lulworth has been a ruin for a good while and in its small way it is something of a folly, having been built in the early 17th century in castle-style as a fad. Its well-known triangular North Lodges (not so much triangular as trefoil) don't really make the folly grade, although for us they are respectable enough, being built on what is the special and particular folly groundplan. John Tasker probably designed them, in 1785

Lulworth Lodges

for Thomas Weld, mirroring Lulworth itself. They have recently been restored.

The real folly here is Clare Towers, to the west of the lodges, against the backdrop of a wood. The twinned circular towers, a narrow arch between them, again by John Tasker, were possibly intended as an eyecatcher. Clare was Clare Arundell, who had married the then owner of Lulworth, Humphrey Weld, in 1641.

Melbury Sampford

Prospect Tower (c.1540)
ST 570 060

The earliest recorded folly still existing in Britain is generally agreed to be Freston Tower in Suffolk, which is beautifully sited with a still lovely view on the banks of the Orwell. It was built in 1549. Ten years earlier John Leland, visiting Melbury Sampford in Dorset, wrote:

> Mr Strangeguayse hath now a late much buildid at Mylbyri quadrato, avauncing the inner part of the house with a loftie and fresch tower.

The 'fresch tower' is now nearing its 450th anniversary, which makes it the earliest surviving building intended solely for pleasure—a prospect tower—in the country. Because it is part of a house, it is difficult to take in isolation, but had the house been demolished and the tower left, as has been suggested happened at Freston, Dorset may well have boasted Britain's first folly.

Milborne St Andrew

Obelisk (1761)
SY 810 965

In 1761 Edmund Morton Pleydell built a brick obelisk on the site of Weatherby Castle, an Iron Age hill fort a mile or so south of Milborne St Andrew. He put a copper ball on the top. Pleydell was an affable fellow. Gibbon dined with him and noted that he was very good-natured and ready to do whatever his guests pleased, while his wife was 'a little ill-natured thing that seems to torment him continually'. The visit took place a year after Pleydell had built his obelisk; perhaps she hadn't forgiven him. The Pleydell house was demolished in 1802, and the obelisk has been neglected from then until 1989, when it was restored.

Milton Abbas

Sham Chapel (early 19th century)
Eyecatcher (mid-18th century)
ST 090 020

Another Dorset folly on the edge of a wood is the sham chapel, now a school, at Milton Abbas. It was built by the Earl of Dorchester, who had demolished the old market town because it interfered with his views (the village and its site appear to been designed by Lancelot Brown and William Chambers). The desire to build a sham chapel in the woods when you already have one of the largest parish churches in the county and have razed the local town can only be described as bizarre; especially when at the time there was already a genuine ruined Norman chapel—St Catherine's—in the grounds. A design for the sham, by an unknown hand, survives in the RIBA drawings collection. It is rather good, with somewhat severe side turrets and small castellations, but it is now in a very sorry state.

Delcombe Manor, which is a couple of miles north of Milton Abbas, has been cobbled together from genuine medieval bric-à-brac from the abbey (a datestone says 1515) around the middle of the 18th century and serves as an eyecatcher.

Morden

Charborough Tower (1790–1839)
ST 929 976

North of the village of Morden is Charborough Park, the seat of the Drax family. The park is large, impressive and private, made so by altering the course of the main Dorchester–Wimborne road so that it travels in a semicircle around the northern perimeter of the park instead of through the middle as it did until 1841 (the tower had just been rebuilt), when J.S.W.S. Erle Drax had the road closed to the public. He was sued for the reopening of the road by a Dorchester man, who lost, and the triumphant Drax had a gloating plaque erected to commemorate his victory, which he prudently placed on the park side of his entrance lodge so it couldn't be seen from the new road. The old road must have passed close to the foot of

Charborough Park Tower, one of the finest folly towers in Britain.

The approach to the tower from the house is grand: a long, wide grassy avenue is flanked by monolithic plinths—empty, of course; what real folly builder would dream of putting statues on bare plinths?—leads directly to a balustraded bridge crossing nothing in particular, then up a flight of steps to the tower. It has been likened to a factory chimney, but we think it is one of the most perfect of folly towers. Gothic (of course), it appears to have five storeys, octagonal, with buttresses rising two storeys (a pinnacle fell off in 1973 and has not been replaced). Inside the tower, we can see at once it has been loved and protected. Yet from the outside there is a perceptible southward list. A plaque on the ground floor records its history:

THIS TOWER WAS BUILT
BY EDWARD DRAX, ESQUIRE,
IN THE YEAR 1790, DURING
THE SHORT TIME HE
WAS THE POSSESSOR OF
CHARBOROUGH. IT WAS
STRUCK BY LIGHTNING
ON THE 29th OF
NOVEMBER 1838, WHICH
SO DAMAGED IT THAT
IT BECAME NECESSARY
TO TAKE DOWN THE
GREATER PART. IT
WAS REBUILT IN 1839
BY JOHN SAMUEL
WANLEY SAWBRIDGE
ERLE DRAX ESQUIRE

Charborough Park Tower

WHO CARRIED IT FORTY
FEET HIGHER THAN IT
WAS ORIGINALLY BUILT
MAKING THE PRESENT
HEIGHT UPWARDS OF
ONE HUNDRED FEET.

A grotesque bearded head—Edward Drax?—greets the visitor on the banister rail at the foot of the stairs. For a folly, the staircase is superb. Most prospect towers were thrown up in such a hurry that a permanent staircase was very much a secondary consideration, and the cheapest option was usually chosen, if indeed the stairs were remembered at all. At Charborough the Draxes were building for posterity, and they have left their heirs an excellent example of a geometrical open-well staircase, stone built with iron balustrades supporting a wooden rail. What makes it exceptional is that whereas the open string is naturally a geometrical spiral, the wall string has had to follow the octagonal exterior of the tower. The unknown architect handled the problem with confidence, and the result makes the stairs easy and comfortable to climb, unlike almost every other folly tower. The staircase is unlit—the five storeys do not exist—until the room at the top, which gives panoramic views over four counties. A short wooden staircase leads from the prospect room to the roof, from where the views and the wind are literally breathtaking. This is always assumed to be the tower in Thomas Hardy's novel *Two in a Tower*.

Safely down again, the folly is looked at with a new sense of respect, for its style, quality and condition put it a rank above most other follies. It has 28 blank windows, with prominent hood moulds and label stops with faces of bears, grimacing prelates, monkeys and devils, and only five real windows. A Drax family legend says that a white stag in the deer park presages the birth of an heir to Charborough. Let us hope that white stags appear frequently enough to ensure the survival of this magnificent folly.

The tower has recently been restored. In the grounds too is a grotto of around the same period as the rebuilding of the tower, and the lodges are especially good.

Moreton

Pillar (1785–6)
SY 810 880

Near the village of Moreton, lost in the trees, is another crumbling folly. This is, strictly speaking, a pillar, for the proper definition of an obelisk is a four-sided pillar that tapers to

Moreton Pillar

the top and is crowned with a pyramid. The Moreton pillar, set on a massive plinth, tapers to about two-thirds of its 75ft (23m) height, then rises vertically to its flat top, which is crowned by an Adamish urn. A now vanished marble tablet was inscribed:

Erected by Capt. John Houlton as a public testimony of his gratitude and respect for James Frampton Esq. of this place.

It was built between May 1785 and September 1786 by James Hamilton of Weymouth. The entire hilltop was surrounded by a low brick wall, now largely vanished.

Nottington

Spa House (1830)
SY 660 830

Nottington is a completely forgotten spa, yet the sulphurous spring still works, and the building itself also remains. Modelled on the Temple of the Winds by Robert Vining, a builder from nearby Weymouth, it was deemed not fashionable enough and business petered out.

Portesham

Hardy Monument (1844)
SY 620 870

Come out of the woods; Dorset is a county of panoramas. The finest view in the whole county is to be had from Black Down near Portesham, and, appropriately enough, Hardy's Monument crowns the ridge, for Hardy is the best loved name in Wessex, a writer whose love of Dorset pervades every line he wrote. The views are tremendous, although it might be regretted that the people of Dorset could not have chosen a more dignified memorial than a 70ft (21m) sink plunger for their greatest man of letters. In fact, they didn't. In the winter it would be difficult to imagine a colder or more exposed place. It was winter when we visited it. Numb with cold, we read the inscription above the locked steel door, only to find it had no connection with Thomas Hardy at all. This delightfully ugly chimney, designed by A.D. Troyte, was built when Thomas Hardy was four years old, erected by public subscription to commemorate 'Admiral Sir Thomas Masterman Hardy Bart, CCB, Flag Captain to Lord Nelson on HMS Victory at the Battle of Trafalgar'. So it's the Hardy of 'Kiss me, Hardy' fame—what a thing to be remembered by. Sir Frederick Treves saw factory chimneys all over the county, for this, as well as Charborough, reminded him of one, but this time he was more accurate. The monument has also been compared to a chess piece, a peppermill, a candlestick telephone and, most accurate of all, a factory chimney with a crinoline. Nevertheless it survives, having been under the care of the National Trust since 1900, one of their earliest properties.

Sherborne Castle

The Folly (18th century)
ST 660 160

It is called The Folly by the locals. To us it is a sham ruin. No date, no nothing. Lancelot Brown designed Sherborne's park in two phases, in the 1750s and 20 years later, in the mid-1770s. Near to the house are some interesting amenities: the Gothick dairy (now a tea-room containing a Roman mosaic discovered in 1836 on a nearby site and removed to Sherborne), an ice-house and a game larder on stilts. The walk follows the western contours of the lake and visits such pleasing trifles as Raleigh's Seat and Pope's Seat (with castellated front) and leads up to the sham ruin in Monks Walk, bordering the walled enclave of the ruins of the old castle. The Folly, so near to the real ruins, must have been planned as the false outposts to the old castle. The sham ruin is really a screen with the shell of a round tower and a section of crumbling wall. There are no castellations and only a few arrowslits. It is not the kind of thing Brown would have recommended, so it is possibly later.

Stalbridge

Obelisk (1727–1836)
ST 740 160

Just south of Stalbridge, in the north of the county, is the Thornhill Obelisk, the earliest in Dorset and certainly the most graceful. Tall and slender and in an excellent state of preservation, it was first put up by Sir James Thornhill to celebrate the accession of George II and Queen Caroline—'Master Of Britain, France And Ireland'. A storm blew it down, and it was re-erected in 1836.

Swanage

Burt's Follies (late 19th century)
SZ 030 780

Portland Bill is an obvious site for an obelisk, and sure enough there one is, but let's pass on to another Dorset obelisk, which introduces us to a great folly character, George Burt of Swanage. Bursting with Victorian civic pride and supplied with the means to do something about it, Mr Burt set about improving Swanage in every way he could. He would, one imagines, have regarded himself as economical as far as his buildings were concerned; nearly every one of them originated in London before he bore them home to Swanage.

On the top of Ballard Down, between Swanage and Studland, stands a small obelisk erected by George Burt to commemorate the introduction of 'pure water from the chalk formation into Swanage'. But he cannot resist adding: 'The granite was taken down from near the Mansion House, London, and re-erected here.' This presents a rare example of a folly being demolished and rebuilt in modern times; in 1941 it was taken down to prevent it being used as a point of reference for enemy aircraft. It was returned in 1973, shorter than before, because part was found to be cracked and was therefore mounted next to it.

The water had been supplied since 1883, but George Burt waited for the right time to mark the occasion. Even if there wasn't an occasion Mr Burt would find some way of commemorating it. In his time he gave Swanage:

- a clock tower (with no clock)
- two massive Ionic columns
- a 40 ton globe
- a castle
- a new front to the Town Hall
- an archway from Hyde Park Corner
- two headless statues of Charles I (or II)
- a Chinese pavilion complete with dragons
- assorted iron columns from Billingsgate
- floor tiles from the Houses of Parliament

and probably much more. He managed much of this through his uncle's firm, John Mowlem, which is still flourishing today. In the Victorian era, Mowlem's did a considerable amount of construction, and consequently demolition, in London, and Burt was never slow to appropriate items that he felt could enhance Swanage. A granite obelisk commemorating a naval battle of 877, fought between Alfred the Great and the Danes in Swanage Bay, was erected by Burt's uncle John Mowlem in 1862.

The magnificent clock tower, now in the grounds of the Grosvenor Hotel, originally stood on London Bridge, where it had been erected in 1854 as the Wellington Testimonial Clock Tower. With its blank clock windows staring blindly out over the Channel, it stands as a testimony to Burt's Folly rather than Wellington's Glory. Two Ionic columns stand forlornly in the hotel car park. The statues, the Chinese Pavilion, the archway and the iron columns are all to be found in the garden of Purbeck House in the High Street, now a convent.

Out on Durlston Head, to the south, of the town we find Burt's finest and most original efforts. No removals here—this is all original, and very impressive it is too. Durlston Castle was a commercial venture and, though fanciful, it was built as a restaurant and remains one today, so it cannot be regarded as a folly. The Weymouth architect G.R. Crickmay built it for Burt, as he did Purbeck House and the Swanage water tower of 1886, which looks a lot like Durlston. But Burt's enthusiasm had to find some outlet. Suspicions are aroused with the three pillars marked 'DURLSTON HEAD CASTLE' with the third one marked 'ABOVE SEA 215 FT'. All along the side of the castle on the path down to the sea are educational inscriptions on geographical and astronomical detail: we learn that the time in Swanage is eight minutes before the time in Greenwich, that the longest day in Hamburg

The Great Globe at Swanage

lasts 19 hours, that when it is 5.54 in Calcutta it is 7.04 in New York. To help orientate the holiday-maker a relief map of the district at a scale of one inch to one mile (carved in stone) is provided.

All this goes a little way to prepare us for the Large Globe. It is surprisingly big: a diameter of 10ft (3m) sounds small enough until you get close. It weighs 40 tons and appears, unlike the earth, to be a perfect globe. Surrounding it are plaques with pious, educational and exhortatory inscriptions incised on every available space, but by far the most touching inscription in the whole collection is to be found on the two stones at the entrance where Burt, fearing the attentions of like-minded souls, requested: 'Persons Anxious to Write Their Names Will Please Do So On This Stone Only.' And, to the credit of Swanage and its visitors, they have in the main honoured George Burt's

One of George Burt's Pavilions

wishes. The Large Globe and its environs are innocent of graffiti, while the two large stones specifically provided for that purpose are completely covered. Perhaps Burt arranged for them to be periodically renewed; perhaps latter-day town planners and housing experts could take his example. In any case, the stonemasons of Swanage must have sincerely mourned his passing.

There is possibly one folly-like building in Swanage that has nothing to with Burt: a disused water tower of 1886. It is rather squat, with small castellations, and is offset by a tiny turret on one corner.

Wimborne Minster

Kingston Lacy Obelisks (c.150BC; 19th century)
ST 980 020

Near Wimborne Minster, at the National Trust's Kingston Lacy, three more obelisks can be found, including the real thing. This obelisk, although only erected in 1827 in Dorset, has been dated to c.150BC. It was erected by the priests on the island of Philae to record their exemption from taxes, a sensible waste of tax-free money. There is also an Egyptian sarcophagus in the park, as well as two more obelisks, one commemorating Queen Victoria's jubilee and the other completely plain.

Wimborne St Giles

Sham Gateway (1740s–50s)
Grotto (1740s–50s)
SU 030 120

As the Bonds of Creech Grange gave their name to Bond Street, so the Shaftesburys of Wimborne St Giles gave their name to London's Shaftesbury Avenue. The park is dank and overgrown. At one time it contained a grotto, a large gazebo, an Ionic temple and a sham gateway, but a recent search failed to find the gazebo and the temple. (The gazebo has surfaced again, at SU 045 109, on a hillock: it is the so-called Philosopher's [Shaftesbury himself] Tower, but is still a low, two-storey gazebo, dating from the first half of the 18th century.) The grotto, a particularly fine example, is well protected against the vandals who would have the idiotic drive to seek it out, but the gateway close to the house is a more obvious target. It is a very satisfying folly in all but siting; two sturdy, round, castellated, two-storey towers with vermiculated banding flank an arched gateway no more than 6ft (1.8m) wide, leading imposingly to a ditch. The structure is solid, and the casement windows remain, but neglect takes effect.

In the 19th century the grotto was believed to be the work of an Italian 'who would never allow anyone to see him at work', but in reality it was by a Mr Castle of Marylebone, no doubt a specialized workshop. It is covered with shells, and the exterior is of rubble, picturesquely assembled to form a low pavilion with side wings. It was restored in 1959, but left to rot again. Grotto and gateway were made for the 3rd Earl, between about 1745 and 1754.

DURHAM

Durham did badly out of the new county changes, losing a large northern chunk to Tyne and Wear and a hefty bite from the south to Cleveland. We have gallantly reinstated them here. On the map, Durham promises to be a county well-endowed with follies, for around the beautifully sited city of Durham the names of several hamlets indicate an eccentric inventiveness that bodes well for our quest. Battles (always a fertile loam for folly growers) are commemorated by the villages of Quebec and Inkerman, while more personal fates are remembered in Pity Me and Unthank.

Towards the east Quaking Houses, Running Waters and Deaf Hill would seem more at home in an Indian reservation. The Durham follies are a continuation of the style set in North Yorkshire: a Gothick that is both quirky and imaginative yet looks sturdy enough to resist any marauding hordes of Picts.

Barningham

Grouse Obelisk (1872)
`NZ 088 100`

Barningham Moor borders North Yorkshire, and here at the old family residence of Barningham Park, Sir Frederick Milbanke re-erected the granite obelisk that formerly stood on Wemmergill Moor. It records his shooting in 1872 of 190 grouse in 20 minutes. The normal number for a day's shoot at that time was about 150 brace.

Bishop Auckland

Deer House (1767)
Gatehouse
`NZ 216 304`

Bishop Auckland has one the finest of the ecclesiastical follies so typical of northern England. Bishop Richard Trevor had his palace embellished with a gatehouse designed by the dilettante architect Sir Thomas Robinson: a Gothick confection of battlements, finials and quatrefoils, the centre

Bishop Auckland Deer House

acting as a clock tower.

What concerns us more here, however, lies ten minutes walk through the park and across a valley facing the bishop's walled garden, now obscured by rich English trees: a veritable castle of a Deer House. It consists of an arcaded, square-walled, double enclosure, with pinnacles marking the corners and a taller square tower inside the west wall, beautified with more pinnacles, cross arrowslits and quatrefoils. This spectacular Deer House was built seven years after the palace gatehouse, for which both Robinson and Richard Bentley had submitted designs.

Burn Hall

Cow House (1783)
NZ 260 387

What is it about the climate of Durham that makes the people want to build lavish dwellings for their cattle? At Burn Hall the banker George Smith employed John Soane to build him a great house, but for some inexplicable reason Soane started with an ice-house and a highly ambitious cowshed. It was built in 1783 as a neo-classical, semicircular temple with two pyramid-roofed side pavilions. Soane had tried out a similar design for a cow house in Marlesford in Suffolk, another of Smith's estates, and later built the mansion at Piercefield in Gloucestershire near Chepstow, a place of pilgrimage for those in search of the picturesque. In 1793 Smith's bank collapsed, which may have been a reason for Soane's reticence in not completing Burn Hall, but by the turn of the century Smith's finances had recovered sufficiently for Soane to be employed in the redecoration of his London house. The cow house has now been converted into a human house.

Chester-le-Street

Riverside Park (1997)
NZ 265 515

No follies here, but a happy collection of new garden buildings and sculptures, funded with £99,000 of National Lottery Fund money. A sun temple with a 'copper effect' dome (good grief) has been inspired by Thomas Wright and the local parish church, and the dome is pinpricked to provide the effect of a celestial panoply by day. By night it simply leaks.

Cleadon (Tyne and Wear)

Cleadon Chimney (1860)
NZ 384 624

The Cleadon Chimney is not a chimney; it is another of those Italianate towers so dear to the Victorians and to builders of pumping stations in particular. This one is made the more spectacular by its splendid siting on a west-facing ridge, high above the other buildings in the complex, all built in the same deep red brick with soot-blackened stone quoins. It is a darkly impressive ensemble, which was created by Thomas Hawksley, the civil engineer who also worked at Rivington Pike in Lancashire. At the time of writing, the Grade II* listed pumping station was redundant and deserted, and as commercial access is not easy up the rugged track that leads to it, its future is uncertain.

Coatham Mundeville

Hallgarth Deer House (18th century)
NZ 290 203

By golly, here's another deer house, this one at the Hallgarth Hotel, but smaller and slightly more restrained—Gothick, of course,

Hallgarth Deer House

with corner turrets decorated with the anticipated cruciform arrowslits, a double-arched Tudor entrance and a stepped gable. One of the prettiest of all the deer houses, it now stands rather forlornly on a golf course, where deer are not welcome.

Darlington

Clock Tower (1874)
Grotto
NZ 280 150

Darlington's greatest claim to fame is as the world's first railway terminus, so it is fitting that its baronial clock tower should have been built by a railway man, the Quaker promoter and industrialist Henry Pease. Designed by Alfred Waterhouse, the tower's shaft has double lancet windows, with a clock-face on the superstructure, on the corners of which are small turrets. A church-like spire tops the lot, and at the foot are the initials H.M.P. (not, sadly, for Her Majesty's Prison) and the date 1874. Tower Road, together with the tower, once formed part of the Pierrepoint Estate, where only a grotto remains of the elaborate early Victorian gardens.

Morton Park Mallard (1997)
NZ 326 154

One would think that 185,000 bricks and £750,000 are enough to build anybody a reasonable house (or a small block of flats), but Morrisons Supermarkets and Darlington Borough Council decided to use lottery funding to build a 120ft (36.6m) brick train to house bats. 'Train', designed by David Mach, is loosely based on the famous steam speed record holder, *Mallard*, and commemorates the world's first scheduled railway service between Stockton and Darlington.

One can't help feeling there may be a touch of intercity rivalry here, with Darlington and Gateshead competing to see who can build the bigger folly—and remember that in our context the word is used in admiration. This is in direct descent from the 18th-century rivalries among the great landed estates to see who could build the tallest tower or longest eyecatcher. On this basis, Gateshead is a wing ahead.

Durham

The Count's House (1820)
Needle's Eye
NZ 273 418

Shortly after the French Revolution a Polish dwarf visited the city of Durham, unsurprisingly liked what he saw and decided to spend the remainder of his 97 years in these parts. 'Count' Joseph Boruwlaski, of noble birth but without actual right to the title, had wandered around Europe for much of his life, displaying his 39in (99cm) stature in society. He became quite a success— Voltaire, Maria Theresa of Austria and George III all took an interest in him but the novelty inevitably wore off, and Boruwlaski was obliged to keep himself alive by giving concerts, a poorly disguised means (given his musical talents) of begging for alms. In 1788 he wrote his memoirs in French; they were translated into English and German and were still in print as late as 1820.

The Prebendary of Durham donated a residence called the Bank's Cottage to the Count. It was later demolished, but on the banks of the Wear below South Bailey, a small Doric tetrastyle temple, with Doric columns and one room, still carries the name the Count's House. Together with an ice-house, which is reached by a muddied flight of steps behind the temple, it stood in the grounds of the cottage where the Polish dwarf lived, looked after by the Ebdon sisters until his death in 1837.

In recent times the temple has found a

David Mach's 'Train'

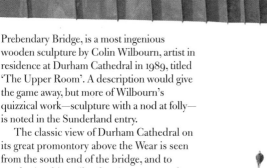

The Count's House

reasonably convincing role as a backdrop to open-air productions of ancient Greek plays, presumably after being cleared of the detritus of broken glass, discarded needles and rubber goods all remote urban sites accumulate. Somehow one expects more of Durham. On the way to the temple, to the east of

Prebendary Bridge, is a most ingenious wooden sculpture by Colin Wilbourn, artist in residence at Durham Cathedral in 1989, titled 'The Upper Room'. A description would give the game away, but more of Wilbourn's quizzical work—sculpture with a nod at folly— is noted in the Sunderland entry.

The classic view of Durham Cathedral on its great promontory above the Wear is seen from the south end of the bridge, and to emphasize this a pile of ancient masonry has been re-erected as a cone to give a needle's eye view of the Cathedral.

Salvin Obelisk (1850)
NZ 267 428

In Obelisk Lane, near North Road on the other side of the river, is a tall, needle-thin obelisk that, according to its inscription, was built as the north marker for the Salvin-built observatory a mile or so to the south. A hole in the middle of the obelisk was presumably used for sighting purposes, another Needle's Eye in the city. A plaque reads

WLW
ASTRONOMIE
DECAVIT
MDCCCL

Gainford
Edleston Hall Column (1750)
NZ 170 170

This column celebrates the Treaty of Aachen, which ended the war between England and France in 1748. The column, together with a classical summerhouse, was brought over to Gainford from Stanwick Park in North Yorkshire, and was originally commissioned by Hugh Smithson Percy, 1st Duke of Northumberland, whose more famous follies were built at Alnwick (see Northumberland). The column and summerhouse were moved to Edleston Hall when Stanwick, a William Kent house, was demolished in 1923.

Gateshead (Tyne and Wear)
The Angel of the North (1998)
NZ 266 578

The Angel of the North

Much local invective was directed against Gateshead Council when it announced it was planning to erect an £800,000 monument for the millennium entitled 'The Angel of the North' on the site of the Team Colliery's old pit-head baths, on a prominent hill south of the town overlooking the A1. More than 4000 residents signed a petition decrying it. Described by its detractors as an up-ended Messerschmitt fighter (any swipe at the Germans is always populist) and by its promoters as resembling Rio de Janeiro's Christo Rei (they can't half play football, those Brazilians), the 65ft (19.8m) high figure with a wingspan of 175ft (53m) was finally erected in February 1998. The figure's outstretched 'arms' are indeed remarkably reminiscent of the old Gustav's wings, but the rest of the body is based on sculptor Antony Gormley's own torso. The idea had been germinating for some time: a 1988 photograph of Gormley by Snowdon shows the sculptor standing beside a mould of his body with outstretched arms. Whatever the public opinion, it has become a highly popular destination, with cars parked all along the side of the A167 to get a closer look, attended by the inevitable ice cream vans and 'Buy Your Angel of the North Key Rings Here!' Small children run excitedly round the base of the massive erection, screaming confusedly about the Angel of Death. The only 20th-century eyecatcher to rival it for motorway visibility is the Ashton Memorial in Lancaster.

Greta Bridge

Rokeby Hall Cave, Urn and Grotto (1797)
NZ 083 138

Rokeby Park and its romantic surroundings provided the setting for Sir Walter Scott's eponymous epic, although a remark in an old guide book questions Scott's validity as an admirer of nature: 'it will probably strike every visitor that the popular poet has somewhat erred in the direction usually taken by irresponsible writers: exaggeration.' 'Rokeby' was conceived on Scott's visits to the house between 1809 and 1812, and the actual writing of the poem is supposed to have taken place in a natural cave in the grounds, which was further excavated and roofed over in Scott's lifetime. A rustic table inside provides the hermit touch. Not far from the grotto near Mortham Tower, also part of the estate, is a sepulchral urn of stone with iron handles. The inscription reads:

To the long try'd love of a sister
J. B. S. M. inscribed this monument,
July 5 1797

The initials are those of John Bacon Sawrey Morritt, owner of Rokeby and a friend of Scott's.

Hamsterley

Pinnacle (1930s)
Summerhouse (1930s)
NZ 142 556

Heading north on Medomsley Road, Consett, will soon bring you to Hamsterley Hall, where the last outpost of civilization and democracy is represented by a tall pinnacle from the Houses of Parliament, brought down to the Hall in the 1930s. At the same time, a domed summerhouse from Beaudesert in Staffordshire was removed to Hamsterley. R.S. Surtees, the sporting novelist, Gothicized some of the surrounding buildings when he took over the Hall in the early 19th century.

Hawthorn

Sailor's Hall Tower (mid-18th century)
NZ 430 467

Between them, Cleveland and Tyne and Wear have reduced Durham's official coastline to a minimum. The short stretch that remains has a solitary folly to show for itself: a small, heavily battlemented tower, standing north of Hawthorn in a field above the livery stables at Kinley Farm. Built for Admiral Mark Milbanke, who had built the nearby Sailor's Hall, his summer seat, it is a stoutly constructed little tower, with oversized battlements, which has withstood the howling gales from the east for nearly two centuries. Sailor's Hall has now gone, and its Gothic replacement, Hawthorn Tower, built in 1821, is rapidly following.

Peterlee

Pasmore Pavilion (1963)
NZ 422 396

'Folly!' cry the locals. 'Masterpiece!' cry the conservation societies. 'Sod off!' cry the vandals. This graffiti-stained bridge, designed by the fine arts professor Victor Pasmore with an uncompromising concrete modernism, has been listed by English Heritage, but it has so persistently been targeted by local saddies that it has become a deeply scarred, deeply unpleasant environment, fit only for demolition. The vandals and the locals share a healthy contempt for the cutting edge of modern architecture, but it was ever thus— although this particular cutting edge would have looked distinctly blunt had it been erected in Utrecht 30 years earlier. The Peterlee residents were the beneficiaries or victims, depending on one's point of view, of a brave new experiment in post-war social housing, a New Town to wash away the depression and the squalor associated with miners' housing. The idealistic architect Berthold Lubetkin was appointed as master planner, and he assembled a team of internationally known designers and architects. Their Ville Universelle was universally hated by its residents, and the design team was riven by the dissensions and resignations only idealists can truly enjoy.

When architects describe their own creations, they frequently fall into the trap of Pollyanna optimism: the Pasmore Pavilion was designed to be: 'an architecture and sculpture of purely abstract form through which to walk, on which to linger, and on which to play.' The structure has now become a shabby dump; English Heritage wants to list it; Easington Council wants to demolish it. 'Nobody here wants it,' said one local. 'If English Heritage wants to list it, they should take it somewhere else and list it there.' 'It used to be nice when we first moved here but now it's horrid,' said another girl. 'They should knock it down.'

If there was once access to the upper level it has long been blocked off. With the wind howling through it and rain lashing the concrete it is not difficult to see this as one of the more depressing sites of 'modern' British architecture. You can easily smack your head walking underneath—was Pasmore a very short man? What if they simply painted it and tidied it up? Instead of the drab uniformity of white, why not step back three-quarters of a century to its original inspiration and paint it

in the simple primary Rietveld colours of red, blue and yellow? Then see how the good people of Peterlee like it.

Rowlands Gill (Tyne and Wear)

Column of British Liberty (1750–57)
NZ 178 591
Gibside Banqueting House (1751)
NZ 182 586

South of Whickham, near Rowlands Gill, is the Gibside Estate, owned from 1721 to 1767 by George Bowes, a Whig MP and member of an old-established Durham family, who made their fortune from coal. It was mining that paid for the glamorous estate, but the wheel turns, and mining subsidence caused the ruination of almost all the Gibside buildings. Gibside Chapel, the Palladian mausoleum built by James Paine between 1760 and 1766, was rescued in 1965 when it was given by the 16th Earl Strathmore to the National Trust, along with the Grand Walk, a glorious three-quarter mile avenue of English trees uncluttered by the multiculturality of conifers. The National Heritage Memorial Fund gave £309,000 to the Trust in 1993 for the purchase of the remainder of the estate.

The Column of British Liberty, representing 152ft (46m) of whiggery, with a statue of the self-same British Liberty carved *in situ* by the fearless Richardson on top of the Doric column, seems not to have been threatened by the mining activities. This monument, facing the chapel, took £2000, seven years (1750–57) and two architects (Daniel Garrett and James Paine, who took

The Pasmore Pavilion

over Garrett's practice in the 1750s) to build, and £72,000 to restore in the 1990s. The Hall was abandoned in 1885, burned down in the 1920s but makes an impressive ruin at an angle to the Grand Walk. The Palladian orangery, also by Paine, is now in ruins.

Against all odds however, Gibside's most fanciful edifice has been saved. The Gothick Banqueting House, built in 1751 by Garrett, had already lost most of its interior decorations and a spire on top of its two-storey bow when the Landmark Trust began restoration in 1980. The Banqueting House is a charming embattled and ogee-windowed affair, standing high above a pond overlooking the park. Its most prominent feature is the bow, facing the lake with quatrefoils and topped by three gables, each ending in pinnacles. It bears a fair resemblance to a bishop's mitre.

The Friends of Gibside have been struggling like Bellerophon against the chimaera of dereliction, commercial forestry and corporate apathy. The visual destruction of Gibside was vigorously assisted by the Forestry Commission, which carpeted much of the landscape park with quick-growing conifers. A splendid touch of whimsy was lately offered by the use of the neo-classical stables as a piggery, their owner of 20 years having been thwarted by local planners in his attempt to convert them into luxury houses. Such individuality cannot be countenanced for too long, particularly when the National Trust has a master plan for the salvation of the whole estate, and so a compulsory purchase order was drawn up by Gateshead Council. It is rumoured that it plans to convert the stables into luxury houses, but at the time of writing the pigs are still in residence.

Sedgefield

Hardwick Hall Folly Group:
Temple of Minerva (1754–7)
NZ 343 291
Buon Retiro (mid 18th century)
Gothic Ruined Gateway (1764)
NZ 346 288

Hardwick Hall is now a restaurant set in a country park, which caters for the varied interests of the Sedgefield constituents. There are woods to walk in, and a motorcycle scrambling track. Deep in the woods is a lake, if the sounds of splashing and screaming were anything to go by. Hardwick Hall itself seemed rather pedestrian—perhaps it has gone, as the building that now houses the restaurant seems a sad little affair, scarcely

The Column of British Liberty

more worthy than a bailiff's house.

John Burdon, who came into possession of the Hardwick Estate in 1748, started by celebrating the Palladian style. The now demolished Banqueting House was the showpiece, with busts of Vitruvius, Inigo Jones and Palladio himself. The Doric bath house has also gone. The superb Temple of Minerva (1754–7) is the last of the classical buildings to survive, albeit only just. It was a stunning domed octagon, with an Ionic square surrounding colonnade of which the major part has been deliberately dismantled, leaving a blank bricked-up box crouching in a copse. The columns lie unnumbered and untended in the undergrowth.

Strangely enough, the Gothick style was welcomed with equal fervour at Hardwick. Of these follies, a seat and a grotto have been destroyed. The Buon Retiro, a hermitage incorporating a sham library (the shelves were painted with dummy books) and two corner towers, is a ruin.

The Gothic Ruined Gateway, built here in 1764 for John Burdon by James Payne, has been consolidated by the council and now serves as a faintly unconvincing sham castle backdrop for a wooded picnic site. Its arch, partly made out of fragments from the medieval Guisborough Priory, has a round towerette to one side. There are plenty of notice boards to tell people that it is a folly and to relate what is known of its history, but the magic has been lost in the preservation of the building. Here is the eternal dilemma: once follies are made safe and secure, they lose the very air of raffish danger that makes them so appealing in the first place. But that

The remnant of the Temple of Minerva

must be better than losing them completely, mustn't it? In the 1970s a local Sedgefield councillor reflected the general attitude of local councils throughout England when he exclaimed: 'Let them rot!' A report in the *Northern Echo* in 1979 had the council justifying its decision to let the follies in the park fall to pieces because 'to return the three existing monuments… to their original standards' would cost hundreds of thousands of pounds. Ten years later, in 1989, the plan was to restore the buildings completely, and another councillor announced that 'this was an excellent example of the way organizations can work together to achieve something really worthwhile'. It doesn't take long for public opinion to swing in the opposite direction.

Another ten years on, and the folly remains only partly restored, although more funds were raised in 1993 towards the restoration of the Serpentine Bridge, which won a Civic Trust commendation in 1994. The local MP really should be able to do something if he has any influence.

All the buildings, Palladian and Gothick, were designed by James Paine between 1748 and 1764, and John Bell, a Durham builder who was Paine's chief assistant in the region, did the construction work. Now that Painshill, Surrey, formerly thought to be past

redemption, has been carefully and imaginatively restored, a similar undertaking to preserve the gardens and buildings at Hardwick should be considered. The follies at Hardwick were the finest group in Durham, and they need to be saved.

Shildon

Pigeon Palace (1991)
NZ 230 253

The Northeast's obsession with animals continues gratifyingly unabated, with Kevin Alderson building this 60ft (18m) long fortified façade surmounted by a rickety 30ft (9m) tower to provide a suitable home for his pigeons. Two extremely grubby English and Scottish flags flap above it. 'We don't normally mind people building pigeon lofts,' commented a worried planning officer, 'but this one is rather substantial.'

South Shields (Cleveland)

Marsden Grotto (1782)
NZ 399 649

> *By the rocks of old Marsden come wander*
> *   with me*
> *And view Allen's Grotto that borders the*
> *   sea*
> *Here fifteen apartments by magic arise*
> *And gaol, ball and dining rooms wake*
> *   our surprise*
> *See the sweet smile of Peter's loved*
> *   daughter invite us*
> *Then we gaze on the portrait of Allen*
> *   and sigh*
> *That with travails complete he should*
> *   sicken and die.*

It gets to a pretty sad state of affairs when the weather gets so bad that the dog refuses to get out of the car, but that's what can happen in the Northeast. No wonder they make Barbours here. In the late 18th century the locally celebrated Peter Allen, a mining contractor, hollowed 15 rooms out of the cliff of Marsden Rock and created a house, now a pub, called The Grotto. It is accessible from the beach by a steep flight of steps or, alternatively, a lift, a monumentally industrial chimney-like affair perched on the roof of the pub. It faces a sheer rock a hundred yards offshore, which had a picturesque natural arch until storms blew it down in 1997. The pub is now a popular haunt of the young women of South Shields and their potential partners. The rough rock ceilings and walls are greased with years of dark brown nicotine stains and the taint of cheap cooking oil.

Staindrop

Raby Castle Folly (18th century)
NZ 127 231

The 1st and 2nd Earls of Darlington
embraced the Gothic Revival with great
enthusiasm. In the architectural free-for-all
that followed, the family seat of Raby Castle
was Gothicized by Daniel Garrett, James
Paine, Sir Thomas Robinson and John Carr.
Between them, these architects were
responsible for submitting a remarkable
number of designs, many of which were
executed. Among these are Garrett's arcaded
Gothick seat, the bath house (also ascribed
to Robinson) and Paine's Raby Hill House
and Park Farm, two of several castellated
farm buildings in a severe but effective style.
Near the house, Paine erected the Gothic
screen on a hill top; it has five bays and a
central gateway with battlements and
arrowslits as prescribed by the art of military
fortification.

The screen is repeated, in a slightly
different shape, as a huge eyecatcher façade
on the top of a hill behind the castle, clearly
marked on the Ordnance Survey map as
'The Folly'. This differs only marginally
from Paine's original design, the most
noticeable deviation being that the
battlements on the right hand side are not
ruinated. The façade consists of a screen
wall with square, low towers at the ends and
a gateway with a Norman arch. Over the arch
is a blank *trompe l'oeil* window, perhaps an
afterthought since it does not appear in the
original design. The archway is flanked by
two towers, ending in truncated obelisks.
Battlements, quatrefoils and arrowslits are
strewn liberally over the façade. The whole
edifice is in a shocking state, ignored as if it
were an embarrassment to the family. There
were two cottages behind the terminating
towers, but these are completely ruined.
Unintelligent planting has obscured the
front of the eyecatcher, and lower down the
hill a stand of trees completely blocks its
original view from and of the castle—out of
sight, out of mind. This wonderful,
enormous folly can and should be saved,
perhaps by a Landmark or Vivat Trust.

Washington (Tyne and Wear)

Penshaw Monument (1844)
NZ 334 544

The Penshaw Monument, built by local
architects John and Benjamin Green, a father
and son team who specialized in churches,
bridges and monuments, is a smaller copy of
the Athenian Temple of Theseus—essentially
a roofless, longish, Doric temple supported
by pillars with no walls. The Grade I listed
monument, one of the best known follies in
the Northeast, is visible from miles around,
blackened with industrial soot from the many
surrounding collieries and factories, a satanic
response to the pure white Hellenic ideal. It
was erected in 1844 as a memorial to John
George Lambton, 1st Earl of Durham and
Governor of Canada, who died in 1840. The
honeycomb of mine-workings in the area

The Penshaw Monument

have seriously undermined the foundations so that now the building is unstable; once a staircase inside one of the massive columns led up to the roofless parapet walk to allow visitors to enjoy the view.

The National Trust spent over £100,000 in restoration in 1996, but the original cast-iron cramps that reinforce the structure have corroded to twice their original size and have buckled the masonry as a result. It is planned to replace them with stainless steel cramps bedded in lead. Scaffolding on the building would appear to be permanent. The Trust took the applauded decision not to clean the smoke-blackened stonework as it 'reflects the area's industrial past'.

Victoria Viaduct (19th century)
NZ 320 546

Below the Penshaw Monument is the Victoria Viaduct, which spans the River Wear. Another classical copy, this is a railway bridge inspired by the Roman Alcantara viaduct in Spain.

Westerton

Westerton Folly (1785)
NZ 241 310

On a grassy knoll in the trim little village of Westerton is a small, round, stone tower with tiny buttresses, cruciform arrowslits, a rather martial-looking doorway and a commemorative plaque: another minor folly in a land well blessed with them. This one, however, is special—it was built as an observatory by one of the 18th-century's finest folly builders, the enigmatic Thomas Wright, Wizard of Durham. Wright was a mildly eccentric polymath, which is perhaps why his perfectly serviceable stargazing observatory should have acquired the honorarium of folly early in its life. Or it may have been because construction started the year before Wright died, so he had little time to enjoy its use. Whatever the reason, its importance has been recognized locally with the formation of a society to honour Wright's achievements—although too late to save his house, which was arbitrarily demolished in the cynical sixties. The plaque reads:

This observatory tower was erected by
THOMAS WRIGHT
born at Byers Green 1711, died there 1786
To commemorate his treatise
THEORY OF THE UNIVERSE
published 1750, this tablet was placed here
by the University of Durham 1950

Years ago we heard that the observatory formed part of Wright's scheme, like Henry Holland's in Kent, to erect a copy of Pliny's famous villa together with vast and elaborate gardens at nearby Byers Green, his birthplace. Now research at the University of Durham suggests that the tower was intended by Wright to be the nexus of Heliopolis, with radiating avenues dividing the landscape into zones of the zodiac. More research, please.

Whickham (Tyne and Wear)

Long John atop his Monument

Long John Monument (1854)
NZ 208 613

At Whickham, south of Newcastle, stands a monument to Long John English, a Victorian stonemason and wrestler who is supposed to have sculpted his own bust on the top of the column.

I ENGLISH
1854
Donated by
BELLWAY to
Whickham Village
MCMLXXVII
This monument
formerly stood in
Woodhouses Lane
Fellside

The Angel of the North follows this tradition of sculptors sculpting themselves.

Whitburn
(Tyne and Wear)

Barnes's Folly (1860)
NZ 406 617

In the back garden of a bizarre Victorian fantasy, Whitburn House, stands a 30ft (9m) high Perpendicular medieval window. It was originally part of St John's Church, Newcastle, which was demolished in 1848. Thomas Barnes, a brick-maker, acquired it and re-erected it in his garden as a conversation piece; now it has become a conservation piece. Local legend claims it for a genuine monastery, with a secret tunnel leading to the church for smugglers, of course, but the tunnel turns out to be the coal hole for Whitburn House. The sham ruin was erected in 1860, when the front of the house was coated with its strange half-timbering effect. The present owner replaced the mullions some 30 years ago using the same source of stone, and they are beginning to weather in harmony with the rest of the window.

Barnes's great friend George Foster, thrice Lord Mayor of Newcastle, spent much of his time at Barnes's house, so much so that he remains there to this day—his gravestone lies in the lawn by the window.

By the church in pretty Whitburn village is Barnes's earlier house, the Red Cottage, which is a red brick fancy to rival Massey's Folly in Hampshire. He is said to have used every kind of brick available in its construction, including in the chimney one shaped like a cricket bat.

Witton Castle

Lodges (1811)
Dovecote Tower (1811)
Gazebo (1811)
NZ 154 307

The lodges to Witton Castle, west of Bishop Auckland, are all castellated to a greater or lesser degree, but the south lodge was given

Unnecessarily fortified lodge to Witton Castle

the full treatment as a large gatehouse with turrets and arrowslits. In the same style, and probably of the same date, is the Gothick three-storey tower beyond the castle, the top of which is used as a dovecote. The ground floor of the tower is arcaded and an embattled summerhouse is attached. The estate is now a leisure complex.

Wynyard Park (Cleveland)

Obelisk and Temples (1827)
NZ 421 268

The old Durham part of Cleveland has in Wynyard Park a small group of garden buildings and one folly. Charles William Stewart, 3rd Marquess of Londonderry (1778–1854), had the Wynyard mansion built by Philip Wyatt in 1822–9. Wyatt was later sacked because of incompetence, and later the other Wyatts took over. The marquess had £80,000 a year to spend because of his successful investments in Durham collieries, an even more successful marriage and his undertaking the development of Seaham, further north. The result was a house whose interior was generally agreed to be in rather vulgar taste. Some particular aspects shocked the Princess Lieven, who described in a letter the four-poster bed she had seen in Lady Londonderry's bedroom. Its posts were formed by 'large gilt figures of Hercules, nude and fashioned exactly like real men'. It is now occupied by a Japanese electronics company; presumably the offensive bed has been removed.

The buildings in the grounds were not as daring or as original, however. There were a Greek and a Roman temple by Benjamin Wyatt, who also designed the classical Lion Bridge. The only folly is the 127ft (38.7m) high obelisk, erected in 1827 to commemorate the Duke of Wellington's visit to Wynyard. The marquess, a hot-tempered man, considered himself a close friend of the Iron Duke, but Wellington's feelings towards Londonderry were ambivalent—in letters and despatches from the battlefield he sometimes referred scathingly to the marquess. Originally the obelisk bore the inscription 'WELLINGTON FRIEND OF LONDONDERRY', but when the marquess was refused a seat in Wellington's 1828 Cabinet, the inscription was altered to plain 'WELLINGTON'. Londonderry had his final revenge in 1852, when the Order of the Garter that had become vacant with Wellington's death was bestowed upon him.

ESSEX

Essex is a schizophrenic county, urban yet rural, industrial yet also a holiday centre. Places like Southend and Clacton have long been a playground for London's East Enders, but the county also caters for the more refined trippers, who go to Frinton and Brightlingsea. The western end, where it abuts London, is a seemingly endless factoryscape; the road through East London, through Dagenham and Rainham and out to Gray's Thurrock and Tilbury would be an easy winner for the Most Depressing Drive in Britain competition.

Little Walden · Saffron Walden · Pentlow · Colne Engaine · Audley End · Belchamp Walter Hall · Middleton · Fingringhoe · Stansted Mountfitchet · Halstead · Alresford · Great Dunmow · Colchester · Hatfield Forest · Brightlingsea · Harlow · Layer Marney · Clacton-on-Sea · Loughton · Upshire · Chelmsford · High Beach · Epping · Thorndon Hall · St Osyth · Theydon Mount · Brentwood · Tolleshunt Major · Chingford · Hockley · South Weald · Southend · Little Thurrock · Canvey Island

We've lost two good hermitages in Essex: the one at Whitleys on the hill outside Baythorne End, which was sufficiently well known in its day to have been the subject of a popular engraving, and the hermitage on the lake at Braxted Park, to the west of Witham, which was an 18th-century ice-house crowned with a summerhouse, where a hermit is said to have lived for a year and a day. Hermitages can be rebuilt, but a more permanent loss is the folly garden at Matching Green, a front garden packed with concrete effigies of animals and people, poured by a cantankerous old man who was the son of the village blacksmith. Decaying and overgrown, they were there in 1973 but have since been destroyed. Ramsey had its own folly castle made from the right materials – rocks and bottles and broken glass – by a Mr Littlewood. It was, however, destroyed in the 1980s.

Around 1960 the two concrete folly towers of 1873 at Heybridge were demolished to make way for a housing estate.

Alresford

Fishing Temple (1772)
TM 070 220

Rural Essex is a delight, but the beauty of villages such as Finchingfield and Dedham has been their own worst enemy, with coachloads of tourists descending on their inadequate resources all summer long. There are many other beauty spots, less well known, where the voice of the tourist is seldom, if ever, heard in the land. One such is Alresford, which is reached through unprepossessing roads bordering the mudflats of the River Colne, southeast of Colchester. The Quarters at Alresford is a

The Quarters

Audley End's Teahouse Bridge

Chinese Fishing Temple, built in 1772, according to a builder's mark found on the roof, by Richard Woods, the landscape gardener. It is a pity that Woods's work is not better known, for he created here one of the most tranquil scenes to be found in the English countryside. The Quarters, standing on the shore of its little lake at sunset, is one of the most beautiful artificial compositions in England. Woods was commissioned by Colonel Rebow to build the Chinese Temple at a cost of £343 13s 6d, and it seems probable that work actually started in 1765. The delight of the building is the roof, a double-curved, concave, copper-covered affair, which, to an untutored Western eye, appears Chinese without there being any architectural precedent for it being so.

In 1816 the Colonel's successor, General Isaac Rebow, commissioned John Constable to paint the temple. The picture, now in the National Gallery of Victoria in Melbourne, shows the veranda of the cottage jutting out over the water to provide a fishing platform; nowadays it stands a few feet back from the water's edge.

Audley End

Garden Buildings (18th century)
TL 530 380

Most of the large Essex estates have been broken up or have disappeared, some swallowed by ever-encroaching London, some just abandoned and decaying. Fortunately, one of the finest remains intact, although it is but a shadow of its former self.

Audley End at Saffron Walden was one of the largest houses ever built in Britain. It was designed by the Earl of Northampton and Bernard Janssen for Thomas Howard, Lord High Treasurer, and built between 1603 and 1616. When James I saw it, he commented: 'it is too much for a King, but it might do very well for a Lord Treasurer.' Shortly afterwards, Howard was a guest at the Tower of London, accused of defrauding the king of £240,000.

The house itself was the size of a small town, and in 1707 Vanbrugh was called in to demolish the major part of it. What remains is, of course, still magnificent, but what concerns us here are the works in the park after Lancelot Brown landscaped it in 1763. Robert Adam was appointed to design a bridge that same year, and went on to design the Temple of Victory on Ring Hill (1772), a circular Ionic temple to commemorate victory in the Seven Years' War (1756–63) and a Palladian bridge with a summerhouse on it by the cascade in 1782–3. The Springwood Column of 1774—Doric and surmounted by an urn—was dedicated to Lady Portsmouth. All these were commissioned by Lord Braybrooke. The only piece not by Adam is the rectangular Temple of Concord, with unfluted Corinthian columns, which was designed by Robert William Brettingham in 1790 as yet another premature celebration of George III's recovery from madness.

Audley End is clean, well-preserved, safe and slightly antiseptic; the park's embellishments are too sane to deserve full folly status.

Belchamp Walter Hall

Eyecatcher (late 18th–early 19th century)
TL 820 410

West of Belchamp Walter Hall is a tiny, ivy-covered folly gateway. It is very thin and slender and with all kinds of openings in all sizes.

Belchamp Walter Hall's Eyecatcher

Brentwood

Pagoda (1980s)
TQ 600 940

The Hammond family of Brentwood call their house The Magnolias because … yes. And not only that, along one of their ponds they have constructed a tiny wooden Chinese temple, a three-decker pagodette.

Brightlingsea

Bateman's Folly (19th century)
TM 090 150

Bateman's Folly on the front at Brightlingsea is too insignificant, a gently leaning, 25ft (76m), two-storey tower used for rigging practice. It is said to have been built by Mr Bateman as a freelance lighthouse.

Canvey Island

Dutch Cottages (1618; 1621)
TQ 770 830

There are two Dutch cottages on Canvey Island, at Hole Haven Road and Northwick Corner (Northwick is no doubt a bastardization of Noordwijk). Both are octagonal, with thatched roofs, and they look rather like truncated windmills. They are supposed to be, and probably are, linked with Dutch land reclaimers. Despite that, they must have been much altered, because if these are typical Dutch houses, I'm a Dutchman.

Chelmsford

Conduit (1814)
TL 710 060

Hylands Park outside Chelmsford has a Gothic cottage, which may have been designed by J.B. Papworth, but Essex has a few good water towers at Epping, Halstead and Colchester, although the one at Chelmsford has gone. Chelmsford's domed, circular, Doric conduit of 1814 must be safe now; it survived a relocation in 1939 from the High Street to Admiral's Park, so it must have municipal protection.

The water tower in Rainsford Road didn't make it, however. Dating from 1888 and built of red brick, it was truncated several decades ago, and the rest was demolished in the early 1980s.

Chingford

Queen Elizabeth's Hunting Lodge
(early 16th century)
TQ 390 950

The splendid timber-framed Queen Elizabeth's Hunting Lodge, a grandstand tower dating from the early 16th century, is, strictly speaking, in London.

On Pole Hill an 1824 obelisk has something

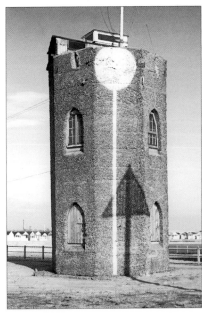

Bateman's Folly

to do with Greenwich Observatory, so it perhaps doesn't really count.

Clacton-on-Sea

Moot Hall (20th century)
TM 180 130

Some buildings are not all they seem, and one such is the wonderfully medieval Moot Hall in Albany Garden West, which turns out not to be medieval at all but merely a re-assembly of 15th-century timbers taken from a barn at Hawstead in Suffolk.

Colchester

Water Tower (1882)
Summerhouses (1747; 1745)
TM 000 253

The county's the most popular water tower (if that concept can be applied to such a structure) is the 105ft (32m) high one at Colchester, the only water tower in our experience to have acquired a nickname. The townspeople call it Jumbo, because it was built by Charles Clegg in 1882, the year in which Barnum & Bailey's famous circus elephant first hit the headlines. Unlike other water towers, it has a pyramid roof capped with a lantern, and the open arches around the tower itself are spectacular. In 1988 a group of evangelists tried to buy Jumbo:

A handful of Christians in Colchester began to meet and pray together. During one of these meetings somebody got a picture of Colchester from the air. As we prayed we got the sense that God was drawing our attention to this tower, the highest point. When Jesus looked down on Jerusalem and wept it was from a high place.

Colchester lays claim to being the oldest town in England, and it could almost claim to have the largest folly in England, too, in the garden of Hollytrees, the best 18th-century house in Colchester and now the town museum. Charles Grey MP, the owner, incorporated in his garden the vast bulk of Colchester Castle keep, the largest keep in the British Isles, to provide, as Pevsner so excellently put it, 'a somewhat Brobdingnagian garden ornament'. Not satisfied with the sheer size of the keep, in 1747 Grey added a circular domed and buttressed summerhouse on the top of the walls, and erected nearby, with total disregard for any attempt at architectural harmony, a small Tuscan tempietto. To the east he built a massive pedimented archway with stones taken from the castle. It would seem likely

that he was assisted in these undertakings by James Deane, the Colchester architect who had already worked at Hollytrees.

In the garden of The Minories, also in the High Street, is an octagonal summerhouse with a mighty castellated brick façade. It was originally built in 1745 at East Hill House but moved here when Thomas Boggis built the new house is 1776.

Berechurch Hall, 2 miles south, has now been demolished, and the little folly we were told was in the grounds can no longer be found.

In 1997–8 a 15ft (4.6m) sham Roman rotunda was built on the Roman Fields

A mighty summerhouse at The Minories

housing estate at Gosbecks, 'to add a bit of visual interest' and in order to refer to nearby archaeological finds.

Colne Engaine

Column (1791)
TL 850 500

Colne Park in Colne Engaine has a column surmounted by an urn, dating from 1791. Its only claim to fame is that it was designed by Sir John Soane for Philip Hills. The urn went missing a decade ago.

Epping

Copped Hall Pavilions (1895)
Water Tower (1872)
Wensfell Pavilion (late 19th century)
TL 450 010

Copped Hall, to the west of Epping, is another stately home that has disappeared. Only the shell remains, but it seems at first glance to be entire: a pleasing, chilling *trompe l'oeil*. It was designed in 1753 for John Conyers by John Sanderson, who also designed a renaissance garden pavilion, which was not built—at least not until 1895, when the architect C.E. Kempe built the two spectacularly beautiful pavilions and the arcade walls to Sanderson's original designs, which seems very odd, because the pavilions are a typical mishmash of High Victorian retro-vignettes. The house was burned down in 1917; the pavilion and the walls remain. Copped Hall has long been maltreated, and much of the statuary and odds and ends have found new homes or have been destroyed. Now, however, Alan Cox's Copped Hall Trust has come to the rescue and the future is looking better.

In Epping High Street is a water tower of 1872, a tall, square, ivy-covered, red brick tower with a thin circular stair turret and white stone castellations.

Wensfell Cottage in Epping Forest has a wooden garden pavilion with two galleried wings and a belvedere on top of the centre bit. Dating from the 19th or early 20th century, it has been well restored.

Fingringhoe

Bear Pit (18th century)
TM 030 100

Fingringhoe Hall, south of Colchester, has a bear pit, a rare survival from more barbarous days. The building, a two-storey tower, has seen more uses, however, and its first function appears to have been as a signalling platform. The bear pit is, of course, at the bottom of the building, the ground floor room was prettified to make it into a summerhouse, and the top storey holds pigeons.

Great Dunmow

Ornamental Cottage (mid-18th century)
TL 610 210
Summerhouse (late 16th–early 17th century)
TL 620 220

Stone Hall, just north of the A120 to the west of Great Dunmow, was built in the mid-18th century as a *cottage orné* by the Maynards of the now-demolished Easton Lodge. It is remote and (unusually in folly architecture) Romanesque, with two turrets and a conical roof, and mullioned 14th-century windows taken from the local church. It has been converted into a desirable residence.

At Bigods stands a delightful brick summerhouse with an ornate doorway and a quatrefoil motif in the centre of its gable.

Bigods was where Frances Evelyn Greville (1861–1938), Countess of Warwick, heir to Easton Lodge, socialist society beauty and animal preservationist, established a school and laboratories around 1900 in order to teach children rural crafts. Little remains.

Halstead

Water Tower (1890)
TL 810 300

The round, brick water tower on Colne Road, its drum surrounded with brick pilasters, was the centre of a planning debate some years ago: it was going to be converted into a house with a conservatory on its top, but locals objected as they felt inhabitants of the water tower house would be able to look into their houses and gardens.

Harlow

Gibberd Garden (1956 onwards)
TL 480 120

Thankfully, follies are still being built in Essex. Sir Frederick Gibberd, who was one of the few 20th-century architects with the courage to practise what he preached (he designed most of Harlow and chose to make his home there, albeit in Old Harlow, at Marsh Lane), enjoyed building landscapes in his relatively small garden, relishing the challenge of the confined space. He added summerhouses, statuary and a log fortress, ostensibly for his grandchildren to play in, but perhaps we know better. There is also a two-column sham ruin, taken from the old Coutts Bank building in the Strand, London (which was re-modelled by Gibberd in 1969).

Best of all is the Prospect Tower, a two-storey concrete building, the bottom half open and the top with a roof supported on columns. After Gibberd's death in 1984, the garden was maintained by the Council, but ten years later house and garden had to be sold. Now its future is secure again—Lady Gibberd lives there.

Hatfield Forest

Shell House (1759)
TL 530 200

There are no grottoes at all left in Essex (the one at St Osyth is much damaged; see below). The closest we can get is the large, elaborate and pretty shell house in Hatfield Great Park, outside Bishops Stortford. It was built in 1759 by Laetitia Houblon on the shore of the artificial lake.

High Beach

Catacomb (1860s)
TQ 400 980

There is a fine catacomb at High Beach in Epping Forest. It is said to have been built in the 1860s, using stones from Chelmsford Jail. The entrance is normal enough—you pass through a circular colonnade—but as you penetrate the earth the architecture goes awry: the columns supporting the ceiling are massive at the top and fragile at the bottom, as at Knossos, the floor is deliberately uneven, and there is a terrible sense of impending collapse. A subterranean folly to make one think.

Hockley

Pump Room (1842)
TQ 840 920

Essex seems to have been fated with its spas. A good spring was discovered at Hockley in 1838, and an attempt was made to capitalize on this in 1842 by James Lockyer, who built a heavy and inappropriate pump room alien to the rest of the village, which then suffered the same fate as Mistley (see below). The redundant pump room lingers on, and most locals are ignorant of its original purpose.

Layer Marney

Layer Marney Tower (1520)
TL 930 170

Layer Marney Tower is one of the glories of Essex: it is a late medieval skyscraper, eight storeys high, which was built in 1520 and complies perfectly with the dictionary definition of a folly. It was intended to be the gatehouse to a magnificent, vast residence for the Marney family, but the 1st Lord Marney died in 1523 and his heir died only two years later, so the mansion was never built.

Why is it not a folly? There are several factors to consider. First, it was built to impress, a prime motive in the building of many follies, but the tower was constructed at a time when the ruling classes were more impressed by militaristic than artistic displays. Second, it is unlikely that the Marneys had not carefully budgeted the cost of their new house, but they assumed the continuation of the line and hence the continuation of the family income. When that stopped, so did the building. So there it stands, confused in the shallow Essex countryside and a harbinger of a building that never arrived.

Little Thurrock

Clock House (c.1873)
TQ 630 770

A beautifully restored house in Dock Road was started c.1873 as a master's house and made, Mr Burnley informs us, of shuttered concrete and flint 'and may be one of the earliest of this type of construction'. The pagoda-like roof of the clock tower is the curiosity here, although it is not a real folly. It contains a bell dating from 1786, which obviously came second-hand.

Little Walden

Cinder Hall (19th century)
TL 540 410

Cinder Hall at Little Walden is a house variously described as Gothic, Tudor and Georgian. It was built of flint and red brick, with turrets and castellations and burned cinders for added decoration—a gallimaufry of styles. Recently, a modern extension in the same eclectic style and materials has been added, tripling the size of the house. The addition has been handled sympathetically and intelligently, and the result is brilliantly successful.

Loughton

Obelisk (early 19th century)
TQ 420 970

At The Warren, off the A104 in Epping Forest, stands the 15ft (4.6m) obelisk to the horse General Grosvenor rode at the Battle of Waterloo.

Cinder Hall

Middleton

Middleton Arch (1841)

TL 870 390

Right on the county border with Suffolk, just by Sudbury, is a small, sweet, unexceptional little folly called the Middleton Arch. It is about 15ft (4.6m) high and stands in a ploughed field north of the church. Built of brick, flint and bits of Lavenham Church, it bears an inscription that, initially, seems puzzling:

PLANTED BY OLIVER RAYMOND . LLB . RECTOR .
OF . THIS . PARISH . IX . NOV . MDCCCXLI . THE .
DAY . OF . HRH . THE . PRINCE'S . BIRTH

The inscription refers, in fact, to the great avenue of oak trees planted by the royalist rector; the arch merely served the ancillary purpose of announcing the avenue. In the interests of improving agriculture (and despite a preservation order), most of the mighty oaks have now gone, and the commemorative arch, with its incongruous carvings of De Vere mullets, is a lonely loyalist testimony.

The lake near the church also has some bits and pieces, classical this time. The motto 'CAVE STAGNUM' may, according to Phil Wisdom, refer to the rector's coach missing the turn and going into the lake.

Mistley

Mistley Towers (1776)

TM 420 320

The Mistley Towers were originally part of Mistley Church, one of the few churches designed by Robert Adam. The church was originally built in 1735, and Adam was called in by the grossly corrupt politician Richard Rigby to remodel it in 1776. He added identical classical towers at each end of the nave, each one square, with eight supporting Tuscan columns and topped with a tall domed cupola with Ionic pilasters. This made for a strange-looking but eyecatching church, which became even stranger in 1870 when the nave was demolished because of dry rot, leaving the towers facing each other like two kings on a chess board. The intention was to use the towers as mausolea, but in the event, the highest they aspired to was temporary service as the village morgue.

The Ten Commandments and fragments of Richard Rigby Sr's will can still be seen in the east tower: 'Richard Rigby Esq by his will dated August 8th 1730 charged a portion of his estate at Mistley to the value of six chauldrons of coal…' The towers are now surrounded by warehouses and are kept locked, but the key can be obtained during reasonable hours from the address given on the notice board outside.

Richard Rigby Jr was out for all he could get. Through connivance, making and breaking alliances, conviviality, treachery and underhandedness, he finally achieved his ambition, which was to became Paymaster General, a lode worked with equal corruption by his one-time mentor, Henry Fox. He died in 1788, leaving (as his best known epitaph) 'near half a million of public money'. Some of that was spent on Gothic and Chinese temples and bridges in Mistley Hall—even Horace Walpole designed a Sino-Indian room for him in 1750—but all has now gone, except for two Adam lodges. Mrs Birch of Brantham Glebe, just over the river in

The Adam Swan at Mistley

Suffolk, wanted to buy one of the lodges and re-erect it in her garden with her modern obelisks and temple, but the Georgian Group stepped in to prevent the sale and, presumably, thereby condemned the building to death, as it is now derelict and fading fast.

Rigby's other ideas for Mistley included launching the village as a spa, but like so many spa enterprises it came to nothing, and the only trace we have left is a stone swan, also by Adam, gazing at its reflection on the circular basin in the centre of the village.

Pentlow

Bull's Tower (1859)
TL 820 450

Essex has a number of folly towers of a more traditional sort, but all are eclipsed by the most terrifying tower in Britain.

Bull's Tower in Pentlow is a rather attractive, unostentatious Victorian brick tower, standing in a rectory garden. When first we called, we tugged on the old bell pull and far away in the depths of the house a rusty bell finally tolled. No one answered. When we stepped back, every window of the house had a white cat sitting in it looking out at us. Nervously, we made our way across the ramshackle lawn to the tower. It is 70ft (21m) high, banded with diapered cross and diamond bricking, with the date, 1859, prominently set above the door. Above that is a narrow window, and then further up are the initials 'AC'i', also picked out in dark blue brick. This stands for Anno Christi, rather than the more usual Anno Domini. A plaque records that:

THIS TOWER WAS ERECTED BY THE REV. EDWARD BULL, M.A. IN MEMORY OF HIS PARENTS ON A SPOT THEY LOVED SO WELL

It is the most frightening building we have ever been halfway up. It was long after we had got away from the tower, tyres squealing, overcome by inexplicable terror, that we sat down to try and rationalize the fear. A little research made it all the worse. We discovered that the Rev. Bull left Pentlow to become rector at another village 4 miles away and built himself a new rectory there in 1865; his Borley Rectory, which burned down mysteriously in 1941, only took a few years to establish itself as the most haunted house in England. Old photographs of Borley show it to be similar in style to the rectory at Pentlow.

No other tower in the county compares with it as a folly. Nothing in Essex equals Pentlow for atmosphere—we hadn't been back since 1974.

Bull's Tower, Pentlow

We finally screwed our courage to the sticking-place and returned, full of trepidation, in 1998. The place was transformed—there were no cats but signs of life in the house, so we knocked, still a little gingerly. 'Oh God,' snapped the exasperated new owner, 'if everyone who said they were writing a book on follies actually got them published there'd be nothing else on the shelves. You can't see it, it's derelict.' And indeed it is, and the new owner appears to be doing nothing about this precious listed building. Perhaps a compulsory repairs notice might help.

Saffron Walden

Railway Mission (18th–19th century)
The Folly (18th–19th century)
Garden Buildings (18th–19th century)
TL 530 380

There are scraps of follies to be found in every county. They are usually too insignificant to get a mention in type, and they lack provenance, authority or protection, so when their time comes, they pass and are forgotten with the rest. Essex has its share; time forbids further researches than to list some that may be threatened in the future, but if local readers are interested enough to look further into the backgrounds of these defenceless buildings, their chances of survival may be brighter.

Saffron Walden, for example, has a castellated laundry (once the Railway Mission), a folly in the garden of Elm Grove, another in the garden of a house called The Folly in Abbey Lane, and an octagonal 18th-century summerhouse, the 'Poets Corner' temple and an arch called the grotto in Bridge End Garden—none merits a detailed description, but they have all brought somebody pleasure.

St Osyth

Grotto (18th century)
TM 120 150

At the western end of the deer park of St Osyth's Priory are the remains of what once was a shell grotto or, rather, a shell house. The building was torched some years ago and the bulk of the shell decoration has gone. There's a rustic hut next to it.

South Weald

Tower (late 18th century)
TQ 570 840

Robert Adam worked at Weald Hall in South Weald outside Brentwood, where he did some interior decoration on the house, which was pulled down in 1951. The architect of the embattled belvedere tower, now in the Country Park overlooking the M25, is unknown.

Southend

Crow Stone (1836)
TQ 857 853
Crow Stone (1755)
TQ 861 787

Essex is surprisingly short of columns and obelisks. The 1836 Crow Stone at Southend marks the limit of the jurisdiction of the Port of London Authority (and is matched by the London Stone on the Kent bank), but the old Crow Stone, an 18th-century obelisk, has been re-erected near Prittlewell Priory, the birthplace of Southend.

Stansted Mountfitchet

Inspection Pavilion (1895)
TL 520 230

At Blythwood Farm, John Campbell informs us, stands a rather vernacular octagonal building, an agricultural folly, with a door at each corner. Inside is a central pier, divided into four columns, which used to have a stove inside. Lord Blyth would sit inside and his prize Jersey cattle would be let in and paraded around this curious pavilion so that Blyth could inspect them—hence the name. There was also a model dairy, now much altered.

Theydon Mount

Temple (18th century)
TQ 480 980

There is a small island temple on the pond at Hill Hall in Theydon Mount (west of Stapleford, Tawney); it was once a women's prison.

Thorndon Hall

Hatch Farm (1777 and 19th century)
TQ 630 920

Thorndon Hall, south of Brentwood, is now a golf course and country park, the house, built by James Paine in 1764 for Lord Petre, having burned down in 1878. Lancelot Brown landscaped the grounds from 1766, and Samuel Wyatt designed Hatch Farm in 1777. It is a neo-classical, red brick building, with a centre gate, colonnades and two-storey end pavilions. Also on the estate there is a mausoleum and chantry chapel by Pugin.

Tolleshunt Major

Gatehouse (1546)
TL 910 120

The gatehouse at Beckingham Hall in Tolleshunt Major dates from 1546, and again seems to presage a grand house, which was never built. Thin, mad and pinnacled, it is invariably associated with the Erwarton Hall gatehouse in Suffolk.

Upshire

Warlies Park Rotunda (1780)
Boadicea Obelisks (19th century)
TL 410 020

Warlies Park at Upshire has a rotunda temple of 1780. Now the headquarters of the marketing company Creative Minds, Warlies also has two obelisks, one, at Obelisk Farm, marking the spot where Boadicea took her fatal draught of poison, the other marking the spot where she died, almost exactly a mile away. It is a continual source of wonder to us how people could be so confident of an historical site as to erect something as permanent as a obelisk—there are three at Naseby to commemorate the battle, all far, far apart. And we can't be having all this Boudicca nonsense.

GLOUCESTERSHIRE

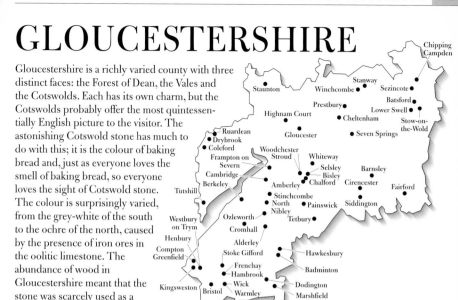

Gloucestershire is a richly varied county with three distinct faces: the Forest of Dean, the Vales and the Cotswolds. Each has its own charm, but the Cotswolds probably offer the most quintessentially English picture to the visitor. The astonishing Cotswold stone has much to do with this; it is the colour of baking bread and, just as everyone loves the smell of baking bread, so everyone loves the sight of Cotswold stone. The colour is surprisingly varied, from the grey-white of the south to the ochre of the north, caused by the presence of iron ores in the oolitic limestone. The abundance of wood in Gloucestershire meant that the stone was scarcely used as a building material until Tudor times, and surprisingly few of the county's follies take advantage of its natural warmth.

The Vale of Berkeley and the Vale of Gloucester are the central low-lying lands bordering the mouth of the Severn, Britain's longest river. The land is fertile and suitable for growing towns and motorways. The Forest of Dean is a land apart.

Alderley

Banqueting House (c.1770)
ST 770 910

Upper House was demolished in 1859, but its banqueting house is still there on top of a hill. Built in mimicry of a small fortification, it nevertheless can't really choose between the Gothick and the classic. We have had flying sheep (Temple Mills, Leeds), plummeting cows (Burton Pynsent Steeple, at Curry Rivel, Somerset), but no horses yet. Here it is: in 1947 a horse climbed onto its top and fell through the roof. Needless to say, the folly deteriorated after that, but in the early 1990s it was restored and converted into a house.

Alderley Grange has a modern summerhouse in the grounds, although Verey says it is 18th century.

Amberley

Eyecatcher (late 18th–early 19th century)
SO 850 020

Rodborough, Amberley, Inchbrook and Nailsworth are strung along the valley and hillside south from Stroud. The Amberley eyecatcher, a house called The Gateways in St Chloe, was built by the wonderfully named Sir George Onisipheros Paul, who died in 1820, as an eyecatcher to

Rodborough Manor, which burned down in 1906. Two round towers with Gothic windows are joined by a battlemented arch, now filled in. The architect was probably Anthony Teck, although the whole structure looks Sanderson Miller-ish. The best view of it comes from the A46 below, but it is difficult to see it on a sunny morning as it hides against the hillside. The eyecatcher also goes under the name Rodborough Lodge, and a c.1906 postcard showing it in unspoilt state, is subtitled 'The Hermitage Manor House'.

The Amberley Eyecatcher is intended to be seen from the other side

Badminton (Avon)

Folly Group (18th century)
ST 800 830

For some reason, everyone who writes on follies appears to deprecate the Badminton follies, and so did we in this book's first edition. The follies in the great park of Badminton are mainly by Thomas Wright, and although the Ragged Castle is a triumph of rustic romanticism, some of the others have something of a pattern book feel about them, as if the Duke of Beaufort had been told that he should embellish his park and, at a loss to know what to do, had handed the commission over to Wright with orders to get on with it.

The lodges are decorated. Two have battlemented or pyramidal roofed turrets at each corner; another has Gothic windows and overhanging eaves; Bath Lodge is in the classical style; and Castle Barn has two massive towers each side of a screen wall with a crow-stepped gable in the centre, now obscured by a prefabricated Atcost barn. The Root House is the splendid exception, of course. This superb hermitage shows the mysterious Wright at the height of his powers: thatched and riddled with worm, but still eerily standing, solitary in the deer park. The buildings were all erected between 1748 and 1756, and for a thatched building made out of unworked roots and lumps of diseased trees still to be standing after two and a quarter centuries is an achievement in itself.

After another visit, we now feel that there is more to Badminton. Let's face it, there aren't that many folly groups by Thomas Wright, and here are all these delightful lodges and castellations—one would hope for every second farm building in the land to be decorated in this way, but instead, decorated and ornamental farms are disappearing at an alarming rate. As a group, the silly agricultural forts at Badminton are pure pleasure. In the luscious green of summer the Ragged Castle was almost unfindable and certainly in an extremely bad state once found—however, the remainder are still looking fairly fit.

At Wrest Park, Bedfordshire, Archer's great baroque pavilion takes the prize, but then it didn't have much competition. At Badminton it must, despite the pleasures of the many follies, be Kent's awesome Worcester Lodge that comes out on top as an eyecatcher. Built in 1746, two years before Kent died and Wright succeeded him as garden building designer here, this lodge is more of an eyecatcher and belvedere in one. A rusticated lower storey is surmounted by a temple front and topped by a cupola, the whole flanked by two pyramid wings. It is in the vista from the house, although a long way away from it, presents a stunning view and can best be seen from a tolerable distance—from near the Ragged Castle, for example, when its scale appears enormous.

Barnsley

Alcove (late 18th century)
Grotto (1980s)
SP 070 050

Barnsley Park is off the A433 out of Cirencester; the house was built from 1720 by an unknown architect, who did a magnificent job and gave us one of the most beautiful houses in the county—but there are no follies, only the name Pepper Pot, which led us here in hope but turned out to be an octagonal lodge by Nash.

Barnsley House, the old rectory that was built for the same Bourchier family who owned the Park, has, however, two delightful garden buildings: an elegant Gothick alcove (more of a miniature cathedral front), and a Doric temple built in 1787. Both were removed from Fairford Park in 1962 by the writer of Gloucestershire's two 'Pevsners', David Verey. Simon Verity created a small shell grotto here in the 1980s.

It is difficult to pin down what makes the village of Barnsley so satisfying until the total absence of overhead wires, telephone cable and street furniture is pointed out. All necessary services are buried underground or hidden behind houses, rather like Lacock in Wiltshire and an example we wish could be followed everywhere.

Batsford

Japanese Garden (1880s)
SP 190 330

Lord Redesdale found fame through his garden. A man as talented as he could have reached the top in any of his chosen fields, but it is for his arboretum and Japanese gardens that he will be best remembered. As a diplomat he spent four years in Japan, coming away with an admiration for the country that he had an opportunity to convert to reality when a cousin died, leaving him his estate and his fortune. The garden at Batsford Park, near Moreton-in-Marsh, reflects Redesdale's enthusiasm for trees and for Japan: there are scattered Buddhas and a pretty red and white tea-house temple, set on a knoll in the arboretum.

Berkeley

Park Lodge (late 18th century)
Park House (late 18th century)
The Temple of Vaccus (late 18th century)
ST 685 990

In the grounds of Berkeley Castle is Park Lodge, which contains the stables, kennels and the estate offices. As it could have been noticed from the house, however, a Berkeley fortified it violently with black and white stone in the early 19th century, so now it cannot be missed. It is a nine-bay building, the central arch crowned with castellations.

In the deer park is the Tudorish Park House, with four towers on the corners—no doubt a hunting stand. There is a castellated cottage on the B4066 coming in to Berkeley, and in the village is the root hut called the Temple of Vaccus, where Edward Jenner (1749–1823) carried out the first vaccinations against smallpox. It is said to have been designed by Thomas Wright and is made of stone blocks and grizzled tree stumps and has a thatch roof—the sort of building that is constantly set afire by vandals.

Bisley

Obelisk (1721)
SO 900 050

At Bisley there is a 18th-century gazebo at Over Court, and at Jaynes Court there is an octagonal brick and stone cockpit-cum-

Jayne's Court Cockpit

dovecote, of the same century, but later.

In the grounds of Nether Lypiatt Manor is a small obelisk in the woods to the memory of a horse that died in 1721:

> *My name is Wag, who rolled the green*
> *The oldest horse that ever was seen,*
> *My age it numbered forty-two*
> *I served my Master just and true.*

The plaque is a replacement engraved on metal in 1938; the graffiti on the obelisk are old and extensive—1802 W. HUXFORD, G. L. WYATT 1828—they carved rather than scratched in those days. The manor house itself is exquisite: the quintessential small English country house, utterly desirable, perfectly proportioned and of a manageable size. It was built in 1702–5 by an unknown architect.

At Lypiatt Park (Upper Lypiatt) there are sham castle stables and fine gatehouses by Sir Jeffry Wyatville dating from c.1809.

Bristol (Avon)

Cabot Tower (1897–8)
Goldney's Grotto and Tower
(mid-18th century)
St Vincent's Priory (c.1810)
Tower (1729)
Cook's Folly (1693–1858)
Follies (20th century)
ST 570 730; ST 560 740

Bristol has a prodigious number of follies, almost every kind imaginable. Many are on the outskirts or in surrounding villages (Brislington, Warmley, Henbury, Hambrook and so on) and will be dealt with there (see also Somerset).

On Brandon Hill in the heart of Bristol, the 105ft (32m) Cabot Tower is a pink stone manifestation of Victorian confidence and assertiveness. Designed by W.V. Gough, who was also responsible for the inappropriate Port of Bristol Authority building, it was built in 1897–8, at a time when architects were not afraid of decoration. Like St Pancras Station, the Cabot Tower has enough detail to keep the eye occupied for some considerable time, but its primary function was to look from, not at. As a municipal tower in a public park, it is carefully maintained and usually open to the public for a small fee. John Cabot was the Venetian who set off from Bristol to discover America in 1497, and the somewhat belated monument to him reflects civic pride as much as pride in the city's most famous adopted son.

Thomas Goldney was another Bristol merchant of high repute and, if we can judge by what he has left us, a rare and elegant taste. His follies—just on the folly side of garden ornament—are small, well preserved, elegant, carefully looked after and quite enchanting. Goldney House is now a hall of residence for Bristol University, and the grounds are not open to the public. The natural site offered an obvious opportunity; the garden runs along an escarpment overlooking the Avon Gorge at Clifton, with all the panoramic benefits that suggests. At one end is a castellated circular summerhouse, built in 1757, unusually enough in the Jacobean style. It stands above a carefully manicured bastion, running 30 yards (27m) beyond the end of the garden and guarding the sympathetically designed student's quarters.

Back along the terrace walk from the summerhouse there is a most remarkable statue of an ancient Greek god playing baseball in the shadow of the small but satisfying folly tower. The tower has three storeys above a low entrance room, with extremely narrow Gothic windows on each storey, an open arch on the second storey and a porthole window at the top. Castellations and pinnacles complete an architecturally unimportant but oddly fascinating little tower. At around 40ft (12m) high, it is smaller than the trees that surround it.

Hard by the tower is the celebrated Goldney's Grotto, started in 1737, finished in 1764, and one of the best preserved and most remarkable of 18th-century grottoes. Notwithstanding several Folly Fellowship outings to visit this grotto, through force of circumstance these writers have never managed to be there when it has been open, but from all accounts it is spectacular, the walls lined with the most fantastic shells and mineral formations, and an extraordinary cascade. It is possible, when the entrance is

LITTLE EGYPT

Some Pyramids

NETHER WALLOP
Hampshire

———

FARLEY DOWN
Hampshire

———

BRIGHTLING
Sussex

———

BLICKLING
Norfolk

———

NOSTELL
West Yorkshire

———

KINKELL
Ross & Cromarty

———

CASTLE HOWARD
North Yorkshire

———

COMPTON WYNYATES
Warwickshire

———

GOATHURST
Buckinghamshire

———

TONG HEN HOUSE AND
RANDZ DES VACHES
Shropshire

———

BIDDULPH
Staffordshire

locked, to go down a Stygian passage on the right of the entrance (the passage on the left is a dead end) and venture along it as far as your courage will take you. In our case, without a torch, it was not very far.

St Vincent's Priory on Sion Hill, Clifton, is considered a folly, but its owners are much more interesting than the house itself, which was built around 1810 but looks a lot younger. It is tall and narrow, its main feature being the extraordinary bay windows, three on top of one another, leaving almost no wall space. The gambolling ladies serving as capitals to the uppermost bay window's columns leave no doubt that the ecclesiastical lettering above the entrance to the house and the florid cross topping the roof are a spoof, an impression confirmed by the little sphinxes above the entrance. In the house there are quasi-papal glazed windows, but again accompanied by classical faces. A bricked-up 'grotto-like room' was discovered late this century, but appears now to have gone. No doubt this must have been a fake monastery, like the ones the members of the Hell Fire Club liked to lounge in. This was once, in the mid-19th century, the home of 'Sir Richard Smyth', a mountebank and horse thief whose real name was Tom Provys and who claimed ownership to the Ashton Court Estate; he was eventually sentenced to 20 years' transportation.

In 1967 the property was bought by George Melhuish, an 'aesthete, artist, writer, agnostic and philosopher', so there must be something fishy there—yes, it turns out Mr Melhuish would don top hat and cane and peruse Clifton for able-bodied girls, and other things unmentionable in family reading. On his death in 1985, Melhuish left his house and contents as a museum to the City Gallery, but they turned it down—a shame. His bequest also appears to have included a £10,000 fee for any author 'deemed capable' of writing Melhuish's biography. Ah! now you're talking—look out for our next work. There was a row over the will, but apparently in the 1980s a memorial service was held in Bristol Cathedral for the totally agnostic Melhuish, with the Lord Mayor declining the invitation. It is claimed that gifts to the non-existent Brothers of St Vincent are still left on the pavement.

Close by the Clifton Suspension Bridge is a small tower with Beckfordian connections: an observatory (others say a windmill) built in 1729, but probably only embattled in the 1830s or 1840s, when Benjamin West, who designed a stained glass window for Fonthill Abbey (now in a Bristol church) turned it into a camera obscura.

Another, earlier, Clifton character had something to say about the other folly in the neighbourhood. Montague Summers (1880–1948), the noted occultist, Gothic novelist, Roman Catholic cleric and paedophile, tells the story of Cook's Folly in his autobiography *The Galanty Show*. It was built in 1693 by a man called Cook (John Cook, a wealthy merchant) as a belvedere or observatory, but the story Cliftonians will believe is that Cook had been warned by a gypsy that his son and heir would die by violence before reaching his 21st year. In order to prevent the prediction from coming true, Cook built his two-storey tower and immured

his son in it, although every imaginable luxury was catered for and food and drink were hoisted in with a rope and pulley. On the eve of the feared 21st birthday, the boy received bundles of faggots to keep him warm for the night—next morning his father at last entered the tower and found his son dead—the faggots had contained a hidden viper. Mrs Emma Marshall published a shocker about it in 1886, *The Tower on the Cliff*.

In 1783 it was described as 'a pleasure house', owned by a Mr Jackson. Further researches were carried out by Jonathan Holt and he has 'excavated' the building, which everyone thought had long gone: its place (on Cook's Folly Road!) is taken by a castellated house of 1858. Yet, the house is still reputed to be haunted because of a variant to the story above: a girl was imprisoned in the tower because of an unwanted relationship. One day the father found the suitor on a ladder. He fired a pistol, but instead of killing the young man he hit his daughter who had thrown herself in front of her lover.

On to more wholesome follies, dug up by Peter Godfrey. St Werburgh's City Farm on Mina Road has a retro café by Graham Caine, who fashions plywood into organic forms, which always tend to turn into Art Nouveau once you work with them. It is a very fine building with some of the greyish exterior looking like the 'cement rustic' that was so favoured by the French and Belgians between the wars. The interior has a veritable forest of Caine's half-faked wood, and the artist's own house, on Boiling Wells Lane, is, of course, a showcase for the material and looks rather like a chalet inhabited by Heidi who's been on a Blavatsky weekend.

In Wellington Road, ½ mile or so east of Cabot Tower, Mr McKenzie filled a *jardin imaginaire* with trivia, horseshoes, toys and dolls, the inevitable garden gnomes and hub caps. Things get stolen, are taken away by the owner, but replaced again.

Cambridge

Tower (1980s)
SO 748 038

A small, 15ft (4.6m) high, drystone round tower, with a conical roof stands just off the A38 at Ryall's Lane, constructed from stones left over after constructing a stone wall. It was evidently built for the fun of it, although it holds a clay model of the head of the builder's son.

Chalford

Grotto (late 18th–early 19th century)
Summerhouse (late 18th–early 19th century)
Gazebo (early 19th century)
SO 890 030

In the steep terraced grounds of a house called The Grove are a grotto and a summerhouse with three mighty ogees under a curved pediment, and in the garden of Wickham Grange is an early 19th-century gazebo. The Golden Valley of the Frome is aptly named in Chalford's case; the autumnal trees in the valley make a display worthy of New England, and the golden stone reflects what people have to pay to live in this village of steep hills and steep prices.

Cheltenham

Rock House (mid-19th century)
Caduceus Garden (1960 onwards)
SO 950 220

Rock House, which was destroyed as recently as 1978, was the best building in Cheltenham (folly-wise that is), but we have to have a reason for mentioning a demolished folly: Cheltenham has a small grotto in the grounds of Cheltenham College, mid-19th century.

And now we can safely drone on about Cheltenham's lost grotty house: Oliver Bradbury has researched the history of Rock House, a most delightful little house of *c.*1843 or possibly the 1830s, when it was known as Rockville, only to be named Rock House after the turn of the century. Its outside was of rough tufa, interspersed with light-coloured rocks and individual shells. Its inside had the same decoration, only even more laborious. There is the story that Captain Hardy ('Kiss me, Hardy') lived here or even built it, bringing over the tufa 'on his last voyage'. Bradbury suggests that the actual builder of Rockville may have been a T. Newman, grotto builder at Swiss Cottage, Cheltenham. The College grotto may, therefore, also be Newman's. Eventually, in the spring of 1978, Rock House was ripped down, its tufa blown to bits, its shells crushed. Bastards.

The Caduceus Garden remains, however, a private garden in the area of Cheltenham called Pittville, at Coach House. Created by Linden Huddlestone from the 1960s onwards, it contains statues and urns, but also a grotto, a tiny cattery, a mount and obelisk, a Gothick screen, a false door and various titbits, covering a space of about 25 by 5 metres, Bulwer-Lytton's 'the four

Chalford Gazebo

quarters of the globe in a mole-hill'. The Caduceus Garden is a very conscious joke on landscape gardens and their follies, made from left-overs, recycled material, copies and spoils, with elaborate references to the whole of gardening and building—it is the best fun to be had in Cheltenham. Mr Huddlestone is much involved with the Georgian Society and with Painswick Rococo Garden, so he knows of these things.

Chipping Campden

Sham Castle (1925)
SP 150 370

Going up to the far north of the county, a modernish folly has been built outside Chipping Campden. Sir Gordon Russell built a small-scale sham castle at Kingcombe in the garden designed by Geoffrey Jellicoe.

Cirencester

Alfred's Hall (1733)
Garden Buildings (mid-18th century)
SO 990 030

All roads lead to Cirencester, the ancient Roman capital of Corinium. The park laid by the Earl of Bathurst starts in the middle of town and stretches for 5 miles into the countryside. The house itself acts as the straight arc of a huge circle hedge of yew, as tall as the house, a device repeated by the Ten Rides rond-point in Oakley Wood. Lord Bathurst was the patron of Alexander Pope, and Pope's influence in Cirencester Park is seen everywhere. He helped Bathurst plan it, plant it and develop it with an almost proprietorial enthusiasm, even going so far as to call it 'my bower'.

What interests us most here is Alfred's Hall, one of the first 'romantick' follies in England. An admirable work of scholarship by Michael Cousins for the Folly Fellowship reveals that the present structure was complete by 1733, replacing the Wood House, an earlier structure on the site, which had been rather shoddily built in 1721. This collapsed in 1727, a narrow escape for Dean Swift who had been visiting Lord Bathurst. Mrs Pendarves wrote to Swift in 1733:

> My Lord Bathurst talked with great
> delight of the pleasure you once gave him
> by surprising him in his wood, and
> shewed me the house where you lodged. It
> has been rebuilt; for the day you left it, it
> fell to the ground; conscious of the
> honour it had received by entertaining so
> illustrious a guest, it burst with pride. It
> is now a venerable castle, and has been
> taken by an antiquarian for one of King
> Arthur's, 'with thicket overgrown,
> grotesque and wild'.

So much for antiquarians. Incidentally Mrs Pendarves later became Mrs Delany, whose voluminous correspondence has proved a fruitful source for all students of 18th-century social life, a sort of one-woman *Hello!* Magazine. She it was who wrote the famous letter about the building of the Conolly Folly outside Dublin:

> My sister is building an Obleix to answer
> a Vistoe from the Bake of Castletown. It
> will cost her 3 or 4 hundred pounds at
> least, and I believe more. I don't know
> how she can dow so much and live as she
> duse.

Bathurst had written to Pope the previous year, saying: 'I have almost finished my hermitage in the wood.' It is challenged as the first Gothick sham ruin in the country by John Freeman's ruin at Fawley Court, which was erected 'but a year since' in 1732, but it is unclear just when Bathurst began to rebuild his hermitage. As with the invention of television, inspiration appears to have struck in different places at the same time.

It is big; it was enlarged in 1732 with pieces taken from Sapperton Manor. The interior is wainscoted, with a large, carved chimneypiece. Sadly, part of the folly collapsed in the 1980s and this sham ruin, which has lasted over 260 years, is now in danger of becoming a real one. Despite the

recent collapse, it was carefully made, unlike many of its successors; Bathurst, who lived to be 91, was determined to build to last. Consequently, virtually every embellishment he made to the park survives today, despite the open access granted to the townspeople.

The Hexagon of 1736 is exactly what it says: three heavily rusticated open arches and three blind arches, set on a plinth; Pope's Seat is a little rusticated arch with seats in niches either side of a pedimented gateway; the Round House and the Square House are both cottages with castellated towers added; Ivy Lodge was an eyecatcher folly converted into a house with a square central tower and crow's foot gables at either end of the screen walls—one is merely a façade, decorated with sham windows. The Horse Guards are two Ionic alcoves ½ mile before the Ten Rides rond-point, and the final Bathurst buildings are Queen Anne's Column, built in 1741 with a statue of Queen Anne on the top, and an obelisk on the edge of the Bull Ring. A word of warning to people who stroll up to the park gates in Cirencester: it will take you 2½ hours brisk walking to get to Alfred's Hall and back. We know from bitter experience.

At the time of writing plans are being made for the restoration of Alfred's Hall.

Coleford

Rock House (after 1818)
SO 570 100

The Forest of Dean's most unexpected pleasure is to be found in the town of Coleford, which is dominated by a big Beecham's factory to the south. Coleford is neither particularly beautiful nor ancient, the oldest house being 17th century, but in Newland Street is a 19th-century Gothic sham castle like a pink fairy armadillo, now a dentist's surgery called the Rock House. It has no certain provenance, but speculation leads us to conclude that the architect may have been the Rev. Henry Poole, Vicar of Coleford from 1818. He was passionately fond of building and designed churches at Coleford, Parkend, Bream and Berry Hill.

Clearwell Castle to the south is another very early example (c.1727) of neo-Gothicism in Gloucestershire, but it is a castle, not a folly.

Compton Greenfield (Avon)

Hollywood Park Tower (c.1848–54)
ST 570 820

On the M5 a tall tower can be seen to the west of Junction 17. This is the Hollywood

Park Tower, and it now stands on land owned by Bristol Zoo in Compton Greenfield. The tower is square, with chamfered corners, battlemented and with a taller stair turret. Buttressed at the base and with a relatively small clock-face, it looks more like a church tower without a church than almost any other folly. It was built for Sir John Davis some time between 1848 and 1854, and although the architect's original drawings still exist, they are unfortunately unsigned. Sir George White, the last private owner, believes it may have been Francis Niblett, the church architect, who was active in this area at the time. Davis had purchased the estate, then called Holly Hill, in 1839, but did not retire from the Governorship of Hong Kong until 1848. Sir Stanley White, Sir George White's grandfather, said that Sir John either won or was given the clock, and had to build a tower to put it in. In the early years of aviation it was used by the Whites as a landmark to fly around, and even the *Graf Zeppelin* used to dip its nose in salute as it cruised by when the flag was being lowered.

Cromhall (Avon)

Tower (c.1850)
ST 690 900

Lord Ducie, whose activities at Woodchester and North Nibley are followed elsewhere (see below), commissioned the reviled but prolific High Victorian architect S.S. Teulon to design him a new house at Tortworth, a Viollet-le-Duc derived fantasia. When the house became Leyhill Open Prison the word 'WELCOME' over the archway was removed. The remains of a Ducie-inspired tower are hidden in the undergrowth of Priest Wood by Cromhall, a mile to the south.

Dodington (Avon)

Tower (1764)
Bath Lodge (1802)
ST 750 800

Dodington House has a fine cascade, designed by Lancelot Brown in 1764, complete with a castellated tower like a toy fort and ice-house, although Sylvia Beamon, who is our expert on cold buildings, thinks it may be very much older, but modified. Somehow, although undeniably impressive, it is not as pleasing as the rotunda-like Bath Lodge to the south, designed by James Wyatt in 1802.

Drybrook

Euroclydon Hotel (1876)
SO 640 160

The *Companion Guide to the Shakespeare Country* describes Drybrook as 'probably the most consistently horrible village in the Forest of Dean'. The Euroclydon Hotel, somewhat uncommercially named after a cold, vindictive east wind, is a residential hotel for elderly people, built on a hill above the town. It is a large, unremarkable black and white building, except for a five-storey square tower, which erupts from the south side and is adorned by a wrought-iron balcony looking north over the roof of the house. It was built by a mine-owner, J.B. Brain, in 1876 in order to keep a watchful eye on his workers, so the story goes, and it is now used as a loft for the hotel owner's doves.

Fairford

Obelisk (late 18th century)
SP 150 020

Gloucestershire has a number of inscriptionless columns commemorating some forgotten event or person. At Fairford Park a comprehensive school stands on the site of a 17th-century mansion, demolished in the 1950s. A short but elegant 18th-century column, perhaps by Sir John Soane, who carried out some alterations to the house in 1789, stands in a field to the north.

Frampton on Severn

Orangery (mid-18th century)
SO 750 060

In the Vale of Berkeley we could be entering a different country. The scenery is uninspiring, but the villages are pretty. Frampton Court in Frampton on Severn boasts the finest garden pavilion in Gloucestershire, and one of the finest in Britain, the Orangery. It is a stunning, virtuoso display of Gothick by the Bristol architect William Halfpenny: two two-storey octagons are linked by an entrance bay, with an octagon on top; everything is castellated and pinnacled; every façade is lit by a beautiful ogee-framed honeycomb-paned window; and a cupola crowns it all. It is the most florid interpretation of the Gothick style we have seen and a sheer delight in every part—but the windows are its chief glory. It stands at the end of an ornamental canal in the grounds of the big house of the Cliffords and is, according to the local publican, often let to visiting Americans.

Frenchay (Avon)

Grotto (1820s)
ST 630 770

Frenchay was very much a Quaker community, and here we have a Quaker grotto again, built at Lake House in the early 19th century. The present owner, Stephanie Cawthorn, has not been able to find out anything about the grot, but the thing is relatively complete, with lots of minerals, shells and, of course, ammonites (there must be a huge quarry of these beasts in the Bristol area, because this is where, compared with the rest of Britain, they are most used in grotto decoration), and a terracotta head or mask. It also holds an 'altar'.

Gloucester

Addison's Folly (1864)
SO 840 170

Another of those handy two-in-one follies: Addison's Folly, a small castellated tower next to a house almost as high, was built by the solicitor Thomas Fenn Addison in order to express his appreciation of Robert Raikes, founder of the Sunday School movement, and so that he could have a view of Hempstead churchyard, where Hannah, his wife, was buried.

Hambrook (Avon)

Gerizim (1853)
ST 640 780

Behind Hambrook House is Gerizim, an ice-house with a church steeple on top. The steeple comes from Winterbourne, where it was replaced in 1853 after having been struck by lightning 26 years earlier. The man who took the steeple home was the Rev. John Pring of Hambrook House, head of the Church of England School at Winterbourne. Gerizim is one of a pair of Old Testament mountains, so its twin, Ebal, may also be around.

Hawkesbury (Avon)

Somerset Monument (1846)
ST 770 870

Lord Edward Somerset, one of Wellington's major-generals, had a long and distinguished military career in Europe, as befitted a son of the Duke of Beaufort. He died in 1842 at the age of 66, and shortly afterwards work started on this distantly beautiful tower. It was designed by Lewis Vulliamy, one of the more fashionable early Victorian architects, whose mastery of the Gothic was said to have been 'far in advance of his contemporaries'. It is something of a puzzle, therefore, why the

Frampton Court Orangery

style of the tower and particularly the ornate stonework on the roof seems more Indian than anything else, since neither Vulliamy nor Somerset had any connection with India. As if to excuse this heathen decoration, the top of the tower is surmounted by a large cross. This is a rarity among follies: it is easily accessible, in superb condition, and for a small fee (payable at the tower-keeper's cottage) one can climb it. The view, as expected, is extensive, the wind on the day we visited was phenomenal. 'I reckon you'll be blowed away when you get up the top there,' said the towerman cheerily.

The marble slab inside the doorway records the valiant derring-do of Lord Somerset, and a damp but comfortably solid spiral staircase led up to a balcony, where the wind made it nearly impossible to stand. Not a hint of movement from the tower though; Vulliamy's talent and its continued upkeep have ensured its survival.

Henbury (Avon)

Blaise Hamlet (1811)
Tower (1766)
Rustic Lodge (c.1830s)
ST 560 770

A short way off the motorway in Henbury lies Blaise Hamlet, the picturesque yet eminently practical model village designed by John Nash in 1811 for the retired estate workers of a Quaker, the banker John Scandrett Harford. There was already a folly on the estate, a triangular castle on the hilltop, built in 1766 for a previous owner, Thomas Farr, by Robert Mylne at a cost of £3000. It differs from the standard run of

triangular folly towers in having a circular core, with three slightly taller round turrets on the corners. Today it looks crisp and clean, mantled with a carefully controlled amount of ivy and looked after by Bristol City Museum. Even the entrance doorway is blocked up with matching stone.

The Rustic Lodge is a different building from the rest of Blaise Hamlet—it is of an uncertain date (possibly 1830s) but can stand on its own as a folly, while the hamlet must be viewed as a whole. Made of tree trunks, branches, bark, sticks and, of course, thatch, it caught fire in 1991, but was admirably restored by the aptly named St Blaise Ltd—rustick follies a speciality.

Highnam Court

Grotto (1849)
SO 790 190

Highnam Court has a rock garden by James Pulham Jr, made from clinkers and cement that was poured over picturesquely formed mounds of clinker. Work started in 1849, and the owner, Thomas Gambier Parry, took a keen interest and had more features done by Pulham: a megalithic cave and two grottoes, one of which is called Owl Cave and had a statue of the bird in it. The gardens are now a little worn, but are being restored. Highnam Court also has the usual appendages: lodges, boathouse and embattled stables.

Kingsweston (Avon)

The Loggia (c.1714)
Brewhouse (c.1714)
ST 540 770

Vanbrugh worked here and designed, among others, a very neat classical building, almost Italian in flavour, the Loggia, as well as the Echo, a banqueting house of which now only the walls stand. Almost everything at Kingsweston had to do with the consumption of either liquids or solids—the enchanting Penpole Gate, a gazebo and 'breakfast lodge', was demolished in 1952, but the brewhouse or alehouse remains. Now that would have been a country house that *should* be made into a restaurant!

Lower Swell

Spa Cottage (1807)
SP 170 240

Lower Swell near Stow-on-the-Wold was another village with aspirations to become a

Spa Cottage, Lower Swell

spa, after a chalybeate spring was discovered there. A cottage at the east end was built in 1807 as the Spa Cottage; it is probably surprisingly large inside, but from the outside the central section is tiny. Like a child's drawing of a house, the front door is in the middle with a window on either side, and two more windows on the next floor. The door is surmounted by a solid stone, carved canopy, and the windows with their large diamond-patterned paning have Gothic ogee surrounds. The parapet frieze is ornately carved, and the dormer windows have concave gables, immediately giving the cottage an oriental flavour. The double windows in the side extensions have attractive shell fanlights.

The only thing against this charming cottage is that it stands right by the main road. It is supposed that the materials used in its construction were overs from Sezincote, so it may possibly have been designed by Samuel Cockerell, although Lower Swell has a much more vernacular air about it.

Marshfield (Avon)

Three Shire Stone (1736)
Grotto (18th century)
ST 790 720

Marshfield used to be on the border of Somerset, Gloucestershire and Wiltshire, so somebody at the Rocks erected a sham tetralithon in 1736 on the Roman road to Batheaston and called it the Three Shire Stones. Nearby, set in the park wall, is an elaborate spandrel-arched doorway, blocked up with massive stones. In Beek's Lane is a stone pillar with a ball finial and a badly weathered inscription—'over the hill' are, suitably, the only words we could decipher.

The Rocks consists of the ruins of a 19th-century sham castle and Rocks East Woodland was its park, now a forest. A cave and a grotto have been discovered in the undergrowth, as well as the remains of a 17th-century pond. The whole is now being surveyed, and perhaps, in the near future, we can witness the emergence of yet another lost folly garden.

North Nibley

Tyndale Monument (1866)
ST 742 955

Gloucestershire's tallest tower monument is S.S. Teulon's Tyndale Monument, 111ft (34m) high on Nibley Knoll above North Nibley and visible for miles around. It was as good an excuse as any that William Tyndale had been born in North Nibley 382 years before the monument was built, and convenient that there happened to be a perfect site for a tower, clearly visible from

The Tyndale Monument, North Nibley

Lord Ducie's new estate in Tortworth. It was opened by Lord Ducie on 6 November 1866, a tall, tapering belvedere tower with a pyramidal roof:

ERECTED A. D. 1866

IN GRATEFUL REMEMBRANCE OF

WILLIAM TYNDALE

TRANSLATOR OF THE ENGLISH BIBLE

WHO FIRST CAUSED THE NEW TESTAMENT

TO BE PRINTED IN THE MOTHER TONGUE

OF HIS COUNTRYMEN

BORN NEAR THIS SPOT HE SUFFERED

MARTYRDOM AT VILVORDE IN

FLANDERS ON OCT 6TH 1536.

Also in attendance on that inaugural day was the vicar of North Nibley, Rev. David Edwards. We shall come across Mr Edwards again in Stancombe Park (see Stinchombe, below). Biographical information on people from the 15th century being what it is, there is a strong suspicion that the William Tyndale of North Nibley was not the same as the William Tyndale, 'born on the borders of Wales', who translated the Bible, in which case the monument is pure folly.

The monument is one of those rare towers that can be climbed; the key can be obtained from a house in the village, and the address is given on a notice board at the beginning of the path to the tower. To help spot distant landmarks, there is a topograph near the tower, erected to commemorate Queen Elizabeth's 1977 Jubilee.

Ozleworth

Parsons' Folly (1980s)
Lodges (1832; c.1820)
ST 781 931

Robert L. Parsons from Texas has been restoring Newark Park for over 20 years and is praised for it in Verey. He has discovered several garden buildings in the undergrowth, restored them as well, but had to do without one particular eyecatcher sham castle, which had long been lost. So he decided to construct his own as well as he could: it is a picturesque construction of castellated walls, towerettes, ruined Gothic windows and arches.

The Reform Lodge to Newark Park is Gothic and must be from about 1832.

Ozleworth Park has a large, round bath house temple, with a cold bath. Built in an odd classical style with small oval windows in its dome, it probably dates from around 1800.

At nearby Combe a very pleasing folly on top of Rushmire Hill has disappeared, demolished in 1925 or 1926. It was called The Towers, and that was exactly what it was—four fat, cemented, be-quatrefoiled and embattled towers, linked to form the tollgate house. It must have dated from 1820, when the nearby Ridge House was built. A lodge survives. On the opposite site from Wotton-under-Edge stands another one, just circular and embattled, but of approximately the same date.

Parson's Folly, Ozleworth

Painswick

Garden Buildings (1730s–40s)
SO 876 970

North of Stroud is Painswick, a sleek, wealthy little town. The M5 has taken much

The Eagle House

of the holiday traffic away, but the A46 running through the town remains a busy road. Painswick House is to the northwest. Built in the 1730s, it was originally called Buenos Ayres, and Bishop Pococke visited it in 1757:

> Mr Hyett built an house of hewn stone, in a fine situation, and made a very pretty garden; before it is a court with statues and sphynxes, and beyond that a lawn for the grand entrance; the garden is on an hanging ground from the house in the vale, and on a rising ground on the other side and at the end; all are cut into walks through wood and adorn'd with water and buildings.

Some of the buildings still remain. There is a classical seat with rusticated columns, the classical Pigeon House, a rather uninspired Gothic alcove with proof that hooliganism is hereditary—graffiti reads 'B. Perrott 1952' and elsewhere 'Gary Perrott 1973'—a rustic alcove by a bathing pool, two pavilions, the beautiful Gothick Red House and the Eagle House.

The garden, which became derelict after the war and is now undergoing extensive replanting and refurbishment, is convincingly attributed to Thomas Robins, who also built a castellated stable barn with quatrefoil and

diocletian windows out of the beautiful honey coloured Cotswold stone (which he then painted red) on the other side of the Painswick valley. No longer red, it now stands opposite Greenhouse Court, but it was originally the stable to Pan's Lodge, a vanished pleasure house of Hyett's.

Since this was written, the restorations at Painswick have come to a close, with the whole park now marketed as Painswick Rococo Garden, which it is, a remarkable survival-cum-reconstruction of that most interesting phase, the transcendence from formal to informal. The Gothick Eagle

The Red Barn before its conversion into a house

House, built above a grotto-arch, has made its entrance again (the top part was missing) and so has the Exedra, while small cascades and pools are all about the place. An enchanting little park.

Prestbury

Remains of Grotto Tea Gardens
(19th century)
SO 970 230

There is a fine Gothick house on Cleeve Hill as we come into Cheltenham from Winchcombe, but there is nothing grand now left to see in Gloucestershire. The Grotto Tea Gardens with a Chinese temple and, of course, a shell grotto ('in the Gothic

Stile') at Prestbury a mile along the road were the height of fashion in the late 18th and early 19th centuries. Towards the middle of the 19th century, however, they acquired a liquor licence, and the pleasure grounds quickly became disreputable and licentious. Local opinion put a stop to these activities when the grotto was demolished in the 1860s. Not completely though—a diligent search in the undergrowth behind the hotel can reveal a 5ft (1.5m) plinth for a lamp, the sad remnant of forgotten fun.

Ruardean

Tower (early 19th century)
SO 620 160

At Ruardean the Bishop's Wood valley is bisected by the Hereford–Gloucestershire border. There are now forestry roads, wide and red, cutting up the valley but here and there are echoes of a grander past—a South Lodge on the main road with a coat of arms, the remains of what may have been an ice-house, two overgrown lakes, but the memory of what used to be has been excised from local minds: all except for The Oldest Inhabitant. 'Yes, there used to be a big house here, but it must have been demolished oh, over eighty years ago—before I was born!' he grinned. It was owned by Sir George Bellew, whose crest with three bees was on the lodge wall, and previously by a Major Macalman, who achieved much success with a racehorse named Isinglass. In fact, the house here was built for John Partridge by Sir Jeffry Wyatville in 1820, in the Gothick style, and burned down in 1873. The most tangible relic is, amazingly, a splendidly preserved folly tower, perhaps somewhat pedestrian in its architecture, certainly a copy of the work of earlier, more innovative designers and thus dated to the early 19th century—it must have been built before Wyatville's house.

It is a standard folly tower pattern, octagonal, battlemented, with a taller stair turret. The windows are modern because it has been converted into a house, with an extension, hesitantly castellated to blend in when seen from the Ruardean road, added at the back.

Selsley

Column (18th–19th centuries)
SO 830 020

Below Selsley, southwest of Stroud, is an Ionic column on a plinth standing anonymously in a field under Stanley Park.

Seven Springs

Thames Monument (19th century)
SO 969 171

The Thames Headstone at Coates was a statue of Neptune, which sat in a meadow to mark the source of the Thames. It was put there by the Thames Water Authority in 1958 and removed 15 years later because of vandalism. Nowadays there is nothing to see, not even in the Thames Head pub nearby.

There is however a plaque at Seven Springs, where it is claimed that the Thames emerges in the guise of the River Churn:

HIC TUUS O TAMESINE PATER
SEPTEMCEMINUS PONS

Reginald Dixon writes that the nearby round house was built by William Hall in 1840 as an early parcel office.

Sezincote

Sezincote House (1805)
SP 170 300

Sezincote must be recognized as Samuel Cockerell's masterpiece. Built for his brother Sir Charles Cockerell in 1805 in the 'Hindoo' style, it still impresses today because it comes as such a surprise, rather like a Cotswold Brighton Pavilion. In ruins, it would unhesitatingly be described as a folly; as a sturdy, well-cared for and very private country house it can only be described as an eccentricity.

Siddington

Tower (late 18th century)
SP 050 973

Just south of Cirencester are the villages of Coates and Siddington. The Round House at Siddington is castellated and looks like a converted 18th-century windmill, although the occupier swears it never was but instead was built by a Dutchman. Why that should serve as an explanation we cannot imagine.

Stanway

Pyramid (1750)
SP 050 320

On Lidcombe Hill above Stanway stands a tall pyramid, which was built by Robert Tracy in 1750 to commemorate his father. The beautiful Tudor manor house of the Tracys sits peacefully in the valley, guarded by its remarkable gatehouse, but the pyramid is even more remarkable. Some 6oft (18m) high, it is probably the largest pyramid in the

British Isles. It stands on an open arched base and forms the centrepiece of the cascades and water gardens that tumbled down the hill. The high-level canal no longer exists; as the owner of Stancombe Park remarked, playing around with waterworks is the quickest way to go bankrupt.

Under the aegis of Lord Neidpath, the glorious cascades are now being restored again, together with the canal, which was filled in in 1824 when a publican's wife drowned in it.

Staunton

Columns (18th century)
SO 790 290

Staunton on the Worcestershire border has some Ionic columns set up in a garden on the B4208.

Stinchcombe

Stancombe Park Follies (19th century)
ST 740 980

Stancombe Park in Stinchcombe is just north of North Nibley. Too recent to be a legend, the story of the Vicar's Secret Garden smacks more of rumour and the Sunday papers. In the mid-19th century Miss Purnell, who owned Stancombe Park, married the Rev. David Edwards, vicar of North Nibley. He set

about building a romantic garden far from the house where, so the local story goes, he could have assignations with the gypsy woman who was his one true love, without being observed. It is difficult to see how he could have managed this, as the garden would have been constantly filled with workmen building paths, cascades, grottoes, temples, waterworks and all the other impedimenta that Mr Edwards felt were essential to the creation of a mood. However, the mood he eventually achieved was romantic in the extreme; any gypsy with fire in her blood would have capitulated immediately.

The house is a jewel. It looks earlier than 1840 but is actually later; the 1840 house was burned down and mostly rebuilt in 1880. The site, at the head of one of the most beautiful, naturally-landscaped valleys in England, is magnificent. An iron-fenced path winds gently downhill underneath the immaculate main garden, looking high and over the valley to the Tyndale Monument, and down to a small lake in the valley with an island reached by a Chinese bridge. As the path gives way to steps, so the mood changes from serenity to mystery; we are aware of the sound of rushing water, the air becomes humid, the atmosphere torrid—even in March! Massive replanting is going on; the owners are justifiably proud of their remarkable garden.

The Temple at Stancombe Park

Suddenly it becomes paths—there are stone-flagged paths everywhere, a multiple-choice garden. The main one goes into a tunnel under the old drive, emerges briefly into the light—giving enough time for a huge white stone dog to startle visitors—then plunges into blackness again, a seeming cul-de-sac but for a pinpoint light at the end. The light looks out over the lake, and here the path divides, the left leading around under a pergola-covered lakeside walk, the right to another underground junction. Here, a straight path leads to what is the most memorable part of the garden: a small square court with a plain urn in the centre and a doorway on each side, one a whalebone arch, one a Cretan doorway with curved lintel and the third an extraordinary affair like a keyhole

The Stancombe Ankh

or an Egyptian ankh—straight out of *The Story of the Amulet*. The sense of mystery is dispelled only by the light traffic on the B4060 right behind the hedge—we are a long way here from the house.

The flawless hedges flank a narrow path leading from the keyhole gateway around the foot of the lake and past the Thessalian Boar and a massive whale's skull to the newly restored (1997) Temple, a small golden-stoned Tuscan eyecatcher-cum-summerhouse, ignorant of the punctiliousness of true classical architecture, but freely using its motifs to make a warm and welcoming building. At the end of the

Temple walk are two little leaded glass summerhouses like Tweedledum and Tweedledee, guarding the corner.

Could this all have been built by a love-lorn vicar? The folly garden may be remote and invisible from the house, but it is behind a hedge right next to the road and is flanked by servant's cottages; moreover the old main drive to the house runs right over the garden and is used as a landscape feature. The present owner's theory is that the garden predated Rev. Edwards, and was built by persons unknown in about 1820 who learned the motifs from soldiers who had served in the Egyptian campaigns in the Napoleonic Wars. Stancombe is one of the most satisfying gardens in the country and, although private, it is often open to the public in the summer months. Don't miss it.

Restorations are continually carried out on the buildings, and Mrs Barlow is busy on a Menagerie Walk (a squirrel, a bear, a gorilla and a pig in box), and plans to built a sham ruin near one of the ponds.

Stoke Gifford (Avon)

Stoke Park Obelisk (18th century)
Sarcophagus (c.1770)
Tower (c.1800)
ST 620 790

After Badminton (see above) Thomas Wright appears again as the landscape gardener at Stoke Park, the seat of Norborne Berkeley, now a hospital. All but one of the buildings for which Wright may have been responsible (a copy of the Monument to the Horatii and the superbly named Bladud's Temple of Bladud's Cell among them) have not only vanished but have been forgotten, but there are reported to be an obelisk (dated 1732) to the memory of a Berkeley, and, in the woods, the sarcophagus (1834) of a horse that won the St Leger, although this must surely be the other way round, with the dates mixed up as well. There is a sarcophagus, but this is certainly by Thomas Wright, c.1770, to the memory of the 4th Duke of Beaufort; it is splendidly sited and executed, very antique. Now the temples are to be brought back again—is there no end to folly restitution and restoration?

In Stapleton Road, more in the direction of Bristol itself and wedged between motorway and railway (just beyond the railway bridge, in fact), is a sandstone tower, which belonged to the Easton Estate. The ground floor is squarish, but the two storeys on top of that form the round tower proper, which is embattled, of course. The pointed, bricked-up entrance, does have a Thomas Wright feel to it, but we shouldn't be carried away; it is probably later and not good enough for Wright.

Stow-on-the-Wold

Enoch's Tower (1848)
SP 190 250

In Oddington Road stands a plain, squat, four-storey, castellated building called Enoch's Tower, built in 1848 by a local man, Richard Enoch, who appears to have had a reputation as a philanthropist. The tower housed his private museum of curiosities. Fifty years later it was converted into a house, and more recently an even uglier extension has been built. Three counties may be seen from its top.

Stroud

Rodborough Fort (1761–1869)
SO 850 030

Stroud has The Castle in Castle Street, with a sham 19th-century castle in front of it, which we haven't seen. Much more exciting, however, is Rodborough Fort, which is directly above the town to the south, on the edge of Rodborough Common. It is a massive sham castle, on the scale of Bladon Castle in Derbyshire, and was built in 1761 by Captain Hawker as an eyecatcher (and also to hold cannon to protect the town). Rebuilt as a house in 1869, it is a typical folly of pedestrian imagination: square towers with heavy battlements, a taller stair turret and cross arrowslits. Big and noticeable, but somehow oddly unsatisfying as a folly.

Tetbury

The Folly
Grotto (18th century)
ST 870 950

We haven't yet hunted out The Folly, very derelict, in woodlands near Folly Farm. It may have disappeared. At Upton House, Tetbury Upton, is an 18th-century grotto close to the house.

Tutshill

Tower (18th century)
ST 540 940

The Wye valley, which separates Wales from the Forest of Dean, is beautiful. Across the

Enoch's Tower, Stow-on-the-Wold

river from Chepstow and its great, grand castle is Tutshill, with the ruined shell of a rubble look-out tower on top of the hill overlooking the castle and river. It is only listed Grade II because no one knows what it was and whether it was used as a prospect tower or for military purposes. 'Tut', as in Tutshill, means watchtower in the local dialect, so the owner argues that it must have had a military significance—but there is a fireplace, and would the builder have been that concerned about the comfort of a mere sentry?

Along the road at Parson's Allotment in Tidenham Chase a tall standing stone has been raised to commemorate Queen Victoria's Jubilee—the citizens of the county are punctilious in observing royal jubilees.

Warmley (Avon)

Warmley Gardens Follies (1750s–60s)
ST 680 740

The outskirts of Bristol are tawdry. As in New Jersey, what beauty once lived in the landscape has been erased by indiscriminate ribbon development and indifferent planning regulations. The Kingsway Trailer Park at Warmley is not a pretty site. Row upon row of mobile homes stand hopelessly on a patch of scrubby, unhealthy looking land. In this unpromising locale the sudden appearance of a colossal statue of Neptune towering above the caravans and surrounded with a halo of ivy comes as a real shock. The lady who lived in the mobile home closest to the statue was eager to explain. 'That's King Neptune, that is, he used to have a tripod but now they've taken it away and I'm glad because it used to be ever so scary at night. And a crown, but it's all covered up with ivy.'

Neptune's right or reason to be there was unquestioned. The trailer park is the bed of a drained lake, once the major feature of the estate of William Champion, a Quaker zinc and copper smelter. Neptune stood in the middle of the lake proudly and economically, being built of furnace slag (the merits of this unusual building material are described in the entry for Brislington, Somerset). His cement face has fallen away; indeed, stripped of his trident it is difficult now to make out his shape except for his thunderous thighs. Five times taller than the caravans surrounding him, his calves alone are too big to be encircled with both arms.

Champion's boathouse remains, bridging the carefully tamed stream, which is all that is left of his lake. Built, along with the rest of the estate, in the 1750s–60s when Champion was employing more than 2000 people in his works, it has the typical folly battlements, and once again was built of spelter slag. It has been converted with the utmost lack of understanding into a house. The black slag has been painted white, the white corner stones have been painted black, the building looks like a negative. Compressed round the bottom of the towerlet is a modern timber-clad house, totally unsympathetic to the good Quaker's architectural intentions. What would happen to the remnants of the estate when we first wrote about Warmley was anybody's guess.

Eventually, things worked out better than anyone dared hope for. The Avon Industrial Buildings Trust and Kingswood History Society have pooled resources, and large parts of Champion's remarkable 101 Things To Do With Slag have been discovered and restored: the embattled summerhouse, the boathouse, a wall, tower, ice-house and the weird clock tower (bell dated 1764). The greatest find was probably the grotto—slag and clinker, of course—which used to have cascades, pools and channels and probably originated from an earlier industrial setting.

Westbury on Trym (Avon)

Eyecatcher (1822 or 1828)
ST 580 770

The eyecatcher at The Ridgeway, Brentry, a small housing estate (about £400,000 a house in 1989), looks like the best 18th-century rogue architecture could offer—a screen of rubble stone with a pointed archway, a lovely large traceried window and two turrets, one with its spire still in attention—yes, they knew how to make them, these folly builders, but you can always tell, can't you … Well, we couldn't. This turns out to be a genuine 15th-century ruin, although moved about a bit by the owner in 1822 or 1828 (sources differ). It was part of the Mayor's Chapel at Bristol's College Green, but we are sure things must have been added and 'restored' in the 1820s—the screen looks too good, and the spooky turrets are certainly folly work.

Whiteway

Whiteway Colony (1898)
SO 910 110

Whiteway is a Tolstoyan colony and as a survival is rare enough—all decisions in the community are still taken collectively. It is, of course, not a folly, but some of its buildings must rate as interesting *ad hoc* architecture. The settlers built their own village hall, houses and workshops, trying to be self-sufficient. The colony was founded in 1898 (at the time of writing it is a century old, although we visited in the early 1990s), and some of its inhabitants have been living there since the 1930s. There are still a few corrugated iron huts to be seen, some beautiful, folksy gardens, bungalows with D-I-Y verandas and something labelled Lucifer Lodge.

Wick (Avon)

Gateway (19th century)
ST 710 730

As one approaches Wick, one suddenly comes across the enormous columns at the Gateway to Tracy Park near Doynton, now a country club. At the south entrance they are circular and brick built, with Doric capitals and grossly over-proportioned cornices, which appear capable of holding the mightiest of arches instead of the thin air they do support. At the north entrance the columns are square; more like gate piers, the same overstated size, but this time the cornices are embellished with masonic symbols.

Woodchester Park Tower and Mansion

Winchcombe

Grotto (early 18th century)
SP 020 280

Winchcombe, on the road to Cheltenham, was once the county town of the long-forgotten Winchcombshire; then it was the second most important town in Gloucestershire; next it became the centre of Britain's tobacco plantations. A remarkable history lies behind this little town, which now has a population of only 4000. Bleby House in Abbey Terrace has a small, early 18th-century shell grotto in the garden, which slopes down to the Isbourne, and it is one of the few English grottoes that may have been inspired by religious rather than fashionable sentiments. Winchcombe was the shrine of St Kenelm, and the grotto is said to have been built on the spot where he died. In Hailes Street is a house called The Follies—false alarm.

Woodchester

Woodchester Park Tower (1720s)
Woodchester Mansion (1840s–60s)
SO 840 020

Woodchester Park Tower, in the Inchbrook valley, overlooks Woodchester Mansion, which was planned and built for William Leigh from 1846 onwards. It would seem that if ever house deserved to be called a folly, this one does. On the advice of A.W.N. Pugin, Leigh demolished Spring Park, Lord Ducie's house, where J.A. Repton had been working some 20 years earlier, but jibbed at paying the price Pugin proposed for the new house. He therefore employed Benjamin Bucknall, a local man, and for 15 years the house slowly took shape. The reason for the leisurely speed of building is unclear, but it would appear to be linked with Mr Leigh's parsimony. A datestone on the tower reads 1858; shortly after that time work stopped and the mansion was never finished. It is magnificently built, in the style of Viollet-le-Duc, using solid stone throughout, even for baths and drainpipes. The wooden scaffolding is still in place.

Now to the tower: it is two storeys high, embattled, but very austere, with a tall central chimney, and it commands a fine view over the landscape. The tower predates the unfinished mansion and may, according to Oliver Bradbury, be the hunting lodge, which was built here *c.*1720. A story disputes this and says its function was to act as a watchtower while 'illicit liaisons went on in the Georgian mansion'.

HAMPSHIRE

Hampshire is a big, quiet county with much to boast about but little need to. Two factors have led to its relative peace, inasmuch as any southern English county can be called peaceful: it is buffered from London by Surrey and reasonably poor communications, and it has protected itself from tourists by achieving an almost completely urban, industrial and military coastline. The miles of golden sands so beloved of trippers did once exist in the county, but then Bournemouth was cunningly shifted into Dorset, which caters for that sort of person. We have arbitrarily reinstated it here. What remains as a result is a large county, with very few tourists and dotted with picturesque villages apparently all set in parkland. Here nature anticipated Lancelot Brown.

Real Hampshire is to be found in the villages and small towns. Alton, Petersfield, New Alresford, Lyndhurst are all far more typical of the county than Aldershot, Basingstoke, Farnborough and Portsmouth. Winchester, the first capital of England, is, like all capitals, a law unto itself, while Southampton, which gave its name to the county, took advantage of its superb natural deep-water port and eagerly embraced commerce. The army and the navy have both chosen Hampshire as their headquarters, with the result that the county is packed with retired generals and admirals, while Farnborough and aircraft are indissolubly linked.

But while these towns and fighting men are in Hampshire, they are not part of Hampshire. There is a reserve in the county of which Chesterton would have approved as being quintessentially English. Overlords may come and go, but the rural Hampshire Hog ambles on his way, watching his rulers' antics with patience, condescension and occasional bafflement. In just such a bemused way the natives must have watched their masters as sudden orders were given to run up a little frippery of a building here, an obelisk there, all to no apparent purpose. The final outcome has yet to be decided, for here, far more so than in any other English county, the joy of folly building has not died. Since 1973 several follies have been planned and built, and an already lovely garden has been enhanced still further through the addition of a monumental column (already making its bow on the Ordnance Survey map as 'MON.'), a grotto and other garden ornaments.

Avington

Pavilion (18th century)
SU 540 320

Avington Park has a Doric temple pavilion, now converted into a flat.

Boldre

Walhampton Grotto and Arch
(early 19th century)
SZ 330 950

Hampshire cannot boast folly groups or gardens to compare with Stowe (see Buckinghamshire) or Stourhead (see Wiltshire), but a few estates have more than the traditional solitary Greek temple to offer. Walhampton House, now a school, in the

parish of Boldre (but really much nearer Lymington), has a fine grotto, a marble arch and a mount view, all said to have been built in the 1780s for Admiral Sir Harry Burrard Neale. The building called the Boatswain's Grotto—above ground in a brick summerhouse—is decorated with shell, glass and marble chip representations of lions, dragons, lizards, butterflies and so on, which are said to stand for the names of the ships on which the Admiral served (missing are a *Centaur* and a *Roebuck*, ships on which he actually sailed). As Sir Harry would have been 15 years old in 1780, however, this is fanciful. The grotto was built either by his uncle Sir Harry Burrard or, if one accepts a later date, possibly under the Admiral again, because the legend attached to the original grotto says that it was built by his loyal boatswain, who spent years and years on the grotto and when he finished it he went and drowned himself.

In 1840 an obelisk was erected to the admiral's memory at Mount Pleasant, after he had served as MP for Lymington for 40 years. No monument remains to the unhappy boatswain, except for the grotto-work itself.

The Marble Arch in the middle of the garden is Venetian, built of ashlar stone and, we would guess, by uncle Burrard. The grotto-decoration was originally in a proper grotto—it is very rough with a bit of a

A Shell Lion in the Walhampton Grotto

pointed entrance—but that must have been taken down after the Victorian period and replaced by this brick box on a different site.

A very good rustick house or hermitage, recorded in 1787 (and probably earlier), has long since disappeared, as has the summerhouse that stood on the Mount, and in the 1950s we lost a Chinese boathouse.

Bournemouth (Dorset)

Water Tower (c.1890)
SZ 008 920
Water Tower (late 19th century)
SZ 150 920

Two Dorset towers used to be in Hampshire—no, they weren't demolished and re-erected, they were just given to Dorset when Bournemouth was handed over in the county boundary reorganization. One is a small, heavily castellated and machicolated red brick tower, skulking among the trees at the top of the Upper Gardens and looking like a late Victorian water tower, and so it was. But its original function has long been

forgotten, because during World War II its waterwheel was dismantled, and the pond it supplied with water was filled in.

The other tower is in Seafield Gardens in Southbourne. Big and square, it has bartizan turrets at each corner.

Bramdean

West Meon Hut Stone Circle (1830s)
Apple House (c.1740)
SU 630 270

There is a pathetic little druids' circle on the north side of the A272, between Bramdean and West Meon, where the road forks to Brockwood, the circle on one side of the road, the barrow on the other. The barrow was supposedly built by Colonel George Greenwood of Brockwood Park as a monument to his favourite horse. The stone circle is thought to be genuine, although it has probably been tampered with.

At Bramdean House is a palatial apple house, a fruit store, thought, according to Pieter Boogaart, to have been built by Catherine Venables in 1740. It is complete with clock-face and weathervane and was, first and foremost, a summerhouse.

Calshot

Luttrell's Tower (c.1780)
SU 470 010

The only comparable folly to Peterson's Tower (see Sway, below), is Luttrell's Tower at Eaglehurst near Calshot. It was erected around 1780 by Thomas Sandby. Not strictly a tower, it is described by Pevsner as a 'super-folly' and was built regardless of expense as a genuine high-class smugglers' hide-out. It consists of three storeys, with a very much taller stair turret looking out to sea. The rooms are finely decorated, with exquisite fireplaces, including one in the cellar from where an underground passage (which still exists!) leads directly to the beach. It is quite obvious that this was a smugglers' den, and if one wonders how Temple Simon Luttrell, the owner, got away with such blatant flouting of the law, the answer is that he did his smuggling for the Prince Regent. In 1793 he was arrested in Boulogne and imprisoned in Paris for two years, during which time he was exhibited to the *citoyens* as the brother of the English King. He died in Paris in 1803, but the wonderful folly he left can now be enjoyed by everyone, as it is let out as a holiday home by the Landmark Trust.

Droxford

Tunnel (19th century)
SU 610 170

Studwell Lodge in Droxford has a tunnel joining the upper garden to the lower garden, a favourite early 19th-century romantic device.

East Stratton

Portico (1960–65)
SU 540 410

The stone is older, the architecture is older, but the portico became a folly only when Stratton Park was demolished in 1960 and a new house built in 1965. Only this *porte cochère* of the old house was left standing; it is by George Dance the Younger.

East Tisted

Gardener's Tower (late 19th century)
SU 690 320

The Gardener's Tower at Rotherfield Park in East Tisted is a massive sham castle, in the style of Radway Grange and its imitators but built very late, towards the end of the 19th century. It is also much too close to the main house, separated from it only by the stable road. A great, square, heavily machicolated tower was originally used for hanging game; this abuts a taller, round, three-storey tower, which provided the living quarters, with a taller, round stair turret. Nearby, the laundry

chimney is executed in the same style, with the addition of a conical roof. The Gardener's Tower has now been converted into a luxurious house.

Exbury

Tower (19th century)
SU 424 000

There is a rather grand tower here, but, like the one at Fritham (see below), it is—or was—probably something very functional. It has a clock-face but is without the belvederish aura of Fritham tower.

The Church of St Catherine was built in 1907 but is made partly of folly material, or rather... the old chapel at Lower Exbury was pulled down in 1827 by William Mitford of Exbury House. He built a folly and a pigsty with the stonework. However, when the village church was rebuilt in 1907 by the more pious, down went the folly and pigsty again to provide spoils with which to construct the church. Recycling going full circle.

Farringdon

Massey's Folly (1870–c.1900)
SU 720 350

In the midst of the idyllic scene [at Farringdon], *arises a most appalling horror of scarlet brick and tile, towering above all. It reminded me of a suburban Palace of Varieties, and it might have*

Massey's Folly, Upper Farringdon

been shot down here by some scoffing genii to mock the old church over the way. It is another Hampshire 'folly', and for some 13 years it has been in the building, a most mysterious proceeding it would seem, for only one bricklayer is allowed on the premises by the eccentric owner and deviser.

So says Arthur B. Connor in his *Highways and Byways in Hampshire* (1908)—the 13 years were surely at least 30 years. This is one of Hampshire's most extraordinary edifices.

The locals called it Massey's Folly from the day work started, even though for more than 100 years this crazy structure has served as village school, church hall and general meeting place. Farringdon is a small village divided into two parts, Lower Farringdon on the A32, and Upper Farringdon ½ mile east up the hill. In 1870 the rector, Rev. Thomas Hackett Massey, resolved to build in Upper Farringdon. What he decided to build is still not certain, but what he left us was a very positive statement about something. For a start it is big, wildly out of scale with anything else in the village—more suited to St Pancras than Farringdon; and second, it is red—very red. The village is predominantly thatch and whitewash; Massey's Folly is built of scarlet brick and off-the-peg Victorian terracotta panels. It has towers, battlements, ridge irons—a Chas. Addams delight. So what was it intended to be? The two favourite stories are that it was intended to be tea-rooms for when the London–Portsmouth line arrived at Farringdon (in fact, the line eventually ran to the west even of Lower Farringdon), or that it was supposed to be a theological college, which could have accounted for the 17 bedrooms it ended up with.

The story behind the building of it is as extraordinary as the building itself. Once we dispel any speculation about its purpose—there was none: Massey had the *folie de bâtir*, a condition also known as *furor architecturalis*—we are left with the folly of the construction. The rector and his bricklayer, Mr Gilbert from Farringdon, built the whole thing themselves, without any other help, except, so we are informed by Mr A.H. Gill, who knew them both in their old age, for a young man called Frank Bone who lived in Alton. Mind you, it took them 30 years because Massey would periodically demolish parts of it that no longer appealed to him, and would add others seemingly, and probably genuinely, at random. During his 62 years as rector of the parish his congregation diminished as his folly grew; not because of any unspoken condemnation of his

eccentricity—the English are far too polite for that—but because of the unrelieved diet of hellfire and damnation preached at them Sunday after Sunday. Finally, he was ranting at only two members of his parish, his faithful bricklayer and his washerwoman, the rest of the faithful having decamped to nearby Chawton Church. The Rev. Massey died in 1939, one of Hampshire's great eccentrics. In 1991 half the folly was converted by the Royal Institute of British Architects into their southern regional office—what greater homage could the profession pay to an amateur?

Farley Mount

Pyramid (1735)
SU 400 280

Hampshire's best pyramid is the delightful 30ft (9m) high edifice on Farley Mount, between Winchester and King's Somborne.

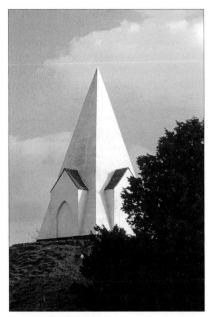

Farley Mount Pyramid

It has three blank porches and one open one: it is possible to go inside the pyramid and shelter from the remarkably cold wind that can blow up along these Hampshire downs and discover the wonderful reason for the pyramid's erection on the tablet inside.

UNDERNEATH LIES BURIED

A HORSE

THE PROPERTY OF

PAULET ST. JOHN ESQ

THAT IN THE MONTH

OF SEPTEMBER 1733 LEAPED

INTO A CHALK PIT TWENTY FIVE
FEET DEEP A FOXHUNTING
WITH HIS MASTER ON HIS BACK
AND IN OCTOBER 1734 HE WON THE
HUNTERS PLATE ON WORTHY DOWNS.
AND WAS RODE BY HIS OWNER
AND ENTERED IN THE NAME OF
'BEWARE CHALK PIT'.
. . . .
THE ABOVE BEING THE WORDS OF
THE ORIGINAL INSCRIPTIONS
WERE RESTORED BY THE RT. HON
SIR WILLIAM HEATHCOTE BARONET
SEP. A. D. 1870

and there really is nothing more that need be said.

Fritham

Tower (19th century)
SU 230 140

There's a mysterious tower here, several storeys high, looking quite industrial or agricultural, but one floor is open with broad arches, making this section into a summerhouse-cum-belvedere, and there's a similar one at Exbury (see above), 15 or so miles away as the crow flies.

Hambledon

Hopton Tower (mid-19th century)
SU 640 150

In the grounds of Folly House is Hopton Tower. Three storeys high and built to watch labourers on the estate, it is embattled and similar to the tower at Shawford (see below). Despite the explanation this one also remains a mystery.

Hartley Wintney

Folly Group (1970s onwards)
SU 750 550

West Green House near Hartley Wintney, a National Trust property, is the home of Alistair McAlpine. Since 1974 Lord McAlpine has been adding garden buildings at the rate of about one a year, using the services of Quinlan Terry, probably the last unashamedly classical architect working in Britain today. Most are elaborate accessories—vases, urns and so on—but the irresistible urge to inscribe has overcome Lord McAlpine from time to time. At the north end of the garden is an exotic, rope-ringed rusticated column, about 50ft (15m) high and surmounted with a device that looks as if it was copied from the top of an

elaborately turned chess piece.

HOC
MONVMENTVM
MAGNO PRETIO
QVOD ALITER IN
MANVS PVBLICAN
ORVM QVANDOQVE
CECIDISSET
AEDIFICATVM EST
ANNO MCMLXXVI R.A.McA

The inscription can be roughly translated as: 'This monument was built with a great deal of money which otherwise some day would have been given into the hands of the public revenue.' In 1979 a classical triumphal arch was planned, flanked by two Ionic columns and female acroteria and topped with a squat obelisk bearing the plaque:

MCMLXXIX
THIS TRIVMPHAL ARCH
WAS ERECTED
IN HONOVR OF
THE FAIRER SEX
& TO MARK THE OCCASION
OF THE ELECTION
OF THE FIRST LADY
PRIME MINISTER
OF GREAT BRITAIN

and then underneath on the frieze:

VIVAT REGINA

Yet another monument was to have 'four traitors… trying to pull down a heroic figure of a women who stands above them'—the Thatcher monument. Never built.

Terry, with McAlpine, has produced some remarkably fine work, notably the *trompe l'oeil* nymphaeum, curving inwards like a Borromini church façade until one gets quite close—when all is revealed as a sham, a flat façade cleverly painted. In a photograph the effect is perfect—it's impossible to believe it's not real. A smoke house heavily influenced by West Wycombe, an elaborate eyecatcher complete with the Ghost of West Green, a Doric lodge, a shell grotto, a birdcage, Chinese cowsheds, an island gazebo and more go to make up this 20th-century folly garden, although the grotto eventually was broken away as the stagnant water began to smell and the shellwork did not stick to the walls—an unintended political comment?

Havant

Folly Group (19th century)
SU 730 100

Hartley Wintney, Havant, Highclere, Hursley and Hurstbourne Priors all have garden ornaments that verge towards the folly, one in

particular being splendidly inexplicable. We
have already dealt with the new follies at
Hartley Wintney; at Havant's Leigh Park we
come across another dedicated builder, Sir
George Staunton. Sir George was fluent in
Chinese and wrote extensively on China; in
1832 he became MP for South Hampshire,
then for Portsmouth until 1852, describing
himself as a 'liberal Tory'. In 1832 he
commissioned Lewis Vulliamy to design him
a library that would stand separately from the

The Library at Leigh Park

house and hold his great collection of
Chinese writings, including his own
publications, such as '*An Inquiry into the
proper Mode of rendering the word God in
translating the Sacred Scriptures into the
Chinese Language*'. Vulliamy provided him
with an octagonal 1½-storey building with
arched windows, which now makes a
pleasing ruin. Sir George was proud of his
ancestors, writing a biography of his father,
an Irish diplomat, and erecting the Staunton
Memorial, a hexagonal garden grotto house
with tablets inside commemorating members
of the Staunton family (Sir George himself
was a bachelor).

The Beacon, a circular domed temple
with eight Doric columns, stands in open
farmland above the old estate, and
Staunton's final offering lies in Havant
Thicket, now barely recognizable but once a
monument to George Canning. The
Corinthian Bridge here was rebuilt in the
1990s, albeit as a wooden façade, but now it
has been torched, although another try at
rebuilding is at hand.

Hawley

Summerhouse (19th century)
Gazebo (1898)
SU 850 570

Minley Manor at Hawley on the Surrey
border has a little 19th-century summerhouse
with a thatched roof and a pebble floor, as
well as a gazebo neatly topping the water
tower, a pragmatic late Victorian compromise,
built by Arthur Castings in 1898. And in 1998
it was sold by Pavilions of Slendour.

Highclere

Heaven's Gate (1731)
Jackdaw's Castle (1743)
Garden Buildings (18th century)
SU 440 570

Highclere, the seat of the Earls of Carnarvon,
is the largest house in Hampshire. The estate
has several useless buildings, but our
favourite is unquestionably Heaven's Gate. It
is hard to describe why some follies appeal
instantly, while lacking any outstanding
characteristics. Heaven's Gate is an
eyecatcher arch, placed on the top of Sidown
Hill (south of the castle), with a central,
round-headed arch and two smaller side
ones, the whole pleasingly overbalanced by a
massive tympanum flanked with curtain walls
sweeping up to the pediment. Somehow, as it
stands forlornly in its rubbly dereliction amid
the uncontrolled undergrowth, it is
immediately appealing, crying out to be
loved. It has no particular feature apart from
its excessive size—60ft (18m) by 100ft
(30m)—but it is a very desirable building.

It was first built in 1731, perhaps designed
by Henry Herbert, Earl of Pembroke, for his
brother Robert but in 1739 it collapsed. An

Heaven's Gate

eyewitness, the Rev. J. Milles, wrote:

> We had not been there above half an
> hour before we saw it cleave from ye
> foundations and it fell with such a noise
> yet was heard at three or four miles
> distant.

Long ago there were tea-rooms and a seat for admiring the view, but these have disappeared. The re-erected arch now stands on firmer foundations, but the fabric is in such poor condition that it cannot survive for many more years, and another delightful folly will have been lost.

A grade listing might help. Another folly at Highclere has been deemed worthy of maximum protection with a listing of Grade I. This is Jackdaw's Castle, a wonderful name for an unexceptional Greek temple, listed probably because it was built in 1743 with Corinthian columns that came from Berkeley House in Piccadilly, designed by John May and accidentally burned down in 1733. The Ionic Rotunda has been attributed to Sir William Chambers, but it was 'improved' by Sir Charles Barry in 1838, who added the drum, the urns and altered the dome.

The Lake House by Milford Lake was built as a serene fishing pavilion and has been variously attributed to the Earl of Pembroke, William Kent and Barry. Barry may well have reworked it, but the interior is by Kent, and the probability is that Pembroke originally designed it. Grotto Lodge, by Ashworth on the track that runs to Heaven's Gate at the top of Sidown Hill, is a strange little flint- and stone-dressed building with seemingly nothing to link it with a grotto. It consists of two round towers connected by a short battlemented curtain wall. The larger tower has three storeys, is naked without its battlements and has a ludicrous little octagonal battlemented chimney placed in the centre of the flat roof. The smaller tower has two storeys, with a conical roof topped with a ball finial. Cruciform arrowslits and tiny round-headed windows complete the picture. The Ordnance Survey map answers the name; opposite is Grotto Copse, where the nine daughters of the Rev. Thomas Lisle of Crux Easton built a long-vanished grotto. Alexander Pope, a friend of the Lisle family, dutifully obliged with some verses:

> Here shunning idleness at once and
> praise
> This radiant pile nine rural sisters raise
> The Glittering emblem of each spotless
> dame
> Pure as her soul and shining as her fame
> Beauty which nature only can impart,
> And such a polish as disgraces art;
> But fate dispos'd them in this humble sort
> And held in deserts what could charm a
> court.

Jackdaw's Castle, Highclere

Recently most of the follies at Highclere have been consolidated.

Hinton Ampner

Temple (1960s)
Obelisk
`SU 590 270`

The original house here was replaced by a new one in 1937, but after a fire it was rebuilt in 1960. The classical temple was also erected around that time, but we do not know whether the obelisk is earlier.

Houghton

Sham Ruin Lodge (c. 1800)
Grotto (1880)
`SU 030 330`

At Houghton the lodge gate to Houghton Lodge—confusing but true, Houghton Lodge itself being a large, comfortable house in the *cottage orné* style, attributed to John Nash—is a flint-built sham ruin. A Gothic doorway leads into an empty grotto-room, with arches giving onto a shaded drive to the house. After a hit-and-run lorry smashed into it, the little building has been repaired again. There's also the remains of an ice-house.

Hursley

The Castle (18th century)
Grottoes (19th century)
`SU 430 240`

Cranbury Park, south of Hursley, holds creeping Chandler's Ford at bay. IBM now owns the estate and is covering as much of it as it can with office blocks and laboratories, but thankfully it has retained the fragments of follies that litter the grounds. First and foremost is the Castle, built in 1770 from fragments of the north transept of Netley Abbey by Thomas Dummer, the owner.

Other pieces left in the grounds include the remains of two grottoes, a shell grotto in a steep bank and Wordsworth's grotto, built over a spring. A tablet bears the inscription:

Written by Wordsworth
on visiting this spring.
Gentle Reader view in Me
An Emblem of true Charity
Who, while my Bounty I bestow
Am neither heard nor seen to flow
For every Drop of Water given
Repaid by fresh Supplies from Heav'n.

George Dance built the Dairy, a colonnaded garden house, and there is also a sundial, alleged to have been designed by Sir Isaac

Hursley Sham Castle

Newton. A tree has fallen on the shell grotto and it is now destroyed.

Towards Otterbourne, across the M3, is a 19th-century Gothic water tower.

Hurstbourne

Monument (18th century)
`SU 440 460`

Hurstbourne Park is another Hampshire estate to see; here is the splendidly inexplicable object we referred to earlier. A small armless leaden statue of a Roman emperor stands on the dome of a curious rectangular structure with four projecting arches opening into blank, knapped flint-lined niches. The whole appears from a distance as if it were built of drystone, crudely positioned. The statue is said to be George III, but it was obviously added long after this enigmatic building was erected. Thomas Archer designed a new house here for the 1st Earl of Portsmouth, and a painting shows a sham castle and a cascade as well, but it is thought that the work was never started. Certainly this folly could never have come from the same hand that designed the pavilion at Wrest Park in Bedfordshire.

Andover Lodge, or the Bee House, on the road from Whitchurch to Hurstbourne Priors, is referred to as a folly, but even to our overenthusiastic eyes it appears to be little more than a house with wilful detailing. It is of the early 18th century and has been converted and extended in the early 1990s.

Hythe
Forest Lodge (early 19th century)
`SU 430 060`

Up Southampton Water from Luttrell's Tower is Hythe, surprisingly screened from the massive refinery at Fawley and still retaining some village atmosphere. Forest Lodge, on the road in from Fawley, had an early 19th-century Chinese garden with bridge, pagoda, observatory tower and boathouse, but although remnants are still said to be visible, everything solid of interest has disappeared. Knightons on the seafront was the home of the eccentric Charles Kelsall, who put up nine terms of great men and a round clock tower with a triple cross on top, explaining in a Latin inscription that it stood for Catholicism, Protestantism and Reformation. It has, however, made way for a supermarket in the 1980s.

Kelsall owned Forest Lodge, and at last a survival has come to light, an inscription in Latin again, presumably from a third house (or just Knightons?), saying that he rebuilt a stone mill and transformed the little garden into something more elegant and embellishing it with statues of famous Britons. The house was given the name Amaltheae in 1849. The discovery was made by Ann Graves, and the Rev. Peter Murphy provided the translation (thank God for local vicars). Mr Kelsall may, when we review the evidence, have left more interesting items, and he certainly sounds a good subject for a local paper.

Lepe
Tower (18th century)
`SZ 440 980`

In the grounds of Lepe House, between Exbury and Calshot, is a round, buttressed and truncated tower, a former windmill we thought, but apparently it was a dovecote. It now serves as a Solent-view belvedere.

Medstead
Jonathan's Folly (1973)
`SU 660 360`

Jonathan Barnes, a pupil barrister then living at his parents' house in Medstead, was the first to go folly in the later 20th century. Jonathan's Folly is a small, circular, castellated tower, built in traditional Hampshire style of brick surrounds and flint infill, constructed, as Barnes freely admits, because he wanted a folly in the garden. A short flight of steps leads up to an open entrance into the one

room, from which a ladder leads up to a flat roof some 20ft (6m) above the ground. It is small but memorable; a little slate plaque at the top of the steps reads 'M.J.B. 1973' and at a glance it already seems to have aged ten years for every one. A villager attending a fete in the grounds sought out Barnes's father to exclaim that although he'd lived in Medstead for over 50 years he'd never known there was a castle in the village before.

Mottisfont
Summerhouse and Fishing Hut
(late 18th–19th century)
`SU 330 260`

Mottisfont Abbey has a Gothick flint and stone summerhouse, small but perfectly formed, as well as a rustic fishing hut along the river.

Douce's Pyramid at Nether Wallop

Nether Wallop
Pyramid (c.1760)
`SU 300 360`

At the west end of Nether Wallop Church is a 15ft (4.6m) pyramid built as a mausoleum for Dr Francis Douce, who endowed a school in the village provided that his pyramid was looked after. The rest of the graveyard has been grassed over, but his pyramid still stands proud on a mound above the west door.

Northington
Sham Castle Lodge (early 19th century)
`SU 560 340`

The Grange at Northington, the magnificent Grecian mansion designed by William Wilkins in 1804, has a small lodge eyecatcher, made up to look like a fierce little Pekinese of

King John's Hunting Lodge, Odiham

a castle, with battlements topping its mighty two storeys and an octagonal stair turret. The Grange itself had much more of the air of the folly about it when we first saw it in 1969, a great gaunt Grecian ruin, derelict and abandoned. It has now been restored by the Department of the Environment.

Odiham

King John's Hunting Lodge (c.1740)
SU 750 510

King John's Hunting Lodge near Odiham is immaculately tended, the mystery of the folly all but gone, but here is this extraordinary home, brick, of two storeys surmounted by wildly exaggerated Jacobean gables every bit as tall as the main body of the house itself. Although a National Trust property, it is not open to the public. It was built in the 18th century as an eyecatcher to Dogmersfield Park. The builder was Paulet St John, of 'Beware Chalk Pit' fame (see Farley Mount, above). Of course, he didn't stop there: a Gothick arch was built, a Palladian bridge, a belvedere and a sham Stonehenge. The follies, Michael Cousins found out, disappeared in 1790: 'Pulling down ornamental buildings in Park £300.'

Petersfield

Eyecatcher (late 18th century)
SU 740 230

Another Grange, another eyecatcher, this time at Petersfield, where Grange Farm House was given a rusticated flint frontage so that it could be an object of beauty from Petersfield House. The folly has long survived the house, which was demolished in 1793. The eyecatcher's prolonged existence is, however, threatened.

Portchester

Nelson Monument (1807)
SU 610 060

Mention must be made here of the extraordinary Nelson Monument on the downs above Portchester. Designed by John Thomas Groves in 1807, it is a mighty obelisk-like structure, 120ft (36.6m) high, with an incused panel running the height of the structure from the tapering plinth, topped with a little hollow arch in which, virtually out of sight from the ground, sits a tiny bust of Nelson.

CONSECRATED
TO THE MEMORY OF

LORD VISCOUNT NELSON
BY THE ZEALOUS ATTACHMENT
OF ALL THOSE WHO FOUGHT AT
TRAFALGAR
TO PERPETUATE HIS TRIUMPH
AND THEIR REGRET
MDCCCV

Groves was a little-known architect whose best work was the pierced obelisk at Garbally, Ballinasloe, Co. Galway.

Portsmouth

Monuments (late 19th century; early 20th century)
SU 640 002

An eclectic selection of monuments can be found in Portsmouth's Victoria Park, Portsea. They commemorate naval men, officers and exploits, so cannot be classed as follies, but they do demonstrate a remarkable motley of style in a very small area. Pre-eminent is a tiny Chinese temple, complete with a solid stone pagoda roof supported by four brown marble columns enclosing a Chinese bell captured by HMS *Orlando* at the turn of the century. 'PERPETUAL FELICITY ACHIEVED' reads the inscription on the pediment, and the plinth carries a translation of the inscription on the bell:

COME PLEASANT WEATHER AND GENTLE RAIN
THE EMPIRE HAPPY, AT PEACE AGAIN.

As one enters the park there is a grey obelisk, a pink obelisk, a pink column surmounted by a lion, another pink column topped with a ball, another larger grey obelisk, a fountain and then the temple.

In Gatcombe Gardens stands a removal-folly: a rotunda temple from Crichel House in Dorset, which was erected here in 1973.

Rockbourne

Column (1827)
SU 110 170

Rockbourne, which lies in a spur of the county surrounded by Dorset and Wiltshire, has a monument erected by the East India Company in honour of Sir Eyre Coote, the Indian Army general who died in 1783. Henry Bankes wrote the inscription, and the monument consists of a regulation 100ft (30m) column on a plinth, with a viewing platform and an urn on top.

Shawford

Belvedere (mid-18th century)
Cromwell's Tower (mid-18th century)
SU 450 240

At Shawford, on the Itchen between Winchester and Southampton, behind the Bridge Inn, is a small brick and flint belvedere, sometimes called 'The Chapel'. A two-storey tower called Cromwell's Tower—for no good reason—stands in the grounds of Shawford Park by the millstream. Probably dating from the mid-18th century, it has a tile roof, flint walls and no history.

John Webb's Pavilion at The Vyne

Sherborne St John

The Vyne Pavilion (mid-17th century)
Lodges (18th century)
SU 630 560

Hampshire has its share of older follies. The Vyne at Sherborne St John, one of the most famous houses in the county, has a beautiful brick garden pavilion by John Webb, dating from the mid-17th century. It is round and domed with cruciform doorways, looking like a debased Roman church, a precursor of Archer's Pavilion at Wrest Park, Bedfordshire. The lodges to the north and south of the house follow a similar pattern, but date from a century later, and indeed the National Trust now uses the pavilion's memorable shape to symbolize the property. The north lodge has a curious addition; it can best be described as an oriel chimney.

Stockbridge

Tower (19th century)
SU 350 340

A round, two-storey, flint, embattled tower stands in a garden at Atners Towers.

Stratfield Saye

Summerhouse (1846)
SU 690 620

Stratfield Saye House has a rustic summerhouse with a pebble floor; it was built to celebrate a visit by Queen Victoria in 1846.

Sway

Peterson's Tower (1879–85)
SZ 270 960

Hampshire's finest folly—the biggest, the most impressive, the oddest—is unquestionably Peterson's Tower at Sway. Andrew Thomas Turton Peterson was born in Yorkshire in 1813 and died in London in 1906. In the intervening 93 years he ran away to sea, became a lawyer, went to India, made a fortune, retired to Hampshire, became a spiritualist and built Peterson's Tower. Even if it isn't quite the tallest folly in Britain, 218ft (66m) and 13 storeys make it spectacular by any standards. When one adds to that its undeniable ugliness, the stories about the ghost of Christopher Wren, the half-remembered stories of the New Forest Shakers, mutterings about 'Judge' Peterson being buried at the top of the tower and its total unsuitability for the New Forest or, indeed, anywhere, one begins to realize how

Peterson's Folly

compelling this wonderful folly is.

When Peterson, an irascible but soft-hearted radical, retired he found two things to occupy his interests. One was a Mrs Girling, who arrived in the area with her religious troupe known as the New Forest Shakers. The other was a very real concern for the plight of the unemployed in the locality. The first started his interest in spiritualism; the second stirred his conscience. He brought back from India an interest in concrete as a building material, and finding a ready source of labour in Hampshire, he set to work to build additions and improvements to his estate at Drum Duan, all to his own design and using concrete. Here he met opposition: as a radical he was concerned with improving the lot of his fellow man; as a rich man he could do something positive about it. So he paid his men far more than they could have earned elsewhere in the district, which aroused the wrath of all the other local employers. Peterson was at pains to stress that he never employed someone who was not genuinely jobless, but suspicions remained.

As the work he had employed his men to do neared completion, Peterson began to worry about their future. But salvation was at hand in the shape of Mrs Girling. By an extraordinary stroke of luck she was able to introduce him to Sir Christopher Wren (via a medium) and he was delighted to discover that Sir Christopher was as keen on concrete as he was. Together they planned the tower, and if the finished design does not recall Wren's work as vividly as one might have hoped, one can only assume that his powers had faltered a little after 200 years or so.

Work started in 1879, employing 40 men and no scaffolding. The tower rose gradually and was not completed until 1885. It was the first major building in Britain to be built from concrete, and although its continued existence owes not a little to the efforts of Paul Atlas, owner until 1992, it remains a triumphant vindication of Peterson's beliefs. The estate at Drum Duan became known as

Peterson's Memorial in Sway Church

Arnewood Towers. Peterson put two concrete slabs in the basement of the tower. When his wife discovered their true purpose she flatly refused to have anything more to do with it, declaring she wanted a good Christian burial like everyone else. So perhaps Peterson was thwarted in an original attempt to build a mausoleum. The rooms were never furnished, and although he apparently intended to install electric lights— the very latest thing—Trinity House forbade him, saying it would be a danger to shipping. It also forbade him from installing illuminated clock-faces in the circular holes just below the second cornice. Peterson's life in India may well have persuaded him that the Indian tower cremation and subsequent interment of the ashes was the cleanest means of disposing of the dead; in any case, his final wish was granted. He was cremated at

Woking and his ashes were placed on the concrete table in the tower.

In 1990 Paul Atlas, who had owned the tower for 20 years, converted the first five storeys into a sumptuous bed and breakfast *étape*, which allowed guests to climb right to the top of the tower and stare over the world.

Warnford

Summerhouse (late 18th century)
Grotto
SU 620 220

The last individual eyecatcher in the country is the Dower House in Warnford, prettified to catch the eye of the passing traveller, built of flint and unbonded brick as a summerhouse for the Earl of Clanricarde rather than a dower house. It was an early conversion from folly to home, turned into the gardener's cottage in 1810. As at Petersfield, the great house in the park has disappeared, leaving the folly behind with its pretty band of quatrefoils and Gothicky-grotticky feel about it, and indeed Warnford also has a flint grotto running through an earth bank.

Weyhill

Jardin Imaginaire (1970s onwards)
SU 320 460

Stanley Norbury's cemented statues and the concrete D-I-Y temple were started in the late 1970s, in the back garden of the bungalow he created out of a disused recreational hall. His garden holds towerettes, animal statuettes, fountains, an Italianate temple and an arabesque little bridge.

Winchester

Temple Screen (1715)
SU 480 290

At the back of Abbey House, in Abbey Garden, is a Doric temple front, which spans the brook in order to obscure the view to the old mill from the house. Originally the screen was larger and was designed by the otherwise unknown William Pescod.

Woodmancott

Tower (late 19th century)
SU 560 420

At the edge of Embley Wood, near the M3 and A33, is a Gothic tower, possibly a water tower—it certainly looks like one. It is built of brick and is round, with machicolations and a much damaged spire.

HEREFORDSHIRE

There are not too many follies here, but several are out of the ordinary. One of its lost follies was a 19th-century brick tower at Ewyas Harold, which was cannibalized by the locals for building materials.

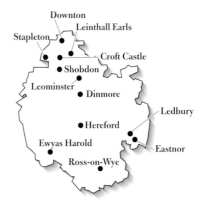

Croft Castle

Gateway (18th century)
SO 450 650

Sanderson Miller is said to have influenced the design of the Gothic gateway at Croft Castle, a National Trust property near Mortimer's Cross in Herefordshire, but to our eyes it looks too clean and finished.

Dinmore

Grotto (early 20th century)
SO 480 510

At Dinmore Manor Richard Hollins Murray built what must surely be one of the first grottoes to use chicken wire for its basic structure. In 1927 Mr Murray bought Dinmore Manor, once the Commandery of the Knights Hospitaller of St John of Jerusalem. Conscious of the religious history of the foundation he had acquired, Murray started to build cloisters and added stained glass liberally throughout. An octagonal court was built at the junction of the two cloisters, and as he wrote:

From this court on the western side is a room with a large Gothic-shaped window which has been glazed with coloured glass depicting an Eastern landscape, the horizon on the window having been measured to coincide with

Part of the gateway at Croft Castle

the true horizon beyond. A grotto effect has been reproduced, the roof being formed with concrete pressed through stout fine mesh wirework and coloured with various earth colours. Two small pools are within, and the effect of the reflection of the window on the lower pool is very pleasing.

Downton

Caves (late 18th century)
SO 440 740

The Rock Hermitage at Downton is in the grounds of Richard Payne Knight's Downton Castle, and as the path to it leads through a suitably creepy tunnel and hugs the cliffside above the picturesque river, it is a reasonable assumption that nature was aided here, perhaps with the ultimate, but unfulfilled, intention of creating a grotto. The walk ends at the ruins of what once was known as the Roman Bath, a sham by the classically inclined Knight (who wrote an infamous thesis on the worship of Priapus). Knight's library was built as a detached tower, almost a folly in itself, and necessary for someone who was known to read for ten hours at one sitting.

Eastnor

Obelisk (1812)
SO 740 360

There aren't many columns or obelisks in Herefordshire. Apart from the expected estate examples, there is only one large obelisk, at Eastnor, outside Ledbury on the A438. It was built to the memory of Earl Somers's son, who was killed at Burgos in 1812, the year

The Wesh and Yemeni Flags fly from Moor Park Tower

Robert Smirke started building the great Eastnor Castle, which is certainly a must for visitors, although without definite follies.

Ewyas Harold

Moor Park Tower (1830s)
Obelisk (1830s)
SO 387 287

Moor Park Tower was built as a 70ft (21m) belvedere by the Bath architect George Philip Manners for the Penoyres of Moor Park. Moor Park went in the 1950s, but the tower remained: a square, battlemented edifice, with some pointed windows and some arrowslits. About ten years ago the artist John Nankivell took possession of it, and although the main fabric of the tower is untouched, he painted the window shutters and installed in the interior much of what has remained from the Ilfracombe Hotel's Arabian Nights decor. A committed flag fanatic, Nankivell needs no excuse to fly pennants and standards from the tower on any occasion. There is also an obelisk.

Hereford

Obelisk (1806–09)
Urn (c.1800)
SO 520 390

Hereford has a huge Nelson Column by Thomas Hardwick, and just outside the city at Longworth there is an urn to commemorate a racehorse. Prospect Farm and Tower Hill to the west are just names on the Ordnance Survey map; whatever they referred to has long gone.

Ledbury

Hope End (1810–15)
SO 730 420

Some 2½ miles northeast of Ledbury is the site of Hope End. It was demolished in 1867, and its Victorian successor was burned down in 1911, but the stables to the first house still remain—and what stables! If it wasn't for the utter Englishness of the surrounding countryside one would expect to have stumbled on the crumbling *fata morgana* of an emir's palace. Hope End was built between 1810 and 1815 by the landscape gardener and publicist J.C. Loudon for Edward Moulton-Barrett. Barrett declared that: 'If I thought that there was another such [house] in England I would pull it down.' There wasn't.

Of course, Brighton Pavilion and

A minaret at Hope End

Sezincote were being planned or built at the same time, but although Hope End was in the same Indo-Moresque style and much smaller, its stark individuality ('coarsely designed,' thought Colvin) set it apart from the others. Elizabeth Barrett Browning remembered her childhood home as 'crowded with minarets & domes, & crowned with metal spires & crescents, to the provocation (as people used to observe) of every lightening of heaven'. The stables, now converted into an elegant private hotel, are still there to amuse the visitor. The block itself is straightforward enough, if one ignores the tall oriental columns on the corners, but the gateway-cum-clock tower looks thoroughly Moorish, even if the four pinnacles surrounding its dome have gone as well as the clock and bell, which now find themselves in Jamaica. The nine-year-old Elizabeth wrote a poem about the clock. The stableyard wall has seven squat columns, also oriental in design.

Near the stable block is a minaret topped with a crescent, very much like the one in Knutsford, Cheshire.

Leinthall Earls

The Folly (1961–6)
SO 440 670

The Folly was built at Gatley Park, near Leinthall Earls, between 1961 and 1964 for Mrs Victor Willis. The architect was Raymond Erith, who deliberately harked back to 18th-century models to build this very odd house. It is circular and three storeyed, with a domed roof and central chimneypot. Arched ground-floor windows are flanked by low wings, which look more like buttresses, the whole making a decidedly unusual effect, rather like an old-fashioned beehive or a jelly mould.

Leominster

Grotto (1870s)
SO 490 190

At Buckfield Keep a most charming grotto-fernery-rock garden survives, most of it in Pulhamite stone.

Ross-on-Wye

Kyrle's Follies
(early 18th century; 19th century; 1975)
SO 600 240

Most of the folly paraphernalia in Ross seems to have been started by John Kyrle (1637–1724), Pope's 'Man of Ross', and all the rest reflects in some way his aims and intentions. Kyrle was a philanthropist, amateur architect and gardener, who saw the beauty of what was later called The Prospect, a parkscape around the church with views over the Wye (the gate to The Prospect is dated 1700). One folly due directly to Kyrle (at least according to legend) is in the garden of Kyrle's house in the Market Place, where there is some grotwork and a swan, all made of horse's teeth, and a summerhouse with a Gothick entrance and a castellated wall behind. This is all very early if it is supposed to date from the first quarter of the 18th century.

The summerhouse is a delightful conceit: a tiny, pinnacled, three-bay houselet, apparently far too small to live in until one steps inside. The house becomes L-shaped— the side wall extends back to form the kitchen beyond a surprisingly spacious living room, and from the hall a spiral staircase goes down into the depths of the earth. It turns out to be a three-storey house, built into the side of a small cliff, rather like the House in

The Folly, Leinthall Earls

the Rock at Knaresborough, and the entrance is on the top storey. The garden is equally delightful, with winding paths, tunnels, frail bridges and arches leading down to a door in the wall, which opens onto the back alley where one discovers the base of the summerhouse.

After Kyrle the Ross Turnpike Trust took the development of the town in hand, and for some reason it started erecting crumbling city walls in the medieval style around the new Wilton Road, as well as a tall, round tower with rather small castellations. This appears to date from either 1833 or 1836. Hotels started to develop as well; the Royal Hotel, above the tower, dates from 1837. There is another tower in the Valley Hotel grounds, possibly built in 1774, and the Merton Hotel has other bits and pieces. A foreign element was introduced in 1975, when a Chinese kiosk appeared in Ross.

Shobdon Arches

Shobdon

Shobdon Arches (1752)
SO 400 630

Herefordshire has one of the loveliest
eyecatchers in the country at Shobdon, a
spidery edifice standing at the end of a long
and wide grass walk up the hill. Unusually
for an eyecatcher, it is three-dimensional,
with the two side arches set back from the
central arch and joined to it by curtain walls
with doorways. The columns and arches are
decorated with cable mouldings and
chevrons, remarkably ornate for mid-18th-
century folly work and also extremely
weathered. The tympana above the side
doorways are barely discernible through
weathering, suggesting a date much earlier
than 1752, when it was set up—indeed, the
whole structure is a picturesque re-erection
of pieces of the original Norman church at
Shobdon, put up by Lord Bateman when he
demolished it to build the existing church.
This may be regarded as 18th-century
vandalism, as the only Norman church in
Britain comparable to Shobdon was Kilpeck,
southwest of Hereford, but he replaced it
with a unique creation, a Gothic-rococo
symphony in pale blue and white; it is an
extraordinary and beautiful church. The
architect is unknown, although it is attributed
to Richard Bentley, a member of Walpole's
Committee of Taste, and it had, of course,
been Walpole who claimed to have converted
Bateman 'from a Chinese to a Goth'.
Bateman's correspondence with the
unnamed architect has survived, and by 24

March 1752 he wrote him to 'pray go and
examine the ruin on the Abbey and send me
word if it stands well', 'the Abbey' being the
supposed site of the old priory of Shobdon
on which the Arches were erected.

A quarter of a mile to the east of the
church, on a hillock, stands a small classical
temple, four Ionic columns supporting the
pediment, in a weak condition.

Stapleton

The Sulking House (c.1908)
SO 320 660

Bryan's Ground is in Howards Ends near
Stapleton and Presteigne. The house dates
from 1908 when Molly and Elizabeth
Dorning Holt, sisters and heiresses from
Liverpool, went to live a happy and busy life
here. Things went terribly wrong when
Lizzie upset arrangements by marrying a
clergyman. The sisters quarrelled and lived
separately, although still next door. They left
notes on the hedges dividing the two
properties, and relations improved only
when Elizabeth's husband was obliging
enough to die in World War I. We are not
told whether the Sulking House has anything
to do with their quarrel, but the name would
imply so. It is a very pretty summerhouse,
Gothic, but with stepped gables at the ends,
and one can imagine one of the sisters sitting
in there after a hard day's a-feudin' and a-
fightin'. The lovely gardens also house a
mock lighthouse (a mental memento from
Liverpool), which contained the gasworks for
house and estate.

HERTFORDSHIRE

Isn't it strange how Londoners of all sorts and types agree on one point: that foreigners (to put it as politely as possible) begin at Calais in the south and Watford in the north. Why the whole of Hertfordshire should thus be arbitrarily dismissed as containing a race of lesser beings while Kent and even Dover are granted equal status can be explained only by the fact that while Kent is the Garden of England, no Londoner goes to Hertfordshire unless he has to. To bring in beer, Kent was famed for its hops (labour intensive) and Hertfordshire was famed for its malt (labour hardly needed). As a holiday centre, it has little to offer. As a place to live, it has plenty, so Londoners reserve for Hertfordians that special contempt all city-dwellers reserve for their country brethren. It doesn't seem to worry the natives overmuch; they are aware of the existence of the metropolis but they are far from awed by it, preferring to keep their obstinate independence.

Pragmatic and sensible, the Victorian Hertfordians were as unlikely to put modesty skirts on table legs as their descendants are to change what must be one of the two most unfortunate village names in the British Isles—Nasty. The other contender, Ugley, is only 10 miles away across the Essex border.

But despite the sense and sensibility of the inhabitants, the county is surprisingly well blessed with follies, including five top ranking examples. There are some good stories, a wide variety of shapes, dates and sizes and a refreshing paucity of obelisks.

Abbots Langley

Ovaltine Dairy (1931)
TL 080 010

The county has three dairies that have been specially treated and may count as follies. The best known is the Node Dairy of 1927 at Driver's End (see below), but the idea was copied four years later at Abbots Langley for Ovaltine, which managed to cram half-timbering into the design but didn't go so far as to thatch everything in sight (which is what they did at the Node)—only everything that could be seen from the main London to Birmingham railway, thus purveying an image of wholesome country goodness to train travellers for over 50 years. An inspired piece of advertising.

Aldbury

Bridgewater Monument (1832)
SP 970 140

This tower is a column, which may seem like a contradiction, but a column can act as a tower while a tower cannot act as a column. If you are confused, there's worse to come. We define a tower as a free-standing structure, taller than it is wide, which was designed to be climbed; a column, on the other hand, whose original function was to serve as a structural support, cannot be climbed. Therefore Nelson's Column in Trafalgar Square is just a column, whereas the Monument in the City, also a column, is at the same time a tower.

IN HONOUR OF
FRANCIS THIRD DUKE OF BRIDGEWATER
'FATHER OF INLAND NAVIGATION'.
1832

It is a National Trust monument, a Doric column by Wyatville, topped with a copper urn, sometimes open to the public (there are 172 steps and a fine view) and a focal point for motorists for miles around. It is not a folly for solitude. Ashridge is always packed with picnicking families, screaming children, giggling girls and pimply youth—the 3rd Duke would have been appalled. By all accounts he was an unpleasant piece of work—fat, stupid and a misogynist to boot, whose commemoration owes more to his self-interest than to his altruism. His sobriquet was given because he constructed the first completely artificial waterway—in order to carry his coal from his Lancashire mines to his docks in Manchester. One can sense his reluctance to commission non-essential works such as landscaping, so it was not until after the duke died in 1803 that Repton was employed at Ashridge; the flower garden was laid out in 1815 for the 7th Earl of Bridgewater, and there is a grotto built from huge boulders as well as a Gothic conduit, attributed to Wyatville.

Aldenham

Aldenham Abbey (1802)
`TQ 140 990`

Protected from Watford by the M1, Wall Hall College at Aldenham is an oasis in encroaching suburbia. At the beginning of the 19th century George Thellusson, son of one of the richest men in England, built a house at Wall Hall to which he grandly added a Gothick façade. He sold the estate in 1812 to Admiral Pole, who, not to be outdone, constructed a ruined abbey, decorated his park with other Gothick trivia and renamed it Aldenham Abbey.

Sly's Castle (19th century)
`TQ 140 990`

South of Aldenham is Hilfield, built at about the same time for George Villiers by Jeffry Wyatville. It is not a folly, but a somewhat bizarre Gothic house, which used to be called Sly's Castle—hence our erring ways.

Ayot St Lawrence

Eyecatcher Church (1778–9)
`TL 190 170`

The most outstanding eyecatcher in Hertfordshire is a church. Time and again we have promised that churches, being built for a clear purpose, have no place in a book on follies. Time and again we come across an exception that begs for inclusion, and one such is the New Church at Ayot St Lawrence, which merits its position here through style, substance and story.

Sir Lyonel Lyde, the lord of the manor, decided to pull down the old 13th-century Church of St Lawrence and replace it with something more harmonious. In 1778 he commissioned Nicholas Revett (of West Wycombe and Shugborough fame) to design him a startlingly modern church in the Grecian style that Revett and 'Athenian' Stuart had so successfully popularized. The Bishop of Lincoln, in whose diocese Ayot St Lawrence then was, came to hear of the demolition and promptly suspended further work, leaving us in the 20th century with a picturesquely ruined church, traditionally sited opposite the village pub.

Meanwhile, across the fields to the west of the manor house, Revett's temple was taking shape: a Doric portico with two colonnaded

The New Church, Ayot St Lawrence

wings, terminating in two small pavilions each side. The east front, facing the house, was stuccoed; the back was left as plain brick.

There is no shadow of a doubt that the primary function of the new church was to serve as an eyecatcher from the house. At that time, for a parish church to be built in the Grecian style was revolutionary, and it is still extremely rare today—but not as rare as turning the church the wrong way round so that the altar is at the west end rather than the east, in order for it not to interfere with the Grand Design. But beyond the church's outrageously fashionable design for its time, beyond the bishop's ban, beyond the eyecatcher façade, lies perhaps the true reason for Sir Lyonel, a traditionalist in every other way, to build such a revolutionary church. The pavilions at the end of each colonnaded wing running north and south from the main body of the church contain, respectively, the sarcophagi of Sir Lyonel and his wife, whose marriage was apparently less than blissful. 'Since the Church united us in life,' rumbled Sir Lyonel, 'she can make amends by separating us in death.'

Barkway

Obelisk (18th century)
TL 380 370

At Newsells Park, to the north of Barkway, stands a middle sized, plain, unadorned, uninscribed, undated but prettily sited obelisk.

Barley

Homestall (1920s)
TL 400 380

Homestall was the house of wealthy Dr Redcliffe Nathan Salaman (1874–1955), whose father, Myer Salaman, founded the family fortune on ostrich feathers (so it's not the meat that will make you rich). Our Dr Salaman was named after the family's London address in Redcliffe Gardens. He gave up medicine in order to become an authority on the potato, and early in the century he bought himself this house in Barley and conducted all his potato experiments in its garden. His fame rests on two books: *Potato Varieties* (1926) and the indispensable *The History and Social Influence of the Potato* (1949).

Homestall apparently started out with some South African influences (no doubt because of the ostriches), but it must have been changed later to include its most

striking feature: a central water tower that also served as belvedere. It is brick, with concrete detailing, and culminates in an impromptu chinoiserie roofline. The chimney stack next to it vies for our attention and is, from ground level to top, almost as high as the belvedere. A house as interesting as its former owner.

Barnet

Obelisk (1740)
TQ 250 970

The tall obelisk at Monken Hadley is the Hadley Highstone Memorial, which was put up by Sir Jeremy Sambrook (whom we shall meet again; see Brookmans Park, below) to mark the spot where Warwick the Kingmaker fell in 1471.

Benington

Sham Ruin (1832)
TL 300 240

The Lordship in Benington is a large house built next to Benington Castle, which was destroyed by King John in 1213. This so fired the imagination of George Proctor, the 19th-century owner of The Lordship, that he embarked on a full-scale romanticization of the remaining ruins and his house as well, employing a gardener called Pulham as architect. This was James Pulham, who later

The Sham Ruin at Benington Lordship

invented Pulhamite artificial stone, and in the year he died, 1838, Pulham created a rock garden made of this material at Hoddesdon Hall. At Benington in 1832 they added a huge gatehouse, which overbalances the scale of both the house and the original ruins. Incorporated into the gateway are a shrine to Buddha and a Trojan inscribed stone. The sheer bulk and treatment of the ruins is grandiose, and Pulham made this into the architectural equivalent of a rock garden: bits and pieces are distributed about the screen walls in a picturesque manner, as if time had mellowed them. A technical survey of this folly might bring some surprises. Benington Lordship has one of the best contrived follies in county and country.

Tower House (19th century)
TL 250 030

A former Victorian water tower for the house has been converted into a tall, slender private house.

Brookmans Park

Folly Arch (c.1730)
TL 250 030

There are two outstanding folly arches in Hertfordshire; one was moved there and one was left there. The one that was left is known as the Brookmans Park Folly Arch, although when it was built it had nothing to do with Brookmans Park. There was once a village called North Mymms, and in that village was an estate called Gobions, once the seat of Sir Thomas More's family. Around 1730 the owner was Sir Jeremy Sambrook, and he employed James Gibbs to build him a mock medieval castellated gateway. A hundred years later the owner of Brookmans, another North Mymms estate, demolished Gobions to enlarge his park, and in 1891 Brookmans itself was burned down. Brookmans Park then became a nice middle-class housing estate, and through all this the Folly Arch (change and decay in all around I see) abided in peace.

There is a story, a long way from being disproved, that a farthing was placed under each brick. Another story says that the arch commemorated a visit by Elizabeth I—150 years earlier? Particularly interesting as one of the first sham medieval follies, the design is reminiscent of Vanbrugh's Claremont Belvedere (see Surrey). One striking touch that makes the Gibbs attribution probable is the different treatment given to each side of the arch. Flanked by two square, castellated, three-storey towers, the side facing the road

Brookmans Park Folly Arch

is straightforwardly presented, with brick quoins and a brick keystone. But the park side has a massive Gibbs surround, somewhat uncertainly handled as the whole structure—battlements, mouldings, windows—is brick built. Much of the arch's effect has recently been spoilt by a new building close by.

Cottered

Japanese Garden (1905 onwards)
TL 320 290

In recent years the Japanese garden at Cottered has seen more excitement than was good for it. History first: the garden was created by Herbert Goode (1865–1937), a porcelain importer who, after a trip to the Far East, decided to recreate in Hertfordshire the gardens he had seen in Japan. He worked for over 20 years on the garden, and the end result is considered reasonably authentic, which is, of course, a pity. But the Cottered garden certainly is beautiful, with a pretty tea-house made out of rare woods and a mini-mountain complete with waterfalls, cascades, bridges and ornaments.

By the 1980s the garden had been acquired by Mr Graeme Woodhatch, who owned a roofing company and who, according to his wife, was at the time 'living beyond his means and spending excessively'. By 1992 Woodhatch had removed most of the movables and immovables from the garden to auction them off at Sotheby's, but it was discovered just in time that the contents of the Japanese garden were listed, so fortunately the sale was aborted. Shortly afterwards Woodhatch was assassinated by the hired New Zealander gunnette Te Rangimaria Ngarima. All the items belonging at Cottered have been returned and the new owners have begun to restore the garden to its original state.

Driver's End

Node Dairy (1927)
TL 210 190

The Node Dairy at Driver's End was built in 1927 by an American, Maurice Chesterton, and although it was built as a working model dairy, it is so fantastic in concept and execution that it has to be seen. The main building is essentially a circular wall enclosing a circular courtyard, the diameter of the courtyard being the same as the turning circle of a 1926 Foden milk lorry. Vehicles enter the courtyard through an arch set in a massive gable, repeated at the rear, and four wings one room deep jut out from the circle. From the air the thing must look like an OXO advertisement. The roof, which contains the second storey, is extremely steeply pitched. A mock Germanic medieval tower disguised a silo, but the really staggering thing about the building is that it is entirely thatched—even the tower. It is said to have been the biggest thatched roof in the world at the time, and as we cannot imagine why anyone should wish to build a bigger, we suppose it still is. Now it is elegantly maintained and used as offices. In 1996 part of it burned down, but restoration work was started immediately. Visit it—it is the most remarkable 20th-century building in Hertfordshire.

Gilston

Sham Porch (1820s)
TL 440 130

At the end of the A414's mad scurry in all directions through the county is the tiny village of Gilston, just north of Harlow. Gilston Park was built in 1852, and in the garden is an apparently authentic Elizabethan porch dated 1583, which Pevsner says came from the previous house on the site, New Place. But the jingoistic inscription round the bust of Elizabeth I is remarkably legible and unworn:

FEAR. GOD. OBAYE. THE. RIAL. QUEEN.

Spaines Rod; Romes Rvine; Netherlandes

Reliefe; Earthes joy, England's gemme, World's Wonder, Natvres Chieffe.

As there is no record of the existence of this little porch before it appeared on a John Buckler drawing of 1830, we suspect it could be a Piltdown porch, a clever sham built by the owner of New Place in the 1820s.

Great Amwell

Monuments (1800; 1818)
TL 370 130

The most beautiful spot in Hertfordshire is the New River at Great Amwell, and if that sounds too sweeping, go and see it. The little village has a number of attractions for the folly-hunter, including a modern unroofed rotunda in a garden that doesn't appear to be attached to a house and an avenue consisting of different types of concrete lamp-post, put up not unexpectedly by a retired lamp-post manufacturer.

The Mylne family, nine generations of architects, made Amwell. Robert Mylne, architect to the New River Company, also built Blackfriars Bridge, and a column from the bridge stands in the garden of Flint House, which was built by Robert's son William in 1842–4. Robert Mylne's crowning achievement in our eyes is the Elysian plot at the end of the hill, below the church. It is dark and shaded, but not gloomy. A small dam in the river has created a tiny lake, no more than a pond, with two manicured, lushly turfed islets. One has a weeping willow, with a white Coade stone urn as a monument to Sir Hugh Myddelton, who constructed the New River in 1609 to bring water to the capital:

From the Spring at Chadwell 2 miles west and from this source of Amwell the Acqueduct meanders for the space of XL miles conveying health, pleasure, and convenience to the metropolis of Great Britain … an immortal work since man cannot more nearly imitate the Deity than by bestowing health. This Monument was dedicated by Robert Mylne, architect, Engineer in 1800.

On the same islet is the source stone, inscribed

O'erhung with shrubs, that fringe the chalky rock
A little fount purr'd forth its gurgling rill.

The second, smaller islet has a yew tree and another monument to Myddelton dated 1818 with lines from John Scott's poem 'Amwell':

AMWELL, perpetual be thy stream

*Nor e'er thy spring be less
which thousands drink who never dream
whence flow the streams they bless.*

The islets are linked by delicate little bridges, and the whole ensemble is so peaceful, so calm, that if sublimity can be found within an hour of London, it is here.

Hatfield

Tower (late 18th century)
TL 240 090

There is a late 18th-century pavilion tower at The Vineyard in the Home Park at Hatfield House, but most interesting were the projects proposed by the architect David Bliss for the Marquess of Salisbury. Apparently the talented Mr Bliss couldn't stop designing features for Hatfield, and he produced numerous designs for gazebos, obelisks, fountains and 'a gatehouse bigger than Marble Arch'. This was not what the patron had asked for and litigation followed. The same thing had happened with Bliss when he worked at Highgrove. A clear case of *furor architecturalis*.

Hemel Hempstead

Charter Tower (19th century)
TL 050 080

Another tower: a squat little two-storey affair called Charter Tower in Gadebridge Park, Hemel Hempstead, stands near St Mary's Church. It is, in fact, a porch, removed here from a long-demolished Elizabethan house.

Knebworth

Sham Ruin (1840s)
TL 040 210

A scrap of a sham ruin was built by the novelist Lord Bulwer-Lytton, author of *The Last Days of Pompeii* (1834), at Knebworth: a church window is set in a rough stone screen wall, with a brook running under it. The rather mannered house and park constitute a fine example of High Victoriana, so for Lord Lytton to erect the ruins of 'Queen Anne's Chapel', as he called his folly, must have been a conscious looking back to an earlier, more romantic era. By this time the fashion for follies was definitely on the wane. The good old days always ended with the previous generation. Perhaps Lytton was poking fun at himself, as trendy people deliberately put gnomes in their gardens, because in his novel *Pelham* (1828) he described a London garden with:

Knebworth's Sham Ruin in the 1960s

a pretty parterre here, and a Chinese pagoda there; an Oak tree in one corner, and a mushroom bed in the other; and above all, a Gothic ruin opposite the bay-window! You may traverse the whole in a stride; it is the four quarters of the globe in a mole-hill.

The last time seen, the whole folly was nothing more than a pile of rubble and any trace of the window has gone.

Little Berkhamsted

Stratton's Observatory (1789)
TL 295 082

Towers are scarce in Hertfordshire, but just the other side of Hertford, in the variously spelled village of Little Berkhamsted, is Stratton's Observatory, probably the best known folly in the county, which was converted from a ruin into a private home in the late 1960s by the architect William Tatton Brown.

The antiquarian John Meyrick noted, *c.*1799, next to a drawing of 'Prospect Tower at Little Berkhamstead':

At Little Berkhamsted is a very handsome Tower, built with bricks of a circular form with an octagon base, the top is a lead flat with battlements from which are fine prospects. It was built for a pleasure House, and has several apartments in the different stages of altitude.

It is a rare example of a Georgian tower, and one glance is sufficient to see why the Georgians generally preferred to use any

Stratton's Observatory pre-plastic

ships in the Thames from it. The tower is 97ft (29.6m) high, 359ft (109m) above sea level and 17 miles from the Thames. Might the story for once have been true? It is mathematically possible, especially with the powerful telescopes all admirals appear to have ... but John Stratton, despite legend, was no admiral, and the observatory appears also to have been called The Monument, and the house that is now The Gage was Monument House—did this have something to do with erecting a monument to William the Conqueror who accepted the surrender of London at Little Berkhampsted? A mystery remains. On the road to Stevenage, near Watton-at-Stone, are farm buildings with similar blind arcading.

Despite the superficial protection of its Grade II* listing, the tower has been vilely disfigured by having its elegant Georgian windows replaced by lamentable PVC frames with flat, lifeless plate glass. The plastic window company did make a stab at reproducing the round windows on the third floor, but failed calamitously. Glazing bars are mimicked by wedging strips of white plastic between the double glazed panes, a device that can only fool at the very first glance. It must be agony to live with it. For rectangular windows this may be effective; the bars hold each other in place. Not so with one of the round windows in the observatory—the *oeil-de-boeuf* was created by surrounding a circular pane of glass with ten spokes to make a larger circle. The false glazing bars in the PVC round window have been unequal to the challenge posed by the stresses and movements of a late 18th-century building, and the spokes have slipped down inside the sealed double glazed unit to huddle hopelessly at the bottom like ugly white spillikins. The central, circular 'glazing bar' has slipped only slightly, giving the tower a wall-eyed look. The unit is sealed. The bars cannot be repositioned. The whole window will have to be taken out and replaced.

This is an awful warning of the consequences of an ignorant marriage between late 18th-century architecture and late 20th-century marketing. We managed to halt the stone-clad uglification of historic houses—now we have to press out these offensive plastic windows. There are no gains without panes. And protect your driveway too, quickly now, before someone sells you Main-T-Nance-Free EZ paving that rolls in a strip off the back of a lorry. It's a constant battle. Be ever vigilant.

other style than their own to build their towers. The cool elegance of Georgian architecture, so much admired nowadays, is never as successful on the vertical plane. Stratton's Observatory is a round, battlemented, brick tower set on an octagonal base, and the fenestration differs on each storey—square, arched gallery, round, portrait. The whole edifice looks like a Soane scribble of four unequal parts, the least successful being the blind arcading punctuated by the gallery and round windows, which looks like early industrial architecture.

But, like Just William, its plainness is endearing, and when we learn that it was built in 1789 by the leisured John Stratton, son of Samuel Stratton, a rich linen draper from Leadenhall Street, we immediately forget about the observatory name and assume that he wanted to be able to see his

Patmore Heath

Pavilion (1984)
TL 440 260

In 1984 the architect Peter Foster built a Chinese pavilion here for Lady Brigid Ness.

St Albans

Arch (1773)
TL 150 070

In the garden of a house in Prospect Road, St Albans, is a sturdy, top-heavy classical arch placed onto a Victorian back, with a dovecote in the roof. Quite how it came to be there no one knows. It was obviously part of a now-vanished house, but for the moment it keeps its secret from us.

St Paul's Waldenbury

Temples (18th century)
TL 180 220

St Paul's Waldenbury has been the home of the Bowes Lyon family for over 250 years—

the Queen Mother was born here—and the tranquil garden, occasionally open to the public, is studded with pavilions and temples, none of which would qualify individually as a folly but, when taken together, contribute the essential whimsy and unexpected beauty that make the English garden admired throughout the world. The gardens were remodelled in the 1950s by Geoffrey Jellicoe, the planner of Hemel Hempstead New Town, and as late as 1961 a 'new' temple was added:

IN 1773 THIS TEMPLE WAS DESIGNED BY SIR WILLIAM CHAMBERS ARCHITECT AND WAS REMOVED FROM DANSON PARK KENT AND RE-ERECTED 1961

(The inscription runs round three inside walls of the temple on the skirting board.)

A large circular plaque on the back wall repeats the date together with the initials of David Bowes Lyon, one-time President of the Royal Horticultural Society. The Doric temple occupies a picturesque position on the shore of the little lake, facing another removal, a temple by Jeffrey Wyatt from

The Doric Temple at St Paul's Waldenbury

Copped Hall on the Essex–Hertfordshire border (see Epping, Essex). The vistas in the garden are beautifully devised, one of them ingeniously incorporating the low tower of All Saints, the parish church. A hidden glade has a terraced theatre and another small temple, and finally there is an octagonal pavilion dated 1735, called somewhat obscurely The Organ House. There is no longer a grotto, and there appears never to have been a pyramid, although it was mentioned by both Barbara Jones and Pevsner.

South Mimms

Spoils (1874)

TL 230 020

Wren, typical Londoner that he was, is the attributed architect of only one house in Hertfordshire—Tring Park—and that has been altered almost beyond recognition. We thought that the genius of Britain's most famous architect had passed Hertfordshire by entirely. Not quite: since 1975, when Hertfordshire acquired South Mimms, it also acquired some of Wren's work. As Forest Hill in southeast London has the spire of Wren's City Church of St Antholin, so Clare Hall Sanatorium had bits of St Antholin's built into its wall and gate after the church was demolished in 1874. These fragments were, however, recycled for a second time: some 15 years ago the sanatorium was demolished to make way for the Imperial Cancer Research Centre, and the wall has been renewed, but the fragments are safe.

Stanstead Abbots

Eyecatcher (19th century?)
Water Tower (20th century)
Sham Ruin (1832)

TL 390 120

Just off the A414 is Briggens Home Farm, which was Gothicized with ogee windows to provide an eyecatcher from Briggens.

On the south side of the road, rotting in the woods, is a splendid water tower with an octagonal clapboarded 'house' disguising the tank, rather like a modest House in the Clouds.

In Hunsdon itself is a small sham Gothic ruin in the garden of Longcroft, probably built for the Rev. Calvert in 1832 as a garden ornament to his rectory, now Hunsdonbury.

Tring

Obelisk (18th century)

SP 930 110

The largest obelisk in the county is a monument to Nell Gwynne on the old Rothschild Estate at Tring in the far west of the county. It is straightforward enough except for the ball finial. Nearby is a summerhouse.

The obelisk at Tring

Wadesmill

Obelisk (1879)

TL 360 170

The smallest obelisk in the county, and that is very small indeed, is interesting historically rather than architecturally. It is tiny, no more than 6ft 6in (2m) tall, but the inscription tells all:

ON THE SPOT WHERE STANDS THIS MONUMENT IN THE MONTH OF JUNE 1785 THOMAS CLARKSON RESOLVED TO DEVOTE HIS LIFE TO BRINGING ABOUT THE ABOLITION OF THE SLAVE TRADE.

It was erected on 9 October 1879 for Arthur Giles-Puller of nearby Youngsbury and cannot be classed as a folly, even though it appears as such in all references. Raising an obelisk to a dead canary is folly, but Clarkson's cause deserves rather more serious recognition. The only other monument to his memory is in his home town of Wisbech. Of course, the little obelisk no longer stands on the spot of resolution, as it was moved 9 yards (8m) for a road widening scheme in 1972.

Across from Youngsbury stands the ruined tower of old Thundridge Church, set on a little mound on a copse (*feuillée*) by the River Rib. Lancelot Brown was at work here a hundred years before Giles-Puller came, and it is tempting to conclude that the master had not resisted the capabilities offered by the romantic tower. Another event of world importance took place in this area nine months before Clarkson made his vow, and this, too, was commemorated by Giles-Puller. The man had the potential to be a folly builder, but his promise faded fast, whether through lack of money or lack of interest we cannot tell. A large sandstone boulder in the hamlet of Standon Green End, a mile north, has a plaque affixed by Giles-Puller which reads:

> *Let Posterity know, and knowing be astonished, that on the Fifteenth day of September, 1784, Vincent Lunardi of Lucca in Tuscany, the First Aerial Traveller in Britain, mounting from the Artillery Ground in London and traversing the Regions of the Air for Two Hours and Fifteen Minutes, in this Spot revisited the Earth.*

Waltham Cross

Temple Bar (1672/1878)
TL 350 020

Early as Brookmans Park Folly Arch is, the other Hertfordshire arch is even earlier, although it has graced the county for only around a hundred years. Driven from town by traffic congestion, this arch made its home in rural (as it was then) Waltham Cross. Now a highway roars past a couple of hundred yards away, and there is again talk of removing the arch back to London. For this is the famous Temple Bar, one of the old entrances to the City of London, now enjoying a tranquil retirement in a Hertfordshire wood.

The architect is popularly supposed to have been the great Sir Christopher Wren, although there is no conclusive evidence for the attribution. It was actually built by Joshua Marshall and Thomas Knight, both master masons, and, as Marshall was a monumental sculptor as well as contractor, it is quite possible that he designed the building. The archway was originally erected in Fleet Street in 1672; by the busy 1870s it was hopelessly in the way of traffic, so Sir Henry Meux and his actress wife, Susie, had it dismantled and re-erected on their Theobalds Park Estate in 1878, presumably as a conversation piece at their lavish parties. The parties may have spilled over into the park, because the building is fitted with a primitive central heating system, and an additional wing is dated 1889. We are thankful that it has been preserved, for despite being roofless and vandalized it is not beyond restoration.

Now it is one of Hertfordshire's best surprises; to walk down a woodland bridleway and suddenly—suddenly because it really can't be seen until one is very near—

A postcard of Temple Bar in 1904

come across Temple Bar, a grand, overstated, baroque and quintessentially urban piece of architecture, is a highly enjoyable experience. Even having seen photographs beforehand, it is much bigger and more solid than one expects, despite its poor condition due to shameful neglect. This building has been listed Grade I, but few seem to care. In 1984 a media fuss started about a proposal to resite the Bar in the shadow of St Paul's, where it would be dwarfed into insignificance, but 15 years later nothing has been resolved and the arch continues to moulder quietly away in its rural resting place.

Pulhamite Walling (late 19th–early 20th century)
TL 360 000

Hertfordshire is Pulhamite country: James Pulham *père* worked at Benington and other places, and Pulham *fils* developed the idea of Pulhamite stone and operated from Broxbourne. So it is fitting that the Pulhamite walling that was in Ponsbourne House Hotel, Newgate Street, has been removed to another Hertfordshire site, Capel Manor near Waltham Cross, next to junction 25 on the M25.

Ponsbourne has now had its folly heart ripped out, so the small dairy still there is of no great interest. Regarding the Pulhamite, one would think it was the idea of the banker James William Carlile, who built Ponsbourne Park in 1876, but doubts have been cast upon this and it may be early 20th century, although the notion that the reverend sisters who stayed here until the 1970s actually made it (as some sort of Lourdes grotto?), has to be wrong: this is definitely Pulhamite.

Capel Manor, now a horticultural centre, has other recent attractions: some classical temples, a small sham ruin and a maze.

Ware

Scott's Grotto (1734–73)
TL 370 140

There is an excellent grotto in Ware, adjoining 28 Scott's Road, although the dank, bedraggled entrance does not promise much. It was started in 1734 by Samuel Scott, a Quaker linen-draper, and finished in the summer of 1773 at a purported cost of £10,000—a phenomenal sum—by his son John Scott, a popular contemporary poet, and his brother-in-law, Charles Frogley. It is difficult to see how it could have cost £10,000, as the grotto is not large and, as befits a Quaker grotto, somewhat austerely decorated. The layout is, however,

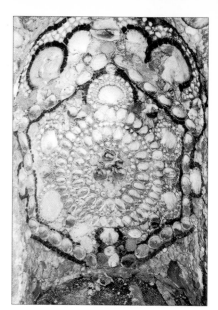

Scott's Grotto

sufficiently complicated, and the various little caverns and chambers are endowed with portentous names—two Committee Rooms, the Robing Room, the Consultation Room, the Refreshment Room and the Council Chamber. The Robing Room, furthest from the entrance, is 70ft (21m) into the hillside and 34ft (10.4m) from the surface, but the air inside is surprisingly fresh and dry.

Dr Johnson, a friend of Scott's, who had little time for grottoes, called the grotto 'a fairy palace', so perhaps he appreciated the austerity or perhaps it was never properly finished. Scott obtained his shells from a Mr Turner in Exeter, and there are some splendid conches, but restraint is everywhere. Now it is owned by the local council, which has done an excellent job of restoration using James Howley, and it is looked after by the Ware Society, which will show visitors round by appointment.

Japanese Garden (1901–05)
TL 370 160

There is a precursor to Cottered's Japanese garden: the garden at Fanhams Hall, north of Ware. The theme is, however, mixed up with that of the Alps. Mrs Croft had Fanhams Hall converted around 1900, and then, with the help of a Mr Inaka and Professor Suzuki, she started on the garden. It contains two tea-houses, the ubiquitous bridges and lanterns, a miniature Mount Fuji, but also an Austrian pavilion that came from the 1901 exhibition and faintly resembles a Swiss chalet.

ISLE OF MAN

The Isle of Man is a strangely unsatisfactory island. It's as if God had scooped up the ugliest examples of English architecture and dumped them all on a rock out of sight of England and Ireland, where they grew and festered. Wild and wonderful scenery surrounds depressingly ordinary bungalows; PVC window salesmen must have thought they had found paradise. The island's semi-independent status makes it a popular tax haven as well as a cheap holiday resort, so we have the curious sight of the double-glazed Mercedes-Benzes of the locals nosing their way between depressed crowds of pinched and windswept holiday-makers. One is reminded of Bishop Heber's old hymn about Ceylon:

Though every prospect pleases
And only Man is vile.

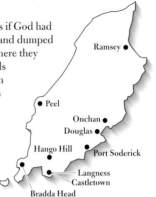

Bradda Head

Milner's Folly (1871)
SC 184 699

Milner's Folly is simply spectacular: a gigantic tower perched on a massive headland dominating the little town of Port Erin. The basic structure is of a square tower with a circular stair tower attached to the east wall, but it is so designed as to imitate the shape of a key, the reason being that William Milner was a safe manufacturer. A plaque above the doorway reads:

Erected by public subscription to
WILLIAM MILNER
in Grateful acknowledgement
of his many charities
to the poor of Port Erin
and his never tiring efforts
for the benefit of the Manx fishermen
A.D. 1871

Milner's Folly

The doorway is open, and a solid stone spiral staircase beckons, and yes, you can actually climb up safely, past an empty, gloomy room, on up to the flat, high-parapeted roof of the big tower. The wind screams—the high parapets are necessary to avoid being plucked off the roof and hurled into the Irish Sea—but you look at Port Erin as though from an aeroplane, and across to the Calf of Man above the gulls and terns.

Mr Milner made his fortune in Liverpool, and if you penetrate to the back of your solicitor's office you may find the deeds to your estate still tied up in a Milner safe. He retired to Port Erin, and immersed himself in local affairs, becoming the benevolent benefactor of the area. Locally it is said that the public subscription raised just about enough to pay for the plaque above the door, so Milner, touched by the thought, graciously contributed the remainder to build the tower. Whatever the truth, he has left us a memorable and beautiful folly tower. Who was the architect?

Castletown

Smelt Memorial (mid-19th century)
SC 262 675

In addition to the Tower of Refuge in Douglas Bay (see below), Sir William Hillary had a hand in another Manx building enterprise, the Doric column outside Castle Rushen in Castletown. Known as the Smelt Memorial, it was erected to commemorate Governor Cornelias Smelt, who lived at the castle from 1805 to 1832. Again there was a public subscription; again it was underwritten by Sir William, but this time building work reached the plinth, faltered,

The Tower of Refuge

continued up the column and finally petered out at the capital, without sufficient funds to pay the £40 required for the statue of the good governor. Sir William was not to be drawn; the capital remains bare to this day.

Douglas

Marine Drive Archway (19th century)
SC 387 745

Douglas boasts some of the ugliest buildings in the British Isles. On Douglas Head is the castellated and rotting 19th-century Douglas Head Hotel, with its thoughtless concrete extensions and concrete trellis balcony. There are three other castellated houses in the area and a wonderful stretch of road heading south around the headland to Port Soderick (don't take it—you'll see why later) through a large castellated archway bearing the words 'Marine Drive 1891'. In what seemed to be the remains of grounds to a long-demolished house there was an odd tower, which could well have been the remains of some garden building or even a folly. It was reminiscent of the remains of Princess Amelia's Tower at Gunnersbury Park, London.

Douglas also has a remarkable Victorian camera obscura, apparently the only one of its particular type in Europe. It is owned by an elderly lady who opens it when she is able, and it looks rather dilapidated. The Island claims to know the value of this gem and is trying to buy it and restore it. It will be a tragedy if it is allowed to decay, although seeing what the island has done to some of its Victorian heritage makes one fear the worst.

The Tower of Refuge (1832)
SC 388 756

The Tower of Refuge was built in 1832 at the instigation of Sir William Hillary, the founder of the RNLI. In 1830 the mail packet had been swept on to Conister Rock at the harbour entrance, where it foundered, and but for the brave work of the 14 men of the Douglas lifeboat, with Sir William among them, 62 lives would have been lost. For some reason this made Sir William decide to build a castle on this low rock, where shipwrecked sailors could shelter in safety. The fact that at low tides it is possible to walk to the rock from the Loch Promenade did not deter him a whit. As his architect he chose 22-year-old John Welch, whose first commission this was. Welch produced a miniature turreted and battlemented fantasy, twin round towers fronting a larger single round tower and a comparatively tall square tower behind to catch the eye. An anonymous writer simply called 'A Stranger', who wrote 'A Six Days' Tour through the Isle of Man' in 1836, described it thus:

The edifice was built agreeably to the designs, and under the superintendence of, Mr John Welch, architect, and seems at this moment to defy the shocks of every sea that rages, and every wind that blows. There have been so many lives lost on this dangerous rock, in times of shipwreck, the sea breaking over it like a swollen torrent over its stony bed; it was deemed desirable to erect a tower, as a place of refuge in which the shipwrecked mariner might outlive the storm, This benevolent object was carried into effect, principally through the persevering agency, and in a great measure from the pocket of Sir William Hillary, president of the Isle of Man District Association, and founder of the Royal National Institution, for the preservation of life from shipwreck. The superstitious will have it that at the present time, whenever a tempest rages, the moaning of the spirits of those who have been lost here is heard from the shore; and that in the 'noon of night' pale corpses are seen to look over the battlements of the round tower into the sea, pointing to their own watery graves.

It was revealed in 1939 that the anonymous author of this romantic piece was Mr John Welch, Architect. In fact, his self-congratulation turns out to be justified; his tiny castle still stands as squat and solid as it ever did. The trick of scale and distance very nearly makes it appear much mightier than it is; not until a herring gull lands on its battlements and assumes the proportions of a rukh is the illusion broken.

Hango Hill

Summerhouse (17th century)
SC 276 678

A lump on the seashore, with the scrappy ruin of a 17th-century summerhouse, was built by the 4th Earl of Derby.

Langness

Herring Tower (19th century)
SC 285 657

The curious round tower you can spot from the air on arriving at Ronaldsway turns out to be a Herring Tower, with a vertiginous unrailed circular stair rising up the inside wall. Apparently, a beacon was lit on the top to guide home the herring fleet, so it served as a primitive lighthouse. The Huer's House in Cornwall performed the same function, but in reverse.

Onchan

Cat Castle (1986)
SC 400 780

If we define a folly as a misunderstood building, this cannot be folly. Its name describes its function, and why shouldn't *Felis catus* have castles, if they are ingenious enough to get *Homo sapiens* to build them on their behalf? That's just what happened here at Woodland Towers, where Mr

O.F.W. Fisher designed an octagonal 10ft 6in (3.2m) high castellated Cat Castle to house rescued cats, 'who would be savagely attacked by Pangur Ban, the resident Sacred Cat of Burma', presumably Mr Fisher's mog. The Cat Castle, built by local builder G. Murray and his son, reflects the design of Woodland Towers. The owner claims it to be the only folly to be built on the island since Victorian times. There is no mention of a cat flap.

Peel

Corrin's Folly (1839)
SC 233 931

On a high ridge between the road and the sea south of Peel stands Corrin's Folly, a tower built in by Thomas Corrin, a 34-year-old farmer. Corrin, a dissenter, had his wife and daughters buried in unconsecrated ground

The Cat Castle

near the tower at the top of Peel Hill, marking the graves with small obelisks. When he himself died he was buried in St Patrick's churchyard, but his fellow dissenters removed the corpse and hid it for two days until they could re-bury it with his family by the tower. Despite demands by the church authorities for the cadaver's return, the nonconformists remained resolute, and finally, to save further feuding, the ground around the tower was consecrated. It is a plain, square, three-storey tower about 50ft (15.2m) high, surmounted by a small, white pyramid. It is a forbidding structure with bricked-in windows and a blocked-up entrance.

Near the tower is the burial place of Corrin's wife and their two children, with two obelisks on each side. On one of the obelisks the slab at the top is engraved on each of the four sides. The inscription is now very worn:

> North side:
> *CORRIN'S PILLAR 1839*
> *This pillar is erected sixty*
> *feet distant from the base of*
> West side:
> *this mount and within*
> *the enclosure upon its top*
> *rests the mortal remains of*
> South side:
> *ALICE CORRIN and her*
> *two beloved children. This*
> *Pillar, Tower and Monument was erected*
> East side:
> *by Thomas Corrin to*
> *perpetuate her memory until*
> *reanimated by the grace of God.*

It is all most strange and atmospheric.

Port Soderick

Resort (late 19th century)

`SC 347 727`

According to Jonquil Phelan, this was a booming small resort in Victorian times and again during the post-war period, until people deserted it for Spain. It has a castellated arch and the sad remains of a miniature railway, paddling pool and large club bar. Marine Drive originally led all the way from Douglas to Port Soderick, but the road has partly collapsed into the sea and the village is now only accessible on foot or bicycle. British seaside resorts are strange, lonely places at the best of times, and when the road collapsed, so, finally, did the enterprise. There is a massive car park for the hundreds of vehicles that never came, but since it is no longer fashionable to sport a sun tan, or even to eat and drink, there may still be a future for this sad little corner of Britain. At least there's plenty of room to park the bike.

Ramsey

Albert Tower (1847)

`SC 453 934`

Above Ramsey (not a pretty town) stands the
> *ALBERT TOWER*
> *erected on the spot where*
> *H.R.H. PRINCE ALBERT*
> *stood to view*
> *Ramsey and its Neighbourhood*
> *during the visit of*
> *Her Most Gracious Majesty*
> *QUEEN VICTORIA*

Albert Tower, Ramsey

> *to Ramsey Bay,*
> *the XX of September M:DCCCXLVII*

It is a dumpy, square, grey, battlemented tower, with cornerstones and machicolations in a lighter stone, and poky little viewing windows on the top floor. The tower is superfluous to the view, which is indeed splendid, though not as grand as that from Milner's Folly at Bradda Head.

The rather pleasant story behind its construction is hinted at in the inscription, which records Victoria's visit to Ramsey Bay, rather than to Ramsey itself. What happened was that the royal yacht, returning from Scotland with Victoria and the Prince Consort aboard, hove to in Ramsey Bay to allow the queen to recover from a violent bout of sea-sickness. Albert hopped ashore and was met by the local barber who took him to the top of Lhergy Frissel overlooking the town, to admire the view. Meanwhile a horseman pelted down the road to Douglas to alert the governor and his circle to prepare for a full state visit with all the trimmings. As they chafed in their formal attire, another messenger arrived to tell them that if they wanted to see the queen they had better make it to Ramsey with all possible speed. The island's upper crust crested Lhergy Frissel just in time to catch a glimpse of the royal yacht steaming over the horizon.

One feels that the gleeful townsfolk of Ramsey erected the Albert Tower more to crow over the injured notables of Douglas than to honour the Prince's visit.

ISLE OF WIGHT

The Isle of Wight is a distillation of the beauty of the English countryside: picture-book villages, chocolate-box scenery and the disadvantages that the obviously picturesque attracts—trippers.

Apart from the vandalized and subsequently dismantled Shakespeare Temple, of which at least bits remain, one particular folly has disappeared completely: Cook's Castle on St Martin's Down at Wroxall. It would have been such an interesting find, as even nowadays people can't decide whether this was a late-medieval embattled tower or a folly of much later date, possibly built by Lancelot Brown. Our Solomon's Judgement on the debate is the following: it was medieval, albeit heavily adapted to become a proper belvedere, so, yes, later on it was a folly, but by no means a Capable one (Cook's Castle was much too heavy-handed).

Appuldurcombe

Obelisk (1774)
SZ 540 790

Only a plinth remains of the 70ft (21m) obelisk to commemorate Sir Robert Worsley above ruined Appuldurcombe House, ruined not through time but through a misplaced World War II bomb. There are two plaques:

TO THE MEMORY OF SIR ROBERT WORSLEY BT
WHO DIED UNIVERSALLY LAMENTED
JULY 29TH 1747 ON THE 77TH YEAR OF HIS AGE
THIS OBELISK WAS ERECTED ON
THE HIGHEST EMINENCE OF HIS LATE PROPERTY
AS AN EMBLEM OF
THE CONSPICUOUS CHARACTER HE MAINTAINED
DURING A LONG AND EXEMPLARY LIFE
AND AS A MONUMENT OF GRATITUDE
BY HIS SUCCESSOR SIR RICHARD WORSLEY

The other plaque states that the obelisk was struck by lightning in 1831 and severely damaged—no mention of World War II nor of its restoration (part-restoration, as it is still only a plinth) by General Sir Richard Worsley 'with the help of the Isle of Wight County Council and the people of Godshill Parish'.

Bembridge

Obelisk (1849)
SZ 640 850

Along the east coast, on Culver Down, is a squat but massive obelisk, visible for miles around, which was erected to the memory of the Earl of Yarborough who founded the Royal Yacht Squadron at Cowes. This is another Pelham's Pillar, for the Yarborough family seat was at Brocklesby in Lincolnshire, where the famous Pillar commemorated the planting of more than 12 million trees.

Blackgang

Shakespeare Temple (1864)
SZ 491 762

The south coast of the Isle of Wight is falling into the sea. We followed the signs from Blackgang to a house called South View, down a rutted road to the entrance gate piers above the sea—or rather gate pier, for the right-hand one has fallen down the cliff, leaving the left balancing unsteadily on the edge. Naturally, the drive disappears down the cliff, but on the left along the remaining road is the smallest rotunda ever built, a minute temple to Shakespeare on a little bluff in the woods. Six fluted columns support a modillion cornice, the whole edifice being

The Shakespeare Temple

just large enough to admit one person inside.

On the road below is a little spring head, with an indecipherable inscription from *The Two Gentlemen of Verona* around it, while in the temple a tablet that bore lines from *Cymbeline* has now completely disappeared. This charming, tiny temple was built in 1864 by Thomas Letts of Letts Diaries.

Since we wrote this 20 years ago, strange things have happened to this wonderful temple. Reports filtered through about destruction by 'some lads on scooters' and the subsequent removal of the remains to Godshill. Others said it was still there in the undergrowth but collapsed. The last report, however, was that it was, indeed, continually under attack by vandals, but the owner of the temple eventually took it down himself and removed it to a garden in Ryde, although the base is still in its place. Also the temple is now believed to date from the 18th century, and was erected by a Professor Letts, of the same family as Letts Diaries, but never directly connected with the firm. He was a professor of literature at Oxford. The memorial must have been rebuilt in 1864. Much ado about such a small temple.

Pepper Pot (14th century)
Salt Cellar (1785)
SZ 491 762

Talk of the Salt Cellar and the Pepper Pot on Niton Down, just above Blackgang, leads the enthusiastic folly-hunter up a stiff climb to discover a genuine 14th-century lighthouse called St Catherine's Tower, which, with its splayed foot buttresses and pyramidal roof, looks uncannily like a medieval rocket. It is octagonal outside and square within, and is known locally as the Pepper Pot. In 1785 Trinity House started to build a new lighthouse here, 150 yards (140m) away, but the attempt was abandoned when it was discovered that the top was perpetually shrouded in mist. The derelict tower was inevitably christened the Salt Cellar, and it stood unused for nearly 200 years until the Ministry of Defence built a radar station in it after the war.

Bonchurch

Smuggler's Haven (early 20th century)
SZ 570 780

Blessed with several alternative names—plain 'The Tower', 'Landskip Look-out' and 'Smuggler's Haven Look-out'—the small, rough stone, castellated tower or, rather, gazebo at Upper Landslip is indeed just a belvedere, although nowadays trees are in the way of a good sea view.

Grotto (1868)
Pyramid (1773)
SZ 567 781

The island-loving Jonquil Phelan wrote to us about these two items: a prim Victorian affair … more akin to a chapel complete with water tap inside. It bears a modern metal plaque:

> *This memorial was commissioned in 1868 by Mrs Margaret Huish as a memorial to her late husband, Captain Mark Huish, who followed a military career by becoming a railway magnate before retiring to Bonchurch where nearby in Mitchell Avenue, opposite the bowling green, he built several houses, he also initiated the local geological collection.*

Nearby is another oddity, a stone pyramid set in the wall and also with a modern plaque:

> *This pyramid of stone was erected in 1773 and is an example of stone quarried in the vicinity. This was at the time shipped from Bonchurch to be used at Portsmouth Harbour.*

Both these curiosities have been preserved by the Ventnor Town Council—to their credit.

Calbourne

Swainston Temple (late 18th century)
SZ 430 870

When we first found Swainston Temple it was a Greek Doric temple on a slope just south of the B3401, between Calbourne and Carisbrooke, hidden in trees and undergrowth at the edge of a wood, forgotten and abandoned but magnificent in decay. As Greek Revival temples go, it was somewhat large, but it actually served as a labourer's cottage for many years. When we saw it, the dwelling had collapsed, leaving only three or four walls and a staircase leading to the sky, while the mighty portico remained. Surrounded by undergrowth as it was, it was almost impossible to photograph, but the temple was rolling in atmosphere. It was built in the late 18th century for Sir John Barrington, perhaps by William Pordern (who was remodelling Swainston at the time), as a belvedere over the Solent and as an eyecatcher from the house. The trees had grown up around it and the temple stood forgotten. But not any longer—down have come the trees, up have gone the temple walls, it has been rescued, renovated and restored. Why, then, are we sad? For we are.

Swainston Temple

Chale

Hoy's Monument (1814)
SZ 490 770

After a strenuous hike up one of the more isolated hills on the island to visit a National Trust folly, we were greeted at the top by an elderly lady with a stick, self-appointed guardian of the tor, who enquired coldly: 'You do realize you have come up by an animal path? The proper path runs around there. Please to keep to it on your way down.' Suitably chastened, we hung around, taking

Hoy's Monument

surreptitious photographs of the inoffensive column, then crept back down the hill, following the designated human animal path. The folly in question was Hoy's Monument on the north spur of St Catherine's Down, which was erected to commemorate the visit to Great Britain of His Imperial Majesty Alexander I, Emperor of All the Russias, in the year 1814 and in memory of many happy years' residence in his dominions by Michael Hoy of The Hermitage (a suitable name) nearby. The plaque has now gone, and has been replaced by a small plastic label with the relevant details. On the south side of the pillar is another plaque, added in 1857 by Lieutenant William Henry Dawes, in memory of the fallen at the Battles of Alma and Inkerman in the Russian Crimea. The monument itself is a plain, unadorned column, 72ft (22m) high, surmounted with a ball and commanding magnificent views over the island.

East Cowes

Shell House (1916–26)
SZ 510 950

In Cambridge Road, just off the Promenade, is a rarity in England, a *jardin imaginaire* in a style more popular in France. In 1916 the fishmonger Frederick Attrill, then 78 years old, began to decorate the outside of his modest semi-detached villa with shells. He had earlier been given the house by Queen Victoria for being so brave as to smack one of the princes for being naughty. When he died ten years later the house had become a tourist attraction, covered on front, side and back with myriads of shells, plates, mosaics, fragments of porcelain, figurines—anything he could lay his hands on. Much has disappeared in the 60 years since then, but the East Cowes Shell House is still a sight worth seeing, unlike its Scottish counterparts in Leven and Buailedubh.

Swiss Chalets (1853)
Albert Barracks (1862)
Bric-à-brac (1860)
`SZ 520 940`

Queen Victoria's much-loved seaside palace has a number of odd buildings—not follies, but worth a look—in the grounds. A Swiss chalet was imported as a playhouse for the royal children and proved so popular that another was built to house their anthropological and archaeological collections. The children built Albert Barracks with their own hands, and even made the bricks themselves. They were also allowed a thatched toolshed, while the Queen herself had an alcove from which to see the sea and a boating-cum-tea-house with a central two-storey tower, now a private residence. Osborne House is open in the summer months for an admission charge, rather like the island itself.

Kingston

Gazebo (18th century)
`SZ 480 820`

Billingham Manor, near Kingston, lies in serenity in a fold of the downs, secluded in its walled garden, complete with an odd little thatched gazebo, topped with a dovecote and a weathervane, now tumbling gently down.

Ryde

Appley Tower (mid-19th century)
`SZ 580 930`

Views are inescapable in the Isle of Wight. With the rolling scenery of southern England, but entirely surrounded by the sea, it cannot fail to stir the sight. Little hills suddenly open out magnificent land and sea prospects to all sides, and it seems surprising that more prospect towers weren't erected. There are only a few, including this one at the far east end of the promenade at Ryde. After the road finishes and the walk continues into the seaside pine woods, stands a little castellated prospect tower at sea level, right at the water's edge, giving in an island of superb viewpoints nothing more than the view across the flat sea to military Portsmouth. Appley Tower was part of the Appley Estate, and the coat of arms remains above the first floor entrance, with a lapwing surmounted with the motto 'VOULOIR EST POUVOIR'.

Designed by Thomas Hellyer, the round, three-storey tower is heavily castellated, with a splayed base and an oriel window looking out to sea.

Shanklin

Grotto (early 19th century)
`SZ 579 809`

Jonquil Phelan again informs us about a grotto, this time in the grounds of the Fernbank Hotel. The hotel dates from *c.*1850, but the grotto is seemingly older and probably originally part of the grounds of a larger estate. Sadly, little remains of the shell and fossil lining.

Belvedere (18th century)
`SZ 583 793`

Another hotel, another folly. At Luccombe Chine Hotel, surrounded by flowers and on a small mound, is a perfect little tower—it is round, with very awkward battlements and pointed windows and entrance, and it was used by the Customs and Excise men to keep a look-out, the same story as the nearby Smuggler's Haven tower at Bonchurch. Both are primarily just belvederes.

Totland

Tennyson Monument (late 19th century)
`SZ 330 850`

The western half of the island has little in the way of follies, but the great, high, granite cross on Tennyson Down above Totland, commemorating the poet, makes a fine objective for a walk from the chalk pit by the High Down Inn—the views over the island and north towards Hampshire are spectacular.

Appley Tower at Ryde

KENT

The Garden of England is a wonderfully evocative appellation, which Kent still, perhaps surprisingly, deserves – half the orchards in England are to be found here. London has swallowed a good part of the northwest of the county, and several follies that were built in rural Kent are described in the London chapter. There is still a good variety, however, evenly scattered, with not too many obelisks, some genuine eccentricity, a good folly group and a real mystery!

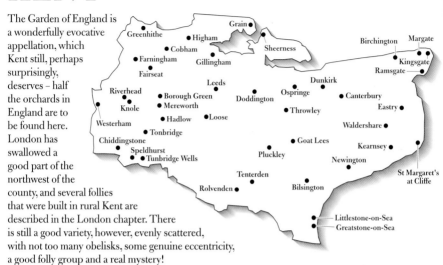

From the hundreds of demolished follies that we have had to ignore, we chose Vavasseur's Folly at Knockholt, on the London borders, which was demolished during World War II. We mention it because of its dual function as belvedere tower and communal house chimney—the only existing example of this kind that we have discovered is at Osmaston in Derbyshire.

Bilsington

Obelisk (1835)
TR 040 340

There is a curious atavistic sensation on reaching Bilsington, after crossing Romney Marsh, that one is finally on dry land. Over 1000 years have passed since this was sea, but the strangely comforting feeling that comes as one drives up the first hill cannot be denied. At Bilsington is the most pleasing obelisk in Kent; not just because it looks nothing like an obelisk, having been half-sheared away by a bolt of lightning in 1967, but for its very existence, prominent in its insignificance. It was built by George Cooper of Canterbury in 1835, and the weathered inscription is still legible:

> AS A TRIBUTE OF RESPECT
> TO THE MEMORY OF
> SIR WILLIAM RICHARD COSWAY KT.
> THIS MONUMENT WAS ERECTED
> BY HIS FRIENDS AND
> THE REFORMERS OF EAST KENT
> IN THE YEAR MDCCCXXXV

Cosway was killed in a coaching accident here that year, and as a reformer along with Kent's other obelisk candidate, Charles Larkin at Higham (see below), he won the respect of his countrymen.

Birchington

Waterloo Tower (1819–20)
TR 310 680

The Isle of Thanet, no longer an island since the Minster and the Chislet Marshes silted up hundreds of years ago, is still reachable only by crossing water, but modern travellers are unaware of this as they cross the Stour or the tiny but enjoyably named River Wantsum. It seems an unlikely spot for follies, but here they abound, and they rank among the finest—certainly the most mysterious—in Britain. Quex Park at Birchington is the home of the Powell-Cotton Game Museum, a fascinating if gruesome collection, occasionally open to the public.

In the grounds is a large copse with an unbelievable sight: a white Eiffel Tower poking out above the treetops. This is the Waterloo Tower, built in 1819 as a bell tower, as a mausoleum, and now one of the most famous follies in a county of famous follies. It is completely ringed by trees and is difficult to picture properly. Four-storey, square and built of red brick, it is castellated in cast iron and has four octagonal corner turrets, but the most remarkable thing, the beauty that transcends workaday architecture and can make a folly into an object to be remembered

The Waterloo Tower with pre-Eiffel topping

for a lifetime, is the spire. It is an Eiffel Tower but more graceful, more ethereal; it is made of white-painted cast iron, with each of its four, convex bowed legs (not concave like Eiffel's) firmly planted on a corner turret. John Newman says it was inspired by the tower of Faversham Church, but although there is a similarity in concept, the execution is totally different. The architect is unknown, but William Pocock, the author of *Architectural Designs for Rustic Cottages, Picturesque Dwellings, Villas, etc.* with appropriate scenery, did some unspecified work at Quex between 1806 and 1809 and may have been called back after the reprint of his book in 1819. If so, the Waterloo Tower is his masterpiece. The compilers of the Department of the Environment List of Buildings of Special Architectural or Historical Interest list it Grade II, but say the spire is a later addition. It was certainly planned from the start; J.A. Parnell wrote in *The Gothic Traveller*:

Mr Powell will have a lofty spire on his Tower thirds of Cast Iron and to be sprung from four quarter circle arches— then it will be a noble seamark being only one mile from that briny fluid.

Briny fluid? The base of the tower consists of two single-storey rooms making up the mausoleum, with the inscription

This tower was restored and the mausoleum was dedicated to the memory of Henry Horace Powell Cotton by his son 1896. The whole edifice is in remarkably good condition, and the local bell-ringers use the 12-bell carillon regularly. Hazel Basford, a member of the Quex Park Society of Change Ringers, informs us that the name of the head carpenter at Quex appears on the iron legs, 'John Clark Ramsgate 1820', and a year before that he was paid to take a model of the spire to London. The casters were probably W.& J. Mackney from Sandwich, millwrights and iron-founders.

A smaller brown brick tower in the same park, called the Gun Tower, was built in 1812 to mount a gun to signal out to sea. Circular this time, it is again of four storeys, with circular and round-headed windows.

Borough Green

Sham Ruin (1960s)
TQ 600 570

Around the 1960s Roderick Cameron started to build the ruins of a monastery in Borough Green, so that he could have a monastery garden.

Canterbury

Dane John (1803)
TR 140 970

Dane John, a linguistic corruption of 'donjon' or dungeon, is the name of a curious mound in the centre of Canterbury, now part of a public park. It is surprising that in this closely

Canterbury's Egyptian Temple

studied patch of land its original function has not been discovered, but theories for its existence include the suggestions that it was a Roman burial mound and a defensive fortification. The park used to be private, but since the 15th century the citizens of Canterbury have ignored the ownership and taken it for their own, and it is said that an alderman who tried to reverse the practice lost his head (literally) at the hands of the said citizens—a rather strong reaction to the closing of a park. With this memory in mind, another alderman spent £1500 on slicing off the top of the mound:

> *This field and hill were improved, and these terraces, walks and plantations, made in the year 1790, for the use of the public, at the sole expense of James Simmons, Esq., of this city, alderman and banker, to perpetuate the memory of which generous transaction and as a mark of gratitude for his other public services, this pillar was erected by voluntary subscription in the year 1803.*

The inscription is on one side of the Dane John monument, a strange, white stone, tapering column topped with an urn, standing on a large square pedestal, with a niche and inscriptions in each side. The other inscriptions record various improvements made to the gardens at various times throughout the 19th century.

Egyptian Temple (1847)
TR 140 970

Synagogues and the like on the mainland of Europe were often built in the Moorish style or some other vaguely Oriental style. To have one in full-blown Egyptian is exceptional. King Street has a building that was erected in 1847 by Canterbury's Jewish citizens, although we do not know that it was a synagogue, nor do we know its architect. In 1982 the King's School took it over. It is in the form of an Egyptian temple, with two delightful obelisks as gateposts.

Chiddingstone

Garden Buildings (early 19th century)
TQ 490 440

Chiddingstone Castle has the full set—Gothic gazebo, ruined Gothic orangery, Gothic sham bridge, Gothic water tower—all from the same building campaign that changed High Street House into Chiddingstone Castle. There is one exception: a rock grotto may have belonged to the earlier gardens. The Streatfeild Mausoleum in the churchyard dates from 1736.

Cobham

Garden Buildings (late 18th–early 19th century)
TQ 670 680

In the grounds of Cobham Hall, especially when you are on your way to the splendid Cobham Mausoleum, you may now and again encounter Charles Dickens's ghost, revisiting old haunts as he walked his many furious miles from Gravesend's Gad's Hill Place. The author himself may or may not have encountered three other ghosts at Cobham: that of Richard Dadd's dead father; the ghost of Peggy Taylor, the maid; and the 5th Earl Darnley's ghoul, he of Toe Monument fame. To some visitors, Cobham Hall is a park where you can find pretty little follies. To us, however, it is Death's Landscape. You are told—a finger points in the appropriate direction—of the spot where Peggy Taylor hanged herself when she found out she was pregnant by one of the Darnleys at the house. It's Peggy Taylor's Hill where you want to be.

You are not told, but will know, of

Wyatt's Mausoleum in Cobham

Paddock Hole, subsequently named Dadd's Hole, which has disappeared because in 1964 it was filled in. Here Richard Dadd, the celebrated Victorian painter of elves and goblins, lured his father from London, took out his knife, specially bought for the occasion at Mosely & Co. of New Street, and slashed his father's throat. Why? Because he had been commanded so to do by the Egyptian god Osiris.

And you will not find the Toe Monument. In 1835 the 5th Earl Darnley visited the wood near the Mausoleum and found there two wood-fellers, who were fiddling about with their axes. 'I'll bloody show you two how to do a tree!' said the earl, swinging the axe, and in one mighty crush cut off two toes on his own noble right foot. Abed at the Hall—bandages, brandy, rest, darkness… tetanus. Dead on 11 February, at three o'clock in the afternoon. The Toe Monument was erected to commemorate the event. There should be yew trees at the spot, yew trees and an iron fence. You can't wait to find it: What will it look like? A boring urn or a trophy made out of axes, toes and sad little angels? Or perhaps it will be an enormous toe. Shrubs, rhododendron seedlings to the left, right, back and front; everywhere yew trees; everywhere remains of iron fences; everywhere the Toe Monument.

Cobham's other monument to Death is

the Mausoleum by James Wyatt, 1783. It has died itself. Black boots trudge through the damp clay and snow, past dead hedgerows, slipping, cold and shivering, over a sinister landscape that lies rotting and stinking beneath its blanket of snow. It is classical, with a pyramid on top, earthen walls around it. The doors have been smashed and a burned-out car dragged half into it. There are bottles, weeds, cold.

Among the rhododendrons she says: 'I want to cut you up.' A penknife is produced. She cuts my left hand, the small knife is blunt and frays a broad, superficial wound. Back at the Mausoleum, I say it's due to a fall among the shrubs, and she ties a handkerchief around the hand. We laugh.

Oh, and at Cobham there are also a Gothic pumping house, Repton's Seat, the Aviary, the Ionic Temple, an ice-house, a Druid's Circle, Merlin's Cave, a ruined orangery and a 1795 Gothick dairy. Pretty little follies.

Doddington

Alexandra Oldfield Monument (1997)
TQ 940 570

Strange to say, but the tower-cum-pavilion at Doddington Place, which commemorates the death from cancer of Mrs Alexandra Oldfield in 1995, is a much more pleasant folly than those at Cobham. There are nastier things to be remembered by. It is a well-turned-out brick, embattled tower, broad and square, of which the lower storey is filled in with knapped flint, Gothic windows and doorway. It acts as both a seat and an eyecatcher and has two plaques 'Remember Alexandra' and 'Et In Arcadia Ego'. The whole was devised by her husband, Richard Oldfield.

Dunkirk

Dawes Folly (19th century)
TR 080 600

Clearly marked on the Ordnance Survey map at Holly Hill, north of Dunkirk on the A2, is a tower. Barbara Jones described it as:

A dumpy little hexagonal tower, two storeys high, made of flint dressed with stone, and the inside of brick; there is an iron spiral staircase running up to a small hexagonal turret on the roof.

Traces remain of a carefully landscaped wood, with walks and rhododendrons and arbours, but two attempts to find the tower have failed. An unhelpful resident meets all enquiries with a repeated, 'It's private property. Don't you understand?' so whether the tower still exists or not we could not say.

Its survival was, however, later confirmed and two stories were given. It was built by Mr Dawes, a ship-owner, who used it as a belvedere to see his ships come in on the Medway; alternatively, it was built in the late 19th century by Sir Edwyn Dawes of nearby Mount Ephraim as a summerhouse, although we were told by the Dawes of Ephraim House that the tower had been built by W.C. Dawes around 1900. Take your pick.

Mount Ephraim also has a room devoted to England's last battle, which took place on 31 May 1838 at Bossenden Wood, north of Dunkirk, when The Messiah, alias Sir William Courtenay, alias John Thom, together with some 20 followers, waged war on a troop of a hundred soldiers. It was intended to be Armageddon and the beginning of a new world. Instead, John Thom and some of his followers were shot. The case aroused tremendous interest at the time, but nowadays almost no one has heard of it. At Mount Ephraim we have seen a photograph of Thom's heart (!), his watch, his portrait, his swords and his standard. The Red Lion Inn at Dunkirk also has Thom connections—his body was put there after the battle.

If the Holly Hill tower is not in remembrance of the occurrences of 1838 at Bossenden Wood, this should be rectified immediately by building a new folly or placing an obelisk at Dunkirk.

Eastry

Foord's Folly (c. 1900)
TR 310 550

Tunnels were dug by the Foord family at the turn of the century under the garden of Beckett's, a house in Gore Road, consisting of rooms, lots of stairs and the tunnels themselves. Its walls are decorated with a Gothic window, a Viking and sham medieval paintings (including 'the foule murder of the two Princes atte the Palace of the Kings of Kent atte Eastrie'). The tunnels may be the result of lime digging and then later improved upon.

Fairseat

The Folly (late 19th century)
TQ 620 610

The folly in Gravesend Road in the hamlet of Fairseat looks like a Swiss pagoda on ecstasy or, rather, it looks like nothing one has ever seen, and the building is understood only (and then only partly) when it is undressed mentally. It is a conical, shingled spire, with a round room. The spire is pierced on all sides (yes, this cone has sides) by fretwork dormer windows. There is a weathervane on top, of course. No date could be found.

Dawes Folly

Farningham

Sham Bridge (18th century)
The Folly (1790)
TQ 550 660

Travellers to Folkestone in the 18th century often found Farningham, 20 miles from London, a convenient coaching stop, and its neat prosperity dates from that time. Luckily, its architecture remains intact, thanks to the A20 bypassing the village early in this motor century, and now the M20 bypasses the A20, and Farningham has settled back into welcome obscurity. The River Darent flows through the village, and northeast of the bridge is a peculiar screen across the river, looking like the remains of an older bridge. It was probably built for a mundane purpose— a cattle-trap, perhaps, or to protect the ford before the road bridge was built in 1773—but the local builder couldn't resist tarting it up a little. There are three segmented arches in red brick and flint, rusticated, with brick and flint piers at the ends and pointed brick cut-waters. It is a smart sham bridge.

The Mill House in Farningham has three octagonal turrets in the grounds, flint and brick again, one with a ball finial, one plain and one crenellated, standing in a row, with a summerhouse on the right. The summerhouse has an inside wall lined with cockleshells, and beneath the buildings are two chambers dug out from the hillside, with brick arched entrances set in a flint wall. Was this to be the start of an ambitious grotto? One chamber has a small cistern dated 1790; it has been suggested that the chambers were used to store grain for the mill. If that is the case, the three turrets and the shell-lined summerhouse were certainly surplus to requirements. As a local said: 'It's always been called The Folly, I don't know why.'

Gillingham

Clock Tower (1934)
TQ 780 670

Rochester, a pre-Roman city, is now caught up in the depressingly anonymous agglomeration known as Medway, which includes Chatham and Gillingham. This part of north Kent is grey and ugly, a landscape of pylons, mudflats and mean urban housing crouching around the Royal Dockyards, the

Gillingham's unfinished Jezreel Temple before it was demolished in the 1950s

reason for Chatham's existence. One of the most famous former follies in Britain was here in Gillingham, the Jezreel Temple of the Flying Roll, a remarkably advanced building architecturally, which was never finished after the sect, led by an ex-Indian army corporal, ran out of cash in the 1880s. Sadly, the great gaunt shell was demolished in the 1950s. The best anecdote of the many about Jezreel, and sadly untrue, was that the architect forgot the stairs.

Gillingham's contribution to folly architecture is, as might be expected, municipal. England had been at peace with Japan for hundreds of years before this clock tower-cum-fountain-cum-memorial was constructed in 1934 to honour a native of Gillingham who went to Japan in 1600 and became the Shogun's adviser. The clock tower was expensively built out of solid blocks of Portland stone and designed by J.L. Redfern, Gillingham's borough engineer, in a curious mixture of styles ranging from Egyptian to London Underground, but this fraternal memorial was not enough to prevent the Japanese from sweeping into Singapore less than a decade later. Reading the inscription, we can see where the inspiration for James Clavell's successful series of 'Shogun' novels came from:

> WILLIAM ADAMS
> BORN GILLINGHAM A.D. 1564
> DIED JAPAN A.D. 1620
> After service in the English Fleet of Queen Elizabeth, William Adams embarked with a Dutch Trading Expedition, which left Texel, Holland, in 1598. Cast ashore off the coast of Japan in 1600, he was taken into the service of the Japanese Shogun and became his adviser. He constructed for the Shogun two vessels of European design and instructed his adopted countrymen in gunnery, geography, mathematics and the like and engaged on their behalf in foreign trading. A monument erected in Yokosuka perpetuates his memory and his work for the Japanese nation.
> THIS CLOCK TOWER, ERECTED IN THE TOWN OF HIS BIRTH BY PUBLIC SUBSCRIPTION, WAS UNVEILED ON THE 11 MAY 1934, BY HIS EXCELLENCY TSUNEO MATSUDAIRA G.C.V.O. JAPANESE AMBASSADOR TO THE COURT OF ST. JAMES
> ALDERMAN S.O.SUMMERS J.P.
> MAYOR OF GILLINGHAM

A Japanese translation of the plaque is mounted next to it. For a clock tower, the choice of timing for its erection was unfortunate.

Goat Lees

Eastwell Park Gatehouse (1843)
TQ 010 450

On the A251 stands the grand neo-Jacobean gatehouse to Eastwell Park. Built of stone and flint and, according to Philip Neville, almost 'mimicking the Tower of London', it was probably by William Burn.

Grain

London Stone (1858)
TQ 861 875

West of Grain, on the Isle of Grain and north of Wallend, on Yantlet Creek, is the London Stone, marking the southeastern boundary of the City of London's jurisdiction over the River Thames. It is a whitish obelisk on an arched platform. No doubt this replaced an earlier marker. The stone for the obelisk was ordered from Mr MacDonald's emporium in Aberdeen.

Greatstone-on-Sea

Listening Wall (1928)
TR 070 230

There is an inexplicably blank wall at Greatstone. A huge concrete bow, 25ft (7.6m) high and 200ft (61m) long, sits forlornly on the flat marshy sands. It has no reason to be there, but no reason not to be. Its function or purpose is totally baffling, and it would take

The Shogun's Clock Tower

an inspired guess to divine the reason for its existence. Even if one knew its date of construction, one would be none the wiser. Its local name begins to hint at its purpose, which turns out to be the sole, sad justification for its redundant life. It is known as the Listening Post, officially 'The Greatstone-on-Sea Listening Device', and it was the concrete manifestation of a civil defence idea to pinpoint enemy aircraft or airships by acoustic reflection. Needless to say, it didn't work, and so there it stays, now a listed structure, puzzling the inmates of the neighbouring holiday camp.

Greenhithe

Ingress Abbey Follies (18th century; 19th century)
TQ 589 748

The site of Ingress Abbey is under threat of imminent redevelopment as we write. It would be a tragedy of major proportions if this remarkably unresearched site, which has held out against the increasing industrialization of the area for centuries, were allowed to disappear. Indeed, the park started out of industry—what would seem to be a cliff-face at the southern edge of the park is the remains of a chalk quarry dating back to Roman times. We say 'park', but it is hard to tell. From the lodge at the entry to the Ingress Abbey Estate, to the follies, grottoes, tunnels and garden buildings, to the new buildings in the grounds, to the house itself, everything is derelict, destroyed, ruined and abandoned. Add to this its location in one of the most dismal quarters of the county, and you have a deeply depressing prospect.

The former park is a tangle of wild garlic, ground ivy and brambles. Sudden cliffs reveal themselves dangerously at the last moment. Getting through the undergrowth is an achievement in itself—this would not make an ideal site for the Folly Fellowship's annual summer garden party. But here and there are traces of what it might have been like: on the right-hand side of the drive (now a concrete slip road for heavy lorries), near the ruined lodge and set below the present road level, is a tripartite flint grotto, probably dating from the mid-18th century. A little further down on the left-hand side is the Cave of the Seven Heads, so called because there are four heads carved inside and out.

Past an abandoned and rapidly decaying 1970s residential block, dating from the time when the estate was the Sea School 'Worcester', training boys for the Merchant Navy, we come to Ingress Abbey itself. There

was a house on this site from the 14th century, although the present house, horribly ruined but not beyond salvation, dates mainly from 1833. Traces of an earlier building can clearly be seen. The jungle intensifies here. Looming behind the house is a ruined archway-cum-gatehouse, with a large Gothic traceried window and an upper chamber, still accessible by scrambling up the side of a cliff, but so close to the house that we suspect it must have been sited deliberately as an *objet*—which begs the question, was it built as a ruin? If so, it is one of the most substantial folly arches in southern England. It is known as The Grange, and in 1997 it was listed Grade II under that name with a tentative dating of 1833. Other structures at Ingress listed at the same time include the Cave of the Seven Heads, the Monk's Well (which may have been an ice-house), the romantically titled Lover's Arch and the Flint Cave. There are two substantial doorways set in the cliff face, each side of the Lover's Arch and about

The Grange, Ingress Abbey

10 metres apart, doors that are big enough to allow vehicles through. Behind is a tunnel, which goes into the cliff face at an angle, turns through 90 degrees and comes out at the other door. A total distance of about 14 metres. That's all. Why? This is utterly baffling. Another tunnel, now accessible only by scrambling over a pile of earth, runs straight and true for over 100ft (30m) before

beginning a gentle, elegant curve just before it finishes. Even more perplexing.

Who was responsible? Some familiar names from the folly canon begin to emerge. Sir William Chambers worked here in the 1760s. John Disney Roebuck bought the estate in 1788 and gave it to his son, Henry, the gambling builder of Midford Castle or Roebuck's Folly (see Midford in the Somerset chapter). The rebuilding of the house in 1833 by the architect Charles Moreing was carried out for James Harmer, a London alderman. We know a little of the history of the Abbey, but nobody has discovered who or why these baffling structures were built. Was Harmer responsible? In the conventional sense they are not follies. They are archaeological puzzles, and someone must be able to come up with a reason or an explanation for them, given time. But there is no time. The Council, the heirs of successive councils that have permitted this part of Kent to be turned into one of England's least lovely places, is eager to press on with the development. It was not ever thus. At the beginning of this century the Shah of Persia was asked what he thought of the River Thames. 'The only thing worth mentioning,' he said, 'was at Greenhithe where there was a mansion standing amid trees on a green carpet extending down to the water's edge.' There is no longer a Shah; there is no longer a Persia; but there is still an Ingress Abbey. It could yet be saved.

Hadlow

May's Folly (1838–48)
TQ 640 500

Samuel Bagshaw's *History, Gazetteer and Directory of the County of Kent* (1847) describes it as follows:

> HADLOW CASTLE, *the residence and property of W B. May, Esq., is a superb mansion, recently erected, and a fine example of architectural embellishments. An octagonal tower at the east end rises ninety feet high, built partly with stone and partly with brick, cemented, from which the level nature of the country can be seen at a great distance This tower exhibits a unique specimen of diversity and beauty; another short tower decorated with pinnacles, rises from the body of the building, to which costly appendages are constantly being added.*

May's Folly can be seen from miles around, and its silhouette is familiar to every traveller in the area. It was built between 1838 and 1848 (the tower, originally an afterthought, was

May's Folly just before the lantern was taken down

finished first, in 1840) by the architect George Ledwell Taylor for the rich squire Walter Barton May, and has been the source of several good folly stories. First, May's wife left him and he wanted her to be reminded of him wherever she went in the county; second, May wanted to see the ships in the Thames but forgot the downs were in the way (a common excuse); third, May had a rivalry with William Beckford and wanted to out-Fonthill Fonthill (the tower does, in fact, bear a remarkable resemblance to the Fonthill tower, which fell in 1822); fourth, he wanted to be entombed above ground so that an old prophecy that the property would pass out of the family when he was buried would never come true. Strangely enough, May's wife did leave him, and he built a 39ft (11.9m) top turret after her departure. The tower is spectacular—its final height of 170ft (52m) made it one of the tallest follies in the country.

May's actual house, Hadlow Castle, was demolished in 1951, and the tower has outlasted it and assumed its name. By any standards, it is an excellent piece of Gothic architecture, phallic in the extreme, and it is interesting to note that the architect Taylor was four times married and had 11 children by his first wife. Perhaps there is something in it after all.

A storm in 1987 severely damaged the tower, and May's Folly is now in the doldrums. The lantern has been removed to prevent further accidents, scaffolding is up, but there is an impasse. At the time of writing, Tonbridge and Malling Council has won over £1 million of grant aid for its renovation and restoration, but the owner refuses to leave, provoking newspaper headlines such as 'Council lays siege to topple tower man'. It is one of the World Monuments Fund's 100 most endangered monuments.

Higham

Obelisk (c.1833)
TQ 710 720

A good obelisk is to be found at Higham, on Telegraph Hill, between Gravesend and Rochester. It is tall and solid, said to be of brick plastered over, but it has been restored and neatly pointed to give the impression it has been constructed from massive 3ft (90cm) square blocks of stone. There used to be an inscription:

> *The Friends of Freedom in Kent*
> *erected this to the memory of*
> *Charles Larkin*
> *in grateful testimony of his Fearless and long advocation of*
> *Civil and Religious Liberty*
> *and his zealous exertions in promoting the ever memorable measure of*
> *Parliamentary Reform*
> *A.D. 1832*

This has disappeared during the obelisk's renovation, and has been replaced by a modest plaque, which simply says:

CHARLES LARKIN

(1775–1833)

PARLIAMENTARY REFORMER

which is more than the *Dictionary of National Biography* has to say about him.

Kearnsey

Sham Ruin (early 19th century)
TR 280 430

At Kearnsey Abbey is an elegant little sham ruin built from genuine medieval fragments, probably in the early 19th century. The two pointed window openings appear to be genuine. One stone used in its construction is dated 1609. The pretty walled garden is generally open to the public.

Kingsgate

Lord Holland's Follies (18th century)
TR 380 710

The Margate grottoes (see below) may have something to do with Henry, Lord Holland, who was the only really rich man in the Isle of Thanet at the right time. He was busy building his own follies a mile or two away from Margate at Kingsgate on the North Foreland. The superbly named Hackemdown Tower, the Arx Ruochim, the actual King's Gate, Kingsgate Castle, the Whitfield Tower—these are the remnants of a once-extensive collection of publicly funded follies, although the public was not aware of that fact at the time. Henry Fox (1705–74), an able, treacherous, self-seeking man, was appointed Paymaster-General after a stormy political career, during which George II had asked him to form a government. This was the opportunity he had been playing for, and by the time he was forced out of office it was alleged that over £250,000 had found its way into his pockets. The poet Thomas Gray was one of his fiercest critics; in a poem entitled 'Impromptu, suggested by a View, in 1766, of the Seat and Ruins of a Deceased [sic] nobleman at Kingsgate, Kent' he wrote:

> *Old, and abandoned by each venal friend*
> *Here Holland form'd the pious resolution*
> *To smuggle a few years, and strive to mend*
> *A broken character and constitutions*
> *Here mouldering fanes and battlements*
>   *arise*
> *Turrets and arches nodding to their fall*
> *Unpeopled monast'ries delude our eyes*
> *And mimic desolation covers all.*

Holland's building works at Kingsgate were said to be an attempt to recreate Tully's Formian Villa; how close he came is best left to the imagination. Most of Holland House

Kearnsey Abbey Arches

Kingsgate Castle

has been demolished, although a small part remains staring out to sea, converted into terraced houses. The biggest folly still standing is Kingsgate Castle, but this has been radically changed. Originally, it was built as stables for the house in the style of an Edwardian Welsh castle, but the skill of Edward's master masons was lacking and it soon collapsed, leaving only a large, round tower standing. What one sees today is the Castle Keep Hotel, a 19th-century reconstruction by Lord Avebury, built around a quadrangle on the cliff edge, grey against the white of Holland House. Across Joss Bay is a pub called the Captain Digby, crenellated, not a folly, but mentioned because it was built specifically to put up 18th-century visitors who came to see the follies. Then it was called the Bede House and was apparently a house of some licentiousness; at any rate half of it fell into the sea during a storm or an exceptionally good party, and what remained was rebuilt and renamed 'The Noble Captain Digby' (after Lord Holland's nephew and drinking companion) in 1809.

The Arx Ruochim, or Neptune's Temple, was a small-scale copy of one of Henry VIII's renowned concentric forts, such as Deal or Camber. There was a red brick tower in the middle, faced with chalk, and a statue of Neptune together with an inscription, which hopefully claimed that the monument had been erected by Vortigern in the year 448. Most of it has collapsed; only the 10ft (3m) high plinth remains.

The Whitfield Tower on Northdown Hill, the highest point in Thanet, is another

rebuilding. It collapsed in 1818 but by then had become a useful landmark for sailors, so Trinity House re-erected it. With a square bottom, two octagonal upper storeys and an onion-shaped ball finial, it was built: 'To the memory of Robert Whitfield Esquire. The ornament and under Thomas Wynne Esquire, the adorner of Kingsgate.' Whitfield had sold his land at Kingsgate to Holland, then acted as his agent and builder. As everything he built collapsed within a few years, he must have been a man of singular personal charm to have had a client build him such a memorial.

Until 1683 Kingsgate had been known as St Bartholomew's Gate, but after King Charles II landed here, the name was changed. To commemorate the event Lord Holland built an arch, the King's Gate, at the gap in the cliff where the King landed, and covered it with suitable inscriptions in Latin and even Saxon characters, explaining the reason for the change of name as from 30 June 1683. A stone eagle, crowned plaques, entwined 'Cs', a 'Y', 'God Bless Bath'lem's Gate' complete the picture. Inevitably, the arch collapsed in a gale in 1819. It was re-erected (the residents are proud of their notorious follies) in the grounds of Port Regis School.

The final Holland folly still standing is also in the convent grounds; this is Hackemdown (some prefer Hackendown; not us) Tower. In the 1760s Lord Holland excavated a barrow on his estate and assumed from the quantity of bones he found inside that he had discovered the site of an ancient battle between the Saxons and the Danes. Accordingly he built this tower—flint, circular, castellated—which is set in the middle of a circular wall that repeats the tower's style and castellations. It used to be set on a base of ogee arches on Doric columns, but these have been removed. A clock was added later, and a Latin inscription reads:

Danorum & Saxonum hic occisorum
Dum de Solo Britannico (Milites nihil a
se alienum Putant) Britannis Perfide &
crudeliter olim expulsis luter se
dimicaverunt HEN de HOLLAND
Posuit Qui Duces quaelis hujus Praelii
Exilus Nulla Notat Historia Annum
circiter DCCCL evenit Pugna Et
Pugnam hanc evenisse Fidem faciunt
Ossa quam plurimo Quae sub hoc &
altero Tumulo huic vicino Sunt sepulta.

which (roughly translated) says:

To the shades of the departed and in
memory of the Danes and Saxons who
were killed here while fighting for the
possession of Britain (soldiers think
everything their own), the Britons
having been cruelly and perfidiously
expelled, this was put up by Henry
Holland. History does not record the
names of the leaders or the result of the
action. It happened circa 850 and that it
happened here seems true from the
quantity of bones buried in this and the
nearby tumulus.

With the huge amounts of money at his disposal and his enjoyment in creating monuments purporting to come from ancient times, Henry Holland would seem to be the likely begetter of the Margate grotto. The lack of documentation blurs the issue, but the lack of a better candidate points to him or his wife, who, as the daughter of the Duke of Richmond, grew up with a shell grotto at Goodwood House.

Knole

Birdhouse and Sham Ruin (1761)
TQ 540 540

Knole at Sevenoaks is more a village than a house. In its huge park is a little octagonal Gothic building, dating from 1761, known as the Birdhouse, now a gamekeeper's cottage, and next to it is a sham ruin, which was built about the same time with pieces acquired from Otford Palace. It was in the Birdhouse that Lord Amherst kept the pheasants that now bear his name, which he brought back from China, where he had been ambassador.

Leeds

Leeds Castle Grotto (1986–7)
TQ 840 530

'The best 20th-century grotto' will not be much of a superlative for Leeds Castle grotto (although recently the very best restoration work has been done on old grottoes and very good new ones arrive nearly each month to please us), but perhaps 'and also one of the best 18th-century grottoes' would be merely sufficient. What architect Vernon Gibberd, *rocailleur* Diana Reynell and sculptor Simon Verity have achieved here is out of this world. Really. The grotto is billed as just a tourist attraction, the centre of a maze, but it is much more. You enter the Underworld, where things are upside down, where fish swim, swans parade, the Elements are personified, the Styx is crossed, and where you finally stand before the Mask of Fire. The final attraction is the Hermitage, designed by yet another superb craftsman, Julian Bannerman. One hesitates between describing the grotto in detail—every crystal, shell, coral, blue john and tufa of it—or giving the reader and potential visitor some space to experience the very best 20th-century grotto building we can

Grot work at Leeds Castle

offer. This grotto sparked a grotto revival, and the above-mentioned artists are now all busy making Britain a place of crystals and tufa. Our only other advice is to go to the Underworld at Yorkshire's Forbidden Corner (see Tupgill), compare the two and see which you prefer (we are omnivores, so we like both).

Littlestone-on-Sea

Water Tower (1890)
TR 080 240

Many years ago we had the best meal in Kent at the Blue Dolphins Hotel in the silted-up

Cinque Port of New Romney, and we saw a tower raise itself laboriously from the distant shoreline and asked what it could be. 'It's not a folly,' said mine host knowledgeably. 'It's a water tower. A bloke built it at the end of the last century, only he found that the water he pumped up into it was always brackish, so it was never used. Somebody turned it into a house, but it's supposed to be haunted.' Wonderful. We rushed down to the chilly Littlestone coast, and the tower is as ugly and as municipal as one would expect a Victorian water tower to be. It's a big, six-storey, red brick, white-banded tower, immaculately preserved, despite the biting wind from the Channel. In 1886 Littlestone was going to be 'a marine town', so the water tower must have been part of the project.

Loose

Double-decker Grotto (early 19th century)
TQ 770 410

When Grot Secretary Vernon Gibberd of the Folly Fellowship was told by his wife Diana that she remembered playing in the grotto of Boughton Mount as a child, he started to investigate. And not only did a ha-ha, a crinkle-crankle wall, a barn-cum-water tower disguised as a classical sham church and a Greek temple seat with ditto inscription come to light, the grotto itself proved to be most interesting: a double-decker one. The list of owners of Boughton is almost folly enough:
- before 1820: John Allchin, who built something called Clock House;
- 1820s: John Braddick, a West Indian

nabob, who became an avid horticulturist, improved the estate and built a new house, first called Wychden;
- 1890 onwards: George Foster Clark, the custard magnate who also marketed 'Eiffel Tower Lemonade Crystals' and who changed the garden into an Edwardian one. It was Foster Clark who built the sham church. The house itself was damaged by a flying bomb during the war and later demolished.

The grotto is now believed to be early 19th century. It is on an artificial mount, and from the side there is a large entrance arch, rubble round it and on top, and on the mound itself is a grotto-alcove, square with rough pinnacles on the corners. Originally, the alcove had whale bone decoration, but this has gone. Inside the grotto's main chamber there appears to have been a fountain. Thanks to Gibberd and the charity Macintyre, the grotto, the only double-decker grotto we know of in Britain, now has a safer future.

Margate

Grotto (late 18th century)
TR 340 690

Margate has the greatest folly mystery in Kent. In 1835 a schoolmaster called Newlove and his two sons were digging out a disused well on Dane Hill when they broke into a passage leading to an underground chamber. They found torches and entered; what they saw dumbfounded them. Carved out of the solid chalk was a passage leading to an oblong chamber, then two semicircular

The double-decker grotto at Loose

passages opening out into a central domed room. The walls were packed with tiny shells, shells of every sort—it has been calculated that there are 28 different varieties, most of them foreign, covering an incredible 2000 square metres of wall in the most wonderful mosaic patterns—then admiration gave way to puzzlement. Who could have built it? And when?

Investigation showed that the cement with which the shells were stuck to the walls

Inside the Margate grotto

contained fish oil and crushed shells, a method frequently used by the Romans. Portland cement came into common use only after the Napoleonic Wars, after the great grotto builders had finished their work. The extraordinary patterns made by the shells included abstract geometrical designs favoured by Indian, Phoenician, Greek, Egyptian and Roman civilizations from more than 2000 years ago, as well as floral patterns more at home in 18th-century England. Small anomalies were ignored. In popular imagination it became a Mithraic Temple or a Phoenician shrine to the moon goddess Tanit (Tanit = Thanet?)—several of the patterns show the sun, moon and stars. There are, however, traces of modern bricks used in the building of one of the Gothic shaped arches, and it seems unlikely that if the grotto had been built 2000 years ago that, first, it would have survived undiscovered and, second, the Phoenicians would have used 18th-century bricks. But people still seem to be no wiser as to who built it or when. All the evidence would seem to point to the end of the 18th century, but the amount of work it must have

taken, and the time—Scott's grotto in Ware took 30 years to build and is spartan in its comparative simplicity—and the money—grottoes, especially incorporating all those different varieties of foreign shells, were never cheap—would surely never have passed unnoticed by the citizens of Margate. And yet, and yet… ever willing to spoil a good story, we suspect Lady Holland, daughter of the Duke of Richmond (see also Kingsgate, above, and Goodwood in Sussex), to have had a hand in it somehow, and, warming to our conspiracy theory, the later owners and 'discoverers' of the grotto have carefully destroyed any evidence connecting it to Lady Holland in order to increase its mystery and therefore marketability. Please prove us wrong.

Mereworth

Arch (1723)
Aviary (1960s)
TQ 669 522

Along the road to Maidstone is Mereworth Castle, which has a fine but deteriorating triumphal arch of 1723 on a wooded hill to the south, the same feel as the much bigger Heaven's Gate in Hampshire but not as appealing. It is loosely based on Titus's Arch in Rome, and the designer may have been

Mereworth Castle Arch

Colen Campbell, who built the house.

There is also said to be a Gothick aviary designed by Lord Snowdon in the 1960s, radically different from his Grade II* listed aviary at London Zoo, but as the present owner of Mereworth refuses even Snowdon access, we have not been able to see this. The arch can be seen from a public road.

Newington

Eyecatcher (18th century)
`TR 180 370`

Temple Cottage, a castellated square house with a cupola and medieval bits, need not detain us. It was probably built as an eyecatcher to Beachborough House.

Ospringe

Sham Ruin (19th century)
`TQ 990 600`

Syndale House was burned in 1961. Its remains and some outbuildings house the Syndale Park Motel, and in the garden is a small sham ruin, a crumbling arch of flint and burned brick only about 8ft (2.4m) high. By

Ospringe Arch

coincidence, Syndale Park used to be called Judde's Folly, after Daniel Judde of Faversham, who produced gunpowder for Cromwell's army. Judde prospered and in 1652 started building himself a grand country house near Ospringe, and when the house was finished in 1660, Charles II had returned and Judde, a staunch Parliamentarian, was driven from his Ospringe residence.

Pluckley

Tower (1992)
`TQ 920 419`

Victorian values have been resurrected at what is now the Madrona Nursery, Pluckley. It started life as a quasi-'agricultural-building-for-storing-a-tractor-to-be-built-in-the-form-of-a-traditional-Kentish-Oast-house-with-attached-barn'. It is, of course, a folly, but you only get planning permission for a.b.f.s.a.t.t.b.b.i.t.f.o.a.t.K.O.h.w.a.b's

nowadays. The folly was built by Liam MacKenzie and is made in the most beautiful coloured brick diaperwork. The tower is its real glory, topped by a copper spire and the Kentish arm-with-sword as a bronze lightning conductor. Luckily, it doesn't resemble an oast house in any way and is much more like a church tower, which in a sense it could have been—it was first going be the chapel of rest for a pet cemetery (a nice change from planning a golf course), but on second thoughts was turned into a garden centre, but still looks suspiciously like a mid-19th century Teulon church.

Ramsgate

Obelisk (1821)
`TR 390 640`

An 1821 granite obelisk stands on the Ramsgate harbour front, floridly recording the departure of George IV from the port.

Riverhead

Shepherd's Watch (c.1770)
`TQ 510 549`
Obelisk
`TQ 512 550`

Thanks to a study by Adela Wright, we now know everything and more about the dilapidated summerhouse at Montreal Park, Salter's Heath. Major General Jeffrey Amhurst built Montreal Park after his campaign in Canada. The house has gone but, as so often, the other buildings remain. The summerhouse, or Shepherd's Watch, is rather simple—rubble with dressed quoins and a stepped gable—and a large arch as entrance. Inside are painted quotations from Ambrosius' *De Officiis* and from Pliny's *Historia Naturalis*, all referring to agriculture and soldiery and how well the two combine. The obelisk records all of Amhurst's victories. An ice-house stands to the north of both summerhouse and obelisk.

Rolvenden

Gnome Garden (20th century)
`TQ 840 310`

From Tenterden towards Rolvenden is a gnome garden to make other gnome gardeners creep home in shame. But beware, the gnomes are taken inside into the warmth in winter, so you may find an empty garden.

St Margaret's at Cliffe

Garden Buildings (late 18th–early 19th century)
TR 350 460

There aren't many apiaries in the country, but there *is* one at Oxney Court, more of a bear pit, octagonal and sunken; there's also a summerhouse and a folly sham ruin. Robert Lugar worked here around 1816, and we may have to put that date on the garden features.

Sheerness

Ship on Shore Grotto (c.1830)
TQ 930 740

Some people may love the scenery of the Isle of Sheppey, but most find it frankly boring. Even in sunlight it has a sort of hopeless utilitarianism, which one can imagine permeating the very souls of the inhabitants, rendering them stolid, flat and unimaginative. Preconceptions such as these are dealt a mortal body blow when we come across a building like the grotto at the Ship on Shore public house in Sheerness. It is sheer fun and built in a genuine spirit of serendipity with whatever building materials came easily to hand. Fortunately, the nearest material to hand was concrete—in 1830 a ship carrying barrels of cement was wrecked on the north shore. Naturally, the barrels leaked, water got in and the cement set hard in barrel-shaped blocks. A local farmer, spying his opportunity, carted the barrel blocks away and built this gorgeous little grotto, piling the barrels six high and filling in the gaps with rubble, flint and burr bricks, shaping the whole to form a sweeping parapet with a succession of curves. The building is L-shaped, with three arches facing the pub car park and two arches facing the road, now planked in and forming the windows and doors. At the moment it is used as the games arcade for the pub, and local youths bleep and buzz and gobble on video games and fruit machines, stolidly oblivious to their surroundings.

Speldhurst

Tower (c.1876)
TQ 550 420

Late in the 1980s we visited David Salomons's tower at Broomhill and discussed whether this was a folly or not. It's a clock tower, a water tower and used to be an observatory as well. Our gut feeling said, of course *folly*, but you never know how the neighbours might react. In 1991 Alan Terrill researched its history, and although we knew a little about

Salomons, the man himself became possibly more interesting than his tower.

David Salomons was a Jewish emancipator, whose merchant father married a Dutch woman. Salomons was one of the founders of the London and Westminster Bank, wrote books on financial matters and became the first Jewish Lord Mayor of London. In 1873 he left his money and estates to his nephew David Lionel Salomons, who was later knighted. The nephew was scientifically inclined, although somewhat fickle in his tastes, and experimented with electricity (for some reason, these are usually good folly builders, as they require towers and the like) and was an early car owner (he was the one who saw to it that cars need not be preceded by a man carrying a red flag). Apparently, he started building the Speldhurst tower (together with palatial

David Salomon's tower

stables of the 1890s and a castellated fruit store) as soon as he got his inheritance, and it was finished in 1876. On top was an observatory. He then changed that to an enormously powerful light in order to brighten the surroundings, got rid of that and brought in meteorological instruments before ending up by throwing all this paraphernalia out as well and filling the tower with water.

The tower is round, castellated, of course, with a slender and higher turret next to it. The house has a museum devoted to the Salomons family, although it is not normally open to the public.

Tenterden

Gazebos (early 16th century)
Gatehouse (1853)
Tower House (19th century)
TQ 880 330

There are two early 16th-century gazebos in the grounds of Hales Place in Oaks Road. They are red brick, octagonal, now roofless, with castellated parapets and Tuscan columns by the doors. Heronden Hall, south of Tenterden, has a Gothic gatehouse, probably built by the house's architect William John Donthorn, but it was severely damaged in the 1995 storms.

The best item is Tower House on Ashford Road, particulars unknown, but next to a house totally different in style leans a square tower, castellated but not really Gothic. One must have been there before the other.

Throwley

Grotto
Sham Chapel (c.1820)
New York (c.1780)
TQ 880 560

Inland Kent is far more attractive than the coast. About 15 miles from Sheerness is Throwley, south of Faversham—it could be on a different continent. This is the perceived image of rural England, with soft rolling hills, wooded glades and the distant summery sound of leather on willow. Belmont Park was reconstructed between 1787 and 1792 by Samuel Wyatt for George Harris, the first of a long line of distinguished public servants, who was ennobled in 1815. The Harrises were punctilious to a man: correct, reserved, polite, hard-working, honourable—one of them even captained England at cricket in the days when they used to win—but somewhere in the family (perhaps in George's wife Ann) was an exuberant sense of frivolity, which manifested itself in an untypically Harris-like form. Behind the house in an enclosed garden is a wonderful grotto constructed with enormous ammonites, tufa and 70 sarsen stones, with one upright stone at the entrance.

The Coronation Walk leads from the house to the cricket field, and at the end of the avenue is a sham chapel made of flint. It is part Gothic and part Indian, a curious but suitable mixture of styles, because Harris's chosen title was Baron Harris of Seringapatam and Mysore. If the name of the avenue refers to the coronation of George IV, this would propose a realistic date of 1820.

Belmont sham chapel/tower

Between Belmont and Throwley itself is New York, mentioned by John Newman as 'a pair of cottages in the American style, *c.*1790 by John Plaw who published them in his *Ferme Ornée* (1795)'. Here is how Plaw describes Plate 17, 'American Cottages':

> *These Double Cottages are built (on the plan and in the style of some in America) at Throwley near Feversham* [sic] *in Kent, by Colonel Montresor. I saw them soon after they were completed, and for their extreme singularity introduced them in this work…*

which means that they are not by Plaw, then. Newman's date is a good guess, although they are probably about ten years earlier. Colonel James Gabriel Montresor of the Royal Engineers fought in the American campaigns and died in 1776 in Teynham, 4 miles northwest of the New York cottages. Curiously however, it is probably his son John who would have built these cottages. He was also a Royal Engineer and actually fought at Hell Gate near New York and had Montresor Island named after him. From around 1780 he lived at Belmont Park and coincidentally also bought Syndale House, Ospringe (see above), and he fancied himself as something of an architect. He died in 1786. Although he was only a major, this must have been Plaw's Colonel Montresor.

Tonbridge

Grotto (late 18th century)
TQ 590 460

Bordyke is near Tonbridge, and at The Cedars in Bordyke, on the A26, is a small grotto in the grounds of a house, probably dating from the late 18th century.

Tunbridge Wells

Gazebo (19th century)
TQ 580 400

Much of Tunbridge Wells reeks of follies—
you expect one around every corner. It is the
right period and has the right sites, but until
to date the harvest is simply a tad
disappointing. At the originally solid
Methodist area of Mount Ephraim is Mount
Ephraim House, with a small tower-gazebo
and a Gothicky entrance porch to the house
itself. Dunarlon Park was the site of a large
house and has a summerhouse near its lake.

Waldershare

Belvedere (1725–7)
TR 280 470

The house at Waldershare Park near
Eythorne burned down in 1912, watched with
great interest by Lord North, who seemed
unusually chipper as he dashed in to rescue
selected items that had not been previously
stored off site. It turned out that the noble
lord was heavily insured, and shortly
afterwards a massive new house by Sir
Reginald Blomfield arose on the site.

By far the most interesting building on the
estate is the even uglier belvedere, which was
built for Sir Robert and Lady Arabella
Furnese in 1725–7 at a cost of £1703 7s 4d and
possibly inspired by the most fashionable
architect of the period, the Earl of Burlington.
Its design seems to have been based on one of
the mausolea at Palmyra. Built unassumingly
of red brick (some of it older brick; there may
have been another garden building on this
spot), it was nevertheless conceived on a

grand scale: three storeys, Palladian, 60ft
(18.3m) tall in a double-cube plan, with
boarded-up Venetian windows on the first
floor, once used as a music room. Now rather
sad and derelict, it was not one of
Burlington's more graceful works—in fact it
was never completed.

Restoration work for the Vivat Trust by
the Folly Fellowship's Vernon Gibberd and
Andrew Plumridge began in 1995, but after
some high-handed intervention by English
Heritage work has stopped, and when we last
visited in 1988 the belvedere looked even
more forlorn than before.

Westerham

Belvedere (1730s–40s)
TQ 430 530

Kent's final folly is the belvedere at Squerryes
Court, Westerham. Frustratingly little is
known about this roofless, ruinous building,
romantically associated with Henry VIII and
Anne Boleyn, but it would appear to have
been built in the 18th century as a prospect
tower or hunting lodge. Oddly enough, it is
built of rubble masonry instead of the
ubiquitous north Kent flint and brick, which
shows it to have been designed as a building
of some consequence. It had two floors and a
basement—there are still remnants of
plasterwork—and it may have been built by
John Warde 'as a shelter from which to watch
the training gallops', although this may be
mistaken for a small gazebo, equally ruinous.

Woodchurch

Tortoiserise (1990s)
TQ 929 363

As far as we know, Alan Terrill's first effort at
tortoiserie was the Ruined Chapel
('Damaged in the Great Storm of 1987'), a
deliberately ruined Gothick church of brick
and slate, but all tortoise-sized. Terrill,
family and tortoises moved house, taking the
Ruined Chapel with them, and they have
now devised a second tortoiserie: the male
tortoises got an Egyptian-Gothick temple,
topped, of course, by the philosopher
Tortonimous III. Terrill has also fashioned
an island in his garden pond, with a bridge
leading to it, and an obelisk in remembrance
of his father and grandfather, as well as, in
other parts of the garden, a dry bridge and a
wooden summerhouse. He is planning a
folly tower to put his stained glass windows
in next, and of course he won't stop there.
We hope.

Waldershare Belvedere

LANCASHIRE

Strangely enough, Lancastrian follies tend to be concentrated in the industrial south; the rural north has few follies, apart from the string of pearls in Furness, snaffled by the creation of Cumbria but properly reinstated here. Their quality is not of the highest, with the notable exceptions of Lord Leverhulme's replica of Liverpool Castle at Rivington and, of course, Lancaster's fantastic Ashton Memorial.

Allithwaite (Cumbria)

Kirkhead Tower (early 19th century)
SO 394 759

An embattled early 19th-century tower on Kirkhead Hill, just south of Allithwaite, is said to have been built by the Cavendishes of Holker Hall, although the Hall is some miles away on the other side of the peninsula.

Barrowford

Waterloo Plantation (1819)
SD 846 386

Lancashire can claim a living folly, a vegetable folly, in fact. At Barrowford, in order to leave a remembrance of his part in Napoleon's downfall, Colonel Clayton of Carr Hall planted an avenue of trees near the house. The avenue is in the shape of his regiment's formation on the eve of the Battle of Waterloo. Trees standing away from the avenue represent the officers, but no one can remember which one stands for the gallant Colonel Clayton.

Blacko

Stansfield Tower (late 19th century)
SD 859 421

Deep inland at Blacko is the tall and slender Stansfield Tower, built prominently on a nab by a businessman who wanted to see the sea. A cottage at the seaside would certainly have cost him less, but then we would have been denied the pleasure and puzzlement of trying to understand his motives.

Blackpool

Tower (1891)
SD 306 360

After the 1889 Paris Exhibition imitations of the Eiffel Tower sprouted all over Europe. A small copy even found its way into a public park in Prague. Of the few *epigoni* to survive, the Blackpool Tower is perhaps the best known. These 2500 tons of steel were erected by Maxwell & Tuke between 1891 and 1894, after sufficient time had elapsed for Eiffel's masterpiece to prove its safety.

Britain's traditional suspicion of ideas first propounded by Europeans remains ingrained to this day. Blackpool Tower, at 568ft (173m), is only about half the height of its model, but it achieves a similar dominance over the landscape—for not even the most ardent Lancastrian would claim that Blackpool could rival Paris architecturally. The tower was built by a consortium led by Sir John Bickerstaffe, sometime Mayor of Blackpool, as a strictly commercial undertaking, and as such it has been successful, so why include it here? First, because it is a spectacular eyecatcher, and catching the eye has always been a prerequisite of a folly. Second, the Tower Ballroom is one of the sights of northern Europe, a must to see both for the decoration and for the ritual dancing. Then, because of the megalomania of the undertaking, because to see it with a fresh pair of eyes is to see how bizarre the very idea is (most Britons are so familiar with its image that they have never actually looked at it properly), because it is a wonderful, useless structure if one forgets the money motive. Anything secular, over 500ft (152m) tall and begun in the 19th century should come within our remit, and even more so if it tries to get away with plagiarizing an older building. Even though the tower has been dressed up with ballrooms, playgrounds and boutiques, it remains essentially a megalomaniac belvedere, a monstrous look-out tower—the kind of building we immediately pronounce as 'folly' if erected by some landowner. Finally, the Grade I listed Blackpool Tower will be with us for a long time to come, unlike its similar but vanquished, vanished rivals at Wembley (begun 1889, never completed, demolished 1907), Isle of Man (abandoned 1890), Morecambe (completed but demolished as dangerous the same year) and New Brighton, (completed 1898, demolished 1919). We are thankful for Blackpool Tower's happy preservation.

Broughton-in-Furness (Cumbria)

Gilpin Obelisk (1810)
SD 213 875

An obelisk in the Market Square is to the memory of John Gilpin, who in 1766 donated the land for the market.

Burnley

Monk's Well (1992)
SD 854 309

A pile of stones in Towneley Park, Burnley, was rebuilt as a Gothic arched folly in 1992. It started life as a wellhead called the Monk's Well, built by Charles Towneley. The British Trust for Conservation Volunteers proposed to rebuild it at no cost to the local council, which nevertheless demurred, thinking of future maintenance costs. Then a happy compromise was reached—why not rebuild it as a ruin, which would need less supervision? Nice one.

Capernwray

Gamekeeper's Tower (late 18th century)
SD 541 714

Capernwray Hall now houses the Capernwray Missionary Fellowship and no longer has any interest in its former Gamekeeper's Tower, with its tiny, lancet-arched windows, ruinous on the edge of a copse at the top of a hill some way to the east. Slowly advancing up the hill towards the slighted tower are the serried ranks of

caravans and trailer homes (the lingering scent of PVC fills the air), but one feels the tower will resist the final assault. It must have been occupied within living memory—as the cheap replacement fireplaces and the wooden window frames testify, and there is still paint on the bedroom walls—but the roof and the floors have collapsed, and a crack is widening in the wall. The massive stone quoins and the shelter of the surrounding trees will hold it together for a while yet. Perhaps there is still hope?

Clitheroe

Turret (1937)
SD 742 415

Clitheroe is a bustling little market town, and in the public park below Clitheroe Castle a turret stands in a rose garden. It came from the parapet of the Houses of Parliament, and was given to the Borough of Clitheroe by Captain Sir William Brass MP to celebrate George VI's coronation.

Conishead (Cumbria)

Conishead Priory (1821 onwards)
Sham Chapel
Braddyll Mausoleum (19th century)
SD 297 751
Priory Tower (19th century)
SD 301 761

The train but not the car can cross the Leven viaduct, where Lake Windermere empties into Morecambe Bay, and on the western side is Conishead Priory, built from 1821 onwards by the inefficient Philip Wyatt for Colonel

Braddyll Mausoleum

Conishead Priory

turret. Roger Fisher, a local racehorse trainer, elegantly restored it in 1990 and now a training track for his horses winds up to it. It is fitted out with a refrigerator, a couple of chairs and two glasses, a most civilized folly. A 1932 map shows another tower next to this, which has now disappeared. There was also a hermitage—only the base is discernible— and a grotto, a man-made tunnel through the hill with decaying entrances.

The best conceit here is the Mausoleum, on a hill above Bardsea, now on the edge of a golf course. It is triangular, set on a round base, which once had railings, with buttresses on the corners, corbel, little pyramids topping each corner, and a cupola with a lantern light. In each side of the building is a pointed niche, with sepulchral urns remaining in two of them. The inscriptions are almost illegible:

Obiit 23rd November 1773

Sarah Giles 1774

John Cale Esq. 1814

The weathered folly seems to be descended from the wilder Irish buildings of the 18th century, especially Thomas Wright's Tollymore follies, and evidently predates Braddyll and Wyatt.

T.R. Gale Braddyll. The house is one of the more astounding monuments of the Gothic Revival. Eventually, it cost the Colonel over £140,000, and the estate had to be sold in order to meet the bill. The Priory is now the Manjushri Mahayana Buddhist Centre.

During the 15 years it took to build Conishead, Braddyll diverted himself by building a few follies. A medieval chapel on Chapel Island, Cartmel Sands, was transformed into a sham ruined eyecatcher which, for its own part, has now fallen into genuine ruins after a storm in 1984. Nearer to the house, but now part of the Great Head House Estate, is a small tower on the top of Hermitage Hill, octagonal and machicolated, with cross arrowslits and a tiny bartizan

Dalton

Ashurst's Beacon (1798)
SD 500 083

A couple of towers have settled east of Ormskirk, among such delightfully named villages and hamlets as Dangerous Corner, Hunger Hill, Stormy Corner, Ring o' Bells and Robin Hood. North of Skelmersdale is

Ashurst's Beacon

Ashurst's Beacon, built in 1798 during the Napoleonic Wars and giving its name to the nearby pub. A tall, slender, pyramidal spire sits on top of a square plinth, once a room but now with all the windows and door blocked up. In 1962 it was presented to the corporation of Wigan by Florence Meadows in memory of her husband.

Darwen

Jubilee Tower (1897)
SD 680 215

On top of Darwen Hill stands the Jubilee or Victoria Tower. A buttressed octagon, decorated with shields above the open arched base, supports the octagonal stone tower; the shaft is pierced by elongated windows, and the embattled parapet serves as a crown. Inside, 65 broad stone steps lead up to a platform before a further 17 steps of rattling metal spiral staircase reach up to the lantern, where the wind instantly attempts to pluck the climber over the parapet.

Royal sentiment was not the only reason this tower was built: in 1878 five men were served with writs by the local squire after a provocative Sunday afternoon stroll on Darwen Moor. He argued that the men were trespassing on private property and frightening game—the men fought the case together and won, thus opening the moors for public enjoyment. With good Lancastrian

Darwen's Jubilee Tower

economy, the tower serves to celebrate both the Jubilee and the walkers' victory.

1897

THIS TOWER

WAS ERECTED (AND A SUM OF £650

DEVOTED IN AID OF THE

NURSING ASSOCIATION)...

TO COMMEMORATE THE

DIAMOND JUBILEE

OF THE REIGN OF

HER MAJESTY

QUEEN VICTORIA

OPENED SEPTEMBER 24TH 1898 BY

THE REV WILLIAM ARTHUR DUCKWORTH MA

LORD OF THE MANOR

then the extensive committee, all named, with their honorariums, and right at the end:

R W SMITH-SAVILLE, BORO ENGINEER & HON

ARCHITECT

RICHARD J WHALLEY, BUILDER

There is a 1996 plaque commemorating the centenary of the granting of public access to Darwen Moor, and a 1997 plaque commemorating the start of the building of Darwen Tower. We arrived too early in the year to see what they had planned for 1998.

India Mills Chimney (1859)
SD 693 218

While in the wallpaper town of Darwen itself, one cannot fail to notice the immense polychromatic tower chimney at India Mills on the south side of town. Built between 1859 and 1867, the cotton mill's tall tower is one of a variety of tower chimneys that came into being with the publication of several tracts on chimney building in the 1850s and 1860s. Leeds may have finer examples, but for sheer nerve of design and robustness the Darwen chimney holds its own. India Mills seems permanently to be for sale, while its Grade II* tower stands as erect as an impoverished aristocrat.

Elswick

Stable Screen (1819)
SD 435 385

There are miscellaneous Gothicisms all over the county, including a castellated stable screen of 1819 at Elswick.

Far Sawrey (Cumbria)

The Station (1799)
SD 378 955

Halfway up the lake a ferry runs between Far Sawrey and Bowness. Don't even think of trying to use it on a bank holiday. On the Far

Sawrey side is the castellated Gothic Station Cottage. The more interesting folly is above it on Claife Heights, most of which is owned by the National Trust. Here is the Station, a summerhouse built by the Rev. William Braithwaite, who originally named it Belle View. Braithwaite planted about 40,000 trees on his newly acquired land, much to the chagrin of Wordsworth, writing in one of the Lake Guides:

The Pleasure house is happily situated, and is well in its kind, but, without intending any harsh reflections on the contriver... it may be said that he, who remembers the spot on which this building stands, and the immediate surrounding grounds as they were less than 30 years ago, will sigh for the coming of that day when Art, through every rank of society, shall be taught to have more reverence for Nature.

Wordsworth may rest assured that Nature is busily engaged in getting her own back from Art, for the Station is dilapidating fast. The pavilion is made of different kinds of stone and built on an octagonal ground plan. Several towers are attached to the two-storey core, and this may have been done by its second owner, J.C. Curwen, who bought the place two years after Braithwaite built it. The window openings and the doors are rectangular, the towers are castellated. Originally, the upper windows contained stained glass, 'giving a good representation of the manner in which the landscape would be affected in different seasons...'. Apparently this worked like a giant Claude Lorraine glass. From the building a short stretch of wall with an arch and cross arrowslits runs off into the rock.

Finsthwaite (Cumbria)

Pennington Tower (1799)
SD 364 872

In the woods near the village of Finsthwaite, at the southern end of Lake Windermere, is a tower raised by James King of Finsthwaite House. An inscription gives his reasons for building Pennington Tower:

To honour the officers, seamen, and marines of the Royal Navy, whose matchless conduct and irresistible valour decisively defeated the fleets of France, Spain and Holland, and promoted and protected liberty and commerce...

Perhaps Mr King, when pressed, would stress 'commerce'.

Finsthwaite Spire

Finsthwaite Spire (17th century)
SD 356 865

A squat, rectangular rubble obelisk hides mysteriously and effectively (we couldn't find it) in Spire Wood, surely erected by James King for some pressing but now forgotten reason.

Hampsfield Fell (Cumbria)

The Hospice (1846)
SD 398 794

High on the fells above Grange-over-Sands is a well-preserved, plain, square building with an external staircase to the roof, rather ambitiously called The Hospice. Above the entrance is the inscription 'ΡΟΔΟΔΑΚΤΨΛΟΣ ΗΟΣ' in Clarendon Greek, and indeed it does face east towards the rosy-fingered dawn of Homeric renown. It, together with a curious but effective direction indicator on top, was erected 'for the shelter and entertainment of travellers over the fell' by Thomas Remington, the vicar of Cartmel. The simple interior is covered with inscriptions:

THIS HOSPICE AS AN OPEN DOOR,
A LIKE TO WELCOME RICH AND POOR;
A ROOMY SEAT FOR YOUNG AND OLD,
WHERE THEY MAY SCREEN THEM FROM THE COLD.
THREE WINDOWS THAT COMMAND A VIEW
TO NORTH. TO WEST, AND SOUTHWARD TOO;
A FLIGHT OF STEPS REQUIRETH CARE,

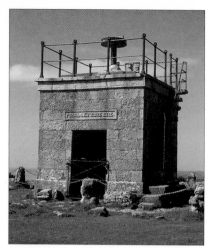

The Hospice

THE ROOF WILL SHOW A PROSPECT RARE:
MOUNTAIN AND VALE YOU THENCE SURVEY,
THE WINDING STREAMS AND NOBLE BAY:
THE SUN AT NOON THE SHADOW HIDES,
ALONG THE EAST AND WESTERN SIDES:
A LENGTHENED CHAIN HOLDS GUARD AROUND.
TO KEEP THE CATTLE FROM THE GROUND;
KIND READER FREELY TAKE YOUR PLEASURE,
BUT DO NO MISCHIEF TO MY TREASURE.

and to praise the fabulous view:

O God! O good beyond compare!
If this thy meaner works be fair…
How glorious must those mansions be
Where thy redeemed dwell with thee.

and to allow a certain fatalistic cynicism:

TAKE NOTICE

All persons visiting this Hospice by permission of
the owner, are requested to respect private
property, and not by acts of wanton mischief and
destruction show that they possess more muscle
than brain. I have no hope that this request will
be attended to for as Solomon says 'Though thou
shouldest bray a fool in a mortar among wheat
with a pestle yet will not his foolishness depart
from him.' G. REMINGTON, Cartmel 1846

which we were delighted to discover has not
been borne out in later years. The Hospice
stands untouched by graffiti or the
ubiquitous spray can, which is not unduly
surprising as the place is busier than
Piccadilly Circus at rush hour. Parties of
ramblers keep arriving in groups of twos and
threes, like the No. 19 bus, and we were made
to feel distinctly underdressed in our
unbranded clothing.

Below the ridge to the north is a small,
two-storey castellated tower, roofless and
gutted, perhaps as a tea-house for the
Longlands estate.

Hare Appletree Fell

Jubilee Tower (1887)
SD 542 573

On the moorland southeast of Quernmore
stands this plainest of castellated towers. It is
presumably solid, as there is no trace of any
window or entrance, with external steps
leading to the roof 15ft (4.6m) up, from where
the view is virtually identical to the view from
ground level. A fast-eroding plaque by the
steps reads:

THIS TOWER
WAS ERECTED BY
JAMES HARRISON
OF HARE APPLETREE
IN COMMEMORATION OF THE
JUBILEE OF HER MAJESTY
QUEEN VICTORIA
ANNO DOMINI 1887

This is ten years older than the vastly more
impressive Jubilee Tower at Darwen; we tend
to forget that Victoria celebrated two
jubilees.

Hartshead (Greater Manchester)

Hartshead Pike Tower (1863)
SD 961 024

Hartshead, on the northeastern periphery of
Manchester near Mossley, has a short tower
on a big hill. It serves well as an eyecatcher, in
the distance looking like a nipple caught by

Hartshead Pike

surprise. Closer to, it looks more like a sharpened pencil stub, with the lantern at the top taking the lead role. All the windows and the door have now been bricked up, and the fat little tower has a perceptible and worrying backwards tilt. It is at least the third tower on the site; only the plaque remains of the previous occupant:

> *Look well at Me Before you Go*
> *And see you Nothing at Me Throw*
> *This Pike was rebuilt by*
> *Publick Donations*
> *Anno Domini 1751*

What better reasons for its reconstruction than to mark the Prince of Wales's marriage to Alexandra of Denmark in 1863 'and to restore the ancient landmark of Hartshead Pike'? Originally the tower was to have been 85ft (26m) high, but lack of money or stamina prevented completion, so the edifice was declared finished as it stood and capped with a conical roof. The architect was John Eaton.

Higher Tatham

Clearbeck House Pyramid (1989)
SD 605 694

Built as part of a metaphysical garden by Peter Osborne, this 12ft (3.7m) high breezeblock pyramid, sprayed with dung to encourage a wide variety of ivies, represents death, with the grotto passage through the centre leading through to a pool and a hidden garden. Should we not be walking through this backwards? But no, the builder tells us that if the Pyramid, with ivy, shells and bones in its grotto, signifies Death, then water is the transition, and the garden Hope.

Hoghton

Brindle Folly (early 19th century)
SD 505 106

Buried in a private wood close to the Preston–Blackburn railway line is a mysterious little round sandstone tower with an octagonal cap. Walls with Gothic arches flank the tower, and on one of the stones is a primitive carving of a fish, which has a feeling of great antiquity. Of course, this is probably all cod-Gothic—there is also said to be a datestone of 1634, but we could not find it. Other stones are deeply carved with diagonal lines, and we conclude that the little folly may have been constructed from recycled materials. A narrow spiral staircase of just 34 tiny steps leads to the open top of the tower and a view—well, a glimpse—through the wood to the railway.

Hornby

Claughton Hall (1930)
SD 575 660

An impressive feat of architectural engineering was the removal of Claughton Hall, near Hornby, from its original site to a hilltop a little way to the north along the A683. It was moved by Esmond Morse in the 1930s for the benefit of the view, but he forgot part of it, and the lost property is now called Claughton Hill Farm.

Ince Blundell (Merseyside)

Pantheon (1802)
Temple (1780)
Column (1780)
SD 327 030

Ince Blundell is rural Merseyside, almost a village, threatened by Liverpool. The house belonged to Henry Blundell, who in 1802 erected his mighty domed Pantheon with an Ionic tetrastyle portico adjacent to his house as a fitting depository for the famous collection of antique sculpture he owned. It is still used as an art gallery, fortunately for sculpture rather than paintings, which are less likely to be damaged by the leaking roof.

In the garden are a Tuscan temple, also built as an art gallery, with a massive oversized face on the pediment, and a matching column crowned with an eagle. Both are by William Everard, whose portrait shows him with the design for the temple in his hands.

Knowsley (Merseyside)

White Man's Tower (early 18th century)
Summerhouse
SD 454 943

Knowsley Hall, still home of the Earls of Derby but now with a popular safari park in the grounds, is right on the edge of the city. House and park form a bastion against an urban pincer movement. Above the park's generous lake is an early 18th century tower, remodelled from round to square but now ruined. This features in a description of 1766, illustrating the finer points of park-breaking:

> *At Knowsley-house, having by fair words*
> *and a small bribe, prevailed upon one of*
> *Lord Derby's grooms to get the keys to the*
> *gate, we passed through the park, thus*
> *making a short cut to Prescot, where we*
> *intended to dine… On top of the highest*
> *eminence in this delightful park is a very*
> *neat summerhouse with four arched*

White Man's Tower

*windows opening on as many elegant
and extensive prospects. These landscapes
are painted in the arch of each respective
window, but they are mouldering away
and no care is taken to renew them.*

This description is hard to reconcile with the park today, for the 'highest eminence' is decisively crowned by the ruined square tower, while a summerhouse, which otherwise fits the description, is down by a gate at the side of the drive, still intact, but the paintings, of course, have long gone.

Lancaster

Ashton Memorial (1907)
SD 488 613

England's most spectacular folly was erected as the *pièce de résistance* of Williamson Park by the thrice-married linoleum manufacturer James Williamson II, Lord Ashton (1842–1930), allegedly to commemorate one of his wives. A brass plaque inside makes no excuse for the folly:

> THIS BUILDING WAS ERECTED BY
> THE RIGHT HON. LORD ASHTON
> AS A MEMORIAL TO HIS FAMILY AND
> PRESENTED TO THE INHABITANTS
> OF LANCASTER A.D. 1907

So dearly did Ashton love his family that he eventually died intestate, with an estate valued at £9.5 million. The park had been given to the city by Williamson's father in 1880. At its peak, their factory employed a quarter of the working population of the City of Lancaster; the company is now a subsidiary of a Swiss corporation.

This vast edifice, a pumped-up Wrest Park pavilion built on the same principles as the American personal coupé in the 1950s (gigantic on the outside but with virtually no usable interior space) is obviously heavily influenced by St Paul's and St Peter's. It is reached by an elaborate flight of stairs and is a confection of domes, cupolas and columns. The four gigantic buttresses glorify Science, Art, Commerce and Industry. It was designed by John Belcher Jr, in partnership with J.J. Joass, whose hallmark was a resplendent neo-baroque style. The memorial cost Williamson the then-staggering sum of £87,000.

The monument was finally opened without fuss or fanfare on 23 October 1909. It was raining and just two of the inhabitants of Lancaster were waiting outside. Their immediate, and as it turned out only, concern was to get inside to shelter from the rain. For years the folly was boarded up, as it was in desperate need of repair— among other things, the enormous dome was declared unsafe. In the mid-1980s a public appeal raised £600,000—this before lottery cash gave every fund-raiser tunnel vision—and after restoration work in 1985-7 was carried out by Charles Wilson, the Lancaster City architect, this astounding

A model of Ashton Memorial inside the Ashton Memorial

monument was opened again to a more appreciative public in 1989, and is now licensed for weddings.

On another hill a couple of hundred yards away stands a tall and enigmatic square white stone pillar, elegantly carved. The holes to support a roof halfway up the shaft reveal its purpose; this was the Pavilion, also designed by Belcher, but now it has lost its canopy and only the central pillar remains.

Music Room (c.1730)
SD 475 617

The entire city of Lancaster appears to have been washed. Everything is clean and appetizing, apart from the sound of the northern suburb of Slyne with Hest, which leaves a nasty taste in the mouth. Until recently the Music Room, a summerhouse built c.1730 for Dr Marton, vicar of Lancaster, was in danger of being crushed between encroaching houses, sheds and garages. The building was bought by the Landmark Trust, which demolished the buildings in front of the Music Room, thereby providing much-needed breathing space. The building is square, three storeys high and has a belvedere balustrade on the roof. The classical façade is decorated with pilasters, but the best feature is the music room itself: chock-full of intricate and highly detailed plasterwork, most of which was saved and restored. Only the Muse Terpsichore had to be replaced by a modern rendering. Considering the building's vicissitudes—at one time in the 19th century it formed part of a lighting and heating works—its survival is nothing short of a miracle.

Lee

Lower Lee Gazebo (18th century)
SD 566 552

There is such an immaculately restored slate grey gazebo here on the garden wall that it looks brand new.

Lindale (Cumbria)

Obelisk (19th century)
SD 418 803

Castle Head, the residence of John Wilkinson, the eccentric engineer and inventor, stands above the estuary of the River Kent. Many firsts in the iron trade can be credited to Wilkinson; among others he launched the first iron ship and installed the first large French steam engine. He was a personage of such wealth and importance that he had his own money coined, which

circulated freely at the time. Tantalizingly, the *Dictionary of National Biography* notes that his 'domestic arrangements were of a very peculiar character' but does not elaborate. After his death in 1808 the great iron-master was buried as he directed, in an all-iron coffin. From then on a wearying time set in for the corpse; until it found a final resting place in Lindale churchyard the body was moved no fewer than three times.

There is a big obelisk at Lindale, iron plate of course, which has almost as moving a story as John Wilkinson's body. After some years it ended up in the River Winster, was re-erected, but lately it has been damaged by lightning. Somebody up there does not like Mr Wilkinson. The black (formerly red) painted obelisk is held together with iron straps and carries a medallion with Wilkinson's profile and a tablet with an inscription:

JOHN WILKINSON

IRON MASTER

WHO DIED XIV JULY, MDCCCVIII

AGED LXXX YEARS

HIS DIFFERENT WORKS

IN VARIOUS PARTS OF THE

KINGDOM

ARE LASTING TESTIMONIES

OF HIS UNCEASING

LABOURS;

HIS LIFE WAS SPENT IN

ACTION

FOR THE BENEFIT

OF MAN;

AND, AS HE PRESUMED

HUMBLY TO HOPE,

TO THE

GLORY OF GOD

and then on the base of the plinth:

LABORE ET HONORE

Liverpool (Merseyside)

Obelisks (c.1800; 1909)
Gateway (late 19th century)
Tunnels (19th century)
Towers (1848; 1855)

Liverpool itself has more follies than one might expect. Two obelisks endure in the suburbs: the one at Allerton Hall dates from about 1800, and the second, at Sefton Park, is a memorial to Samuel Smith. Mr Smith made a bundle of money in the cotton trade and, having amassed the necessary wealth, embarked on a new career in philanthropy, dabbling a little in politics the while. This very Victorian state of affairs gained him no title, which in cynical retrospect he would seem to have been seeking, but it did gain him this handsome obelisk, erected by the grateful citizens three years after his death in Calcutta in 1906.

Forty years earlier the architects Lewis Hornblower and Edouard Andrée built the weird gateway to Sefton Park. The roof looks like an inflated, tapering chimney in the Tudor Style. The saddest discovery is inside the park, where a gigantic octagonal Palm House that would grace Kew Gardens stands glassless, derelict and forgotten. It is owned by the local council.

Towers are useful in areas where space is limited (as Manhattan demonstrates so spectacularly) but so are tunnels, as the London Underground reveals. In the 19th century Joseph Williamson, a man of initially ample means, engaged workmen to excavate a system of tunnels beneath his native city. There doesn't appear to have been any reason for the project, which must have cost a large fortune, and the tunnelling had to stop when the railway came to Liverpool. Now most of the tunnels have caved in or been filled in. When the first edition of this book was published there were still rumours of a long blocked-off entrance at 44 Mason Street, but we were fortunate enough to find one still open behind an Edge Hill council depot in 1990. Hidden behind a line of Portakabins is a high, double-arched access entrance, more of a slice across the tunnel than a formal entrance. Now the threat to build student housing on the hill above has triggered the formation of two Joseph Williamson societies to protect his molecular activities.

For better or worse redevelopment is endemic in Liverpool. It has cost us the city's most famous icon of modern culture, the Cavern (perhaps once part of Williamson's tunnels?), and the essential redevelopment of the appallingly decayed dockland area is threatening the existence of the works of Jesse Hartley. Hartley was Surveyor to the Liverpool Dock Trustees from 1824 to 1860, a methodical, reliable, conscientious type of man who would have shuddered at the very thought of building follies; such frivolities were alien pleasures. He approved of solidity and scale, but above all he liked building. He liked building a *lot*. Dockland is his memorial; the whole place is conceived on a massive plane, with gigantic walls and piers, everything rather larger than necessary. Two individual pieces deserve special mention: at the entrance to Salisbury Dock looms the Victoria Tower of 1848, a many-sided clock tower with a tapering base, machicolated and embattled, a giant guarding the docks. The low tower at the entrance to Wapping Dock dates from 1855 and resembles a Hun's hut— a conical shape, with sides flattened towards the top, something like a more barbaric version of the Sefton Park gateway. Hartley's follies deserve to survive.

Manchester (Greater Manchester)

Heaton Park Screen (1912)
SD 830 040

Heaton Hall, in the northern reaches of Manchester itself, offers a good view of the city from the largest municipal park in Europe. It was a beautiful clear sunny day when we were there, not a rain cloud in sight, but then when we went to Chicago it wasn't windy. Rain is endemic to Manchester, but that day the portico of the old Manchester town hall, built by the pushy architect Francis Goodwin between 1822 and 1825 and removed here in 1912, glowed yellow and dry in the sunset. Although what remains is but a mere snippet of the original colonnaded front of the town hall, in its parkland setting it is positively huge. Four massive Ionic columns support the architrave between the two endbays, and it sits grandly in front of the lake, basking in the rare sunset.

The Grand Lodge, an impressive Doric archway lodge to the park, and the Smithy Lodge of 1806, an octagonal curio with heavy Doric columns on each angle under deep overhanging eaves, are both attributed to Lewis Wyatt. The Smithy Lodge, formerly a craft shop and information centre, is now empty and prey for vandals. There is also a large domed rotunda, presently concealed behind corrugated iron sheeting, but frankly when you've seen one large domed rotunda, you've seen them all.

Nuttall (Greater Manchester)

Gothic Screen (1874)
SD 796 159

The Nuttalls of Nuttall Hall were an important family in this locality. A Gothick screen was erected at their home farm in order to hide some ghastly barn or pigsty. The screen, with a large central arch and Wrightesque arrowslits, deteriorated as the farm was converted into a dyeworks and later switched back again to its original use. This part of England was enthusiastic about screening disagreeable objects or turning them into eyecatchers; the influence of Cheshire with its many Gothic farm buildings is strong.

Ormskirk

Bath Lodge (1819)
SD 425 092

Now very derelict and in desperate need of salvation, Bath Lodge off Dark Lane was used by the Earls of Derby in the 18th century as a hunting lodge. Underneath the thick cloak of ivy one can just make out tall and splendid Gothic windows. For sale, ruinous, at £80,000 in 1992, its fate was still unresolved at the time of writing.

Cedar House Temple (1995)
SD 410 080

Templum Petri is constructed of an eclectic selection of Lancastrian materials, including the bottom half of a fibreglass septic tank, a window from Strangeways Prison, the entablature from the demolished Preston Public Hall and some reproduction Ionic columns, all assembled for under £1000.

Sister's Folly (16th century)
SD 413 084

The parish church at Ormskirk has both a square tower and a tower with a spire, packed tightly together and donated by two quarrelsome sisters who refused to agree on which to give the church—so both were built. This is a famous story, repeatedly proved to have no foundation, but it always gets trotted out when Lancashire follies are discussed. The towers actually date from different centuries—the bell tower was built around 1540 to house the bells from Burscough Priory, while the spire tower was erected about a century earlier. A good folly story should disdain mere facts.

Over Kellet

Gothic Convenience (1819)
SD 524 693

At Kirkhouse, a working farm opposite the church to the south of the village has a structure in the garden with blind Gothic arches, which we were told was yet another

Over Kellet Gothic Convenience

farm building—in fact, a pigsty—which had been disguised and beautified. Ever assiduous, we checked, and discovered that under the debris of an ordinary garden shed it was a two-seater privy.

Padiham

Arbory Lodge (1794)
SD 787 341

A forest of castellations—even on the absurdly elongated chimneys—trail along the roofline of this peculiar double-diamond-shaped lodge by an unknown architect and carry on right over the pointed arch at the former entrance to Huntroyde Hall. The drive to the Hall is now bisected by the A6068, which runs immediately behind the lodge. The building was offered for sale for £5 in a local newspaper competition in 1991, which was evidently its salvation, because one half has now become a smart little house with '1794' picked out in stained glass on the

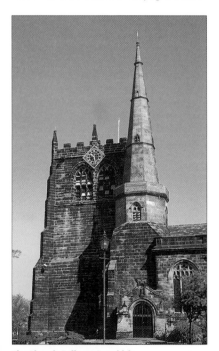

The Sister's Folly at Ormskirk

Arbory Lodge, Padiham

back door. The other half remains as an opportunity to continue the restoration—in other words, it is derelict.

Parbold

Parbold Bottle (1832)
SD 505 106

By a quarry, with a sweeping view across to the Ashurst Beacon, stands one of Lancashire's biggest folly disappointments—the Parbold Bottle. Somehow its euphonic name led us to expect a substantial eyecatcher like White Nancy, but instead we parted the undergrowth and there it lurked, more of a hand bell than a bottle, just a small pillar with a crinoline base, erected to commemorate the Reform Act. The little plaque simply reads:

REFORM ACT

1832

COLUMN RESTORED

1958.

Ramsbottom (Greater Manchester)

Peel Tower (1852)
SD 776 164

The continuing process of decay and regeneration common to all urban areas naturally means that any outlandish or derelict follies have been swept away, and no money is available for the restoration of the few that remain. That's what we thought, but we underestimated the Mancunian capacity for sentiment. Sir Robert Peel was born near Bury, then in Lancashire but now in Greater Manchester. In 1850 he was killed in a riding accident in Hyde Park, and the following year the citizens of Ramsbottom began to erect the Peel Tower, a monument on the southern spur of Holcombe Moor a few miles from his birthplace in Bury. The 128ft (39m) tower was designed, in true northern fashion, by a committee (which wanted battlements) and it cost £10,000. A plaque inside carries an extract from his resignation speech in 1846:

'IT MAY BE THAT I SHALL LEAVE
A NAME SOMETIMES REMEMBERED
WITH EXPRESSIONS OF GOOD WILL
IN THE ABODES OF THOSE, WHOSE
LOT IT IS TO LABOUR...'

and a new, unbeautiful concrete open-well staircase climbs its dizzy way to the top.

The path that separates follies and monuments is suitably narrow, and there will be many readers of this book (we hope) who will splutter 'But that's not a folly!' on discovering some favourite structure included here. Not for them, perhaps, but there are stout defenders of even the most blatant folly, and we would respectfully remind readers of our original definition, that folly lies in the eye of the beholder, and of the general catch-all nature of this book. Eyecatchers, dovecotes, pillars, garden temples: all structures whose architecture outweighs their function may be considered worthy. You may also have noticed that we enjoy an anecdote, and there are two pleasant stories about the Peel Tower, which turned out to be true. The first is that the tower was erected on Holcombe Hill using gritstone quarried from the same hill without the permission of the landowner, the Duke of Buccleuch. One can picture the duke returning to his property after some years travelling abroad and being not a little surprised to discover a massive stone tower on the top of one of his hills. He cannot have been too upset, for in 1868 he granted the trustees of the tower a perpetual lease on 21 acres (8.5ha) of the moor. The second story is more typically English: the East Lancashire Railway Company organized a special train to run from Salford to Ramsbottom for the grand opening celebrations. It arrived shortly after the celebrations had been brought to a close.

Inevitably over the years the square stone tower suffered the usual depredations of vandals and the weather, and by 1947 it became clear that the internal staircase was no longer safe. So the tower was blocked up (stage three in the life of a folly), and people sat back to await its eventual collapse. But in 1984 Bury Council put forward a £50,000 scheme to restore the tower to its former glory, and it was re-opened to the public in 1985. Another folly rescued? We hope so, but when we went back to check again in 1998 it seemed rather firmly closed, the single word PEEL in raised slab serif lettering above the door staring blankly back at us. The tower dominates the surrounding towns and countryside.

Ramsbottom had another, lesser known monument in the splendid high Gothick Grant's Tower, which commemorated the philanthropic Grant brothers, who personified all the positive aspects of the Victorian era. It was through their industry that Ramsbottom developed from a small agricultural community into a thriving township. The two inseparable brothers were immortalized as the benevolent Ned and Charles Cheeryble in *Nicholas Nickleby*, although Dickens based them in London. The tower collapsed in 1944.

Rivington

Liverpool Castle (1916)
SD 628 130

On the banks of the Rivington reservoir in Lever Park is a sham ruin replica of Liverpool Castle. The real castle used to stand where Derby Square now is, but was demolished in 1720 for a very 20th-century reason: to make way for the city's increasing traffic. Sufficient detail must have survived to inspire Lord Leverhulme's enthusiastic start on the full-size replica in 1916, but the noble soap-maker's zeal flagged somewhat in later years, for the castle still hadn't been completed by the time of his death in 1925. Nevertheless, the folly he concocted on the desolate moorland 20 miles from Liverpool is quite spectacular. This is so much more than the common or garden sham castle. Castles by their nature are seldom small, but this really does impress by its sheer size. There are roofless rooms, corridors to explore, a very solid spiral staircase, a little tower or two and excitingly unsafe parapets. It is reached by long, imposing avenues and, like the surrounding countryside, is usually deserted. The architect is thought to have been Thomas H. Mawson, the landscape gardener who laid out Roynton Gardens (now Lever Park) and had a long and fruitful association with the then William Hesketh Lever. Although the masonry and detailing

Roynton Gardens Watch Tower

Rivington Pike—perhaps a hospice?

are very similar in style to the various garden buildings at Roynton, Mawson was no longer working for Lever by 1916 and makes no mention of the replica in the list of works he undertook for him. As Mawson commented in his autobiography that working for Lever merely involved implementing detailed orders, the plans for the castle may well have been drawn up by the energetic viscount himself.

After his death an auction in 1925 offered: 'Lot 1280 A model of Liverpool Castle in mahogany. Square case, glazed top and sides on four cabriole legs, 15½″ square, 42″ high. Lot 1281 Four Emu eggs laid at Rivington, in mahogany glazed case.' Where are they now?

The last word on this amazing building has to be left to the 2nd Lord Leverhulme. Writing in 1927 he said:
Already the newness is wearing off… the uninitiated will not know that the replica is not a genuine ruin. As a bold experiment in landscape design it has certainly succeeded. Future generations will be grateful for this careful reconstruction of a piece of bygone Liverpool.

Roynton Gardens (1906–21)
SD 639 143

When we first visited Roynton Gardens, or Lever Park, it was the wonderful ghost of a grand garden. The Bungalow, or Roynton Cottage, Leverhulme's bijou mansion, planned on the side of Rivington Pike, had long been demolished, but the plan of the garden, scored so hard into the inhospitable hillside, remained. Walks, lakes, seats,

terraces—all were there in a state of suspended decay as if it only needed a team of enthusiastic gardeners a couple of weeks to put things straight, but it was all an illusion. The garden was not beyond reclamation, but we felt that the cost was certainly beyond any private and most municipal pockets. Shortly after our second visit, funding for a restoration project was put in place.

The Watch Tower at the top of the garden, built in 1906 in the contemporary style—with echoes of Webb, Voysey and Mackintosh—was derelict, and a new roof was needed. It is a square, three-story tower, with a steeply pitched roof and a chimney rising from the third floor; presumably the lower two floors, not affording such extensive views, were unheated.

The Cottage was at first a wooden bungalow, which was burned down by suffragettes. In 1927 it was replaced by the stone-built bungalow. The gardens were largely designed by the brilliant, unsung landscape architect Thomas Mawson, unfairly overshadowed by the team of Jekyll and Lutyens, who also designed The Hill in London's Hampstead for Leverhulme. Beginning in 1900 with 50 acres (20ha) of barren windswept hillside, 'without a tree or shrub to give it homeliness', he created a masterpiece, which was raised, razed and restored all within a century.

As for the garden buildings, the Out Look Tower, gatehouses and glass roofed pergola were in place by 1906, and the new gatehouse and a romanesque bridge were built by 1912, at which time Leverhulme sacked Mawson for not giving him sufficient personal attention, although he was later reinstated. Leverhulme's main contribution, apart from providing the funds and donating 360 acres (146ha) of the land to his home town of Bolton as a public park, was to fence off some of the parkland to provide paddocks for deer, yak, buffalo, wallabies and emus. 'Of all the gardens which have ministered to my professional enjoyment,' wrote Mawson, 'none comes into comparison with Roynton. Everyone prophesied failure.'

Rivington Pike (1733)
SD 642 137

On top of the Pike, above the gardens, is a small—very small—square tower built by a Mr Andrews in 1733 as a shelter and belvedere. There is some mild early Gothick decoration, and, of course, all the windows and doors have been blocked up. Visible from miles around, the little 'tower' is only about 15ft (4.6m) high.

Sawley

Eyecatcher Arch (1819)
SD 776 465

Two abbey ruins have been improved by additions—at Whalley (see below) and at Sawley, where an arch was rebuilt from bits and pieces at the entrance to the abbey.

Silverdale

Lindeth Tower (1816)
SD 461 742

Silverdale, in the top northwestern corner of the county, has yet another tower: the 1816 Lindeth Tower. It is square and has three storeys, with four trim battlements, as plain as plain can be, and stands in the garden of Tower House, opposite Gibraltar Farm. Mrs Gaskell wrote several of her works in this tower, which was a beloved holiday retreat for the popular Victorian novelist. In the summer of 1852 she wrote: 'We have fixed to go to the Tower house at Silverdale 3 windows being made to open wide viz., two little bedrooms and staircase.' Mrs Gaskell, whose memorial tower in Knutsford (see Cheshire) is one of the rare Arts and Crafts follies in this book, mistakenly took it for a medieval pele tower, whereas it had been built a few years earlier by Mr A.P. Fleetwood, a retired banker from Preston, as a belvedere.

A tower on the shore, clearly visible from across the sands, turns out to be a copper smelter's chimney, with the remains of a tiny jetty and miniature narrow-gauge railway.

Stretford (Greater Manchester)

White City Gates (1992)
SJ 810 955

These mighty gates were erected as the entrance to the greyhound stadium, which has since been demolished to make way for a retail park. The gates remain, renovated by the developers but now standing ineptly among the Pizza Huts and supermarkets.

Thornton

Hulton's Folly
SD 350 425

Hulton's Folly, on the corner of Skippool Road and Tarn Road, Thornton, failed to reach its reserve auction price of £20,000 in September 1994. It appears to be a barn.

Tottington (Greater Manchester)

Tower Farm (1840)
SD 775 132

Joshua Knowles's industrial Tottington Mill of 1840 was later converted into a farm. It is now known as Tower Farm, because it incorporates an embattled 6oft (18m) high tower, the surviving part of the original calico print works. We could not find it.

Lindeth Tower

The railway bridge gazebo at Turton

Turton

Railway Bridge Gazebo (1840)
SD 729 152

When James Kay bought the variegated Turton Tower, a half-timbered extravaganza attached to a castellated medieval pele tower dating from 1420, he began to carry out extensive modernizations. In 1840 the London to Brighton railway was driven through the grounds, but Kay battled to get the company to design a footbridge in a manner appropriate to the architectural style of the Tower. As this incorporated most known designs to date, the builders had a relatively free hand and opted for a splendidly heavy Gothic. The reason for adding a flight of steps up one of the turrets to make a look-out post remains unclear; anyone standing there when a train passed would have been engulfed in acrid smoke. Still, there's no accounting for taste.

Turton Tower is now owned and run as a museum by Lancashire County Council, and the printed guide enthusiastically describes its every outbuilding and stretch of wall as a folly. There is, however, an elegant and surprising garden building, no longer part of the estate, which stands like a miniature Lyveden above the road and river to the east of the house. It is a four-square Jacobean summerhouse, with rich mullioned windows around the first floor, built in a beautiful honey-coloured stone, ruined yet crisp and almost new—and it is a total sham, having been built by James Kay in 1840. This lovely building has now been reduced to the role of pony shed.

Ulverston (Cumbria)

The Hoad (1850)
SD 295 791

North of Ulverston (or Ooston, as the locals call it) on Hoad Hill, stands the immense monument commonly known as The Hoad. Erected in 1850, it commemorates the Under-Secretary to the Admiralty, geographer and miscellaneous writer Sir John Barrow, who died two years earlier. This remarkable and striking folly is a 100ft (30m) high, landlocked copy of the Eddystone Lighthouse, decked out with inscriptions and emblems relating to Sir John's career. Designed by Andrew Trimen, it has naturally never served as a lighthouse, although Trinity House stipulated when it was built that it should be capable of being used as such should the need arise.

Some £35,000 was spent on restoration in 1990–92, and it was then opened to the public for a 25p entry fee on summer Sunday afternoons and bank holidays when the red flag is flying—so says the notice at the top of the hill. Why not put the notice at the bottom? The council advertised for a custodian and received over 100 replies, including one from a prisoner in Strangeways who lost interest when he discovered he would not be able to live there.

Whalley

Baby House Towers (1780s)
SD 751 368

Half a mile from Clerk Hill Hall stood these mysterious ruins, one an octagonal, castellated tower with quatrefoil windows at the top. Mysterious, because the earliest printed reference to them, in 1902, supposed that 'it was customary

for such towers to be erected for the purpose
of observation in time of war or rebellion'.
Clearly the memory of their purpose lasted
little longer than the builder's life. On 24
June 1792 a Mr Torrington noted in his
diaries that:

> *a new and well-made road carried me
> from Whalley, near Mr Waller's house
> and grounds, who has, with miserable
> intention, built some strange ruins upon
> an hill-top;—being probably ignorant of
> the splendid ruins* [Whalley Abbey] *at
> the hill bottom.*

Mr Waller was the occupant of Clerk Hill in
1780, so it is reasonable to suppose the folly
dates from then. The curious name may be
explained by an old Lancastrian idiom—to
'play at babyhouse' meant to act foolishly, like
a child. It seems superfluous to suggest that
the name was not coined by Mr Waller. The
towers have suffered an ignominious fate; one
owner was an enthusiastic Territorial Army
volunteer who acquired some blasting
materials, and to prove his commitment and
abilities he dynamited his towers. He was
taken to court and fined for his actions.
Expecting to find nothing as a result, we were
delighted to find that the new owner has
begun the slow and lengthy process of
manual reconstruction, a little at a time. The
dressed stone and elegant quatrefoils of the
original are still some way away, but the 100ft
(30m) width of the first layout can clearly be
seen. The folly now consists of three circular
stone walls—the bases of the towers—each
about 5ft (1.5m) high and connected by
flanking walls, giving a strong impression of
Iron Age brochs.

Wheelton

Church Top (1776)
SD 603 217

The top of Wheelton Church now stands in
the garden of Prospect House. Divested of its
former function it makes a good garden
temple: a domed rotunda on a six-column
base.

Whitewell

Browsholme Spire Farm (early 19th century)
SD 682 465

The common concept of a spire is an
elongated cone, capping a church tower, but
pedantically it can be said to be any elevated
structure serving to catch the eye. This is the
use of the word at Spire Farm in
Browsholme, which has, not a spire as we

The rebuilding progress at Baby House Towers

expected, but a tall, thin wall with three
inadvertent castellations on top. It is attached
to a moorland farmhouse, a superfluous
erection 'put up because it looked nice, I
suppose'. The Parker family lives at
Browsholme Hall in the valley below, and
were probably responsible for this.

Worsley (Greater Manchester)

Ellesmere Memorial (c.1870)
SO 734 009
Chimney Top Fountain
SO 750 004

The Ellesmere Memorial is a neo-Gothic
shrine, dating from c.1870, on a hill above the
motorway. We have not managed to see this,
although it is under threat of demolition. It
was sold in 1992 for £100, with a compulsory
repairs notice of about £60,000 hanging over
the building.

When the canal and mining empire of the
Duke of Bridgewater was demolished, the
arched top of one of the factory chimneys
was re-erected as a fountain at Worsley.

Browsholme Spire Farm

LEICESTERSHIRE AND RUTLAND

Long Whatton
Loughborough
Belvoir Castle
Burton on the Wolds
Ravenstone
Measham
Market Bosworth
Swithland
Clipsham
Barsby
Exton Park
Bradgate Park
Scraptoft
Rutland Water
Lowesby
Leicester

LEICESTERSHIRE

There is much to regret about Leicestershire. It is foxhunting country, beautiful if you live there and love it, home of the Quorn and the Belvoir. The landscape favours the sport, being flat or gently rolling, but as we write this it seems possible that this ancient country pastime may soon be banned. From our selfish point of view it has the fewest follies of any major county in the United Kingdom; from the view of Leicester's heritage it must surely regret the failure of the Rev. William Hanbury's grandiose plans to establish a collegiate academy in Church Langton, with a church spire to top Salisbury, a museum, observatory, library, hospital and every other public building to reflect the greater glory of God—or perhaps the Rev. Hanbury. None of it was built. Not even his mausoleum survives.

Gone, too, are the garden buildings (and the house) at Gopsall Park, where there was a grand tour of eclectic motifs—a Chinese bridge, an Ionic temple and a Gothick seat, among others—although five columns of an octagonal temple from 1764 can still be found, cowering among rhododendrons and brambles. Much excitement attended its rediscovery in the 1990s. Charles Jennens, who owned Gopsall, was Handel's friend and librettist, and it was immediately assumed that the *Messiah* had been composed in the temple. Shortly afterwards documentation surfaced showing that the temple had been built in memory of Edward Holdsworth in 1764. Handel had died six years earlier. The

ruin sank back into its protective undergrowth.

Loughborough has a mighty 150ft (46m) carillon tower, built by Sir Walter Tapper in 1922, the second major carillon in Britain after South Kensington's Colcutt Tower. Ragdale New Hall has an overdefensive façade.

Barsby

Godson's Folly (19th century)
SK 698 091

Godson's Folly was originally intended as a mortuary chapel, but nobody got round to consecrating it, so now it serves well as a small if gloomy house.

Belvoir Castle

Grotto (early 19th century)
Dairy (1810)
Temple
SK 821 335

Belvoir Castle, pronounced Beaver in a deliberate attempt to mislead foreigners, is situated in the northern tip of the county, by the Lincolnshire border. In the summer it is the scene of olde medieval jousting contests, as sham as the castle itself, which is an early 19th-century job by James Wyatt and an amateur architect, the Rev. Thoroton. Near the castle is a conical grotto of rough stone, with pointed arches and a rustic hut placed carefully on top. Wyatt added a Gothic dairy in 1810.

The follies were probably the result of the Duchess of Rutland's enthusiasm for matters architectural. The castle itself seems to have been as much her creation as it was the architects'. She also landscaped the park, painted 'in the manner of Claude', and was described by Mrs Arbuthnot as 'a woman of genius and talent mixed up with a great deal of vanity and folly'. She died young, in 1825, and was buried in the Norman Mausoleum, built by Benjamin Dean Wyatt.

Bradgate Park

Old John (1786)
SK 525 112

Leicestershire's best known folly is Old John, an eyecatcher in Bradgate Park, a well-designed prototypical sham ruin built on a low hilltop. The story connected with it is rather good and therefore almost certainly untrue. Old John, a miller in the employment of the 5th Earl of Stamford, was killed when a flagpole, stupidly the centrepiece of a bonfire to mark the coming of age of the Earl's eldest son, inevitably toppled and brained him. The folly was subsequently erected on the spot in memory of the unlucky servant. Old John's mill was said to have been sited here, and the ruined arch attached to the castellated round tower does give the passing impression of an old mill, though its provenance is more likely to derive from Randle Wilbraham's folly at Mow Cop in Cheshire.

John Hope, a Cheshire architect who had worked for Wilbraham, also worked for the Earl on his Enville estate in Staffordshire; it is not impossible that he was the author of both follies.

Burton on the Wolds

Shell Room (1790)
SK 591 208

Burton on the Wolds has a shell grotto combined with a dairy in the Gothic 'chapel' of Burton Hall. The house was built in 1790, and the chapel must date from the same period.

Long Whatton

Whatton House Gardens (early 19th century)
SK 493 242

The gardens here are more important than the garden buildings, which removes any dignification of folly, but it is instructive to see the importance of architecture in the creation of an artificial landscape. Here is a Chinese garden, emphasized with Chinese artefacts; there are also a Doric bark temple and a Gothick alcove.

Loughborough

Garendon Park (early 18th century)
SK 498 191

Garendon Park is sandwiched between the M1 and Loughborough, polluted by motorway noise and town vandals. From 1729 until he died in 1737, the estate was owned by Sir Ambrose Phillips. His travels in Italy won him membership of the Society of Dilettanti. Like the Shugborough monuments by James 'Athenian' Stuart, the buildings at Garendon are reproductions of what their designer, or rather their copier, had seen on his travels. The circular Temple of Venus is a copy of the Temple of Vesta, and the Triumphal Arch, aligned with the

The Temple of Vesta, Garendon Park

temple along a grassy avenue, is an imitation of the Arch of Titus, both in Rome. The drawing for the arch is in the RIBA collection, inscribed by Phillips: 'A Design of My invention for a Gate for a Park.' Although it is scarcely of his invention, it is a tight, pleasing essay, enhanced by the feeling of discovering Marble Arch in a garden. The quality of the design and construction speaks well of Sir Ambrose's scholarship, and this has been recognized by its Grade I listing. The small rooms inside the arch have now been blocked up, but the gamekeeper's wife remembers meeting an old man some years back, who as a child lived in the arch with his parents and six brothers and sisters.

Sir Ambrose's other creations included a classical summerhouse and an 8ft (24m) obelisk. The old Pugin house in the park, built on the site of a Cistercian monastery, was

The Arch of Titus, Garendon Park

demolished in 1964, leaving a stub end, now used as a shooting lodge, standing forlornly next to an elegant white stuccoed clock arch, formerly the entrance to the stables.

The garden buildings lounge around the park, elegantly dressed as visitors who have turned up for a party to find the host gone. Completely lacking the insanity to be found in the true folly, the buildings at Garendon merit notice through their builder's dramatic appropriation of known classical motifs as his own invention. The Gothic gatehouse on the drive towards Hathern, red brick with crow-stepped gables and a tall, thin octagonal stair turret, came a century later, and is the work of William Railton, a local architect.

Lowesby

Thimble Hall (1816)
SK 723 074

Sir Frederick Fowke gothicized his lucky porter's lodge to celebrate the birth of his son and heir.

Market Bosworth

Bosworth Park Belvedere (late 19th century)
SK 409 029

A three-storey belvedere tower stands as part of the kitchen garden.

Measham

Mr Talbot's Gothic Cathedrals (1939)
SK 338 123

Measham is a large village just south of Ashby de la Zouch. Since the mines closed, a blanket of depression seems to have settled over the community, only mildly alleviated by the restoration of one or two of the more presentable buildings in the High Street and the opening of a new furniture warehouse on the outskirts. It is a solid, no-nonsense, down-to-earth sort of place, which makes the 13 model cathedrals built in Bill Talbot's garden decidedly unusual. Actually, any cathedral in one's front garden often leads to un-neighbourly speculation on one's motives, but Mr Talbot, a miner, was unabashed. Lichfield, Canterbury, York Minster and Coventry (the bombed one, not

Mr. Talbot's Gothic Cathedrals

the Basil Spence version), all are neatly labelled. He just liked to build Gothic cathedrals, mixing the cement himself, and as long as they didn't harm anybody else he didn't see why he shouldn't go on building them, he said in his solid, no-nonsense, down-to-earth sort of manner. He started his project before the war and never really finished, death interrupting his stately progression in 1980. A late innovation was the installation of a loudspeaker under Lincoln Cathedral, with a wire running up to a gramophone in his bedroom upstairs. This enabled him to play choral music, which was adequate until his grandson finally managed to track down a sound effects recording of church bells—Bill Talbot died a happy man. The west front of Lichfield Cathedral is engraved on his gravestone.

Ravenstone

Sham Windowed Almshouse (1784)
SK 402 139

The almshouses at Ravenstone, between Measham and Coalville, date from 1711. There should be nothing of the folly in an almshouse, but when the place was enlarged in 1784 two identical, bow-fronted pavilions were added, one for the master's house and one for the chapel. For some reason (perhaps the window tax?) virtually every window in the chapel by the road is false— both storeys in the roadside wall and the upper storey of the bow front. They have been cleverly picked out in white and grey, so the effect is realistic enough—but why couldn't they have been real in the first place?

Scraptoft

Grotto (mid-18th century)
SK 648 057

A small mound in the grounds of Leicester Polytechnic covers a grotto with scanty remains of shell decorations, which was probably built for Lady Laetitia Wigley. There used to be a Chinese pavilion on top of the mound, which would date the ensemble to *c.*1740.

Swithland

Gazebos (17th century)
SK 548 131

A pair of granite gazebos in the High Street are all that remains of the Old Hall.

RUTLAND

We would have included Rutland as a separate county anyway, but it is good to see that England's smallest county has now officially been reinstated. It has largely been flooded to provide water for Leicestershire; a few follies balancing gaily along the abyss of decay, neglect and vandalism stand wetly on the scant acreage remaining.

Clipsham

Mr Wheatley's Folly (1990)
SK 968 169

There was great excitement when we heard that Clipsham, just off the A1, had a modern folly built by a Mr Wheatley. It turns out to be a mildly Gothicized pumping house for a swimming pool.

Mr. Wheatley's Folly

Exton Park

Fort Henry
Bark Temple (c.1811)
SK 949 122

An excellent folly in Rutland, the Hermitage Sanctuary of the Hermitage Finch at Burley-on-the-Water, was destroyed by youths setting fire to it in 1965 (they'll be about 50 at the time of writing—we wonder how they feel now?), and another sad loss in this rapidly diminishing category of naïve wooden buildings is the collapse of the Bark Temple at Exton. Other follies remain on the estate, probably dating from 1811, when Sir Gerard Noel-Noel's house was built. Sir Gerard's

Fort Henry, with the Bark Temple in the background, before its collapse

architect, John Linnell Bond, is known to have designed a Moorish room in Southampton Castle and as the Bark Temple has, or had, prominent Moorish features, Bond could well have been the designer.

Exton's buildings range from a stupendously pinnacled octagonal dovecote and a game larder built as a circular temple with a thatched roof to the Gothick gimmickry of Fort Henry. This is a splendid lakeside pavilion in excellent condition, a model folly, crenellated and enhanced with ogee windows, the building trailing off into short stretches of wall. The best view can be had from the public footpath running along the other side of the lake, from where it appears to float upon the water like a little Gothick battleship. The public footpaths on the Exton estate are very clearly marked, and all other parts of the estate are even more clearly marked PRIVATE—NO ENTRY, reinforced by the distant crump of land mines claiming another hapless rambler.

The Bark Temple here was probably the largest and finest example in England of this most fragile building style. Little remains but for a pile of rotting timber and one small end portico of four columns drunkenly clinging on to life. It stood right behind Fort Henry; it could be and should be re-erected. But what hope can there be for a forgotten, collapsed and rotting wooden pavilion when whole villages were drowned in the making of Rutland Water?

All that remains of the Bark Temple

Rutland Water

Normanton Church (1976)
SK 338 123

When the River Gwash was dammed to create Rutland Water, one of the largest post-war reservoirs in England, it was realized that the shoreline would run through the aisle of Normanton Church. This was generally agreed to be a Bad Thing, so an embankment was constructed around the church to save it from partial immersion. Obviously it can no longer be used for regular worship, so now the little church just floats on the edge of the lake, looking like an ecclesiastical submarine breaking the surface.

LINCOLNSHIRE

Not just Skegness but the whole of Lincolnshire is so bracing, which is advertising talk for a remorseless east wind, which scythes through as many layers of clothes as you care to put on. The winters are even worse. Flat counties usually seem to deter follies, but there are a fair number here, mostly in the slightly warmer and surprisingly beautiful west. There is much in the way of monuments and obelisks and bits and pieces attempting to be sham ruins, but now and again a really remarkable folly, a building of national significance, appears—like The Jungle at Eagle.

Ashby Puerorum

Arch (20th century)

`TF 314 725`

Some recent removal follies—a particularly popular pastime in Lincolnshire—can be found at Ashby Puerorum, where the garden of Holbeck Manor contains pieces from Denton Manor and an arch from Sir Cecil Wray's Eastgate House in Lincoln.

Aswarby

Column (mid-19th century)

`TF 065 396`

The A15 dog-legs through the village of Aswarby, where a pale imitation of the Virginia Water Leptis Magna columns ornament a large roadside garden—enough to puzzle passing motorists, not enough to stop them.

Belton

Bellmount Tower (1749)
Sham Ruin (c.1740)

`SK 949 388`

Belton House, just north of Grantham, has one of the county's most spectacular follies, the Bellmount Tower. Set on a hill as a hunting lodge, it was originally attributed to the little-known landscapist William Emes in 1750, whom we accused of using motifs from as many different architectural orders as he could. Following a total restoration, it now appears to have been built from 1749 by the master mason William Grey and master builder and joiner Samuel Smith. A round-headed arch pierces the bottom half of the

tower, making it look more like an overbalanced arch than a tower, topped with blind Venetian windows, obelisks at the side and curious angled windows set in the corners of the stepped side buttresses. At the top a four-angled roof slopes up to a flat balustraded level, once presumably accessible, but when we first saw it the balustrading hung tiredly over the edge of the roof and the whole structure was in poor condition—dilapidated rather than ruinous. A less successful marriage of styles was difficult to conceive. The National Trust completed the restoration of the tower in 1990, a few years after acquiring the property, and on Sundays in August it is now possible to climb up to the single room above the arch

"Lord Brownlow's Britches" before restoration

by a spiral staircase, although one perspiring summer visitor emerged muttering that it wasn't worth the effort.

The blame for its inept proportions can be laid at the door of Philip Yorke, who suggested to the 1st Lord Brownlow that the original flanking arches, which gave the composition greater integrity, should be demolished:

> *Belmount may be well clipped its two wings; they are the most offending members, and I think sh'd be cut off.*

The resulting absurdly elongated solitary arch inevitably acquired the nickname 'Lord Brownlow's Britches'. The original eyecatcher design can be seen in the distance in a 1750s painting by John Harris, which hangs in the main house. It shows a tall arch flanked by lower arches, with a painted iron cupola, topped by a gilded star and a wooden balustrade on a hipped roof.

Another of Lincolnshire's sham ruins made from medieval pieces is nearer the house. We originally speculated that it could have been by one of the Wyatts, but it was already built by 1742 and is mentioned in a letter of April 1745 from Viscount Tyrconnel to his nephew and heir, John Cust:

> *a grand Rustick arch finished with vast Rough Stones over ye Cascade of ye River, and two Huge Artificial Rocks on each side, Design'd and executed, as I think, in a taste superior to anything that I have seen.*

Also on the estate is a 'Tudor Alpine' boathouse by Anthony Salvin in 1821. It awaits restoration while architectural historians grapple with the concept of marrying Tudor and Alpine styles (but then the owners of Belton never troubled themselves with stylistic precision). There is also a classical temple. Salvin's Hermitage, also dating from 1821, was destroyed in the 1970s when a yew tree fell on it. The village has an obelisk that serves as a pump, also probably by Salvin, who built the pretty estate village in a good overblown Harlaxton style in 1828–29.

Belton

Bellwood Lodge (late 18th century)
Obelisk (late 18th century)
SE 799 079

Just a castellated lodge and 40ft (12m) obelisk remain of the Bellwood estate at Belton, bisected by the M180 on the Isle of Axholme. The obelisk is, economically enough, a memorial to both a favourite horse and two favourite dogs. When his horse died, the owner grieved so much that he vowed to quit

hunting, and as he had no further use for his hounds he shot them and erected this obelisk in their memory. In our experience dogs usually have to make do with plaques or urns, so in a sense this is a promotion. The house at Belton burned down years ago.

Boston

Freemason's Hall (1860–63)
TF 330 442

The fashion for pharaonic architecture lasted for a mere dozen years after Napoleon's Egyptian campaign, when, with an imagination that remains startling to this day, he took artists, surveyors and historians along with his armies. Their discoveries galvanized Europe in much the same way that Howard Carter's discovery of Tutankhamen's tomb in 1923 electrified the world, but not for long—the Egyptian style, which endured virtually unchanged for two

Freemason's Hall, Boston

millennia, has been reduced to fad and fashion in the last 200 years. Britain's finest example is in Penzance (see the chapter on Cornwall), built in 1811 and rounding off the first flush of enthusiasm, after which only isolated pockets of Egyptiana broke out, a curio rather than a movement. In the 1840s came the Temple Mills in Leeds (see Yorkshire), then there was nothing of note for 20 years, until this astonishing little revival, built in a Boston back street for the freemasons of the town.

The Egyptian façade, monumentality in

miniature, screens an ordinary, functional building. One wonders if the clients deliberately specified a pre-Christian style of architecture? There must be an innate public resistance to the style; on London's Hampstead Road a huge office block, formerly Carreras House, then Greater London House, was built in the style of an Egyptian temple. The owners, having difficulty letting space in the building, cravenly erased every trace of individuality until it became another anonymous monolith. It was soon filled with companies owned by Robert Maxwell, (but we are delighted to report in 1999 that the old Carreras building has been re-Egyptianised).

Boultham

Hartsholme Hall Column (1902)
`SK 944 693`

Lincolnshire, famous for poachers, has a peculiar interest in commemorating unusual anniversaries. At Boultham, a southern suburb of Lincoln, a neglected column in the grounds of the now-demolished Hartsholme Hall was erected to commemorate the establishment of the Lincoln Waterworks in 1846.

Branston

Mr Lovely's Bizarre Gates (1850)
`TF 013 676`

Past Dunston Pillar a road turns off to Branston, where a Mr Lovely built a strange house called Stonefield with wonderful gates. On top of gate

There's a monkey on Mr. Lovely's bizarre gates

Sophia Aufrere's Mausoleum

piers made out of rubble and decorated with masks lurk monkeys that look as if they were used on the set of *The Hunchback of Notre Dame*. They don't do anything, they just look at you. Unusually, Pevsner tells us the story: 'There'll be a good monkey (mortgage) in that house,' said one local. 'I'll show them where the monkeys will be,' says Mr Lovely. There are also a couple of Lovely houses in Silver Street.

Brocklesby

Grotto and Root House (1770)
`TA 137 106`

Lancelot Brown undertook the new layout of the park in 1771; the grotto and the root house would seem to be earlier. The grotto, tufa-coated with one room and a tunnel, serves as a focal point for the root house, and vice versa. The root house has an entrance like a whalebone arch and is built from rough stones and branches. A hermit is alleged to have lived here, but the plain brick back of the hut establishes it as pure ornament. Genuine hermitages can normally be stalked from all four sides.

Arabella Aufrere's Temple (1786)
`TA 138 103`

Away from the wilderness is Arabella Aufrere's Temple, which is possibly by Brown. It consists of a central pedimented arch, flanked by brief colonnades with balustrades on top. Much of the balustrading is missing, presumed vandalized, and the temple's columns are now assisted in their function by supporting wooden props.

Mausoleum (1794)
TA 133 089

The beautiful Sophia Aufrere was buried in James Wyatt's stunningly lovely mausoleum, perhaps his finest work, which also holds a full-length figure of Sophia by Nollekens. It is so far from the house that it is actually in the next village.

TO THE MEMORY OF

SOPHIA

THE WIFE OF C.A. PELHAM

WHO DIED

JAN XXV MDCCLXXXVI

AGED XXXIII

Holgate Monument (late 18th century)
TA 138 112

Wyatt was also responsible for the Holgate Monument near the Orangery, another Coade stone sculpture of an urn on a triangle supported by three tortoises. There are three similar monuments in Britain and Ireland; this one was erected by the 1st Earl of Yarborough to the memory of George Holgate of Melton, who died in 1785 'a tenant and friend, who as a mark of gratitude bequeathed to him a small estate at Cadney…'. That must be worth an urn of anybody's money.

Newsham Lodge (1790)
TA 126 127
Memorial Arch (1865)
TA 116 109

Newsham Lodge on the edge of the estate is a Georgian cottage attempting to look like a medieval relic. The Tenants and Friends of the 2nd Lord Yarborough erected a Memorial Arch straddling the B1234; but the best known Yarborough folly is Pelham's Pillar, 5 miles away near Caistor (see below).

Also in the park is a dry bridge, the result of the draining of the lake.

Caistor

Pelham's Pillar (1840–49)
TA 129 037

This Pillar

was erected to commemorate the Planting

of these woods by

CHARLES ANDERSON PELHAM LORD

YARBOROUGH

who commenced planting 1787

and between that year and 1828 placed on his

property

Pelham's Pillar

12,552,700 Trees

The Foundation of this Pillar was laid in the Year

1840

by his Son and the Building was finished by his

Grandson

in 1849

The monument—more tower than pillar or column, being square with a lantern top and ogee roof—was designed by Edward James Willson, who was paid 100 guineas for the plans. It cost £2,395 4s 3d and was visited by Prince Albert on its completion. The Pelhams would appear to have been meticulous record-keepers. The tower is always locked, but entry is possible: a key can be obtained during reasonable hours from Keeper's Cottage, Pillar Lodge.

Cleethorpes

Ross Castle (1885)
TA 308 087

Shrouded in ivy above the promenade in this gay seaside resort are the remains of some substantial fortification, built, one assumes, to repel Scandinavian invaders. It has been consolidated by the council, and a path winds up to a viewing platform at the top. There is nothing to indicate that it is all a sham, built by a Mr Ross, the financial director of the Yorkshire, Humber and Lincolnshire railway, as an incentive to lure holidaymakers to visit Cleethorpes, a town effectively created by the arrival of his railway.

Coleby

Temple of Romulus and Remus (1762)
Roman Gateway
SK 975 609

On a westerly ridge south of Lincoln (not all the county has been ironed flat), Coleby Hall has a Temple of Romulus and Remus built in 1762 by William Chambers for his friend Thomas Scrope. The house has the view; the circular domed temple with two side apses is hidden away in the woods to the east. Unfortunately—and expensively—restoration and maintenance have to be continuous; damp has now penetrated around the base of the coffered dome, despite a comprehensive restoration programme a few years ago. It still looks wonderful.

The Temple of Romulus and Remus

Not to be outdone by Chambers, Scrope, who fancied himself as something of an architect, designed himself in 1770 an expedient wooden Temple to Pitt, with a crescent moon finial on the concave roof, which was in a state of extreme decay when we last saw it and now seems to have disappeared for good.

The only folly here is the Gateway, which was copied stone for stone from a ruined Roman arch in Lincoln, which Scrope had tried to prevent being demolished. Perhaps the imitation was built to advertise the worthy cause or to provide a record once the original had finally disappeared. It stands in the middle of one of the darkest avenues we have seen—one needs headlights to drive down it in high summer.

Denton

Grotto (late 18th century)
SK 864 324

Not long ago Grantham was voted the most boring town in England, a title that it probably came close to winning for years. At any rate, local squires seemed to find solace and amusement in folly building; there are plenty in the area. A mile from Harlaxton is the Welby's Denton Manor, where an old porch makes an agreeable object in the park. Near the lake is a grotto on a hillock. The room behind the cyclopean arch is decorated with shells and fossils, and inside a barely legible text reads:

Approach you then with cautious steps
To where the streamlet creeps
Or Ah! too rudely you may wake
Some guardian nymph that sleeps.

This appears to be a rendering of the *Huius Nympha Loci*, but differing from Pope's translation in the grotto at Stourhead.

Dunston

Pillar (1751)
TF 009 620

If on a winter's night a traveller in the 18th century dared venture up Ermine Street towards Lincoln without protection, he ran a greater risk of getting into trouble than a 20th-century stroller in the seamier streets of London. Footpads—bucolic muggers—were scarcely the romantic figures of legend; it was all too easy to get lost on the featureless heaths of Lincolnshire, and if one took a fancy into his head to make a little extra on

The truncated Dunston Pillar

the side then it was all over for the traveller. Sir Francis Dashwood of West Wycombe and Hell Fire Club fame owned an estate at Nocton, 7 miles southeast of Lincoln, and in an unusual gesture of public spiritedness he paid for a Land Lighthouse to be built, to guide travellers safely across the heath. The inscription testifies to the tower's use:

COLUMNAM HANC UTILITATI PUBLICAE D.D.D.
F.DASHWOOD M.DCC.LI

and the 92ft (28m) tall Dunston Pillar, as it is known, guided travellers safely for over 50 years. One young messenger boy was given strict instructions to keep the light to his right as he journeyed to Lincoln; he was found the following morning a mile away from the pillar, having walked round it in circles all night. It was also widely believed that the fire that lit the beacon came directly from hell (although no one ever quite summed up the courage to propose the theory directly to the mercurial Sir Francis), so in 1810, after his death, the beacon apparatus was removed and replaced by a Coade stone statue of George III by Joseph Panzetti. It was the King's Golden Jubilee, and a mason named John Willson was employed to put the statue in place. His tomb in nearby Harmston churchyard refers obliquely to the subsequent accident:

He who erected the noble King
Is here now laid by Death's sharp sting.

George III stood there for the best part of a century and a half until World War II, when he and the top 60ft (18m) of the tower were demolished as a hazard to the RAF. The top half of his torso can still be seen in Lincoln Castle, and the truncated pillar has since served as a chicken coop and bicycle shed, dominating the garden of its very proud owner.

Eagle

The Jungle (1820)
SK 883 685

Out-loveleying Mr Lovely is the extraordinary house called The Jungle at Eagle, southwest of Lincoln and by the Nottinghamshire border. Set in the middle of nowhere, this sham ruined castle appeared to be uninhabitable, but the ordinary house at the back shows how Samuel Russell Collett was able to live here in the 1820s. He kept a zoo around his Gothick bungalow, with kangaroos, goldfish, buffalo, American deer and pheasants—hence The Jungle. The façade is unbelievable: jagged outlines, burned brick, creeper, rusticated stone… and yet this well-proportioned sham was obviously carefully thought out.

It is now—well, it always has been—a private house. In 1976 the rear was completely rebuilt as a luxurious seven-bedroomed house in a concrete moderne style, like a west London office block, a clever contrast with the wit, spirit and idiosyncratic genius of the façade. It was sold for £600,000 in 1996, complete with matching double garages for his 'n' her Roller and Merc. The fabulous façade, now cheaply screened by a dense and vigorous British leylandii hedge, can no

The Jungle, Eagle

longer be seen from the road. Worse is the planting of ornamental trees right up against the façade, so the new building is thrown into prominence by comparison. It is as if the owners were ashamed of their unique home.

Fillingham

Gateway (1760)
SK 968 867

Sir Cecil Wray, a much-ridiculed 18th-century politician, had been the owner of Eastgate House in Lincoln. Irritated by the noise from a smithy opposite, he built a new house at Fillingham, 9 miles north of the county town on Ermine Street, which he called Summer Castle from his wife's name, Esther Summers. In the Gothic style, it was

Fillingham Gateway

possibly built in 1760 by John Carr, although Colvin doubts this. In the park is the so-called Manor House, according to Pevsner a 17th-century cottage later 'done up with pointed lights' and serving as an eyecatcher. Summer Castle was given two Gothic archways. One is a little sham fort, pressed hard against the long, straight Roman road of Ermine Street, now the A15, impressively guarding a grassy avenue sweeping to the house in the distance. The other, somewhat larger, has been restored and still stands by the side of the B1398: two square towers flanking the arch in between, with triangular lodges. Redbourne Hall, 10 miles to the north, has a similar but duller gateway, dating from 1773, for Robert Thelwell, which also has been attributed to Carr.

The Shatoo

Gate Burton

Shatoo (1748)
SK 830 835

Gate Burton is almost in Nottinghamshire. The Shatoo is a miniature stately home which makes Ebberston Hall look like Castle Howard; it is a temple designed by the 19-year-old Yorkshireman John Platt for Thomas Hutton in 1748. The delightful name is a Lincolnshire rendition of Château. It is now leased by the Landmark Trust, which has reverted to the name Chateau and describes the interior as having 'little space to swing a cat'. It sits comfortably on a mound facing Gate Burton Hall, now screened from it by trees, and overlooking a small lake. Limping sheep graze round the mound (injured by falling down rabbit holes), and it would be an idyllic English country scene, were it not for the cooling towers of Cottam power station dominating the skyline on the other side of the Trent.

Greatford

Folly Gardens (1930)
TF 088 119

Greatford, near Stamford, in the plump underbelly of the county, has several weird ornaments decorating the village. They are all the work of Major C.C.L. Fitzwilliam, who was also responsible for the famous roof garden on top of the old Derry & Toms department store in Kensington. The items in themselves are negligible, but cumulatively they are effective and amusing. Obelisks, huge stone crowns in cottage gardens, statues, stone sofas, mushrooms, pillars, capitals and Gothic bric-à-brac are all

The fantastical Harlaxton Manor

scattered throughout the village—not only in the Major's garden—as if the Gnomic rising had taken place. The village exudes prosperity, and it is not surprising that they have secured a grant from the Millennium Fund for the restoration of their trim little church. People who know how to make money also know how to put in successful grant applications. Don't seem fair, do it?

Grimsby

Dock Tower (1852)
TA 279 112

This is astonishingly tall—309ft (94m) high—slender and elegant, designed by J.W. Shaw and clearly inspired by the Torre Mangia in Siena. Unfortunately for us as collectors of follies, it was also built for a practical purpose: to provide water pressure for the hydraulic works at the docks. A few years later it was discovered that water in a pressurized tube would do the job equally well and there was no need for such immense height. The tower became redundant, so we can squeeze it in. Full marks to the citizens of Grimsby for preserving it; it is a stunning tower in a superb location. All we need now is a bareback horse race round the docks, for a banner perhaps?

Harlaxton

Harlaxton Manor (1832–54)
SK 895 323

Previous editions of this book have mentioned Harlaxton and then passed on, because it was designed and built as a house, was used as such and is still occupied and cared for, although now by an American university rather than as a private house. What purists we were. The constraint of definition has to be flung aside when one first sees this ethereal masterpiece rising like a new Jerusalem out of the plain Lincolnshire countryside. It is a jaw-droppingly magnificent sight, on a par with Ludwig II's castles in Bavaria, predating them by over 30 years and all the more spectacular by contrast with the uniformity of its surroundings. This was one man's obsession: Mr Gregory Gregory was his own architect, although four professionals in succession, Salvin, Bryce, Blore and Burn, 'whispered in his ear', as the bibliographer T.F. Dibdin discreetly put it. Gregory had been planning the palace for years before the first stones were laid, making architectural pilgrimages around the great houses of England, such as Knole, Hatfield, Longleat, Kirby and Hardwick, and as far afield as Constantinople and the Crimea. He had no family, few friends, just his house. He set out to build himself a palace, and his folly is that he succeeded. He enjoyed the house for a mere three years before he died.

Holbeach

Black Knight's Tower (early 20th century)
TF 381 249

This tiny octagonal red brick tower on the corner of Branches Lane and Fleet Road would almost be too small to notice were it not for the 8ft (2.4m) metal knight with upraised sword poised behind the battlements. The tower used to house the cash desk for a small garage. The owner was given a stained glass window of the Black Knight and was inspired to make a plaster statue. Lincolnshire weather being what it is, the statue soon dissolved, so a new, improved knight was crafted out of metal. That, too, was removed in 1997, and the tower is now hidden by leylandii, which screen the plot of land, up for sale when we visited.

Lincoln

Merryweather's Observatory
(late 18th century)
SK 972 719

Governor Merryweather added an observatory tower to the medieval Lincoln Castle, a rather futile gesture.

Londonthorpe

Bus Shelter (19th century)
SK 953 380

The 19th-century builder of the Londonthorpe bus shelter did not understand the classical vocabulary of architecture (with Bellmount nearby anything was possible), but he must have leafed through some books and picked out the elements he liked. The shelter is a heavily rusticated arch with a horse on the roof. This must have started life as something more dignified.

Louth

Vicarage Spire (1844)
Priory Sham Ruin (1818)
Broadbank Folly (1859)
TF 326 874

The market town of Louth has no fewer than three 19th-century follies. The top of the church spire, which came down around 1844, now stands appropriately in the vicarage garden, where a hermitage used to stand before the vicarage was built in 1832. Another religious removal is at The Priory, a Gothic house built by local architect and antiquarian Thomas Espin. Scraps from the 12th-century abbey were pieced together to make the sham ruin in the garden, probably by Espin himself. When he died in 1822 he was buried in his Gothic mausoleum near the ruin.

Broadbank House has a peculiar shellwork screen. Castellations, Gothic windows and turrets make up the folly; the whole is decorated with shells and fleurs-de-lis.

Elsewhere in the town a little tempietto covers a drinking fountain, recording the gift of the Hubbard Hills Estate to the local council in 1902, in memory of Aanee Pahud.

Brackenborough Hall Sham Ruin (c.1850)
TF 330 906

A little north of Louth, near Little Grimsby, is Brackenborough Hall, which has another ruined sham ruin, this one built by a Mr Ellis out of Gothic leftovers.

Marston Hall Gazebo

Marston

Marston Hall Gazebo (1962)
SK 894 437

The Thorolds have lived in Marston for over 600 years. Marston Hall, a little jewel to the northwest of Grantham, is the site of a precious folly. A summerhouse in the garden, originally an 18th-century gazebo, was rebuilt in 1962 for Henry Thorold by John Partridge. Barbara Jones did the murals; her painted birds are inside—penguins, a

The Barbara Jones mural inside the Gazebo

phoenix, flamingos and her trademark owls, including an Owl and the Pussycat above the door—but it is the exterior that gives it away, as splendidly brittle and artificial as crispbread, a thin façade with its crenellations and fantasy pinnacles like Emmett out of Williams-Ellis. It is an object to be coveted. The grounds are often open to the public on weekends in June.

Saltfleetby St Peter

Saltfleetby Folly (c. 1812)
Round Windowed Houses
`TF 435 8961812`

In the grounds of the one-time rectory of Saltfleetby St Peter is a neo-classic tower, two square blocks, the upper slightly smaller, surmounted by an octagon with round windows, about 40ft (12m) high. It may well have been designed by Sir Jeffry Wyatville, who is recorded as having built a tower in Lincolnshire in 1812, and it is marked on an 1820s map as a gazebo. The house was built by Thomas Oldham, who also built two extraordinary houses next door—their fenestration consists purely of round windows, producing a most comical effect. One eight-windowed house stares at the road like a big double four domino; next door the owners presumably lost their sense of humour, blocked up the round windows with discrepant bricks and substituted conventional rectangular lights instead. Some people are no fun.

Saltfleetby Folly

Skegness

Sham Castle Façade (1933)
`TF 571 640`

Next to Gwrych Castle, Abergele, this is the longest sham castle façade in Britain, running for 200ft (61m) along the side of an artificial boating canal and ineffectually trying to conceal the AstroGlide rollercoaster. It was built out of reinforced concrete purely for pleasure.

Skegness Sham Castle

Sleaford

Westgate Walling (mid-19th century)
TF 064 456

Along the path leading from Northgate to Westgate is a wall into which has been built a number of Perpendicular windows complete with their tracery. Apparently, they do not come from the demolished Sleaford Castle, nor from the church's restoration in 1884 or 1853. Their provenance remains a mystery, although the builder was named as a Charles Kirk.

Somerby

Somerby Hall Pillar (1770)
TA 061 068

At Somerby Hall, near Caistor, a pillar crowned with an urn marks 29 years of happy marriage between Edward and Ann Weston.

Spalding

Tower House (mid-19th century)
TF 249 220

Down a lane off the Cowbit Road stands this castellated freak of a red brick Victorian building with a pleasant mystery. The enthusiastic owners are unable to find any of its history—who built it, why, when. All they could find out was that it used to belong to a local brewery called Soames; it was very run down when they bought it in 1982. Restoration finally began in 1993, and now it

Spalding's red brick fantasy

makes a most curious and individual house, rather like a smaller version of Massey's Folly—bricks crisp, even and sharply defined like a giant Lego construction.

Stamford

Bath House (1760s)
TF 040 060

Burghley House and its park, the great house of the town, are now in Cambridgeshire, although Stamford itself is, of course, in Lincolnshire. Lancelot Brown was at work here from 1756 onwards, but his Bath House probably dates from the 1760s, after Walpole had said in 1763 of Brown's other (Gothick) additions that he didn't find them in keeping with the house. The Bath House is one of the first Jacobean revival buildings in the country—so faithful, in fact, that one might question whether it was a revival or a hangover. He also produced a gamekeeper's lodge, a dairy and a Gothick greenhouse.

Stoke Rochford

Obelisk (1840)
SK 918 281

In 1840 Christopher Turner of Stoke Rochford Hall near Grantham commissioned the architect William Burn to build 60ft (18m) of praise to Sir Isaac Newton. Stoke Rochford Hall itself is passing strange as a building, like the crazy Harlaxton Manor—but the architecture in the village provides real amusement, giving a flavour of the bizarre Manor.

Swinstead

Vanbrugh Pavilion (1725)
TF 022 225

Sir John Vanbrugh was commissioned by the Duke of Ancaster in 1722 to rebuild Grimsthorpe Castle. He worked here for four years, so it is quite possible that this summerhouse on the edge of a field on the Ancaster Estate is his work. The massive building, first noted in 1725, also bears a resemblance to Vanbrugh's Claremont Belvedere (see Surrey). The tall, three-storey central pavilion is flanked by taller towers, one with a stair turret, and there is a sympathetically designed two-storey extension at the back. In the 19th century J.B. Papworth drew up plans to convert it into a mausoleum for the 4th Duke. These were never carried out, and the summerhouse became housing for estate workers, then a water tower for

Vanbrugh Pavilion, Swinstead

Swinstead Old Hall, until it was finally abandoned in 1966. Some 25 years of neglect followed, until this Grade I listed building was rescued and restored in 1992. It is now an elegant and very covetable private house.

Tealby

Castle Farm (1836)
TF 147 914

Bayons Manor was a folly to rival Harlaxton, begun at the same time and also attributed to Anthony Salvin. It was torn down in 1965, but fragments of the glory that was remain, such as Castle Tealby Farm, on the Viking Way footpath. Here a stone stockade has been decorated with battlements and turrets to imitate a castle, probably as an eyecatcher for the Manor. Bayons was described by Lincolnshire's Property Services Department as having 'good claims to have been the most ambitious and thorough-going Romantic Folly of them all. It had towers, barbican, inner and outer bailey and keep'. And it had a mighty drawbridge, which never worked. It was a distressingly large house, built to placate the vanity of Charles Tennyson d'Eyncourt (he added the d'Eyncourt to claim a spurious aristocratic ancestry). Starting with his father's house, an unpretentious Georgian edifice called Tealby Lodge, he added a library wing, a Great Hall, a battlemented tower, then—when he failed in his bid to be elevated to the peerage—

turned the house into a full castle, with keep, moat and no fewer than six gatehouses. His descendants somehow managed to sustain the fantasy until just before World War II, when they moved out, the Army requisitioned it and the decay that led to its demolition set in.

Woodhall Spa

Wellington Memorial (1844)
TF 199 652

At Woodhall Spa, east of Dunston, Colonel Richard Elmhirst erected the Wellington Obelisk in Waterloo Wood, 29 years after the battle. The monument, a tapering, octagonal column with a bust of the duke, marks the planting of the wood from acorns sown there after the battle. For some unaccountable reason it did not occur to the brave colonel to plant the oaks in Waterloo battle formation, as in several other sites around the country. The inscription is now virtually illegible, but it read:

WATERLOO WOOD
RAISED FROM ACORNS SOWN
IMMEDIATELY AFTER THE MEMORABLE
BATTLE OF WATERLOO WHERE VICTORY
WAS ACHIEVED BY THAT GREAT
CAPTAIN OF THE AGE HIS GRACE THE
DUKE OF WELLINGTON COMMANDING
THE BRITISH FORCES AGAINST THE
FRENCH ARMS COMMANDED BY NAPOLEON
BONAPARTE. THE 18
OF JUNE 1815 WHICH MOMENTOUS VICTORY
GAVE GENERAL PEACE TO EUROPE
THIS MONUMENT ERECTED BY RD.E. 1844

Wootton

Castellated Pigsty (early 19th century)
TA 088 162

There was a crenellated façade to a pigsty in the elegantly maintained grounds of the former vicarage in the pretty village of Wootton, but the sty to house pigs has now been replaced by a bungalow to house the mother-in-law. The façade remains, apparently much diminished, for years ago locals remember more extensive walling and rooms inside the structure, which is now just a screen wall with sham round arched windows and a small turret at one end. Before the house became a vicarage it had been a coaching inn, and the main road ran along what is now the drive to the house. The screen may date from that time, but looks early Victorian to us. It is heavily screened itself by extensive planting.

LONDON AND MIDDLESEX

An astonishing number of follies and architectural curiosities survive within the boundaries of Greater London. Whimsical houses, over-elaborate monuments, grottoes, towers, arches— London has more follies to the square mile than anywhere else in the country. The quantity is unexpected; the quality is not. Few of them would excite much comment outside their urban environment, but their very survival, the tenacity of a useless scrap of brick and mortar holding out against the

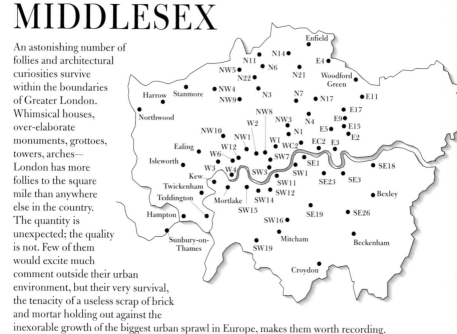

inexorable growth of the biggest urban sprawl in Europe, makes them worth recording.

London's follies and allied structures can be divided neatly into two types—the pampered and the ignored. The pampered ones are well known, sometimes even loved; the ignored have no known history, and unless they happen to be lived in or otherwise used, neglect and vandalism accelerate the deterioration. Many are lived in, or were built as individualistic houses, a cry for identity in a uniform street. The housing shortage in London, as in all big cities, usually means that if a building can be lived in it will be.

Lots of London follies have, of course, been lost, especially 19th-century ones. North of the Thames, the Regent's Park Colosseum was an enormous art gallery, built by Thomas Hornor to display his bird's eye views of London, complete with the first passenger lift in the city, but the money ran out, the building wasn't finished, and Hornor fled the country, leaving behind him vast crowds of visitors, who paid a fortune to gawp at Hornor's Folly.

Another delight would have been England's answer to the Eiffel Tower in Wembley, proposed by Sir Edward Watkin, chairman of the Metropolitan Railway. In the early 1890s building reached 100ft (30m), about a tenth of the intended way, then interest was lost and the rusting hulk stood there forlornly for a number of years until Watkin's Folly was demolished in 1907, and later Wembley Stadium was built on the spot. In 1904 there was a 300ft (91m) Ferris wheel near what is now Chelsea's football ground; it was never intended to be a permanent structure, but the sheer size was awe-inspiring. Go and see the Collcutt Tower in South Kensington and try and picture a wheel of which the diameter was 20ft (6m) taller. You may get the chance if the proposed Millennium wheel is erected on the South Bank.

The Euston Arch was demolished in 1962 and thus became the supreme martyr of Victoriana—most famous preservation battles after that were fought with the icon of Euston Arch in mind. But, thanks to diligent research by Dan Cruickshank, the final resting place of the arch became known recently: the majority of the debris was used in strengthening the Prescott Channel and is still to be found, although under water. So the Euston Arch could be re-erected using much of the authentic material. It would have been a fine Millennium project, but we are to get a Dome instead.

London has been arranged differently from other counties. For obvious reasons we have followed postal codes without using Ordnance Survey grid references. Outlying areas follow in alphabetical order.

E2

Arch (1845)

East London, carefully ignored by almost every tourist and every guide book, has its share of curiosities. There is a large lancet arch flanked by taller buttresses at the entrance to Meath Gardens, freshly painted in white with the shield bearing the inscription 'V.P.C. 1845'. What it guarded we did not know, nor why it remains intact between the scrubby little recreation grounds and the dismal council flats, but we have since found out that it was a cemetery gateway—Victoria Park Cemetery—and all those council flats were built over the former graveyard. Hmm.

E3

Gateway (early 18th century)

A removal folly, the rustic arch by William Kent came originally from Northumberland House, which was demolished in 1874, and now rests in Bromley Recreation Ground, St Leonard's Street.

E4

Obelisk (1824)

On Pole Hill in Chingford is a granite obelisk, some 11ft (3.4m) tall. The inscription reads:

THIS PILLAR WAS ERECTED IN 1824
UNDER THE DIRECTION OF THE
REVEREND JOHN POND M.A.
ASTRONOMER ROYAL.
IT WAS PLACED ON THE GREENWICH
MERIDIAN AND ITS PURPOSE WAS TO
INDICATE THE DIRECTION OF TRUE
NORTH FROM THE TRANSIT TELESCOPE
OF THE ROYAL OBSERVATORY.
THE GREENWICH MERIDIAN WAS CHANGED
IN 1850 & ADOPTED BY INTERNATIONAL
AGREEMENT IN 1884 AS THE LINE OF
ZERO LONGITUDE, PASSES 19 FEET
TO THE EAST OF THE PILLAR.

We would have thought that here is an unmissable opportunity to erect another pillar 19 feet away.

E5

Craven Tower (1840s)

Down the road in Hackney—'Britain's Poorest Borough', as it delights in telling its long-suffering residents—is an astonishing survival, a genuine squire's burned brick folly tower and arch covered in ivy, jutting into the parking area of a block of council flats. It was built in the 1840s by Arthur Craven as a prospect tower for his house Craven Lodge, set in 70 acres (28ha) on Clapton Common, the highest point in Hackney. The block of flats, built in 1957, was named Tower Court after it.

Portico (1823)

On a fine day the driver who glances down Linscott Road while motoring along the Lower Clapton Road runs the risk of being severely distracted from the job in hand—at the end of yet another East London mean street towers the Acropolis, glowing in the sun. In fact, it is the enormous, 13-bayed shell of the London Orphan Asylum, designed by the 23-year-old architect William Southcote

The portico of the London Orphan Asylum

Craven Tower, Hackney

Inman and built in 1821–3. Later it became a Salvation Army Congress Hall, but was demolished in 1975. Now only the façade remains, a massive four-column portico, flanked by open distyle colonnades four bays long. Set on a hill in the country this would make the finest eyecatcher in Britain; lost in the back streets of London it has become a golden, forgotten folly.

E9

Stone Poem (1980s)

A housing estate in Ballance Road has an interesting oddity—the complete text of Lewis Carroll's 'How doth the little crocodile' set in a paving stone in the walkway between Ballance Road and Hassett Road.

Victoria Park Fountain (19th century)

Despite the admirable work of the Fountain Society, London has few fountains of any note, but there are one or two amusing drinking fountains—a far more practical idea. The one at George Green, E11, will be dealt with a little later, but Hackney's Victoria Park has a rather elaborate fountain, built by Baroness Angela Burdett-Coutts in charitable mood as a gift to the impoverished East Enders. Made of porphyry and marble and complete with clock, it cost a whopping £8000. The clock has stopped at ten past one and the water has long been turned off, but the edifice is still too awesomely grand to deface.

E11

Wanstead House Grotto (18th century)
Temple (18th century)
Gazebo (18th century)

Viscount Castlemain's Wanstead House was one of the 18th century's most fashionable houses. Demolished in 1824, it is now an unkempt public park, but the mighty grotto head remains on the lake shore, carefully protected from the attentions of vandals by a fearsome and highly visible steel fence. It has been attributed to Kent, but only on the grounds that he decorated the ceiling of the Great Hall there in 1721. The Temple or banqueting hall in the park is of roughly the same date.

The best folly in Wanstead Park has long since gone—Ilford Castle, or Raymond's Folly, named after Sir C. Raymond, who lived in Wanstead House around the 1760s and built himself a mausoleum that looked nothing like a mausoleum but exactly like the common-or-garden triangular folly tower, with three round towers with narrow connecting walls between them. Of course, the tower doubled as a belvedere, and it was never consecrated as a mausoleum, let alone used.

Wanstead House Grotto

Remains of Wanstead Grove are also extant. There is a ruined brick 18th-century gazebo, used as a gaming room, in the garden of 20 The Avenue, which has lately been restored. A temple said to be by Colen Campbell was built *c.*1730 for Matthew Wymondesold, one of the successful South

Sea Bubble speculators, and it now finds itself lurking in the back garden of a conventional semi-detached house at 14 The Avenue.

George Green Fountain (19th century)

On the way to Wanstead Park, on the corner of George Green, is a tiny Rumpelstiltskin of a Jubilee fountain. At the time of writing, it was going to be moved to another corner of the green, because of building work.

E15

Obelisk (19th century)

Right in the middle of the main road in Stratford is a big obelisk to the memory of Samuel Gurney, but when you are in the area do not on any account miss the extraordinary monument in the churchyard behind.

E17

Lighthouse (1892)

Markhouse Road has an engaging curiosity, built with faith and passion. It is a land lighthouse; quite useless, of course, in landlocked Walthamstow but built for symbolism rather than practicality. 'I am the Light, the Truth and the Way' was taken literally by the builder of this remarkable folly—perhaps a Captain King, who laid the

Markhouse Road Lighthouse

keystone in 1892. It was built as a United Methodist Free Church, and such it remains to this day, proudly labelled 'THE LIGHTHOUSE'. The logic cannot be faulted; as a beacon to save lost souls the tower has an undeniable presence, but to come across this memorable edifice bursting out of even-terraced East London, with its carefully delineated ramp staircase and steeply pitched tiled roof surmounted by a large glass lantern, is enough to make anybody gasp and stretch one's eyes.

Turkish Kiosk, Bishopsgate

EC2

Turkish Kiosk (1895)

Last time seen, this was the Gallipoli Restaurant in Bishopsgate Churchyard, complete with belly dancers, who tried hard to steam up our glasses. We were, of course, more impressed by the architecture. It was the entrance to Nevill's Turkish Baths and designed by S. Harold Elphick. The brothers J. and H. Nevill also owned the now-demolished Charing Cross Turkish Baths. The juxtaposition to the City's modern high-rise office blocks makes it even more wonderful. The outside is Moorish, with the crescent on top and beautifully coloured bricks and tiles. The souterrain, now the Sri India restaurant, still has most of its tiled pillars and arches, but the place must have been decorated with exotic tiles everywhere—perhaps they are to be found under the carpets. Stuart B. Smith, director of the Ironbridge Gorge Museum, informed us that the tiles were produced by Craven Dunhill and were made to look rather like those at the Alhambra.

N1

Crumbles Castle (1991)

The noticeboard guarding Crumbles Castle in Bingfield Street, Islington, manages to take away almost all the fun of the place:

This playground is open to all children aged between 5-14 years regardless of ethnic background, appearence [sic], sex, sexuality, religion, ability or first language.

The fact that someone has thought of all these things in relation to children makes it all rather sad and pathetic. Sex? Isn't that illegal for 5 to 14 year olds? We could however fault the council on one major piece of political incorrectness: ageism. Crumbles Castle itself is a delight: a sturdy fort made of old and rejected bricks, with towers, towerettes, castellations, machicolations, the lot—great fun. Oops. Doesn't this encourage militarism?

N3

Avenue House Follies (1860s)

Finchley's Avenue House Park, along East End Road, has an oddly unpleasant atmosphere, close and suffocating. It owes its name to a curious house with some

The Bothy

interesting details, built by an architect named Robineau in 1887 for the ink manufacturer H.C. Stephens, and it contains in the grounds a large kitchen garden known as the Bothy, walled in on all four sides and made to look like a huge fort. The gardeners used to live in one of the walls. The heavily overgrown Bothy is castellated and crudely Gothic, surely not by Robineau, whose touch with the Avenue House is deft and assured. The excitement here is that this could be the first post-Roman concrete building in Britain—we await the verdict of the scholars, who will judge the rival claims of the Bothy and Peterson's Tower at Sway, Hampshire. On the edge of the park is an ivy-covered water tower and wash house, again in the fortress style. This is the one supposed to have been demolished shortly after World War II, or was there yet another water tower? More must have gone.

Stoke Newington Pumping Station

N4

Stoke Newington Pumping Station (1854)

The Stoke Newington Pumping Station in Green Lanes is just as spectacular as the London Orphan Asylum in its own way, but it has a claim to be excluded from folly consideration because it was designed as a working building and remains so to this day. However, its architecture is so outlandish that it forces its way into the book. Set between Clissold Park and a row of self righteous, mock-Tudor houses, an enormous, grim castle thrusts turrets of varying shapes and sizes indiscriminately into the air. There is a different design of tower at each corner of this heavily buttressed building. The architect, William Chadwell Mylne, secure in the knowledge that he had already served 43 years as surveyor to the water company and that they couldn't sack him now, allowed his imagination to run riot, loosely basing his designs on the admired Stirling Castle. It is a splendid, eye-stopping building, tremendously sited even today, high on a mound dominating Green Lanes. It is now an indoor climbing centre, but what will happen to it when this fad goes the way all crazes go?

Mylne's son Robert was the last of this remarkable family to practise architecture—nine generations, the longest dynasty of architects in Britain, beginning in Dundee in the 16th century—and Mylnes feature elsewhere in these pages, in Great Amwell, Hertfordshire, where serenity contrasts markedly with the aggression of Green Lanes.

N6

Grotto (late 1930s)

A garden in Stormont Road, Highgate, has a nice 'gardenesque' grotto, which the owner believes dates from the 1930s, although the type is much more that of three to six decades earlier.

N7

Clock Tower (1855)

A wonderful survival lingers on in Clock Tower Place—the old clock tower and carillon of the Caledonian Metropolitan Cattle Market. This tall, Italianate, white stone tower by J.B. Bunning, with open-arched buttresses at the base, was the centrepiece of one of London's busiest markets, closed since 1939. It was built in 1855 on the site of the 17th-century Copenhagen Tea House, and now stands just to the south of a housing estate, towering over the new buildings but now silently guarding an empty playing field, all that remains of the market.

N11

The Turrets (1887)

In New Southgate, in Friern Barnet Road, is a pub called The Turrets, an unremarkable building except for the two spidery thin conical-roofed bartizan turrets flanking the façade facing down Station Road. A crudely lettered plaque reads 'AD 1887 WWW'.

N14

Miniature Buildings (late 20th century)

Just across from the entrance to the ASDA Superstore is a garden filled to the brim with miniature buildings—too prim to be a *jardin imaginaire*, but fun nonetheless.

Caledonian Market Clock

N17

Tower (19th century)

There is a mystery tower in Tottenham's Lordship Lane at Bruce Castle—red brick, battlemented, blind arches and hollow. Pevsner puts it as 16th century, but it would appear to be far later, early 18th century at the earliest. At 21ft (6.4m) in diameter and 30ft (9m) high, it is too short to be a prospect tower (anyway, there could never have been a prospect) and too austere to be a summerhouse. There is a small window at the top of one of the arches, and one blank quatrefoil. A good and accessible enigma.

N21

Water Tower (19th century)

Far to the north of the river, in Quaker's Walk, an architect has carefully converted an old Victorian water tower into his home. There is a glass wall at the top to take advantage of the southerly views.

Bruce Castle Tower

N22

Mushroom Cottage (early 19th century)

The *cottage orné*, too common on country estates to merit a mention unless interpreted in a particularly eccentric fashion, is obviously rare in London. There is an almost forgotten example in North London. In Woodside Park on Wood Green High Road stands a little round house with central chimney and slate roofing. It has recently been meticulously restored, but is not yet lived in, so the vandalizing has started again.

Obelisk (19th century)

In Bounds Green Road there is a pleasant granite obelisk-cum-drinking fountain (dry):

Erected
in affectionate remembrance of
Mrs CATHARINE SMITHIES
of Darlham Grove, Wood Green
founder of the Band of Mercy Movement
and presented by the family and friends
for the use of the public

accompanied by texts from the scriptures exulting the virtues of temperance and of drinking water.

NW1

Fountain Grot (1878)

Just outside Regent's Park in Gloucester Gate, opposite the Prince of Wales's Institute of Architecture, is a drinking fountain in the shape of a formal grotto, set up by the Drinking Fountain Association in 1878. The convenient cave at the back of the sculpture is currently occupied by a Knight of the Road.

NW3

Swiss Cottage (late 19th century)

Public houses have good reason for bedecking themselves in architectural splendour—anything that sets them apart from their neighbours must do something for trade—but, perhaps surprisingly, few London pubs have chosen to do so. The best known is of course The Swiss Cottage, which has given its name both to a district and to an underground station.

Kenwood Sham Bridge (19th century)

North London has no folly estate to speak of. There is an attractive sham bridge at Kenwood on Hampstead Heath, white-painted wood, but nothing else that merits inclusion. Dr Johnson's summerhouse was nearly the authentic thing, but it went up in flames years ago.

NW4

Obelisk

There is an obelisk to Shakespeare in Manor Hall Avenue.

A house in Holly Village

NW5

Holly Village (1865)

Holly Village, off Swain's Lane, is a model estate built by the philanthropic Baroness Angela Burdett-Coutts (1814–1906), who also carried on her good building works in Hackney's Victoria Park and the village of Heath and Reach in Bedfordshire. Holly Village is her coronet; a tiara of tiny Gothic cottages sprinkled around an enclosed green, like refugees from Highgate Cemetery over the road. The architect was H.A. Darbishire, and the intention was to provide a pleasant living environment for the baroness's staff, along the lines of Blaise Hamlet in Avon. Where Blaise succeeds through its tranquillity and serenity, Holly Village exudes gloom and pointed despair. The lightheartedness intended by some Victorian Gothic architects does not seem to have been passed down to us.

NW8

Crocker's Folly (1898)

Crocker's Folly in Aberdeen Place was more properly known as the Crown Hotel, and at first glance it looks like an elaborate Victorian pub with little of the folly about it. A closer look reveals the almost Byzantine elaboration of the pub's decoration, especially its interiors, and its sheer size, surely unnecessary when catering for a small catchment area—there are not many streets in London without a pub on the corner. The story when it comes is truly satisfying and the perfect material from which follies are made.

Frank Crocker knew—just *knew*—that the terminus for the new railway was going to be in Aberdeen Place, so in 1898 he speculated with all his available cash to build an emporium that would be an irresistible magnet for thirsty travellers alighting from the trains. As work progressed on his gin palace, so work progressed on the railway, and Mr Crocker watched in horror as the navvies dug relentlessly past his pride and joy to finish up at Marylebone. Even if the story isn't totally true—and who is to say it isn't?—we are still left with a glorious, enormous Victorian pub in a quiet backwater, now properly rechristened Crocker's.

Chas. Addams House (late 19th century)

John Adams-Acton's house in Langford Place is a sharp, crouching little house, more at home in a Chas. Addams cartoon than in St John's Wood. Its most startling feature is a bay window like a scarab beetle, and its oddity is set off by the sober town houses that surround it.

Langford Place house

NW9

Trobridge Houses (1920s)

Why not go the whole hog, as the nearly forgotten architect Ernest Trobridge did in Kingsbury after World War I. Encouraged and financed by the success of a prefabricated house he had exhibited at the Ideal Home Exhibition in 1920, Trobridge bought 10 acres (4ha) of Kingsbury and set about building his own ideals of popular housing. Being a concrete human being rather than an abstract architect, the houses

Two of Ernest Trobridge's houses in Buck Lane

he designed were and still are highly popular with their inhabitants, despite (or perhaps because of) looking like medieval castles with mighty battlements, arrowslits, moats and machicolations. Those were just the flats—the individual houses were variations on the Anne Hathaway's Cottage theme, mostly thatched, with low ceilings, the Southern English dream house. Start at the corner of Buck Lane and Highfield Avenue to immerse yourself in Trobridgeshire.

NW10

Hindu Temple (early 1990s)

Neasden's vast Hindu temple is a wonder—and before the world's Hindus rise up and march upon the publishers, it merits its place in this book as a spectacular eyecatcher. It is officially called the Swaminarayan Temple and would have been remarked upon even in India. Some 2000 people worked on it, half of them donating their time gratis. Some of the decorations came prepared from India, but most were done on the spot, and the whole mind-boggling complex is a true gathering-of-nations: the Carrara marble came from Italy, of course, the limestone from Bulgaria, and the oak from England. No steel was used, because it would interfere with meditations. They are pleased to show respectful visitors around the temple.

SE1

Oxo Tower (1928)

The Oxo Tower is a familiar landmark to most Londoners, sited in a prominent position overlooking the Thames on the South Bank. We are not certain quite why public imagination has classed it as a folly, but there it is. We see it as a permanent advertisement, a clever ploy by the directors of Oxo and their architect Albert Moore. When plans for the five-storey tower on top of the Oxo warehouse in Coin Street were submitted in 1928, the London County Council objected on the grounds that advertisements could not be placed over a certain height; the architect successfully argued that it was not an advertisement but that the windows in the tower just happened to be in the shape of Os and Xs. The plans were allowed through, and now the tower is a fashionable restaurant.

SE3

Pagoda House (1780)

Away from the classical vocabulary of architecture, the adoption of another nation's vernacular style to build a house, pub or office would seem to be a peculiarly British weakness. It would be difficult to envisage a row of semi-detached villas in Peking, so why does it seem any less strange that a pagoda house should be built just off Blackheath? Like Swiss Cottage, a pagoda is sufficiently unusual to lend its name to the area—the road this particular one is in is called Pagoda Gardens. The house itself is Chinese only in the exaggerated upswing of the eaves and the peculiar horns at each end of the roof. Apart from this, its most obvious feature is an enormous oval window on the second floor. It was built in 1780 for the 3rd Duke of

Buccleuch. As we struggled to take a photograph over the high wall that surrounds the house, legs flailing in mid air and lenses dangling either side of the wall, two children walked past us and muttered 'Perverts'.

SE18

Rotunda (1814)

A gigantic rotunda in Woolwich, off Repository Road, houses the Museum of Artillery. John Nash built it originally in St James's Park for the Year of Peace in 1814 as a mock tent. Like Crystal Palace, it was too huge to ignore, and it was re-erected here in 1819. It is unmistakable, with its huge, concave roof sweeping up to the lantern at the top, the entire structure being nearly all roof supported only by a low, yellow brick wall. This is not circular as we expected, but polygonal, although we failed to agree on the number of angles. This is a wonderful, eyecatching building, which not only deserves to be better known but also, surprisingly, does not seem to have given rise to any legends.

Severndroog Castle (1784)

The folly towers of London are more common than might be expected. Any large, dangerous structure is more likely to disappear here than in some remote corner of the country, so the preservation of those that remain seems assured. The majority date from the 19th

Severndroog Castle

century, but the earliest and the best is Severndroog Castle, built in 1784 in what is now Castlewood Park, on Shooter's Hill.

This Building was Erected MDCCLXXXIV by the
Reprefentative
of the late
WILLIAM JAMES Bart.
To commemorate that Gallant Officer's
Atchievements in the
EAST INDIES
during his command of the Company's Marine
Forces in thofe Seas
And in a particular manner to Record the
Conqueft of
The CASTLE of SEVERNDROOG off the COAST of
MALABAR
which fell to his fuperior Valour and able
Conduct
on the 2nd Day of April MDCCLV

The tower is a beauty—a classic triangular, brick folly tower with hexagonal corner turrets, all in superb condition, gently Gothick, but above all Georgian in its elegance and refinement. The trees have been allowed to grow up all around it, so preventing its use as a belvedere. Greenwich Council, which now owns it, seems at a loss as to what to do with it or how to deal with it. Perhaps the council should donate it to the Folly Fellowship as its headquarters.

As befitted a Company man, the tower was designed by the Company's Surveyor, Richard Jupp, who had designed Painshill House in Surrey for the Hon. Charles Hamilton the previous year but who was otherwise an architect of little originality. The 'Reprefentative' was in fact Sir James's widow. The massive water tower nearby, which can be seen 14 miles away in North London, was built in 1910.

SE19

Prospect Towers (early 20th century)

Numbers 73 and 75 Belvedere Road have glazed brick prospect towers added to make a show among their neighbours. No. 22 has Castle House in its garden, a building that is just as it sounds.

SE23

Bayer's Folly (late 19th century)

In Honor Oak, one of those London areas like Stroud Green that everyone has heard of but no one can quite place, the owners of 23 Liphook Crescent have the great good fortune to have inherited a folly in their garden, a splendid 19th-century, octagonal, brick and

The folly tower in Liphook Crescent, in better days

stone tower. It was built on the top of the hill as a prospect tower for Tewkesbury Lodge in Honor Oak Road and survived when the house was demolished in the 1930s. The views over London from here are just amazing.

SE26

St Antholin's Spire (17th century; 1874)

The spire of Sir Christopher Wren's City Church of St Antholin makes a very acceptable substitute for an obelisk, especially when it is removed and mounted on a plinth in a respectable housing estate in Round Hill. It has been here since 1874, but no one seems to know why.

Dinosaurs (1854)

Crystal Palace would have been a delight, but there are still dinosaurs to be seen in Crystal Palace Park. Not of flesh and blood, but of bronze and paint; nevertheless, they are lifesize and lifelike and built in 1854 by B.W. Hawkins and Professor R. Owen. To celebrate their completion, a dinner for 12 was held in the belly of the brontosaurus.

Sham Ruin (19th century)

In Sydenham Hill Wood, north of Crystal Palace Park and wedged in between SE26's Crescent Wood Road and SE21's Cox's Walk, is a sham ruin that must have belonged to one of the Victorian villas demolished in the 1960s.

It is a good area for finding follies. To the

rear of 1 Crescent Wood Lane is a small grotto, although not of very great interest.

SW1

Shell Houses (1950)

Outside Victoria Station in Grosvenor Gardens are two little shell houses, rather improbably built by the French Government after World War II to house gardeners' tools for looking after the triangular garden dedicated to Marshal Foch.

SW3

Izba (early 20th century)

The least expected ornamental architecture to be found in London must be Russian, but there is an *izba* in The Vale. A real *izba* is a Russian peasant's thatched hut, with pink or whitewashed walls; this one is substantial, no thatch, black clapboarding, not a peasant to be seen, but still called the Russian House. Huts do not come cheap any more—the Russian House was recently on the market for £1.5 million. To some this might seem a bit steep for a left-over from one of the international exhibitions in the early 1900s, but then this is Chelsea, not Sverdlovsk.

Flowerama (1990s)

Great fun this! Provisionally called Flowerama by its discoverer, Vernon Gibberd, the name stuck, despite an indignant protest by its owner, Baroness Wynne-Jones. What is it? A piece of garden bricolage just off the King's Road, in Elystan Place. Sticking to a former farm cottage, this has become a haven for exotic birds ('rainbow paraqueets… crested fire birds… the golden song bird of Paraguay… the fairy blue bird of Australia, rose finches and emerald linnets…'), which fly in and out the tiny little jungle created from 'four apple trees, two Himalayan cherry trees, a May tree, a pink horse chestnut tree and an aspen', which have gone completely wild and are mixed with silk flowers, apparently in order to encourage the 'homing' of this weird and wonderful collection of birds. There are also a pair of artificial swans and several bird-houses.

SW7

Colcutt Tower (1886–92)

This tower is really huge, free-standing and far too grandiose for its simple purpose as a carillon, and it is almost unknown to Londoners, despite being in the middle of

South Kensington. At 287ft (87m), the Collcutt Tower easily outstrips folly giants such as the 218ft (66m) Peterson's Tower at Sway, Hampshire, or the 275ft (84m) of Wainhouse's Tower in Halifax, but hidden among the buildings of Imperial College in Imperial Institute Road it is almost ignored. True, there was a successful campaign to save it from demolition about 30 years ago, but since then it has been keeping a low profile, if such a thing can be said about the tallest folly in Britain.

It was designed by Thomas Edward Collcutt as part of the Imperial Institute exhibition centre in 1886 and was saved when the Institute was demolished in stages in the 1950s and 1960s to make way for the new Imperial College buildings. The tower was also known as the Queen's Tower, as it was to serve as a monument to 50 years of Victoria's reign in 1887. Institute and tower were finished by 1893 (the tower itself was finished on 17 November 1892). The tower now stands alone in its glory, which we suspect may have been Collcutt's intention all along—he was particularly fond of towers in his early years, as seen by his design for Wakefield Town Hall in West Yorkshire.

Albert Memorial (1865–76)

The Albert Memorial represents the finest flowering of Victorian Gothic. It cost £150,000 and took 12 years to build, using materials of biblical sonority—agate, onyx, jasper, cornelian, crystal, marble and granite. The architect, George Gilbert Scott, regarded it as his masterpiece and would no doubt have been horrified by the derisive attitude of Londoners towards it a couple of generations later, when it was vilified as a hideous monstrosity. In our own lifetimes, public opinion has gradually shifted, and more people now approve than disapprove, but there are still those who find it an eyesore of the first magnitude.

Fitzgerald Avenue Coach House

The memorial has just undergone extensive restoration. The original gilding has been replaced (the statuary was blackened during World War I as it was believed to attract bombers) with near-blinding goldleaf, so public opinion will no doubt have its say again. Lovers of trivia will be interested to hear that the book lying open on Albert's lap is the Catalogue for the 1851 Great Exhibition.

SW11

Peace Pagoda (1985)

On the banks of the Thames in Battersea Park, halfway between the Chelsea and Albert Bridges, is a gross, alien intruder—another Peace Pagoda, like the one at Willen in Milton Keynes, and built by the same Japanese Buddhist sect of Nipponzan Myohoji. This one is the height of an 11-storey office block, set in the middle of the only wooded river bank in town. It was finished in the summer of 1985, to the astonishment of Londoners who never dreamed that such a folly could be granted planning permission in a London park.

SW12

The Orangery (1793)

HIC VER ASSIDVVM ATQVE ALIENAS MENSIBVS ÆSTAS

This was designed by Dr William Burgh of York as a calm and peaceful retreat in the grounds of Thornton House, which has long ago made way for a housing estate. It is a perfectly reasonable and functional building with nothing of the folly about it, apart from the fact that its life-support system has been cut off, and it stands lost, bewildered and perplexed in the middle of high density urban Clapham. This is a remarkable survival.

SW14

Coach House (late 19th century)

DOMUS ESTA MIA DOMUS ORATORIUM
(This is my house; A house of prayer)

One of the most eccentric houses in London is the Coach House in Fitzgerald Avenue, a hotchpotch of red brick, Ionic pillars and turrets, assembled seemingly at random from discarded elements of older building by the builder of the Rylett Road Stables (q.v.). The lintel above the door is dated 1696, but the overall structure seems to be mid-Victorian.

SW15

Obelisk (1784)

At Tibbet's Corner on Putney Heath is the Fireplates Obelisk, which commemorates the fireproof house built here in 1776 by David Hartley. It had iron and copper plates sandwiched between the floors.

Tower (late 18th century)
Grotto (late 18th century)

Barn Elms Playing Fields are the remains of the Ranelagh Estate, before that known as plain Barn Elms, rebuilt for Richard Hoare in 1771. It has been roughly dealt with, the house mostly gone, as well as a small tower, a flint grotto and a much damaged ice-house on a mound.

SW16

Garden Buildings (1835)

St Michael's Convent is north of Streatham Common. Originally Park Hill House, it was built for William Leaf, a rich draper, and the grounds were ornamented like a country estate in miniature, with a Doric temple, a rustic seat and a sunken rockery garden, which winds the width of the estate to a small octagonal folly tower with gateway, all built by John Papworth in 1835—and they all survive, cherished and preserved by the Sisters of the Congregation of the Poor Servants of the Mother of God who put the estate on the market for £2 million in 1999.

SW19

Sham Castle (1822)

No. 84 Phipps Bridge Road is a real folly, a

The Sham Castle in Phipps Bridge Road

mighty flint and stone sham castle incorporated into a terraced house. Pevsner suggests a date of *c.*1875, built 'from stones from London Bridge'. In fact, however, it was built by a Mr Everett, owner of nearby Wandle Villa, who over the years had been constructing a terrace of cottages for his estate workers. The terrace, built on the flood-plain of the Wandle, was on the verge of completion when it was discovered that the last house was rapidly sinking into the ground, like a torpedoed cathedral. Everett quickly found a solution, building this externally massive and internally minute castle as an extremely exotic buttress on the end of the terrace. This is one of the lesser known National Trust properties; the ochre-coloured Gothick cottage with a small tower at the other end of the terrace was built by the Trust a dozen years ago.

The timber framed toolshed in Soho Square

W1

Toolshed Ornée (1876)

The practice of disguising urban toolsheds cannot be praised too highly: it has given us one of London's best known follies, the half-timbered Tudor mini manor house in the middle of Soho Square, built by S.J. Thacker. It does not, as has been suggested, hide a ventilating shaft.

Berkeley Castle (1930s)

Berkeley Castle is a dullish, over-restored, late medieval brick house with castellations, in Mount Row, Mayfair, at the back of some other houses. The only thing is, it can't have been put there to blend in, so it must have been somebody's whim. It is still dull.

While in Mayfair we should mention the

Roman Baths built by Constantinides in the year MCMLXXXVIII. They are under the garden of a private residence, but we can't give you the address. We are not being difficult, we simply aren't allowed to know. The architect's brief was to construct a 'basement rock grotto feature', and out came a magnificent underground temple, with carefully distressed columns, holding up a roof with roof-light and set in a limestone 'quarry'. The whole is as splendid as can be, and Mr Constantinides of St Blaise has done a well-thought-out job, but why do rich people always have to have things like this as a swimming pool feature? It would have provided a much better sitting room.

W2

Leinster Gardens Façades (late 19th century)

There are strange houses to be found all over big cities—sometimes they aren't even houses. Nos. 22–24 Leinster Gardens look to all appearances like the grand stuccoed town houses terraced on either side of them. But there are no curtains at the windows; in fact, there are no windows. The two are mere façades to stop an unsightly gap where the Circle Line railway runs between the houses.

W3

Gunnersbury Park Follies (18th–19th century)

Most of the estates that ringed London are now little more than memories perpetuated in street names—Tottenham Court, Stapleton Hall and so on. Some were large enough or held out by virtue of the owner's position or wealth against the encroaching houses for long enough to become public parks, and it is in these few areas that we find oases for follies. Gunnersbury Park, for example, has a rather distinguished pedigree. Princess Amelia, the second daughter of George II, started it, rivalling Kew, yet she never coveted the Chinese and Moorish quirks across the river. Amelia's follies were classical and Gothick, but most have disappeared, leaving only the Doric temple-cum-dairy facing the Round Pond, whose builder is said to be William Chambers.

Princess Amelia's Bath House suggests another survival, but the building appears to be of a later date. The Bath House is near Gunnersbury House (now a museum) and is half-hidden by municipal planting. It is a Gothick pavilion with battlements, corner pinnacles and putti carved in the lintels. Through the barred windows one can just make out the actual bath room and the remains of a shell room. Right in the middle of the park is the Farm, plain but ornamented with Batty Langley-style windows.

In the 19th century Gunnersbury Park was divided into three parts. Nathan Meyer Rothschild bought the largest section in 1835 and started building stables in the northeastern corner, hard against the

Pocock's Gothic Screen at Gunnersbury Park

The Doric temple-cum-dairy at Gunnersbury Park

property of a certain Thomas Farmer. Rothschild's grandiose stables dominated Farmer's carefully conceived garden, so Farmer re-employed the architect W.F. Pocock, who had built lodges and gates to his estate in 1834, to erect a Gothick screen to conceal Rothschild's obtrusive white stable range. Farmer was so pleased with the result that after Pocock's death in 1849 he employed his son, William Wilmer, to carry on building the ruins, tall mouldering arches like the remains of some once great abbey. The ruins themselves have become ruinous, particularly the tower, which has been made safe by cutting it to such a low height that only a few steps can be climbed to a low parapet. There is some good sham Anglo-Saxon detailing. Rothschild was not to be outdone by his tiresome neighbour. In 1861 he acquired the southern part of the park, and where the M4 now flows he built castellated lodges, which still survive under the flyover. An old claypit was transformed into Potomac Pond, with matching rockery and boathouse. From the boathouse a boarded-up and castellated octagonal tower rises, with all the required details (brackets in the form of heads of medieval kings) in the required places, so the whole effect is convincingly old.

Obelisk

In East Churchfield Road is an obelisk to the Earl of Derwentwater, who was executed for taking part in the rebellion of 1715.

W4

Chiswick House Garden Buildings
(18th century)

Chiswick House was the home of a trendsetter in style, design and architecture, Lord Burlington. The house and its grounds now lie between the pincers of two major roads, the A316 and the A4; although its survival is ensured, its serenity has gone for ever. Not that Burlington searched for serenity. His 1725 house was as shocking in its time as the International style or neo-brutalism was in this century, an uncompromising architectural statement, an essay in Palladianism. When the 4th Duke of Devonshire acquired the property, he demolished the old house and added two large wings to the little villa. These were finally demolished in 1952, and the house we now see is as Burlington intended it. Before starting work on the house, however, he had begun the garden with the help of, first Bridgeman and then Kent. It is the garden that opened the way for the great flood of creativity in English landscape design, a true break with the past, and although to modern eyes it may look episodic and indecisive, it gives that impression only because it was the first attempt at a new look for landscape. The grounds, carefully maintained by the council, are crammed with statues, the centrepiece being the exedra by Kent. There were obelisks, a grotto seat, a cascade, columns, busts, terms, a temple, a rustic house. Many still exist and still more have been replaced or rebuilt by the enlightened council.

W6

Grotto Cottage (1838–9)

The true folly—and here we include such items as towers, commemorative obelisks, grottoes and shams—when found in London is a delightful puzzle. Is it the palimpsest of some half-forgotten, vanished country estate, years before cheap housing wrote its indelible mark on the landscape? Is it a more recent effort at townscaping? Has it 'always been there'? The Grotto Cottage in Stamford Brook Road is one such example. An ordinary little house has been given an excellent grotto façade—by its owner or by someone who wanted a little eyecatcher to see from a bigger house? No, it was actually done in 1838–39, by the speculative builder James Cubitt (possibly a relative of the better known Thomas and Lewis Cubitt, but we do not know). Cubitt lived in Starch Green, behind Rylett Road, and owned a brick field. Spare clinker? Warped and unsaleable bricks? I'll build myself a grotto cottage! As soon as the house was finished, he sold it to Charles Brown, another builder.

The Grotto Cottage in Stamford Brook Road

W12

Rylett Road Stables (late 19th century)

Rylett Road itself has some bizarre, Gothick stables, once facing each other across the road. Now terraced housing has sprung up on either side of the road, concealing the castellated Gothic screens. The western one remains ruinous at the time of writing, abandoned and overgrown, while the eastern one was restored in 1992 by the architect Peter Faggetter, and it now makes an excellent pavilion of splendour. Before the 'ideal' suburb of Bedford Park was built in the 1870s, the estate belonged to the Dukes of Bedford. The stables appear to have been built by Jonadab Hanks, who created the equally eclectic Coach House in Barnes.

Renovation, reconstruction and rebuilding at the Rylett Road stables

WC2

Toolshed Ornée (1852)

In Lincoln's Inn the gardener's hut is a tiny fantasy of crow-stepped gables.

Obelisk (c.1000 BC/1877)

London is as scattered with obelisks as it is with clock towers; to list them all would take up more space and patience than we or you possess. For the dedicated obelisk hunter we have selected a few of the more amusing or the more remote—in areas, that is, where there is little else worth seeing. The real thing, of course, is on the Victoria Embankment: jestingly called Cleopatra's Needle when it arrived in London in 1877, the name stuck. It has weathered more in the last hundred years of its life than it did in the previous 3000.

Trafalgar Square Globular Lights and Police Station (19th century)

The curious globular lights on either side of the square in line with Nelson's Column are interesting in two ways. First, for the theory that, like a diamond, a lamp globe with 40 facets would cast a more brilliant light than a regular globe (it didn't, which is why there are only two); and second, for the fact that the pedestal on which the east light stands is Britain's smallest police station—room for one copper and a telephone, to keep an unnoticed eye on demonstrations and disturbances in the square.

Beckenham

Siamese Petrol Station (1930s)

There is an excellent and amusing Siamese petrol station on the Wickham Road roundabout, startling with its double eaves and upswung ridge culminating in a tiny pagoda. It was built as a garage in the 1930s and is in excellent condition, well looked after by Texaco.

Bexley

Bath House (18th century)

At Vale Mascal, along the River Cray, stands a splendid and forlorn bath house in the back garden of a 20th-century house. It contains a cold bath and, sensibly, a fireplace. The bath house resembles a chapel, is made of flint and brick and is dated by English Heritage as 18th century, although we would have gone for the 19th century. It did receive a Grade II* listing, though.

The sham chapel on Blackfen roundabout

Sham Chapel (mid-18th century)

Another lost, lonely and blighted folly is huddled by the side of the Blackfen roundabout in a desert of dual carriageways, D-I-Y superstores and flyovers. At first sight it unequivocally proclaims 'I am a Folly'; then doubt sets in. It has the aspect of folly, with a tiny, cheap-looking castellated tower at one end and a vainglorious steeple at the other, crowding the three-bayed nave with Gothick windows. Surely no real chapel ever had a central door? But all this is fevered imagination on our part, for at the southern end of the chapel is a table tomb, inscribed but impossible to decipher—and surely the rest of the graveyard is buried under a concrete road system. It is genuine after all. We leave, faintly embarrassed at our over-enthusiasm.

Then comes comfort and confirmation that we are not so dazed by folly that we see it everywhere. The conservation officer for Bexley confirms that the sham chapel—oh joy—was built as an eyecatcher for Danson House, a little jewel of a miniature stately home (recently restored by English Heritage), sitting in a nearby public park. But what about the tomb? 'Oh, that's a sham,' comes the airy reply. 'It was built to conceal a wellhead.' A sham church with a sham tomb? Ah, paradise. This is the only sham tomb we have discovered in Britain.

Croydon

Water Tower (1867)

As well as the water tower on Shooter's Hill and the Water House in Carshalton, there are two other London water towers particularly worth seeing, one in Croydon and one in Southall (see Ealing, below). Both are remarkable because of their prominence and because, their primary function finished, they survive thanks to public acclaim. The 100ft (30m) high Norman tower in Croydon was built in 1867 by Baldwin Latham and was decommissioned in 1971. Perched on the top of Park Hill—in Watertower Road, naturally—it is such a familiar Croydon landmark that its existence after it ceased to be functional was never seriously threatened.

Ealing

Southall Water Tower (19th century)

The resurrection of the Southall water tower is little short of miraculous. A familiar sight to Paddington commuters, it long ago became surplus to the requirements of the neighbouring gasworks. Luckily, its bizarre appearance—hexagonal, mighty machicolations, angle turrets and a great spindly stair turret—resulted in its being listed Grade II, and eventually a housing co-operative bought the shell for £38,000 in 1978. £1,100,000 later there were 37 flats inside the old hulk, and the first inhabitants moved in in 1984.

Enfield

Jardin Imaginaire (late 20th century)

Chase Side has a recent house in the front garden of which is 'a wide variety of everyday items such as weighing scales, paraffin stoves, all most neatly arranged'. Sounds exciting, but we have not been able to visit yet, and it may have disappeared by now.

Hampton

Huck's Chalet (1899)

We come across the Swiss influence again at Hampton Court, where Huck's Chalet on Hampton Court Road was built in 1899 as the offices of a marine engineering company. The building is, in fact, genuine, imported from Switzerland and joyfully and inappropriately re-erected here on the banks of the Thames. As with pubs, it acts as a good advertisement for the company.

In the late 19th century eager customers from all over Europe imported ready-made hunting lodges from Norway and Russia, log cabins from Canada and Swiss chalets from, of course, Switzerland, although most appear actually to have come from one or two specialized manufacturers in Paris, among them a firm called Seiler, which was advertised as an *établissement gigantesque pour la fabrique de chalets et maisons suisses*. Charles Dickens ordered his own Swiss chalet (in 94 prefabricated parts) in 1865 from Paris, possibly from Messrs Seiler. This was presumably much cheaper than having your chalet built by craftsmen brought over from Switzerland, which appears to have been the case in Attre, Belgium.

Inside the grotto at Hampton Court House

Hampton Court House Grotto (1767)
Ice-house (1767)
Fernery (19th century)

Hampton Court House (not Palace) is no longer in limbo—it used to be a children's home and at the moment of writing is for sale for an ambitious £8 million. Certainly in the summer of 1998 it was buzzing with builders, who nearly outnumbered the rabbits. The existence of its main feature is announced early on by some undefinable grotto-like excrescences on one or two walls along the drive. The park of Hampton Court House has just arrived at its most romantick stage: uncared-for and bleak, it houses a marvellous grotto, prefigured by a smaller, circular edifice, which has always been called the ice-house, although it looks like a summerhouse, enough of an eyecatcher on its own although buried in undergrowth. But it is the large grotto that really stirs the soul. In the same style, it sprawls its amazing bulk over the earth—there are steps and arches, minerals, flint and slag, everything looking very weird but eventually one finds this is a classical building underneath. The grotto has been identified by Eileen Harris as very much by Thomas Wright, and resembles his published *Designs for Arbours and Grottos* (1755–58). In fact, Wright also designed Hampton Court House. The grotto must date from about 1767, and was mentioned in 1769. In the 1980s it has been admirably restored by—who else?—Diana Reynell and Simon Verity. In went new shells and other ornaments, and the ceiling received its typical Wrightian starry sky again.

The pond in front of the grotto was originally heart-shaped and still has a dilapidated grotwork fountain head at the other end. It is being restored as this is written.

Beside the house are the remains of what must have been a winter garden or a fernery, dating from about a century later than the Wright grotto. There is the usual array of miniature fake rockwork, but it has been declared '*not* Pulhamite', which makes a change.

Shakespeare Temple and Grotto Passage (c.1758)

On the river side of Hampton Court Road, opposite Garrick's house, is the Shakespeare Temple, now restored by the Temple Trust. It is an octagonal building with a Greek portico, built for Garrick by L.F. Roubillac to hold his sculpture of Shakespeare. The original statue is now in the British Museum, and the Temple Trust is installing a £50,000 replica. The temple was linked to the house by a Pope-influenced grotto passage under the road. Now in private hands, it is wonderful and dark, and restored by Diana Reynell in 1997.

Harrow

Tooke's Folly (1862)

Tooke's Folly in Pinner Hill Road is a very pleasing one. We drove straight past this at first, thinking it was a real chapel, then came slowly to the realization that real chapels don't stand in farmyards and came back. There was the tower, and there was the nave, but the roof of the nave had Velux windows, looking far too up to date. An indecipherable plaque on the tower would appear to read 'The Tower of A.W. Tooke'; the date 1862 can be seen.

The owner told us that this was not Tooke's Folly—that name was given to his mansion of 1864, a huge baronial Belgian chateau tower, properly known as Woodhall

Tooke's Folly

Towers, now demolished. Arthur William Tooke was the son of the first President of the Society of Arts, but other than that seems not to have distinguished himself in any way, apart from his fine 'chapel'.

The sham chapel used to be the stables to Woodhall Towers (and served as a tolerable eyecatcher into the bargain, despite being built two years before the house). The present owner wanted to make it habitable but the council refused permission, saying it couldn't be a house as it hadn't got a garden. So it became an office.

Isleworth

Grotto (18th century)
Summerhouses (1780)

The grotto at the National Trust's Osterley Park is actually inside the house under the staircase; the rest of the house is more interesting.

The park itself has two summerhouses designed by Robert Adam in 1780, but again and again one is distracted by the sight and sound of the M4 carving through the exact centre of the huge park, an incredible piece of planning.

Kew

Kew Gardens Follies (18th–19th century)

On 5 July 1761 Horace Walpole wrote to the Earl of Strafford: 'We begin to perceive the tower of Kew from Montpellier-row; in a fortnight we will see it in Yorkshire.' Montpelier Row is 2 miles from the Pagoda in Kew Gardens, which remains one of the great landmarks of south London. It was designed by Sir William Chambers for Augusta, Dowager Princess of Wales, and a plaque inside describes it further:

> It is 163 feet High and has Ten Storeys, the lowest being 26 ft. in Diameter and 18 ft. High. Above this each storey decreases by One foot in Diameter and one in height from the next Storey below.
>
> The Building was formerly rather more spectacular in appearance than it is at the present day, each Angle of the Roof was decorated with a Guardian Dragon. These Dragons were covered with a film of Multi-Coloured Glass which produced a dazzling reflection.
>
> Each Roof was covered in Sheets of Varnished Iron in varing [sic] Hues. The Decoration at the top being gilded.

The Pagoda is still a spectacular sight; it must have been truly magnificent. There were also bells on each roof angle—80 of them—which chimed in the wind, so in a breeze the whole building would have harmonized with itself in gentle tones reminiscent of the chink of porcelain tea-cups, which was presumably one of its few functions. It is not open to the public because the staircase, which takes up most of the interior space, is wide enough to allow only one person to ascend or descend at a time.

But Kew, besides being the finest park in the London area, has other delights to offer

The Temple of Bellona

the folly-hunter. It is not, of course, really a park at all but a botanical garden, which is open to the public, and the varieties of trees alone makes it worth a visit. Botanists may find that amusing—they can spend 25 years there and never notice the follies—but we are concerned here primarily with misunderstood buildings.

The Dowager Princess allowed Chambers free rein, and in rapid succession he produced a Mosque, a Gothic Cathedral, the Alhambra (these three inspired by J.H. Muntz, an associate member of Walpole's Committee of Taste, and the designer, in 1764, of the first Gothick building in the Netherlands), the Temple of Aeolus, the Temple of Arethusa, the Temple of Bellona, the Temple of Victory, the Temple of Pan, the Temple of Solitude, the Temple of the Sun, the Temple of Peace, the Ruined Arch and probably the Queen's Cottage, as well as several galleries and a theatre. Lewis Goupy, the fan painter, added another Chinese building, the House of Confucius, and for George IV Sir Jeffry Wyatville built the Pantheon in 1837. Ten years later Decimus Burton supplied a folly with a function—the Italian campanile, which is the only building in the gardens that can be seen from the Kew Road, is a disguised chimney for the heating beneath the Palm House.

Much of this has disappeared, otherwise there would have been more buildings than trees, but enough remains. Chambers's Ruined Arch, which marks the division between the Botanical Garden and the Park, was built in 1760 out of Act of Parliament brick, the result of an attempt to standardize the size of building materials. Walpole commented acidly that this showed that 'a solecism may be committed even in

The Pagoda in Kew Gardens

architecture'. Now Brussels has taken up the challenge for standardization on our behalf—what Walpole would have said is unthinkable. The Pantheon, or King William's Temple, survives on a mound in the park, as do Chambers's Temples of Aeolus, Arethusa and Bellona. All the rest have gone.

Mitcham

Ruined Sham Ruin (18th century)

Ravensbury Park off Morden Road is the remnants of the Throgmorton Estate in the 16th century, later part of the Carew Estate. The pile of rubble in the park is all that remains of a 18th-century sham ruin.

Mortlake

Burton's Tent (1890)

A bizarre memorial is in the Roman Catholic cemetery at Mortlake, in North Worple Way. This is a stone tent to the memory of the explorer Sir Richard Burton, who died in 1890. The mausoleum was designed by his wife, and the Muslim star and crescent frieze around the tent is incongruously surmounted by a cross.

Northwood

Rotunda (19th century)

In Duck's Hill Road a little rotunda nearly overhangs the road, incongruous in leafy suburbia. From the outside it is an unremarkable garden gazebo, colonnaded on the garden side, walled to the road. Its joy is in the wooden domed interior, finely carved with 20 ribs culminating in a huge central boss of diminishing circles. The ribs spring from 20 carved faces of saints, kings and angels, all different. The rotunda was originally part of the grounds of Northwood Hall, built in the mid-19th century by Daniel Norton, a timber merchant from Uxbridge. Northwood Hall is now Denville Hall, a home for retired actors, and the grounds have been parcelled off to make large—and interesting—gardens for the neighbours.

Stanmore

Obelisk
Temple (18th century)

There is an obelisk to Julius Caesar in Stanmore, and Cannons Park has two classical summerhouses, one dating from the 18th century, placed back to back and providing an odd temple.

Sunbury-on-Thames

Arnussi (1923)

Not everyone who has been on holiday to some exotic location is liable to build his next house in the style of the country visited, but in the 19th century this was not uncommon for old soldiers, discoverers and collectors, who were rather well acquainted with one particular area of the world—but perhaps this applies only to visits to warmer climes. People who had been to the North Pole usually did not tend to build igloos, but made do with houses resembling ships. The explorer Percy Stamwitz had spent some years in the Middle East during World War I (he had also been to the Arctic), and later on he secured a job at the Natural History Museum, not so much out of financial necessity but so as to have something to do in later life. In his spare hours he kept himself busy with building his dream house, Arnussi. Together with his son, he designed and built the house, mostly of ferro-concrete. Arnussi is usually referred to as 'in the Egyptian style', but it is better to use the catch-all description 'Moorish', although the interior does have many Egyptian mementoes: murals depicting scenes from archaeology, as well as a genuine mummified cat set in a niche. The house is a riot: little domes, small minarets and oriental castellations, with only the rather austere windows dating it in the 20th rather than the 19th century.

Teddington

Obelisk (1900)
Cottage Orné (late 18th–early 19th century)

At Sandy Lane in Hampton Wick is an obelisk to a shoemaker who fought to preserve a public right of way; there is also an earlier *cottage orné*.

Twickenham

Pope's Grotto (1718–30)

Grottoes are the most fragile, the most susceptible to damage of all buildings, so it is remarkable that so many have survived. Fortunately, one of the earliest and most important grottoes in Britain remains intact. Alexander Pope's grotto at Twickenham (St Catherine's School at Cross Deep) started the fashion that swept the 18th century, and although his villa was demolished in 1807 and the gardens have been built over, his celebrated grotto remains. Frankly, it is a disappointment, a garden ornament better read about from contemporary accounts than visited in the 20th century. Pope was the acknowledged King of Twickenham, and when in 1718 he dared to reject the previous formality of garden design and embrace the natural look, the beau monde followed. Grottoes and gardens sprang up imitatively all over Twickenham and spread around the rest of the country in the succeeding years.

Marble Hill Grotto (1740)

The Countess of Suffolk at Marble Hill, Horace Walpole (the successor to Pope's crown) at Strawberry Hill, James Johnstone at Orleans House—all followed the lead set by Pope, though, of course, Walpole was to extend the boundaries of fashion further than anything Pope dreamed of. But Pope's Grotto was the catalyst, and Twickenham was the retort. The Countess of Suffolk had two grottoes at Marble Hill Park; one has disappeared and the other has only just been rediscovered and is being excavated by the GLC's Historic Buildings Division.

It was first mentioned in a letter to the Countess from George Grenville in 1742, in which he *'sends his compliments to the inhabitants of the Grotto which, I hope, goes on prosperously'*. A 1767 description of the grounds notes that *'there is an Ally of flowering shrubs, which leads with an easy Descent down to a very fine Grotto; there is also a smaller Grotto, from whence there is a fine view of Richmondhill'*.

'Pope's Other Grotto' (c.1762)

This area drives one wild: there is Grotto Road, Pope's Grotto Inn, Upper Grotto Road, Pope's Grove, talk of yet another grotto, but the best catch in the area is not Pope's Grotto itself, nor any of the others, but 'Pope's other grotto', a misnomer

The figure is a later addition to Pope's Grotto

because this one was built after the poet's death by Sir William Stanhope, who took over Pope's villa and made extensive changes to the gardens. The grotto, or rather cave, tunnel or 'subterraneous passage', is situated in the garden of a house in Radnor Road and dates from around 1762. In the late 18th century an inscription was noticed inside the tunnel, but this has certainly gone:

> *The humble roof, the garden's scanty line*
> *ill suit the genius of the bard divine;*
> *but fancy now displays a fairer scope,*
> *and Stanhope's plans unfold the soul of Pope.*

One was to emerge from the passage into the renovated garden itself, but nothing remains now, and after about 60ft (18m) or so the tunnel abruptly ends, blocked up with brick and earth. The remainder does, however, survive, under Radnor Road. So to the tunnel itself.

Forgetting to bring a flashlight when visiting grotto-tunnels is always a good idea. The gaping mouth of the tunnel is announced by a cladding of quartz, coal, slag and other materials. It is strangely pleasing—utterly dark and inhabited by huge spiders who take bungee-jumps at any humans entering. Gradually, the eyes get used to the darkness that is relieved only by a spluttering candle or two, and the rather naïve patterns on the tunnel walls become visible: butterflies and peacocks have been picked out in the pitch dark walls by using whitish minerals.

Radnor Gardens Gazebo (18th century)

Just across from Pope's Grotto Inn is Radnor Gardens, and after a struggle in the late 1980s this small park was saved and the wooden gazebo restored. This used to be the bath house, and is Gothick, with ogee arches, but for some reason has a Chinese feel to it, perhaps the ghost of all the Chinese follies along the Thames that were lost.

The Octagon (1720)

The Octagon at Orleans House was designed by James Gibbs around 1720 and from the outset has always been more or less attached to the main house. One can see, however, that it was conceived as a rather grand garden ornament, a banqueting house. The interior was stuccoed by Swiss craftsmen, Artari and Bagutti, and is still intact.

York House Fountain (1904)

Further along the river, in the grounds of York House, now the Twickenham council offices, is a gigantic Italian fountain, far too large for its site, picked up by Prince Ratan

The Octagon at Orleans House; nothing beside remains

Tata in 1906 from the effects of the suicide Whitaker Wright of Witley Court. The egregious Wright and his extraordinary follies are described in the Surrey chapter. The most immediate impression a Londoner has on visiting Rome is the number and variety of fountains; the York House fountain, so blatant in suburban Twickenham, would barely be noticed in Rome. But what joy—the naked ladies border on the obscene, frolicking away on the artificial rocks. The unofficial story is that the goods were damaged—they literally fell from the back of a lorry—and Tata bought them. The official story is that Wright had never even unpacked this fountain.

Strawberry Hill (1749–66)

Twickenham's most important building is too well described elsewhere to need a full description here, but unfortunately it is not open to the public (even to watch the England Rugby XV in training), so a brief account is needed. Strawberry Hill was the first significant house wholeheartedly to embrace the Gothick style, and coming from such a society figure and arbiter of taste as Horace Walpole (1717–97), its repercussions were felt as far away as Northumberland and a hundred years. Walpole's Committee of Taste and the brilliant designers and architects with whom he surrounded himself combined to produce the epitome of light-hearted Gothicism. In later, less sure hands the style took on a barbarity more appropriate to the marauding hordes that unknowingly lent their name to this most delicate style of architecture—in general the Goths preferred demolition to construction, as Walpole himself admitted:

'the Goths never built summerhouses or temples in a garden.' Walpole's Gothick was a joyous affair, architecture from the heart rather than an accurate historical recreation of the fine medieval ecclesiastical architecture that formed the inspiration for the Committee of Taste.

Here it might be as well to reiterate our definitions of Gothic and Gothick. For the purposes of this book—and in real life—we work on the belief that Gothic was essentially a medieval style of architecture prevalent in the 12th and 13th centuries; Gothick was the revival of certain elements of that style— notably the pointed and the ogee arch— which lasted for about a hundred years from 1720; and the Gothic Revival was a more

The Chapel in the Woods, Strawberry Hill

serious, academic and austere architecture, which led into the Victorian age and the flamboyant excesses that are gradually returning to favour. Strawberry Hill is indisputably Gothick. In 1747 Walpole wrote to his cousin General Conway:

> Strawberry Hill is a little plaything-house that I got out of Mrs Chenevix's shop, and is the prettiest bauble you ever saw. It is set in enamelled meadows, with filigree hedges.

William Robinson made the first alterations to Strawberry Hill in 1748, closely followed by John Chute of The Vyne in Hampshire, who was largely responsible for the elevation. Walpole purchased the house in 1749, and in 1751 Richard Bentley, another member of the Committee of Taste, started to design the hall, the chimneypieces, the stairs and much else, until he had a spat with Walpole in 1761. Bentley was a prolific designer of follies, few of which survive: we must regret the Triangular Chinese Building he designed for Lord Holland in Thanet. Strawberry Hill remains his major work. Later, Walpole called in Robert Adam to do a Gothick ceiling and chimney piece in 1766–67. Ever a pioneer, Walpole anticipated a more learned approach to Gothicism, and in 1776 he employed James Essex, who designed a gateway and the Beauclerk Tower. Essex was probably the most accurate Gothic architect at the time, having studied it as an antiquary. Walpole's final commission before he died was given to James Wyatt for the Offices in 1790.

The prestige and influence of those who worked at Strawberry Hill was immense, but the house, although the inspiration for many follies, cannot be remotely considered one. Walpole, who positively advocated ornamental building, had little time on his estate for follies. There were, indeed, garden buildings, but these were the expected ornamentation of the time: a shell seat, an ornamental bridge, a rustic cottage—nothing particularly exciting—and they have now disappeared. There is one survival, the sham Chapel in the Woods, a tiny octagonal building with portico in antis, designed by John Chute in 1772 and built by Thomas Gayfere in 1774 to hold Walpole's collection of stained glass. As Strawberry Hill is now a Roman Catholic college, a chapel that was not a chapel was held to be a bad thing, so it was restored and consecrated after nearly 200 secular years.

Egyptian Mausoleum (1854)

Along St Margaret's Road is an Egyptian mausoleum for Francis Jack Needham, 2nd Earl of Kilmorey—that is to say, for his wife Priscilla, who died in 1854. Kilmorey joined her 26 years later. It was designed by Henry Edward Kendall Sr, to be put in Brompton cemetery at a supposed (and absurd) sum of £30,000. In addition to being a general architect, Kendall was something of a funerary specialist, building several mausolea and publishing his designs for Kensal Green Cemetery in 1832. Pink and grey granite were used, and the result is a very satisfying Egyptian temple, a retake of several mausolea in Kensal Green. The mausoleum was removed from Brompton cemetery in 1862 to Woburn Park, Weybridge. Six years later Kilmorey again moved house (he was an inveterate house buyer) and again took the mausoleum with him, and put it in its present site. A.C.B. Urwin, who researched the Kilmorey Mausoleum, tells us that the earl not only spent most time of his life doing up new houses and then buying new ones, but was also rumoured to be member of a Hell Fire Club and had an abhorrence of socks. There are also rumours of a tunnel Kilmorey had built from Gordon House to the mausoleum in order to have his body moved over (or rather under) his own land when the day had come. Contrary to so many of these legends, there was indeed a tunnel, but it went under the present Kilmorey Road only and was later bricked up. The earl also took to trying out his coffin, which he had prepared years before, and thus reclining in what was to be his final resting place, he was pushed again and again by servants to and from the mausoleum.

Crane Park Tower (1828)

Opinions differ about the purpose of Crane Park Tower, listed Grade II. It has an attitude problem, looking as it does to all intends and purposes as a folly tower. Its other name, the Shot Tower, suggests that it had direct dealings with the powder mills, but it may also have been an industrial water tower. The date of building is certain—1828. The 80ft (24m) tower, which has recently been restored, is made of brick and is cone shaped.

Woodford Green

Sham Ruin (18th century)

The former Harts Hospital in Woodford Green, on the Essex border, was said to contain a sham ruined abbey in the grounds, but it turns out to be no more than an L-shaped sham ruin wall, accompanied by a rough pillar and a serpentine watercourse.

NORFOLK

Norfolk is strong on church towers, and we were tempted to include a few but managed to restrict ourselves to one splendid example. For aficionados of things octagonal, the 15th-century Red Mount Chapel at King's Lynn is a must.

We arrived too late to see the Reffley Temple in South Wootton, outside King's Lynn, with its sphinxes and obelisks set on what once may have been a little moated island, but the best folly to have been lost is perhaps Randall's Folly, on the beach at Salthouse. It was built by Onisipheros Randall, who was born in nearby Clent-next-the-Sea in 1798, went to London and made his fortune as a speculative builder (*onisipheros* literally means 'profit-bringing', and it is not a unique name; see Amberley in Gloucestershire). The folly, a very strange and large box of a building with some superfluous battlements, pinnacles unlike any other and an illogical positioning of the windows (he must have been his own architect), was a summerhouse, and here he used to entertain ladies of easier virtue than most. As a result the building acquired a local nickname of which we were kept in ignorance, for reasons of decency. The front of the house had double doors through which Onisipheros could drive his coach, no doubt packed with a blast of strumpets. Randall died in 1873 (the folly may date from around 1850), and the tower was subsequently used by the coastguard as a storeroom for flares – hence the later name, the Rocket House (although the pinnacles may have had something to do with that as well). It was later extended and used as a private house, but in 1953 it was swept away by floods.

Blickling Hall

Pyramid (1794)
Grandstand (19th century)

`TG 177 287`

Within 10 miles of Blickling Hall there are eight follies, one of the most concentrated areas in the country. Unfortunately, none is what one might call a classic, although they all have their own distinctive charm. Blickling itself is one of the National Trust's leading properties. It was the first major house to be made over under the Country House Scheme, meaning that the Trust owns the house and opens it to the public, while the family is allowed to remain in occupation, thus ensuring the building's preservation as a home rather than as a museum.

The finest pyramid in England can be found here. It is the mausoleum of John, 2nd Earl of Buckinghamshire, and his two wives. Built by Joseph Bonomi in 1794, it has weathered exceptionally well, and even the massive entrance porch and the side windows seem to harmonize with the regularity and superb workmanship of the 45ft (13.7m) pyramid.

In the gardens themselves, the three-bay Tuscan temple is probably by Thomas Ivory of Norwich, while the Racecourse Stand, a square, two-storey, castellated, red brick Gothic building, with a much higher circular stair turret some way from the Hall, is unattributed. It is now a private house, and on the hot summer's morning when we visited it, it was actually living up to its name: 'And a clear round for Spellbinder ridden by Laura Buxton,' echoed from the field in front of the Stand as the gymkhana sweated its way through the sultry day.

Brettenham

Grotto (19th century)
TL 940 830

Shadwell is a corruption of St Chad's Well, and in the grounds of Shadwell Court is apparently a medieval spring, once a place of pilgrimage, which was beautified by one of the Buxton family to make a grotto, with statues in niches and stone seats. We weren't allowed to see it, however, and got a very cool reception indeed from a manservant when we asked for permission at the house. There is also a scrawny little distyle temple at the edge of the woods.

Brettenham Grotto

Briningham

Belle Vue Tower (16th–18th centuries)
TG 040 350

A mile north at Briningham is the fat, circular, five-storey Belle Vue Tower, which was probably built as a 16th-century look-out tower (described by Pevsner as a 'standing'), but chopped and changed over the years so that the octagonal bottom storey is dated 1721, and the wooden superstructure was eventually rebuilt in brick by Sir Edward Astley in the 1770s. It has been used as an observatory, a signalling tower and a dwelling; this last is where its future lies, as it was up for sale in 1998 for £395,000. From a distance it looks more like a stray grain silo than a folly.

Burgh St Peter

Church Tower (late 18th century)
TM 490 940

Burgh St Peter's Church stands isolated to the east of the village, backing on Lowestoft. If one wants an English ziggurat, this is it: it lacks a spire and consists of a medieval base on which someone had stacked four storeys

Burgh St. Peter's church tower

of brick boxes, diminishing in height and width at every next stage. The corners have been buttressed, and each side has a pointed window to itself. Is this just vernacular architecture, or was there some squire around who had tremendous fun in changing what must have been a perfectly respectable if worn steeple into an object of ridicule?

Corpusty

Last Follies (1974 onwards)
TG 110 400

What the Last brothers, John and Roger, have done at Mill House, Corpusty, is what we would really like to see everyone do. This is not the neo-neo-classical, which for the last two decades has been so popular with architects and home-owners alike, but most of the Lasts's new follies are done in the Gothick taste (although they do fabricate classical buildings as well).

They started in 1974, when follies were still decidedly unfashionable, with a belvedere, some 15ft (4.6m) high, built of rough local stone and with a narrow Gothick entrance, cross arrowslits and some good painted decoration inside. A three-chambered grotto followed, decorated with river gods and fossils. Then came the Gothick Greenhouse, which looks like one of the Rendlesham lodges on the rebound and contains a Victorian reredos from a demolished church. Next came the classical, or rather the Palladian, pavilion of flint, which is accentuated by greyish-blue brick and has a domed roof, classical statue and busts and two side pavilions, which act as repositories for compost. A small grotto is at the back.

The Gothic bits and pieces introduced by the Earl of Orford in the 19th century at Mannington Hall provided the Last brothers with yet another building: The Ruin, which was built in 1985. A stone archway from Mannington was set in a flint wall, and yet another sham ruin screen was built from local stone.

They can't stop, of course, and other buildings are being erected, among them a classical garage at John Last's house in Pakefield, Lowestoft. This has an Apollo set in the pediment and squat, fluted columns, the moulds of which were borrowed from Peter Foster.

Oh, and the plants here are a wonder, but we are not interested in those, are we?

Costessey

Tower (19th century)
TG 170 120

At Costessey Park (also known as Cossey Hall), in the woods near the ruins of the house itself, a castellated round tower has been reported by Pevsner.

Crimplesham Hall

Sham Chapel (19th century)
TF 660 040

The finest folly in Norfolk is unquestionably the Chapel at Crimplesham Hall. It is a remarkable edifice, which bears little relationship to any chapel built anywhere else but by the Brothers Grimm. A tall, spidery bell tower is the most prominent feature, and at first glance that is all there appears to be. A closer inspection reveals that this is merely all that can be seen of a rather substantial building, so encrusted in ivy and creeper that it is hard to make out the overall shape. It is not known if it was built as a ruin or if the undergrowth has acted as architect, but the overall effect at the moment is near perfection. Any further botanical encroachment and the structure will be threatened, any less and it will lose much of its brooding mystery.

Three masses of ivy mark the roofless walls of the main building, which is dominated at the back by a large traceried

Crimplesham Sham Chapel

window. An entrance porch, also assembled from medieval fragments, stands to one side. Behind the bell tower is the much shorter main tower, which has one room per floor; the room on the first storey is remarkable for the mosaic on the floor—it is made from horses' teeth. The staircase leading to this remarkable sight is now blocked up, but the owners assure us that the floor is still there and showed us a photograph of it. A bell still swings precariously in its wooden cage at the top of the bell tower, but it is no longer rung, for safety's sake. The tower, capped with a pointed roof, looks romantically Germanic; any moment one expects Rapunzel to appear at the top and let down her golden hair.

When last seen, the chapel had been saved from the ivy's stranglehold, although some of it has been retained—a commendable state of affairs.

Denton

Grotto (1770)
TM 270 880

Grottoes are not common in Norfolk, which is rather strange for a county with such a long shoreline. The one at Denton near Bungay, with gables and arches, is said to have been made with coral and shells from the Great

Barrier Reef; not surprisingly it is the best in the county.

Nearby is a re-erected church window forming a romantic Gothic ruin. A pagoda, possibly of the same date, has long since gone.

Didlington

Kate's Castle (19th century)
TL 780 970

The Shell Guide says of Didlington Hall: 'A tower and colonnade are all that remain of the vast hall whose once famous garden… has been devastated in the name of State Forestry.' But Didlington has proved that there's still some life in it. The Hall was demolished in 1950. Beside it was a flashy museum, which contained the collection of Egyptiana belonging to William Amhurst Tyssen, 1st Baron Amherst [sic] of Hackney, whose father made his fortune in property development in Hackney. Lord Amherst was a keen book-collector and Egyptologist, but by 1906 his solicitor had bankrupted him and he had to sell his books; the collection and the house went later. Amherst died in 1909, a disillusioned man.

The lakes at Didlington were dug to give employment, and a turn-of-the-century colonnade still stands beside one of them. On the shore of another lake is Kate's Castle (we couldn't find the reason for the name, but it was probably named after one of Amherst's daughters). It is a late 19th-century sham castle-cum-summerhouse of brick and flint, castellated, of course, a polygonal pavilion (the roof gone) with a large octagonal tower attached to it. Strange how the follies always seem to survive when the main house has disappeared.

Great Yarmouth

Nelson's Column (1817–20)
TG 530 050

The 144ft (44m) Nelson's Column at Great Yarmouth would not normally merit inclusion in a book such as this if it were not for the fact that the Coade stone figure on the top is Britannia, not Nelson, and she is looking inland rather than out to sea. The column was built to the design of William Wilkins, and it predates the 1ft (30cm) taller Trafalgar Square column by some 20 years. The sadness from a folly lover's point of view is that the competition for the Great Yarmouth monument was not won by Francis Chantrey, who proposed a 130ft

(40m) floodlit statue of Nelson at the end of a pier 'on a pedestal made of the bows of vessels taken from the enemy'. The EU would have made us take it down by now.

Gunton Park

Gunton Tower (1840s)
TG 239 349

The exuberant early Victorian Gunton Tower, a sort of combination lodge-cum-eyecatcher-cum-observatory to Gunton Park is a memorable building to discover in the rolling Norfolk countryside. It looks like no recognized style of architecture—19th-century municipal or railway English is the nearest one can get. It has three storeys topped by a flagpole. The top storey is a glass-walled observatory room with two interior levels; the second storey is a single large room with two tall, round arched windows in each wall (the staircase to the top floor meanders uncertainly through the air, ignoring the safety of the walls, before latching itself to the south side wall for the last few feet of the climb); and the ground floor has a tall arch through which the drive to the main house runs. The accommodation on the ground floor is in the wings, which curve out at both sides to give a symmetrical appearance.

The tower was converted into three apartments in 1986, but although they were proud of the work they were doing, the

The splitting wings of Gunton Park Tower

builders were not envious of the prospective tenants. 'We've worked up here through two winters, and we know what it's like,' commented one. But the view, they admitted, was indeed superb. 'The only place in Norfolk where you can see the sea and Norwich Cathedral from the same room,' said the other proudly. When they started work, every pane of glass in the building had been smashed, and the floors were rotten. Now the tower looks as if it has just been built—an excellent preservation job for an excellent folly.

Heydon Hall

Tower (19th century)
TG 120 270

Heydon Hall has an obelisk and a tower clearly marked on the Ordnance Survey map, but the tower is so tiny among the encircling trees that it is very difficult to spot. When it is found it seems hardly worth it: the smallest, plainest type of look-out tower, octagonal, brick with flint infill, and only about 40ft (12.2m) high. The trees tower over it.

Holkham Hall

Monuments
TF 880 430

Holkham Hall, west of Wells-next-the-Sea, is the seat of the Earls of Leicester. There are no true follies here, just monumental scale. The Leicester Monument, the house, the obelisk and the triumphal arch are all exactly aligned over a distance of 2.8 miles. The road itself is straight only between the arch and the obelisk, which is just over 1.6 miles, and curiously there is a Roman road less than ½ mile away.

Leicester Monument (1845)
TF 884 436

The Leicester Monument is a 120ft (37m) Corinthian column, using cow's heads for the helices, a neat touch by the designer W.J. Donthorne, because Thomas William Coke, Earl of Leicester (1754–1842), can lay strong claim to being called the father of modern agriculture. Coke of Norfolk was the way this prodigious man liked to be known, and in addition to pioneering a revolution in agriculture, he had an interesting married life. His wife died in 1800, and 22 years later his god-daughter proposed to him, which enabled him to go on to sire five children after the age of 70. There was a 52-year age difference between his eldest and his

youngest child. The monument has four extensions from the plinth, which are aptly labelled:

BREEDING IN ALL ITS BRANCHES
LIVE AND LET LIVE
SMALL IN SIZE BUT GREAT IN VALUE
THE IMPROVEMENT OF AGRICULTURE

with statues of cows, agricultural implements and sheep, in case anyone missed the point. On three sides of the plinth are elaborate friezes; on the fourth (north) side a lengthy and fulsome inscription.

Obelisk (1729)
The Temple (1734)
TF 882 420

Near the obelisk, inscriptionless and allegedly erected in 1729 before the building of the house, is the temple, which is supposed to have been designed by William Kent but was erected, with alterations, by Matthew Brettingham some time after 1734. It is not a successful design. The grandeur of the Tuscan portico is lessened by the wings at either side with their lean-to roofs and the rather hesitant dome on a drum with Diocletian windows.

Triumphal Arch (18th century)
TF 882 395

Neither is the triumphal arch a triumph of architecture. The central arch carries more masonry above it than one might reasonably expect, probably so that it could clearly be seen from the obelisk.

Hunstanton

The Octagon (c.1655)
TF 690 420

The Octagon is just that: an old brick summerhouse of eight sides, castellated with stone dressing and a pedimented entrance and windows. Possibly the work of the mason William Edge, it is a superb little temple or gazebo, built for Sir Hamon Le Strange of Hunstanton Hall around 1655 so that his wife, Alicia, might practise her violin here, on a small island in a lake—presumably the infernal noise was not tolerated in the house itself.

Andrew Plumridge found out that this is the original for the building at the fictional Woollam Chertsey in P.G. Wodehouse's story 'Jeeves and the Impending Doom'. Wodehouse frequented Hunstanton and was charmed by this little pavilion.

three blank circles), it has a smaller top storey with louvred doors and a little domed roof. Clustered around the bottom, like the wings of a Greek church, are four, once-identical, two-storey cottages with chimneys at the front. It certainly has the style of mid-Victorian industry—it is not a pretty sight, but undeniably a memorable one.

Melton Constable

Bath House (late 18th century)
`TG 030 320`

There is a splendid bath house at Melton Hall in Melton Constable, an estate that pops on and off the market with confusing rapidity. From the back it is a plain two-storey cottage in which an old couple have lived for the past 18 years, but from the front it is a wonderful celebration of Gothick, with a three-sided, three-storey tower as the centrepiece, giving the impression of a church from the big house. The windows were originally much larger, and the tower's top storey is sham. The sad thing is that the occupants aren't allowed into the park to see the front of their house—the tall gate giving access to the deer park is permanently locked.

To the north of the house a stand is reported, with changes in 1721.

Norwich

Plantation Gardens (19th century)
Towers (19th century)
Pulhamite Conservatory (19th century)
`TG 200 080`

The Plantation Gardens, at The Beeches Hotel, Earlham Road, on the outskirts of Norwich, are being restored to their former glories. Which means the pleasing decay of the place must by now have disappeared. Never mind.

The gardens were planned by Henry Trevor of Norwich, who invested much of his work and capital in them and placed all sorts of odds and ends there. After he died in 1897 the gardens slowly fell to pieces. A church window is placed—apropos of nothing—against a slope, and there are several monuments, among them a fountain, which looks like a pinnacle on steroids, assembled from leftovers after a good day's demolishing and recycling small traceried windows, corbels, bricks and pieces of stone.

The rest of Norwich enjoys some other follies. There are two towers, both in Thorpe, east of Norwich. Pine Banks along Thorpe Road has a large Gothic 19th-

Hunstanton Octagon

Langley

Lodges (1784)
`TG 350 010`

Southeast of Norwich an eyecatcher pops up to the east of the A146, near Langley. On closer inspection it becomes a small, elegant archway with two lodges attached: 'Designed by Sir John Soane 1784, Restored by Capt. & Mrs R.D. Hutton 1980.' It was built for Sir Thomas Beauchamp-Proctor long before Soane was knighted. On top of the lodges are greyhounds rampant on shields above the motto 'TOVIOVRS FIDELE'. It is too small ever to have been used as a lodge; its function must simply have been to catch the eye. Soane published the design for these four years later, together with the unbuilt version, which includes a triumphal arch.

Letton Hall

Summerhouse (early 19th century)
`TF 970 060`

A year after the lodges at Langley, Soane built Letton Hall near Shipham. Perhaps some time later the reported summerhouse at Letton came into being, using three traceried windows from the church that had been demolished. There is also a restored dovecote.

Little Ellingham

Clock Tower (c.1855)
`TM 010 990`

If the finest folly in the county is at Crimplesham Hall, the oddest one must be the clock tower at Little Ellingham. A tall, square tower with one large clock-face (and

century tower, as well as some other folly-work. Tower House to the south, in Bracondale, has another tower in the gardens, although the name Tower House refers to the core of the main house.

Colney Hall, a few miles to the west, has Pulhamite grotwork in its conservatory. Doubtless hundreds of other houses still have it, but these winter gardens and ferneries are getting rarer.

Potter Heigham

Helter Skelter House (early 20th century)
TG 420 200

The Helter Skelter House is a holiday home, and there are two conflicting stories about how it got here. What is sure is that The Mat, as it was known, originally stood on Britannia Pier, Great Yarmouth (it came from Holland—but then, anything inexplicable in these parts seems to come from there). The first explanation tells how the suffragettes fire-bombed Britannia Pier, the Helter Skelter suffering damage. A bookie bought the remains and had them removed to Potter Heigham. The alternative explanation says that the Helter Skelter was used as a range-finder by German gunboats in 1916 when they shelled Great Yarmouth from the sea. It was taken away and bought by a furniture store owner, who had them removed to Potter Heigham.

Now, one of these stories has to be false. You can even switch bits of them around and see what you get next. What really amazes us is how these local stories have all the right

and utterly convincing details about them. There is material for at least two novels in there, as well as an Ealing Comedy.

Raveningham

Milestone (1831)
TM 380 970

There is a curious cast-iron milestone on the edge of a field of gladioli at Raveningham. It was made by John Thomas Patience in 1831 (praise be to artists who sign their works!) for Sir Edmund Bacon. It is a 10ft (3m) high, octagonal, Gothic turret, like a chimney, set on a crumbling plinth. Most of the distances and places have now disappeared, and all that is left on the three front faces is:

RAVENINGHAM

MILES TC 4è

III

Any guesses?

Saxthorpe

Removals (1860s)
TG 450 330

Some 2 miles northeast of Saxthorpe is Mannington Hall, with its beautifully tended gardens. Walpoles live at Mannington, and when we heard there were follies… but they are the tiniest scraps, removals of small columns, an arch, fragments of this and that, brought from Norwich *c.*1860 by Horatio, 4th Earl of Orford, and clustered around the old ruined church.

The only original structure seems to be a small, circular, red brick building, once

Mannington Hall follies

thatched but ruinous since at least 1902, as shown by an old photograph. It was too delicate to be a tower, and too small for a summerhouse. Could it have been a Gothic toolshed?

Most astonishing, perhaps, were the blatant manifestations of Orford's misogyny, which were expressed on the walls of his house, although perhaps not in the way that Horace 'Strawberry Hill' Walpole did. The later Orford sounds as if he had been cruelly disappointed in love, as he claims a great insight into women—which usually means he was interested in only one woman. Next to the door he put these inscriptions:

> *Trust your bark to the winds, do not trust your heart to girls. For the wave is safer than a woman's faith. There is no good woman, and if one attains to any good I know not how an ill-made thing becomes good.*

Not very snappy, though. The next is much better as a slogan:

> *A tiger is something worse than a snake, a demon than a tiger, a woman than a demon, and nothing worse than a woman.*

And positively abusive is a long Latin inscription that goes on about what woman is and is not (she's an animal, insatiable, a scourge of the house, an adulteress &c &c). Poor man.

Upper Sheringham

Repton Temple (1812–1975)
TG 139 419

A good mark of a folly is the delay between conception and completion, like the Jefferson Monument in Washington, D.C., the world's tallest obelisk. We cannot imagine a longer delay, however, than the Repton Temple at Sheringham Hall. It was designed in 1812 and built in 1975—a gap of 163 years. The reason is that Abbot Upcher, who bought the estate in 1811 for 50,000 guineas (at the age of 26), died suddenly in 1819 before the house and grounds were properly finished, and his wife was too heartbroken to carry on with the plans. The temple was finally built by the trustees of the estate as a 75th birthday present to Thomas Upcher, the direct descendant of the abbot.

The temple differs from the one planned by Repton in that it is hexagonal, not circular, and built of Portland stone rather than brick with flint infill. The property now belongs to the National Trust, which was advertising for tenants in 1998.

Westwick

Tower (c.1800)
TG 293 263

Mistakenly called an 'obelisk' on the Ordnance Survey map and by the locals and clearly visible from the railway, the tower tries to hide in a corner of a wood, shambling in the undergrowth. It stands on a square, red brick plinth, with heavy flint rustications on the corners and around the now bricked-up, round-arch doorway. There is an Alice in Wonderland type doorlet let into the brick, through which one can see the extant wooden spiral staircase. The tower is a heavy, round, brick rendered column, with porthole windows and a projecting, octagonal, flat metal roof. The evidence lying on the ground suggests that it used to have a conical spire, but that was taken down because, according to an old lady living in one of the lodges, the top was unsafe. As the tower appears to be on the direct flight-path for the runway at Coltishall fighter base, we would imagine the USAF had a say in the matter.

Excursions Through Norfolk (1818) sheds some light on the tower's purpose, yet also insisting on calling a belvedere an obelisk:

> *At a little distance from the house is an obelisk, ninety feet high, with a room at the top neatly fitted up, from whence there is a remarkably fine prospect…*

Westwick Tower

NORTHAMPTONSHIRE

Many of Northamptonshire's fine
Elizabethan houses antedate English
mannerist architecture. Some of these
houses border on follydom themselves:
the glorious ruins of overdecorated
Kirby Hall at Deene, or Burghley
House with its preposterous chimneys
giving it a bizarre silhouette. Castle
Ashby even has a lettered balustrade,
the whole forming a pious inscription.
In this shoemakers' county the follies
are far from pedestrian. There are
relatively few, but this is neatly balanced
by their importance.

Althorp

Temple by the Lake
The Falconry (early 19th century)
SP 680 647

Althorp was another of Britain's great
heritage of stately homes and parks, splendid
but not outstanding among its peers, with the
expected obelisk standing in the landscaped
park. Then Lady Diana Spencer was born
here and is now buried here on an island in
the lake, like Rousseau, heavily guarded and
inaccessible. At one stage in her too-public
lifetime she considered The Falconry on the
Althorp estate as her get-away-from-it
residence after her divorce from the Prince of
Wales; the press discovered it, found it to be
mildly Gothic in style and immediately
pronounced it to be a folly. No wonder she
chose to live elsewhere.

Boughton Park

Folly Group (mid-18th century)
SP 751 659

Boughton Park just north of Northampton
has the greatest diversity of follies in the
county, all built for William Wentworth, 2nd
Earl of Strafford (1722–91). Like Montagu,
Wentworth was a dilettante in architecture,
usually a guarantee of first-class follies.
Wentworth, however, was not entirely

Althorp's Temple by the Lake

original. Several of the Boughton buildings closely resemble those at Wentworth Castle in South Yorkshire, built by his father Thomas.

The 1764 obelisk, south of the house, is definitely one of the younger Wentworth's creations. The Hawking Tower along the A508 is essentially a copy of Steeple Lodge at Wentworth Castle, and it serves as the park's main entrance lodge. Built in or before 1755, it is three storeys high, with ogee and quatrefoiled windows and an outer staircase. Nearby are two similar castellated archways, one leading from the village into the park, the other into the kitchen garden. The castle style is carried on in the park, although the 1770 Newpark Barn has been decastellated. Bunker's Hill Farm, inscribed 'S 1776', retains its castellations, with quatrefoils in the façade facing the house. Strafford was a friend of General Howe, who led the attack on Bunker Hill in 1775 in the American War of Independence.

The Spectacles

The Spectacles (mid-18th century)
SP 768 659

Towards the village of Moulton is another cluster of Boughton follies. Holly Lodge, a pretty castellated house adorned with putti, is the centrepiece. A tall clock tower, dating from *c.*1861, rises to the back of the lodge. Two other follies belong to the same period as Newpark Barn: one of them has been christened The Spectacles, facing Spectacle Lane, the other remains nameless. Both consist of an arch between slender, castellated turrets. Again, these follies have a common ancestor at Wentworth Castle: the

archway of the sham Stainborough Castle, but they most closely resemble Sanderson Miller's eyecatcher arch at Wroxton in Oxfordshire. There is no evidence that Miller was employed here.

Brigstock

Lyveden New Bield (1605)
SP 983 853

See RUSHTON

Brockhall

Ivy House Eyecatcher (19th century)
SP 618 625

One end of a working barn has been topped with a small castellated wall, pierced with a Gothic window, presumably to be seen as an eyecatcher from Brockhall Hall.

Castle Ashby

Garden Buildings (mid-18th century)
SP 863 592

The follies at Castle Ashby tread the narrow line between garden buildings and true follies. Lancelot Brown, who worked here in the 1760s, let himself go only when the mood took him. No such mood took him here, for his buildings are classical: a temple-fronted dairy and an aviary/menagerie, which has now been turned into a house. It has a central dome resting on Doric pillars, and two end bays with Soane-like windows. Pretty, but no pure follies. Knucklebone Lodge and Nevitt's Lodge are better, although they come too late to make convincing candidates. Both share a Victorian rusticity, the thatched Knucklebone Lodge owing its name to the knucklebones that pattern the floor. The floor has recently been restored by the leading thatchers, Raffles, and readers of a nervous disposition had better skip to the next paragraph. These knucklebones come from sheep, and as one sheep's knucklebone covers only half a square inch, 12,000 were needed to make the star-shaped pattern on the floor. That's 6000 sheep—you can only use the front knucklebones. It is labour-intensive work, but at £50 per ton the materials are relatively cheap.

Later than these two are the buildings by Sir Matthew Digby Wyatt, among them a water tower of 1867-8, in the hybrid style peculiar to the era, and a screen of nine bays in the Renaissance style, a favourite motif of Digby Wyatt's. The lettered balustrades surrounding the house itself remain Castle

Ashby's main attraction, although they have been strangely neglected and were cited in a 1998 English Heritage report as being severely at risk. They must have been the inspiration for the oversized lettered balustrading reading 'FOOTSHAPE BOOT WORKS' on the Barratt factory of 1913 in Northampton.

There is also a rusticated dairy and another Gothick lodge near Ferry House, but somehow all this energetic building lacks the required lunacy; it is too studied. In 1995 the old Ferry House lodge was partly re-erected elsewhere in the grounds after it made way for a new bypass—the Gothic façade and the 19th-century cottage wing have thus been rescued.

The Garden House at Easton Neston

Castor (Cambridgeshire)

Garden Buildings (18th century)
TL 150 990

Outside Peterborough, the Milton Park Estate at Castor has all the necessary ingredients for a folly estate, but never quite makes it. The garden was designed by Humphrey Repton in 1791, and the various garden buildings include the tetrastyle Corinthian temple by Sir William Chambers, built in 1774–6, the orangery and the elegant Gothic lodge, built by William Wilkins in 1800, which is near the entrance by the motorway roundabout.

But the best, or rather the most folly-like, piece of work on the estate is the Kennels, also attributed to Chambers and built in 1767 as a sham medieval gatehouse. It has now been painstakingly restored—a good squat tower with a gigantic buttress, a curtain wall with arrowslits and a Gothick arched door, terminating in a round, cone-topped tower.

Easton Neston

The Gazebo (19th century)
SP 702 494

The plight of the garden buildings at Easton Neston was highlighted in *Follies* Magazine in 1990, but the gazebo and garden house remain seriously threatened.

Fawsley

Badby Lantern House (early 19th century)
Preston Capes Arches (early 19th century)
SP 574 546

Daventry has a slightly hopeless air about it; as with Jane Austen's opinion of Birmingham, there seems to be something depressing about the whole concept. Yet the High Street is pretty, cresting a small hill with Felicia 'The boy stood on the burning deck' Hemans's house a highlight (now a pet food store) and nicely finished off with a quirky Gothic façade at Sheaf Street. As with so many

English towns, it's the drab uniformity of the suburbs that brings it down. Still, the surrounding villages could model for an English tourist office brochure, particularly those to the south, such as Newnham and Preston Capes, which bask in the rolling English countryside like sleek, contented cats.

Dovecotes and windmills are often Gothicized, as usually only a few battlements are needed to transform them into convincing medieval castles. The private gardens of Newnham Hall, buried behind the village of Newnham off Poet's Lane, are noted for their splendid but labour-intensive topiary. The Hall has a Gothicized 19th-century dovecote tower on an islet in the small lake, hardly the handiest position for collecting squabs and evidently putting appearance above convenience. It is now a tiny, ivy-clad sham ruin, complete with towerette.

Fawsley Hall stands alone in the countryside between Badby and Preston Capes, a substantial Tudor house protected from the narrow country lane behind it by its outbuildings. At the time of writing it was being converted into a country house hotel. A mile or so to the north, on the surprisingly busy A361, is a former lodge house to the estate, widely known as the Lantern House from its central chimney, which is perched on top of an octagonal pyramidal roof. Formally called Fawsley Lodge, it was restored and extended in 1981 to make a double octagon,

Badby Lantern House

with help from the County and Daventry District councils. Although rare, octagonal lodges are not the least common building type in Britain, and the renown of the Lantern House must owe much to its prominent location and curious name.

Looking north towards the same Hall are a couple of castellated cottages in the middle

Preston Capes Eyecatcher from the sunny side

of the village of Preston Capes, two on each side of a battlemented arch, built to act as a silhouetted eyecatcher from the Hall and now occupied as separate houses. They were designed by Lady Knightley, the wife of Sir Charles Knightley. Given their architectural merit, it is unlikely that she was assisted by Thomas Cundy, who made some alterations at the Hall between 1815 and 1816. The Lantern House may possibly be Cundy's; it shows a far more assured touch than the red brick eyecatcher cottages, which are simple in both concept and execution.

Finedon

Folly Group (late 19th century)

The follies at Finedon near Wellingborough speak of the grief of the village's last squire, William Mackworth-Dolben, who lived to see all three of his sons die. The now-vanished *Volta* Tower was dedicated to the memory of a son who was lost when the ship *Volta* sank in September 1863. The high Victorian memorial was a gigantic folly, a massive, circular, polychromatic brick tower, diapered and with crosses round the parapet, packed into a farmhouse with at least six gables and a crazily varied roofline. The whole mad concoction had pairs of Romanesque windows dotted seemingly at random over the façade. But the tragedy continued—in 1951 it collapsed, killing the owner.

Ice Tower (1864)
SP 910 720

Mackworth-Dolben decorated a substantial part of the village in his particular style, a picturesque mullioned vernacular with titling—all the village buildings are captioned, their names in blackletter on florid scrolls. Thingdon Cottage, Exmill Cottage, the Vicarage, a school, the pub—all are neatly labelled. The Ice Tower is not labelled, but it is indisputably in Mackworth's style. It is a tall, slender, battlemented, stone tower with Romanesque window arches, now firmly attached to a modern house on the housing estate that fills the park of Finedon Hall. The owners are justly proud of their bizarre excrescence, and beneath it is a large, dry cellar, which presumably once held the ice. We know of no other ice tower in the country.

Exmill Cottage (early 19th century)
SP 907 725

Exmill Cottage is typical. A more modern house has been attached to the truncated ex-

mill a little way out of the village, which with its heavy castellations and finials makes a convincing piece of medievalism. There is the name scroll, and the Mackworth-Dolben shields, and a millstone proudly displayed on the side of the tower with the letters REST where one might expect NWES.

> BEAR YE ONE ANOTHERS BURDENS
> AND SO FULFIL THE LAW OF CHRIST

reads the lettering on the eaves of what may have been a lodge. Finedon, the scene of much sublimated anguish, still shows itself as an elaborate memento mori.

Wellington Tower (1815)
SP 934 750

Between Finedon and Woodford, a familiar sight on the A510 to Thrapston is the Wellington Tower. Short, fat and circular, with a conical roof and a railing round the central chimneystack, it carries a large cruciform plaque under a round window reading:

> PANORAMA
> WATERLOO
> VICTORY
> June 18
> A.D.
> 1815

The tower was built by Charles Arbuthnot, MP and Secretary to the Treasury, whose friend Wellington pointed out the local landmarks that reminded him of Waterloo

Ice Tower, Finedon

Wellington Tower, Finedon

from the top of the tower. Others maintain that the Iron Duke pointed them out with his feet firmly on the ground, the tower being built afterwards to commemorate the occasion. With added wings, it has now become a farmhouse.

Geddington

Boughton House Chinese Tent
(mid-18th century)
SP 901 815

There are two Boughtons in Northamptonshire, each consisting of a Boughton Park and a Boughton House. We concern ourselves with the House near Kettering and the Park near Northampton. Boughton House was built in the latter half of the 17th century and is often referred to as a miniature Versailles. Its builder, the 1st Duke of Montagu, had served as Ambassador to the French Court. John Montagu, the 2nd Duke (*c.*1688–1749), apparently tried to improve upon this: in order to link Montagu House, his London residence, with Boughton, he proposed a 70-mile avenue of elms to run in a straight line between the two houses. The plan did not take root, although several elm avenues survive in the immediate vicinity. Montagu thoroughly enjoyed an innocent bit of fun, as his mother-in-law implies in a letter:

(His) talents lie in things natural to boys of fifteen, and he is about two and fifty.

To get people into his gardens and wet with them with squirts, to invite people to his country house and put things in their beds to make them itch, and twenty other such pretty fancies.

The old lady obviously had to endure many of the duke's little amusements.

Montagu kept a portable folly in the garden of his London house: a Chinese Tent, that most elusive of garden ornaments. A Chinese (or Turkish or Moorish) tent can mean anything from a real tent (General Hill brought one over from Arabia to Hawkstone in Shropshire) to a pagoda or mosque— hardly portable. Britain is still dotted with molehills called Tent Hill. The Montagu tent is one of the rare survivors. It was eventually transported from London to Boughton and there, on special days, it rests on the lawn. It is made of oilskin, is 12-sided and has a curved roof. The interior is painted with fiery dragons, which have started to show some craquelure, nevertheless making it the sort of tent Genghis Khan would have coveted. Even its provenance has been established; it comes from a workshop in no less an exotic place than Knightsbridge. The house itself has a Chinese staircase, which, together with the tent, makes the duke an early China fancier. Sir William Chambers's Designs for Chinese Buildings (1757), made pseudo-Chinese edifices fashionable:

The trav'ler with amazement sees
A temple, Gothic, or Chinese,
With many a bell, and tawdry rag on
And crested with a sprawling dragon,
etc.

(Lloyd's *Poetical Works*, 1774, i. 45)
The duke also seems to have been one of the first to embrace the castellated style of farm building, although most of his commissioned designs or those prepared by the duke himself as an amateur architect have come to nothing.

Holdenby

Holdenby Arches (1583)
SP 692 678

Two lonely arches in a field are the sole survivors of a gigantic house that ended its life here in 1651. Were they just forgotten or were they even then considered to be of value as agreeable objects? The Holdenby Arches stand forlorn in a horse pasture with just themselves for company, having run out of polite conversation years ago. They are twins, one standing behind the other. Each consists of the actual arch, flanked by two arms, of which the upper part has been brick infilled, the lower containing niches. On top of the arches is some uncertain scrollwork with a label and the date 1583. Messrs I. Davis and C. Wright have each scratched their signatures in the sandstone with accompanying dates—1850 and 1868. Even graffiti become interesting with age.

The Holdenby House that now stands here is about ½ mile from the arches, and it has a similar-style entrance arch, although dated 1659. It is said that the present house is merely part of the north side of the northwest courtyard, and that the old house extended all the way to the arches.

later classical garden temple which, converted into a house, was sold for £420,000 in 1994.

Naseby

Battle Memorials (1936)

SP 693 784

Flanking the B4036 is the Battle of Naseby Memorial. That should read Memorials, for there are two monuments, and there ought to be at least three. The official memorial, erected in 1936, is in the form of an inscribed column, announcing that from near this site

The Menagerie, Horton

Horton

The Menagerie (c.1740)
The Arches (18th century)

SP 826 542

Horton Hall was demolished in 1935, and the Menagerie, a splendid low, wide building with a central bow, was left to rot. It was saved from destruction by the late Gervase Jackson-Stops, who recreated the stunning interior plasterwork—we saw traces of plaster violins when we visited it as a near ruin—and they have since been fully restored. He made it into a delightful private house. It is one of the few Thomas Wright buildings to survive, resembling the Castle Ashby menagerie although the Horton façade is much broader. The heavy rustication shows a singular vermicelli pattern.

The second folly at Horton is The Arches, a triumphal arch acting both as an eyecatcher and a lodge. The likely builders were Thomas Wright or Daniel Garrett—if Wright, then he may have been inspired by the arch at Shugborough in Staffordshire, where he also worked. Near The Arches is a

Oliver Cromwell led the cavalry charge that decided the issue of this battle and… that of the Great Civil War. The rogue memorial that marks the wrong battlefield is to the north, an obelisk on a plinth, both firmly standing on a rough stone base. The plaque asserts in language less prosaic than that of the 1936 memorial that the outcome of the battle

LED TO THE SUBVERSION OF THE THRONE,
THE ALTAR, AND THE CONSTITUTION
AND FOR YEARS PLUNGED THIS NATION
INTO THE HORRORS OF ANARCHY
AND CIVIL WAR:
LEAVING A USEFUL LESSON TO BRITISH KINGS
NEVER TO EXCEED THE BOUNDS
OF THEIR JUST PREROGATIVE,
AND TO BRITISH SUBJECTS,
NEVER TO SWERVE FROM THE ALLEGIANCE
DUE TO THEIR LEGITIMATE MONARCH.
THIS PILLAR WAS ERECTED
BY JOHN AND MARY FRANCES FITZGERALD
LORD AND LADY OF THE MANOR OF NASEBY
A.D. MDCCCXXIII

Of late, the site of the 1936 memorial has been disputed, so we can hope for yet another monument.

Rothwell

Market House (1575)
SP 818 813

See RUSHTON

Rushton

Triangular Lodge (1595–97)
SP 830 831

If it be demanded why I labour so much in the Trinity and Passion of Christ to depaint in this chamber, this is the principal instance thereof: That at my last being hither committed, and I usually having my servants here allowed me, to read nightly an hour to me after supper, it fortuned that Fulcis, my then servant, reading in the Christian Resolution, in the treatise of Proof that there is a God, &c., there was upon a wainscot table at that instant three loud knocks (as if it had been with an iron hammer) given; to the great amazing of me and my two servants, Fulcis and Nilkton.

—undated letter from Sir Thomas Tresham, *c.*1595

Sir Thomas Tresham's buildings at Rushton and Lyveden may not be the oldest British follies, but his Triangular Lodge of 1597 has a strong claim to be the purest folly in the country. With Tresham, building loses all pretence of function; it is a means of expressing an idea, an obsession.

The mind that thought up these remarkable structures can perhaps best be explained in terms of family history. The Tresham family seems to have had a standing order of bad luck—they inevitably seemed to pick the wrong bankers. Sir Thomas's great-great-grandfather got himself murdered in 1450 by some servants in what appears to have been

Rushton Triangular Lodge

a politically motivated attack. His son Thomas, robbed and wounded on the above occasion, was beheaded 21 years later after the Battle of Tewkesbury. Sir Thomas's grandfather threw his lot in with Queen Mary, but unusually died of natural causes. As his son predeceased him, Sir Thomas inherited directly from his grandfather. His son, Francis, was deeply implicated in the Gunpowder Plot, ending up with his head stuck on a pole in Northampton. The tumultuous family died out in the mid-17th century, apparently the only way out of the Tresham curse.

Sir Thomas Tresham himself spent the best part of his life in gaol, largely due to the state's interest in his religious beliefs. Nominally brought up in the Church of England—it was a criminal offence not to be—he became a recusant at the age of 15, and for the rest of his life, although fiercely loyal to the Crown as head of state, he waged an unyielding battle against the religious intolerance of that time. Catholicism was the passion of the Treshams; Sir Thomas transmuted that passion into stone. Fuller, in his *Worthies of England*, found it hard to say whether Tresham's delight in building was greater than his skill, adding that he was 'more forward in beginning than finishing his fabricks'. Tresham's fortune was considerably depredated by fines for his resolute recusancy and for hiding the Jesuit Edmund Campion in 1581 (the year of his execution), he was sentenced to seven years imprisonment. Tresham was taken to Fleet

prison, followed by house arrest at Hoxton Hall, after which he was finally removed to Ely prison. Here on the walls of his cell he worked out the mottoes, emblems and symbols that were to result in his magnum opus, the Rushton Triangular Lodge.

Before working on the Triangular Lodge Tresham had begun the Market House at Rothwell. This was started in 1578, but whether because of gaol sentences or the excitement of a new project, he never got round to completing it, and it was not roofed until late in the 19th century. The Rothwell building was a precursor to the lodge in so far that its walls were used as a gallery for a large number of Tresham coats of arms— family pride burned strong in his breast. In the year 1593, the date he later put on the Lodge, Tresham took the firm intention to build his monument to the Trinity in the grounds of Rushton Hall, northwest of Kettering. Work started on the Triangular Lodge—originally known as the Warryners Lodge, presumably because the rabbit keeper lived there—the following year. The Tyrell family were engaged as masons, while a man called Parriss was employed on much of the fancy work. John Thorpe has been credited as the architect, largely because he was certainly involved in the building of Rushton Hall in 1595, and one of the few buildings that has been confidently ascribed to him is the triangular Longford Castle in Wiltshire. However, as Thorpe has been credited as the architect of almost every house of any importance in Britain at this time, it is more

Lyveden New Bield (see p.382)

likely that the strong-minded and obsessive builder Tresham was his own architect.

The format is quite simple—as soon as one overcomes the initial shock of seeing what is unquestionably the oddest building of its period in the country, one understands the gist of it. The brick building has three sides, each measuring thirty-three feet, three storeys, three gables on each side, and a total of nine gargoyles. In addition, the exterior is littered with trefoils, three to a row, and the crowning (solitary) central chimney has, inevitably, three sides. All this stands for the Trinity, but Tresham himself also comes into it: above the door (only one door) is a text reading:

TRES.TESTI
MONIVM.DANT

below the Tresham coat of arms. This is a biblical quotation (John 1:5–7): 'For there are three that bear record (in heaven).' The TRES stands for Tresham as well, a word play quite acceptable to Elizabethans. Biblical quotations are carried on as a frieze along the outside walls of the lodge, each text consisting of 33 letters. They can be interpreted to reflect on the persecution of Catholics in England:

QVIS.SEPERABIT.NOS.A.CHARITATE.CHRISTI.
CONSIDERAVI.OPERA.TUA.DOMINE.ET.EXPAVI
APERIATVR.TERRA.&.GERMINET.SALVATORVM

[Who will part us from the love of Christ? I have looked on thy works Lord and am afraid The earth opens and brings forth salvation] There are still more mottoes on the walls, gables and chimney, together with some singular ciphers, which have been attributed to a presumed interest in the Cabbala and Black Magic. The ciphers also prove to be biblical in content, however. Above the door, for example, is the number 5555. If one puts the date of the Creation at 3962BC (as more than one 16th-century cleric did) the date turns out to be AD1593. The other numbers 3098 and 3509 are significant Old Testament dates.

Lyveden New Bield (1594-1606)
SP 974 853

Lyveden New Bield (New Building), a National Trust property set in the surprisingly remote rolling Northamptonshire hills between Brigstock and Oundle, is much larger than the Triangular Lodge. The first impression is astonishment: one expects a ruin and discovers an unfinished building, and the two are very different. As it comes into sight over the crest of the hill, the New Bield looks

immaculate, almost literally new; apart from not having roofs or windows it looks as if it has just been built and is even now awaiting completion. In the silence it seems as if a 16th-century bank holiday is taking place, and tomorrow the builders will be back at work with the hammering of nails, the rasp of the saws and the creak of the winches. But work has stopped here for nearly 400 years. The second impression is that, apart from its condition and situation, this is no different from the normal run of Elizabethan country houses, but closer examination shows that the New Bield is Rushton's logical heir. Lyveden was started in 1594 and is represented, along with hundreds of other houses, in John Thorpe's famous book of plans and elevations now at the Soane Museum. For a long time Lyveden was ascribed to Thorpe; anything was possible from an architect who designed his own house basing the ground plan on his initials. The actual builder of Lyveden was Robert Stickells: there is a drawing in the British Museum of the lantern that was intended to top the house. This was not executed for there was never a roof on the New Bield, although around 1750 plans were made to palladianize the unfinished shell.

Lyveden New Bield is planned in the shape of a Greek cross, each wing ending in a bay window, and set in the remains of a garden constructed at the same time as the house, which was doubtless a part of Tresham's emblematical intentions. Lyveden's symbolical content is that of the Passion and the Mater Dolorosa. There are inscriptions and emblems of the Passion to confirm this. The number symbolism is that of 3, 5, 7 and 9. The bay windows are five-sided and five feet long, each wing has a frieze inscription of 81 letters (9 x 9; 3 x 3 x 3 x 3), and the emblems of the Passion are sevenfold. The number three and nine signify, as we have seen, the Trinity. Five is the Five Wounds on the hands, feet and side of Christ, seven stands for the Seven Sorrows of Our Lady, the Seven Instruments of the Passion, the Seven Stations of the Cross, the Seven Last Words of Christ, the Seven Gifts of the Holy Ghost and, perhaps the personal touch, Tresham's seven years in gaol for his faith.

Stoke Bruerne

Stoke Park Pavilions (17th century)
SP 741 494

There are substantial pavilions and a colonnade designed by Inigo Jones.

NORTHUMBERLAND

There is something strangely familiar about Northumbrian scenery between the moors and the sea. The whole countryside looks like a vast park for some unimaginably huge stately home or, worse, a golf course. Then one realizes that this is where Lancelot Brown, the most famous landscape designer of all, was born and where he lived until he was 23 years old. You can take the boy out of the country, but you can't take the country out of the boy. Throughout all his works he helplessly, unconsciously reproduced the natural scenery of his native land: grassland sweeping down to lakes, clumps of trees. You can walk through the landscaped business parks of Silicon Valley in California or any golf course in the world and see Brown's influence spanning 5000 miles and 250 years.

Architecturally speaking, this is the land of the Goth, for apart from the menacing Seaton Delaval mausoleum, a handful of obelisks and a garden temple or two, Northumberland has few neo-classical follies. England's northernmost county is now innocent of Moorish and Chinese conceits. Peers and gentry alike have embraced the only possible folly style to befit this weathered and rugged area: Gothick. It has been adapted for every type of building, from towers, façades, sham castles and summerhouses, to dovecotes and kennels. It need not be brutal—a tiny, pretty Gothick summerhouse with a decorated ogee-arched doorway, flanked by quatrefoil windows, was recently unearthed during the clearance of undergrowth at Chipchase Castle in Warton-on-Tyne. Its provenance is a mystery for the moment. Because of the horrendous east winds no one seems to have bothered with coastal follies, despite a romantic shoreline; most of the follies are inland, and are Georgian rather than Victorian.

Alnwick

Alnwick and the Percys are synonymous. For nearly a thousand years this family has dominated the north of England: where Percys led, others followed. The impetus for the Gothick movement in northern England came from the rebuilding programme at Alnwick Castle, an undertaking that spanned most of the latter half of the 18th century. In the 1750s the immensely rich Hugh Percy Smithson, 1st Duke of Northumberland, started the restoration of Alnwick, until that time a ramshackle collection of castle walls, towers and corridors, most of it in a more or less ruined state. At first, James Paine started on the tremendous task of redoing both the interior and exterior, but later the Adam brothers were called in. After some years the castle began to look presentable, and the duke had Lancelot Brown fashion the park. As his labours took effect, the duke turned his attention to the construction of a few follies, even going so far as to plant rather incongruous acroteria on the parapets of the medieval barbican.

Among the earliest ornaments was the Lion Bridge of 1773; three embattled arches with arrowslits and quatrefoils and the lead statue of a lion on one side of the parapet. Denwick Bridge, leading to the northeast, also came in for the Gothick treatment. The Percy lion formed the staple part of the decorations on the estate, and a quarter of a century later the duke was lampooned in a pamphlet called 'Wood and Stone: or a Dialogue between a Wooden Duke and a Stone Lion'.

Brizlee Tower (1777)
NU 158 149

Alnwick's finest and most famous folly stands on top of a 600ft (183m) hill to the north, variously known as Brizlee, Brislaw and Briesley Hill. Mackenzie's *View of Northumberland* claimed that the original model for Brizlee Tower was made of pastry by a French cook. His Grace was so pleased with this ingenious design when it was placed upon his table that he ordered all the proportions to be strictly observed in erecting this tower. Two years later, in 1827,

Brizlee Tower

Parson & White's Gazetteer of Durham and Northumberland spoiled the fun by revealing that the patissier had created the dessert only after the tower had been built.

Despite stories of the duke having been his own architect, the tower, a tremendously ornate architectural pudding, was almost certainly designed by the Adam brothers in 1777. This concept of pastrycook as architect is not entirely without precedent; in 1815 the renowned chef Marie Antoine Carême published *Le Patissier Pittoresque*, which included designs for all sorts of follies to be executed in more or less edible materials.

The Grade I tower, completed in 1781, is about 80ft (24m) high, starting from a broad base with pointed arches and canopied niches. Above this is a balustrade with fancy open-work battlements of an intricate design. From here the shaft supplies three more stories of pointed windows and niches; 129 steps up to the top is another balustrade and a battlemented octagon on which is an iron cresset with little trefoils on the rim. The ground floor has been boarded up to prevent vandalism, and although compared with most folly towers it has led a favoured and pampered life, English Heritage was recently still prepared to describe its condition as poor—'slow decay, no solution agreed'— much to the irritation of the Percys. On the external walls some of the bas-relief plaques of the duke and his family have weathered so badly that their inscriptions can no longer be read, although a small plaque immodestly recording the 1st Duke's achievements in planting trees in the area remains legible:

CIRCUMSPICE

EGO OMNIA ISTA SUM DIMENSUS

MEI SUNT ORDINES

MEA DESCRIPTIO

MULTAE ETIAM ISTARUM ARBORUM

MEA MANU SUNT SATAE

The duchess's interest in her own family's history was responsible for the restoration of the Malcolm Cross, recording the death of the Scottish king Malcolm II seven centuries earlier.

Ratcheugh Observatory or The Gazebo (1784)
NU 225 146

A couple of miles northeast of the castle is Ratcheugh Cliff, on top of which sits the spectacular gazebo, built about 1784 by Robert and James Adam as part of an

Ratcheugh Observatory

uncompleted grand design. 'Gazebo' is an utterly inadequate word for this magnificent erection. The eyecatcher strides along the crest of the hill, one of the mightiest sham castle screens in the country. Windows all round the gazebo, poised above the long screen wall of pointed arches and battlements, earned it the name of Ratcheugh Observatory, and the single square room, flooded with light from north, south, east and west, has views to St Mary's Isle in the Firth of Forth, views beyond even the expanse of the Percy demesnes.

In the town itself is Pottergate Tower, built in 1768 around a medieval core. The tower was paid for by the Borough, but the duke evidently had his say in the affair and the folly is obviously the product of the castle workmen and architects.

Hulne Park, northwest of the town and improved by Lancelot Brown and Robert Adam from God's very promising raw material, is encircled by a 9 mile long, 8ft (2.4m) high stone wall. Near the entrance to the Park is the tiny monument to William the Lion, King of Scotland, erected *c*.1860 by Algernon Percy, the 4th Duke. The arched square on a plinth commemorates the capture of William after an unsuccessful siege in 1174.

Also in the park are the ruins of Hulne Priory. Here in 1776 both Adam and Brown improved the medieval ruins for the junketaceous 1st Duchess to use as a picnic site. Tradition has it that Adam did the interior of the Lord's Tower, set amid the ecclesiastical remains, while Brown designed the exterior. The Gothick windows and door are, indeed, in Brown's style, except for a niche in the side wall, which is more related in its ornamentation to Brizlee Tower. The façade has two white, round, portrait plaques of the duke and duchess, set in two quatrefoils made in 1773 by the relatively unknown George Davy. The Peace of 1814 was commemorated by the 2nd Duke with the Peace Column, complete with small bell on top, a Tuscan column in the woods on the golf course.

The Farmer's Folly or Tenantry Column (1816)
NU 192 131

The 2nd Duke's folly fame lies not with the Peace Column, however, but with a column he did not build. The Farmer's Folly, near the station, is impressive—a sort of Trafalgar Square rurally resettled. Amid four lions, a fluted column on a broad base rises 83ft (25m) to a drum, on which an aristocratic lion is perched. Its official name is the Tenantry

Column, and it was built in 1816 to the designs of David Stephenson, the architect shared between the Percys and Sir Matthew Ridley of Blagdon Hall. It was raised by the duke's tenant farmers to express their gratitude to him for reducing their rents by 25 per cent after the catastrophic fall in agricultural prices after the peace of 1814. Pragmatically, the duke felt that if they could afford to make such a tangible expression of their gratitude, they could afford to pay higher rents, so he upped them to the old levels.

Clayport Eyecatchers (1823)
NU 181 124

Two Gothick improvisations serve as landscape enhancements at St Thomas Farm and Swansfield Park. At the farm, the rear of an outbuilding has been Gothicized with castellations and arrowslits, and further south the same treatment has been effected to the park wall.

Bedlington

Obelisk (1997)
NZ 256 8203

The Market Cross at Bedlington (where the terriers came from) in the old industrial district northwest of Seaton Delaval can hardly be called classical as the obelisk is built from very rough-cast stone.

Belford Hall

Gazebo and Grotto (mid-18th century)
NU 510 340

The formerly derelict house has now been converted into apartments, which accounts for the excess of PRIVATE—KEEP OUT notices to replace the estate workers who would courteously enquire as to how they could assist you. There are the remains of a Gothick summerhouse by James Paine, and a grotto and a gazebo are said to exist but we failed to find them. The grotto may have been mistaken for the ice-house, which is adventurously connected to the kitchen block by a tunnel.

Belsay Hall

Romantic Gardens (1817)
Bantam Folly (1757)
NT 088 784

Belsay Hall is a remarkable house built by Sir Charles Monck, who changed his name from Middleton in 1799 in order to inherit his maternal grandfather's estate. This chaste

Bantam Folly

One curious effect of the garden is the sensation of plunging deeper into a savagely overgrown chasm—in fact, the ground remains roughly level while the sides of the gorge grow higher, an illusion aided by judicious planting.

This powerful garden was created more than 50 years after the toyshop Gothick of Bantam Folly, an eyecatcher farmsteading built by Sir Charles's ancestor Sir William Middleton. Drawings survive of the original plan for Bantam Folly, which has a central castellated square tower with quatrefoil moulding flanked by two ruinous pavilions. A spire was planned, 87ft 11in (26.8m) high, but when built it turned out much shorter: 'it was only a small thing,' says an annotation to the drawing. Instead of demolishing the folly, which by the early 19th century was hideously passé, Monck merely took down the spire. The central tower is now 29ft (8.8m) high. It says much for his liberal classical romanticism that he allowed this architectural solecism to remain in his grand scheme; indeed, the contrast between the high geometrical perfection of the house and the wild informality of the quarry garden testifies to his rare breadth of appreciation. Sir Charles's second journey to Italy in the 1830s prompted a row of curiously broad-arched cottages in the village, but for the village school in 1842 he finally chose Gothick.

Greek Revival house was built between 1807 and 1817, its owner acting as his own architect with the practical help of John Dobson, a Newcastle architect who 'had the secret of keeping out the cold', an invaluable asset in the northeast. Such a purist was Monck that his Greek Revival has echoes of Egyptian temples in its austerity; it is said that he calculated the measurements to three decimal places. Monck married his cousin Louisa Cook in 1804, and received his architectural inspiration from a two-year honeymoon spent travelling through Germany to Athens and back by sea via Portugal, *à trois* with Sir William Gell of Hopton Hall in Derbyshire, an eminent dilettante whom we meet in the chapter on that county. His diary reveals his primary interest during his honeymoon. In Berlin he examined the Brandenburger Tor and noted: 'The architecture is pretty correct except that the columns have bases.'

Monck transfigured the quarry that had yielded the stone for the building of Belsay into a garden closely following Richard Payne Knight's and Uvedale Price's precepts on the Picturesque. The valley walks and high bridged underpasses illustrate a particular passage in Price's 'An Essay on the Picturesque' (1794):

> such [i.e. picturesque], *for instance, are the rough banks that often inclose a bye-road or a hollow lane: Imagine the size of these banks and the space between them to be increased until the lane becomes a deep dell,—the coves large caverns,—the peeping stones hanging rocks, so that the whole may impress an idea of awe and grandeur…*

Berwick-upon-Tweed

Wilson's Folly (1854)
`NT 994 534`

Berwick-upon-Tweed's status has been unclear for years. Until 1746 it was effectively a free town, owing allegiance to neither England nor Scotland. This has persisted in public imagination until it was firmly believed that Berwick was left out of the Treaty of Versailles that ended World War I. We were told in all seriousness that, as the town was still formally at war with Germany, the Ambassador had to be summoned to Berwick in 1966 to sign a final peace treaty. We even have his words, no doubt remarked as he recapped his fountain pen and let his monocle slip: 'The good burghers of Germany will sleep easy in their beds tonight.' Likewise, Arsenal and Manchester United have little to fear: Berwick Rangers play in the Scottish League.

Fronting 11 Railway Street is a conventional late Georgian house. Just walk around the corner to 48 Tweed Street and feast your eyes on a house that appears to

Wilson's Folly, Berwick-upon-Tweed

have been built out of fish scales. Every stone has been carved with an abstract repeating pattern, and each window is topped with a carved head (although one was missing when we visited). This was wreaked by the sculptor William Wilson, perhaps for show as a vast trade card or master piece? But then in the district of Spittal we come across more of Wilson's cascade of decorations in Main Street, where number 178 is a substantial house with even larger fish scale carvings, also adorned with acroteria and sculpted heads above each window, and we have to conclude that he did it purely for his own pleasure.

Spittal's Main Street is a rare example in England of an unmodernized, ungentrified, uncommercialized high street; not particularly shabby or run down, simply overlooked. It retains a strange, elderly charm.

Bolton

Crawley Tower (mid-18th century)
`NU 069 165`
Jenny's Lantern (mid-18th century)
`NU 119 153`
Shepherd's Law (mid-18th century)
`NU 087 166`

Crawley Tower, now a farmhouse, is a genuine 14th-century pele tower, which was 'improved' with battlements and crow-step gables on the southwest side in the 18th century to serve as an eyecatcher from the Hargrave family's Shawdon Hall, along with Jenny's

Lantern and Shepherd's Law.

These are all reworkings of existing buildings, enhanced to serve as economical eyecatchers. Jenny's Lantern, above Bolton, derived its name from the light hung out by the eponymous Jenny to guide her husband back from the pub each night. The story is better than the building, which is a plain, three-walled ruin on a remote hilltop. Don't bother walking up to it for architectural interest, although the exercise will doubtless benefit you. Shepherd's Law is the most visually distinctive of the trio, with its two blocks of great blind arcading, which now conceal a monastery. Law is a dialect word for a hill.

Branxton

Cement Menagerie Garden (1962)
`NT 894 376`

John Fairnington retired from his joinery business at the age of 80 on 31 December 1961, and to amuse his handicapped son Edwin he began to make life-sized concrete and cement models of the world's animals. Edwin enjoyed this, and so his father was encouraged to proceed. By the time he died in 1981, Fairnington had had to acquire additional land to extend his garden to contain this vast menagerie of more than 300 animals, the great majority life-size, including two giraffes. Surely only financial considerations must have prohibited the construction of an elephant or blue whale.

There is a nod towards other sculptors, with a copy of William Brodie's Ram Fountain at Moffat in Dumfriesshire. This is not just a rare example in England of a *jardin imaginaire*, it is also one of the largest collections of Art Brut or outsider art, as this style of folly building is variously called, anywhere in the world. Holy Land USA, in Waterbury, Connecticut, takes up more acreage, but its buildings are puny compared to the exuberance of Fairnington's animals. Inscriptions, verses, dedications and homilies abound, as one would hope, but curiously we could find no mention of the most momentous event in these parts, the bloody battle of Flodden Field just ½ mile away.

John Fairnington and his dog?

Brinkburn Priory

Manor House Hermitage Tunnel
(late 18th century)
NU 117 983

Here is an L-shaped tunnel, said to have
housed a hermit during the Age of
Romanticism.

Cambo

Wallington Hall Arches (mid-18th century)
Griffin Heads (mid-18th century)
NZ 030 843

The main gardens are to the east of
Wallington Hall, on the other side of the
road. At the China Pond, where a long-
demolished piece of 18th-century chinoiserie
once stood, is now a standing stone, pilfered
from a nearby stone circle. In the 1760s
Lancelot Brown, who went to school in the
village, worked for Sir Walter Calverley
Blackett of the Hall, which is now a National
Trust property. A new, large and impressive
stable block was built, and the old stable arch

the Jacobite troubles: a stretch of walling
ending in two squat machicolated towers with
a third tower in the centre. Its rather fancy
decorations of cross arrowslits, pointed doors
and windows, blind arches and the
whalebones (these last have now disappeared)
suggest a perfunctory use, although it was
most likely to have been used by Sir Walter, its
builder, for refreshments while hunting.

Codger's Fort (1769)
NZ 044 901

Thomas Wright's sham castle known as
Codger's Fort, also built for the industrious
Sir Walter, crowns a redoubt a little way to
the north of Rothley Castle. It is more
sparsely decorated and repeats the same plan
with some variations, mainly in roofing the
end bastions with pyramids of rough stone.

Thanks to the Countryside Commission's
stewardship scheme, Rothley and Codger's
Fort, owned by siblings Elizabeth and John
Walton, are now free to public access. 'I like
people to get out into the country,' drawled
Elizabeth.

Codger's Fort from the defender's point of view

and screen were re-erected in the fields
½ mile to the north to serve as an elegant
eyecatcher from the gardens.

By the house are four griffins' heads set in
the lawn bordering the road. These came
from Aldergate, London, and were said to
have been brought to the north as ballast on
Blackett's coal barges. The heads were first
placed on top of Daniel Garrett's Rothley
Castle but were later removed to the
immediate vicinity of the house.

Rothley Castle (1755)
NZ 044 888

The meandering sham Rothley Castle,
designed by Daniel Garrett, was erected on its
hilltop position in about 1755. It is reputed to
have been intended as a point of defence in

Capheaton Hall

Sham Chapel (mid-18th century)
NZ 037 804

Lancelot Brown was born in Kirkharle in 1715
or 1716, went to school in Cambo, and worked
at Kirkharle Hall. A clump or two in the
grounds of Capheaton Hall are said to have
been planted by Brown, and it is tantalizing to
think of the small, Gothick, sham ruined
church in the park as one of his creations.
Sadly, Brown was not involved; the
Swinburnes say there is no record of his being
employed at the Hall. They should know, as
they built it in 1690 and have lived there ever
since. We were guided to the folly by a small
child. 'What's your name?' we enquired
winningly. 'Swinburne!' he bellowed.

One of the sham castle gates at Ford

Eglingham

Cockhall Folly (1800)
NU 101 198

This is tiny but very pleasing. The gable end of a stone barn in a very ripe working farm has been prettily Gothicized to serve as an eyecatcher from the road. A blind, triple-pointed arch window in the facing wall is surmounted by a hood moulding, and the roof end is punctuated by three small obelisks and slanting battlements. Everything else is pure farmyard.

Ford

Castle Gates (1773; 1801)
NT 945 374

Ford Castle, now the headquarters of the Northumberland Health Authority, has a pair of high quality Gothick gates of such exuberant pretension that they cry out to be classed as follies. The South Gate (1773), the entrance to the gloriously sham ensemble, is a creation of James Nesbit, the architect of the ill-fated Twizel Castle, and it consists of a thin castellated arch with rustic archway, tiny quatrefoils and pretty rusticated—almost frosted—quoins, built for Sir John Hussey Delaval. Its charm lies in its fragility; no cannonballs would be needed to blow this arch down, just a huff and a puff.

As if to compensate for this frail gateway, Alexander Gilkie's huge and splendid East Gate (1801) is in the Sturdy style and takes up one entire side of the castle keep. A sham portcullis provides the centre, with the gateway flanked by two three-storey towers that are decorated with blind and open quatrefoils, blind niches, with a tiny clock-face

lurking in the right-hand tower and a dovecote in the left. Walls with cross arrowslits and the inevitable castellations connect the embattled end pavilions. This is one of the finest sham castles in the country, almost on a par with Ralph Allen's in Bath (*see* Somerset).

Haggerston

Tower (1900)
NU 042 437

Haggerston Tower between the A1 and the sea is, as might be expected, neo-Gothick,

Haggerston Tower

albeit a turn-of-the-century, Artsy Craftsy interpretation of the style: a tall, thin, dressed stone tower with a stair turret. It was the final addition to an enormous 18th-century house, which had been rebuilt in 1893–97, burned down in 1903 and rebuilt again, and the last to be left standing after the rest had finally been demolished in 1933. It was designed, first, as a belvedere and, second, as a water tower for Christopher John Leyland by R. Norman Shaw. Now the centrepiece of a thriving holiday resort, it is ignored by thousands. It towers over the unheeding holidaymakers, who pay it scant notice as it forms no part of their entertainment. One half expects camps to have watchtowers.

Hartburn

Dr Sharp's Folly (1756)
Grotto (1750s)
NZ 089 862

John Sharp, vicar of Hartburn from 1749 to 1792, was a keen antiquarian. His campaigning efforts brought about the restoration of Bamburgh Castle in 1757, and about this time he built a tower house at Hartburn, some 3 miles from Codger's Fort. The little house's most attractive feature is the north façade, which is castellated, with crow-stepped gables and ogee windows. It was originally built to house the village hearse, so was known as the Hearse House; then the parish clerk lived there and it was called the Clerk's House; then the first-floor room, reached by an outdoor staircase common to Northumbrian bastle houses, was used as a schoolroom, and eventually it became one of Britain's more intriguing post offices, before being converted to a private house. It is now called the Tower House, but through all its changes of name and many different functions it has always been known as Dr Sharp's Folly.

A small Gothic arched bridge spanning a rivulet a couple of hundred yards to the west of the house once led to Sharp's Gothic rock-cut grotto, but now it is easier to cut down straight to the burn and tramp along its muddy banks to the grotto. This was a natural cave, which Sharp assisted with a pointed arch and fireplace inside; two niches above in the rock face once held statues of Adam and Eve. A short tunnel, not much higher than a drain, leads from the grotto to the bathing pool in the burn, locally known as the Baker's Chest because the villagers used to hide their valuables in the baker's chest and sink it in the pool during periodic

Scottish incursions. The tunnel was said to have been built to preserve the ladies' modesty as they scampered from the grotto to the pool. The ladies must have been both short and hardy; the water in the pool comes straight from the icy Northumbrian moors, and the fireplace in the grotto was no luxury. The fireplace is still used by the people of Hartburn, who gather at the grotto for summer picnics and barbecues. Swimming is a seldom chosen option.

Haugh Head

Dovecote (late 18th century)
NU 004 257

This octagonal Gothick dovecote with blind quatrefoils sits on a sudden hill south of the hamlet of Haugh Head. It was built for a former pub called Surrey House, now an

Haugh Head Dovecote

empty private house, unforgivingly close to the busy road. The interior is decorated with rib vaulting, which seems a little grand for pigeons and suggests it was also used as a gazebo. It is now in such a sorry state that even the birds have deserted it. Who said follies were functionless? Many have at least one use.

Holystone Grange

Garden House (1933)
NT 966 003

The Garden House (quite different from a summerhouse, for there is one here as well) was re-erected here in 1933 after the sale of the remnants of Haggerston (see above).

Horton

Bebside Old Hall Grotto (mid-18th century)
NZ 278 807

This is a massive limestone block grotto without the house, which was demolished in the mid-19th century.

Kielder

Kielder Castle (1772–75)
NY 632 934

Another of the 1st Duke of Northumberland's buildings is a fair way from Alnwick even in these days of flyovers, motorways and such; it is nearer to Cumbria and the Scottish border. Kielder Castle is a fashionably Gothick castellated hunting lodge, which was built by William Newton between 1772 and 1775. It is now the Forestry Commission headquarters for Kielder Forest, and although Kielder is a bustling tourist attraction it still retains a pleasing remoteness.

The original entrance to the hunting box is masked by a more conventional Victorian extension, which now serves as a tea shop, and only round the back can one appreciate the frowning battlements and fancy corbelling of the original façade with its tiny arrowslit windows.

Kirkley

Obelisk (1788)
NZ 147 769

Another classically inspired obelisk can be found at Kirkley Hall, now the Northumberland College of Agriculture, where Newton Ogle erected a needle with an eroding Whig motto:

> VINDICATAE LIBERTAS PUBLICAE
> ANNO CENTESIMO
> SAPUTIS MDCCLXXXVIII
> NEWTON OGLI

Above the inscription is a bas-relief of a Jacobin cap on a pole. Ogle's sympathies were not hidden.

Lanton

Obelisk (1830)
NT 919 316

At Lanton we meet Alexander Davison, the merchant who raised the self-important Nelson Obelisk at Swarland Park (see below). Here Davison has his own memorial: another obelisk, erected by one of his sons high on the sweeping moor above the village to commemorate his death in Brighton in 1829. There is a certain lack of imagination in this family, we fear, although the situation is splendid.

Lemmington

Column (1928)
Façade (18th century)
NU 124 110

Lemmington Hall, a convent near the B6341 leading from Rothbury to Alnwick, has a Soane-designed column in its grounds. This tall Doric monument originally stood at Felbridge Place in Surrey, where it was erected for James Evelyn in 1785 in memory of his parents, Edward and Julia. An urn is on top of the column, and a snake, carved by Soane's sculptor Edward Foxhall, coils round its base. The column was moved from

Kielder Castle's Victorian entrance

Homilton Tower, Little Bavington

Surrey to Northumberland in 1928.

Nearby Lemmington Branch Farm has a very broad, Gothick façade. The centre gable, walls and end gables are all castellated, with cross arrowslits and ogee windows. William Newton, who built the temple at Heaton Hall and may have been responsible for the Gothick work done at Simonburn and Nunwick, could also be credited with this superb eyecatcher—he designed Lemmington Hall and was well versed in the Gothick idiom, as evidenced by his Kielder Castle (see above).

Little Bavington

Homilton Tower (18th century)
NY 975 782

On a bare hill above Homilton Farm at Bavington Hall, west of Belsay, is a terrific ruined eyecatcher. It is castellated like a fortress, and the keep inside the walls once acted as a dovecote.

In the grounds of the Hall itself are a dull little Ionic temple and the remains of a rock grotto.

Newcastle-upon-Tyne
(Tyne and Wear)

Grey's Monument (1838)
NZ 248 645

There is scarcely a bleak moorland in England that doesn't have its simple rough-stone tower to commemorate the Reform Act of 1832, which enfranchised the middle classes, but here is the Official Site. Grey's Monument, one of the city's major

landmarks, is a Doric column tower with 164 steps. It stands at the north end of Grey Street in Newcastle and is one of the country's many memorials to Charles, 2nd Earl Grey, who was Prime Minister when Lord John Russell's bill went through Parliament. It was erected during the earl's lifetime although he had withdrawn from active politics. Grey's statue on top of the column was sculpted in 1837 by Edward Hodges Baily, RA. The 135ft (41m) column was another work by the Greens who built the Penshaw Monument (see Washington in the Durham chapter).

Nunwick

Kennels (1768)
NY 880 742

The Gothick kennels were built in the grounds of Lancelot Allgood's Nunwick House, which is still lived in by the Allgood family. The kennels were constructed on a rectangular plan, perhaps as an adaptation of an old watermill, and they are battlemented and have pointed arched windows. They serve as an eyecatcher to the house. We called to see it without warning at a most inopportune time and were unsurprisingly given short shrift by the owner, so this is purely hearsay.

Near the house is a spiral shaft originating from the 13th-century St Mungo's Church in Simonburn (see below). The architects William and Robert Newton restored and rebuilt the church in 1762–63. Perhaps they were also called in to design Allgood's eyecatchers.

Otterburn

Percy Cross (c.1777)
NY 877 937

Between the village and the junction of the A68 and A696, an obelisk in a dark green strip of wood commemorates the Battle of Otterburn (1388), better known as Chevy Chase. The Percy Cross, which dates from about 1777, is named after Hotspur, Sir Henry Percy. The commander of the Scottish side, the Earl of Douglas, fell in battle, and the cross is supposed to mark his grave, although it replaces an earlier medieval cross.

Seaton Sluice and Seaton Delaval (Tyne and Wear)

Octagon (1761–4)
NZ 339 768
Starlight Castle (late 18th century)
NZ 334 761
Obelisk (mid-18th century)
NZ 327 758
Mausoleum (1766)
NZ 328 765

The exception to the landlocked Gothick style shared by most of Northumberland's follies is Seaton Sluice: it has a harbour, which was the start of the Delaval family fortunes. An embattled octagonal structure (called the Octagon and recently converted into a private house) with faintly Gothick windows seems to date from the time the harbour was rebuilt between 1761 and 1764.

The delightfully named Starlight Castle, a Gothick gazebo built for Lady Delaval, is a little way up the dene. The name comes from the very probable story that Sir John wagered he could build a castle overnight; he had the toy fort prefabricated and erected above the burn by starlight so that when his mocking friends arrived to collect their winnings, there stood the castle as promised. Unfortunately for the story, a 19th-century map names the little folly, now diminished to an arched window in a mere scrap of wall, as Stirling Castle.

Seaton Delaval, a mile inland, together with Blenheim Palace and Castle Howard, forms Vanbrugh's famous triad of country houses. The ringed shafts of the portico and the rustic centre block of the façade in Vanbrugh's original design give it a precocious Ledoux-like tinge. It is hard to believe that much of the house is ruined. After a great fire in 1822 the centre shell was reroofed and refenestrated but internally left ruinous and at first, even second, glance it appears to be intact. The books must be

Starlight Castle

wrong, one thinks, but no. Only the west wing is still habitable.

The grounds contain an obelisk and a crouching black mausoleum like a squat, seven-bayed country house in an overgrown wood. When we first saw this eerie erection, the lead or copper that once sheathed the dome had been stripped off, leaving the bare wooden framework rising above the portico like an Eiffel dome, but even that has now rotted and collapsed. It was built in 1766.

Despite the menace pervading this gloomy structure, life at Seaton Delaval was far from despondent. John Delaval, one of the occupants of the mausoleum, was an early victim of political incorrectness. He died in 1775 at the age of 20 'as a result of being kicked in a vital organ by a laundrymaid to whom he was paying his addresses'. Sir Francis Blake, one of the later owners and builder of the proto-folly Twizel Castle, enjoyed an occasional practical joke: unsuspecting house guests were plunged into a cold bath by means of a mechanical device attached to their beds. What fun that must have been.

Simonburn

Eyecatcher Castle (1766)
NY 872 737

South of Wark-on-Tyne Lancelot Allgood Gothicized both his estates: Simonburn Castle and Nunwick (see above). The ruined medieval castle, which is hidden in a wood at Simonburn and of which only a small part still stands (it was razed by villagers convinced that a treasure lay buried in the ruins), was enhanced with Gothick fragments to make a feeble eyecatcher. Now, little more than a mound remains at the side of a farm track. There are fragments of Gothick arches round the back, but restoration would be futile.

Stannington

Blagdon Hall Folly Group
(18th and 19th centuries)
NZ 217 768

Blagdon Hall, with its beautiful gardens set in a wooded area along the A1 near Stannington, was built for the Ridley family. At least four generations used the same name—Sir Matthew White Ridley. It was the 2nd Baronet who donated a conduit, the Cale Cross (also known as the Scale), which was built by David Stephenson in the early 1780s, to the Corporation of Newcastle. It was removed from its original site in 1807 and returned to Sir Matthew. He re-erected the open temple in the grounds of Blagdon House, where it still stands, an elaborate frieze with urns on top, resting on four columns and four pillars. Another open temple, which has lost its dome, came to Blagdon from another property of the Ridley's, Heaton Hall in Newcastle, where it had been built by the local architect William Newton in 1783.

An imposing 19th-century stone road bridge, with two statues by J.G. Lough at each end, crosses high over the lake, and on the north bank are two small Gothick sham ruins, one built with stone from the medieval Hartford Bridge Hospital, the other of brick.

In front of the larger sham ruin is the stone-cut tomb of a child. The Mole Hole Club meets in an underground room beneath the garden bridge, but beware—they are self-confessed pirates.

There are urns and plinths dotted in the woodland; a triple-arched alcove near the roofless temple has three bas-reliefs. A new axis cut through the woods has an anniversary arch inscribed 'MWR 1953 1993 AR' and the Ridley bull, aligned with a arch on the main road.

Sunderland (Tyne and Wear)

St Peter's Sculpture Project (1997)
NZ 400 575

Curios on the river front: along the Wear the sculptor Colin Wilbourn has built and carved three works of art, which make even the most blasé passer-by stop and ponder for a moment (see also Durham). A flight of stone steps leading down to the water is enhanced by a patterned stone carpet, with stone shoes at the top and stone boots at the bottom. Nearby is the Red House, a sculpted red sandstone ruin, together with a pile of sculpted books to commemorate the ancient learning that first brought renown to the region.

Swarland

Nelson Obelisk (1807)
NU 174 029

A solid and very well-preserved obelisk stands in a thicket off the old A1, north of the village of Felton. It was put up to the memory

A sham ruin at Blagdon Hall

Twizel Castle—never completed

of Horatio Nelson, and the builder was Alexander Davison, merchant and army contractor, who particularly specified on the obelisk that it was erected to mark their private friendship, rather than Nelson's feats in battle—a case of reflected glory. It is amusing to see how little basic human nature has changed: today's obelisks to secret friendships take the form of columns of newsprint, in which aggrieved chums pour out their hearts to the widest possible audience. Placing a 30ft (9m) obelisk hard by the side of the main coaching road from London to Edinburgh would appear to be a reasonable early 19th-century equivalent.

The contractor does indeed seem to have been the Admiral's intimate friend, but his acquaintance with the highest circles of government and the military did not prevent corruption charges being levelled against him two years later. Eventually, he spent 21 months in Newgate prison.

ENGLAND EXPECTS EVERY MAN TO DO HIS DUTY
VICTORY 21ST OCTOBER 1805
NOT TO COMMEMORATE THE PUBLIC VIRTUES
AND HEROIC ACHIEVEMENTS OF
NELSON,
WHICH IS THE DUTY OF ENGLAND
BUT TO THE MEMORY OF PRIVATE FRIENDSHIP
THIS ERECTION IS DEDICATED BY
ALEXANDER DAVISON
SWARLAND HALL

Davison's house was demolished in 1947, leaving its predecessor Swarland Old Hall still standing, with its east gable end Gothicized with triple blind arches and castellations (one poorly concealing a chimney) to answer the view from the vanished mansion.

Twizel

Twizel Castle (c.1770)
Blake's Folly (1770–1812)
NT 883 434

Sir Francis Blake rampaged across the county like a Northumbrian King Midas in reverse—everything he touched turned to folly. Twizel Castle looks like a hundred other ruined castles, yet it virtually defines the folly. It is a magnificent, huge, impossible building, the product of a building mania never satisfied. Men worked on this house for nearly 50 years to no purpose—it was never finished, never inhabited. Sir Francis was the onlie begetter, but little more is known about Twizel except that work started c.1770, that it was designed by the unremarked James Nesbit whose other work mentioned in this book is the gate at Ford Castle (see above) and that George Wyatt was working there in 1812. Find your way to beyond, then go to the back of it, and you will discover Twizel Castle sitting on the steep north bank of the River Till, just before it flows into the Tweed. Five floorless storeys were built before work was abandoned. Nothing disturbs the castle, now indistinguishable from a genuine ruined castle, save a few incurious cows at the back.

Meanwhile, Sir Francis was equally occupied in building Tillmouth Park nearby (now an hotel), which he actually completed. Doubtless shocked by this unaccustomed turn of events, he started on a bridge over the River Till (the Tweed was thought to be too ambitious, and anyway there might have been Scots at the other end), but loss of interest or some other equally valid excuse forced him to abandon the project after only one arch had been built. This is called Blake's Folly. Later his son demolished the only building his father ever completed, and the new building (by Charles Barry Jr, 1887) now stands in Sir Francis's original grounds, with his tunnel, arches, alcoves and lesser bridges.

Warton-on-Tyne

Chipchase Castle Gothick Summerhouse
(18th century)
NY 883 757

A tiny, pretty Gothick summerhouse with a decorated ogee-arched doorway, flanked by quatrefoil windows, was recently unearthed here during clearance of undergrowth in the private gardens. Its provenance is a mystery for the moment, but the owners have begun restoration, rebuilding the back of the little folly and reroofing it with stone slates. Avenues are being made through the garden to focus on it. Its preservation seems assured.

Whitton

Sharp's Folly (1720)
NU 058 009

Thomas Sharp, archdeacon of Northumberland, lived in an old pele tower in Rothbury and was the father of Dr John Sharp of Hartburn (see above). Around 1720 he is said to have assembled the unemployed masons of the village and set them to build him an observatory: a 50ft (15m) high tower, round and castellated, with classical doorways and windows instead of the Gothick (this was a decade or two too early). How many unemployed masons can one small village sustain? Considering its date, Sharp's Folly makes an early but not entirely convincing eyecatcher.

Sharp's Folly at Whitton

Proposals for its restoration in 1993 attracted suggestions for a more functional use for the structure; among the more printable ones were an electricity-generating windfarm, a Deugar watch observatory and a launch pad for the Rothbury Space Probe, but the programme has faltered save for a small plaque giving the date of building. The little tower stands derelict but unforgotten.

Wooler

Ewart Park Tower (1787)
NT 964 315

In the second half of the 18th century Ewart Park was owned by a Colonel Horace St Paul, who started alterations in 1787. What he created is not so much a house as a stage set for some 18th-century Lloyd Webber's production of *The Castle of Otranto*. It is all show, and gimcrack at that—Petticoat rather than Drury Lane. Everything is castellated, and the third storey abutting the tower isn't

The eerie Ewart Park Tower

really there at all: it is just a crenellated wall with sham Gothick windows painted on. The main tower is circular and four storeys high, with a prominent arrowslit quatrefoil, machicolations and battlements; it pretends to be medieval and is said to have been inspired by Twizel Castle, the astonishing folly right on the Scottish border. The whole affair was built cheaply, then poorly maintained; it is little short of astonishing that is has survived these two centuries. This underfinanced, desperate striving for effect should evoke sadness and pity rather than denigration. The house has long been abandoned, and its empty silence heightens the atmosphere of hopeless ambition.

NOTTINGHAMSHIRE

Nottinghamshire means Sherwood Forest, Robin Hood, the Trip to Jerusalem, tobacco, the prettiest girls, the tallest men, closed pits, D.H. Lawrence, rows of depressing red brick mining villages and the once fashionable Dukeries. Sherwood Forest itself is now little more than a theme copse, a few stunted, dead oaks by a car park, encircled by a vast army of the Forestry Commission's implacable evergreens, marshalled like sheriffs. However, it's a great county for digging in: dukes, aldermen and miners alike have all tried their hand. The strangest and most powerful house in the county is Nottingham's Wollaton Hall, built by Robert Smythson for the coal king Sir Francis Willoughby in 1580–88. The bulk of the house is conventionally Elizabethan, but it is topped by a gigantic and apparently functionless clerestory room, which has puzzled architectural commentators for centuries. Mark Girouard ingeniously argues that it was an attempt by the notably devout Willoughby to create a replica of Solomon's Temple as described by contemporary scholars.

Bestwood

Bestwood Pumping Station (1870)
SK 555 475

Our first ducal folly stands a little north of Nottingham. The Pumping Station is typical of those genuine working buildings like Mr Bliss's Tweed Mill in Chipping Norton, Oxfordshire, and the Green Lanes Pumping Station in North London, which are architecturally so over-dramatic when their mundane function is recalled that they have to be classed as follies. In the early 1870s the Duke of St Albans granted a permit for the 150ft (45.7m) tower to be built on his land. Architect J. Witham could start work on the water tower on condition that Bestwood would be ornamental rather than starkly functional. In tune with the times, a classico-Gothic skin was grafted onto the tower. Pevsner dismisses it as 'a tall, tasteless tower', but it is immaculately preserved and cared for, surrounded by manicured lawns. It will be many years before it completes the folly cycle, gracefully bowing its balconied head and collapsing overnight in approved Beckfordian manner.

Budby

Budby Castle (1807)
SK 621 699

The Thoresby estate has a charming model village called Budby. Budby Castle is a castellated and whitewashed folly house, set in a small copse of trees on a knoll to the east of the village, apparently synonymous with Castle William, designed by John Carr *c.*1789. On the estate, which has eight listed garden buildings, are several Gothic farmhouses, of which at least one was built by P.F. Robinson, the best known early Victorian cottage and farm architect.

Bunny

Bunny Hall Belvedere (1723)
SK 584 297

Sir Thomas Parkyns, Greek scholar, Cornish wrestler, Latin scholar and amateur architect, here adorned the walls of the village schoolhouse with improving texts, scorning the vulgate for the purity of the original tongues:

SCIENTIA NON HABET INIMICUM NISI

IGNORANTEM
DISCE UEL DISCEDE
NEMO HINC EGREDIATUR IGNARUS
ARITHMETICES

the final stone, with the inscription 'tices', has been renewed. Above the main door is a list of Parkyns's charitable works, finishing with a bequest by his younger daughter, Anne, for apprentices aged 14, 'who must first be well educated in true Reading Legible Writing and Vulgar Arithmetick'.

Not content with all this, the wrestling baronet then built himself an idiosyncratic—outstandingly ugly—five-storey high belvedere on the end of his house, with a huge, semicircular arch on the first floor, blind windows and a 1723 datestone. With great delight we spotted a pineapple, the archetypal folly fruit, on Sir Thomas's oversized coat of arms. Given that later generations always find fault in their ancestors' taste in architecture, only to be reconciled to it three or four generations down the line, it is comforting to come across one piece of Georgian architecture that has remained deeply unattractive for nearly 300 years. It is also encouraging to discover that hideousness is no barrier to a Grade I listing, although the listing itself, designed to protect buildings at risk, has not been particularly effective here, as the Hall is currently vacant and decaying.

Clipstone

Duke's Folly (1842)
SK 607 658

There are three ducal follies in the county. One of these is simply known as the Duke's Folly, and is buried in the forest between Edwinstowe and Clipstone. Archway House,

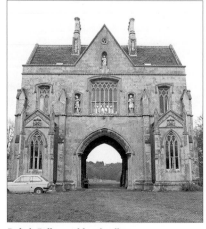

Duke's Folly, astride a ley line

to use its more prosaic name, is a Gothic, buttressed building erected by William Hurst and William Moffat for the 4th Duke of Portland in 1844 as, for some obscure reason, a copy of the Worksop Priory Gatehouse. A light-hearted element is added by statues in niches of, not saints, but Maid Marion, Robin Hood and the cause of their rebellion, Richard Lionheart. In fact Duke's Folly is only 2 miles from the ruins of the royal hunting lodge or King John's Palace, as it is called locally. Evidently the 4th Duke preferred to throw his lot in with the buccaneers of the forest. A crest on the west wall reads:

SEPULCHRI IMMEMOR STRUIS DOMOS
AD1842
DP
AET 74

and on the east wall

TU SECANDA MARMORA LOCAS
SUB IPSUM FUNUS

The 'DP' was thought to refer to the Duke of Portland, but no duke of that line died in 1842.

Bas-reliefs of hares are carved in the tympani above the bay windows. Two families live either side of the archway, which is said to straddle a ley line. Formerly friends, the families no longer speak to each other, which is a pity, for the avenue through the forest behind the arch is called The Neutral Ground.

Clumber Park

Temples (18th century)
SK 626 746

After Welbeck and Thoresby, the National Trust property of Clumber Park is the third member in the Dukeries triumvirate. The house has vanished, leaving a splendid Victorian church and nearly 4000 rolling acres of woodland and lakes. But the expected follies have all disappeared or, Robin Hood-like, have secretly melted into the undergrowth. All we are offered are two classical temples and a Palladian bridge.

Elston

Middleton's Folly (1872)
SK 747 483

Elston Towers on the Foss Way is a house that, like Bladon Castle in neighbouring Leicestershire, has been a folly from the start, setting itself aside from lesser dwellings. It is called Middleton's Folly because of the enormous outlay Robert Middleton made on his house: Elston Towers was built between 1872 and 1874 at a cost of over £30,000. Mr

Middleton indulged in the peculiar hobby of preaching. He performed in strange attire, the oddity of which was heightened by his circular frame, and being able to afford his indulgences he also built himself a chapel to seat 300, although locals privately doubted that he would be able to fill it. A small building connecting the chapel to a cellar is said to have been used by Middleton so that he 'never needed to sit through the sermon without a cosy nip', which, of course, is plainly illogical if he were the preacher.

Another feature at Elston is the bell tower connected to the mansion, famed for being able to perform 28 different tunes, ranging from 'There's no luck about the house on washing day' to an array of more conventional hymns.

Middleton's house-warming party went on for several days and the whole village was invited to take part in the consumption of six sheep and an enormous bullock. Small wonder the party was gatecrashed by people from as far afield as Newark and Grantham in Lincolnshire. In the 1960s Elston Towers enjoyed a modest degree of fame as one of Britain's more important bluebottle breeding establishments, a fitting pinnacle of achievement for a folly.

Gunthorpe

Gunthorpe Hall (19th century)
`SK 679 444`

This very strange, cream-stuccoed Gothick house has castellations, arrowslits, quatrefoils and two thin pilaster turrets, rising like minarets flattened against a church tower. It is as if a traveller from an antique land had once in his life, many years ago, glimpsed a church, and this was his half-remembered interpretation of the sight.

Linby

Castle Mill (c.1785)
`SK 535 509`

Façade architecture is in evidence at Castle Mill, a couple of miles south of Newstead. Castle Mill should be part of Papplewick rather than Linby, as it originally belonged to the Hon. Frederick Montagu's property there. The mill was built before 1785, because in that year James Watt installed the first cotton spinning steam engine here. Because of the vile working conditions of that period, the churchyard is full of children's graves; we counted 163, dead from starvation, exhaustion and the occasional accident. The

The weird Gunthorpe Hall

mill, now it has been converted into flats and softened with tasteful planting, looks a little more pleasant than it used to—but it is impossible to look at this folly without being reminded of how grimly appropriate its whimsical militaristic architecture was: a dungeon for children with a toy castle façade. Only the front towards Papplewick has been embellished—there are corner towers, pointed windows and a door, quatrefoils sprinkled in between.

Milton

Newcastle Mausoleum (1832)
`SK 715 731`

Incongruity is one of the finer elements of folly, and sufficient incongruity can grant folly status to a building that may well have been conceived with conventional aspirations. Finding a substantial urban Greek temple alone in a field is a purely pleasurable folly experience, even when it turns out to be a mausoleum to Georgiana, Duchess of Newcastle, who died giving birth to twins in 1822. It was designed by Sir Robert Smirke, and at the west end he added a church to replace the old parish church at Markham Clinton, which was made redundant. In its turn, the new church has now been made redundant, and the worshippers have returned to the old All Saints.

Newstead

Sham forts (1749)

`SK 538 539`

The 5th Lord Byron, the Wicked Lord, was at least as mad, bad and dangerous as his heir the poet. On his Newstead Abbey estate, now a large public park owned by the City of Nottingham, Byron, still in his twenties, built Folly Castle, where he presumably held orgies in Hell Fire Club style. The building became so disreputable that it was later torn down. Probably at the same time two Gothick façades were erected, confronting each other across the lake. These sham forts took part in mock naval battles with a 20-gun boat on the lake manned by Byron's luckless servants. The larger one, on the stable block side of the lake, has now been converted into a private residence, hidden by a tall hedge, and can best be seen from the other side of the lake. The smaller fort is buried in saplings and undergrowth and is hard to reach in summer. Once found, it is a delightful folly: compact, small, sparely and purposefully designed. Its folly comes from its purpose. Shooting one's servants for sport is no longer widely condoned. The fort has two angled and castellated bastions, flanking a central semicircular one, with small, stone-domed sentry boxes at each end. Beneath are Gothic arched niches, presumably to act as magazines, and a handkerchief dock for a pocket battleship.

In 1765 Byron killed his cousin William Chaworth in an after-dinner scuffle. Being a peer, he was not convicted, but public disapproval thereafter virtually confined him to Newstead, where he became more and more of a recluse, living in only a small part of the house (like the Duke of Portland a century later) and letting the rest fall into disrepair. Many of the rooms were used as stables, while the woodlands were deforested in an apparent attempt to irritate the rest of his family. A monument to a pet dog was sacrilegiously placed on the site of the high altar in the old priory. Byron died in the scullery, which had for some time been his bedroom, being the only dry room in the house. The property was sold in 1817.

North Clifton

Pureland Garden (1980)

`SK 825 721`

A small pagoda built from scrap metal, a corrugated iron bridge, a Japanese tea-house and British garden plants combine to create Nirvana in Nottinghamshire, a Zen garden lovingly created over 20 years by Buddha Maitreya, formerly a bloke from Newark.

Nottingham

Alderman Herbert's Tunnels (1856)

`SK 574 404`

Alderman Herbert of Nottingham drove a tunnel from the cellars of his house in Rope Walk to facilitate entry to his garden on the other side of the street. This was probably only an excuse because the tunnel itself

The frowning battlements of Lord Byron's toy fort

seems to have captured most of Herbert's interest. A series of figures were hewn out of the stone—there is the Lion's Den, with Daniel flung in between the lions, his body twisted in an oddly expressionistic way, which can doubtless be blamed on the sculptor's ineptitude; along the same biblical path an Egyptian Temple was devised, with sphinxes substituted for the lions. The figures of some pre-Christian druids are to be found, but alas no Buddhas or Aztec Sun Gods. A pity.

Pagoda
SK 580 400

Also in Nottingham is a mid-Victorian pagoda of little consequence with some aviaries at the Arboretum in Waverly Street, a sort of provincial Kew Gardens. Radford Folly in Radford Street, often mentioned, has long disappeared; in the last stages of its life it was little more than an octagonal post where the Radford Tea Gardens used to be.

Nuthall

Nuthall Temple (1759)
SK 515 446

The suburb of Nuthall is northwest of Nottingham, and here, until 1929, Thomas Wright's glorious Nuthall Temple stood—not a temple, but a magnificent house in the style of Palladio's Villa Rotonda. It now comprises the hard core for Junction 26 of the M1, and all that remains is a Gothick gazebo, stylistically also by Wright, and so tucked

Nuthall Temple

away that even the locals are unaware that it still exists. This is a scary summerhouse; a huge ogee arch with two empty patera (or niches that may once have held bas-reliefs), flanked by tall circular towers, give the impression of a blinded giant, a Bomarzo from Easter Island. The datestone is buried in the earth on the right-hand edge of the first step up to the entrance. There is evidence that there was once an upper floor, which was used as a dovecote, but forget the practicalities—this is real folly.

Papplewick

Tempietto (1787)
SK 548 517

Papplewick Hall was built about 1787. Robert Adam has been tentatively put forward as the architect, although Samuel Stretton, a local man, may have been involved. Stretton made a speciality of designing industrial buildings, so Castle Mill at nearby Linby (see above) may be his, however tempting it may be to ascribe a Gothick folly to the affected, elderly Scotsman. Thomas Gray and William Mason were cronies of Montagu in Cambridge, and he honoured them by erecting an urn and a Tuscan tempietto to their respective memories in the grounds of Papplewick. Mason, whose ecclesiastical career had been considerably furthered by Montagu, wrote part of his long-winded but contemporaneously influential poem, 'The English Garden' at Papplewick. Did he inspire Castle Mill or did Castle Mill inspire his famous lines:

> *Let every structure needful for a farm*
> *Arise in castle semblance!*

Scarrington

Horseshoe Pile (1945–78)
SK 735 416

The M1 skirts Nottingham to the west; 2000 years ago the Romans skirted to the east with the Foss Way, now the A46 running from Leicester to Newark. In the village of Scarrington, just off the old Roman road, George Flinders, the Scarrington blacksmith, got into the habit of throwing discarded horseshoes on one spot—50,000 of them—until by 1978 the spot had reached a height of 17ft (5m), and a millwright had to be called in to straighten the dangerously leaning edifice. It weighs about ten tons. Real fans of horseshoe piles should hasten to North Grimston in Yorkshire, however, where there are three of them.

The Underground Ballroom at Welbeck lit by skylights from above

Welbeck Abbey

Underground Ballroom (1860)
Tunnels (1860)
`SK 563 7451860`

Easily the finest of Nottingham's ducal follies is Welbeck. The greater part of the 5th Duke of Portland's underground (and overground) mansion, incorporating some of the most bizarre construction work in Britain, was long ago taken over by the army as a sixth-form college, and the only way to visit it is to exert considerable influence in the upper echelons of the Ministry of Defence. Many of those who have been there say disappointedly that the legend is greater than the reality, but we are not among them. The legends have been inflated, but the actuality is unique.

The man behind it all is the prime motive for a visit, even if his much-vaunted underground follies may disappoint. William John Cavendish Bentinck-Scott was born in 1800. He inherited the title of 5th Duke of Portland in 1854 and became an eccentric of the first order, in a country that prides itself on its eccentrics. He refused the Order of the Garter because it would have entailed presenting himself at Court. Preferring to keep his own company, he had a string of underground rooms dug at Welbeck; this subterranean refuge consisted of three libraries and a chapel, which was later converted into a ballroom-cum-picture gallery—a strange choice for a man with such a horror of socializing. All his underground rooms were painted pink, and they opened into the Rose

Corridor, a conservatory. Few of these constructions were true tunnels, however, being constructed on the cut-and-cover method, with light coming in from the glass roofs at ground level. No member of his staff was allowed to acknowledge his presence if he was surprised in one of his nocturnal forays. Withdrawing into just five of the hundreds of rooms in Welbeck Abbey, he communicated with the outside world (which included his servants) by means of a letterbox.

Although he had served in Parliament as a young man, the only cause to stir him from his reclusivity was antidisestablishmentarianism, remembered today merely for being the longest word in the English language. He was in the habit of wearing several coats at the same time, and assuming a number of dismally ineffectual disguises. He was said to be disfigured, which accounted for many of his less lucid actions, but other sources say he was astonishingly good-looking. He carried an unrequited infatuation for the singer Adelaide Kemble, the Judy Garland of the day.

Periodically, in what seems to have been his only really unpleasant characteristic, the duke had stacks of paintings burned because he didn't like them. Food was supplied by a small railway—trains were another of the duke's little foibles. Even a reclusive duke has to emerge occasionally, so in order to get to London unobserved, he had another tunnel dug to take him and his private railway carriage the 3 miles to Worksop station, where he could be coupled to the London train. Needless to say, a vast workforce was needed to answer Portland's demands adequately. All accounts of Welbeck mention the 15,000 men, each of whom, before they started the day's work, was equipped with a donkey and an umbrella.

There is a core of truth in all this, but as with stories of Atlantis everything has been exaggerated a hundred-fold—there were few more than 150 workers, but they were, indeed, supplied with donkeys and umbrellas. The scene must have been picturesque, if noisy. There are none of the habitual folly stories about the works being undertaken to relieve local unemployment—the duke had to import labourers to fulfil his fantasies, and because digging was involved, so were the Irish. The navvies were housed (when they were housed) in an estate ghetto called Sligo, and contemporary accounts are full of the fighting that took place. The 15 miles of tunnels shorten to about 3 miles under closer scrutiny. The stories of state rooms bare of all furnishings but for 'a convenience in each,

quite exposed and not sheltered in any way' are put down to malicious gossip from his cousin, Lady Ottoline Morrell. The tunnel to Worksop Station is fantasy; there is, indeed, a mighty tunnel entrance with a railway running into it, but it runs for less than 2 miles to the edge of the estate—the exit is now lost. His trips by underground train to Worksop and thence to London are more likely to have been undertaken in his usual coach, carried on rails through the tunnel and then on by natural horsepower to Worksop station to be loaded on to another bogie. He built dozens of estate cottages, and in each of them he had the kitchen and the lavatory put underground.

What is true and what is fantasy? This much is true: the great underground ballroom is now the school gymnasium and examination hall. There is nothing of the bizarre about it, apart from there being no windows in the walls. The skylights above make it lighter than a conventional room. As it was constructed by cut-and-cover, the room is clearly visible from the outside, with the skylights at ground level or a little higher. The disappointment that some people feel on visiting it lies in its normality. It was restored in 1995 at a cost of over £1 million, and it is painted blue rather than the pink favoured by the 5th Duke. But read this: it is huge, a single room of over

Two entrances to the Welbeck tunnels

10,000 square feet (929 sq m), measuring 160ft (48.8m) by 64ft (19.5m), with the largest unsupported ceiling in Europe, and the great bulk of it is underground. In the duke's day, food was delivered to the room in heated trolleys running on rails. A painting by Sir Joshua Reynolds now hangs at one end of the room and serves as an involuntary backstop for a basketball hoop.

At the time of his death, Portland was excavating a truly gigantic underground room further to the west, known as the Bachelor's Room. Unfinished, it was later adapted as a sunken garden, and now has a black wooden temple, a pergola, fishponds, rose gardens and tennis courts hidden at the distant end. A tunnel, now blocked at either end although the centre section is still accessible from the sunken garden, led 1020 yards (933m) from the ballroom to the great riding school block. Walking briskly by torchlight, it took us nine minutes to get from end to end. The tunnels were lit by rooflights (now blocked) during the

Above: a fireplace in one of the tunnels
Left: Dark, damp and despairing, a futile tunnel stretching to infinity

day and gaslights by night. Portland spent a prodigious £113,000 with one foundry for water pipes and gas fitments, and he had a gas and water fitter living with him at the Abbey at the 1871 census.

The duke was aware that his gloomy tunnels did not appeal to all tastes. His horror of the public gaze caused him to try to get a right-of-way over the estate diverted without success, so he plunged it deep into the earth so that 'it is possible to travel the entire length of its detestable interior without catching the slightest glimpse of the lofty pleasure-dome above it'. One broad tunnel, approached under a curved glass roof prefiguring Nicholas Grimshaw's Eurostar terminal at Waterloo, but now collapsed, has a huge fireplace by the entrance. The Riding School, although sadly for us built above ground, is another building of gargantuan size, 400 by 108ft (122 × 33m).

The Duke of Portland was an awkward man, but he was compassionate towards his servants and workers and a generous giver to charity. With liberal hindsight, we can now say he exhibited all the characteristics of repressed homosexuality. Read Mick Jackson's remarkable novel *The Underground Man* to get a different perspective on this human enigma. The truth of Welbeck may be more prosaic than the legends, but the reality remains astonishing.

Wiseton

Griff Inn (late 18th century)
SK 718 897

After building Wiseton Hall in 1771 Mr Acklam worked hard on improving his estate. He placed ornamental farms on the tops of the surrounding hills and enhanced the White Swan Inn, now the Griff Inn, on the banks of the Chesterfield Canal, to serve as an eyecatcher from the Hall. The design is based on Askhill House at Richmond in Surrey. The heavily rusticated doorway of the pub is carved out of chalk.

OXFORDSHIRE

Part Cotswold, part Chiltern—
Oxfordshire seems to have a little of
everything in its make-up. Is it the
southernmost northern county or
the northernmost southern county?
There is an equal uncertainty about
its follies, which follow no particular
trends, although the best in the
county are both eyecatchers.

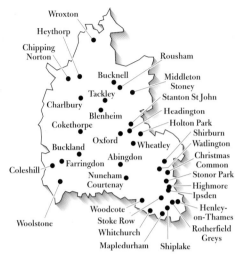

Wroxton
Heythorp
Chipping
Norton
Bucknell
Rousham
Middleton
Stoney
Tackley
Stanton St John
Charlbury
Headington
Blenheim
Holton Park
Cokethorpe
Shirburn
Oxford
Watlington
Wheatley
Buckland
Abingdon
Christmas
Farringdon
Common
Coleshill
Stonor Park
Nuneham
Highmore
Courtenay
Ipsden
Woodcote
Henley-
on-Thames
Woolstone
Stoke Row
Whitchurch
Rotherfield
Greys
Mapledurham
Shiplake

Abingdon

Sham Ruins (c.1860)
Grotto (19th century)
`SU 510 960`

The ruined abbey cloisters at Abingdon
deceive many visitors and probably one or
two of the residents. Easily accessible in a
public park behind the council offices, they
are large, elaborate and fraudulent. Parts of
the extensive ruin are indeed medieval,
genuine fragments of the dissolved abbey, but
in about 1860 a Mr E. Trendall gathered
them all together and built this fine fake
abutting the wall of his garden in Abbey
House. The archway at St Helen's Church is
probably also a creation of our Mr Trendall.

A little, domed, rough stone grotto was
saved here near the Vernon Gibberd-
designed Youth Centre. The county council
wanted the grot destroyed, but Gibberd
fought like a lion, and although a huge oil
tank has now been violently inserted into it,
the building is still there.

Blenheim

Column of Victory (1727)
`SP 430 150`

Blenheim is gigantic, its conception and scale
so great that they preclude follies: the spirit
of the place is national rather than personal.
Hawksmoor's 130ft (40m) Column of
Victory, the closest contender, is the product
of a committee rather than the caprice of a

Abingdon Sham Ruins

single mind. There were possibilities in such
buildings as the Temple of Diana, the Temple
of Health (built, prematurely, to celebrate
George III's recovery from lunacy), Lancelot
Brown's picturesque Ranger's House or
High Lodge, the Swiss Chalet, the
Shepherd's Cot and, especially, the
Springlock Boulder, a massive boulder that
blocked a path but moved aside when a
hidden lever was pulled, but the whole estate
was generally too worthy and serious to trifle
with architectural eccentricities; it impresses
by size rather than surprise.

Buckland

Ice-house (18th century)
SU 340 980

Buckland House is built on a much more
human scale but again lacks any real follies,
although there is a pleasant rotunda,
probably built by Romaine Walker in 1910,
which contains a memorial plinth and urn to
the 20th-century Knights of Kerry. It is most
famous for its ice-house, the finest in
Oxfordshire, built as a tufa and stone temple

The thatched Ice-house at Buckland

with grotto overtones, but there is particular
pleasure to be had in comparing the
solemnity of the big house with the
architect's own description of himself when
applying for membership to Liverpool's Ugly
Face Clubbe four years earlier, in 1751:

*A stone colour'd complexion, a dimple in
his Attic storey. The Pillasters of his face
fluted. Tortoise-ey'd, a prominent nose.
Wild grin, and face altogether resembling
a badger, and finer tho' smaller than Sir
Christopher Wren or Inigo Jones's.*

Sadly, John Wood does not seem to have
been commissioned to design any follies; a
man with such self-deprecating sense of
humour would have enjoyed a stone joke.

Bucknell

Water Tower (1905)
SP 550 240

It's an essential building: brick arches on
four sides, with two sides filled in, a
balustrade around its top and a weird
roofline. Of course, it's a water tower, built in
1905, so John Hearn told us, to supply
Bucknell. It is also one of those buildings that
grab everyone's attention because it is now
situated on a motorway, between the M40's
junctions 9 and 10. The real folly of the thing
is its mere existence. When the M40 was
under construction, the county council was
made aware of the tower's state of repair—it
could collapse any moment and would be a
danger to passing motorists. Instead of
pulling down an interesting and satisfying
piece of architecture, as every sane authority
would have done and has done so for the last
hundred years, the council restored it. Now
there's a council with its heart in the right
place (and it has made up for wanting the
Abdingdon grotto destroyed).

Charlbury

Lodge Farm (18th century)
Temples (18th century)
Grotto (18th century)
SP 390 210

Ditchley Park, northwest of Charlbury, was
laid out by James Gibbs in the 1720s and

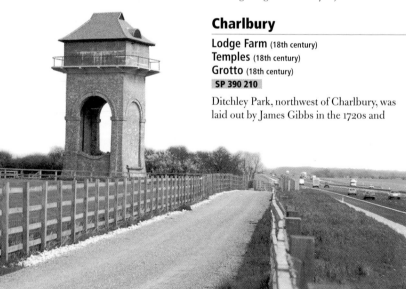

Better known as the M40 Tower, this is the Bucknell Water Tower

Ionic Temple, Ditchley Park

reworked by Brown in 1770. William Kent worked inside the house rather than in the garden, although Lodge Farm, built as an eyecatcher to the south, has some qualities of his strained Gothick. The façade facing the house has three arches in the centre—formerly open but now filled with door and windows—Gothick traceried windows in the side wings and five quatrefoil windows on the first floor. A barn to the west also has arches and quatrefoils.

There are two temples in the park itself: a Tuscan temple originally built by the lake but moved nearer the house in 1930, and a round Ionic temple, which was built by Stiff Leadbetter in 1760 but which has also been attributed to Henry Holland. There is a three-arched stone grotto at the head of the lake.

Chipping Norton

Bliss Tweed Mill (1872)
SP 310 250

Bliss & Sons' Tweed Mill in Chipping Norton is a fine example to start or finish arguments about how follies should be defined. This was a factory, built in 1872 and operating continuously until it closed in 1982. By most standards this excludes it from candidacy. But the driver who on leaving Chipping Norton and seeing the mill for the first time doesn't narrowly avoid driving off

the road in shock is blind to the delights of architecture. It was designed by the Lancashire architect George Woodhouse in the style of a French château, with balustraded parapets punctuated by graceful urns, apparently to blend in with the non-industrial countryside, but the imposition of a gigantic Tuscan factory chimney erupting out of the domed bay front to twice the height of the building is shattering in its effect. One can only stop and gape at such obtrusive camouflage. Listed Grade II*, the building has been subject to successive failed redevelopments, but has finally been successfully converted into flats.

Christmas Common

Christmas Common Tower (1967)
SU 720 940

In the woods near Christmas Common is the moated tower Lord Esher built for himself in 1967. He wanted a house 'dark in colour and picturesque in outline, so it would loom up out of the woods', and it is now six storeys high (an extension of the original four storeys, or have we miscounted?) with a turret not containing the stairs as usual but, sensible man, a lift. It is not a folly, but folly-like and as Sherwood and Pevsner wrote: 'it has some of the best qualities of Early Victorian architecture.' It was sold in the 1990s.

Coleshill

Strattenborough Castle (1792)
SU 230 930

Strattenborough Castle Farm near Coleshill, right on the Wiltshire border, is a splendid sham façade on the back of an otherwise unremarkable farmhouse. Some 20 years ago the owner was claiming it to be a genuine castle dating from the 11th century and refurbished in the 18th, but the claim has now been relinquished. The stone front is charming, with its mock windows, turrets and battlements, but the most convincing part is the brick infill, without which the western wall of the front would crumble away to ruin—intentional or otherwise? The two main walls are high and level with it; the remains of the battlements can be seen on the top. Incorporated in a team wall are the remains of a massive round-arched window, and underneath, set into the wall, is the carved figure of a man on a horse, which looks early medieval and is probably a spoil. Coleshill Park lies a mile away across the valley; from the famous house that stood there until 1952 Strattenborough must have appeared as a vanquished rival in picturesque decay.

Cokethorpe

The Fish House (18th century)
SP 374 066

South of Witney the quaintly named Fish House at Cokethorpe also received the eyecatcher façade treatment to make a viewpoint from Cokethorpe Park. The square mill-house was battlemented and ornamented with heavily crocketed pinnacles in the centre and at the corners of each wall, gargoyles and Tudor windows. It is three storeys high and carries a datestone of 1723 ('17 AI 23' and another stone says 'REPARD'), which, as Jennifer Sherwood points out, is too early for this treatment. It is much more likely to have been modified later in the 18th century—the tower includes masonry taken from Stanton Harcourt manor, which was demolished *c.*1750. Basil Harley, who has researched the building, believes it may be the result of the 2nd Earl Harcourt's meddling with the original 1723 building—he was the amateur antiquarian who also busied himself on Nuneham Courtenay (see below), and the spoils that were used in the embellishment of Fish House might have also come from the church there.

Faringdon

Lord Berners's Folly (1935)
SU 290 950

In 1974 Oxfordshire acquired one of the most famous folly towers in Britain, when the town of Faringdon was transferred from Berkshire. Lord Berners's Folly, as it was known from the start, is the last major folly tower to have been built in Britain. It was completed in 1935 despite strenuous local opposition, Gerald Tyrwhitt-Wilson, 14th Lord Berners (1883–1950), a talented musician (who drove around with a harpsichord built into his Rolls Royce), being a good deal too obviously unmarried for the fulminating generals and admirals who lived in the

Lord Berner's monstrous erection

region. When the council met to decide whether to grant planning permission—a factor that never troubled the original folly builders—one furious old salt bellowed that it would totally destroy the view from his house. When counsel for Lord Berners pointed out that the proposed tower could only possibly be seen from Admiral Clifton Browne's house with a telescope, the sailor retorted that being an admiral he only ever looked at the view through a telescope. Nevertheless, Lord Berners won his battle, and the 110ft (33.5m) tower, designed by Trenwith Wills and Lord Gerald Wellesley, later the 7th Duke of Wellington, was finally built. Much amusement was caused by an old soldier contemptuously referring to it as 'Lord Berners's monstrous erection'. The building provided diary editors and social pages with their bread and butter during 1935, culminating in a grand party and firework display on 5 November and the release of hundreds of doves dyed red, white and blue.

Alas, the tower itself is plain rather than ugly. Apparently, it was originally colour-washed cream; now no trace remains. Gaunt ribbed bricks rear up 100ft (30m), with two tiny wood-framed windows, devoid of ornament, on each side. At the top is a smaller square belvedere room, with three arched windows on each side. On the top, an octagonal-pinnacled room, with elongated oblong windows, stands as the only decoration on the tower.

When we first visited it, the tower was ruinous and derelict. The mortar had fallen from between the bricks, the glass had gone, and, worst of all, the entrance was firmly and finally blocked up. But times and attitudes change, and what was once a matter of shame is now a source of pride. In the glorious summer of 1989 the freshly restored folly tower was formally reopened, and for the first time we were able to climb to the top. Claims that the Bristol Channel could be seen on a clear day were disproved by Christopher Hayhurst-France, the estate manager. There was also no trace of the famous note from Lord Berners, which read: 'Members of the public committing suicide from this tower do so at their own risk.' (There was also a sign in the grounds saying: 'Anyone throwing stones at this notice will be prosecuted.')

The first building in Faringdon is a pub called The Folly, but it has no connection with the wicked lord's tower: it was called The Folly long before 1935. The clump of trees (*feuillée*) on the hill was planted in the 18th century by Henry Pye (1745–1813), the half-remembered Poet Laureate, who wrote a poem about the site called 'Faringdon Hill'. The site has been known as Faringdon Folly for at least 200 years.

Robert Heber-Percy, who lived with Berners at Faringdon, donated the tower in 1983 to the people of Faringdon. He himself had added to Faringdon House an embattled swimming pool, ditto bath house (its floor covered with inlaid old penny pieces) and two antique wyverns.

Headington

Headington Shark (1986)
SP 540 070

When it comes to planning battles and complaining neighbours, the late 20th-century equivalent of Lord Berners's Folly is also in Oxfordshire: Bill Heine's Headington Shark. Visitors to Oxford's dreaming spires hurry through Headington, on the eastern outskirts of the city, in the formerly correct assumption that there was nothing worth seeing. How wrong they now are. Just off the High Street is a row of undistinguished terraced houses, industrial south midland housing at its least inventive. The monotony is

The Headington Shark

broken by the carcass of a 25ft (7.6m) basking shark, which has plummeted through the roof of No. 7, impaling itself in the upstairs bedroom. It is an astounding sight; the shark's body and tail in frozen flail emerge from the roof like a downed jet fighter.

Heine, a cinema owner who had a chat show on Radio Oxford, was the bane of local councillors, and although he claimed that his beloved shark was merely a sculpture (and so a work of art and not, therefore, subject to planning permission—he even changed the name of his house to 'Plinth'), it was fairly to be expected that the planning officer would tend to disagree. The battle raged for years and calmed only when the civil servant quit under the stress and moved to a new job in Brighton. There he found that Heine had just bought a house… .

It's better to observe these wars from a safe distance; there is very little fun in getting involved on either side. We are, however, pleased to report that the Shark is still proudly erect after 14 years, and that far from the neighbours objecting, one has renamed her house 'Shark View'.

Henley-on-Thames

Friar Park (1896)
SU 760 830

Oxfordshire's most bizarre building is the French Gothic mansion of Friar Park, set in 42 acres (17ha) of grounds behind the Town Hall in Henley-on-Thames. It is now the home of the former Beatle George Harrison, and as visitors are not allowed in this description has had to be assembled from other books and a dash of hearsay. It was built in 1896 by a solicitor, Sir Frank Crisp, and his architect, M. Clarke Edwards. Crisp gave full rein to his fantasies not only in the house but also in the park, constructing a range of sham Swiss Alps, with a scale model of the Matterhorn (complete with cast iron chamois) by the gardener Philip Knowles, underground caverns and lakes lit by electricity. Such models were no exception at the time—Mount Fuji was represented at the Japanese garden at Fanhams Hall near Ware, Hertfordshire, and in Hull's East Park Edward A. Peak (*nomen est omen*) created a model of the Khyber Pass. There are several caves: the Blue Grotto, the Ice Grotto, the Vine Grotto, the Large Cave, the Wishing-well Cave, the Skeleton Cave, the Gnome Cave and the Illusion Cave. They were made by the rocailleur firm of T.B. Harpham in London's Edgware Road, while the firm of Pulham was responsible for the rocks above ground, together with James Backhouse & Son from York. All these caverns were decorated and electrified in such a way that the visitor passing through them could be treated to a display of conjuring tricks from a Victorian Disneyland. Electricity was still very much a novelty at the time, and to see a crocodile with flashing eyes was genuinely shocking. There was an artificial underground rainbow, faces—not your own—staring back at you from sunken pools, a skeleton that jumped out at you—all the fun of the fair.

In the house all the bells and light switches were model friars: the noses were turned to switch on the lights. Lady Ottoline Morrell, who visited in 1905, couldn't decide if Sir Frank was 'colossally simple and really thought these vulgar and monstrous jokes beautiful and amusing'. Gradually, the monstrous jokes fell into decay. Until 1969, when Harrison bought it, the Order of St John Bosco used it as a Roman Catholic school and presumably had little interest in maintaining jokes at the expense of friars or in perpetuating models of walled-up clerics in the caverns. However, it is rumoured that the ex-Beatle has spent £1.25 million renovating the garden with its amazing private fun-fair; it would be wonderful to see it. How about it, Mr Harrison? Go on, George!

The long barrow in Henley Deer Park was another pure practical joke, but much earlier and only to be enjoyed fully long after the practitioner had died. In 1932 a Colonel North excavated the mound, expecting to find evidence of a Bronze Age burial; instead, he discovered an urn and a tiled chamber of chalk blocks containing a Latin inscription etched on a piece of glass to the effect that 'This mound was built by John Freeman of Fawley Court, 1731' (see Berkshire).

Heythrop

Grotto (late 19th century)
SP 360 260

Heythrop House, southeast of Heythrop, has a three-arched grotto in the grounds, overlooking a pond and built after the renewal of the house in 1871. It was built to 'house the skeleton of the Northern Bottle-nosed Whale', which had been presented to the millionaire Albert Brassey. It is situated in one of those rockeries so popular in the late 19th century.

Highmoor

Sham Castle (1942)
SU 690 840

On the road from Stoke Row to Nettlebed is a tiny, easily overlooked curiosity by the side of the B481—a model country house/castle no more than 2ft (60cm) high, built, so the inscription tells us, by '343 ENGNRS US ARMY 1942', as a three-dimensional replica of their corps insignia.

Holton Park

Earthworks (17th–18th century)
SP 600 060

In Holton Park is a curious octagonal ditched earthwork, said by some to be a Civil War battery emplacement and by others to be the site of a long-vanished folly, Holton Park being a Gothic house of 1815. Unsurprisingly, we prefer the latter theory.

Ipsden

Stone Circle (1827)
SU 640 830

Across the road from Ipsden House in the surprisingly bleak village of Ipsden stands a sham druid's circle, with stones no more than 2–3ft (60–90cm) high. It was built in 1827, and in the same year, in a field a little way to the north, near a dissenters' chapel, stands a small pyramidal monument, erected to John Reade, who died in India. Nearby Braziers Park of 1799 is a Goth's delight.

Mapledurham

Old Palm (18th century)
Arch (mid-18th century)
Fernery (early 19th century)
SU 650 750

Hidden in the woods by Mapledurham House is a little statue on a grossly over-elaborate plinth; it is hard to decide whether

Old Palm

the statue was intended to decorate the plinth, which looks like a chimneypiece without a house, or vice versa. It is known as Old Palm, and on Christmas Eve the statue climbs down and passes through the village, spreading good cheer. And if you believe that, welcome to the Folly Fellowship.

In the north wall of the kitchen garden are an ornamental arch, originally part of a mid-18th century summerhouse, and a Gothick fernery of the early 19th century.

Middleton Stoney

Lodge (1749)
SP 530 230

En route from Middleton Stoney to Weston-on-the Green are a small Gothick tower lodge and a barn, dating from the same time, to which strips have been applied to the gable end to form a large traceried blank arch. Until now it has been dated *c.*1815, like The Rectory of 1812–15 by Henry Hakewill and Thomas Cundy, on the same road, but it appears that the lodge is much earlier—1749—and by Sanderson Miller, according to Mowl and Earnshaw.

Middleton Stoney Lodge

Nuneham Courtenay

Carfax Conduit (1770s)
Grotto (1770s)
`SU 540 980`

Beneath an ivy-covered stump on the side of a hill at Nuneham Courtenay is an old wooden seat with a plaque on top reading:

> Thif Tree
> Waf planted by one Barbra Wyatt who
>   waf fo much
> attached to it that at the removal of the
>   Village of
> Nuneham Courtney fhe earneftly
>   entreated
> that fhe might remain in her olde
>   habitation
> her requeft waf complied with and her
>   Cottage not
> pulled down till after her death. Anno
>   1760.

and then the back of the seat below has a 36-line poem painted on it which ends:

> Hear this ye great, whose proud
>   pofsefsions spread
> O'er earth's rich surface to no space
>   confin'd
> Ye learn'd in arts in men in manners
>   read
> Who boast as wide as empire o'er the
>   mind
> With reverence visit her august domain
> To her unletter'd memory bow the knee:
> She found that happinefs you seek in vain
> Bless'd with a cottage and a single tree.

If the rhythm and metre of this poem seem familiar, it is not surprising: it has been proved to most people's satisfaction that Nuneham Courtenay is the Sweet Auburn of Oliver Goldsmith's *Deserted Village*. The poem itself is by another forgotten Poet Laureate, William Whitehead (1715–85).

Simon, 1st Earl of Harcourt, demolished the village of Nuneham Courtenay in 1760 to create a magnificent park and landscape. We visited the park one beautiful spring morning, and it would not be easy to disagree with Horace Walpole's assertion that the landscape is the most beautiful in the world, a remarkably lovely scene, with daffodils and cherry blossom clothing the hill, which slopes softly down to the Thames from the church—or, rather, the eyecatcher basilica—which Harcourt designed with 'Athenian' Stuart and built in 1764.

The 2nd Earl, Harcourt's republican son, mellowed with age and employed Lancelot Brown in 1778. He designed a Gothick tower, which was never built, because in 1787 Harcourt acquired the magnificently ornate Carfax Conduit, which originally stood in Oxford's High Street, and erected it on the tower's chosen site as an eyecatcher. This splendid building, excellently preserved, stands on a high ridge overlooking the Thames and its former home. It is square, with an ornate, carved parapet with 'O N', for Otho Nicholson, the builder of the conduit, repeated all round, and is topped by an even more elaborately carved octagonal turret

Carfax Conduit

Cauldwell's Castle

supported on four legs, with carved figures in niches, on the columns and on the top of the little dome.

The grotto at Nuneham is very dilapidated and was included in a fernery and rock garden. Mavis Batey and Oliver Bradbury have done research on this grotto and found the remains of a rock arch, a plaque with a quote from Milton and the grotto itself, a small affair with the remains of fossils, shells and minerals. Water used to flow through the grotto. There is also a tunnel. A letter of 1778 to Whitehead from Harcourt explains:

> *The cave is not near compleated and will be a tedious and costly business; to have it well done and to secure the brains of those who will most frequent it (for they have brains as well as skulls) I have been obliged to send for a person on purpose, who has been employed in making artificial rocks… It is lighted from the top by a bell glass, blown flatter on purpose than usual.*

Who was the builder? Joseph and/or Josiah Lane? Wiltshire, their homeground, is not too far away. A bark temple also remains in the later stages of decay, and it is possible to discover here and there fragments of former glories of these urn-bestrewn gardens, like a Temple of Flora of the 1770s. The house is now a conference centre, so the park will be cared for as a facility for delegates.

Oxford

Folly Bridge
Cauldwell's Castle (1849)
Summerhouse (early 18th century)
SP 510 050

Folly Bridge in Oxford is famous, but not for being a folly; the nearest thing to a folly to creep into that architectural paradise is Cauldwell's Castle (or Isis House) next to the bridge. It is a castellated house with statues set in niches, built in 1849 by Joseph Cauldwell, an eccentric accountant, who wanted the house built as a castle to withstand attacks made by rioting undergraduates, a perpetual fear. As is so often the case, it was Cauldwell, the imaginary victim, who proved to be the aggressor, shooting and severely wounding a student who had tried to make off with one of his brass cannons.

Also in the town is an early 18th-century domed garden-house behind 16 St Giles' Street, formerly known as the Judge's Lodging House.

Oxford could, however, have had the biggest folly in the world. In 1975 John Madden, an undergraduate, submitted plans for a 450ft (137m) pyramid to be built in Christ Church Meadow. The submission was properly drawn up and presented: it would have been necessary to freeze the Thames over for seven and a half years in order to excavate the 100ft (30m) deep foundations; then a further 16½ years and 18 million tons of stone from Headington Quarry would be needed to build the thing. Labour was no problem—there was to be compulsory secondment of second-year undergraduates—but the question of finance was delicately avoided. The intention was that the pyramid should serve as Mr Madden's mausoleum, and his application got as far as the City Planning Committee, where it was defeated by the narrowest of margins—five votes to four—after the city engineer pointed out that street lights would have to be kept on all day because the sheer bulk of the monument would keep the city in perpetual darkness. The pyramid would have been finished exactly by the time this new edition of *Follies* came out. Instead we have the Millennium Dome.

Rotherfield Greys

Greys Court Garden Buildings (20th century)
SU 720 820

The extremely ancient National Trust property of Greys Court in Rotherfield Greys has a delightful 20th-century addition to the garden—a full moon gate; this is complemented by a Chinese wooden bridge over a ha-ha and a turf maze dedicated by the Archbishop of Canterbury. Lately a Gothicky wooden arbour and gazebo have been added, designed by the architect Roger Barnes for Lady Brunner.

Rousham

Folly Group (18th century)
SP 480 240

William Kent produced Oxfordshire's most notable eyecatcher (but wait for the one at Wroxton) for General Sir James Dormer of Rousham House. Starting in 1738, Kent remodelled the house and landscaped the relatively small garden nestled in a bend in the Cherwell to such effect that it became a blueprint for succeeding landscape architects and is generally regarded as his masterpiece. His paths, walks and cascades overlaid the Charles Bridgeman designed garden of 20 years earlier and remain substantially unaltered to this day. Kent's stroke of genius lay in opening up vistas outside the garden to involve the surrounding landscape. Aware that a view needed to be answered, he erected two structures to catch the eye. One was the transformation of an old mill into the Chapel of the Mill, complete with flying buttresses, stepped gables, pinnacles and a quatrefoil window. The other, a straightforward eyecatcher and the first ever built, stands a mile to the north, on a hill to the east of the village of Steeple Aston. It is a large tripartite arch, buttressed, with blank side wings and a curved pinnacled top. Close to, the basic structure is seen to be severely rectangular, the curved top seeming to be a later infill; there is no record to show if this was Kent's original

Rousham Eyecatcher

intention, although the eyecatcher was intended to be a triumphal arch celebrating General Dormer's victories in Spain.

There is no need to list all the temples, terraces and statues in the garden itself, but mention must be made of the elegant arcade and the cascades in Venus Vale, which echo, perhaps unconsciously, the eyecatcher, but the name (and layout!) also implies more erotic connotations. In front of the bottom cascade is a memorial inscription to Ringwood, 'an OTTER-HOUND of extraordinary Sagacity', with an exhortation to local otters ('Tyrant of the Cherwell's Flood') not to pollute his tomb. The Gothick Cow house, also by Kent, is of a stark yet very effective design but sited a little out of the way of the usual walk round the garden.

Crowsley Park Grotto

Shiplake

Crowsley Park Grotto (late 18th century)
SU 730 790

A fine grotto is in the grounds of Crowsley Park at Shiplake, now largely a wireless transmitting station but still retaining an excitingly gloomy yew walk to a hollow in the woods, where the flint façade of the grotto looms, like an ogre's mouth. Inside it is plain and friendly, a vaulted roof with *oeil-de-boeuf* centre and ribs running down to the corners, terminating in smiling faces. The four niches either side may once have held busts, but nothing now remains, not even a shell. Surprisingly, it is warmer inside than out. The owner credits the building to the Earl of Uxbridge and Lord Dungannon, two dissolute members of Dashwood's Hell Fire Club; West Wycombe is only about 10 miles away.

Shirburn

Lodge (1807)
SU 690 950

The Gothick lodge, although by John Nash, is not really a folly but a ruse to mention here the very early neo-Gothic of Shirburn Castle (1716–25) by Thomas Parker, Baron Macclesfield, a privy councillor, who had started as an attorney and judge and who was a favourite of the king. In 1725 political enemies found out that he had spirited away huge sums of money belonging to his clients, as well as practising every type of corruption known to man. Parker was stripped of his many titles and situations, resided awhile in the cells of the Tower of London and returned to Shirburn. The castle, with its sham Gothic on a medieval core, had provided him with the house that equalled his stature. There is a later temple in the grounds.

Stanton St John

Belvedere (1990s)
SP 570 090

Bob Nimmo has erected a cupola that stood on the roof of Culham's European School in his garden. It is hexagonal and stands on stilts, with a weathervane on top.

Stoke Row

Maharajah's Well (1863)
SU 670 840

Stoke Row is a neat, tidy and safe suburban settlement in the countryside, but it has one of the more curious gifts to be offered to this

Inside the Maharajah's Well

country by a foreigner. Known as the Maharajah's Well, its oriental design and cosy English situation appear incongruous to modern eyes. Things were very different in 1863, however; at that time Stoke Row was 'a number of cottages scattered around a melancholy common' on the chalk Chilterns, and the water supply was sporadic, with empty claypits being used as reservoirs. Edward Reade of Ipsden House, Lieutenant-Governor of the Indian Northwestern Provinces, was friendly with the Maharajah of Benares and pointed out to him the similarity between the Chilterns and a part of his estate, as well as the similar suffering caused by the lack of water. The Maharajah endowed a charitable trust to supply a well at Stoke Row, and the unusual maroon, gold and blue wellhead was erected above a 368ft (112m) deep borehole. The well was used up until World War II. It is beautifully painted and maintained and could still be used for drawing water if required.

Stonor Park

Stone Circle (19th century)
SU 740 880

Druids seem never to have caught the Oxford imagination to any great degree, possibly because in the Rollright Stones they had the real thing. We have, however, mentioned the sham druid's circle in Ipsden, and only some 10 miles to the northeast are the stones at Stonor Park, which are approximately the same size. Could they be by the same hand?

Tackley

Grotto (late 18th century)
SP 470 190

It is felt that the grotto at Hill Court (formerly Tackley Court, a 17th-century house demolished 40 years ago) owes much to the grotto cascade at Rousham only 5 miles away. It is three-arched as well, similarly sited and is thought by local historian Charles Stiller to have evolved in stages from a bridge into a grot.

Watlington

White Mark (1764)
SU 690 930

This is, take your pick, a triangular obelisk or spire-shaped hill figure on the slopes of Watlington Hill. Steve Graham unearthed the story, Lawrence Duttson the maker and the date. Edward Horne (the family's mausoleum

is in the church) found the sight of his church tower at Watlington without a spire to be unsatisfactory, and as he was not able or willing to spend any money on providing the required spire, he instead carved this hill figure as a backdrop, so that from his house he could enjoy a gleaming white spire. Hill figure enthusiasts would interpret the elongated shape as a phallus, but of course we know better.

Wheatley

Gothick Temple (1734)
SP 570 060

Shotover House on the outskirts of Oxford, can boast the survival of a nearly complete, early 18th-century garden. Rousham has the first eyecatcher; it is very likely that the Gothic Temple at Shotover is the second or third Gothick Revival garden building in Britain. Once again the credit goes to Kent, the building having previously been variously attributed to Vanbrugh, Hawksmoor, Gibbs and Townsend, but recently Kent's own

The Gothick Temple at Shotover

drawings for it have been discovered and sold to the United States. As a model, it could scarcely be bettered. Despite Walpole's acid comments on Kent's ability with the Gothick touch, this early Gothic folly has almost all the requirements. It is large, gabled, battlemented, pinnacled, turreted, mysterious, enigmatic and old. In Bickham's bird's-eye view of Shotover, dated 1750, it appears well settled into its environment, squarely facing the house along the formal east–west axis. In 1734 General James Tyrrell commissioned Kent to improve his landscape, and here the first tentative steps away from the formal garden and towards a more picturesque appearance were taken. Instead of rigid straight lines, rectangular canals and formal ponds, Kent laid out serpentine paths in the woods between an obelisk and an octagonal, domed temple, which he built on an artificial mound. The reduced circumstances of later proprietors of Shotover have largely been responsible for the preservation of these gardens in the face of rapidly changing fashion.

Whithurch

The Baulk (c.1900)
SU 650 760

A very late and very pleasant eyecatcher, the Baulk has a brick and flint façade on one end, with two pyramidal towerettes, so that it could be mistaken for a church from a distance. It was built for Sir Charles Rose of Hardwick Court. There used to be other follies here, dotting a picturesque walk.

Woodcote

The Folly (20th century)
SU 640 820

The Folly at Woodcote sounded promising, but it turned out to be a house called 'The Folly' on a housing estate, with a narrow enclosed avenue running back towards a plinth that may once have held a statue.

Woolstone

The Tower (1877)
SU 290 870

Lord Berners's Folly at Faringdon is the only tower in Oxfordshire. The building called 'The Tower' in Woolstone, in the Vale of the White Horse, is only a three-storey house with fanciful brickwork, and 'A. N. 1877' picked out boldly on one gable end and 'W. N.' but no date on the other.

Wroxton

Eyecatcher (c.1750)
SP 430 420

At Wroxton Abbey there is an obelisk commemorating a visit by the Prince of Wales in 1739, as well as a classical temple and a dovecote trying to look like an ancient Gothick tower, but the real joy to be discovered here is the beautiful eyecatcher (possibly by Sanderson Miller) on a hill a mile away, south

Wroxton Eyecatcher

of Drayton. Trees have now grown up, concealing the eyecatcher from the abbey, but like all Miller's work it is equally enjoyable close to. This was his country: his estate of Radway is only a few miles away, and he knew the land and its stone. To see Wroxton's eyecatcher on an autumn evening with the sun slanting across the golden field on to its golden stone is to be captivated by this extraordinary cul-de-sac of architecture, in which buildings made with no thought for posterity have somehow survived and given untold pleasure to succeeding generations. Its stone and its situation make it memorable.

There is evidence that Miller designed the eyecatcher, but he worked on Wroxton Abbey for the Earl of Guilford, producing a now-demolished Gothick temple and a new tower for the 14th-century church. We must always remember that Miller was an amateur architect; when Horace Walpole visited he commented:

> the tower is in a good plain Gothic style, and was once, they tell you, still more beautiful, but Mr Miller, who designed it, unluckily once in his life happened to think rather of beauty than of water-tables, and so it fell down the first winter.

Walpole described also the chinoiserie—the first recorded chinoiserie—with which Wroxton's park was decorated:

> There are several paltry Chinese buildings and bridges, which have the merit or demerit of being the progenitors of a very numerous race all over the kingdom; at least they were of the very first.

Unfortunately, not a trace remains.

SHROPSHIRE

Shropshire is a large, sparsely populated
and rather beautiful county, which has
remained surprisingly unspoilt. A wealth
of half-timbered building, lovely scenery,
which presages the savage grandeur of
Wales, and an almost entirely rural
aspect make it difficult to realize that
this was the first industrial area in the
world. Shrewsbury, with a population of
only 60,000, was by far the largest town
in the county until it welded
Wellington, Oakengates, Dawley and
some other townships together to
create the inchoate but well-named
Telford. The new town still has the
ability to deliver some surprises: the
headquarters of ENTA Technologies has
been built in the style of a Chinese palace,
set in a chinoiserie pleasure garden. The climate
for follies in Shropshire must have been like a damp,
warm cellar is for mushrooms – good countryside with rolling hills, lots of money coming in at
the prime time for folly building – so it's surprising that there aren't more. They are, however,
varied – perhaps more so than anywhere else in the country – and they are generally of a high
standard, even if their preservation leaves something to be desired. Unlike many other counties,
the Shropshire imagination did not stop working as soon as someone came up with the idea of
building an obelisk.

Acton Burnell

Grotto (18th century)
SJ 534 019

There's a beehive-shaped grotto room here,
set upon the hill, with its 18th-century
decorations still intact. The lady of the
manor must have spent her idle hours in
here, season after season patterning quaint
little shellwork vases, faces and flowers on the
walls. At one point she was presented with
some Delftware tiles, which line the lower
part of the room.

Sham Castle (18th century)
SJ 544 016

An absolute gem—a little known and very
lovely, Gothick triangular sham castle, set on
a small wooded knoll three fields away from
any stranger's gaze. It is much in the style of
Blaise Castle north of Bristol, but it is
compromised by the addition of a two-storey
lean-to at the back, which is necessary to
make it habitable by two people. Blaise

Acton Burnell Grotto

Castle, being an uninhabitable ruin, escapes
such visually inappropriate accretions.
Unlike Blaise, much of the original interior
plasterwork and decoration of the Sham

Acton Burnell Sham Castle

Castle remains intact. It was put up for sale at £180,000 in 1993, and any intelligent isolate with the cash in hand would have been heartbroken not to have snapped it up.

Atcham

Attingham Eyecatchers (early 19th century)
SJ 542 093

A few miles east of Shrewsbury lies Attingham Park, a superb Humphrey Repton creation. The approach is from the village of Atcham, which is still graced by some remains of a projected model village by John Nash. There is an ice-house and an 18th-century wooden bee house in the park, but the follies consist of two cottages flanking a side entrance to Attingham; a churchy edifice called Western Lodge, probably by Nash; and an eyecatcher lodge. It is a fairly half-hearted attempt at catching the eye: a narrow façade with an elongated cross for a window has been put onto the projecting part of the lodge. The rest of the house is untouched. Both buildings can be dated at *c.*1800.

Bache

Tower (1830)
SO 473 818

At the bottom of Corve Dale a small, square, castellated tower house sits on a low rise, built for the Colwinston Estate as a shepherd's shelter, where they could use its three storeys to scan the dales and edges for lost sheep.

Bridgnorth

Dracup's Cave (1981)
SJ 720 930

A natural sandstone cave has been improved over the years by artist Antony Dracup, who has embellished it with columns, arches and vaulting until the entire ensemble resembles a small cathedral crypt.

Fort Pendleton (mid-19th century)
SJ 724 943

A mile north of the town, between the River Severn and the A442, is a castellated part factory, part warehouse, with three small turrets, prickly and aggressive but half-buried

Bache Tower

among small workshops. It was up for sale in 1995 at £80,000, but stands empty and derelict at the time of writing.

Gazebo (18th century)
SJ 727 928

The Governor's House in East Castle Street has a Gothick gazebo looking east, high over the Severn, but sufficiently well hidden not to be seen from the Castle Walk running beneath it.

Callow Hill
Flounder's Folly (1838)
SO 461 850

Mr Benjamin Flounder of Ludlow decided to build himself a tower on top of Callow Hill, east of Winstantow. It marked the boundary of four different estates. As he seems to have been sufficiently well-off, he built the tower up to some 80–90ft (24–27m). One morning in 1838 Mr Flounder drives up from Ludlow in a carriage-and-four. The scaffolding has just been removed. His dilettante's eye does not notice the inauthenticity of his castellations. He opens the door, which bears his initials and the date of construction, and climbs the staircase. On the parapet he is met by his steward and the head mason. 'Fine view. Fine view indeed. But—what's this?' His two companions notice Mr Flounder's face getting quite purple. There's a hill obstructing the view towards his own estate! Mr Flounder works himself into one of his tantrums. 'I won't have it! Take it down!' The steward is worried about the extra cash that will have to be found for the demolition of the tower, and all this on top of the preposterous sum already squandered on this silly project. Suddenly he points to the north. There, in the hazy distance, a silvery stretch of water can be seen. 'Look sir—the Mersey!' And Flounder decides to keep the costly tower and use it for observing the ships going in and out of port. He must have had sensational eyesight; the Mersey is over 60 miles away as the crow flies.

Eyton-on-Severn
Summerhouse (1607)
SJ 572 061

This was never built as a folly, but through time and isolation it has achieved folly status. An octagonal gazebo, with a taller octagonal stair turret, it was built purely for pleasure and amusement while more serious business was conducted at the great house. Now the

house has wasted away and vanished, and all that remains is the frivolity in the park, laughing longest. The Vivat Trust lets it out for holidays.

Hadnall
Waterloo Windmill (c.1820)
SJ 524 212

Off the A49, just before entering Hadnall from the north, is the Waterloo Windmill. It was built for General Lord Hill, who lived at the now-demolished Hardwick Grange, on which estate the mill is. The house was built c.1820 by Thomas Harrison, and the folly is probably of the same date and by the same architect. Harrison was something like the

Waterloo Windmill

family architect: the Citadel at Hawkstone was altered by him, and he also worked on the Hill Column in Shrewsbury (see below). Harrison was a monumental specialist: the obelisk at Moel Fammau, the column at Llanfair P.G. and the Memorial Arch at Holyhead were all his work. Waterloo Windmill, of course, commemorated Lord Hill's heroic deeds on the battlefield; it is supposed to be a replica of the Waterloo headquarters. Its arrowslits and Gothicized windows, however unlikely in a field HQ, assure one that it is not just another converted windmill. The surrounding woods were planted in order to indicate the position of the armies at the start of the battle. The

The Grotto Arch at Hawkstone

story sounds very *déjà entendu*: a similar story is told about the woodlands at Woodford, Northamptonshire, and in Lancashire and so on and so on. It could, however, represent a so-called battle garden (or, in this instance, a battle park)—an arrangement of earthworks and/or plantations so that they resemble in miniature the location of a famous battle. A good example has come to light at Kilwarlin, County Down, which recreates the Battle of Thermopylae during the Graeco-Turkish wars of the 1820s.

Hawkstone

Easily the most coherent group of follies in Shropshire exists at Hawkstone Park; it is also one of the best preserved British parks in the Picturesque vein. The sum total of atmosphere, follies and landscape provides for an unforgettable experience.

The Citadel (1780–1825)
SJ 571 285

A couple of hundred yards from the village of Weston there is a building looking like a fortress, trefoil-shaped, with a terrace in front, which may be used for installing batteries of cannon. Of course, it's all just for fun. The Citadel was built some time between 1780 and 1800, with additions in 1825, and it was used to house the steward of the Hill family, the owners of Hawkstone. The design for the Citadel was apparently taken directly from the Hill coat of arms.

Many of the park's attractions were completed in the 1780s by Sir Rowland Hill. After that Sir Richard Hill took over, and building went on well into the 1850s. When we first visited Hawkstone in the 1970s it could not be visited without the services of a guide, to be contacted through the Hawkstone Park Hotel. The hotel is now mainly for users of the golf course, which winds its way through the park. It started, however, as the Hawkstone Inn, *c*.1800, which was built to accommodate the growing number of sightseers. Hawkstone in a way can be said to be the inspiration for Longleat, Woburn and all the other stately homes that attract visitors; one could pay for a day out at Hawkstone 200 years ago.

Without a guide one was liable to lose one's way or even fall into an unexpected crevasse, as several people have done these last few years. The guide was Mr J.T. Jones, in his sprightly seventies, and the last of four generations of Jones guides at Hawkstone. He led us through the park, up the very steep hill and down the valley—to be repeated an exhausting three times. But Mr Jones's services are no longer required, because Hawkstone has been reborn as a model of how to refurbish an 18th-century park to suit 20th-century tastes without compromising its integrity or authenticity. It is signposted as a Folly Park from 20 miles away—unthinkable 20 years ago, and splendidly the owners have resisted the temptation to turn it into a theme park. Of all the restorations that have been carried out since we first began to write about follies 20 years ago, this is the one that has been carried out with the most love and imagination, and the astonishing thing is that it has been done by a private, profit-making company, not by the National Trust or some grant-aided, tax-exempt charity. The company deserves our fullest praise, and a visit to Hawkstone is essential for anyone who wishes to understand the 18th-century conception of the sublime. The following description is based on the route as taken by the guide; nowadays the walk is done in reverse. Maps are supplied at the octagonal visitor centre, another intelligent addition to the park, carefully screened from the rest of the landscape.

Red Castle (late 18th century)
SJ 583 293

The first stop is the Red Castle, to be approached through junglish paths. It is a beauty of a folly. People usually mistake 18th-century towers for the well-worn remains of some medieval burgh. This time it is the other way round, for the castle is real, dating from the 13th century. All this has led to genuine confusion—Pevsner describes 'a grey circular tower which is original medieval work', but the Shropshire Standard Records point out that the tower is in a non-defensive position and yet has narrow, ornate window slits. 'There appears to be no purpose for a tower in this position unless it was erected in an attempt to add to the natural beauty of the place.' One detects the faintest whiff of disapproval. Our interpretation is that the medieval tower, built out of the solid rock, was topped up in the 18th century to improve the scenery, but the 'improvements' have now fallen down. They don't build like they used to. Its natural defences and unassailable position must have made an attack on it sheer hell. So will be the walk up there if one is too eager and makes a dash for it.

At the foot of the hill is a large opening through which one enters the rock and peers down the Giant's Well, again cut out of the solid rock. A feeling of sublimity may have taken over at this point and is likely to remain on our tour. Nearby is the Lion's Den: a neat gorge that ends with the den itself, a half-circular opening. The bars that once were there have been broken away and the huge, sculpted head of the fearsome lion lies meekly at your feet. It was possibly sculpted by John Nelson, who also provided the statue on top of the column and two sphinxes for the park. The vandalization of much of Hawkstone appears to date from World War II, when the park was turned into a POW

A rustic bridge into Little Switzerland

camp. The second large rock is called Grotto Hill; its apertures and eyecatcher arch are admirably viewed from Castle Hill.

The Grotto (late 18th century)
SJ 573 297

The Grotto is stupendous. Tunnel, chambers and galleries whirl and twirl on top of the hill. Conflicting claims are made as to who excavated it: Roman miners and/or early Brits, or the Hills (that is to say their labourers). On our visit, Mr Jones had 'forgotten' the torch and we were advised, on entering an innocent enough looking hole, just to follow him and keep in touch with the wall. Ten yards later is was impossible to turn back as all the light had gone. This went on for a very long 90 metres; meanwhile, we were pathetically groping the wall and claustrophobia had set in. At last a little light fell on our whitened hair, and we entered the part of the grotto that is decidedly 18th century. Unfortunately, this is one part of the restoration where safety regulations have now diminished the pleasure of the visit; the law has demanded that the Stygian passages be lit, albeit dimly.

A thorough job has been done on the grotto room: shells, minerals, roof, stained glass—all has been destroyed, apparently by two cyclists who were refused refreshments at the hotel after the war. Their delirium might be understandable if they had cycled up the hill. The 1807 Description of Hawkstone aptly remarks that the grotto is:

without any thing of that diminutive or formal decoration and petitesse, by which Grottoes are usually rendered more like artificial baby-houses* than grand natural and romantic caverns.

The stained glass that has now disappeared represented 'The Four Seasons' and a 'Philosopher at his Studies', done by a Mrs Peirson. A pity that such things are always the first to go. A rhododendron-lined path will see one safely down again, near the remains (now rebuilt) of the Victorian Gingerbread Hall or Temple of Patience, a thatched hut backed by the rock, where in olden days Martha Higginson sold ginger beer and gingerbread to hungry and thirsty tourists.

An underpass, made in 1853, sends the visitor uphill again, *en route* to the column. But first, here were the scanty relics of the hermitage, covered in undergrowth. Reports of a hermit living here around 1800 seem to be false, but there was a papier-mâché one.

* For another interpretation of this phrase, see Whalley in Lancashire.

At this point on the tour, the guide would leave his group and enter the hermitage through a secret back door. While the visitors were peering into the hut, discerning only the dim outline of the bearded hermit, a skull on the table in front of him, the guide would work some levers. The hermit's eyes could roll at will, he would rise to greet the people at his door, and his mouth would mimic words spoken by the guide. The manikin fell apart years ago, but as befits our wired age we now have a Virtual Hermit to take his place—a sublime reinterpretation. Much was made of the hermit's existence: at the coming-of-age party of Lord Hill in 1851, as the clock struck 12, the then guide entered the ballroom dressed as the hermit. Presumably he delivered some wise and well-meant eulogy.

Inside the White Tower

White Tower (early 19th century)
SJ 578 291

From the site of the hermitage one can walk towards the White Tower, which is, of course, red. It was formerly very difficult to reach, and frankly we were disappointed by the little dullard. It was only meant to be seen from a distance.

After the restoration work, the face-lifted tower has become much more handsome, particularly the interior, which has an elegant white oak floor, and its *raison d'être* becomes clearer—its windows admirably frame the view.

After and before restoration—   the 'Obelisk' at Hawkstone

The Obelisk (1795)
SJ 579 292

The path leads on to the Obelisk, which is not an obelisk at all, but a 112ft (34m) tall column. Upon this stout Tuscan fabric stood the statue of another Sir Rowland Hill, who was the first Protestant Lord Mayor of London. When we first saw it, only his feet remained—the rest of him had descended some years earlier. Full marks to the present owners of Hawkstone, who have re-erected a replica of the statue. The railings around the top of the column had gone as well, and the restoration architects tell spine-chilling stories about stepping out on to the narrow, unguarded parapet on their first inspection only to find it was coated in a thick sheet of ice… Anyone with enough breath left can climb the spiral staircase inside the column and gulp the equally breathtaking views. The building of the column seems to have served for giving much needed employment to locals, who were also put to work digging the enormous stretch of Hawkstone Lake.

A Dutch scene on the lakeshore has gone. It would have made an interesting change from the semi-Chinese, Italianate and druidical landscapes normally encountered in parks. It consisted of a Dutch house called Neptune's Whim, which was inappropriately decorated with Swiss landscapes, a whalebone arch and a windmill in the Dutch style. The whole set was designed to remind one of a Ruysdael painting.

The Menagerie (early 19th century)
SJ 576 290

Also gone are a Tahitian hut, Murad Bey's tent (brought over from Egypt in 1801 as a trophy by Colonel Hill), a Gothick menagerie (although scraps of its ruins remain at the above grid reference), a fortified vineyard and some more towers. Yet there remains enough of the Hawkstone follies, and above all the landscape, to be able to enjoy the risk of falling off columns and precipices, getting stuck in tunnels or even being hit by killer golfballs.

Hodnet

Column Eyecatcher (1970)
SJ 610 288

Just before leaving the A442 there's a splendid view on the left of the ruined

Hodnet Columns

columns in a field opposite an entrance to Hodnet Hall. They were acquired by Brigadier Heber-Percy from the demolished Apley Castle in 1956, and were put up in 1970, a fairly arid time for follies. It is a good piece of neo-classicism before plunging into the wonders of Hawkstone Park.

Ironbridge

Severn Wharf Building (mid-19th century)
SJ 668 036

The fires have now all died down at Ironbridge, the much publicized Cradle of the Industrial Revolution, but its Gates of Hell, the furnaces, the foundries and the warehouses, where work never stopped, like some Moloch needing fuel day and night, have been well preserved by turning Coalbrookdale into a string of museum areas. In the middle of it, near the world's first all-iron bridge, squats the red and yellow brick, Grade II* listed Severn Wharf Building, which was built in the 1840s for the Coalbrookdale Company. Minerals were off-loaded from the boats moored here and taken into the warehouse on carts. The grooves for the rails can still be seen on the wharf. Some whim of the owners saw to it that the building was castellated, and two hilarious towerettes were put up in front, flanking a Gothic apse. As in Germany, industrialists

often had the insolence to compare themselves to medieval barons. Minstrels on the battlements could have provided the Music While You Work, but apparently bad taste didn't stretch that far. It is now the Visitor Centre for the Ironbridge Gorge Museum Trust, the valley's museum complex. Because of its fire and brimstone connections, this must be one of the least pleasurable follies in the country.

Lilleshall

Sutherland Obelisk (1833)
SJ 729 156

This 70ft (21m) obelisk on the hills above Lilleshall is to the memory of the well-loathed 1st Duke of Sutherland, who owned a good proportion of the county and by dint of a careful marriage acquired a good proportion of the rest of England and Scotland and consequently a dukedom, which he enjoyed for six months before he died in 1833.

Llanyblodwell

Summerhouse (18th century)
SJ 262 228

Perilously close to Wales for most Englishmen, the owner of Blodwell Hall still found enough peace in the 18th century to build this pretty summerhouse in the garden for his family.

Longden

Gazebo (mid-19th century)
SJ 473 818

There is an octagonal gazebo in a sorry state on the corner of Summerhouse Lane at the south of the village.

Market Drayton

Pell Wall Lodge (1828)
SJ 920 104

Decaying for years, Pell Wall Hall was largely destroyed by fire in 1986. Applications were made to demolish it, fortunately without success, and the house has now been passed into the hands of a Preservation Trust, which will at least consolidate the structure, although it may not have the funding in place to complete the restoration. The house was built by John Soane in 1822–28 for his friend Purney Sillitoe.

In 1778 the architectural publisher John Taylor had published Soane's *Designs in Architecture*, a work devoted to garden buildings and, according to a letter from

Soane:

> *intended to form a set of designs to please the different tastes in Architecture and to render the work generally useful and immediately calculated for execution.*

In essence, it consisted of an idiosyncratic collection of projected follies; in later, grander years, Soane disassociated himself from the book. Nevertheless, Taylor published a reprint in 1790, and Soane, despite himself, never really lost his taste for the *outré* as we can see from the contents of the Soane Museum and the fact that at Pell Wall, the last substantial commission he undertook, is a lodge very much in the vein of his *Designs*.

At the entrance to the north drive stands this tiny triangular lodge. It was the sort of folly to take home and cuddle, proof that a folly builder, however grand, ultimately cannot deny himself. But it is no longer cuddly; lodges were built to house gatekeepers, and gatekeepers were housed to open and close gates, not to raise families, buy Range Rovers, go on holidays abroad and have neighbours round for dinner. Consequently, a gatekeeper's lodge is much too small for today's living, just as the country house is much too big. So in an attempt to make Pell Wall Lodge viably habitable in today's world, it has been extended by a blind architect living in Vladivostok who was unable to pay a site visit. There can be no other explanation for the hideous extrusion that evidently holds the living quarters. The worrying thing is that, if the lodge was listed after the extension was built, the eyesore itself will be protected

by the listing: one of the anomalies of this otherwise splendid legislation.

In its original form this was a very remarkable building, and if Soane had had a greater influence on his immediate successors this could have changed the face of Britain. It is highly unusual for an artist working late in life to break new ground: most radical work is achieved before the age of 40. This lodge was built when Soane was in his seventies, but who can tell when he dreamed it up? The mass of Victorian architecture stemmed from a diluted Gothic revival. Pell Wall Lodge combines the Temple of Dendur with Le Corbusier; it is old, it is new. Nothing built before or since has looked much like this; like Simon Conway-Morris's extraordinary lost phyla from the Burgess Shale, this is a cul-de-sac of architecture. It could have been a contender—which makes the utter banality of the new attachment even harder to come to terms with, like nomads camping in the ruins of lost and greater civilizations.

Much Wenlock

Shirlett Obelisk (19th century)
SO 665 977

There are only two noteworthy obelisks in the county. One is at Shirlett High Hall, near Much Wenlock. It is battered and braced and said to be erected to the memory of a golden retriever, which fell down a mine shaft. As two golden retrievers have now played a large part in our folly expeditions, we have to say we are not unduly surprised.

Pitchford

Tree House (late 17th century)
SJ 527 041

South of Atcham is Pitchford Hall, probably the finest half-timbered house in the county. The tree house deserves mention, first, because of its age—it was heavily restored around 1760 when it was already ancient— second, because it is the only Grade I listed tree house in the country, and third, because it illustrates one of the meanings of the word folly—, or a hut made out of tree branches. This one, in fact, is 11ft (3.3m) up in an ancient lime tree, with the wood painted in a brick pattern and the whole embellished by ogee Gothick windows. The interior is spectacular, with rich Chippendale Gothick plasterwork. In 1992 the owner tried to interest the National Trust in the property, but without success; it was sold on the open

Pitchford Tree House

market, and at the time of writing this beautiful house was empty and starting to decay. Such an important house will never be allowed to disappear, but its current steady deterioration need not be happening.

Quatford

Watch Tower (early 19th century)
Quatford Castle (1829–30)
SO 739 910

Downstream, past Bridgnorth, the village of Quatford has two follies to show for itself, both built by the same man. The red brick, castellated Watch Tower on a crag north of

Quatford Watch Tower

the church is as picturesquely sited as Quatford Castle, a sham, built as a home for John Smalman in 1829–30. Smalman was a local builder, and in Colvin's words he had 'pretentions to gentility, and claimed descent from the Smalmans of Wilderhope .'(whoever they may have been). What does a builder who claims gentility do? He builds himself a castle. Apart from his two follies, he rebuilt the village itself. This earned him the admiration of George Griffiths, who dedicated his poem 'The English Village' to the builder. Smalman was something of a poetaster himself, writing verse of a 'somewhat eccentric character'. The Salopian McGonagall? He sounds the man to have built more follies, but none have come to light.

Shrewsbury

Hill Column (1850)
SJ 507 122

At Shrewsbury, we come across Hill of Hawkstone connections again; the huge column with its statue of General Hill really does catch one's eye. As it should, for it is said to be the largest Doric column in the world; 133ft 6in (40.7m) of stone record Hill's 18 battles, but he was 'not more distinguished for his skill and courage in the field or during the arduous campaigns… than for his benevolent and paternal care in providing for the comforts and supplying the necessities of his victorious countrymen'. The Salopians seem to have been happy to provide the funds to build the column and toasted a hearty 'Hills of Shropshire; may they last as long as the Shropshire hills' to it. The statue itself is made from the mysterious and seemingly everlasting Coade artificial stone, ensuring that General Hill remains on his perch for a good time to come.

Shoemaker's Gateway (1679)
SJ 490 120

The Quarry, a park by the river, consists of folly odds and ends: architectural fragments, statues, a summerhouse and a removal folly, the Gateway of the Shoemaker's Arbour. Its date is 1679; exactly 200 years later it was taken from Kingsland and re-erected here in the Dingle, the park's main area. There is also an obelisk with Gothic decorations, transported from the station square where it had been placed in 1874.

Laura's Tower (1790)
SJ 495 128

In the grounds of the neatly manicured Shrewsbury Castle, on the mound, is a small, red sandstone, octagonal turret called Laura's Tower. Between 1787 and 1790 Sir William Pulteney engaged the young Scotsman Thomas Telford to make the castle habitable again. For decoration, he contrived this turret, which sits on the site of the medieval tower, and named it after Pulteney's wife. Through Pulteney's influence Telford acquired the position of Surveyor of Public Works for Shropshire, and an illustrious career thus started by building a folly.

Stanton Lacy

Downton Hall Lodge (1760)
SO 524 792

Not precisely a folly, but fun to find—we have

Downton Hall Lodge

a soft spot for anything that combines ogee arches with Venetian windows. It is so much of its time.

Tong

Durant's Follies (early 19th century)
SJ 795 075

Hard by the church porch stood the home of Little Nell in *The Old Curiosity Shop*, and the church porch on which Dickens is supposed to have based it is Tong. 'There are few parishes in England that bear more marks of the ownership of a family than Tong does of the Durants,' stated G.H. Boden's *History of Tong Church, College and Castle* (*c*.1910). Today we have to change the verbs in the above sentence to 'have been', 'bore' and 'did'. Few folly groups can have suffered so many casualties.

The first George Durant amassed his wealth in 1762 'at the plunder of Havana'. Part of the village is still called Tong Havana. He chose to retire to Tong, bought the medieval castle (which was allegedly originally built by Merlin the magician for Hengist) from the Vernon family and had it altered into a spectacular piece of Gothick-Moorish fantasy by Lancelot Brown. It was pulled down in 1954. The second George, happily for us, was mad. During his reign pillars and urns were strewn about Bishop's Wood, a hermit called Carolus was installed in a cave, a round house was built in the village and a circular dovecote was erected in the park. All this sounds like the common or garden insanity of so many folly builders, but the best was yet to come: the second George

developed mottomania. The wheelwright's shop in Tong Norton was fitted out with the shape of a coffin and the words 'In Mortate Lucrum' (In Death Is Gain); a well on the estate received a plaque reading 'Adam's Ale, Licensed to be Drunk on the Premises, 1838'; a coal house was inscribed 'Mausoleum'.

Gates and walls held a special interest for Durant. He started with the old entrance near the church. Crosses and Xs were carved into the still existing wall, and the iron fence posts were adored with the motto 'Beati Qui Durant'. He was only just beginning. Two jaw bones of a whale spanned the drive to the castle and were inscribed 'Death The Gate Of Life' and 'A Haven After So Many Storms'. Near the castle was an elaborate gateway with pillars upon each of which 'an Aeolian Harp denoted sweet music to unappreciative animals'; the animals in question presumably being the hounds in the nearby kennels. If the Aeolian harps actually functioned, the dogs must have been driven beserk by the ceaseless, vacant harmonies. Here again there was a plaque, with a poem

Egyptian Aviary—the Pyramidal Hen House

that began 'Harp of the North! that moul'dring long has hung…'. No wonder he called one of his sons Ossian.

Durant could not be satisfied with so few gates. He had another built, with an adjoining cottage called Convent Lodge. The Lodge still stands. The gate piers in front must have been the most bizarre pillars this side of the Channel; they are very fruity, with

lots of flowers and vegetation, a pineapple—
the folly-builder's favourite fruit—topping
the lot. The Gothick niches showed the east
and west views of the castle, the whole set off
by thick stone ropes and tassles. The iron
gates themselves came from the
Coalbrookdale Works, and the whole
astounding, unique, irreplaceable flight of
fancy was torn down to facilitate works traffic
for the M54. The lodge appears to have
suffered from deliberate neglect. It doesn't
seem particularly remarkable until one has a
closer look; there are queer patterns on the
walls and a plaque that reads

No more to Chiefs and Ladies bright
The harp of Tara swells
The Chord alone that breaks at night
Its tale of ruin tells.

Ruins indeed! From the lodge a stretch of wall
leads into a small valley. One plunges in the
exuberant growth of grass and nettle, holding
the camera above one's head. The jungle
closes in. It's worth the trouble. Large
butterflies, crowns, shields, crosses and other
emblems are hewn out of the wall. It is very
slippery indeed underfoot. Eventually the
dingle is reached. There's the brook, spanned
by a small stone bridge. Carolus the Hermit
could have resided here; the grounds look
promising enough. The path is getting too
slippery for comfort, so this will have to keep
for later. Returning along the wall, past
Gothic seats, one discovers the lower part of
the Pulpit, which is settled on the wall and is
almost totally overgrown. Eight years ago the
Pulpit was in perfect condition; it must have
been destroyed deliberately. According to the
History of Tong, Tara again was featured here:

The harp that once through Tara's halls
The soul of music shed
Now hangs as mute on Tara's walls
As if that soul had fled.

Judging from an old photograph, the Pulpit
appears be a copy of the medieval refectory
pulpit in the grounds of Shrewsbury Abbey.

Another example of the Tong mottomania
is the Egyptian Aviary at nearby Vauxhall
Farm. Covered with ivy but still going strong
and cared for, it is an elongated pyramidal
shape, set on a rectangular base, advertising its
use by the egg-like openings in the top. The
motto here is 'AB OVO', still visible under the
openings. Most of the other mottoes are no
longer to be seen—the brick has weathered
badly—but a list of them reads as follows:

EGYPTIAN AVIARY 1842

LIVE AND LET LIVE

TRIAL BY JURY

SCRAT BEFORE YOU PECK

TEACH YOUR GRANNY

CAN YOU SMELL

GIVE EVERY DOG HIS DUE

HONESTY IS THE BEST POLICY

TRANSPORTATION

BETTER COME OUT OF THE WAY LOVE

Mr Wynne, the farmer, told us that each
centre brick on the pyramid was carved to
represent a local area. The only one still
distinguishable in the 1980s—and that very
faintly—was a lizard, representing the copse
on the hill opposite, which is in the shape of
a lizard. Hence the name of the neighbouring
village over the border in Staffordshire,
Weston-under-Lizard.

The pyramid spawned another similar
building, also designed for Durant. It is
about 2 miles away in a cottage garden at
Bishop's Wood in Staffordshire, but as it is so
clearly a Durant folly we will cover it here.
This time he built a pyramidal pigsty, smaller
than the Vauxhall Farm pyramid and so
belying the inscription 'TO PLEASE THE
PIGS', as they must have been cramped for
space. Nearby is a Tudor-Gothic stable, also
none too large, with the text 'RANDZ DE
VACHE', which sounds like a bastardization
of 'cow-ranch.'

Even towards the end of his life George
Durant indulged his peculiar sense of fun.
On 19 September 1839 a Water Tournament
was held on the now-drained Tong Lake. A
cannon shot started the champions, who
stood in small boats and were armed with
jousting lances. The winner received a gold
purse from the Queen of Love and Beauty, a
prettier title than Miss Tong 1839. One of his
buildings was destroyed the very night
Durant died, in 1844. Boden, our verger and
village historian, tells the story:

Mr Durant had a monument erected on
Tong Knoll to commemorate his victory
in a law suit against his wife.
Presumably this was his first wife and
mother of his children, Maria Eld of
Leighford. In 1830 he married again,
this time to Celeste Lefeore or Lavefue—
Boden and the epitaph in Tong Church
disagree. It caused great annoyance to
his sons, who on the very night their
Father died took two barrels of gun
powder, and blew up the whole structure,
the report being heard many miles away.

Durant's ice-house escaped destruction by
kin, time or motorway planners, and found a
loving home at the Avoncroft Museum of
Building in Worcestershire.

On first sight the follies at Tong present a
riddle as to what Durant might have intended

Quinta Circle

with his buildings, decorations and mottoes. Their only reason for existence appears to be their owner's eccentricity, but one wonders whether there may be something deeper to Tong; an iconographic programme, in a rather perverse manner, of mocking religion, chivalry and nobility—the Durants were nouveaux riches, and their closest neighbours were the Earls of Bradford at Weston Park—maybe also a celebration of death and decay.

Suddenly it starts to get grim, this obsession with harps, walls, ruins and crosses; the fear and hatred of the children who destroyed mad George's gloating monument on that night of his death—at what point does a sense of humour decay into insanity?

Uffington

Haughmond Castle (1780)
SJ 537 138

Two circular towers and a battlemented connecting wall were constructed in an ancient hillfort on the top of Haughmond Hill so that a flag could be flown when John Corbet of nearby Sundorne, who was Master of the Warwickshire Fox Hounds, was hunting in the area. Did this serve as a general warning or was it mere egotism? One of the towers and most of the walling collapsed in June 1931.

Westbury

Whitton Hall Folly (18th century)
SJ 345 091

A ruined folly on top of the hill faces the house.

Weston Rhyn

Quinta Circle (mid-19th century)
SJ 281 364

Near Weston Rhyn, on the northwestern edge of Shropshire that hugs the Welsh borders, some slabs of stone stand about in a field, trying hard to fool visitors that this is an ancient stone circle. It is not. It was actually built by a Major West between 1830 and 1840, to be seen from the nearby Quinta House. Why are there never runic inscriptions on these sham Stonehenges, waiting to be deciphered by touring professors from Leipzig or Breslau, who would find encoded Bovril advertisements? Perhaps the Quinta Circle was another example of squires trying to alleviate unemployment by devising labour-intensive projects.

Woore

Bridgemere Nursery Mow Cop (1990)
SJ 725 448

Mow Cop is in Cheshire as any fule kno, but in the great tradition of smaller copies of greater buildings (*vide* Corris, Blackpool, Lichfield, Kiparrissia) there is a model sham ruin inspired by this most famous folly in a garden centre outside Woore. It was built by John Bailey for John Ravenscroft's Bridgemere Nursery stand at the 1990 Chelsea Flower Show and was so appreciated there that it was re-erected at the garden centre and 'improved' by the addition of a moat and a medieval gateway.

SOMERSET

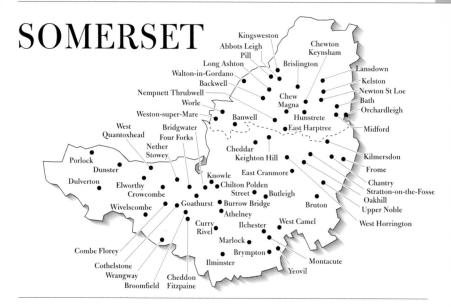

Abbots Leigh (Avon)

Boathouse (18th–19th century)
ST 540 740

There is a dilapidated boathouse or cave on the edge of Abbots Pool at Rayne Thatch in Leigh Woods, together with a cascade.

Athelney

King Alfred's Monument (1807)
ST 346 293

No trace remains of the great monastery of Athelney, over Stan Moor. A farmhouse now occupies the site, together with a peculiar squat memorial signposted 'To King Alfred's Monument'. It really is a disappointment. 'A short plain truncated obelisk of no architectural merit,' says Pevsner precisely. It was erected in 1807 by John Slade, a local farmer (and Lord of the Manor of North Petherton), to commemorate King Alfred fleeing past the spot one thousand years earlier, in 807. From the little monument one can see Burrow Mump Sham Church and, to the south on a ridge, the Burton Pynsent Steeple.

Backwell (Avon)

Larcombe's Folly (1990s)
ST 490 680

The folly of this construction lies largely in the care taken to annoy neither neighbours nor council. Stan Larcombe of Backwell, southwest of Bristol, has made pretty sure his building didn't reach over about 6ft (2m) in

height, otherwise it would have needed planning permission, and after it was finished, he planted around it so thoroughly that even the neighbours can't see it. This *maquisard* of a folly, which pretends to be a Romanesque ruin, 'the first in a line', consists of pinkish painted walls made of breezeblocks, blind arches and some carvings—and it has lots of rectangular plant boxes, making it look rather like a gimmick thought out by one of the lads at the local garden centre.

Banwell (Avon)

Folly Group (early 19th century)
ST 400 590

A hill like a submarine shelters the village of Banwell from the south, a long, dank, overgrown ridge diving down to the M5. In 1780, while they were prospecting for lead, two local men discovered a large cave; no lead being found, they closed it up again. It was reopened in 1824, and the bones of several prehistoric animals were found, some unidentifiable. The then Bishop of Bath and Wells was a keen palaeontologist, and he soon built a small house, a fashionable *cottage orné*, at Banwell in order to pursue his interest more closely.

An interest in bones leads naturally to a keener sense of mystery and drama, and Bishop Law built a dramatic garden. The site, a high, sunbathed south-facing ridge, was perfect, but the Bishop made his garden on the damp north side, with the moss and the slugs. The paths are now heavily overgrown with skeletal, light-starved, frondy plants, which brush wetly against your face as you slide on the greasy steps that lead inconsequentially away up the hill. Low stone walls border the paths, and unnatural shapes can dimly be made out through the bony overgrowth. Suddenly, in classic folly fashion, a tiny alcove appears. It is difficult to imagine it could ever have been intended as a seat as it is perpetually damp.

Directly above is a little building covered in tiny pebbles, roofless and very derelict, with three arches facing west. It was built for meditation and tranquillity, but by a trick of the land, the noise of the motorway is particularly intrusive here. The gloomy paths intertwine, climbing and descending the hill

The Druid's Temple at Banwell

randomly. One descends more steeply than the others, becoming steps and spiralling down, down into a tunnel, barred by a rotting but still functional wooden door. Is this the entrance to the bone cave? It is very dark and very wet, and a powerful stench of decaying vegetation is everywhere. The slugs are plentiful, huge and juicy. This is the end. There is nowhere else to go.

Up on the backbone of Banwell Hill, the sun is shining. It has been for hours, and there isn't a cloud in the sky. The Stygian pathways fall behind, and the ridgeway ride passes through two 10ft (3m) gate piers near a large, ugly watertank. The piers are made of tufa, ossified rock, and large blocks of it line the path at regular intervals up to the Monument. The Monument is a folly tower, octagonal, with three storeys and in the process of restoration. Once it had a parapet and a spire, but their remains lie on the ground at the bottom of the tower, and the drum that supported the spire stands naked, like the fuse on a banger. The stairs, strangely, are still intact; at least it was possible in 1983 to climb to the second storey

and look at branches instead of a view, because the trees have overtopped the tower. The Monument (to what?) is architecturally quite different from anything else on the Bishop's estate. It is squat and assertive and looks out at the world, while the garden is introspective and quiet. It was finished in 1840, when the Bishop was aged 79 and no longer active in the diocese—although bishops never retired—suffering from a 'gradual decay of mind and body'. It is far more likely, therefore, that it was built by his son, Henry Law, rector of Weston-super-Mare, who assisted him with the gardens from the start.

The inscriptions and exhortations that once graced the gardens—they were once intended to be open to the public—have now almost all disappeared. One remains, difficult to read in the afternoon sun, on the Druid's Temple at the foot of the hill; it was built by real druids say the locals.

Here, where once Druids trod in times of
yore
And stain'd their altars with a victim's
gore,
Here, now, the Christian ransomed from
above
Adores a God of mercy and of love.

It is a low-roofed shelter, semicircular, with five pointed arches, pebble stone facing, a circular wooden table inside and a little pebble pyramid on the top.

Anyone wishing to know the full and complete history of the Banwell follies, should read Michael Cousins's article in *Follies* Magazine, 1991, but we wanted to give you the smell and the feel of the site.

Leaving Banwell on the A371, the most extraordinary sight unfolds in front of you at the top of the rise outside the village. A full blown Gothic castle, immaculately kept, with portcullis, gate-tower, pinnacles, castellations, crenellations, towers—a child's full-size toy fort. It was actually built as a house in 1845 by Joseph and Amelia Sampson, but within ten years they went off to rebuild Banwell Abbey. The castle has been continuously occupied ever since, and is described as 'very comfortably arranged' by the present owner, but the obvious handicap of living in such an extraordinary edifice was summed up by a notice on the gatehouse which read:

BANWELL CASTLE
Built in the 19th century and
of no historic interest. Kindly observe
that this Englishman's castle is his home,
and do not intrude.

Ralph Allen's Sham Castle

Bath (Avon)

Ralph Allen's Sham Castle (1762)
Prior Park Follies (mid-18th century)
Pinch's Folly (1853)
Vellore House Grotto (1850s)
Crowe Hall Grotto (c.1860)
Sheridan's Grotto (18th century)
ST 770 630

Bath is the most beautiful city in England, even if sometimes it wears its beauty a little self-consciously. Its site, its stone, its sudden discovery as a fashionable spa town at a time when English architecture was at its most elegant, have combined to make it a fortunate city. The 18th century belonged to Bath; in modern terms it was a Gstaad or a Mustique.

One of its most elegant inhabitants was Ralph Allen, who augmented his fortune as a quarry-master by an income of £12,000 per annum through revising the postal system, or what we may nowadays call sleaze or cronyism, depending on one's political persuasion. A little of that huge fortune was spent on building what is now one of the best loved and best known follies in Britain—Ralph Allen's Sham Castle. Set high on the slope of Bathwick Hill (you reach it by taking the road to Bath Golf Club), it looks proudly down on once glittering Bath, the perfect example of an eyecatcher. When it was built, alone on its hillside, it was sited so as to be seen from Allen's town house in Old Lilliput Alley. Now, with new houses springing up all along the hill, it is difficult to pick out the sham from the town, so at night the City of Bath, which was given the castle in 1921, proudly floodlights it.

It is not a big building, but it is remarkably well done. The design has always been attributed to Sanderson Miller, and indeed he drew up plans for a sham castle for Allen in 1755, but the actual building is now known to have been designed and built in 1762 by Richard Jones, Allen's clerk of works. Allen was evidently not easy to get on with from an architect's point of view; he dismissed John Wood the Elder from his villa Prior Park and let Jones finish the job. Jones responded by

The Monument, Prior Park, Bath.
Erected by Bishop Warburton in Memory of Ralph Allen.

The late lamented Prior Park Monument

providing a magnificent copy of a Palladian bridge, and although he may not have been an architect of great original talent, he had an eye for mass and effect that made the sham castle one of our most successful follies.

The 'castle' is two dimensional, Disneyesque even. Two 'round' towers are, in fact, semicircular, and the smaller square towers at each end of the façade offset the bulk of the central gatehouse. The whole edifice, with its blank windows and blank arrowslits, looks blindly out over Bath. It is no more than 40ft (12m) high and 100ft (30m) long, and its air of cardboard frivolity and excellent state of preservation make it seem like part of a recently abandoned film set, rather then a building two and a quarter centuries old.

Prior Park itself we have not seen after it was restored in the late 1990s, but there was

of the grotto has now been excavated. Priory Lodge, near the house, is in a very decent Gothic.

Pinch's Folly in Bathwick Street is a baroque gateway leading, like the sham castle, nowhere. The story goes that it was built in 1853 by a builder's merchant called William Pinch, who wanted to stop coal carts making a short cut into his yard. Its style, however, suggests that it is the re-erection of an entrance gateway from a forgotten house.

The area is certainly rich in follies. Pevsner mentions the Sydney Hotel, which in the 19th century had a sham castle in the grounds, cast-iron Chinese bridges, umbrellos—the whole panoply of Victoriana in any half-decent vauxhall. In Sydney Road is the Bath Spa Hotel—it used to be Vellore House—where General Augustus Andrews dreamed of the Vellore, Madras, he had

The Palladian Bridge at Prior Park

quite a lot still there, albeit in ruins, when we visited it in the late 1980s. Of course, the famous Palladian bridge, some way down the grandiose grassy downhill sweep towards town, is the only reason why Prior Park is ever mentioned—always in connection to the triumvirate of bridges at Wilton House, Stowe and Prior Park. The triangular Gothick tower monument to Ralph Allen, erected by Bishop Warburton, was demolished in 1953, and lots of other features have also disappeared. But the remains of Pope's grotto (he had a hand in it), which had a statue of Moses on its top, are still here, although there is only a tufa arch, and the brick, classical sham bridge nearby was in a bad way. Apparently, the mosaic floor

earlier left. In the 1850s Andrews had a grotto built in his garden, costing more than £1000. The grotto is a very rough, spiky long chamber, which was, as anyone taking notice of the date it was erected must have already guessed, used as a fernery and has water flowing in it. The new owners of the hotel originally wanted to bulldoze the lot, but went through a Saint Paul conversion after Dave Ellis of Acorn Renovations drew their attention to it.

Southeast of Bath is Crowe Hall, with a 19th-century (1860 has been mentioned) rough stone grotto in the hill. It is furnished with stone steps and tunnelling, shells and the grotto-fossil *par excellence* in these parts, ammonites—this kind of decoration is rare for such a youngish grot.

In the centre of town is a minimal grot, the 18th-century antithesis of the romantic grotto. It is more of a chamber or two in the stone banks along the Avon but associated with… we can't remember. Was it John Gay? Was it the one Pevsner says is in the garden of 14 North Parade? And what was that thing we saw in the distance? Oh, for our long lost notes! Found them: it is Sheridan's grotto, at North Parade Bridge. It is more of an alcove where love letters were left by Sheridan for his lady friend(s)—and vice-versa—to be collected later.

For William Beckford's follies, which are mainly in Lansdown, see that entry below.

Batheaston (Somerset)

Batheaston Villa (1765)
ST 772 672

Two miles east of Bath, on a hill overlooking the river Avon, an Irish heiress, Lady Miller, built a house from which she intended to launch herself upon Society. Horace Walpole described her villa and grounds as 'a very diminutive principality with large pretentions'. One of the charming pretentions is a Bath stone rotunda in the form of a classical 8-column temple. Batheaston Villa was famous in the 1770s for its poetry contests in this domed-roofed *tempietto*. A partial exedra exists to the N. of the temple making an informal viewing gallery.

Bridgwater

Castle House (1851)
ST 300 370

Castle House is a showcase for the uses of concrete. It must have been built by someone who was promoting the sullen material, much like the terracotta fantasies one sometimes encounters. Castle House is magnificently ugly, decorated with what looks like breezeblocks and with the walls in imitation stonework and spiky concrete castellations on top. The interior details are mostly also in poured concrete. Last heard of, the Somerset Building Preservation Trust was looking for sponsors from the concrete industry to preserve this bizarre house. We hope they succeed—there's nothing else like it. Its equivalent in iron is the Chateau de Fer in Ath, Belgium, which was built as a showcase for the uses of cast-iron panels, and it vies with Castle House in ugliness.

Brislington (Avon)

Black Castle (1764)
Arnos Gateway (1769)
ST 630 710

A folly converted into a pub is a mixed blessing. On the one hand, its preservation is ensured and one can get a drink; on the other, it loses the mystique of the true folly because the design departments of the breweries are irresistibly tempted to turn the whole thing into ye olde medieval theme pub, with age-blackened plastic beams and

The Black Castle , Brislington

other fitments as remote from historical accuracy as was the original building.

The Castle Inn at Radway, Worcestershire, is an important folly because it was one of Sanderson Miller's earliest works; the Ship On Shore in Sheerness, Kent, was originally built as an alehouse and has become a folly, but after The Grotto at South Shields (see Durham), Brislington's Black Castle is perhaps the strangest of them all. To begin with, it is much larger, more obtrusive and more bizarre than the others. Then again it is built out of this extraordinary spelter slag, a type of purplish-black stone, which looks as if it has been boiled. These are cut blocks of the slag left from copper smelting, and, being strong, light and impermeable, they make an excellent building material.

The Black Castle sits in confused perplexity in the middle of an industrial estate on the outskirts of Bristol, surrounded by cars, lorries and cash 'n' carries. William Reeve, another Quaker copper smelter, like William Champion (see Warmley, Gloucestershire), built it as the stables to his house at Arnos Court in the 1760s (one of its pinnacles bears the date 1764). Incongruous though this black and white castle looks in its present surroundings, it was so out of place in rural Brislington in the 18th century that the startled Horace Walpole called it the Devil's Cathedral, a name by which, together with Arnos Castle, it is still known. It is a famous folly, and yet, and yet… it was built for a purpose, it has been in continual use for well over 200 years, it was remarkably cheap to build, because the material used in its construction was free, an otherwise useless by-product, and there is no sign that the fabric is deteriorating. None of the classic parameters apply in this case, although it is indisputably a folly. It is thought to have been built for Reeve by James Bridges, but it does have striking similarities to Ralph Allen's 1762 Sham Castle in Bath (see above), which was conceived by Sanderson Miller in 1755 but actually designed and built by Richard Jones in 1762. Which influenced which?

Mr Reeve built several other little 'conceits' on his estate, which is now bisected by the A4. The best of these was the bath house, now safely preserved at Portmeirion, Sir Clough Williams-Ellis's home for distressed gentlebuildings. The elaborate gateway still gets its daily shaking from the A4 juggernauts and still stands bravely up to it. It adjoins Junction Road, which leads to the Black Castle, and to passing travellers no doubt looks authentically medieval. Reeve, so Mike Jenner informs us, bought two medieval statues in 1769 and either the gateway must have been already there or they were meant as features in the yet to be erected folly. The statues came from the genuinely medieval Lawford's Gate in Bristol. In 1770 he added another couple that came from Newgate Prison. Arnos Gateway remained unfinished because of Reeve's bankruptcy in 1774. The gate was moved in 1911 for a road widening scheme, and the fact that everyone believed it to be the real thing saved the building. The gate was restored in 1994, and replicas of the statues were set in its niches (in 1898 the figures had been removed to St Nicholas's Church).

Broomfield

The Folly (19th century)
ST 222 321

At Fyne Court two embattled small, round towers, coupled by a wall (collectively called The Folly), survived the fire that destroyed the house in 1894, obliterating most of the scientific experiments held here by Andrew Crosse (1784–1855), who is said to have been the inspiration for Dr Frankenstein. Most of his direct family having died, Crosse was left with Fyne Court in 1805 and began a solitary life mainly investigating electricity and its phenomena (although he eventually got married, he never took to it, even though he fathered seven children and married for a second time). Crosse was denounced by the local rector as a wizard, and Mary Shelley got to hear of his experiments and used Crosse's reputation in her 1818 book. The two towers may have been used in Crosse's atmospheric electricity trials. Nowadays they house bats, which is just how Bela Lugosi would have liked it.

Bruton

Chequers Towers (late 18th century)
ST 686 325

A very good eyecatcher gateway crosses a path at Pitcombe, the result of a proposed visit of King George III to nearby Redlynch House. For the occasion, the owner of Redlynch wanted to alter the somewhat pedestrian approach to his house, and he built himself this gateway at a site called Chequers: two round towers with castellations (of course), quatrefoils and pointed and traceried windows and doors,

Chequers Towers

flanking the pointed and embattled arch, with heraldic devices added to it. So much money was poured into this rich decoration that no money was left to lay out the new drive to pass through, so the gateway was never used. Henry Flitcroft produced designs for Redlynch House around 1755, but that seems much too early for the gateway.

Grotto (1990s)
ST 720 390

Cannwood Farm belongs to Andy and Polly Garrett and he and the designer Julian Bannerman have created a great grotto, constructed from burr elm, which makes an amazing natural gargoyle. It looks rather like an enormous, scruffy and overgrown tree stump in a sort of round room-shape, with new trees growing within the structure. Inside are flints and ammonites and there is actually a stove with a little chimney, so you feel you have just entered fairy wonderland.

Brympton

The Alcove (1723)
ST 520 150

Brympton D'Evercy house is built of Ham stone, and it is difficult to imagine any more beautiful building material when looking at Brympton in the late afternoon sun. In the garden on the west front is a peculiar, useless little building built from older assorted parts—an archway and a tiny belfry—it looks at once like a lych gate, a dovecote and a summerhouse. On the other hand, it looks so natural in its setting, so at peace with its environment that it could not be bettered. Known as The Alcove, its function as a shelter seems purposeless when the house is

only 20 yards (18m) away. Like most good follies, it is beautiful, useless and pleasurable.

Burrow Bridge

Burrow Mump Sham Church (18th century)
ST 35 30

The hills and views of central and west Somerset diminish to the southeast into a flat, fertile plain, relieved occasionally by peculiar island-like lumps in a green and yellow sea. Islands they were: at one time nearly the whole area was water or marshland and mumps such as Glastonbury Tor were genuine islands. A child spending holidays in Somerset in the 1950s remembers feeling a little cheated that the tower of St Michael's Church on Glastonbury Tor was not a folly. It had all the necessary attributes, except it is genuine. Luckily, 10 miles and 200 years away

Burrow Mump Sham Church

someone else felt the same way. Although Burrow Mump at Burrow Bridge lacks the grandeur and sheer size of Glastonbury Tor, it still rises almost as abruptly out of the flat surrounding countryside, and it still has the stepped ridges encircling the hill, gouged out, it is said in Glastonbury, by the tail of the dragon defeated by King Gwyn long before recorded time. It seems they had a second bout at Burrow Mump. But Burrow Mump, unlike Glastonbury, didn't have a tower, an irresistible challenge to an 18th-century Englishman. There had been a church here, but it was destroyed in 1655 when Royalist troops held it as a fortress. Like Glastonbury, it was dedicated to St Michael. Work started on repairing it in 1724 and again in 1793, but it never saw completion, although the ruined parts were carefully accentuated and capped. Major A.G. Barrett gave it to the National Trust in 1946, as a memorial to the men and women of Somerset who died in World War II.

Galleon's sterns on the Hood Monument

Butleigh

Hood Monument (1831)
ST 502 316
Obelisk (1852)
ST 502 317

In Yorkshire there is a column to Admiral Keppel, who was courtmartialled after the Battle of Ushant. In Somerset—never outdone—there is a column to the memory of Admiral Sir Samuel Hood, who falsified his ship's log and testified against Keppel. Hood's monument was built nearly 50 years after Keppel's, in 1831, by William Beckford's protégé, H.E. Goodridge. It stands in Butleigh Wood, south of Street. Once there was a way up to the top from where there would have been remarkable views to Glastonbury Tor, but now the entrance has been traditionally blocked up. On our visit we could dimly make out the shape of a galleon's stern at the top of the column. We were above cloud level and visibility was poor, but what was seen was seen to be good. The galleon's stern is said by those who have seen the monument on clearer days to be merely a stone shield, but we prefer, for an

admiral's sake, to see it in the mist.

Nearby, in Copley Wood, is a small, pinkish, stone obelisk, which was built in 1852 or thereabouts to record a hunting accident. It takes a long time to find, even with the help of the Ordnance Survey map, and is eventually not worth the finding, because we are going to tell you the inscription in full:

HERE FELL

MORTALLY WOUNDED

BY THE ACCIDENTAL DISCHARGE OF A GUN

WHILE SHOOTING WITH SOME FRIENDS

OCTOBER 30th 1852

HUNGERFORD COLSTON D.C.L.

ONLY SON OF

WILLIAM HUNGERFORD D.D.

RECTOR OF WEST LYDFORD

THIS OBELISK ERECTED

BY HIS ONLY SISTER

Chantry

Grotto (late 18th century)
ST 720 470

A grotto to smoke opium in, or at least that was what the local gossip presumed when the 'disreputable owners' of Chantry House built their grotto in the 18th century. Some of it has collapsed, but the thing is a little wonder: water flowed through it and it is still quite a complex structure, a set of arched colonnades, with dark tunnels and several rooms. The rough stone grotto could, indeed, be of the period mentioned, but the house dates from around 1825 and was built by James Fussell, an iron-master.

Cheddar

Rowland's Tower (1906)
ST 570 540

The best view of Cheddar Gorge is supposedly from the metal tower at the top of the 322 steps that constitute Jacob's Ladder, a tower built by the entrepreneur Rowland Pavey. The entrepreneurial spirit still survives and they charge for the climb. We bought a postcard instead and later regretted it, as Rowland Pavey turned out to be an interesting man: he owned several of Cheddar's tourist attractions but was also an adept of water divining and 'published a book explaining his methods of unassisted flight and demonstrated this to an expectant crowd by jumping off Pulpit Rock on several occasions, always fortunately landing in the trees below'.

Cheddon Fitzpaine

Hestercombe Mausoleum (18th century)
Witch House
`ST 250 280`

Hestercombe, northeast of Cheddon, is
known for its Lutyens garden. Our interest,
however, goes out to Hestercombe's startling
mausoleum in another part of the grounds,
which was designed by Somerset's own
Sanderson Miller, Coplestone Warre
Bampfylde (1719–91), owner of Hestercombe,
amateur architect and painter. Bampfylde was
a friend of Stourhead's Henry Hoare, and he
erected an urn to both Hoare and Charles
Tynte of Halswell House. He was also
influenced by a visit to the Leasowes. In 1761
the following features were recorded:
Cascades, a Root House, an Octagonal
Summerhouse, a Chinese Seat and a Gothic
Seat, a Witch or Root House, a Tent and the
Mausoleum.

Hestercombe is another successful valley
garden, like Hackfall or Hawkstone. The
buildings have all suffered neglect and
damage, some have completely disappeared,
but since 1995 sterling work has been
undertaken by Philip White to restore the
18th-century pleasure grounds. The arched
mausoleum is of brick with vermiculated
rustication and topped by a pyramid with an
urn. The Doric temple was added in 1786, and
the Witch House is being restored at the time
of writing. Other features will no doubt follow.

Chew Magna (Avon)

Chota Castle (1848–64)
Chew Tower (c.1770)
`ST 570 630`

Also known as Chew Manor, this is a 17th- and
18th-century house, with castellated additions
in 1848 and 1864, the latter by John Norton.
The house is called a folly, but wrongly so.
The real folly, the castellated Chew Tower of
c.1770, to the south of Chew Magna has been
submerged in the Chew Valley Lake,
according to Barbara Jones, but another
source claims it is still there, to the north, on
Dundry Hill. We discovered this reference too
late to hunt it out for this edition.

Chewton Keynsham (Avon)

Wolery or Owl Hoot (early 20th century)
`ST 650 650`

Wolery is the local patois for Owlery, which
is pleasant. It is, however, more usually
known as the Owl Hoot or Owl's Tower at

Chewton Owl Hoot

Chewton Place, one of those follies that
bring the rocket to mind. It is leaning
daringly over the river beside it and may fall
at any moment or, as is the way with such
things, only in the next two or three
centuries. Built by an untrained hand, it is
tall, with corner buttresses, a pointed
entrance and lots of small windows,
apparently for the owls to nest in, but
inhospitable nevertheless. Heated
discussions went on as to when this was
built, and we now veer towards the above
date. It comes with a small rockery.

Chilton Polden

Chilton Priory (1840)
`ST 380 400`

Cock Hill, a National Trust property on the
road from Street to Bridgwater, overlooks
Sedgemoor, the site of the last battle fought
on British soil, between Monmouth and
James II in 1685. On the north side of the
hill, set slightly below the road, is an
immaculately kept sham church, originally
built for the antiquarian William Stradling as
a house in the first half of the 19th century
(possibly by either John Westlake
Wainwright or the craftsman William
Halliday). Still a private house, its only
drawback is its proximity to the main road.
On a clear day the view is spectacular; you
can see across smoky Bridgwater and the
motorway to—if you look in the right

direction—a village called Goathurst, 9 miles away as the crow flies (see below).

Combe Florey

Winter's Folly (1790)
ST 150 320

Winter's Folly in Combe Florey was, legend goes, used by Henry VIII to imprison one of his more recalcitrant wives. The truth, sadly, is more prosaic, but still vaguely unsatisfactory. It was built in the late 18th century as a keeper's cottage, probably by John Francis Gwyn, the grandson of 'Rotchester's Gwine'. But if that was the case, why build it five storeys high and make it look, as Jeboult said in 1873, like 'a very debased attempt to represent a church tower'? The building is, sadly, rather ugly, except for the colour of the red stone used in parts of its construction. Above the front door is an arched window with a trefoil on a wooden batten, but the rest of the fenestration is utilitarian cottage casement.

It was obviously used as a house. When we first visited there was a large fireplace on the ground floor, plastering on the walls and remnants of room partitions on the first and second floors and part of a staircase. The top three storeys were rendered, and inside, the top two showed no sign of even having had floors. So why build so high? By the time Mr Jeboult visited, 'the tenants seemed ignorant for what purpose this unseemly tower was erected'. His exasperation shines through

Winter's Folly

bright and clear.

A brick on the ground marked 'W. Thomas and Co. Wellington' would date the tower to the first half of the 19th century.

Since the conversion of the tower from a ruin to a house in 1990 more information has come to light, although we are still left with two conflicting stories: it was built by John Winter in 1790, either as a hunting lodge and banqueting house or (and we prefer this) in order to spy on his neighbours, the Lethbridges, in Sandhill Park, with whom Winter frequently engaged in legal battles, which cost up to £20,000 in lawyer's fees. Unfortunately for the developer, his project coincided with the worst recession Britain suffered until the 1930s, so the tower sagged on the market, the price falling by dribs and drabs until it was finally sold for less than it cost to restore. An awful warning to would-be developers of follies.

Cothelstone

Seat (early 19th century)
Tower (early 19th century)
ST 180 320

Getting lost in the Quantock or Brendon Hills in midsummer without a timetable to keep must be close to heaven. The follies at Cothelstone, Elworthy, Combe Florey and Crowcombe are good places to get lost near. Cothelstone is the strangest of the four: two tiny follies, no more than a hundred yards apart, on a ridge overlooking the vale of Taunton Deane. One is an astonishing half-headless figure, with half an upraised arm, perched on top of an alcove seat positioned for contemplating the view. No one seems to know what it was supposed to represent.

The other is breathtakingly beautiful, by accident rather than by design, for the beacon tower that stood here has now collapsed to a paltry 10–15ft (3–4.6m) in two piles of masonry, overshadowed by a well-shaped Scots pine. Lancelot Brown could not have contrived a better landscape.

Crowcombe

Sham Ruin (late 18th century)
ST 140 370

On private land behind Crowcombe Court is a part sham, part genuine ruined castle of sandstone and ironstone. The genuine Gothic fragments were taken in the late 18th century from the demolished chapel of Halsway Manor, just up the combe. It owes its continued existence rather more to the binding of undergrowth than mortar, and now the estate has been parcelled off, its future is uncertain.

Curry Rivel

Burton Pynsent Steeple (1765)
ST 991 441

Burton Pynsent Steeple is a deservedly famous folly. It is large, it crumbles, it has a suitably spectacular setting, its purpose was properly pointless, and it has an amusing story attached to it. A Tuscan column with the obligatory drum and urn on top, it was built in 1765 by Lancelot Brown to the instructions of Sir William Pitt, who was so admired by Sir William Pynsent that he left him his estate. Pitt, who never met his benefactor, returned the compliment by leaving us this 140ft (43m) column: 'Sacred to the Memory of Sir William Pynsent. Hoc saltem Fungam inani munere.'

After the exploits of a cow in the late 1940s, it is no longer possible for us to enjoy the view from the top of the column. Barbara Jones wrote that a cow twice managed to climb the spiral staircase to the top, and was shooed down backwards. (How did the cowherd ever get past her?) The third time, as in all good rural legends, she managed to get to the top and fell off the parapet. The door was then blocked up. Nowadays it is as much for our protection as the cows'. The masonry at the top of the tower is jutting out dangerously, and urgent work needs to be

Burton Pynsent Steeple

carried out to preserve this wonderful, archetypal folly column.

Dulverton

Tower (late 18th century)
SS 937 286
Pepperpot Castle (early 19th century)
SS 989 288

A once-castellated round tower, of rough stone and traces of plaster, has a pointed door but no windows. This tower is situated in a dense plantation of Norway spruces, in Pixton Park, along the River Barle at Louisa Gate, and it may have been intended as either a shelter or an eyecatcher. Nearby is Lady Harriet's Drive, 'constructed in honour of the great bravery of Lady Harriet Acland who rescued and looked after her wounded husband, Colonel Acland, when he was captured by the French during the war in America'. And Louisa Gate appears to come from Lousy Gate, which means pigsty in Somerset-ese.

The Dulverton tower earns its points through its dismal appearance and utter loneliness. Pepperpot Castle near Upton comes top of the list however, because of its design and cheeriness. It is one of these follies on a triangular ground plan, rendered white, with slender-looking hexagonal towers on its corners, with lancet windows and pointed windows in its core. Oh, and we nearly forgot the castellated part. Jutting out from the connecting walls are low, bungaloid extensions, a necessity and something one could get used to. Pepperpot Castle used to be plain Haddon Lodge and acted as lodge to the above mentioned Lady Harriet Acland's Drive, which went all the way from Pixton Park where her daughter lived, through Haddon Hill along the River Haddon and on to Wivelscombe, where Lady Acland lived in widowhood from 1778 to 1815.

Dunster

Conygar Tower (1775)
Folly Arch (1775)
Jardin Imaginaire (20th century)
SS 991 441

Dunster is very much a National Trust interpretation of an estate village, quaintly pretty with the castle perched over it, a middle class bastion against the encroachment of the cheap and cheerful holiday resort of Minehead. The castle of the Luttrells, improved by Salvin, is well hidden, however, and the most obvious landmark in the village is the folly tower on the holly-decked Conygar Hill. It is a hollow, circular tower, 66ft (20m) tall and 26ft (8m) in diameter, designed purely as an eyecatcher by the artist Richard Phelps for Henry Fownes Luttrell, at a cost of £75 11s 0½d. Accounts were carefully kept: £4 2s 6d was

Conygar Hill Tower

allocated for scrumpy for the builders, and a further £2 5s to 'An Entertainment' for them when it was completed. As a piece of architecture it is unexceptional; as an eyecatcher it is magnificently successful, visible from miles around.

A further surprise awaits the explorer on Conygar Hill. Apart from the risk of falling down one of the abandoned quarries buried in the berried undergrowth, there stands at the western end of the escarpment another work for Fownes Luttrell, a splendid and substantial sham ruined gateway, two arches still standing, curtain walling, round bastions, all beautifully mantled in ivy and elegant in its forgotten decay—the folly and the ivy.

The village nestles at the foot of Conygar Hill, and as we come down St George's Street there is a delightful *jardin imaginaire* behind Spears Cross Hotel. On a steep bank above the lawn are at least 25 model houses, the majority half-timbered, with two churches of wildly differing scales, and a rather token representation of a castle. The overall effect is delightfully surprising, the more so because no real attempt has been made at verisimilitude.

East Cranmore

Tower (1863–65)
ST 690 440

There was a very dilapidated, tall, square, Italianate tower at East Cranmore, built between 1863 and 1865 by W.H. Wyatt for John Moore Paget. Cranmore Tower peers above the trees to the north of the A361, deceptively close to the road. The climb to the tower up a green lane in the hamlet of Dean is invigorating, but allow yourself an hour to get there and back. From a short distance, the tower looked well preserved; it's only when you are right up close that its dereliction became apparent. The tower is much bigger than expected, at least 100ft (30m) tall, and the facing stones on the east side had sheared off in bulk, leaving huge areas of exposed fabric from the base to just under the top. Still roofed, the top of the tower looks deceptively solid from a distance. Inside, the greater part of the wooden staircase survives. It was very sturdily built, and only total neglect has allowed it to decay to this extent, but to climb it now needed a degree of stupidity we thankfully do not possess. In 1984 a Glastonbury farmer bought it with the intention of restoring it and opening it to the public, at the same time building himself a four-bedroomed house at the base. The local newspaper gleefully seized on this and headlined it 'Mr Beaton's Folly'. It remains a good, creepy folly, a totally unnecessary building.

Cranmore Tower

East Harptree (Avon)

Tunnel and Grotto (early 19th century)
ST 570 550

At Harptree Court are stretches of tunnelling, clad in stone blocks, that lead you to a Hermit's seat, a waterfall and a grotto. Furthermore there is a reproduction rotunda temple and an ice-house. The tunnelling was uncovered only in 1991, having been blocked up by a previous owner. Date unknown, but the house was largely changed, so it appears, in 1802–4 and the Bath architect Charles Harcourt Masters also designed a new park in 1802 (he may have built the house as well). It all sounds rather delicious, but we have not yet seen it.

Elworthy

Willett Tower (1820)
ST 095 335

The last of the Quantock Quartet is another sham church tower, this time on Forestry Commission land and blessed with views to equal those from Hardy's Monument in Dorset. To be geographically accurate, Willett Tower is on the Brendon Hills, but it doesn't have the Exmoor mood. It is visible from miles around, is clearly marked on the maps and is impossible to find once you start walking. A good brisk walk from the bottom of the hill—and what looked suspiciously like a red squirrel darting past—and we eventually came out of the gloomy alien conifers through a low encircling wall into the cheerful alien rhododendrons.

The folly itself is built of the local slatey stone with red mortar and red brick trimmings, which give the whole tower a red sandstone appearance. It looks like a cardboard church tower; an effort to bring Glastonbury to Elworthy. It was built in 1820 by a Mr Belmerton, a member of the Blommart family, probably as an eyecatcher to be seen from Willett. The wooden staircase inside was probably installed later to take advantage of the view or to look out for forest fires. Enid Byford, however, has another origin for the tower: it was erected in 1774 by subscription, with a Mr Bernard, Lord of the Manor of Crowcombe, coughing up £80 of the required £130. But why would several people club together to pay for what is so evidently a folly, not a memorial?

Four Forks

Agapomene Chapel (mid-19th century)
ST 233 370

At a certain point in his career, the Rev. Henry James Prince went ape. Prince was the curate at Charlinch, and while the parish priest, the Rev. Samuel Starkey, was away for a while, Prince discovered that he was actually the reborn Messiah himself and informed the church-goers accordingly. This and the rest of the remarkable story is told by Enid Byford in *Somerset Curiosities*. Soon Prince found himself with a new congregation, Starkey among them. He married the incumbent's sister, Julia, and things started to get even better as wealthy women began to flock to the fake Messiah. With the proceeds Prince built the Abode of Love, Agapomene, a religious commune with a grand house, summer houses, cottages and a chapel, installing expensive furnishings in the chapel as well as a billiards table and comfy chairs. From now on Prince was known as 'The Beloved', and he revelled in the female attention he got. After impregnating several of his female followers, Prince died in 1899, presumably with a smile on his face. The community survived to receive, three years later, a new Messiah—also a soon-to-be-ex-cleric—and things went on much as before. By 1958 the commune had died out, and the property was sold off and divided into flats. Much of Agapomene still stands and the nearby Lamb Inn has information on it.

Willett Tower

Frome

Jardin Imaginaire (20th century)
ST 775 497

A *jardin imaginaire* usually disappears once its builder and owner is no more, but this is still here, at 2 Mount Pleasant, south of Frome centre. It was started by a Mr Hall and is kept in order by the present owners—it is all the jumble one would like, not only models of houses and churches, but also incongruous pieces of statuary and the usual indefinables.

Goathurst

Halswell Follies (18th century)
ST 260 340

The big house at Goathurst is called Halswell. It is not a beautiful building, but it is large and rambling, and from the hill above it gives the impression more of a small village than a private house. The fabric is dilapidated and neglected. The owner has divided the house into flats; the estate hums with life as the old house dies. The residents of Halswell love it; they are attached to its ugliness, its amorphousness and, certainly not least, its exquisite setting. They deeply regret the landlord's indifference to the maintenance of the building, and they share a delight and interest in the remarkable profusion of garden ornaments scattered around the estate. There is no building that

on its own would really qualify as a folly, but the sustained building over a period of years, the stories that have built up around them and the stifled, overgrown atmosphere of the estate make Halswell a major folly group.

'What chiefly attracts the notice and attention of strangers are the decorated grounds,' wrote Arthur Young in 1768, and he lists the following structures that are still to be found: a Doric Rotunda, a temple to Robin Hood, the cascade with bridge, bench and tablet, and an Ionic Portico. Also still extant but not mentioned by Young are a grotto, a stepped pyramid and an unusual bell-roofed dovecote. Most of these were built by Sir Charles Tynte, or Kemeys-Tynte. The Doric Rotunda stands hidden in an overgrown wood to the east of the house, apparently covering an ice-house, still elegant, still intact, but the lead has recently been stolen from the domed roof and decay is inevitable.

Robin Hood's Temple, a wonderful name for a disappointing building, is slowly collapsing at the top of the hill above the house. What remains is a plain oblong building with a ridiculous, 1930s, Bletchley-style central chimneypot and two ogival windows flanking a ruined circular or semicircular prospect room. The views are magnificent, looking across the Bristol Channel to South Wales; it was obviously intended as a dining room with a view. The

Robin Hood's Temple

right-hand window is blanked off and the room behind seems to have been a kitchen. The servants were not distracted from their duties by sharing the prospect. The element of surprise, so beloved of folly builders, seems to have been the thinking behind Robin Hood's Temple. The approach was evidently intended to be made from the back through the woods and up to the great door covered with rustic bark. Arthur Young, who was also an agriculturalist, wrote about the new plantations to the south of the house 'from a dark part of which you enter through a door into a temple dedicated to Robin Hood, upon which a most noble prospect breaks upon the beholder'.

In contrast the cascade, some way over to the west, is still impressive. Five lakes at different levels start from a weird array of alcoves at the highest level, under a rock carved inscription:

> *When Israel's wandering Sons the Desert trod*
> *The melting Rock obeyed the Prophet's Rod*
> *Forth gushed the Stream, the tribe their thirst allayed*
> *Forgetful of their God, they rose and played.*
> *Ye happier swains for whom these waters flow*
> *Oh may your Hearts with grateful Ardours flow.*
> *Lo! here a Fountain streams at his command,*
> *Not o'er a barren, but a Fruitful land*
> *Where Nature's choicest gifts the valleys fill*
> *And smiling Plenty gladdens every Hill.*

An ornate bridge crosses the lake at the second cascade with two statues, one with an absurd false chin, and a new retaining wall, which looks as if it was bought off the shelf at the local garden centre. By the bottom lake is the Ionic Temple, which was built in 1767 and attributed to Robert Adam but is now roofless and appropriated by cows as a makeshift shed. Confusion sets in here, as Pevsner maintained that this temple has been re-erected in Sir Clough Williams-Ellis's Portmeirion; but here it is, and Sir Clough denied having taken any building from Halswell. The Adam attribution comes from Colvin, but John Johnson the Elder is listed as having designed a Temple of Pan for Sir Charles Kemeys in 1788. There is no trace of this building, unless it has been confused with the Ionic Temple. Young describes it as an 'Ionic Portico' in 1768, so, as it was started the previous year, he probably

saw it in a half-built state. One of Halswell's present-day residents called it the Temple of the Virgins, while it has also been referred to as the Temple of Harmony. Could there be three names for the same building? If this is the case, then Johnson's design was never constructed.

More confusion arises over the dating of the stepped pyramid by the side of the house. It is not easily overlooked and cannot, therefore, have been built before Young's visit in 1768. The inscription on the side, now too badly worn to be legible, is said to have been written by Alexander Pope, who died in 1744. The lines on the tablet at the head of the cascade are in Pope's metre but lack his style. The impetus of the Egyptian revival would place the pyramid at *c.*1770, and if we ascribe it to Sir Charles's group we can only marvel at his eclecticism—Greek, Gothic, Egyptian and rococo within one park. The pyramid was built as a wellhead and now serves as a watertank.

At the back of the house there is a very large dovecote with a remarkable bell roof in an excellent state of repair, unlike the grotto in the wood near the rotunda, which is now so overgrown that it is impossible to see it properly. Once there were plaques, inscriptions and memorials affixed to it— one, discovered lying in the undergrowth, reads 'JIM. DIED DECEMBER 30TH 1903. HE WAS FAITHFUL TILL DEATH' and others commemorated a favourite canary and a chicken, but these have now disappeared. One memorial, vanished from Halswell but still existing, is a sarcophagus for a stallion which died winning a wager for its owner.

The Temple of Harmony before restoration

Hunstrete Arches

Until recently it survived in a nearby field; then a tractor knocked it over and the farmer removed it to his garden in North Newton. He had the inscription let into the floor of the changing room for his swimming pool.

Halswell Park lacks only a good prospect tower to make it one of the finest folly groups in southern England. A polygonal hermitage and a druid's temple of 1756 have completely vanished, but enough remains to satisfy nearly every taste. How much will remain for how long is much more of a worry; the owner's lack of interest and the already fragile structure of the follies can only hasten their demise. It would be a pity to lose them. Halswell is unique.

Since the foregoing was first written, things have started happening at Halswell. Slowly restoration work has begun and several of the problems of attribution have been solved: the Temple of Harmony is by Thomas Prowse, and Johnson's Temple of Pan is a farm building at nearby Patcombe, built in 1771 and intended as a bailiff's house. The grotto and some other buildings have also been attributed to Thomas Wright. The restorations started in 1984, when a local farmer and a solicitor bought the estate. But although initial protection was given to some structures, the rot appeared to be unstoppable. Now the Somerset Buildings Preservation Trust has taken over most of the buildings, and at last there is hope for the resurrection of the Halswell follies. Meanwhile the Temple of Pan has been bought by a speculative builder and has been 'restored' and put on the market. It now looks like one of those attempts at Georgian building one finds in things called The Close.

Hunstrete (Avon)

Unfinished Mansion (18th century)
ST 650 630

Hunstrete House off the A368 is now an elegant and expensive country house hotel. In a cornfield to the north stands a plain wall, pierced by five round-headed arches. It is all that is left of an enormous mansion planned by the owners of Hunstrete in the 18th century. The money ran out before the first rooms were properly finished, and the new house was never lived in. The arches stand in a golden field as an awful warning against profligacy.

Ilchester

The Bell Tower (late 18th–early 19th century)
ST 530 240

In Ilchester there is a boring structure to the west of the bridge in the middle of the town. Irrelevantly called The Bell Tower, it has no bells, nor is it a tower.

Ilminster

Lodges (c.1830)
ST 360 150

North of Ilminster, on Bay Hill, are two delightful Gothick gatehouses to Dillington, which were possibly built c.1830 when the house was altered.

Keighton Hill

Lodge (early 19th century)
ST 520 560

Just off the B3134, coming from Charterhouse and in the direction of Keighton Hill is this rather pleasing Gothic, embattled lodge-cum-farmhouse. The dogs were fierce, the drive pleasant, but nothing is known about the lodge.

Kelston (Avon)

Tower House (1835)
ST 700 660

Tower House—although Pevsner found its tower 'shockingly designed'—is hardly a folly. It was built for Joseph Neeld by the little known architect James Robert Thompson, who some say was a pupil of John Britton, while others say he was trained by J. B. Papworth—why not give our Mr Thompson the benefit of the doubt and have him connected with both these men. Thompson was certainly into towers and things high up, as he later probably worked at Vulliamy's office (Somerset Monument) and also, in 1841, designed a 'Doric column to the memory of Sir Walter Scott', which was not executed.

Tower House is in the Italianate manner so popular around Bath. The architect need, however, not detain us any longer, for we have a dishy anecdote. Joseph Neeld, a barrister, had just inherited almost £1 million from his great uncle. He started buying country houses in Wiltshire and had this one built when he was about to be married to Lady Caroline Ashley-Cooper. The marriage lasted for four days. Neeld kicked Caroline out of the house and moved in one mistress and one love child. Sadly, we do not know how the story ended—or we would have told you.

Kilmersdon

Ammerdown Column (1853)
ST 730 530

In Ammerdown Park the Eddystone Lighthouse stands safe from the pounding of the surf, the crash of the waves and the lonely sea mists—it is, as the seagull flies, 27 miles inland from the coast. Quite why the Ammerdown Park Column should have been a replica of the Eddystone Lighthouse is not clear. The designer was Joseph Jopling, an architect not noted for his marine work, and it was erected to commemorate 'the genius, the energy and the brilliant talents' of

Thomas Samuel Joliffe. A long inscription testifies to the 'profound affection' of the anonymous descendant who caused the column to be built, and in order that the point should not be missed, the same inscription is repeated in full in Latin and in French on the north and east sides.

The 150ft (45.6m) column was finished on 6 June 1853. Let's imagine it. A sunny, warm day. The glistening new tower stands surrounded by its low curlicued walls, its lantern tower sparkling in the sunlight. An apt inscription graces the lantern top, below the lightning conductor. Coade stone animals guard the four points of the compass on the plinth. The entrance door opens into a cool, square room with chamfered corners and marbled walls; the tower extends its foot into this room, so in order to climb the stone spiral staircase one enters through another doorway to the stair tower, an unusual and pleasing device. The staircase, regularly lit by ten tiny portholes, winds up to a splendid view from the glass lantern at the top.

Doubtless there is gaiety and celebration, and much gasping at the view—but one heart is black with envy. A Mr John Turner, whose lands abut the Joliffe Estate, goes home determined to outdo the Ammerdown Column. He waited a while though—building started only in the 1880s and was completed in 1890 (a chair in Hemmington Church bears the inscription 'presented to J. Turner Esq. on completion of the Eiffel

John Turner's truncated folly just prior to its total demolition in the 1960s

Tower 1890'). His square Italianate tower at 180ft (55m) topped Ammerdown by some 30ft (9m) and looked even higher, as it was extremely slender and tapered to the top, at which there was a chair (the one that is now in Hemmington Church?), but it was not to last. It was declared unsafe after being hit by lightning, and in 1910–11 a large proportion of it had to come down. Then, true to folly tradition, it was bought by Lord Hylton, the descendant of Thomas Joliffe, and was finally pulled down completely in 1969.

Kingsweston (Avon)

The Loggia (c.1714)
Brewhouse (18th century)
ST 540 770

John Vanbrugh worked here and designed, among others, a very neat classical building, almost Italian in flavour, the Loggia, as well as The Echo, a banqueting house of which now only the walls stand. Almost everything at Kingsweston had to do with the consumption of either liquids or solids—the enchanting Penpole Gate, a gazebo and 'breakfast lodge', was demolished in 1952, but the brewhouse or alehouse remains. Now that would have been a country house that *should* be made into a restaurant!

Knowle

Eyecatcher (c.1846)
ST 330 400

On the crest of the park of Knowle Hall, now the splendid British Institute for Brain Injured Children, was a small eyecatcher sham castle façade, one wall thick, but it has sadly gone, with only a few stone remnants lingering. The folly was built by Benjamin Cuff Greenhill, who had married for a second time in 1846, for his 19-year-old wife, Pelagie, daughter of the Comte de Breville, who looked from the sham castle towards the Bristol Channel in pretence that she looked over the English Channel to her former childhood home in France. The folly could be rebuilt, as a painting and postcards of it survive.

Lansdown (Avon)

Lansdown Tower (1825–26)
Blaine's Folly (1880s)
ST 730 670

Apart from Ralph Allen, Bath's other great folly builder was the extraordinary William Beckford of Fonthill Abbey notoriety. Shortly before Fonthill collapsed, he came to live in

Bath at 20 Lansdown Crescent, driven from his Gothic fantasy by relative poverty and scandal. Compared with Fonthill, his house was like a terraced house in Hackney as against Buckingham Palace, but he did manage to acquire a good-sized garden. Although not very wide, it stretched over a mile in length, all the way out of Bath to the village of Lansdown, where at the end of his garden the impoverished sybarite built himself a 154ft (47m) tower. Unlike Fonthill, this one did not collapse, and it is the finest surviving example of Beckford's work.

Built by his friend H.E. Goodridge in 1825–26, it begins as a very plain, straightforward square tower for about two-thirds of its height, its severity offset by the house, later converted into a mortuary chapel, at its foot. Then comes an

Lansdown Tower in the late 19th century

overhanging parapet, and above that are three still plain-glazed windows on each side. Above that Beckford and Goodridge allowed full rein to their imaginations and built a replica of the Lysicrates Monument in Athens, a favourite theme for folly builders. The columns here are of cast iron, and they have a bluish tinge against the rust red background of the rest of the lantern. At dusk, when the lights are on in the tower, the whole effect is quite chilling. The tower is open to the public in the summer. It is now part of the cemetery at its foot; both Beckford and Goodridge are buried there.

Before building Lansdown Tower Beckford kept his hand in by building an embattled gateway in the neo-Norman style and a Moorish summerhouse in the garden of No. 20, although strangely enough, he said that he did not care for the 'Saracen' style.

Heading north, past the Lansdown Racecourse, there is a small stone monument in a field on the right. To save your trek to investigate, it is not a folly but a war memorial to commemorate the Battle of Lansdown in 1643 and the Royalist leader Sir Bevil Grenville.

Blaine's Folly

Returning to the city limits of Bath, there is a beautiful 60ft (18m) Italianate tower in a field beside Kingswood School, the entrance blocked up, part of the balustrade on its top gone, and the roof collapsed. It is not beyond repair though, and certainly merits attention as it is not only a well turned out piece of architecture, but presents a good example of how the Italianate style remained fashionable (or at least in use) around Bath till late in the

century. The tower, built in the 1880s, is known as Blaine's Folly. Local man Robert Stickney Blaine was a philanthropist so we can safely assume that he was very rich as well. He had this campanile built by 250 workmen, who then proceeded to cultivate a nearby field.

A very good design for a classical rotunda or plain tower, on All Saints Road by Bath architect Edward Nash, was refused planning permission at Lansdown in 1991. It was to be a rather squat round tower, with a heavily rusticated base and a low octagonal roof with a gazebo topping. We hope it will find a site yet.

Long Ashton (Avon)

The Observatory (1922–c.1930)
ST 510 700

In Long Ashton, near Flax Burton (its more westerly mate), is a remarkably ugly house built by someone who knew exactly what he wanted and was quite prepared to sacrifice his aesthetic sensibilities to achieve it. Now called The Bungalow, but previously known as the Observatory, it is square and flat roofed, like the base of a wedding cake. Plonked in the centre of one side, the entrance porch sticks out and is capped with a pyramidal roof. On either side of it, perched on the corners, are round window rooms with absurd conical roofs, which don't even reach the ground floor roof level. Capping it all was a 360-degree glazed lantern with a dome and a weathervane. A foolish building indeed, the lantern being necessary to bring some light into the middle of the house because the walls are too long and the windows are too small for a square house to allow it to be lit naturally. It looks like an over-ambitious prefab.

Jonathan Holt found out that the Observatory was planned in 1922 by Thomas Twigg Humpage, a Bristol engineer and inventor (among his inventions were a new-fangled bike that never caught on and a safety razor that did catch on, but under another firm's name). The house came into being over several years, with Humpage using labour from his engineering works. As might be expected with a house like this, Humpage was keen on astronomy and kept a telescope in the dome. In 1997 the dome was taken down, and the owner is not planning to renew it. It will be a matter of only a year or two and this building will have gone—the owner is certainly keen on the site's potential.

Martock

Little Follys (1960s)
ST 460 190

Not a folly, despite the give-away name.
Richard England had a good name in the
county for the quality of his stonework, so
when it came to building himself a home, he
used his own skill and labour as well as any
spoils he could lay his hands on. The result
was a cottage near Martock that could satisfy
him and superficially looked like the
traditional 17th-century house typical of the
area. Shortly after it was finished he
discovered that it had been listed Grade II as
a fine example of a traditional 17th-century
house typical of the area.

Midford (Avon)

Roebuck's Folly (1775)
ST 750 620

Over the river from the pretty town of
Bradford-on-Avon is the small village of
Midford, where stands a private house called
Midford Castle. It is better known as
Roebuck's Folly, from a story that the present
owners say is completely untrue because it
first surfaced in a magazine over a hundred
years after the house was built. Nevertheless,
it is so plausible that it bears repeating. The
house is trefoil in plan, and the porch on the
east side completes its uncanny resemblance
from above to the ace of clubs. Why should
anybody build a house in the shape of the ace
of clubs?

The most satisfying explanation is that
Henry Woolhouse Disney Roebuck, an
inveterate gambler, staked £100,000 on the
turn of a card. The correct card was duly
turned up—it was the ace of clubs—and
young Roebuck, £100,000 the richer, went off
to build his folly to commemorate his mighty
success. Sadly for the story, a design for a
building very similar to Roebuck's Folly
appeared in *The Builder's Magazine* in 1775,
by an architect called John Carter, who is
generally credited with the building. The Rev.
John Collinson, in his *History and Antiquities
of the County of Somerset*, published 15 years
later, referred to it with admirable self-
restraint as a 'singular construction'; but had
he known of Carter's predilection for
surrounding himself with young female
acolytes dressed in boys' clothing he may
have had something more forceful to say.

In the grounds of the castle stands, just,
the Priory, a real folly but no match for the
talented eccentricity of the main house. As
one might expect, it was built as a gambling
den, and its design is attributed to the Knight
of Glin. Pevsner dismisses it as a
summerhouse, but now, increasingly ruinous,
it has acquired a sort of overgrown charm
and mystery, which makes one wonder
whether the old gambling stories didn't have
a ring of truth. Collinson, still thinking the
best, described it as having 'a commodious
tea-room with offices beneath'. A rustic
hermitage, which stood at the top of this

Roebuck's Folly

steeply sloping site, has disappeared. The Priory, ever more in a ruinous state, is not long for this world.

Montacute

St. Michael's Tower (1760)
ST 500 170

A real tower, one that can be seen for miles, is superbly placed on the top of the conical St Michael's Hill at Montacute, a National Trust property. It was built in 1760 on the site of the first Montacute Castle—never did a hill live up to its name more acutely. Don't take what looks to be the quickest way up unless you have crampons. Skirt round the wood at the

St. Michael's Tower

bottom of the steepest part of the hill and you will discover a track leading up to the flat hilltop and the tower. Here comes the first surprise: the tower is remarkably small for such a visible object, scarcely 40ft (12m) high. It is circular with a conical roof, not unlike an Irish round tower, but with peculiar fin-like protrusions at the top. Above the doorway is the legend is a Greek inscription with the date 1760. Then comes the second surprise: the doorway is not blocked up, the stairs are intact, and you may freely ascend to the top of the tower. A total of 52 steps bring you to a little room with four barred window

holes giving a view—Devon, Wales, Shaftesbury, Lyme Regis, 80 churches and a 300-mile circle—on the right day. The mystery of the strange protrusions is solved; they are the remnants of an external staircase, now thankfully inaccessible, to the flat roof where once there stood a flagpole as tall as the tower itself. Built unashamedly as a prospect tower, it pleases.

Nempnett Thrubwell (Avon)

Nempnett Needle (18th century)
ST 540 600

'Oh, you mean the Needle,' said the numbingly loquacious waitress. Having found someone who actually lived in the enchantingly named Nempnett Thrubwell, we were anxious to find out who built the obelisk, which we hadn't yet seen. But having found a couple who actually wanted to hear her talk, the waitress was not to be denied her opportunity. Midnight passed and still she talked, her sister in Canada, her son in Australia, our minds in the 18th century. No information was offered. But the Nempnett Needle is aptly though inversely named, as we discovered the following day. It is the plainest, unadorned, uninscribed obelisk; alien in its starkness, but with an inexplicable needle's eye at the pointed end. No one seems to know much—or care—about it.

Due north is the parish church of Dundry, its tower the absolute opposite to the simplicity of the Nempnett Needle, for it boasts a skeleton castle in all its fantastic detail on the top, a coronet resembling that of Gloucester Cathedral's. It's not a folly, quite the opposite; a church tower built with an ulterior motive in 1484 by the Merchant Venturers of Bristol—from the Bristol Channel the prominently placed tower is an unmistakable landmark.

Nether Stowey

Toll House (early 19th century)
ST 190 390

Lodges, toll houses, churches… we know they are not supposed to be follies, but sometimes they just are, and again sometimes they are not, but we nevertheless include them. The very good former toll house in Nether Stowey is one such: Gothick, with just the right mellowing to look as if it was a cast-off by Thomas Wright—but it is surely of a much later date, and as it is in the vicinity of Stowey Court, the owners might have had some say in the design.

Newton St Loe (Avon)

Eyecatcher (18th century)
`ST 700 640`

At Newton Park a recent clearing of the undergrowth has revealed an almost intact Lancelot Brown landscape. There are plans to rebuild a Gothick eyecatcher that was destroyed by a falling tree in the 1960s.

Oakhill

Rustic Cottages (late 18th–early 19th century)
`ST 635 472`

In the grounds of the Pondsmead Nursing Home two rustic cottages of some interest have been reported at the time of this book going to print, the one consisting of grotto-like rough stonework, the other has a small tree in or on its wooden door. Sounds very rustic.

Orchardleigh

Boathouse Temple (18th century)
Lodge (c.1816)
`ST 780 620`

The park of Orchardleigh House has partly been destroyed by the groundwork for two intended golf. The house itself went much, much earlier—in the mid-19th century—and was replaced by another. What remains is a now dry boathouse, temple on top. The temple is tetrastyle, but semi-derelict through vandalism and neglect. The unusualness of the ensemble is the large square in front of the temple—effectively the roof of the boathouse, now cracking up and bulging. There are corner blocks, which look as if they were meant to support something—but what? A statue on each? A wooden frame supports one side of the pediment, which is in danger of collapse, and there is a fireplace inside, but this, too, has been vandalized.

Orchardleigh was built by Sir Thomas Champneys, whom Lord Hylton called 'a lesser Beckford'. The Lullington gatehouse at the northeast corner of the estate has a touch of keeping up with the Jones's, for nearby Farleigh House also has a Gothic gatehouse, but nothing in comparison to Orchardleigh's extravaganza.

Pill (Avon)

Gazebo (1760s)
Sham Fort (18th century)
`ST 533 758`

On the banks of the Avon, in the grounds of Ham Green Hospital, is a hexagonal Gothick gazebo. It is built of rubble with dressed stone, spiky windows and entrance, and a very tame set of castellations, which look as if they have been renewed (a band of brick under them certainly has). The Bristol architect James Bridges has been suggested as the one responsible for designing it. Later on, in the early 19th century, the gazebo was used as a laboratory by Dr Richard Bright.

Another structure has made its appearance at Ham Green, almost in the water, but we don't know what it is. There are towers on each end of a wall with an alcove in it, but it does have a navigation light on top. It may be some very sensible nautical apparatus or it may be a mock fort.

Porlock

Tunnels (c.1835)
`SS 850 470`

William King, 1st Earl of Lovelace (1805–93), was Lord Lieutenant of Surrey for nearly 50 years. He married Byron's daughter and 'interested himself in agricultural and mechanical engineering', and he had two tunnels dug near the coastal path from Porlock Weir to Culbone Church in order to prevent unsightly tradesman in their disorderly vans and wagons from spoiling his uninterrupted view from Ashley Combe House to the sea. So they went in at the picturesque gatehouse, and their route would take them up to the house via the tunnels and past a little tower. The house itself was demolished after World War II. He repeated his theme at East Horsley Towers in Surrey (see there).

Stratton-on-the-Fosse

Sham Façade (1883)
Clock Tower (1903)
`ST 660 510`

At Stratton's Manor Farm at least one of the follies is connected with William Beauchamp, a local brewer. The other building has to do with Albert Edward, a visiting prince. Apparently the sham façade was at first in front of the house but later moved, and it gives the impression of being a superior garden shed, with its classical pediment on Doric columns. It also has the Prince of Wales's emblem, the date 1883 and his initials. It commemorates, of course, a visit of Albert Edward.

The clock tower is 20 years younger. It is built of sandstone and is 30ft (9m) high, with a filled-in arch on the ground floor and the

Street Folly

inscription 'WB 1903'. Here William Beauchamp's brewery bell used to hang, but it has gone now.

Street

The Folly (18th century–1957)
ST 480 360

On the outskirts of Street, where once the Bowlinggreen Factory stood, a classical portico in a field terminates an avenue of youngish trees. It comes from Westcombe House at Batcombe, which was demolished in the late 1950s. The owners of Messrs C. & J. Clark's shoe-works in Street moved it to its present location. The portico was re-erected in early 1957.

Walton-in-Gordano (Avon)

Walton Castle (1614–20)
ST 420 730

Walton Castle in Clevedon was built by John Poulett, a Puritan cavalier who hence lived in more interesting times than most. When he was MP for Somerset between 1614 and 1620 he built the castle, ostensibly as a hunting stand, but it is so conspicuously sited on a hilltop, looking out over the mouth of the Severn and across to South Wales, that it is difficult to imagine the site was not chosen with the view in mind—or with an eye to his escapades 20 years later with King and Parliament.

Collinson described the castle as 'octangular', which it certainly is: an octagonal curtain wall with round towerlets at each corner encloses an octagonal keep with an octagonal stair turret. By 1791 it was derelict, the roof and floors had fallen in, and the bailey was used as a dairy by a local farmer. Despite its exposed position, the structure remained, and remained controversial, so while Pevsner in 1957 could describe it as 'remarkable as a piece of ornamental planning', Barbara Jones called it 'not very exciting' in 1974.

Now the difference is astonishing. Walton Castle has been completely rebuilt and is a luxury home, a very desirable residence indeed, apart from the handicap of being surrounded by yet another featureless golf course. A young couple turned the crumbling shell into a unique and unusual house, and they are to be congratulated, not only for their taste but also for preserving one of the oldest follies in the country.

Walton Castle

West Camel

Parson's Steeple (1794)
ST 557 258

Quite inaccessible, this chimney-like object is among the trees on Camel Hill, marking the grave of Henry Parson, who refused to be buried in the churchyard and chose this remarkable monument to be erected and be buried under. Apparently the funeral itself was quite a spectacle.

West Horrington

Romulus and Remus Monument (1940s)
ST 571 489

Even gaolbirds succumb to the county's charms and show their thanks. On the left-hand side of the A39, about 2½ miles before Wells and opposite a tall television mast, is an extraordinary structure built into a low wall. Four square, shingled columns rise 8ft (2.4m) to support a rusticated pediment, on top of which stands a statue of Romulus and Remus suckling their she-wolf. It is a very small folly, but its siting and accessibility make it somehow memorable. The sculptor who made it was called Gaetano Celestra, a Roman prisoner-of-war who was not, as one might imagine, from the third century but from World War II.

Romulus and Remus by the roadside

Weston-super-Mare (Avon)

The Tower (1850s–60s)
ST 320 620

The Tower is a water tower, but do not fear, this one really is a beauty. It is located on Shrubbery Avenue in the area known as The Shrubbery, a site made popular by Sophia Rooke, a very determined and rather eccentric lady, of whom Archdeacon Law said: 'In this world there are two calamities—the Pope and Lady Rooke, and the latter is the greater evil.' Around 1847 Rooke built Villa Rosa (demolished in the 1960s) and installed a bear pit (no doubt for the archdeacon), had some tunnels dug, built a menagerie and eventually saw to it that a tower was built to supply water to The Shrubbery. The tower must have been erected as an eyecatcher belvedere, because it is a handsome, medievalizing edifice—three storeys high, octagonal, rubble with dressed stone, battlements, blind cruciform arrowslits and elongated lancet windows all around.

West Quantoxhead

St Audrie's Grotto (19th century)
ST 110 424

A small shell grotto house near the Gothick orangery at this former girls' school, now the Amitabha Buddhist Centre (Visitors Welcome), used to be kept locked, but the door has been broken down and ineffectual planks attempt to deter the casual visitor.

Inside St Audrie's Grotto

Astonishingly, the interior of the grotto is in a reasonable state of preservation: the shells are crisp and fresh, the colours still vibrant. There are five or six stalactites. whose ends have dropped (or been knocked) off, but here again one or two fortuitously survive intact. This is a great rarity; an unrestored grotto approaching middle age with her dignity intact, needing but a small amount of make-up, judiciously applied. She lacks the formal splendour of a duchess such as Goodwood, but her enchanting rusticity defines the innocent beauty to which all grottoes aspire.

Wivelscombe

Pinnacle (19th century)
ST 080 280

Viscount Boyd was fortunate enough to secure a 25ft (7.6m) pinnacle from Westminster Abbey and have it re-erected in his garden.

Worle (Avon)

Worle Observatory (19th century)
ST 350 620

Worle Observatory was built in the most economical way for an observatory to be built—by adapting an existing tower, in this case a windmill. But to observe or be observed? Faced with white stucco and prominently castellated, it can be seen from all over Weston-super-Mare. It was converted from a windmill in the early 19th century and was given an onion dome roof 'to make it look like Brighton Pavilion', says the present owner, who looks after it lovingly. He re-roofed it with a flat roof several years ago, the dome having collapsed many years before, and the police have now installed a radio transmitter in it, so finally the old windmill has a use again.

Wrangway

Wellington Monument (1817–52)
ST 135 172

The Wellington Monument is familiar to travellers on the M5. This huge obelisk, designed by Thomas Lea Junior in 1817 (but only completed in 1852, to a changed design), dominates the Black Down Hills, which separate Devon from Somerset. It is difficult for us nowadays to realize the adulation given to Wellington at that time. He was a Mandela, a Schumacher and a Diana rolled into one, and he seemed to be well aware of it. He permitted the burghers of Wellington to record the memory of his spectacular military exploits by building this 175ft (53m) obelisk,

now preserved by the National Trust, and embellished with a spiral staircase leading to a tiny chamber at the top. On a clear, preferably windless day the view alone is worth the journey.

Yeovil

The Obelisk (18th–19th century)
ST 559 129
The Fish Tower (18th–19th century)
ST 555 143
The Cone (18th–19th century)
ST 563 142
Jack the Treacle Eater (18th–19th century)
ST 561 148

Somerset's finest folly achievement is the group at Barwick Park. They are as fine as any in the country and for enigma cannot be surpassed. Not large or obtrusive, they impale themselves upon the memory through their pointlessness, and the mystery is increased when research fails to discover much about their history. The four follies are the Obelisk, the Fish Tower, the Cone and Jack the Treacle Eater. The most reasonable explanation for their existence is that they were built by George Messiter in the 1820s 'to relieve unemployment in Yeovil', but Barbara Jones dates them some 50 years earlier, having seen two paintings of *c.*1770 in which two of the follies appear. It is impossible to date them by their architecture, for they have none. Even the normally conventional obelisk is here transformed into something wildly different—instead of the solid, worthy municipal structure familiar to us all, it has metamorphosed into a neurotic stiletto, a tall, beastly thin, crazily tilting rubbly object, as far removed from an urban obelisk as a javelin from a caber.

Just over a mile to the north is the Fish Tower, again in the same rubble stone. It is a plain, unadorned thin tower about 50ft (15m) high with a carved drum top. There used to be an iron cage with a fish weathervane (hence the name), but that has now disappeared. The inside is hollow, wide enough and rocky enough for a man to climb up if the folly is upon him. There are holes for the light.

The Cone is astonishing. There is nothing else remotely like it in Britain. Tall—about 70ft (21m)—and slender, with a ball finial, it stands on a tripod. Three Gothic arches face north, east and south out of the circular base, and the west wall is solid. There are nine layers of square holes rising to the top of the cone as if in a dovecote, but this was never a dovecote. There are traces of what may have been a wooden roof above the arches. Jones describes it to perfection: 'a highly functional structure designed for no function that has yet materialized.' It looks as if it should work.

Due east of the Cone is Jack the Treacle Eater, the most bizarre in name and shape. The by now familiar rubble style makes a coarse, shouldered arch about 30ft (9m) high, but here the rubble is massive enough to climb. On top of the arch is a smooth round towerlet with a conical roof, and perched at the very top is Jack himself, a lead statuette of Mercury. The towerlet seems to have had a door, long ago blocked (but perhaps it was a sham door) with what looks like a short flight of steps leading to it up the shoulder of the arch. Access to the steps can be gained only by climbing the vertical wall of the arch. Perhaps this led to the now famous legend of Jack the Treacle Eater, who lived in the towerlet, trained on treacle and ran messages to London for the Messiter family. Only someone as agile as he could live in such a dwelling. The true story is… not known. We can only fall back on speculation. The Greeks used statues of Hermes as boundary markers, and the Barwick Park follies are said to mark the boundaries of the old Messiter Estate. The Romans used statues of Mercury as garden ornaments. Treacle originally meant an antidote to the bites of wild beasts, and the statue of Jack (Mercury, Hermes) carried a wand or caduceus, which was supposed to have healing or narcotic effects—our heads are spinning and we are no nearer the truth. The most fanciful stories can be devised with so rich and remote a source, and there are few

Barwick Park Cone

follies so calculated to stir the imagination as these. The legends at Barwick should be fostered; the truth may prove to be debilitatingly prosaic.

Barwick's *digestif* is the fifth folly, a conventional one, but when it was visited in the late 1970s it was full of atmosphere: a damp, dripping, rippling, slippery, rough stone, round grotto-room with a circular pond in the middle of the floor and a light-hole above. The grotto is close by the house, which is now in multiple ownership. Who is responsible for it?

Jack the Treacle Eater

STAFFORDSHIRE

Staffordshire stands in the mind's eye for the Black Country and the Potteries, but these are just patches of soot on a rural map. Much of East Staffordshire is largely in the Peak District National Park, just as beautiful as Derbyshire but without the traffic and the ramblers. It has its fair share of follies, with some good garden ones at Shugborough, Enville and Alton Towers.

Ecton
Beresford Dale
Ilam
Alton Towers
Mapleton
Oakamoor
Upper Teane
Tutbury
Biddulph
Kidsgrove
Ipstones
Cheddleton
Cheadle
Willoughbridge
Trentham
Mucklestone
Adbaston
Sandon
Stafford
Tixall
Forton
Admaston
Meretown
Shugborough
Seighford
Brocton
Weston-under-Lizard
Gailey
Longdon
Brewood
Lichfield
Codsall Wood
Fazeley
Clifton Campville
Somerford
Enville
Shareshill
Wombourne

Adbaston

Batchacre Porch (18th century)
Look-out Tower (18th century)
SJ 754 255

A removal folly stands amid the rural solitude of 18th-century Batchacre Hall, near Adbaston. Now a farm, it was once the seat of the Whitworth family, the bachelor politician Richard Whitworth being the last of the line and justifiably tinged with more than a streak of eccentricity.

In the woods to the south of the Hall stands the Porch, which had been taken from Gerard's Bromley Hall of 1584. Nearer to the house is a small look-out tower, while according to 18th-century paintings in the house there was also an island in a vanished lake defended by a mock fort equipped with cannon.

Admaston

Goat Lodge (1849)
SK 049 233

Thomas Trubshaw, grandson of the Trubshaw who acted as master mason for the building of Shugborough's Tower of the Winds (see below), built the Goat Lodge at Blithfield Hall. Pevsner describes it as 'crazily overdecorated', with goats' heads and ornamental chimneys.

The Trubshaw family's contribution to the appearance of Staffordshire was substantial, with at least four generations

working as architects, engineers or masons. Thomas's father, James, won fame as a bridge-builder, achieving feats even Telford considered impossible. (As an aside, the actor David Niven had a great admiration for the clan, making sure that the Trubshaw name was mentioned in every one of his films.) Thomas, a talented architect who died young, designed several garden buildings and churches, the churches, in Colvin's

Blithfield Hall's Goat Lodge

The Druid's Sideboard at Alton Towers

words, 'possessing a perverse originality'.

The lodge commemorates the herd of wild goats that was given to Sir William Bagot of Blithfield by Richard II and that still roams Bagot's Park. Sir William's descendant, another William Bagot, employed Wyatts as well as Trubshaws, and nearly resorted to law when he accused Charles Wyatt of supplying faulty cement for Gothicizing the Hall. With hindsight, the Wyatts seem to have been pretty fly—remember they built the famous self-destructing Fonthill Abbey, even though they had the help of a Trubshaw, the 16-year-old James.

The Trubshaws and the Wyatts raised families by courtesy of Blithfield Hall. The original Hall was built by Thomas's great-great-grandfather, Richard, and a cluster of Wyatts appears to have been involved with building there from the 1760s up to the 1820s. Innocently or racily, we cannot decide which, rooms at the newly decorated Hall were given names such as 'Paradise' and 'Quality Cockloft'.

Alton Towers

Folly Group (early 19th century)
SK 075 435

Alton Towers lives up to its name. Towers, temples and pagodas spring up from the Chumet valley's rocky earth like mushrooms, popping up above the woods to give a craggy skyline. Like Shugborough, Alton is the work of two men. Charles Talbot the Roman Catholic 1st Earl of Shrewsbury, started the

whole thing *c.*1811. He was a single-minded man, set on running his own show alone. J.C. Loudon wrote in his *Encyclopaedia of Cottage Farm and Villa Architecture* (1833):

> *Though he consulted almost every artist, ourselves among the number, he seems only to have done so for the purpose of avoiding whatever an artist might recommend… His own ideas or the variations of a plan that he had procured were transformed to paper by an artist or clerk of the works whom he kept on purpose; and often, as we were informed by Mr Lunn, the gardener there in 1826, were marked out on the grounds with his own hands. The result, speaking of Alton as it was at the time of the late Earl's death and as we saw it shortly before (October 1826) was one of the most singular anomalies to be met with among the country residences of Britain, or perhaps of any part of the world.*

And artists there were: James Wyatt; Loudon himself; J.B. Papworth in 1818–20 for some bridges (including one sham), as well as for Grecian and Gothick temples; Thomas Allason for the landscaping and some of the buildings; and Robert Abraham.

Abraham appears to have been the very man the earl looked for, his reputation resting, according to Howard Colvin, 'on reliability rather than originality as a designer', and this architectural yes-man was responsible for the faintly Moorish conservatories. Around 1814, he built what is often termed the Chinese Temple but is, in fact, a well-designed although slightly old-fashioned wood and iron tower in the Gothic style. His masterpiece is the three-storeyed pagoda, still spouting a 70ft (21m) jet of water, which was completed in 1827, the year of the earl's death. It was called the Duck Tower, and its prototype was the To-Ho Pagoda in Canton, which was illustrated in Chambers's *Designs of Chinese Buildings* (1757).

Several structures with no architect's name ascribed to them survive at Alton and were almost certainly put up by the 15th Earl. The first two are garden ornaments: the Druid's Sideboard, a childlike stack of boulders, and the Corkscrew Fountain, a weird and literally twisted edifice. The Flag Tower, at some distance from the other follies, is exactly what one has by now come to expect of towers: it is simple and effective, several storeys high, with turrets and battlements. It was built before 1830. The Ingestre Courtyard may date from the same period; it is a façade, only to be seen from across the lake, with two squat towers on the corners and a battlemented wall connecting them, and a fortified entrance in the middle. It gives the impression of a medieval fort. Being accustomed to shams, we were prepared for the emptiness that undoubtedly lay behind it, but once inside the contrast between the small utilitarian farm buildings (renovated and turned into bars and toilets) and the exterior remains striking. Alton Towers is now one of the biggest Disneyland-type theme parks operating in Britain, and the Ingestre Courtyard is shown on the guide map as 'Numerous Toilets'.

On Charles Talbot's death in 1827, his nephew inherited the estate. Anybody in his right mind wouldn't have dared carry on where the previous owner left off, but John Talbot, the 16th Earl, with the help of Pugin, finished work on the house, which grew into a web of towers, turrets, chapels and cloisters, making it quite obvious why the suffix of Alton was originally Abbey, not Towers. In the gardens the new earl erected a Choragic Monument (*vide* Shugborough) to his predecessor, complete with the legend, 'He made the desert smile' ('grin' might have been a better word).

Another of his additions was the Harper's or Swiss Cottage, which is unremarkable but cosy. It was built *c.*1835 by Thomas Fradgley and was, predictably, the home of a blind Welsh harpist, who would strum for his supper by entertaining visitors.

Near the village of Alton, John Talbot brought Transylvania to Staffordshire. Not content to have finished Alton Towers, he set to work, again with the aid of Pugin, on Alton Castle, a variation on the Dracula theme. (Pugin also built St John's Hospital, a 'hospitium', for the rabidly Catholic earl.) After the castle was finished in 1852 there was nothing left to do, so John Talbot took to his bed and died. The Shrewsburys sold the estate to a private company in 1924, and the gardens were opened to the public. Now Alton Towers Amusement Park is advertised

The Duck Tower

on television across Europe, one of the few British versions of Six Flags or Knott's Berry Farm and other American pre-packaged days out. The loop-the-loop big dippers and all the other modern paraphernalia are sensibly kept at arm's length from the park. Perhaps at some future time a new Piranesi will produce holograms of the ruins of Alton's Aerial Cable Cars, Scenic Railway, Aquarium, Fun House and Planetarium.

Beresford Dale

Beresford Hall Tower (1674)
SK 128 589

Spotted but not investigated is a 1674 fishing lodge, square with a pyramidal roof, built, perhaps, for the famous Izaak Walton by Charles Cotton.

Biddulph

Biddulph Grange (1842)
SJ 893 591

James Bateman bought a farmhouse at Biddulph in 1842 and immediately started the activities that made him famous: between 1842 and 1869, when he had to sell the place, he created one of the most remarkable gardens of the Victorian era. Biddulph Grange, now completely restored by the National Trust, is first and foremost a garden, with buildings taking a secondary role. Yet the whole concept cannot be called anything other than 'folly'. The sales catalogue of Biddulph gives some impression of the gardens:

> *The prevailing idea in the arrangements of the grounds… is that of a division into classes of Countries, each with its distinctive Plants and their appropriate Soils, and by a clever arrangement of the Surface into Undulations, Rocky Summits, and Watery Dells, Climates and their Horticultural Results are strewn. A clever adaptation of Back-Grounds and Vistas, Yew, Holly and Beech Hedges, artificially designed Tunnels, Rocks, Caves, Mounds, Masses of Roots and Trunks and other 'Material' arranged in 'skilful disorder' and 'picturesque shape' have been some of the means to bring about their present excellence.*

Enough to whet anyone's appetite. The countries represented are China, Egypt and Italy, the last by the Italian Garden, which unfortunately has no particularly striking features. China has pavilions, bridges, grotto tunnels and gates, all delightful, but at least one bridge was later given a simplified pattern, and the enchanting small dragons from the roof of the Pagoda Pavilion have apparently taken wing and flown off towards Stoke. Egypt is represented by yew pyramids and obelisks, stone sphinxes and more gates. Bateman made the most of his few acres.

Although James Bateman appears to have designed most of the gardens himself or with the help of one Waterhouse Hawkins, Edward Cooke RA, a marine painter, was responsible for many of the architectural features, also designing several of the village buildings. Biddulph also boasts Britain's only metaphysical folly, the Great Wellingtonia Avenue:

> *which is a straight walk nearly three-quarters of a Mile long, planted for a considerable length with very healthy and well-grown Wellingtonia Gigantea, Deodars, Chesnuts and Australian Pines, and presenting, through its ascending character and the diminishing Perspective, the curious effect of an upright Obelisk.*

Clearly Messrs Bateman, Hawkins and Cooke gained enormous pleasure in planning their representation of the world in an otherwise forlorn corner of north Staffordshire.

This mysterious and magical garden has been brilliantly and superbly restored by the National Trust, and as a result it is now one

Egypt—waiting for the yew pyramids to grow again

of the Trust's leading attractions in the Midlands. This is good for Biddulph, good for the National Trust, good for the public. It is sad for us, because an intangible aura of enchantment has been lost. There is a beauty in decay, a pleasure in ruins, which is as ephemeral as smoke.

Brewood

Speedwell Castle (mid-18th century)
SJ 883 087

The area north of Wolverhampton, consisting of Brewood, Somerford, Chillington Hall, Weston Park, Gailey and Shareshill, is still remarkably unspoilt, despite the intrusion of the M54. Brewood, a prosperous, small, market town, serves as the area's natural heart, and on the corner of Market Place is Speedwell Castle—a town house, but what a town house! Its ogival windows and doorway offer sufficient exuberance for it to count as a folly on the strength of its decoration alone. To top this, a garden gnome stands above the doorway, flowerpot in hand. The interior of this Gothick extravaganza has a Chippendale staircase in the Chinese manner, and, a local story says, the whole was built from the winnings of the Duke of Bolton's eponymous racehorse, Speedwell. It has now been divided into flats and presents a striking but faintly shabby appearance to the wider world, like an ageing matinée idol down on his luck. We do not know who the architect

Speedwell Castle

was, but a similar Batty Langley-type style can be seen at the Gothick House at Coleshill, Warwickshire.

Brocton

Octagonal Dovecote (1801)
SJ 965 195

Three miles south of Shugborough is Brocton Hall, which was built in 1801 for Sir George Chetwynd, Bt. There is a borderline folly, an octagonal Gothick dovecote in the garden, and also a neat little ruin, consisting of two genuine medieval arches, said to have come from the Priory of St Thomas, but perhaps also the relic of an earlier Brocton Hall.

Cheadle

Hales View Farm (1983)
SK 021 441

Les Oakes is a general dealer; if he worked in a city environment he'd be called an entrepreneur. He'll do a little bit of this and a little bit of that, but what drew him to our attention was his interest in carts. He collects them, and as they tend to be on the bulky side he was faced with the problem of storing his collection. So he erected sheds to house them, but no ordinary sheds—the brick façades are bestrewn with icons, images, architectural salvage, junk, *objets trouvés*… the acquisitions of a life. A building such as this becomes the shorthand diary of the builder's life; every gloss and marginal note or brick will recall an incident, a memory, an anecdote. 'LES'S HOSS & CART' was a significant event in 1983, immortalized under the east gable.

Encouraged by general appreciation of his barn, Les went on to build a second of rather less grandeur in 1989, featuring a corrugated iron wall. When his third barn went up in 1991, closer to the road, the patience of the council finally snapped, despite his hasty inclusion of patriotic inscriptions, and he was ordered to demolish it before it had been completed. Farm buildings are exempt from planning consent, but it was clear even to the most liberal bureaucrat that these were not real barns, rather a burgeoning museum complex. Inevitably a battle ensued, with Les playing the part of the injured little man struggling against monolithic local government. Much to everyone's surprise, he won, and he was allowed to complete his third 'barn,' with another pale brick-outlined cart pulled by two horses over

'19STAFFORDSHIRE91' It is good to see a little individuality is still allowed to flourish in these protected times.

Cheddleton

Basford Hall Bathhouse (1841)
SJ 988 513

The Sneyd family (see Ipstones) owned Basford Hall, which is northwest of Ipstones towards Leek. The Bathhouse here is a rather elaborate, picturesque sham castle, built in 1841. Barbara Jones writes of a 'swimming bath, waterwheel, underground passages, living room and kitchen,' which all add to its mystique.

Clifton Campville

Clifton Campville Hall (early 18th century)
SK 263 097

Mention of a gazebo at Manor Farm draws us to Clifton Campville, before we discover that nearby we have the physical manifestation of the dictionary definition of folly—a huge building begun without reckoning of the cost—but it doesn't look like our preconceptions of folly, just two roofless but substantial ruined houses facing each other. Then we learn that Sir Charles Pye employed the Shropshire architect Francis Smith to build him the grandest mansion in the country—and this is not what remains, but all that was built. The two houses are, in fact, the wings of an enormous house that was never constructed; the central block simply never existed. One wing has now been repaired, while its derelict sibling stands glaring resentfully across the empty courtyard.

Codsall Wood

Chillington Eyecatchers (late 18th century)
SJ 854 053

Eyecatchers and temples abound in the ancient park of Chillington Hall, near Codsall Wood, now blighted by the M54. The Giffard family has owned the land for over 800 years, but this is merely an achievement; nothing must stand in the way of the haulage industry, and so the motorway to Telford thunders through the south of the park. Lancelot Brown, Richard Woods and James Paine worked here for Thomas Giffard in the more peaceful 1770s, and any one of them may have designed the simple Ionic, or Roman, Temple or the Gothick Temple. Little remains of the Gothick Temple, although the Roman Temple, bearing graffiti

from 'Young, J, 1816', was restored in 1980.

The Grecian Temple (which hides the gamekeeper's cottage from view), is listed Grade I and has been attributed to Soane in the 1780s. The fourth eyecatcher, south of the motorway, was originally called The Sham House, but is now known as The Whitehouse. Built as early as 1724 by Francis Smith, it has a classical façade with Tuscan columns and served as an eyecatcher from across the 85 acre (34.4ha) Pool, as Brown's lake is known. Peter Giffard, the present owner, built the mound in front to block out the intrusion of

The remnant of the Gothick Temple at Chillington

the motorway. The five-arched Sham Bridge to the north, designed by Brown and like all sham bridges best seen from a distance, hides a reservoir, which keeps the Pool at a constant level. Water flowing through the sluice out of the lake eventually reaches the North Sea through the Humber estuary.

Ecton

Sham Castle (1931)
SK 097 583

In 1931 someone with the initials 'AR' built a mock castle with a prominent copper spire in the hamlet of Ecton, near the curiously named

Ecton Sham Castle

National Trust property of Ape's Tor in the Manifold valley. This is a lonely, lovely land, and this curious rambling house was carefully crafted with an eye to the picturesque in building and in location. At the time of writing it appeared to be abandoned, with polythene sheeting covering once leaded windows.

Enville

Folly Group (mid-18th century)
SO 824 862

Enville, although well known, is sparsely documented. The most detailed study is by Michael Cousins, Editor of *Follies* Magazine, and remains unpublished. It is part of the triumvirate formed by 'The Leasowes', Hagley and Enville. 'The Leasowes' was the property of gentleman-poet William Shenstone; Hagley and Enville were owned by Lords Lyttleton and Stamford. Shenstone lived in relative poverty, and the grounds of 'The Leasowes' were ornamented with both Taste and the Nearly Always Empty Purse in mind. But Shenstone's taste was much admired, and he began to advise the two lords. In their parks he could tilt at the grandiose without personal financial risk.

Enville's follies appear to exist not so much in brick and mortar as in ephemeral lists of labels; the names of the follies being lost or interchanged. There is one important 18th century source: Joseph Heely's *Letters on the Beauty of Hagley, Envil and The Leasowes* (1777) conjures up 'a small dusky antique building' above the cascade, a boathouse, octagonal, with a 'curious sliding window… adorned with painted glass in whimsical groups of grotesque figures', a rotondo, a Gothick Shepherd's Lodge, a chapel dedicated to Shenstone, a thatched cottage, a Gothick arch, and an 'exceedingly well designed' Gothick Billiard Room, housing a billiard table, an organ, and the busts of Homer and Cicero. After Heely, nomenclature collapsed; the Billiard Room, for example, has been called the Greenhouse, the Summer-house and the Museum. Out of this hotchpotch of descriptions emerge several buildings which have survived to the present day. Others are in a ruinous state, and some have been completely destroyed.

Osvald Sirén in his *China and Gardens of Europe* published a photograph of what he termed 'The Hermitage', a makeshift, octagonal bark-covered hut with stained-glass windows—Heely's original thatched cottage? No—this lies ruined in a wood. Barbara Jones saw Ralph's Bastion, dated 1753, and Samson's Cave, which she mistook for Shenstone's Chapel; although simple, the chapel is not so grubby as to be described as a cave. The Chinese Pavilion—missed by Sirén, mentioned by Pevsner (as a Pagoda)

The Museum, Enville

and seen by Jones still stands, lost in a wood. Gone is a Gothicised farmhouse and the fabulous conservatory with its onion domes.

Confused? You will be, until Cousins publishes his detailed study of the gardens. "No, No, NO!" he scrawled across our original text for the park. Sadly in a general work such as this we do not have the space to record the fate of every fragment; our role is to create the awareness, to spark the enthusiasm that will result in more detailed attention. There is little point in attempting to compress a scholarly paper into 750 words when all we want to convey is the genius of the place.

Nevertheless according to Cousins the buildings which have graced the park at Enville are as follows: a Chinese Temple & Bridge; the Rotunda; the Gothick Greenhouse, Summer-house or Billiard Room; the Gothick Seat; Lyndon Hall and the Shepherd's Lodge; the Thatched Cottage; the Gothick Gateway; the Cascades; the Ruin; the Boathouse; the Chapel; the Fountains; the Conservatory; the Eaglery or Owl & Eagle House; the Pagoda; the Ice-House; Sampson's Cave and Ralph's Bastion.

Of all these buildings the only one which has the power to take the breath away is the now beautifully restored Museum. No, it's not mentioned in Mr. Cousins's list, because this was formerly the Billiard Room. Or Summerhouse. Or Gothick Greenhouse. Whatever its name, whoever the architect, the writers believe this to be the finest piece of Gothick folly architecture in Britain. And it is just because it is so fine that argument has raged—if such an agreeable subject can turn to rage—about its authorship. Timothy Mowl had convincingly argued a case for the Gothicist Henry Keene as architect, and Roger White believed that it was Miller's design, altered in execution by Thomas Farnolls Pritchard of Shrewsbury, who is believed to be the 'Shrewsbury man' of whom J. I. Talbot of Lacock Abbey wrote to Miller in 1754: 'at Enville we saw an Horrid Massacre of a Fine Gothick design of yours: committed by the Hands of some Shrewsbury man…' Cousins has reattributed the design to Miller on the basis that the Museum was originally the Gothick Greenhouse, indisputably by Miller.

There is a beauty in decay, a wistfulness that vanishes when the decay dissolves into disappearance; but how does one freeze an emotion in time? Either Enville is restored, or it is left rotting, defeated, crumbling, mysterious and romantic; to be no more than a memory in 50 years. Who is to choose?

Fazeley

Fazeley Bridge (late 18th century)
SK 203 018

The manor built by Prime Minister Robert Peel's father, a textile millionaire, at Drayton Bassett has now been demolished. A few garden ornaments remain, but the best survival is the small footbridge crossing the canal at Fazeley. Two white, round, castellated towers conceal the spiral staircases that lead on to the bridge, like the footbridges connecting platforms at country stations.

Forton

Sutton Monument (1780)
SJ 759 217

The Forton Monument at Sutton—otherwise known as the Sutton Monument at Forton—on the Shropshire border was originally a windmill but is thought to have been modified to act as an eyecatcher from Aqualate Hall by Charles Baldwyn. A windmill on the site was first mentioned in 1593 in the Post Mortem of Thomas Skrymsher. Joseph Browne's 1682 map of Staffordshire shows sails on the building, and Smith's 1747 map also marks it as a windmill. It was first described as a 'Monument' in *A History of Staffordshire* (1817) by William Pitt.

If anything, it brings to mind Indian architecture as brought to Britain by way of the Daniell cousins' drawings. It is a 25ft (7.6m) high cone, 40ft (12m) in circumference, rubble built on a double layer of sandstone blocks. It was topped by a 5

The Sutton Monument

hundredweight sandstone ball finial, which fell off before World War II and which now serves as a garden feature for a local farmer. The local council rejected a scheme from the landlord of the Red Lion in Sutton to restore the folly and add a two-bedroom cottage at the back with the immortal words of Councillor Cyril Jones of Norbury: 'It's of no use; pull it down, flatten it and let's have an end to it.' May you be long remembered, Councillor. The landlord continued to wage his campaign, despite repeated rejections.

Gailey

Round House (late 18th century)
SJ 920 104

On the A5 near Gailey, beside the Staffordshire and Worcestershire Canal, stands the Round House, a squat tower, which served as the lock-keeper's cottage. It is battlemented and rather dull, apart from a picturesque arrangement of chimney pots.

Ilam

Necessary Tower (mid-19th century)
SK 132 507

At the southern end of the Manifold valley is Ilam, now a National Trust property and once the inspiration for Johnson's Happy Valley (the philosopher in *Rasselas* is called Imlac, a name reminiscent of the place). The village centres on a tall, Gothic cross, which was erected in 1840 in memory of the wife of Jesse Watts-Russell, who built the model village. The small, two-storeyed, acorn-roofed tower in the grounds of Ilam Hall seems, however, to be of a later date—mid- to late Victorian, perhaps. It is now boarded up, but in its time it has served as a Necessary Tower for gentlemen.

Ipstones

Chapel House (1794)
SK 005 499

Ipstones has a construction that turns the concept of sham churches inside out: John Sneyd of Belmont Hall began to build the village church in 1787, but soon afterwards had a serious disagreement with the parson, which led to his building his own church at the gates of the Hall. Like good Christians, they resolved the matter fairly quickly, and the half-finished church, with mighty buttresses supporting a stumpy tower, was converted for use as a cottage. It has now become a sleek house for the type of people who enjoy personalized number plates.

Ilam's Necessary Tower

Kidsgrove

Round Tower (18th century)
SJ 838 541

Here on the Cheshire border, in the colliery town of Kidsgrove, west of Ravenscliffe Road and east of the church, is a Georgian round tower. There is no story, no history, although the County Planning Department describes it as an ex-mill. Someone must have wanted it once.

Lichfield

19 The Close, Grotto (1771)
SK 115 097

A grotto of shells and fossils, built by Charles Howard.

Observation Pavilion (1756)
SK 124 086

On top of Borrowcop Hill, whence came the stone for the building of Lichfield Cathedral, stands the Observation Pavilion, double arches all round its four brick-built sides. It must have been put up by a local landowner who wished to enjoy the view.

Crucifix Conduit (1863)
SK 114 091

This is neither a crucifix nor a conduit, and furthermore it doesn't even stand at the Crucifix Conduit. It is a florid Victorian clock tower, built by a committee with too many surplus funds, with faux medieval zigzag patterning around the doorway, near a well, which a Lichfield bell-founder donated to the Friars Minor in the 13th century. In 1928 it began to get in the way, as things do, and was moved to its new location on the central reservation of a dual carriageway. Still flush with funds, the Conduit Land Trust restored it in 1991, and now it prettily rings the quarter hours to motorists flashing by in their sealed and sound-proofed vehicles.

Longdon

Hanch Hall Cathedral (late 20th century)
SK 100 137

There are now two Lichfield cathedrals, the better known one being in the centre of Dr Johnson's city, the lesser known one in the countryside to the north. It is not the seat of a rival denomination, but rather a large—very large—garden ornament in the grounds of a manor house. Some 40ft (12m) high and tangled in the undergrowth by the lake, it replicates the west front of the cathedral with

Longdon's ephemeral Lichfield Catheral

its three spires.

Replicas of famous buildings may reasonably be expected to be erected by homesick expatriates oceans away from their inspiration, but strangely this is not often the case. Here is the copy of Lichfield Cathedral in Lichfield; the Ritterturm at Machern in Saxony has its tiny disciple in a garden in the same village; Liverpool Castle graces the shores of Anglezark Reservoir a few miles from Liverpool, each basking in the glory of its more famous neighbour. Even the relatively unknown Azerley Tower in North Yorkshire had its own model in front of it.

The problem with this cadet cathedral is that it is an ephemeral folly, built of plywood on a base of breezeblocks for an exhibition and unlikely to last more than a dozen years here in its removal location. The new owner is fond of it, however, and may be prepared to re-create it in a more durable material.

Longton Hall

Pottery Follies

If ever you come across some curiously shaped china with representations of an elongated pyramid, a church, an obelisk, an arch and other essential landscape elements, buy it and ship it to us—it is the rare Longton Hall Folly Pattern. The Hall, south of Stoke-on-Trent, and its follies have long disappeared, although they were still standing in living memory.

The Temple of Pomona

Mapleton

Okeover Hall Temple of Pomona (1747)
Necessary House (1747)
SK 157 481

Northwest of Alton Towers is Okeover Hall, built for Leak Okeover by Joseph Sanders in 1745–8. Two garden temples date from this period. North of the house is the Temple of Pomona, goddess of fruit, with a lovely little statue titled THE DAWN OF LOVE by G. Bergonzoli, while to the east is a building of Useful Intent, the Necessary House, a classical closet in harmony with the Pomona temple. Camouflaged garden lavatories appear to have been as popular as they were useful, although survivals are rare. The folly toilet was the subject of serious consideration—John Plaw, for example, published the design of a rustic 'Wood Pile House' in his *ferme ornée* of 1795. This 'convenience in a park or plantation where the walks and rides are extensive' was realized at Mistley Thorn in Essex and Wootton Court, Kent, while German and Dutch pattern books show a relatively high number of conveniences disguised as rustic huts, sham ruins or even rather daringly as Gothick chapels. The French appear to have been deficient in this respect.

Meretown

The Castle (early 19th century)
SJ 767 194

Aqualate Hall has a Repton park, some quaint lodges and The Castle, a gabled, red brick house with a fortified garden, probably by John Nash and thus another instance of a Repton–Nash collaboration, as at Attingham Park in Shropshire.

Mucklestone

Oakley Folly (18th century)
SJ 715 364

Probably built by the Chetwedes of nearby Oakley Hall, Oakley Folly is another sham church, here concealing a barn. Now very ruined, this sham church still has the power to confuse and mystify. Even minds attuned to the whims of folly builders are ready to see this as a genuine ruin, and the Grade II listing offers no clue, merely commenting on 'a curious 18th-century structure in the form of a church'. It stands north of Hales, near the B5415.

Oakley Folly

Oakamoor

Bolton's Gate Piers (19th century)
SJ 055 450

These mighty gate piers have been transplanted to a grassed area from the Bolton Brothers' copperworks, which stood in the middle of one of the largest industrial estates in the Churnet valley. Now, in our post-Thatcher, post-industrial land, we cannot think of any further use for them.

Sandon

Perceval Shrine (1812)
Pitt Column (1806)
Lord Harrowby's Folly (1912)
SJ 965 201

Dudley Ryder, 1st Earl of Harrowby, managed to become engaged, albeit as a bystander, in some of the political violence that marked the turn of the 18th century. In 1798 he was one of William Pitt's seconds in his duel with Tierney. In 1820 the Cabinet was to have been assassinated by the Cato Street conspirators at a dinner to be held at Harrowby's London house. In between these dates, in 1812, the Prime Minister Spencer Perceval was murdered, and Harrowby felt sufficiently moved to erect a Gothic alcove in the Sandon Hall park, the Perceval Shrine.

Six years earlier he had commemorated William Pitt, who had considerably furthered Harrowby's career, by erecting a 75ft (23m) Doric column with an urn on top.

But the best folly at Sandon owes its existence to the 4th Earl, and is called Lord Harrowby's Folly or the Trentham Tower. Normally this would be regarded as a neo-renaissance pavilion, common enough to merit a passing mention as a garden ornament, but a folly it is, because it is actually the decorative arcading forming a kind of cupola on the top of Sir Charles Barry's Trentham House, built between 1834 and 1849, and demolished in 1912. Harrowby bought the topmost fragment for £100 and re-erected it, stone by stone, at Sandon. We say fragment, but it is a substantial chunk of masonry, more like a loggia—it is square, with three tall, open arches on each side, topped with a gradually disappearing balustrade.

Seighford

Sham Church (18th century)
SJ 875 255

Just west of Stafford, in the grounds of Seighford Hall, is an 18th-century gamekeeper's cottage with stepped gables; it is rather pretty. It has been built on to a 14th-century tower from the former Ranton Abbey, giving the effect of a converted Norman church.

Shareshill

Portobello Tower (1743)
SJ 950 046

On a hill in the spandrel of the M54 and the M6 stands the hexagonal embattled Portobello Tower, which commemorates Admiral Vernon's audacious capture with only six ships of the Spanish fort of Porto Bello in 1739. The Vernons of Hilton Hall belonged to a distant branch of the admiral's family, but they must have decided to capitalize on the jingoism that led to medals being struck in Vernon's honour, pubs named after him and several roads and villages being renamed Portobello; there is even a Portobello in Wolverhampton, some 4 miles away from Hilton.

Richard Trubshaw worked for the Vernons at Hilton in 1743 (in fact, he appears to have been the family architect since 1734), so he may well have been responsible for the rather plain design. The Hall is now the headquarters of Tarmac plc.

Shugborough

Folly Group (18th century)
SJ 992 219

A few miles west of Stafford lies the National Trust property of Shugborough, the home of the Ansons, Earls of Lichfield, for over 350 years. It is well cared for and much visited, and the follies in the garden (as opposed to those in the park) tend to look almost too spick and span.

Two men were responsible for the Shugborough follies: Thomas Anson (1695–1773), a founder member of the Society of Dilettanti, widely travelled (from the Pyrenees to the Holy Land) and ready, by the 1740s, to settle down and display a little of his expensively acquired good taste; and his younger brother, George, who went to sea at the age of 13 and was given command of six ships in 1740. He returned after a four-year voyage having circumnavigated the world, sacked settlements, sunk ships and captured the most glittering of all prizes, the treasure-laden Acapulco galleon. The booty amounted to some £500,000, and a large proportion of it remained with Admiral Anson.

Thomas seems to have been subsidized

quite handsomely by his famous brother. He became MP for Lichfield in 1747 and in the same year work started on converting the house. Two tower-like pavilions were added by the elusive Thomas Wright, designer of some of the best follies in Britain and Ireland, and he may also have done some of the garden work around the house.

Shepherd's Monument (mid-18th century)

The Shepherd's Monument, to the north of the house, closely resembles one of Wright's *Six Original Designs for Arbours* (1755). The centrepiece, now removed, was a Peter Scheemakers bas-relief of Poussin's 'Et In Arcadia Ego', which, with the Ansons' sudden fortune, uncannily echoes the legend of Rennes-le-Château, the Holy Grail and the enormous riches that came to the guardians of its secret. The enigmatic inscription has never been deciphered, only adding to the mystery:

O. U. O. S. V. A. V. V

DM

A twisted arch, resting on two stout Doric pillars, encloses the vacant spot, and this is set into an alcove with abundant classical detail.

The Ruins (mid-18th century)

The Ruins, assembled from fragments of several buildings, including the Bishop's Palace at Lichfield, give a view from the west front of the house. In the 1740s they were more extensive, and incorporated a Gothick dovecote. Nowadays they look faintly ridiculous: too small to impress; too large to ignore. Two arches attempt to sink dramatically into the earth, weighed down with the Piranesian dust of centuries past,

but the immaculately tended turf surrounding them belies the illusion. The statue of a philosopher sits amid the ruins, stoically contemplating these absurdities. A ruined colonnade across the River Sow has disappeared.

William Gilpin, in his *Observations Relative Chiefly to Picturesque Beauty Made in the Year 1772*, was not impressed by his visit to Shugborough, and was moved to comment:

It is not every man, who can build a house, that can execute a ruin. To give the stone it's mouldering appearance-to make the widening chink run naturally through all the joints—to mutilate the ornaments—to peel the facing from the internal structure—to shew how correspondent parts have once united; tho now the chasm runs wide between them—and to scatter heaps of ruin around with negligence and ease; are great efforts of art; much too delicate for the hand of a common workman and what we very rarely see performed.

Besides, after all, that art can bestow, you must put your ruin at last into the hands of nature to adorn, and perfect it. If the mosses, and lychens grow unkindly on your walls—if the streaming weather-stains have produced no variety of tints—if the ivy refuses to mantle over your buttress; or to creep among the ornaments of your Gothic window—if the ash, cannot be brought to hang from the cleft; or long, spiry grass to wave over the shattered battlement—your ruin will be still incomplete- you may as well write over the gate, 'Built in the year 1772'. Deception there can be none.

Chinese House (1747)

Thomas Wright may have had something to do with the actual building of the Chinese House in 1747, one of the first pieces of chinoiserie in Britain. It was copied from a design by Sir Percy Brett, Anson's First Lieutenant on the *Centurion*, and inspired by architecture seen in Canton. The pavilion is surprisingly simple, almost classical, with fretwork windows and rococo-chinoiserie inside. An afterthought in the shape of a small pagoda of 1752 has gone.

Cat's Monument (1768)

The pavilion is linked by an iron bridge, dating from 1813, to a small island, on which the Cat's Monument presents something of an enigma. On a bulky plinth stands a large urn, around the base of which are four rams'

The Shepherd's Monument

heads, perhaps representing the herd of Corsican goats that Thomas introduced at Shugborough. On top of the urn a cat curls its tail. The plinth bears a Coade stone tablet, with a heraldic device in bas-relief. The structure may be intended as a whimsical memorial to nothing in particular, or it may commemorate the cat that accompanied the admiral on his trip around the world, or it could be a memorial for the last of a breed of Persian cats that died at Shugborough soon after 1768. We can date the monument to this time, because artificial stone began to be used in 1767 and Mrs Coade started her famous firm in 1769.

Doric Temple (mid-18th century)

A Doric Temple in the garden links up with the second stage of development at

The Lanthorn of Demosthenes

Shugborough. It is attributed to James 'Athenian' Stuart in the 1760s. Stuart—painter, architect, and also a member of the Society of Dilettanti—had been sent by the Society together with the gentleman architect Nicholas Revett on a 'fact-finding' trip to Greece. The results of this journey were published in four volumes of *Antiquities of Athens*, a seminal work, which precipitated the Greek Revival. George, Lord Anson, had seen to it that Stuart was appointed Surveyor of Greenwich Hospital,

which brought him £200 per annum. Naturally, Stuart would have been delighted to return this favour when some years later he was asked to design several buildings for the admiral's brother.

Triumphal Arch (1762)

It is usually taken for granted that the Greek Revival buildings in the park were financed with Thomas Anson's inheritance, left by the Admiral when he died in 1762, but the Triumphal Arch was started a year before, as is shown by an estimate for its building by John Hooper, Mason, dated November 1761, for £84 14s 1d.

The arch is in Shugborough Park, which for the following ten years was to be the nursery for the Greek Revival in Britain. Designs from the store of drawings made by Stuart and Revett in Athens were taken and constructed, and both the Tower of the Winds and the Lanthorn of Demosthenes found their way into numerous British gardens. The Triumphal Arch, a copy of Hadrian's Arch in Athens, manages in turn to look menacing and light-hearted, serious and frivolous, as it stands on a slope south of the house like a solitary tree. After the death of Admiral Anson, the arch was decorated with

The Triumphal Arch

The Temple of the Winds

states, busts and medallions by Peter Scheemakers, commemorating Lord and Lady Anson.

Rococo Railway Bridge (1847)

If the earth moves as you are contemplating the magnificence of the Triumphal Arch you are not, alas, participating in some supernatural awakening of your artistic sensibilities, but merely standing on top of the tunnel that carries the London–Stafford main line. This also explains the film of black soot disfiguring the marble. The train leaves the tunnel through a medieval fortress to rival Hassocks and Linslade, turrets and all, built in 1847 by Livock. All too often forgotten in the excitement of seeing Shugborough's more famous follies, this ornate railway dry bridge is exuberantly decorated in rococo architectural style. Thankfully, it was recently restored by British Rail, because it's a fair bet no one would have touched it afterwards.

Lanthorn of Demosthenes (mid-18th century)

The second of Stuart's Greek toys, the Lanthorn of Demosthenes (its more precise name being the Choragic or Lysicrates Monument), can be seen in one form or another, on its own or topping columns and towers, at Holkham in Norfolk, the Lansdown Tower in Somerset, the Burns Monument in Alloway, Tatton Park in Cheshire and at Staffordshire's Alton Towers. It has become, like the Tower of the Winds or the Sybil Temple at Tivoli, a stock pattern in European architecture. The Lanthorn is a slightly simplified version of the real thing: a tallish drum with nice detailing and an elaborate trophy above. Originally, this consisted of a metal tripod and a Wedgwood bowl, but these disappeared long ago and were replaced by fibreglass replicas in 1965, setting an honourable precedent for the use of fibreglass in modern follies. The Lanthorn is just the right size to have been used as an arcadian convenience, but this is scatalogical speculation.

Temple of the Winds (1764)

The Temple of the Winds was built in 1764–5 by Charles Cope Trubshaw after a design by Stuart (he was beaten to it by his partner Revett, who built a Temple of the Winds at West Wycombe in 1759). It is hexagonal, with two porticoes and a half-round bulge attached to it that mirror Wright's additions to the house. In 1805 it was converted into a dairy by Samuel Wyatt for Lady Anson. Like the other two Greek edifices in the park, the tower is well sited, although Gilpin found there was—

something rather absurd in adorning a

plain field with a triumphal arch; or with the lanthern of Demosthenes, restored to all it's splendor. A polished jewel, set in lead is ridiculous. But above all, the temple of the winds, seated in a pool, instead of being placed on a hill, is illstationed.

We leave Shugborough with a picture of the world as seen by the Anson brothers. The house itself is full of mementoes of the admiral's voyages, of chinoiserie and classical details, of paintings of the park, the gardens and the buildings (the best are by Nicholas Dall). The buildings reflect the brothers' travels in China, Greece and Egypt (an obelisk on Brocton Hill fell down in the early 18th century); their social and political aspirations; and of course the admiral's vast wealth. The estate is a remarkable example of autobiography expressed in terms of architecture.

But what can that inscription on the Shepherd's Monument mean?

Somerford

Eyecatcher (18th century)
SJ 899 081

Somerford Grange, not far from Brewood, has an eyecatcher façade on the banks of the River Penk, facing Somerford Hall. In addition to the usual PRIVATE notices, the gates are padlocked. We have failed to see this.

Stafford

Stafford Castle (1817)
SJ 902 222

The ancient town of Stafford, though a little dull, is a good starting point for a folly hunt because it sits smack in the middle of the county. It boasts only one folly—Stafford Castle, louring over the side of the motorway and assumed by any motorists who notice it to be a genuine ruined castle. Sir George Jerningham, later Lord Stafford, wanted to build himself a Gothic mansion on the foundations of the ruined medieval castle. His nephew Edward, who had practised by building a chapel in the grounds of Sir George's Norfolk estate, was put in charge of the project. In five years, two towers and one storey of the new castle were erected, but by 1825 the whole fabric had started to give way and the site was abandoned. Slowly the rest of the structure crumbled away and some years ago parts of it were demolished. The remains of the ill-fated rebuilding still make a rather sublime skyline, not unlike Riber Castle in neighbouring Derbyshire.

Tixall

Bottle Lodge (17th century)
SJ 979 228

About 2 miles northwest of Shugborough is Tixall, which has a small octagonal building with an ogee roof; it is aptly named Bottle

Tixall Gatehouse—splendidly oversized

Lodge. It mirrors the corner towers of the splendidly oversized Tixall Gatehouse, a late 16th-century structure now restored to its former magnificence by the Landmark Trust. Needless to say, the gatehouse lacks a house to lead to; it was rebuilt umpteen times before finally being demolished early this century. On a much smaller scale, the Bottle Lodge itself has been completely renovated and returned to a unique if minute house.

Tixall village has some curiosities: an

Tixall Bottle Lodge

obelisk of 1776 doubles as a milestone, and there is an octagonal Tuscan temple of the same period, rescued from the rapidly dilapidating park at nearby Ingestre.

Trentham

Sutherland Monument (1836)
Mausoleum (1807–8)
SJ 868 409

Although Trentham Hall has been torn down and the top transferred to Sandon, the grand entrance to the park and the orangery remain, now derelict and redundant. The appalling Duke of Sutherland owned Trentham, and a Sutherland Monument, one of many in the country, was erected here three years after his death in 1833. The design was provided by local architect, Charles Winks, and the bronze statue of the duke on top is said to be by Chantrey.

Of quite another order is the massive Mausoleum on the A51 leading past the estate. It was built in 1807–8 by C.H. Tatham, an architect proficient in near-follies such as lodges, ornamental cottages, gates,

mausoleums and sundry garden buildings. For Trentham he designed a thoroughly Egyptian greenhouse, apparently never built. The Egyptian influence in the mausoleum was much diluted but is still evident. The building is square, with battered corner pylons and a second storey topped by what can only be described as a drooping cross made out of stone lotus flowers. A recent restoration incentive proposed to allow the ashes of common man to be interred alongside aristocracy—for just £10,000 we would be permitted to share the mausoleum with our betters for a period of ten years. And after ten years? Apparently we would make a very fine mortar.

Tutbury

Julius's Tower (c.1775)
SK 209 291

In the middle of the picturesque and genuine medieval ruins of Tutbury Castle stands a round sandstone building, known as Julius's Tower. This is not another medieval relic; it was built *c.*1775 by the 4th Lord Vernon and rather shoddily at that—when restoration work was carried out at the castle in 1988 the engineers commented on the poor quality of the original workmanship compared to the masonry of the real castle. It is pure folly. Why should anyone wish to build a romantic ruined, sham tower in the middle of a romantic, ruined, real castle?

Upper Tean

Tean Temple (1836)
SK 033 399

This small, domed, rotunda temple was constructed using unfluted Ionic columns from the portico of Heath House, ½ mile southwest, which was torn down in 1836 to be replaced by the present house. It was the focus of a woodland walk lined with rhododendrons, but the woodlands were taken up 'by the government' during World War II and the land turned over to farming, so now the formerly secret little temple stands isolated and exposed.

Weston-under-Lizard

Temple of Diana (1765–70)
Knoll Tower (mid-18th century)
ST 803 092

Before tackling Chillington (see Codsall Wood above), the Brown-Paine duo collaborated a few miles away at Weston

Knoll Tower, Weston Park

Park, Paine building in 1765–70 a Temple of Diana and a Roman Bridge. In addition, there were a Swiss cottage, an observatory, an unmarked obelisk, a sprinkling of boathouses and a later prospect tower, which visually connects Weston with Tong in Shropshire. The Earls of Bradford, who own Weston to this day, probably regarded the loopy George Durant of Tong as very nouveau, but there is an indication that the siting of the tower was carefully chosen to allow a view of both Weston and Tong. It is a straightforward, basic pattern, square folly-tower built from red sandstone quarried at Weston, battlemented and flanked by a slender octagonal stair turret. Its one eccentricity is a plaque, dated 1631, referring probably to a fireplace, not the decidedly later tower. Our guess for an architect would be Thomas Rickman, who worked at Weston in 1830–31. Of the other follies at Weston, only the observatory (now used for parties and conferences, including a 1998 G8 summit of world leaders) and obelisk remain.

By the 1990s the follies and garden buildings in the park were beginning to look and feel their age, and an ingenious scheme was hatched to ensure their preservation. The buildings were offered for sale on a repairing lease—in effect, they were loaned to the occupiers for 21 years, on the proviso that specified repairs were carried out. The lessees gained accommodation at a peppercorn rent, the Weston Park Foundation had its park buildings repaired for free.

Willoughbridge

Bath House (late 17th century)
Hunting Lodge (late 16th century)
SJ 746 403

Northwards along the Shropshire border is another of England's many failed spas. This one became fashionable as early as the last quarter of the 17th century, when Lady Gerrard erected a house called Willoughbridge Wells in order to take advantage of the warm springs here. On the lake's edge stands a small and simple bath house, a reminder of thwarted ambitions. The hunting lodge of some hundred or so years earlier, set on a hill, points to an earlier interest taken by the Gerrards in this particular spot.

Wombourne

The Bratch (early 19th century)
Bearnett House Tower
SO 865 735

Another lock-keeper's cottage, octagonal this time, is at The Bratch near Wombourne, and at Wombourne itself sits a battered, roofless Gothic tower in the grounds of Bearnett House—no date, no architect.

SUFFOLK

Suffolk has possibly the widest variety of follies in Britain, and some are surely the most famous in the country. To top that, it also boasts the one folly generally acknowledged to be the first: Freston Tower.

Barton Mills

Sham Façade (c.1800)
TL 710 730

The Vicarage at Barton Mills has a remarkable façade. Pevsner describes it as dating from *c.*1800, castellated, with a raised centre and a quatrefoil window, but extensive rebuilding has since taken place. The façade remains, much cleaned up, but the Vicarage behind is completely new. The battlements are now cleanly defined in yellow brick, blending rather unhappily with the knapped flint façade, the quatrefoil window has been replaced by a simple round one, while the four Gothic windows remain on the ground floor. The central arched doorway has been blocked up. It is a startling sight when one approaches it from the main road.

Brantham

Obelisks and Temple of Venus (1970s)
TM 110 330

At Brantham, overlooking the Stour, Mr and Mrs Birch built two obelisks and a Temple of Venus in the early 1970s. The brick obelisk, topped with a ball finial, was supposed to have Vestal Virgins dancing around the base, but they hadn't got round to that in the 1980s.

Bungay

Tower (1839)
TM 330 900

Beside the River Waveney, in Bungay's Castle Lane, stands what is described as 'a romantic turret', built in 1839 for J.B. Scott, whose diaries were published in 1930 as *An Englishman at Home and Abroad.*

Regrettably, we have seen neither diaries nor turret, both of which sound delightful.

Claydon

Grotto and Ruins (c.1862)
TM 140 490

When squarson George Drury started to pull down part of Claydon Church in order to improve it (which he did in 1862), he had parts of the chancel re-erected further away in the grounds of the rectory, behind the churchyard wall. A shellwork grotto, which may be of an earlier date, already stood there.

Coddenham

Tower (19th century)
TM 130 530

A mile or so south of Coddenham is Shrubland Park, now a well-known health farm, where Sir Charles Barry did magnificent work on the house and garden in attempting to recreate the Villa d'Este in rural Suffolk. On the edge of one of the few hills in the county is a well-preserved, four-storey, polygonal prospect tower and a higher stair turret. It is heavily battlemented and very private, surrounded by a high barbed wire fence.

Elveden

Elveden Hall (1860s–70s)
TL 830 800
War Memorial (1921)
TL 760 750

The village of Elveden on the A11 is dominated by a folly house in Elveden Hall, acceptably Italianate from the outside (including the essential mid-Victorian water tower) but with a spectacularly oriental interior, converted in the 1860s and 1870s for Duleep Singh, the dispossessed Maharajah of the Punjab, a man much liked by Queen Victoria. Elveden became the Maharajah's marriage gift to his exotic new wife, the half-German, half-Abyssinian Bamba Müller.

Down the main road at the junction of three parishes is a gigantic war memorial (this area was the training ground for the 1916 tank). It is a Corinthian column tower, 113ft (34.4m) high, and topped by an urn; it was designed by Clyde Young in 1921. It is no longer possible to climb the 148 steps to the top because the entrance has, inevitably, been blocked up. The inclusion of a war memorial in a book on follies may reasonably be questioned, but when one considers the most fitting way of commemorating the valiant dead of three tiny Breckland parishes, a look-out tower on the A11 must rank fairly low, especially if we can no longer look out of it. The same amount of money could have endowed a small cottage hospital for many years.

Erwarton Hall

Gatehouse (c.1549)
`TM 230 340`

In the same year that Freston Tower, the earliest folly in Britain, was built, nearby Erwarton Hall produced a gatehouse—but what a gatehouse! Bizarre in the extreme, it long predates any similar follies, but had it been built in the 18th century—it could have

The rockets of Erwarton Hall Gatehouse

been built at any time—it would have been an inevitable inclusion. Architecturally it resembles nine brick Saturn Vs in a square of three by three, with an archway cut through the centre three. The motive was purely decorative, an avenue of architecture that has remained unexplored.

Euston Hall

Temple (1746)
Arch (18th century)
Sham Church (18th century)
`TL 510 780`

On the Norfolk border by Thetford is Euston Hall, which was built on land so poor that, in the words of Robert Bloomfield, the

A peaceful riparian scene—but the church is a sham

poet and author of *The Farmer's Boy* (1800), 'whole fields hereabout get up and blow away'. While they were struggling to make a profit from these miserable acres it is surprising that the Dukes of Grafton had the time or the money for architectural fripperies in the park; but there is a fine and elaborate Temple or Banqueting House by Kent dated 1746, an eyecatcher arch, also by Kent, and a watermill disguised as a church with battlemented tower. As at Holkham, Matthew Brettenham was involved with Kent, although he is not specifically credited with any of the buildings.

Eye

Sham Castle (19th century)
TM 150 740

The site of the not very grand motte-and-bailey castle at Eye was recycled twice, once in the 17th century, when a windmill was erected on the disused castle mound, and again in the 19th century, when it was replaced by a sham castle, but that has also deteriorated. Now the council seeks to make Eye Castle famous again as a tourist attraction by clearing away the undergrowth and improving accessibility.

Freston

Freston Tower (1549)
TM 170 390

Freston Tower, on the banks of the Orwell, has an uncertain history. The date of its construction is given as 1549; some say it was by Edward Latimer, others by Hugh de Freston. Its purpose is equally obscure: whether it was part of a long forgotten house or simply a free-standing prospect tower is not known. One point in favour of the more prosaic first explanation is that the bottom three stories on the south side are windowless, which they would be, of course, if this part of the tower had abutted another building. This side also has the only entrance, a miserable little affair compared with the sophistication of the rest of the building and fit only for an internal doorway (although a turn-of-the-century postcard shows it with a brick arched surround). Finally, there are traces on the brickwork of there having been some other structure joined to the tower at some stage. Nevertheless, the only story one hears with any degree of regularity is that of the education of the lovely Ellen de Freston, for which the tower was built—even the

Freston Tower—England's oldest folly?

curriculum has been handed down to us:

Monday (Ground floor): Charity
Tuesday (First floor): Tapestry
Wednesday (Second floor): Music
Thursday (Third floor): Painting
Friday (Fourth floor): Literature
Saturday (Fifth floor): Astronomy
Sunday (out of the tower): Church

It makes a good story. Other versions have her ending up on the roof in the arms of the builder, furthering her education in a different way.

Great Bealings

Trimurti (1806)
TM 240 480

Major Edward Moor (1771–1848) was interested in two peoples: the deities of India and the inhabitants of Suffolk. Of the first he wrote the authoritative *Hindoo Pantheon*, of the second *Suffolk Words and Phrases*, and in between he published a pamphlet setting out plans on how to reduce Britain's national debt. Moor returned from India a learned man, and when he bought Bealings House, he also built himself Trimurti (signifying the trinity of deities: Bramah, Shiva and Vishnu), a little temple, which the locals supposed was to be the pyramidal burial place of all these statuettes of Hindoo gods he was so conversant with.

Great Saxham

Grandfather's (early 18th century)
Tea House (early 18th century)
Umbrello (early 19th century)
TL 780 630

Grandfather's (no suffix) sounded great, a sort of wendy house for elderly children perhaps. In fact, it turned out to be the Temple of Dido at Saxham Hall, the grand house whose predecessor had a much better name: Nutmeg Hall, thus named by its builder John Eldred who made it big in spices in the late 16th century. It was changed by Robert Adam in 1774 into what a century later would have become the agreed style for lunatic asylums, seaside hotels and stations. Sadly, this house burned down in 1779 and a new one was planned, the present Saxham Hall. Dido's Temple must have belonged to the still unreformed Nutmeg Hall, and dates possibly from the 1730s or 1740s. It is hexagonal and built of brick with bands of vermiculated rustication.

Its sister in the park is the Tea House, which mirrors the Temple's design but was much changed around 1840.

The best building is, of course, the Umbrello, which smacks of Batty Langley's designs but may have been erected as late as the early 19th century. The Coade stone pillars are marked COADE & SEALY/LAMBETH. The Umbrello is octagonal with ogee arches and pyramidal pinnacles on top. It has lost its domed roof, and although Save Britain's Heritage's *Pavilions in Peril* made a case for its restoration, we must say the Umbrello looks much better without than with its roof.

Hadleigh

Sham Ruin (late 18th–early 19th century)
Taylor Monument (1819)
TM 030 430

At the back of 2 Benton Street, Hadleigh, is an undated Gothick sham ruin. It is a

The Ice-house at Heveningham Hall

delightful gimcrack wall, with some spoils introduced into the fabric and extremely slapdash—there is no delicate trailing off of the wall, no crusty spikes along the top; it is not Gothick, more Norman.

Just to the west of the town on Aldham Common is the 1819 monument to the memory of the giant Dr Rowland Taylor, sometime parson of Hadleigh, who was burned to death in 1555 for being a Protestant.

Helmingham Obelisk

Helmingham

Obelisk (early 19th century)
TM 180 570

Near Stowmarket is Helmingham Hall, the estate of the Tollemache family. Some way from the house is a tall and crumbling brick obelisk on an artificial mound beside a pond, which was probably formed when the mound was thrown up. John Nash worked at the Hall in 1800, but locals say the obelisk was built from the remains of a cottage on the mound, which was used as Lord Tollemache's rallying point for the local militia in the Napoleonic Wars.

Heveningham Hall

Temple (18th century)
Ice-house (18th century)
TM 350 740

The northeast corner of Suffolk is almost bare of follies. There is a little temple by James Wyatt in the grounds of Heveningham Hall, a property that is, at the time of writing, in the throes of being restored 'regardless of expense by a furriner' and that also boasts a magnificent thatched ice-house with stepped gables at the entrance, very similar to the one at Holkham Hall in Norfolk. At Huntingfield, northwest of Heveningham, stands a Gothick castellated house, which probably acted as an eyecatcher from the Hall.

Ickworth

Obelisk (1804)
The Round House (19th century)
TL 820 620

SACRED TO THE MEMORY OF
FREDERICK EARL OF BRISTOL
BISHOP OF DERRY
WHO DURING XXXV YEARS THAT HE PRESIDED
OVER THAT SEE,
ENDEARED HIMSELF TO ALL DENOMINATIONS OF
CHRISTIANS
RESIDENT IN THAT EXTENSIVE DIOCESE.
HE WAS THE FRIEND AND PROTECTOR OF THEM
ALL
HIS GREAT PATRONAGE WAS
UNIFORMLY ADMINISTERED UPON THE PUREST,
AND
MOST DISINTERESTED PRINCIPLES.
VARIOUS AND IMPORTANT PUBLIC WORKS
WERE UNDERTAKEN AT HIS INSTIGATION
AND COMPLETED BY HIS MUNIFICENCE
AND HOSTILE SECTS WHICH HAD LONG
ENTERTAINED
FEELINGS OF DEEP ANIMOSITY TOWARDS EACH
OTHER
WERE GRADUALLY SOFTENED AND RECONCILED
BY HIS INFLUENCE AND EXAMPLE.
GRATEFUL FOR BENEFITS
WHICH THEY CAN NEVER FORGET
THE INHABITANTS OF DERRY HAVE ERECTED AT
ICKWORTH
WHERE HIS MORTAL REMAINS WERE DEPOSITED
THIS DURABLE RECORD OF THEIR ATTACHMENT.
THE ROMAN CATHOLIC BISHOP AND THE
DISSENTING MINISTER
RESIDENT AT DERRY WERE AMONG THOSE THAT
CONTRIBUTED
TO THIS MONUMENT

This remarkable inscription is to be found on a big, solitary and hidden obelisk in a field southwest of the National Trust's Ickworth House, outside Bury St Edmunds. Frederick Augustus Hervey (1730–1803), Bishop of Derry, 4th Earl of Bristol, 5th Baron Howard de Walden, was ambitious, enormously wealthy, keen on art, obsessed with building and, thankfully for us, as eccentric as all the Herveys. He was also that rare thing among 18th-century aristocrats, a man blessed with a strong social conscience and a highly developed sense of fair play. Unlike many of his predecessors, he took an active interest in the affairs of his large and prosperous diocese, building new roads and bridges, sponsoring coal mining operations, even appointing an Irishman as his chaplain, an unheard of move for an Anglican bishop. While not going so far as to advocate an independent Ireland—such an attitude would have been rare indeed among the ruling classes—he did believe that the franchise should be extended to Roman Catholics.

But it is his buildings that concern us here, particularly those in Suffolk. The obelisk was erected to his memory, and surprisingly enough that glorious paean of praise would seem to be largely true. What also surprises is that the only other folly on the estate would appear to be Ickworth House itself, one of the very few circular or, more precisely, ovoid stately homes. It was begun in 1796 by the Irish architect Francis Sandys from a design by Mario Asprucci, but as the earl bishop had already started on a circular house in Ballyscullion, Co. Londonderry, in 1787 (which was, in turn, inspired by John Plaw's circular house Belle Ile in Lake Windermere) the origin of the idea is evident. Even earlier, in 1785, Hervey had built the circular Mussenden Temple in Co. Londonderry on a magnificent coastal site. He attracted a certain degree of criticism by naming it after Mrs Mussenden, a notably attractive 22-year-old widow, but she alleviated any hint of scandal by conveniently dying before it was finished. The earl bishop demonstrated his untypical liberalism by allowing the local Catholics to celebrate Mass there.

Back to Suffolk, where the only other interesting building on the estate is, not surprisingly, called The Round House. This is a private house with a conical roof and central chimney, half-timbered under the eaves and well hidden from the main road. It looks too recent to have been the responsibility of the bishop, and we are left to ponder the ambiguity of the 18th-century comment on his eccentricity: 'God created men, women and Herveys.'

Lowestoft

Tower House (1865)
TM 550 930

Pevsner describes the Tower House in The Marina as 'a nightmarish High Victorian house'. It was built in the ubiquitous yellow brick of the town in 1865.

Nacton

Towers (1854; 1859)
TM 220 380

Orwell Park stands on the north bank of the
Orwell, in the village of Nacton. It used to be
the home of Admiral Vernon, nicknamed
'Old Grogram' from his habit of wearing
trousers in that material and cursed by
generations of sailors for decreeing that the
naval issue of rum should be watered down—
hence 'grog'. The house is now a preparatory
school, and in the grounds are not one but
three towers erected by George Tilman in the
mid-19th century. One is an observatory
tower attached to the house, another is an
Italianate water tower, and the third is a clock
tower with a circular stair turret, dated 1859.

Redgrave

Folly Lodge (c.1766)
TM 050 780

Redgrave Hall was demolished after World
War II but, as so often happens, some of the
garden buildings have remained, although
their existence has been a precarious one.
The Fishing Lodge or boathouse will
probably have collapsed by now. It is a
rusticated little building, built around 1766
by Lancelot Brown, who not only designed
park, garden buildings and (demolished)
orangery, but also the main house. Redgrave
has long been a no-hoper, but in 1990 work
started on the restoration of what is
alternately called Folly Lodge, The Folly, the
Round House and the Lodge—it is all the
same building and is neither round nor a
folly, just a brick, octagonal temple with blind
arched windows and a domed roof.

Rendlesham

Woodbridge Lodge (late 18th–early 19th century)
Ivy Lodge (late 18th–early 19th century)
TM 340 540

East of Wickham Market, in the flatlands
known as the Sandlings, is the most amazing
lodge in Britain. Rendlesham as a village no
longer really exists, but 1500 years ago it was
the seat of the kings of East Anglia. Even
Rendlesham Hall disappeared in 1950, but its
lodges survive.

Woodbridge Lodge is confusingly marked
on the Ordnance Survey map as a water
tower, but anything less like any form of water
tower is difficult to imagine. It looks like an
insane chapter house from a madman's
cathedral; from the outside it is impossible to
divine the floor plan without the most
detailed investigation, so cluttered up is the
exterior with buttresses and pinnacles. As the
column was promoted from a mere
architectural artefact (a device for supporting
other parts of a building), into an end in itself
in the monumental column, so here at
Rendlesham we see the same promotion of
the far more exciting flying buttress into an
end in itself. Woodbridge Lodge is little more
than an exercise in flying buttresses and
pinnacles, with a little house crammed in
there among them. Four graceful and mighty
buttresses, enough to hold up a good sized
abbey, fly up to support only themselves; they
are cleverly disguised chimneys. The building
is variously dated between 1790 and 1820, and
it was constructed for Peter Isaac Thellusson,
son of Peter Thellusson, who was thought by
many to be the richest man in England when
he died in 1799. In 1801 Thellusson employed
Henry Hakewill, an architect whose speciality

The bizarre buttresses of Woodbridge Lodge

Stoke-by-Nayland Fishing Temple

was Tudor Gothic, to Gothicize Rendlesham
Hall. The lodge could well be attributed to
Hakewill or it could have been built in 1806 to
celebrate Thellusson's elevation to the
peerage as Baron Rendlesham. Recently a
new theory has emerged: Hugh Pilkington,
the architect who has carried out a
sympathetic restoration and extension of the
lodge, thinks it may have been inspired by
Chichester's market cross, a view of which
appeared in 1806—which would tie in nicely
with the Hakewill attribution.

Ivy Lodge, at the main entrance gate to
Bentwaters RAF base, is so covered with ivy
that it is difficult again to discern its real
shape, but it consists of a ruined tower joined
by an elegant arch, which spans the drive to a
smaller tower. Through the gate the entrance
to the lodge proper, which is in the larger
ruined tower, is through a semicircular
arched doorway flanked by two matching
windows, the whole set in a large infilled
dropped arch. It may be that the ivy supports
the building; certainly in the last five years it
has grown to such an extent that the folly is
currently more vegetation than construction.

Sternfield

Garden Buildings (19th century)
LM 390 620

Sternfield House is a superior B&B, and its
garden appears to contain not only a classical
temple and a rustic hut, but also a tea-house
with Dutch tiles and some grotwork. We have
not seen them.

Stoke-by-Nayland

Fishing Temple (1760s)
TL 990 360

Like Redgrave, Tendring Hall was
demolished after World War II, but the
classical Fishing Temple or Lodge of the
mid-18th century survives in extremely
healthy condition along the grand canal. It
has been attributed to Sir Robert Taylor, who
on his Tour of Europe found it necessary to
disguise himself as a monk—we often find
that need as well. He was a shrewd and able
architect whose bequest of an enormous
fortune to Oxford University was contested
by his son Michel Angelo. The lodge is very
fine, and one can imagine why it is usually
attributed to Soane, who built the house.
Further away a boathouse ('Bavarian Tudor')
of 1854 has been reported.

Tattingstone

Tattingstone Wonder (1790)
TM 140 360

The rather cruel epithet 'Silly Suffolk', which
has oppressed the county for years, is
claimed by Suffolk partisans to be a linguistic
corruption of 'Selig Suffolk', Selig being the
German for fortunate or blessed. Why the
Germans should have chosen this particular
word (which also means deceased) to
describe an English county is not revealed;
the English appellations for places such as
Württemburg or Baden elude us for the
moment. Certainly the blessed inhabitants of

the village of Tattingstone were silly enough in 1790 for the local squire, Edward White, to vow to give them something they could really gawp at. Thus came the Tattingstone Wonder, one of the most famous follies in Britain. Its fame stems largely from its euphonious name, because it is far from being the only one of its type—indeed, there are several follies in Suffolk itself that are more bizarre. Nevertheless, the Wonder is a splendid example of a folly.

It started life as a pair of cottages, until Squire White decided to enliven the view from Tattingstone Place. He built a third cottage on the end and topped it with a square flint church tower, omitting the southern wall because it wasn't visible from the house. The front of the cottages was replaced by a façade with two Gothic windows, and the crowning touch was a large rose window on the southeastern wall.

Since we first visited, the then uninhabited cottages have been converted into a single house, and the valley between the Wonder and the big house has been flooded to make the Alton reservoir, thereby adding a touch of landscaping of which Squire White would surely have approved. However, the 18th-century shock of seeing an apparent church occupied as a house has diminished enormously in the late 20th century because of the spate of church conversions scattered across the land—nowadays it comes as no surprise or wonder to be seen to be living in a church. White's once daring and famous joke has become a commonplace.

Thorpeness

The House in the Clouds (1920s)
TM 470 600

The village of Thorpeness, north of Aldeburgh, is unusual in that it was built in its entirety as a speculative development holiday centre. The old fishing hamlet of Thorpe was acquired by G. Stuart Ogilvie, landowner, playwright and barrister, who proceeded to build what his copywriters variously described as 'the ideal holiday village' and 'the Home of Peter Pan'. One problem was how to supply expected amenities, such as mains water, in the Home of Peter Pan without disfiguring the landscape with an obtrusive water tower. The answer came with the removal of a windmill from Aldringham, the next village, to replace the American 'New Mill', which pumped water into a rusty iron tank beside it. A system of lakes and waterways, called The Meare, complete with a miniature sham fort had been designed by Ogilvie in 1910, but the war intervened and it was not until 1923 that he installed the 'new' old post-mill and cast around for a suitable means of disguising the necessary water tank.

Ogilvie was very fond of dovecotes, and

Now you see a church, now you don't—the Tattingstone Wonder

had already disguised his own water tower at Sizewell Court a mile up the coast as a dovecote in 1908, using the bottom part as a carpenter's workshop. What more natural than to use the same pleasurable idea at Thorpeness, but on a very much larger scale? So The Gazebo was built—a five-storey house underneath the brilliantly disguised 30,000 gallon water tank. The tank was concealed in an everyday clapboarded house with pitched roof, chimneys and sham windows, perched incongruously on top of a 60ft (18m) tower. 'Who on earth would want to live in it with all the water rushing up and down?' was the major objection to the scheme, but Ogilvie had no difficulty finding tenants. Mr and Mrs Malcolm Mason moved

Suffolk on stilts— the House in the Clouds

in, and Mrs Mason loved it. She wrote poems for children, and one, inspired by her house, was called 'The House in the Clouds':

> *The fairies really own this house—or so*
> *   the children say—*
> *In fact, they all of them moved in upon*
> *   the self same day…*

When she recited this to Ogilvie one evening at dinner he was enchanted, and exclaimed: 'The name must be changed to The House in the Clouds—and you are my Lady of the Stairs and Starlight!' So The House in the Clouds it became, and the choice of name, like the Tattingstone Wonder, has helped make this one of the most famous follies in the country.

The success of Thorpeness meant that yet more water was needed, so a 40,000 gallon tank was built in 1929. This was camouflaged as a large, square, faintly Norman tower over an arch in a parade of mock Tudor houses. Thorpeness is now on mains water, and the huge tank in the House in the Clouds has been dismantled. A recent owner put a bathroom in on each floor, overspent and had to sell—the present owners now let it out privately as holiday accommodation with a big difference. Children adore it.

Wattisham

The Castle (late 18th century)
TM 020 500

The Castle is a castellated farm on the Needham Market–Bildeston road—an eyecatcher with towers, traceries and all the rest.

Westleton

The Barn Gardens (1950s onwards)
TM 450 690

The pretty village of Westleton hides one of the most remarkable contemporary garden designs in Britain. Its creator, former Conservative MEP and leading patents barrister Amédé Turner, has been gradually extending his garden since 1952, incorporating many of the odds and ends that have come his way over the years, including the front carriage of the Brighton Belle, African tribal masks, mirror balls, large plastic chains and 78 Art Deco lift doors. 'I like gardens that make you think,' Mr Turner explains. 'Capability Brown doesn't make you think of anything except meadows.' Today the garden's annual open day attracts up to 600 people. 'At first people hated it,' says Mr Turner. 'They used to leave rude messages, and when I first suggested opening it to the National Trust Gardens Scheme they came round and said, "But this isn't a garden." These days, however, people do seem to be genuinely interested.'

The garden is divided into at least ten areas, including the Palace of Nestor, a life-size reproduction of the Greek original; the Blue Stone Circle, a full-size replica of Stonehenge made from lift doors; and the Pavilion, a little acropolis on an artificial mound, also made out of lift doors. The Land Lines are perhaps favourite: a network of sunken paths the idea for which 'came to me in a delirium after eating a poisoned oyster'.

It's all somewhat weird, to say the least, and Turner's own notes and map will serve to deepen the mystery of a man's mind. Weird—but that's how we like it.

Woolverstone

The Cat House (1793)
TM 190 380

The nameless peninsula separating the Orwell and the Stour is the home to two other famous follies as well as Freston Tower and Erwarton Gatehouse—the Cat House and the Tattingstone Wonder. Woolverstone, a popular yachting centre and marina along the banks of the Orwell, is famous for The Cat House, a castellated red brick Gothic cottage, dating from 1793, on the riverside. The east wall is taken up almost entirely by an enormous Gothic window, only partly

real, which formerly (until the trees grew up) overlooked the Orwell. In the bottom left-hand corner of this window sat a painted cat, and the local tale is that the cat was displayed to tell smugglers that the coast was clear. This was the particular pastime of local servant girl Margaret Catchpole, who lived at the house, in order to help her lover, the smuggler Will Laud.

Incidentally, another painted window in the county is at Mulberry House, the old vicarage in Pakenham, near Bury St Edmunds, where an upstairs window has a 18th-century parson in wig and bands looking out. We had hoped to hear that he was put in the window whenever the Devil was around to warn him that the coast was not clear, but there is no local legend here: it was painted by Rex Whistler when he was stationed nearby during World War II.

Worlingham

Castle Farm (c.1800)
TM 440 900

After Ickworth, Francis Sandys must have started on Worlingham Hall for the squire Robert Sparrow, and he may also have been responsible for Castle Farm to the west of Worlingham. It is not in the Gothick mode but in the Norman style, which appears to have been more in favour in East Anglia than in the rest of Britain, probably because of its many surviving church towers. It does stand out among the 20th-century new homes.

Woolverstone Cat House—the cat was painted on a window round the corner to the left

SURREY

Surrey is full of surprises. Whitaker Wright's work at Witley Park is indubitably the most awesome, but there are wonderful gardens, towers and sham ruins to be found all over this much maligned county. The outsider's general attitude is that Surrey was long ago concreted over to make a car park, but although it has a very high population density, there are still some rural, if not remote, spots to be discovered. Surrey does have a splendid quantity of folly towers, far more than one would expect from a county of such unremarkable hills, and at Cobham it

also has the renascent glories of Painshill. With Kew and Richmond now in Greater London, the only estates left in Surrey that concern us here are Woburn Park at Addlestone, Albury Park at Shere and Busbridge at Godalming. The grotto at Oatlands Park in Weybridge, which cost £40,000 to build in the mid-18th century, was demolished in 1948 by the local council and the Ministry of Works. The grotto was said to be unsafe, but could be demolished only with the aid of the Royal Engineer Corps, which had to stack the beautiful grotto with packs of dynamite an blow it up. It was said to be the finest grotto in Britain.

Addlestone

Arches (18th century)
Grotto (18th century)
`TQ 030 640`

All that remains at Woburn Park, once the site of Philip Southcote's experimental, landscaped *ferme ornée* of 1735, are two brick arches by Kent and a grotto, but the importance of Woburn has never been in what it did for follies or garden buildings, but for the development of the landscape garden, although the *ferme ornée*, despite so many pleasant designs, proved a dead end in garden art—a vista that should be opened up again.

Albury

Burmese Temple (19th century?)
Albury Park Grotto (1676)
Tunnel
`TQ 050 470`

Albury is pretty and petite, nothing grand or grandiose in its borders, and despite being such an obvious anomaly in the village, the wooden Burmese Temple or hut in the garden of Rose Hill House manages somehow to look as if it belonged. It is really more like a garden seat, high on four wooden pillars with three sides open and well crafted, and a carved cupola roof. It is well cared for

by the owners and must be 19th century. The pavilion was saved by the present owners, and came from Blackheath, a village nearby. It must have come from somewhere originally— Asia or thereabouts obviously, but after that? A Colonial Exhibition?

Albury Park has 17th-century terraced gardens laid out by the diarist and gardener John Evelyn in 1655 for the Duke of Norfolk. There are no follies as such, but there is an empty grotto dated 1676, and the famous 500ft (152m) tunnel or 'crypta' Evelyn made through the sandstone hill. The Norfolks have been great folly patrons over the years, and this seems to have been the family's first venture into landscape amelioration. A younger brother, Charles Howard, also had tunnels at Deepdene in Dorking, but these disappeared long ago.

Box Hill

Labellière's Grave (1800)
`TQ 170 520`

The remains of yet another expensive military folly are near the grave of Major Peter Labellière, at the bottom of a 100ft (30m) shaft. Labellière was a strange man, who lived on a pension, spent much of it on charity, inhabited Dorking's Hole-in-the-Wall cottage and was nicknamed 'The Walking

Dunghill' because of his personal hygiene and appearance. Yet thousands of people came to Labellière's funeral on Box Hill, on 11 June 1800. On the Major's earlier request the youngest son of his landlady performed a little jig on his coffin, and then the coffin was lowered into the shaft. He was buried head first, because at the Day of Judgement... (see Leith Hill, below).

Broadwood's Folly (c.1815)
TQ 170 520

Compared with the tower at Leith Hill (see below), the one on Box Hill is a much more modest affair. It is a round flint building with a blocked-up doorway, possibly built as a Waterloo monument by Thomas Broadwood, the piano-maker. Box Hill was developed in 1891 as one of the major spearheads against a French and/or Russian invasion. The retired General Sir E. Hamley was convinced an invasion from the sea was imminent, and in the 1880s he developed a scheme in which an early version of the Home Guard would defend London from new forts in the area around the capital. The government went along with the idea, and work on a fort on Box Hill was started, but when Hamley died shortly after, the moving force had gone and all came to nothing.

Caterham

Whitehill Folly (1862)
TQ 327 537

Whitehill Folly is no longer an anonymous flint, stone and brick tower in War Coppice Road, which runs along a ridge called

Whitehill Folly

Arthur's Seat south of Caterham. Andrew Plumridge has found out something more about this castellated tower. It was built in 1862 by a Mr Jeremiah Long, whose house was called Arthur's Seat. It must have been built for the view, but the better story is that Mr Long got interested in views only after one of his sons died at sea, because from the top you actually can see the sea. Somewhere along the way the fourth storey must have been added, probably when the trees around it threatened to obscure the view.

Chaldon

Water Tower (19th century)
TQ 310 550

Willey Farm has a fine water tower of flint and brick.

Chatley Heath

Semaphore Tower (1821–2)
TQ 090 580

One of three surviving semaphore towers in Surrey and forming a line between London and Portsmouth, the tower is just by Painshill. Octagonal and five storeys high, it looks to all intents and purposes like a real folly tower.

Chertsey

Gazebo (1794)
TQ 030 660

As an amateur, Charles Hamilton of Painshill concentrated on his own garden and did little advisory work, unlike his contemporary, William Shenstone of The Leasowes, who was consulted about several Midlands gardens. Hamilton's only outside commissions appear to have been at Bowood House in Wiltshire and St Anne's Hill west of Chertsey, which left other Surrey estates free for the professionals. Charles James Fox's St Anne's Hill has recently lost a Temple of Friendship, a derelict Gothicky tea-house grotto built in 1794, after Hamilton's death, and an octagonal gazebo of the same date, which is now in the grounds of a house called Southwood. The M3 thunders by underneath, all hopes of tranquillity gone.

Chobham

Bell Tower (1910)
SU 970 630

At Westcroft Park northwest of Chobham is a magnificent bell tower, a folly only in that the tower was needed to fulfil a life-long ambition. H.O. Serpell, a biscuit manufacturer from Plymouth, loved the sound of church bells as a child and determined that one day, if he could, he would have his own peal. Biscuits showed him the way to his fortune, and in 1910 he treated himself to a carillon of 25 bells, the largest weighing a quarter of a ton, which he placed in a half-timbered tower in his garden. We have not had an opportunity to ask the neighbours how they feel about it.

Claremont

Belvedere (1717)
Garden Buildings (18th–19th century)
TQ 140 630

William Kent worked at Addlestone, Richmond, Oatlands and Claremont, where Charles Bridgeman and Lancelot Brown also worked. Claremont, just 3 miles away from Painshill, was the only estate that came near to rivalling it for breadth of imagination, yet even with the help of the three greatest names in the greatest period of English landscape gardening, the work of the single dedicated amateur was judged to be the better. How satisfying for the English love of the non-professional.

Nevertheless, and despite having suffered nearly as many changes of ownership as Painshill, Claremont is a splendid estate. Sir John Vanbrugh was the first owner in 1708; he sold it to the Duke of Newcastle, who sold it to Clive of India; it was then bought by the nation as a wedding present for Princess Charlotte and Prince Leopold, who when he became King of Belgium lent it to Queen Victoria; she in turn lent it to the king and queen of France. Then it passed into the hands of the Forestry Commission. Queen Victoria bought it for her son Leopold; when his wife, the Duchess of Albany, died in 1922 the government confiscated the estate, as it would have passed to Queen Victoria's grandson, the Duke of Coburg, who was considered an enemy alien. Instead, it was bought by a director of Cunard. In 1931 it became a girls' school and later passed into other hands again. The National Trust acquired 50 acres (20ha) of the estate in 1949.

The most remarkable item to concern us at Claremont is the Belvedere, perhaps the first true folly, deliberately built for pleasure. Vanbrugh had sold the estate to Thomas Pelham (later the Duke of Newcastle) in 1714, but Pelham called him in to enlarge the house and to build the Belvedere in 1717. It is typically Vanbrughian in design: a massive square central section with four taller square towers at each corner. It is very large and gloomy for a building intended to be light-hearted, partly because of the grey-brown brick chosen for its construction, which is relieved only by Vanbrugh's banding and red brickwork over the round-arched windows, and partly because of its enclosure by heavy, dark trees. Originally it was whitewashed. Several years ago the Belvedere was derelict but still solid; now that a restoration programme has taken place it conveys an air of forced gaiety. It is difficult to imagine that a politician such as Pelham commissioned such a piece voluntarily; it seems more likely Vanbrugh had already designed it and determined its site, then persuaded Pelham to pay.

The stir caused by the Belvedere must have pleased the dour Pelham, for he went on to commission William Kent to build some other little follies in the grounds, including a Bowling Green House and a Temple on an island in Bridgeman's lake. The temple survives, as does a four-arched grotto and a thatched house, but the other buildings have gone. A 19th-century obelisk to commemorate Clive, Prince Leopold and Princess Charlotte also survives, as does a Gothic retreat, designed by J.W. Hiort and John Papworth in 1816 for the princess and converted into a chapel after her death a year later.

Claygate

Semaphore Tower (1821–2)
TQ 150 630

In Telegraph Lane, Telegraph Hill, the three-storey Semaphore Tower, lower than the one at Chatley Heath, has been converted into a house.

Ruxley Towers (1872)
TQ 150 630

Ruxley Towers is best described in Pevsner's words: 'Among later additions one very tall and very bad stucco Gothic tower of c.1830 with a frightening silhouette and gargoyles.' It was, in fact, added as a belvedere to the 1765 house by Lord Foley in 1872. That never stopped it from being Grade II listed, and it has now been converted, winning a conservation award. In the no-expense-spared conversion, there are lead gargoyles on every possible angle. The house was divided into four in 1996, and the developer marketed the four bedroom, six-storey tower without a lift at £1.25 million. The stucco is garish and glaring, and we like it that way.

Cobham

Painshill Park (mid-18th century)
TQ 100 600

In 1738 the Hon. Charles Hamilton, the ninth and youngest son of the Earl of Abercorn, returned from his European Grand Tour with a love of romantic landscape painting and a head full of ideas. He bought a 31-year lease on 200 acres (80ha) of land near Cobham Bridge, formerly part of a deer park belonging to Henry VIII, and set about re-creating in reality the romantic ruined landscapes popularized by Poussin, Rosa and Giovanni Panini. To prepare his canvas, Hamilton first burned the existing heather, then planted turnips which he fed to sheep, then sowed grass over the entire estate. This done, he proceeded to achieve one of the triumphs of 18th-century English landscape gardening. The park at Painshill was lauded by all Hamilton's contemporaries, by people as diverse as Walpole and Wesley; the amateur had succeeded beyond the expectations of professionals, from Kent to Brown. For 35 years Charles Hamilton lovingly created the finest garden in England from unpromising material—Walpole commented, 'he has really made a fine place out of a most cursed hill'—until at the age of 71, crippled by debts and arthritis, he was forced to sell. All the walks, the vistas, the lakes, follies, canals and bridges, were left to

The Grotto before its restoration

moulder away, until after 200 years they had all but disappeared.

But help came from an unexpected source: over the last 20 years Elmbridge Council purchased 158 acres (64ha) of the original estate and a charity called the Painshill Park Trust was set up to attempt to preserve what is left and where possible to re-create Painshill as it was in Hamilton's day. Many of the follies were beyond redemption, but some of the choicest items are undergoing complete restoration or indeed reconstruction from the ground up. The Gothick Tent or Temple is perhaps the best known of these; it now looks brand new, perhaps a little too white and pristine. Nevertheless, it remains a beautiful building: small, decagonal and pinnacled, with ogee arches below quatrefoil windows. It has been

Painshill Park with the Gothick Temple

attributed to Batty Langley, but there is no real evidence for the claim and it is more reasonable to suppose that Hamilton acted as his own architect. Walpole was less enthusiastic:

> In all Gothic designs, they should be made something that was of that time, a part of a church, a castle, a convent or a mansion. The Goths never built summerhouses or temples in a garden. This of Mr Hamilton's stands on the brow of a hill—there an imitation of a fort or watch-tower would have been proper.

The centrepiece of the garden is the artificial lake, 19 acres (8ha) of it, which Hamilton constructed *c.*1760 at some height above the level of the River Mole and fed through an elaborate system of locks and waterwheels. Batty Langley, who died in 1751, had been advertising his services to provide 'Engines for raising Water in any Quantity to any height required, for the service of Noblemen's Seats, Cities Towns &c.', so the possibility that he was earlier called in to advise cannot be discounted. The remarkable thing is that the artificial lake has now become natural. The horse-wheel that Hamilton used to pump up water from the Mole and its later replacement, a massive cast-iron Bramah wheel of the 1820s, are now redundant for the lake sustains itself through rainfall and surface drainage.

In addition to the Tent, Hamilton built a superb grotto, severely damaged by soldiers billeted at Painshill during the war, a hermitage (one of the very few that actually had a live hermit), a Roman mausoleum,

arches, a Turkish tent, designed by Henry Keene, a ruined abbey, a Temple of Bacchus, which is based on the Maison Carrée at Nîmes, and a tall, red brick prospect tower, which is one of England's most visible follies as it overlooks the busy A3. The grotto was intact until shortly after the war, when its roof collapsed after the lead had been stolen. Enough remained to inspire a real sense of awe at the care and dedication that went into the construction. The ruined abbey is surprisingly large, and looks more like an early industrial building than an ecclesiastical one. The house itself was designed for Hamilton in 1774 by Richard Jupp, the architect of Severndroog Castle, but Hamilton had to sell the estate the following year, so it was built for his successor, Benjamin Hopkins, in 1778.

It is an enormous relief to folly lovers—and all admirers of the English landscape garden—that this unique park is being restored with the same degree of dedication as Hamilton himself must have lavished on his garden. Other ghost gardens such as Enville, Hawkstone and Hackfall would indeed be fortunate to be rescued with equal affection and scholarship. The park is now open to the public, as it was in Hamilton's day.

Since the first edition of this book, the awareness of follies and garden buildings has grown and grown. Of course, Hawkstone has been admirably restored, Hackfall is stable at the moment and only Enville awaits further restoration (after a job well done on Sanderson Miller's orangery/museum/billiard room). At Painshill itself, the work

The sparkling Sham Abbey

has been pioneering. The Turkish tent has been completely rebuilt—although sited some 50 metres from its original spot—and Diana Reynell has been working on the grotto. No doubt others will follow. Well done, Painshillians.

Foxwarren Watch Tower (1850s)
`TQ 100 600`

Near Painshill is Foxwarren Park. Its one folly, a garish watch tower built by Frederick Barnes for Charles Buxton, is totally eclipsed by the Painshill follies. Nevertheless, Foxwarren's buildings—lodges, model farm and others—show the full joyous flush of Victorian architectural exuberance.

Compton

Watts's Memorial Chapel (1896–1901)
`SU 960 470`

The reader will have noticed that we permit ourselves now and again to deviate from the subject, either because something is follyesque, remarkable, curious, funny or just plain beautiful. The Watts Chapel is all of those things, although it is a highly serious building. It is a terracotta dream in a mixture of the Italianate, Arts and Crafts, Art Nouveau, Glasgow School and Celtic Revival styles. It was designed by Mrs Watts and has one of G.F. Watts's paintings over the altar. The Watts Gallery next door is less remarkable but still beautiful, and one should search out the gravestones in the burial ground for one or two funereal gems.

Dorking

Stedman's Folly (1828)
`TQ 170 470`

Tower Hill Cottage is a mystery. Its other name is Stedman's Folly, obviously after the owner and builder of this extended flint and brick folly tower, which was sold by Pavilions of Splendour in 1995. We haven't found the location of another nearby 'tower converted into a house' unless it is either a repeat report of Stedman's Folly or the Observatory near Milton, outside Dorking, which was built in 1847–8 by Decimus Burton.

East Horsley

East Horsley Towers (1858)
`TQ 090 530`

The tessellated tower built by William King, 1st Earl of Lovelace, naturally gives the house its name, and it is banded with plaques,

East Horsley Towers

successively depicting stars, horns and grenades (believed to be the devices of Surrey regiments). The round tower stands at the end of the former drive to the house, now unused because the elaborate and extraordinary tunnels through which it passes are said to be unsafe, and it is precisely from these tunnels that the classic, shattering view of the overpowering tower-and-turret is to be had. The most astonishing thing is that the man repeated here what he had done 20 years earlier at Ashley Combe House near Porlock in Somerset (see there), using tunnels so that he did not have to see common folk going about their business.

Also at Horsley are a castellated Gothick dairy, a belvedere, a grotto in the grounds of a pub and a range of over-decorated and castellated lodges, cupolas and farm buildings.

Epsom

Tomb (19th century)
`TQ 210 590`

Epsom very suitably has a tomb to a horse in the grounds of Durdans in Woodcote Road.

Esher

Waynflete Tower (15th–18th century)
Traveller's Rest (1730s)
`TQ 140 640`

It is tempting to include Waynflete Tower, the gatehouse to Esher Place, in a list of Surrey follies. It looks like a folly but it was a genuine 15th-century gatehouse, minding its own business for 250 years until William Kent came along and Gothicized it for the Hon. Henry Pelham, younger brother of the

Duke of Newcastle at Claremont. What we see now owes rather more to Kent's romantic imagination than to the 15th century, like Stafford Castle or Castle Coch. So in it goes.

Pelham was in the right frame of mind in any case: in the 1730s he built the Travellers' Rest in the High Street, a sort of grotto bus shelter, and also a garden temple for Esher Place, which is now in the back garden of No. 36 Pelham's Walk. Both could logically be attributed to Kent.

Gatton

Gatton Town Hall (1765)
TQ 274 524

When we first heard about it, we dismissed Gatton Town Hall almost out of hand for acquiring folly status simply because of its name, reasoning that a town hall, no matter how bizarre, could not really be classed as a folly. We were wrong. Gatton was not a town, nor was it a village. It consisted of a church and one house, and yet this borough was represented in Westminster for nearly 400 years by two members of parliament. Naturally enough, the borough was abolished in the 1832 Reform Act, as the fourth rottenest in the country. In 1765 the owner of Gatton Park erected a Greek temple with iron columns in the park, behind a large urn on which was inscribed:

> Stat ductis Sortibus Urna
> Salus populi Suprema Lex Esto
> Comitium Gattoniense MDCCLXV
> H M Dolus Malus Abesto

Pevsner translates this:

> *When the lots have been drawn, the urn*
> *   remains*
> *Let the well-being of the people be the*
> *   supreme law*
> *The place of the assembly of Gatton 1765*
> *Let evil deception be absent.*

Cynicism or crass stupidity? Sometimes one wonders. Still, with 200 years' hindsight Gatton Town Hall can be seen as an attractive joke, despite the intrusion of modern school buildings close by.

In the park a Japanese garden and a rock garden have come to light, no doubt commissioned by Sir Jeremiah 'Mustard' Colman, who bought the estate in 1888.

Godalming

Busbridge Folly Group (early 19th century)
SU 970 410

Busbridge Hall was remodelled in 1775 for General Sir Robert Barker by John Crunden.

The house was demolished in 1906, but the early 19th-century gardens remained. The estate was split into two and the gardens went with Busbridge Lakes, a house converted from the old stable block. It is hard to believe we are in Surrey, because here are four succeeding lakes, bordered by louring red cliffs, managing to convey the impression we are a thousand miles from civilization. The cliffs, though small, are packed close to the lakes, giving a feeling of much greater size. This Surrey sandstone is easily worked, so there is a profusion of tunnels, caves and grottoes here. A hermit's cave, with pointed doorway and round windows on either side, houses an ice-house and a pillared chamber. Dating from 1756, it is thought to have been an earlier garden feature than the rest. It is a mausoleum for the wife and children of Philip Webb, Member of Parliament and amateur antiquarian, and it has a Roman spoil above the entrance.

A charming, tiny shell and bottle-glass grotto below a crumbling Doric temple carries the date 1810 and the initials of the builder, Henry Hare Townshend. There are two rustic bridges over the lakes, and there were other temples and a tower, but these have now gone. Still remaining are a stuccoed Sino-Gothic boathouse and the Ghost Walk, a splendid path up to the top of the cliff through gruesome fanged arches. Townshend died in 1824; his son Chauncey, unsurprisingly, after growing up in this romantic environment, became a poet.

The Thunder House (1895)
SU 970 410

Munstead, south of Godalming, is to all intends and purposes a villa-settlement of mainly Lutyens houses—if not by Edwin Lutyens himself, then at least the garden is by Gertrude Jekyll (who lived in one of the houses here)—there's Munstead House, Munstead Place, Munstead Wood, Munstead Grange, Little Munstead, Munstead Orchard—no great originality in house-names. But then comes The Thunder House, which was built in 1895 'for Miss Jekyll to watch storms coursing over the Wey valley' and is an overgrown triangular (so in the best folly traditions) gazebo.

Little Fort (18th century)
SU 970 410

Little Fort in Godalming itself is a revamped and extended turret from the early 18th century, built for the owners of Westbrook Place, now Meath Home.

Guildford

Clandon Park Follies (mid-19th century)
TQ 042 512

Clandon Park, east of Guildford, has a simple
flint and brick grotto, which is Kentian in
style, although the grounds were landscaped
by Brown and elevated above the ordinary by
a charming and elegant statue of the Three
Graces. There is also a surprisingly late
circular Ionic Temple of 1838, built for the
3rd Earl of Onslow by the father-and-son
partnership of William and Henry William
Inwood. Coincidentally, these two both died
in March 1843, one in bed, the other on
board a ship that sank in the Bay of Biscay.
The chief joy of Clandon, however, is the
genuine 18th-century Maori House, painted
red and grey, in the garden right by the
house. This was shipped over in the late 19th
century from Te Waioa in North Island, New
Zealand, by the 4th Earl, who had been
Governor there and who liked the country so
much that he gave his younger son a Maori
name, Huia. Poor thing.

Semaphore Tower (1821–22)
TQ 007 490

On Guildford's Pewley Hill stands the last of
the Surrey trio of Semaphore Towers. This
one has a cupola on top, presumably added
later when it was converted into a house.

Moat House (1840)
TQ 000 500

Moat House is an extended 18th-century
quarryman's cottage, which was bought by
Henry Emlyn in 1840. He changed it into a
mock church by adding a tower and steeple
because he wanted to remind himself of
Richmond Church, which he used to see
from his bedroom window when he was a
child. Sadly, the steeple was removed three
decades later, but new Gothicisms were
added. Whether it was at this stage that the
moat was dug around the house is not clear.
We prefer to think it was Mr Emlyn's, to sail
his boyhood boats in.

Booker's Folly (1839)
TQ 989 489

A year before Emlyn bought his dream
home, Mr Booker finished his folly tower.
The Gothic, buttressed, polygonal and four-
storey building stands in a picturesque
corner of Guildford Cemetery, and for its
builder, this was the right place: Mr Booker, a
local dignitary, lost two of his sons in 1824—
one drowned, the other died of smallpox. A

Booker's Folly

certain John Mason was engaged to build the
tower, and he may also have been its
designer. By the time the tower was finished
in 1839, however, its first and foremost
purpose as a memorial to the Booker
children appears to have been somewhat
neglected because Booker dedicated the
opening of it to the marriage of Victoria and
Albert. Cannon were fired, bells rung,
fireworks displayed and there was much to
eat and drink. Andrew Plumridge, who has
researched its history, writes that after the
tower had been taken into use, Booker
entertained his friends there, sitting in its
uppermost storey and surveying the
construction of the Woking railway. After
Booker's death the tower was used in
electrical experiments. Somewhere along the
way the sons were forgotten.

Merrow Grange (19th century)
TQ 017 506

Merrow Grange, in the northeastern suburbs
of Guildford, has Pulhamite wonders: arches
and niches, a mound and a subterranean
fernery as well as walkways, some in
disrepair, and all of the same Pulhamite
artificial stone. An apartment block has been

Pulhamite Grotto at Merrow Grange

Leith Hill

Hull's Tower (1765)

`TQ 140 430`

Surrey has a lot of towers, probably more than any other county, which seems strange in an area where the land never rises above 965ft (295m) without human aid. Admittedly, few of Surrey's towers are good follies. The biggest, the best and the most famous is Hull's Tower on the highest point in southeast England, the 965ft (195m) high Leith Hill. The tower, plain and square, was built in 1765, and the altruistic Mr Hull placed a plaque over the door, proclaiming in Latin that it had been built for Mr Hull's pleasure and for the pleasure of anyone else who wanted to take in the wonderful views from the top. After he died, this privilege was abused and the tower was severely vandalized, so the interior was filled with concrete rubble to prevent access.

When in 1864 W.J. Evelyn of Wotton Hall decided to open it up again, it was discovered that the rubble had set so hard it was impossible to remove, so a new octagonal stair turret was built on the side, incidentally raising the height at the top to 1000ft (305m) above sea level—the magic mountain in English terms. The view was remarkable: with a telescope it was possible to see the

constructed in the middle of the garden, yet much of the rockwork survives. It is well worth saving, and it is at this point that we realize someone ought to be writing a thorough study of Pulhamite and other related grotto materials.

A Bank Holiday at Leith Hill Tower in 1904

English Channel to the south and Dunstable Downs 50 miles to the north. But once again it was vandalized and had to be blocked up. Rumour spread that Hull was buried upside down at the bottom of the tower, so that when the Day of Judgement came and the whole world was turned upside down he would be on his feet to meet his Maker, a story we have come across before on the slopes of Box Hill.

Recently it was decided once again to open up the tower, this time attacking the solidified rubble with pneumatic drills. It was during this drilling in October 1984 that a National Trust workman broke through the bottom of the tower to discover Hull's tomb…

Lingfield

Starborough Castle (1754)
TQ 430 440

Solidly placed in the middle of the moat that used to be Starborough Castle, east of Lingfield, is a Gothick summerhouse, which was built for James Burrow in 1754 from old stones on the island. It is a square box of a building, buttressed, castellated, of course, with pinnacles on each corner, and overlooking the moat is a bay window. It has now appropriated the name of the original castle and was beautifully restored in the avaricious 1980s, just in time for the property slump.

Merstham

Tower-cum-dovecote (1840)
TQ 280 530

There was said to be a small, round folly tower dating from 1840 in the trees north of the church at Merstham, but it turned out to be a dovecote. Now the matter is completely academic anyway, as a falling tree in the storms of January 1990 sliced the tower in two.

Nutfield

Tower (19th century)
TQ 310 500

A small folly tower has been reported in the grounds of the Ewell House Country Hotel.

Peper Harow

Sham Ruin (1841–48)
Bonville Fount (1841–48)
SU 930 430

Sham ruins and real ruins go together to improve the Surrey landscape. At Peper

Harow (pronounced Peeper Harra, although some dispute this) A.W.N. Pugin designed a sham chapel and some farm buildings at Oxenford Grange as eyecatchers to Peper Harow Mansion in 1841–48. There is a beautiful barn, with a steeply pitched roof, looking like a sunken cathedral, and the arch lodge has a stubby tower over a non-existent road. The present owners tell us that the sham ruined chapel is real, only the window tracery being false, but the siting is uncannily perfect for the big house. Some of the walling is genuinely medieval—taken from the old Waverley Abbey Estate—but clearly it has been tastefully rearranged.

The real folly on the estate is the Bonville Fount, also by Pugin, but this has been heavily vandalized, and the owners are worried about its future. They are proud that the man who designed the Houses of Parliament designed their farmhouse, and the buildings are beautifully cared for, the sham chapel set inside an enclosing wall and a carefully tended garden.

Both the 18th-century (William Chambers) and the 19th-century lodges at Peper Harow House and Oxenford are extremely good and bold, and a flint, brick and tufa bath house by the Wey also survives.

Princes Coverts

Pump House (18th century)
TQ 160 610

In Stoke Wood, just outside Oxshott, is Jessop's Well, the pitiful 18th-century pump house remnants of a spa that was going to turn a Mr Jessop into a millionaire; the rival attractions of Epsom overwhelmed the enterprise.

Reigate

Sham Gatehouse (1777)
TQ 250 500

Another arrangement of genuine medieval architecture, like the sham chapel at Peper Harow, took place at Reigate in 1777. After the Civil War, the Parliamentarians demolished Reigate Castle. They left sufficient rubble for a mock medieval gatehouse to be built, and, in case of confusion, the builder, Richard Barnes, announced the deception with two plaques, one in Latin and one in English explaining that in 1777 he had erected the gateway on the site of the old castle at his own expense:

TO
SAVE THE MEMORY

Reigate Sham Gatehouse

OF
WILLIAM EARL WARREN
WHO IN OLD DAYS DWELT HERE
AND WAS
A LOYAL CHAMPION OF OUR LIBERTIES
FROM PERISHING
LIKE HIS OWN CASTLE
BY THE RAVAGES OF TIME

The so-called Baron's Cave was discovered not long ago and seems to have been the 18th-century meeting place of a convivial club of the Hell Fire-variety.

Colley Hill Temple (1909)
TQ 250 500

On top of Colley Hill stands a little temple, built expressly for walkers, with a topograph inside and on the ceiling a mosaic giving the position of the stars and the planets (excepting, of course, as Philip Neville learnedly observed, Pluto).

Obelisk
Chapel Mill (1765)
TQ 250 500

On Reigate Hill is a small, silent obelisk, and on Reigate Heath is a 1765 windmill, converted into a chapel in 1880, for reasons unknown.

Stoke d'Abernon

Decorated Farm (c.1886)
TQ 130 580

Wood Farm on the A245 from Leatherhead has a very good brick façade, partly castellated and with several towers and turrets. It is probably of the same date as Woodlands Park (by Rowland Plumbe, who worked at Hatchford Park), which is late for that sort of decoration.

Sutton (Greater London)

Grottoes (18th century)
Water House (c.1720)
TQ 274 650

Carshalton House and Carshalton Park both have grottoes, perhaps the relics of some forgotten 18th-century rivalry. Carshalton House is now a Roman Catholic convent, and at the head of the lake in the grounds is a five-bayed grotto façade screening a series of blocked-up rooms and passages. It was probably built for Thomas Walpole in the 1770s. The park is on the site of Carshalton

Carshalton House Grotto façade

Leptis Magna Columns at the beginning of the 20th century

Place, demolished over 50 years ago, but the grotto remains, larger than the grotto at the convent but more susceptible to the attentions of hooligans.

There is an earlier 18th-century tower in Carshalton near the grotto in Carshalton House. This was built as a water pump to maintain the level of the lake, but it is so extraordinary that it is certainly worthy of mention. It is called the Water House and was built *c.*1720 in a polychromatic Vanbrughian style. It would appear that the architect was Henry Joynes, who used to work for Vanbrugh.

Virginia Water

Sham Ruins (1785)
Grottoes (1785)
SU 980 690

The oldest rearranged ruins in the county are at Virginia Water. This is an artificial lake, made for the Duke of Cumberland (the Butcher of Culloden) by Thomas Sandby in 1765. The clay and sand dam he built collapsed in 1768, earning him the nickname of Tommy Sandbank, but it was soon rebuilt in more durable materials. Sandby designed the grottoes and sham ruins at the head of the lake in 1785; strictly speaking, these are in Berkshire but as they are part of Virginia Water we include them here. They are by no means as well known as the Leptis Magna ruins.

Leptis Magna Columns (1826)
SU 980 690

The Leptis Magna columns by the lakeside bridges on the A329 were the gift to England from the Bey of Tripoli and re-erected here by Sir Jeffry Wyatville for George IV. Some of the columns stand in triplets, retaining their architraves, some are broken, some lie on the ground, all carefully organized to give the best effect. There are triumphal archways— everything, in fact, the lover of the romantic could desire, but somehow all seeming cold and clinical, an emotionless folly put up out of ostentatious conformity.

Fort Belvedere (1750)
SU 980 690

The most exciting building hereabouts is Fort Belvedere or Cumberland Lodge, which was built in 1750 as Shrubs Hill Tower by

Fort Belvedere or Cumberland Lodge

Henry Flitcroft for the Duke of Cumberland, at the same time as the now-disappeared Chinese houses were built. Once again Surrey can boast a first: this is the first triangular folly tower in the country, the begetter of many, and probably for many of us the triangular Gothick tower on a hill is the archetypal folly image. Flitcroft's Hoober Stand in South Yorkshire (see Stainborough) dates from 1748, but it is a completely different style of triangular building—it has had no successors and therefore remains unique. Shrubs Hill spawned a country of similar towers—Hiorne's Tower, Lawrence Castle, Powderham Belvedere, Broadway Tower, Paxton's Tower, to name a few. The belvedere was castellated and adapted as a house by Wyatville in 1828–29, and in the 1930s it became the Duke of Windsor's favourite residence until his abdication.

Walton on the Hill

Folly Façade (early 20th century)
TQ 230 540

In Deans Lane stands a small folly façade, made of bric-à-brac and spoils. It only came to light when the Methodist Chapel was demolished in the early 1990s, as it was hidden by that building. It is supposed to be the work of a Stanley Woods who lived at the Rise and was done in the early years of this century. The façade is an obvious statement of the delight in handling materials—there's a sham chapel front with a sham window, some low arches, some pillars, walling in different patterns, a bit of roofing, brick, clinker, stone, yet everything is very petite. It was looking desolate when discovered, and one fears for its survival although the locals are aware of it, and the fact that they tore the regular chapel down but left this standing must be a lucky sign.

Wisley

Hatchford Gloriette (c.1906)
Temple of Sleep (1920–21)
TQ 088 582

When Sir Henry Samuelson, son of the more famous capitalist and ironmaster Sir Bernard Samuelson, bought Hatchford Park in 1906 he beautified the surroundings by adding two pavilions and a gloriette, which look like copies from the Elizabethan Montacute House in Somerset. One would be indeed forgiven, after the temple has acquired the necessary patina, for mistaking the gloriette under its ancient tree for the genuine article.

The most remarkable building, however, is the Temple of Sleep, of which the foundation stone was laid in 1920 by a Miss Wall, housemaid at Hatchford. It is an impressive building, and Samuelson had the remains of his family (father, mother and sister) removed from their resting place in Torquay. An inscription pronounces it 'A Temple of Sleep' and the rest of the writing is in Latin and Greek, bar one: 'To the Glory of God, Erected in the Centenary of their Birth in pious Memory of his Father and Mother by their Eldest Son 1920–1921.' Come January 1961, and a couple of men who had stolen the elaborate bronze cover of the coffin and removed it in a lorry were arrested. The coffin was returned, but a few months later i disappeared again—no doubt melted dow by the same crooks.

Witley

Underwater Ballroom (1901)
SU 930 390

Imagine you are standing beside a ta encloses a kitchen garden, 8 acres o garden, the sort of self-sufficiency satisfy a Sainsbury. On the other dirt road is a scrubby wood, der ramshackle and overgrown. In strangely formless holly tree. Y the branches; it has a hollow c middle of the encircling holly something out of a Rupert Bea door. There is nothing else ab just the tree and a door. You g door and find yourself walking a spiral going down into the e very little light. What little the illuminates, on your right, an room lit from above by glass let into the floor of the wood. roughly cut into the wall allov into the room as you walk do Eventually there is a door fro the room. The room is cold a faintly repellent. The ramp c downwards. It gets darker. T gives way to steps. The steps There is now no light at all. You need a torch. You can pi of another room beneath the are now about 40ft (12m) do earth. It is musty. You make through another doorway, an torch is shining into emptine room so large that the beam the other side. Walk carefully rough floor. Don't look in th pleasant lives in them. Walk

The dome of the Underwater Ballroom

comfortable, capable sort of a lake. In the middle of the water is an oblong island, small with a low wall surrounding it. There is a statue in the water just offshore. Row across to the island. It lies about 50 metres from the lakeside and is big enough to take a dance band, if only there were somewhere to dance.

There is somewhere to dance. There is an underwater ballroom, domed and built of iron and glass so you can watch the fish dance around you as you dance. Climb down the stairs to a room directly below the floor of the island; light and airy, nothing to worry about. Down some more steps, through a short tunnel, and you're in the glass ballroom. It isn't very big, but it's big enough and it is completely underwater. You can dance underwater by yourself—not even the Joneses could keep up with this. A lances-arched submarine tunnel leads 40 metres back to dry land and reality.

All this is true. This fantastical place exists—not in crazy California or in sensual Samarkand, but in stolid, suburban Surrey. It was built at the turn of the 20th century by Whitaker Wright, a financier and self-made millionaire who spent £1.25 million—who can guess what that would be worth today?— to improve his estate at Witley Park, southwest of Godalming. He built four lakes, moved a couple of inconvenient hills, planted a forest or two, imported treasures from all over the world (including the head of a dolphin in bronze so big that when they were

...d of the chamber, where you can see a ...nprick of light. There are more steps, steps ...wn to a boat—yes, a boat, moored in this ...ded tunnel fifty feet below ground level. ...bark. Cast off. Walk the boat down the ...nel to the point of light a mile? a hundred ...s? away. It gets brighter.

...ou come out on to a lake, a warm,

The entrance to the wonder of Witley

hauling it up to the estate from Southampton it got stuck under a bridge and they had to lower the road) and then erected a very ordinary, undistinguished house, now demolished, to overlook the lake with the underwater ballroom.

Wright's demise was as sensational as his follies. Sentenced to seven years' imprisonment for fraud, he committed suicide by swallowing cyanide before he could be taken from the Old Bailey, and Witley Park is now a conference centre.

Wonersh

Chinthurst Hill Tower (1920s)
TQ 020 460

Surrey is Lutyens, Lutyens is Surrey. The architect designed the Chinthurst Hill house in the late 19th century, but the tower can be found by climbing the conical Chinthurst Hill itself. Most of the trees there had been felled when we trundled through the mud upwards and upwards, but the reward is there—a strange, three-storey, castellated tower with a fireplace on each level, supposedly built by Lord Inchcape in the 1920s—the date was the subject of tremendous discussion, but we finally agreed, so there it is.

Woking

Mosque (1889)
TQ 000 580

Not a folly, but this earliest mosque in Britain should be searched out by anyone interested in exotic architecture. It's a rather pretty bauble, situated in the suitably named Oriental Road. The Shah Jehan Mosque of the Oriental University Institute was paid for by Shah Jehan Begum of Bhopal and instigated by Dr Gottlieb Leitner, who established the Institute and clearly must have whispered in the ear of his architect, W.I. Chambers, although the two had a widely publicized row once the building work started. Of course, it is Indian rather than Middle Eastern.

Wotton

Wotton House Follies (17th–19th century)
TQ 130 470

Wotton, the home of John Evelyn, has the enchantingly named, but ruined, Tortoise House, where apparently visitors could take tea and watch the antics of terrapins in the pool. This strange building has a four-bayed Ionic portico with an open gallery above, sheltered by a plain tiled pitched roof. It may have been built by the architect Francis Edwards, who worked at Wotton between 1830 and 1853 for W.J. Evelyn. The last time seen it was very ruined, but still in a fit state for restoration.

The rest of the garden has even better buildings. The hill or mound into which the Doric portico temple is eased presents a stunning spectacle. In its slightly desolate state it is halfway to becoming a nymphaeum, Surrey's own Petra. This was built by John Evelyn's cousin George, some time before 1649. And as if that were not enough, there are two sets of grottoes, one, much dilapidated, directly next to the house's west side, and the other in the east corner, in Pulhamite stone and quite delightful. On the eastern hill is an ice-house.

When we visited, the Surrey Fire and Rescue Training College had left the premises (some rooms are in the Burges style), and at the moment Wotton is in a state of rest—there's talk of selling (it may have been bought by a hotel group, and our fingers are crossed that it is Richard Broyd's). This is one of the major folly gardens in the county, the singularly drowsy atmosphere will regretfully disappear once the restorations start, but its importance lies in showing three centuries of garden follies— and what follies they are.

Away from the house the pleasantly picturesque cottage survives, with a bellcote, which, Pevsner says, 'was used when… Evelyn wanted to call his retainers together'. The grotto was Evelyn's retreat where he would 'sulk when displeased'. Much smaller than the 'nymphaeum' but at least in the same manner—shoved partly into the hillside—and on a truly celestial site, is the delightful mausoleum in the Egyptian style, outside the grounds, with some interesting artwork.

Broadmoor Tower (19th century)
TQ 136 455

Just east of Wotton is a delight, and we have forgotten almost all about it: Broadmoor Tower is a round, three-storey, empty shell on top of a wooded little hill, to be approached from an insignificant path leading up through a folly gate—what we do remember are some heraldic devices and the utter loneliness and silence in the woods. Sorry, no date, no builder. And now comes the news that it has been repointed—so someone must care for it.

SUSSEX

'Sussex-by-the-Sea!' proclaimed the Southern Railway's holiday posters in the 1930s, with a degree of accuracy rarely found in advertising. You can't be more than 25 miles from the coast wherever you go in Sussex, and the whole county has a slightly raffish holiday air, a far cry from 'kiss-me-quick' resorts in the North like Blackpool and Bridlington, but none the less with a slightly forced gaiety, leavened by the grim-faced commuters hurrying up

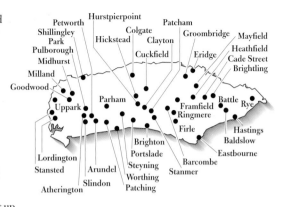

to dirty London from healthy Brighton. Hove, Brighton, Eastbourne, Bexhill, Hastings—no other county can claim so many nationally known resorts on so short a coastline, and the truth is that, facing south as it does, Sussex does get more than the average amount of sunshine for an English county.

Oddly enough, the Sussex climate has not generally attracted the folly builder. Perhaps it has always been too cheerful, lacking the proper grave melancholia so admired in the 18th century. East Sussex has a few pleasant, desultory towers, a little grotto, the egregious Mad Jack Fuller's follies and, of course, the Royal Pavilion at Brighton. West Sussex has fewer follies, but almost all are fine, scattered along the western slopes of the South Downs like vineyards.

Arundel

Hiorne Tower (1787)
Statue Garden (1980s–90s)
TQ 020 070

In the middle of a sweep of Arundel parkland stands the 11th Duke of Norfolk's southern folly. Nowhere near as well known as his

Greystoke follies in Cumbria, it nevertheless plays its role admirably. Triangular—yes; castellated towers—yes; knapped flint—yes; falling to pieces—yes; it is a regulation folly, which now serves to warn visitors of shooting on the nearby rifle ranges. The formidably eccentric duke had Hiorne Tower built as a 'specimen', a sample building by Francis

Hiorne Tower

Hiorne, the architect applying for the position of rebuilding the ruined Arundel Castle. It was built in 1787 to the satisfaction of the duke, but before Hiorne could carry out his work on the Castle, he died two years later, aged 45. The tower now stands derelict in the park, made smaller by the flat pasture surrounding it. In windy weather, a door bangs eerily inside; but this is not a scary building. In front stands a little plinth with an urn, and a plaque relates its history, purpose and reason.

While you are at Arundel search out Vernon Gibberd's Arundel Chairs, which are used in the visitor's restaurant: a good and proper addition to Gothick furniture and fit for the castle itself. And Hiorne Tower has been restored.

At Priory Farm on Ford Road is Geoff Bridges's place where he keeps his version of the Arundel Marbles, a collection of replica statues, added to by his own creations. He has also follified a barn and built a tomb with a Bacchus in top. It is all very weird and wonderful, but the locals weren't too pleased—Bridges had to move from his last location where his statues were vandalized, and now the locals object to his pranks on Priory Farm. Bridges not only looks like the late Edward James, he clearly possesses the same kind of humour.

Atherington

Bailiffscourt (1935)
TQ 000 010

It is now a hotel, but Bailiffscourt, under Climping, was built in 1935 for Walter Guinness and must be one of the most retrograde buildings in the country. It is an exact copy by the architect Amyas Philips, an exact copy of nothing, because apart from the remains of the 13th-century chapel, everything is fantasy, medieval fantasy, but still exact. It made use of old timber and old stone, and the house is as a medieval manor house, perhaps evolving from an abbey, would be like. In fact, it is more than one building—a few cottages and a gatehouse, all genuine, have been thrown in for good measure.

Baldslow

Obelisk (c.1812)
TQ 790 130

At the Beauport Park Hotel is an obelisk that, according to Pevsner and Colvin, is by John Soane, dates from 1790 and is in honour of General James Murray. Strange then to see that the 20ft (6m) obelisk is inscribed:

To The Memory of Ensign Wentworth Noel Burgess of the Coldstream Guards who was killed while leading an assault on the citadel of Burgos 19th October 1812
On the back it just says 'Aged 19'—a recycled obelisk? Erected before the person it commemorates was born?

Barcombe

Shelley's Folly (18th–19th century)
TQ 410 150

A house from the beginning of the 18th century and much changed at the end of the 19th century, but totally 'normal'. The name is explained by the story that the poet bought the house for one of his mistresses and later changed his mind—the Shelley arms are on the house. Henry John Wyatt designed a farmhouse at Barcombe in 1823, but Shelley had been dead for a year by then.

Battle

Tower House (1836)
TQ 720 140

The lodge to Ashburnham Park is some 2 miles west of Battle. It is octagonal and Gothic, of course. The architect is unknown, but according to Philip J. Neville it was based on an Austrian building. In the park of Battle Abbey itself stand a Gothic dairy and a thatched ice-house.

Brightling

Mad Jack Fuller's Follies (early 19th century)
TQ 680 210

Mad Jack Fuller's follies at Brightling and Dallington constitute a major folly group in Britain. John Fuller (1757–1834) was a true British eccentric. Having inherited a fortune at an early age, he not unexpectedly became wilful and autocratic, but these unpleasant traits were redeemed to a great extent by his fierce defence of his county, tenants and constituents. Hilaire Belloc, himself obsessed by Sussex, wrote:

This man Fuller deserves to be famous and to be called, so to speak, the very demigod of my county, for he spent all his money in a roaring way, and lived in his time like an immortal being conscious of what was worth man's while during his little passage through the daylight.
At a time when indigents were accustomed to demanding alms from the servants of great houses (and most households set aside an allowance for this), Fuller issued orders that

Mad Jack's pyramid mausoleum—is he sitting upright inside?

any able-bodied man who came begging should be given work and paid justly for his labours. As a result, the massive wall wandering for miles around Brightling Park came into existence—an actual example of the 'built to relieve unemployment' story that is attached to so many follies. But this was not enough for Fuller. He was the stuff of which legends are made—swearing at the Speaker of the House of Commons, thundering down from London in a carriage with footmen and coachmen armed to the teeth with pistols and drawn swords (how he trusted his fellow man!), refusing a peerage ('I was born Jack Fuller and Jack Fuller I'll die'), drinking three bottles of port a day and indulging in impossible wagers.

He seems to have found solace in folly building after becoming disillusioned with politics on 27 February 1810, when he insulted the Speaker and had to be forcibly removed from the House by the Serjeant-at-Arms. The abolitionist William Wilberforce referred to the incident as 'the interlude of that mad bull Fuller'.

Possibly the earliest of the Brightling buildings is a small Gothick seat in a plantation in the park. It dates from 1803 (so before the Commons debacle) and bears the trademark 'COADE SEALY LONDON'. Also in the park is a brick pillar with a cast-iron vignette on top: a cannon, flame and anchor, a monument to the iron foundries that provided the source of the family's wealth. Another pillar, said to have been a

companion piece marking the site of the grave of Mad Jack's favourite horse, has disappeared. The Rotunda Temple of about 1810, by Smirke, is a strict garden ornament. Fuller was reputed to have held bawdy parties in it. This sounds possible from the man who had Susan Thrale, the daughter of Dr Johnson's friend, followed around by harlots from Tunbridge Wells when she refused to marry him.

Brightling Church is also worth a visit. One wall holds a bust of Fuller by Henry Rouw. On the other walls are plaques commemorating two of Fuller's cronies: the forgotten composer William Shield, who died in Brightling in 1829, and Dr Primrose Blair, 'formerly physician to His Majesty's fleet in the West Indies', who died in 1819. The barrel-organ was a gift of Fuller's, as was the peal of bells named after Wellington's battles. Fuller's pyramid mausoleum in the churchyard was designed by Sir Robert Smirke and built in 1811. Nowadays it's not just the cranks who believe in the ability of the pyramid shape to preserve things—sharpening razor-blades and the like—but then the theory was unknown. Or was it? The story goes that Fuller got permission for his unusual mausoleum from the Rev. Mr Hayley on condition that he would arrange to have his pub, the Green Man, moved from its position directly opposite the church. The pub is now in a converted barn in an awkward corner of the village and is called the Fuller's Arms. The story may be true, but it is not substantiated by the parish register. On 15 November 1810 Hayley made a marginal note:

Be it remembered that John Fuller Esq. of Rose-hill at the beginning of the present year applied for permission to erect a mausoleum in Brightling Churchyard and to lay open the south side of the said Churchyard by removing the old Post and rail fence and erecting a stone-wall: and when he had fixed upon the site for erecting his Edifice he inquired of me as Incumbent of the Living what would satisfy me for the ground it was to stand on: my reply was that as he would be at considerable expense in erecting the Wall would be a good improvement I should not demand any Fee for the other Building. The Wall is now finished and John Fuller Esq. has added hereto a couple of substantial stone pillars & an iron gate way.

And all that beauty, all that wealth e'er gave,
Awaits alike th'inevitable hour,
The paths of glory lead but to the grave.
Rather melancholy—but it was not in Fuller's nature to gloom for long. Smirke's other commission at Brightling was the Observatory; it seemed to have been a genuine attempt at a scientific laboratory.

Fuller's most famous wager gives us probably the best folly story in Britain. One evening at Rose Hill, as Brightling Park used to be known, he was dining with friends and boasting of the view to be seen from his dining-room window: 'You can see the spire of Dallington Church,' he declaimed, and several guests, knowing the lie of the land—the village of Dallington lies in a fold of the downs, although it is only a mile or so from Brightling—rose to challenge him. Fuller accepted all bets. The following morning the curtains were drawn and Jack Fuller gazed

The Rotunda at Rose Hill, or Brightling Park

Fuller is said to be seated fully dressed on an iron chair in the centre of the pyramid, with a bottle of port and a roast chicken on the table in front of him, awaiting the Resurrection. Just in case the Devil came first to claim his own, the floor of the pyramid is strewn with broken glass to cut his hooves. By the time the pyramid was finished, Fuller had the famous ninth verse of Gray's 'Elegy Written in a Country Churchyard' inscribed in the mausoleum's interior:

The boast of heraldry, the pomp of pow'r

out over the rolling woods and fields, across the downs to the sea in the invisible distance, and over the little ridge which completely hid the village and church of Dallington from view. No spire. Fuller would nowadays be known in pop psychological terms as a Right Man, a character unable in his own mind to make a mistake or to be contradicted. No spire? He built one. When the punters came to collect their money they were taken to the dining-room window, and there, unmistakably, was the cone-shaped spire of

The spire of Dallington Church and the Sugar Loaf. We rest our case.

Dallington in the middle distance. Nowadays the folly is called the Sugar Loaf, and at one stage it was converted into a two-storey cottage for a farmworker. A fascinating footnote was added to the story by an article in the *Manchester Guardian* in 1961, reporting the restoration of the Sugar Loaf. The builders found that the original structure consisted of 'nothing more than stones held together by mud', which suggests that the Sugar Loaf had indeed been put up in a great hurry.

The Needle is a rather dumpy, dilapidated, banded obelisk on top of Brightling Down, 646ft (197m) above sea level. There is no record of why Fuller built it, apart from the fact that obelisks were fashionable. In 1985 a row blew up over proposed repairs to it, which would cost an estimated £26,000. The East Sussex County Council narrowly voted to contribute £6800, with one member objecting strongly to spending part of the money available for historic buildings on 'a pile of bricks'—follies still have their detractors. A more sensible objection came from a gentleman who pointed out that if

Mad Jack's observatory

public money were to be spent to restore it, the public should be granted access. The restoration was carried out.

Fuller's last folly was a little 25ft (7.6m) Hermit's Tower in the trees, with a view opening out over Robertsbridge on to Bodiam Castle, which Mad Jack restored at his own expense. The idea of the Hermit's Tower was obviously to house a hermit, but despite assiduous advertising Fuller failed to find one to fit the bill. The requirements were a little excessive: no shaving, no washing, no cutting of hair or nails, no conversation with any outsider for a period of seven years, after which the happy hermit would be made a Gentleman. No takers.

Fuller died in 1834. His obituary in the *Gentleman's Magazine* noted that 'Mr Fuller was distinguished through life by much eccentricity'—a fitting epitaph. Today most of his buildings have been restored and a walk around Brightling Park and its follies is possible.

Brighton

Brighton Pavilion (1786–1821)
TQ 300 040

'It's as if St Paul's had come down to the sea and pupped,' commented Sydney Smith on seeing the cascade of domes, pinnacles, towerlets, arcades, minarets and every imaginable motif of oriental architecture that make up Brighton Pavilion. Completed in the year 1821, it is as much an expression of royal whimsy as of the talent of the favourite royal architect, John Nash. Nash was the third architect to work on the Pavilion. The original building had been put up as long ago as 1786 by Henry Holland (not the eponymous folly-building lord) for the Prince of Wales as the Marine Pavilion; stables, a tennis court and other outbuildings were added in the early 19th century by William Porden; and finally the whole structure was completely remodelled from 1815 by Nash in the oriental style. The place is literally a palace; is it a folly as well? The arguments against say that it was built for a purpose (albeit a frivolous one, but there is a long precedent for that); that it was never built without a true reckoning of the cost; that it was properly finished; that it was well constructed by a master architect; and that it has been perfectly maintained. The arguments in favour merely point out the incongruity of Xanadu-by-Sea, the sheer stark shock of its shape on the skyline. Who is to decide? One can scarcely be objective

about this. Public opinion at the time was far more clear-cut, as is shown by this excerpt from an 1820 satire by William Hone, entitled *The Joss and his Folly*, which, besides showing an amusing liberty of expression unthinkable today even by *Private Eye* standards, is particularly interesting for giving us a very early usage of the word 'folly' in the context of architecture:

The queerest of all the queer sights
I've set sight on;—
Is, the what d'ye-call-'t thing, here,
THE FOLLY at Brighton
The outside—huge teapots,
all drill'd round with holes,
Relieved by extinguishers,
sticking on poles:
The inside—all tea-things,
and dragons, and bells,
The show rooms—all show,
the sleeping rooms—cells.
But the grand Curiosity
's not to be seen –
The owner himself –
an old fat MANDARIN;
A patron of painters
who copy designs,
That grocers and tea-dealers
hang up for signs:
Hence seaboard-taste artists
gain rewards and distinction,
Hence his title of 'Teapot'
shall last to extinction.

After the Pavilion, the other architectural eccentricities in the town might seem to pale into relative insignificance, but recently a whole bunch of weird and wonderful Brighton buildings were researched, and Brighton must now be Britain's most be-follied larger town (excepting the Metropolis, of course).

Baby Brighton Pavilion (c.1827)
TQ 300 040

The Pavilion itself has, indeed, pupped— there is a miniature version of it at Western Terrace, the one-time residence of the Brighton architect Amon Henry Wilds, who built this around 1827. It is a circular, low towerette with a bulbous dome, and it and the adjoining architecture are topped by oriental pinnacles and pilasters with ammonite capitals, a pun on the architect's first name, but, says Raymond Head, 'an idea originally derived from George Dance'.

Sassoon Mausoleum (1892)
TQ 300 040

Another exoticism is the Sassoon Mausoleum, of a much later date, at Eastern

Terrace. It is now a pub but was built in 1892 for the Jewish merchant Sir Albert Sassoon. The Sassoons came from India, which partly explains the chosen style. The building, square with oriental castellations and a tent-like copper dome, was originally in the gardens of the Sassoon house.

Pepper Pot and Others (1830s)
`TQ 300 040`

Patricia Cleveland-Peck has found some more follies at Brighton, among them the Pepper Pot, a very slender, cupola'd ex-water tower (although it is usually called the Observatory) at Tower Road near Queen's Park. It belonged to the now-demolished Attree Villa, and was at some stage in its life converted into a public lavatory. Charles Barry probably designed this in the 1830s.

Another survival of Attree Villa is the Garden Temple (Barry again?) in the central court of a block of modern flats at Cairn Court. It is a square, porch-like structure with Ionic corner columns and a tiled roof topped with a spike.

And still Brighton abounds with follies and follyesque buildings. Also in Queen's Park is another survival: the classical portico of Dr Strüve's mineral water emporium, the Royal German Spa (Strüve hailed from Dresden)—he did what is still, or again, a practice in many pubs and restaurants: making fake bubbly mineral water by passing gas through it.

Tanner's Tower (c. 1850)
`TQ 300 040`

At Carlton Hill is Edward Tanner's Tower, a fat, round, knapped flint drum of a tower, with a much smaller cylindrical turret on top. It was built by a merchant who liked to see his ship come in so he had time to travel to Tilbury and welcome his bounty.

The Rockery (19th century)
`TQ 300 040`

Preston Road has The Rockery, built, according to Cleveland-Peck, 'by Parks Superintendent Captain B. MacLaren to illustrate the story of Willow Pattern Plate'. It is, indeed, a large rock garden, with most of the trappings of a fake Chinese garden, although the tea-house is not at all Chinese, but very rock-like: a thatched structure made from the remains of Lewes police station!

Kemp's Folly (1819)
`TQ 300 040`

It is not known what has happened to Kemp's Folly, or the Temple, in Montpelier Road. Part of it has been demolished, but there are remains of this model of Solomon's Temple, which the speculator Thomas Read Kemp (1781–1844) built as his residence. Kemp was a strange man, very practical and a religious sectarian, a combination not uncommon in the 19th century. He developed Brighton's Kemp Town, but also started a sect, together with George Baring, of which the Temple was a headquarters.

Wagner's Folly (1872–74)
`TQ 300 040`

Religious cranks abounded in Brighton and copy-cats seem to have had a jolly good time of it—after Wilds and Kemp, we come to the Rev. Arthur Douglas Wagner, who in 1872–4 had

Noah's Ark come to rest in Sussex

Edmund Scott build him St Bartholomew's Church in Ann Street; it is also known as Wagner's Folly. Nairn and Pevsner select this church for high praise: 'an unforgettable experience… the most moving of all churches [in East Sussex]… this tremendous church owes its existence to an individual's munificence and devotion.' What they do not mention is that the church was built to particular specifications given by Wagner: the dimensions are based upon those of Noah's Ark (complete with pigeon holes). Even without this knowledge, St Bartholomew's still remains one of Britain's most remarkable churches, with wildly beautiful Arts and Crafts additions to the interior. The Wagner–Scott duo were at it again in 1885–86, building St

Mary's in Buxted, as well as several houses there, but were they constructed to any biblical specifications?

Wayside Museum (20th century)
TQ 300 040

Sadly, Brighton's Wayside Museum is now defunct. It was established by father and son, Stanley and Norman Norris, who started out with the collection of curios formed by Stanley's father Edward James Norris. The Wayside was the family home in 1913 and became through the years a wonderful museum of all that interested the Norrises: old weapons, minerals, shells, skeletons, archaeological finds, things chemical, manuscripts, books, furniture… anything, anything. The museum expanded in the 1930s, with several shacks being built to house the collections. But Stanley also started building, initially to provide models of medieval castles, but soon he became interested in experimenting in cement, and, as Tim Knox tells in his article on the museum, he also dug tunnels and grottoes in the grounds of The Wayside. Although Norman Norris left The Wayside and its contents to the National Trust, it has now proceeded to dismantle the whole collection. One can see the problems there would be with opening it to visitors, but why do away with Britain's Best Private Museum—damn and blast visitors!—this should have been preserved like a 20th century A La Ronde!

Mayhew's Folly (1987)
TQ 300 040

Experimenting with cement appears to be a Brighton speciality—unbeknown to the Norrises, David Mayhew worked with the material for a number of years, and this has resulted in the very entertaining wendy house in the garden of 67 Springfield Road. It is made of ferro-concrete of Mayhew's own devising, and the little cottage is not just a plaything: it is the Shape of Things to Come (if Mayhew had it his way), a precursor of what in the late 1980s he called his 'Cottage of the Nineties'. Regrettably, we are now in the last year of the millennium and still there is no solution to what David Mayhew sees as a very real problem: the building of ever more housing estates. The solution would be recycled material and Mayhew's recipe for compact living: neo-Victorian gingerbread houses in ferro-concrete. Great idea, only the building industry has not yet caught on.

When we arrived in 1988 or thereabouts to see Mayhew's wonderful little cottage at Springfield Road, he was just preparing to lift the house on a very small trailer. The task was absurd, it could never get on the trailer, but if it hadn't been moved by next day, the demolition men would have their evil way with it. After a short stay at the local pub where they refused to serve him, we left Mr Mayhew with a young assistant desperately trying to get the extremely heavy (ferro-concrete!) wendy house on the trailer. Impossible—and we were saddened that we could not be of any help whatsoever. Exit ferro-concrete cottages, we thought. But no, Pieter and Rita Boogaart recently reported seeing the wendy house again, still in its

One of David Mayhew's concrete houses

place at Springfield Road. So the ferro-concrete revolution may take place after all.

Hove has a scrap of a modern folly, a sham chapel wall complete with window tracery in the garden of a house on the corner of Dyke Road and Porthall Road near Booth's Bird Museum.

Cade Street

Cade Monument (18th century)
TQ 600 210

In Cade Street near Heathfield is a little monument marking the site of the assassination of the rebel Jack Cade by Alexander Iden in 1450:

> *This is the success of all rebels*
> *and this fortune chanceth ever to traitors.*

A summerhouse tower at Colgate

Clayton

Tunnel (1836)
TQ 300 130

The most famous railway tunnel entrance in Britain is at Clayton, on the London to Brighton line, where the keeper's cottage above the line is straddled by two mighty machicolated towers built in 1836, but reminiscent of Sanderson Miller at his most whimsical.

Colgate

Summerhouses (c.1823)
TQ 230 320

The now demolished 106ft (32m) Holmbush Tower was built for T. Broadwood by a builder called Summer, assisted by his young son and 'a man named Cox' in 1855–7. The castellated Holmbush House itself was built in 1823 by the architect Francis Edwards for Broadwood, but 30 years later Broadwood realized he still had a lot of bricks and stone left and had the tower built. It was demolished in about 1943. Some summerhouse towers and a fine stag's gate remain, as well as the ruin of a pretty little chapel or hermitage.

Cuckfield

Tower House (1850s)
TQ 300 240

More or less like the Malmesbury observatory tower, this was also erected in the town centre, behind a house, by a Mr Knott, with its glass dome being taken down

before the century was out—but the rest of this round tower stands. Cuckfield Park, to the west, has a very fine gatehouse, which is, alas, the real, 16th-century thing. In the grounds is a modern temple.

Eastbourne

Hermitage (late 18th century)
TQ 580 000

In Eastbourne's Old Town is the Gothick Hermitage, situated near the Towner Art Gallery, which used to be the Manor House. It is not a hermitage though, neither is it Gothick. This octagonal Tartar Tent must have been a summerhouse, and very pretty it is, too, with its thatched roof, ogival door and windows (the ogee arches ending in crescents, hence Tartar) and blind quatrefoils. The building was restored in 1990. There were more garden buildings here, but they all disappeared after Eastbourne was bombed during the war.

Eridge

Saxonbury Tower (1828)
TQ 570 330
Sham Farm (18th century)
Grinhams Tower (18th century)
TQ 563 339

On Saxonbury Hill in Eridge Park, 8 miles north of Heathfield, the Marquess of Abergavenny built a fine Camelotian tower in 1828 to mark the highest point on his estate. It has long been one of our favourite follies, but although it is said to have the most magnificent views, we have never had the courage to climb it. Saxonbury Tower was

The Sham Farm screen at Eridge

Saxonbury Tower

very dilapidated when we saw it, and the stone spiral staircase had been knocked away at the bottom to deter foolhardy climbers; it started about 8ft (2.4m) from the ground. It was always possible for those with nerves of steel to get to the top. Rhododendrons and broad-leaved trees clustered around the base of the tower and flanked overgrown rides, making it one of the most delightfully situated follies. There are the initials 'H.A.' above the door—some say they stand for Henrietta Abergavenny. The tower, opened up to view since the great gale of 1987 removed most of the surrounding trees, has now been restored and serves as a transmitting tower for a cellular phone company, so access is even more out of the question. The aerials are concealed within a bulging white cone at the top of the tower, replacing the previous elegant, slate-covered smaller cone.

The other follies on the Eridge Estate are all screens of some sort; apparently Abergavenny had a violent objection to seeing cottages and farms. At Danegate, on the edge of the woods, the estate office is screened off by a mighty castellated, arrowslitted and buttressed corner tower at an angle of two sham ruin side walls (with some fresh damage), with blind Gothic windows, buttresses, pinnacles, the lot, supposedly in mimicry of Eridge castle itself. (As always the main castle, built by an amateur architect named Taylor in 1787, has gone—taken down in 1938.)

Grinhams Towers is in much the same style and surely of the same date, but it consists of two not too tall towers and bits of screening. These used to hide two estate cottages. The cottages have gone, and now the Nevill Estate wants to rebuild them, but for the moment the planning authorities are reviewing the case.

Firle

Tower (1822)
TQ 460 060

A squat, fat, castellated round tower stands solidly on a ridge at Firle, near Lewes. It was built by Lord Gage in 1822 as a

Firle Tower

gamekeeper's cottage and signal tower, so the gamekeeper could signal with flags to his men on the estate and communicate by telegraph with the keeper at Plashett Park, Ringmer, 5 miles away.

Framfield

Hamilton Palace (1987 onwards)
TQ 493 188

One of the basic folly definitions is that of a huge building left unfinished. Nicholas Van Hoogstraten has taken pains to make sure that this will not happen to him, even if he dies. He has set up a trust that will ensure that should he pass on before work on Hamilton Palace is finished, it will be completed and then sealed up, with his body inside. So there's nothing of the folly about this, then. On completion—should he survive—he intends to throw two huge parties, then close the house. The public— the scum, as he affectionately refers to us— will never be allowed in, not now, not after his death (remember that trust). 'I can't think of anything more disgusting than having scum traipsing around in here, poking at things with their filthy hands and smoking cigarettes,' he told Maev Kennedy.

Hamilton Palace is said to be named after Hamilton Palace Hotel in the Bahamas, but it appears to be more inspired by the Duke of Hamilton's palace in Lanarkshire. Hoogstraten cites his influences as Buckingham Palace, Versailles and some other palace on the Seine; his architect Anthony Browne interprets scrawls from the backs of envelopes. There are plans for a boathouse, a three-storey square building on the edge of a lake, and the main house will have a 600ft (183m) gallery to display the builder's collection of 18th-century furniture. Hoogstraten made his money as a south coast landlord, spending four years in gaol on the way for demanding money with menaces. He seems to have got it. The estimated cost is somewhere between £25 and £300 million, but as the project has been designed to last for 5000 years, talk of money is irrelevant. The palace is being built using reconstituted stone on the site of High Cross, a former Victorian nursing home, which burned down in the 1980s and which was dismissed by Pevsner as being of no architectural consequence. 'It was a beautiful house, and I wouldn't have dreamed of burning it down,' offered Hoogstraten.

Goodwood

Grotto (1740s)
Tunnels
SU 880 090

Goodwood is famous for its racecourse, the most beautifully sited sportsfield in Britain (even more so than Pontypool!), but its shell grotto would be world famous if the public could see it. A description cannot do it justice, and it is sensibly closed to visitors in order to ensure its preservation. This was all worked in the 1740s by Sarah, Duchess of Richmond and her daughters, who mainly made floral patterns out of the shells, and their initials are also there to be seen: CR, SR, CF, EK. In 1739 Captain Knowles of HMS *Diamond* had brought in a shipload of shells for the Dukes of Richmond and Bedford, and over the years many more were contributed from collections made all over the world, particularly the West Indies. The mystery grotto at Margate may have its antecedents here, as one of the Duchess's daughters married Lord Holland; see the description in the Kent chapter. The Goodwood grotto has now been restored by Diana Reynell.

There is a curious system of tunnels running underneath the lawns at the back of Goodwood House, still sound and big enough to walk through. They meander for about 200 yards (183m), ending in a plain brick octagonal room. A mystery.

Groombridge

Penn's Rocks Temples (1938–66)
Groombridge Place Gardens (1990s)
TQ 520 350

The delightfully situated Penn's Rocks (once William Penn's house) has two temples, the classical one of which is called The Folly, but is dedicated to 'The Poets Who Loved Penns', and than we have their names (which one have you never heard of?): W.B. Yeats, Walter de la Mare, W.J. Turner, Ruth Pitter, Vita Sackville West and Dorothy Wellesley, followed by a rather naff 'they learn in suffering what they teach in song'. It was obviously one of those country houses where they kept writers like parrots or monkeys. The other temple, a removal, came from Finchley manor house, which was demolished in 1965, and was brought over the next year.

Technically Groombridge Place is in Kent, but never mind. The gardens here are by Ivan Hicks, who first worked on Edward James's West Dean (see also Stansted below). We do not like gardens or follies to be made by artists, especially not when they are labelled Surrealist from the start—everything to do with Art & Money and Money & Art and nothing with pure and simple folly. But Hicks's works are very tempting nevertheless. Here he's made a Drunken Garden, an oriental one etc. Also a grotto.

Hastings

The Clock House (c.1830)
Wingfield's Folly (1877)
The Piece of Cheese (1871)
TQ 790 080

Hastings is clocks, cheese and wind. We start at St Leonard's, the speculative development of the 1830s to Hastings' west. The builder James Burton was the investor here, and he brought over his son, Decimus, from London in order to develop the seaside resort. The Clock Tower at Maze Hill, a sham chapel, must have been one of its chief attractions. The villa itself is rather tall, like a square tower itself, with a saint's statue nestling in a very Roman Catholic niche. The clock tower next to it is slender and square, with Gothic windows, pinnacles and clocks on all sides.

In St Leonard's Lower South Road, off Bohemia Road, is Tower Buildings or Wingfield's Folly, built in 1877 by Ernest Wingfield, a well-to-do coal merchant and removals man. Wingfield built a Gothic tower on top of the shop front. It is five storeys high with a sundial and, ever the commercial man, a paid-for Bovril announcement. But Wingfield also spared openings near his tower's top in

Weeke's Folly

order to put in clocks, to be paid for by subscription. No one came up with any money, so Wingfield left them empty.

St Leonards had its own Clock House, and central Hastings already had one as well, the Albert Memorial Clock Tower of 1863, so Wingfield's clock tower was wholly superfluous. The tower itself went in 1973, but the rest of the building is still standing, an antiques centre.

Then there is the Piece of Cheese, which looks like a wedge of cheese and was 'built for a £5 bet' in 1871. It is 17ft (5m) across and billed as one of Britain's smallest homes—we are sure every country must have its own 'the tiniest house in the world', so Hastings was modest in its description.

Last, we have a promising house-name in Belmont Road, the Cupola and Tower of the Winds, but we have not seen it.

Heathfield

Gibraltar Tower (1792)
TQ 590 200

Five miles east of Brightling is Heathfield, where the 55ft (18m) Gibraltar Tower was, when we first saw it in 1968, looking very sorry for itself. It was built in 1792 by Francis Newbery to commemorate the exploits of Brigadier-General George Augustus Elliot at the siege of Gibraltar between 1779 and 1783. The walls inside the tower were decorated with pictures of the siege. General Elliot was later created Baron Heathfield. The three-storey, circular tower features in a Turner landscape in the Tate, and in the 1970s it was refurbished to a high standard to form the centrepiece of a new theme park, which opened with a flourish and closed shortly afterwards. It is now neglected again.

Hickstead

Sham Castle (early 17th century)
TQ 260 200

Hickstead, famous for show jumping, has a large, brick, sham castle summerhouse at Hickstead Place which may predate follies—it seems as if it could have been built for a purpose long forgotten.

Hurstpierpoint

Weeke's Folly (c.1800)
TQ 280 160

Weeke's Folly's alternative name is the Tower, and that is just what one finds in West Furlong Lane: round, flint, three-storey and

The terrifying Racton Tower

embattled. The story is better than the building. Richard Weeke was Hurstpierpoint's surgeon during the Napoleonic Wars, and he became convinced the French would invade Sussex, a not uncommon fear in those days. To show Napoleon that Hurstpierpoint was prepared to do battle, he built this little tower and also erected some castellated walls nearby. Some of these can still be seen. The French never did attack Sussex, doubtless thanks to Mr Weeke and his defences. Digression: there is another francophobe folly in the Dutch village of Olst. The owner of its country house had been to Paris in 1870–71 and experienced the Paris Commune. Convinced that the Communards were coming to get him, he built a tower and fortifications near his house, some of which are still there.

Lordington

Racton Tower (1771)
SU 770 080

Along on the edge of the Downs, by the Hampshire border, is the magnificent Racton Tower, or Racton Monument as it is marked on the map. The present owner doesn't want the public to get too close, and quite rightly too: it is horrifyingly unsafe. It lurks in a small wood, surrounded by concrete fence posts, rabbit wire and barbed wire on the top—one expects man traps, but vandals have helpfully removed most of the fencing. Inside, the building is large and louring, and very ruined. Again, it is triangular in plan, but

it differs from the popular triangular folly plan as seen at Arundel and elsewhere. The two-storey bottom section is three-sided, with three circular corner towers. Above the centre section rises a gently tapering, three-storey, round tower to a height of about 80ft (24m). The corner towers have the remains of smaller turrets on top; the whole building is hollow, roofless and floorless. It was built by the 3rd Lord Halifax (his father had changed his name to Dunk in order to get his hands on his fiancée's dowry of £110,000) in 1771, with £10,000 of the money his father had left.

Stanstead or Stansted House, the family home, also has an 18th-century Ionic temple in the grounds called Lumley Seat, after the 1st Earl's father-in-law. Halifax had employed Henry Keene to design the spire of Westbourne Church in 1770, but the elevation of the tower, dated 1772 and titled 'A View of Stanstead Castle, near Emsworth', was drawn by his son Theodosius Keene, who was then aged 18. The drawing shows a splendid building, with castellations on the base and corner towers, castellations on the little corner turrets, quatrefoil windows in the central round tower (now sightless circles), more castellations around the top of the tower and a conical roof surmounted by a lantern, with the Union Flag flying boldly from the flagpole. Was this huge folly really designed by a 17-year-old? Colvin ascribes it to him, but young Keene's father was himself busy two years later designing a folly 5 miles north at Uppark for Sir Matthew Fetherstonhaugh.

Mayfield

Braylsham Castle (1993–8)
`TQ 580 260`

Braylsham Castle is an utter and complete fake, in a county that that already has one or two sham medieval buildings. Built over a five-year period by Jo and John Mew and architect Stephen Langer, this is the ultimate folly castle: in a moat swims a large medieval half-timber hall, to its right is a chapel-like building and again attached to that is a folly tower, which is square with a battlemented round turret next to it. There are secret passages, a minstrel's gallery and a dungeon. All this is a recipe for disaster—the outcome would usually be an ugly concoction of half-understood architecture, Disneyesque at best—but Braylsham is completely different. Partly built from spoils. the only thing that gives it away is the too-good-to-be-true effect of hall, chapel and folly tower. The Mews are not content with this—they are trying for a grotto and an eyecatcher in the grounds.

Midhurst

Obelisk (19th century)
Temple (c.1987)
`TQ 880 200`

The obelisk marked at Cocking Causeway, just outside Midhurst, was erected in memory of Richard Cobden, the free-trader, with an appropriate inscription:

FREE TRADE, PEACE, GOODWILL AMONG NATIONS

North of Midhurst, at Woolbeding Hall, a brand-new rotunda temple with an ogival cupola has just been built by one of the Sainsbury's to commemorate a giant magnolia that did not survive the storms of 1987. It looks an extremely shiny ochre, but that will wear off, no doubt.

Milland

Camel Tower (1988)
`TQ 830 280`

The Camel Tower is at the Burrows, east of the hamlet of Milland, towards Wardley. It was a gimmick used in the television programme by Gerald Scarfe on follies—all the separate items were interspersed with reports on the progress of building this new folly of breezeblocks, and it turned out to be a round, weirdly castellated empty towerette with vaguely oriental windows and a secret ingredient revealed only at the end of the film—the stubby tower at the side of the structure was topped with a head and—lo and behold!—it became a breezeblock camel. The thing has to be seen on its hillock, and despite this tame description it works well as a folly.

Parham

Garden Buildings (19th–20th century)
`TQ 060 140`

Parham House, south of Pulborough, has a few oddments: an early 20th-century wendy house built into the wall of the walled garden, a summerhouse, a boathouse and a temple.

Patcham

The Chattri (1921)
`TQ 310 110`

A war memorial to those Indian soldiers who died in World War I, the white marble chattri looks most exotic here on the Downs. It was designed by the Indian architect E.C. Henriques.

Patching

Tower
Toll House (1820s)
`TQ 080 060`

At Michelgrove, a farm hidden in a fold of the downs above Patching, was a strange tower dovecote, now pulled down and with only the foundations *in situ* (its clock is now gracing J.E. Dell & Loade, Solicitors of Steyning High Street), but there still is a Gothic arched wall with a small tower at one end, the remnants of a house demolished by the Duke of Norfolk in the 19th century.

Along the A280, north of Clapham Wood, is another of Michelgrove's buildings, a toll house, but a good one, whose first function must surely have been that of eyecatcher to the gentry. There is a façade with a large blind arch, castellated and two hollow polygonal towers on the end, with triangular castellations for a change, interspersed with spiky pinnacles. It was built in the 1820s.

Petworth

Upperton Monument (c.1800)
Garden Buildings (19th century)
Pitshill Belvedere and Grotto (1811)
`SU 970 120`

Inside the wall that encircles Petworth stands a tall, plain, stone-built square tower with a much taller octagonal stair turret, which is known as the Upperton Monument. It has now been converted into a luxurious house,

The Toat Monument

with magnificent Turneresque views across the park to Petworth House. Curiously, the garden for the monument is on the other side of the road, enclosed by a high wall. Petworth Park itself has a Doric temple and an Ionic rotunda, and further away, towards Tillington, something that must have been a lodge, it certainly looks like one—a central longish, Gothic block with castellations and buttresses, shored up by two lower versions of the same thing.

In a valley, ½ mile to the west, is Pitshill House, a beautiful Georgian house facing the side of a hill, ignoring the vista that opens out to the south. It holds a belvedere and a shell house, a domed building decorated on the inside by the Mitford sisters in 1811.

Portslade

Grotto (late 19th century)
TQ 260 050

At St Mary's Convent (formerly Portslade's Manor House) lurks something Pulhamite: a fernery-grotto turned into a Lourdes-type grotto by the nuns. They have done no damage, only put a statue of Our Lady of Lourdes in it, turning a perfectly normal Victorian fernery into something religious. On the Continent it also works the other way round, now that most abbeys and convents that were housed in country houses are deserted, the little Lourdes-like grottoes are being converted into garden ornaments.

Pevsner says that the medieval house here 'was pillaged to make up sham ruins a little further up the hill'. Some brick is worked into the grot, but we have not seen any substantial sham ruins.

Pulborough

Toat Monument (1827)
TQ 040 200

The Toat Monument, north of Pulborough, is clearly marked on the map. It stands in a hedge bordering an apple orchard, and if that sounds insignificant it could almost be so—although it is four storeys high and embattled, it remains a very small octagonal tower, erected in 1827 to the memory of Samuel Drinkald, who was killed when he was thrown from his horse on this spot.

Ringmer

Grotto (1810)
TQ 450 130

At Wellingham House a mile or so northwest of Ringmer and built for the brewer Rickman from Lewes, is an amusing grotto or shell house. There is an octagonal gazebo on top of it, with that rare survival: four panes of coloured glass in separate windows, one for each season. We are informed by Adrienne Lawrence that the little grotto was built, or rather decorated, by the Rickman daughters in 1810. Which sounds amazingly like the 1811 Mitford sisters' grotto at Pitshill, Petworth.

Rye

Smuggler's Watch Tower (1768)
TQ 120 200

Little Orchard House in West Street has a little surprise waiting in its back garden—a watch tower for smugglers disguised as a rather substantial gazebo, dating from 1768. From here the sons of Thomas Proctor, mayor of Rye and a smuggler himself, would watch out for any excisemen. One of Sussex's rare classical towers, it is brick with a tiled roof and a weathervane on top of three storeys.

Shillinglee Park

Deer Tower (late 17th century)
SU 970 310

Seen from the road the Deer Tower in Shillinglee Park, northeast of Northchapel on the Surrey border, looks unpromising: a squat, ugly box partly screened by trees, hardly worthy of the appellation 'tower' that is bestowed upon it by the Ordnance Survey map. But walking along the bridleway, across bleak Sussex downland, it assumes a more promising shape. A castellated brick box is stuck on the front of a cardboardy, ur-castle keep, square with a round tower at each corner and colour-washed buff. It is set in a nicely wooded little garden—a dream house for imaginative children. Like so many follies, it was built to serve two roles, and presumably filled neither of them very well. One was to be a look-out tower for the deer keeper, but it is not really tall enough, despite having four floors, and another was to be an eyecatcher from Shillinglee Park House, but it is not pretty enough nor spectacular enough. Now the trees have grown up around the Deer Tower the roles have been reversed: Shillinglee House makes a splendid eyecatcher, but all that can be seen of the tower from the house is a clump of trees on the horizon.

In 1983 the tower was castellated (was there a licence to crenelate?) and extended, and now it looks much less ugly. Inside, the interiors have been done up by a fashionable interior decorator, so as one gazes out over the sweeping downs it feels just like being in the heart of Knightsbridge. Ah, the joys of the country cottage.

Slindon

Nore Folly (18th century)
SU 960 090

The Nore Folly at Slindon is one of the few marked on the Ordnance Survey map purely as 'The Folly'; most are euphemistically labelled 'Tower' or 'Mon'. And a truer folly never was: it looks like no other building anywhere and could never conceivably have served any useful purpose. It has been likened to a railway arch or tunnel entrance, but the resemblance is passing. The National Trust is proud of this one, and the quirks of its builder Samuel Refoy have been meticulously restored with cement and shining flints, so that it gleams in the sun on the edge of its copse. Behind it was once a thatched luncheon room, where the Earl and Countess of Newburgh presumably refreshed themselves and their guests while shooting—how did they explain the rest of the building? Slindon was the family seat of the Countess, formerly Barbara Kemp; it seems most likely that Nore Folly was built between 1749 and 1786, while she was married to the 3rd Earl. The name Nore is puzzling. There is a sandbank of that name in the Thames a little way out from Sheerness; Charles Radclyffe, the Earl of Newburgh's roaring Jacobite father, was captured in the North Sea by the frigate *Sheerness* and taken past the Nore Bank on his way to execution in the Tower in 1746—an extremely tenuous connection but the only one we can make.

Stanmer

Monument (1775)
TQ 330 100

Stanmer House, west of Lewes, has a Coade stone monument erected in 1775 to commemorate Lady Pelham's father. It takes the form of an urn on a triangular plinth, resting on three tortoises, and it must have come from a pattern book—there are three others like it around the country.

Stansted

The Garden In Mind (1990s)
SU 770 100

At Stansted House's kitchen garden Ivan Hicks (see Groombridge above) made The Garden In Mind (hate the name)—it's lots of fun as long as one doesn't think of Art. Everything is too trifling to list one by one, but together they provide a good half hour of pleasure, especially the flowerpot man.

For Stansted's Lumley Seat, see Lordington.

Steyning

Water Tower (1928)
TQ 170 130

There is a remarkable octagonal water tower, well worth seeing, north of Steyning at a

Wappingthorn Helter-Skelter

house called Wappingthorn. It was built by Maxwell Ayrton in 1928 and benefits from the addition of a summerhouse on top. With the staircase wrapping itself around the outside of the tower, the style could best be described as Helter Skelter.

Uppark

Vandalian Tower (1774)
SU 760 170

The Vandalian Tower is now almost totally destroyed (by vandals?), but sufficient pieces remain on its magnificent hill site to gladden us by the pleasure of ruins. All there are to be seen are five or six tall piers for arches or Gothic windows; the original shape can no longer be discerned. Sir Matthew Fetherstonhaugh commissioned it from Henry Keene in 1774 to celebrate the coming of age of his son Harry, and to mark the founding of Vandalia, a new American colony—but young Harry stayed home and partied with a dissolute set, which included the gorgeous 18-year-old Emma Hart, whose 'giddy ways' (she kept getting pregnant by other men) upset Fetherstonhaugh so much he threw her out; whereupon she went on to become Lady Hamilton, Nelson's mistress, and one of the most famous women of the age. Also at Uppark are a Gothick seat, a dairy and a game larder.

Worthing

Castle Goring or The Rat's Castle (1791)
TQ 110 060

Castle Goring along the A27 on the outskirts of Worthing is extraordinary; the only other similar building we can think of is Castle Ward at Downpatrick in Northern Ireland. The entrance front is good strong castle Gothic: massive frowning turrets, heavy castellations and cross arrowslits. Around on the garden side the difference is complete: a pleasant pedimented classical façade, with seven bays with Ionic pilasters. The ensemble was designed—if that's the word—by John Biagio Rebecca for Sir Bysshe Shelley, grandfather of Percy. Shelley it was who was responsible for the schizophrenic layout of the house: not only is one side Gothic and the other classical, but the rooms inside change style halfway through, suddenly becoming vaulted, for example. The staircase is on the opposite side of the house to the main rooms; there is no entrance hall and no corridors; the porch prevents any light reaching the ground-floor rooms and so on. This frightful mish-mash

took 34 years to build, by which time Sir Bysshe was dead, never having lived in it. The locals fondly refer to it as the Rat's Castle.

Tarring Tower (1893)
TQ 110 060

At Tarring in Worthing, at the back of 100 South Street, stands a square, flint, castellated tower, which was built by W. Osborne Boyes a solicitor, as a study in his garden. No doubt he did a spot of star-gazing as well.

Home House Rock Garden (1871)
TQ 110 060

By the time (1871) James Bateman, the famous horticulturalist, left Biddulph

The Vandalian Tower

Grange (see Staffordshire), which he had transformed into a wondrous garden, he transposed himself to Worthing. Here, at his new house in Farncombe Road, he created another rock garden, grottoes, tunnels and, of course, rockeries. Home House was also known as 'Hermit's Cave', and Bateman, whose finances had been stretched to the limits at Biddulph, let the public in for a fee. Today, however, the house and gardens are private. Bateman lived the last days of his life in Springbank, on Victoria Road, and died there in 1897, but we do not know whether Springbank is still there and has yet another rockery.

WARWICKSHIRE

Of all the shire counties, Warwickshire is probably the least affollied. Even allowing for the annexation of the new county of West Midlands, leaving it a largely rural area, there are no more than 20 or so sites worth mentioning (this after some intense scraping of the barrel's bottom)—which is remarkable when one considers this was the home county of Sanderson Miller, one of the most influential folly builders in Britain, although now several half-follies could be attributed to him.

Alcester

Oversley Castle (early 19th century)
SP 093 554

On the far west border of Warwickshire is Ragley Hall, seat of the Marquess of Hertford. Unlike other landed gentry, the Seymours seem not to have succumbed to the fatal fascination of follies, although they bowed sufficiently to fashion to allow Lancelot Brown to do the gardens in 1758. The estate remained folly free until the Prince Regent, visiting Ragley in the early 1800s and playing billiards with his host, looked out of the window and suggested: 'My dear Lord Hertford, your view would be improved by a Castle.' Such suggestions were

seldom ignored, so Oversley Castle was built on top of a hill 1½ miles away, above the village of Wixford. Originally it was just a plain, castellated, square tower, but it has been improved to become a huge and impressive glistening white private house, which engulfed the original folly in 1933.

Arbury

The Round Towers (mid-18th century)
Tower Farm (mid-18th century)
SP 333 910

Good, even splendid Gothick of the Strawberry Hill variety can be seen at Arbury Hall where, dare one say it, the interior is superior to the exterior. Half an architectural

Arbury Towers

Tower Farm, Arbury

dictionary worked at Arbury, but we must confine ourselves to the Round Towers in Stockingford, a suburb of Nuneaton, an exceedingly well-turned-out gateway with lodges, more in the gigantomanic manner than the Gothick: there are no castellations and only a few small round arched windows in each of the towers flanking the roughly-shaped Gothic arch. The arch is made of large rough blocks of stone, and the towers in the same stone but cut smaller. Tower Farm, ½ mile to the west along the B4112, is built in the same style and acted as a farm screen. Both buildings have been ascribed by Mowl and Earnshaw to Sanderson Miller. After this the Griff Lodges of 1776 are, despite their relatively sparsely decorated exteriors, too finicky and unmanly.

Arlescote

Pavilions (16th century)
SP 390 480

Four elegant ogival roofed Elizabethan pavilions terminate the garden walls of Arlescote Manor House.

Burton Dassett

The Beacon (16th–18th century)
SP 390 520

Northwest of Farnborough Park the ridge of the Burton Hills culminates at the Burton Dassett Country Park, a warren of wind-blown, close-cropped, hassocky turf

dropping away to the Itchen plain below. If a good folly is all you seek, then it's hardly worth paying the car parking charge to see The Beacon, a squat little round tower with corbels and a dumpy cone roof. The story is that it was built hundreds of years ago by the wicked Baron Blenknap, who would signal from the tower to other equally wicked barons for help if his serfs looked like revolting, but it looks awfully like a windmill adapted to provide a modest but highly visible eyecatcher.

Charlecote

Mock Jacobean Gateway (1865)
SP 260 560

Charlecote Park, a National Trust property on the road to Stratford-upon-Avon, contains many pieces of furniture and ceramics bought by George Hammond Lucy at William Beckford's 1823 sale at Fonthill. The seemingly genuine Jacobean gate at the west entrance was built by John Gibson.

Chesterton

Windmill (1632)
SP 340 590

The famous windmill in the village of Chesterton arouses more argument about what constitutes a folly than any other building included in this book. Traditionally attributed to Inigo Jones, it seems unlikely that the great man would have stooped to designing a windmill, especially for a mere baronet. So opinion tends to favour the baronet himself, Sir Edward Peyto, as the architect. Nevertheless it is evidently inspired by Inigo Jones's classical style; a circular domed building standing on six open arches, high, mighty and solitary in its splendour. Its design is sufficiently eyecatching, so utterly unlike any other windmill in the country, for many people to question whether it was originally designed as such—including Pevsner, who asks 'was it an observatory, or else a gazebo, or a "standing"?' To us it seems to have been an honest attempt at a working mill from the time it was built in 1632, but Sir Edward, a staunch royalist, was obviously strongly influenced by the king's favourite architect and could not resist the temptation to classicize what he would have regarded as an industrial building. One wonders what the dusty miller, hauling sacks up the ladder that provided the only access to the wheel room, thought of his employer's need to prettify his view.

Combe Abbey

Gateway (1770s)
Belvedere (1770s)
East Loge (1770s)
SP 404 798

Lancelot Brown worked at Combe in the
early 1770s, and the buildings may date from
that time. There is a good gateway and
apparently a rather dilapidated belvedere,
domed and hexagonal and extended into a
house. We made a couple of forays in search
of this, but were seduced by the won, won,
wonderful cod Gothick of the interior of
Combe Abbey, now a romantically bizarre
country house hotel, and we never found it.
Further away, at Brinklow on the A427, is East
Lodge, another conversion, which started as
an octagonal tower in the Gothick taste.

Compton Wynyates

Compton Pike (16th century)
SP 330 420

Compton Wynyates is often said to be the
most typically English house in the country;
it is certainly one of the most beautiful. On a
hill to the south is an elongated, slightly
hipped pyramid capped with a ball finial,
which we would unhesitatingly describe as a
folly, but Compton Pike is authoritatively said
to be a beacon site dating from the 16th
century, for the Armada warnings. It is
strange to see the use of the word 'pike' as a
sharp or pointed structure this far south; in
Lancashire and Yorkshire the word is often
used to describe a pointed hill or the folly
built on its summit.

Coventry (West Midlands)

Cemetery Gazebo (19th century)
SP 341 784

Coventry holds a slightly puzzling piece in
this West Midlands jigsaw: a 19th-century
gazebo, an octagonal, arcaded sandstone
building, reached by a short flight of steps,
topped with a flat roof, looking like a rather
disreputable bandstand for a string duet. It's
not particularly unusual except for its
situation—why should anyone want to build
a gazebo in the London Road Cemetery? A
watch tower against grave robbers, as at
Eckford in the Borders? Whatever the
reason, it has recently been comprehensively
restored, and now looks wonderful and even
more inappropriate.

Edgbaston (West Midlands)

Perrot's Folly (1758)
SP 050 850

This remarkable survival was built by John
Perrott on his country estate. It is a six-storey,
96ft (29.3m) tall, octagonal tower, built of red
brick and with a circular stair turret. It is the
most satisfying folly tower in the Midlands.
Perrott lived at The Lodge in Rotton Park
and was said to have built the tower for the
view or so that his daughter Catherine could
watch the hare-coursing in Smethwick (why
a 96ft tower?) or to entertain friends. There
must be a more tragic reason—and there is, in
a booklet on the Birmingham and Midland
Institute Edgbaston Observatory. It is said
that John Perrott built the monument so that
he would be able to see from the top St

Compton Pike

George Road Bothy

Perrot's Folly

Philip's churchyard in Belbroughton, where his lady love lay buried. Unsentimentally, it has to be said that the only direction that can't be seen from the top of the tower is towards Belbroughton—the stair turret is in the way. By 1922 the old oak stairs had become rotten and were replaced by concrete. Now the old monument (in Waterworks Road, not Monument Road) is surrounded by little houses cuddling up to its base. It is also a listed building in an excellent state of repair; for a hundred years the B. & M.I. used it as a meteorological observatory, for which purpose it is admirably suited. It is now equally lovingly tended by a Christian mission.

George Road Bothy (early 19th century)
SP 056 856

A little distance away in George Road is a Tudor Gothic pavilion, described rather misleadingly as a bothy. Built *c.*1830 of red and blue brick, the polygonal, four-

windowed building forms an attractive composition with a castellated wall joining it to a coach house. Extremely dilapidated, if not ruined, when we first saw it, it has now been lovingly transformed into the centrepiece of a most elegant house, rebuilt around it. The grand Worcestershire coat of arms attached to the façade is particularly pleasing, as this is—or was—Warwickshire, but it is partly justified as the restorers were immigrants from Worcester.

Edge Hill

Edge Hill Tower (1747)
Obelisk (1854)
SP 370 470

Sanderson Miller was born in 1716 at Radway Grange under the lee of Edge Hill, the son of a prosperous Banbury businessman. At 21 he inherited a substantial fortune, which enabled him to lead the life of gentleman architect. He was a trend-setter rather than a technician; his charm, sociability and avant-garde taste won him fashionable friends and commissions, which were drawn up as often as not by his master mason William Hitchcox. Sanderson Miller's practical ideas combined with his romantic imagination formed an unbeatable alliance; to have Miller design you a castle stained, in Walpole's famous phrase, with 'the true rust of the Barons' Wars' was to be in the height of fashion. He had started to Gothicize the Grange six years before Walpole thought of doing the same to Strawberry Hill, and in the previous year (1743) had built a picturesque thatched cottage on the side of Edge Hill, which attracted favourable comment from Dean Swift.

His enthusiasm increasing, Miller launched into his first major folly, Edge Hill Tower, which was completed in 1747 and was

The Castle Inn, Radway

Farnborough

Garden Buildings (mid-18th century)
SP 430 480

Farnborough Hall has a terrace walk laid up the gentle rise of the hill like a fringed tablecloth. With earth and evergreen shrubs a rampart defence has been created, a broad grassy walk sweeping up at the back. The view is to the west, with the gap between Edge Hill and Bitham Hill opening out to Stratford in the plain distance. We first pass a

The slender obelisk at Farnborough

sensationally well received by society for its positioning and its apparent authenticity. It was built on the spot where Charles I raised his standard before the indecisive battle (two monuments on the plain below commemorate the actual battle), and it commanded a magnificent sweep of a view to the northwest, while architecturally it appears to have been based on Guy's Tower at Warwick Castle, with thin, almost fragile castellations surmounting stumpy little machicolations. The tower is octagonal and, judged by the standard of other folly towers, appears commonplace, which is rather like criticizing Beethoven's Fifth for being hackneyed. Edge Hill Tower is a seminal folly by a master folly builder. Later Sanderson Miller was to originate a style of ruined castle that, in its various forms, was to be imitated the length and breadth of Britain.

Whether he tired of improving his own estate or found more enjoyment in new challenges we do not know, but Miller built nothing else at Radway except perhaps the little arched grotto. The slender, elegant obelisk at the foot of the hill was not Miller's:

THIS OBELISK WAS ERECTED BY CHARLES
CHAMBERS ESQ. R.N.
IN 1854 TO COMMEMORATE THE
BATTLE OF WATERLOO
WHERE THE VII INISKILLANE DRAGOONS WERE
COMMANDED
LIEUT. COL. F. S. MILLER
WHO FOR HIS GALLANT CONDUCT
DURING THE ACTION IN WHICH HE WAS
VERY SEVERELY WOUNDED
WAS MADE A COMPANION OF THE MOST
HONORABLE ORDER OF THE BATH

little tetrastyle temple seat with worn composite columns, then reach the gem, an oval two-storey temple of 1756 or before, open at the bottom with Tuscan columns, then at the back a comfortably rising if crude open staircase, visually entirely out of keeping with the rest of the building, leading to a tiny parquet-floored first-floor oval room decorated in Wedgwood blue and white rococo plasterwork, miraculously still intact. The view is very beautiful from here. At the end of the grass walk is a tall obelisk of 1746 or a little earlier, despite being inscribed '1751', and it must have fallen down, because a faded inscription reads 'RE-ERECTED 1828'. These are not follies, but English landscape garden architecture at its most elegant. To have Farnborough Park to oneself on a warm, clear, sunny spring morning is to realize the real beauty of the English countryside, the only intrusion being a sleepy drone not of bees, but of traffic on the M40 below.

Halford

The Folly (1799)
SP 262 454

A house by Thomas Webb in 1799, originally consisting of twin five-storey, octagonal towers, was built, so the story goes, so that Webb could see Stow-on-the-Wold—but for what reason we are not told. The upper two storeys were taken down at the end of the last century, and today the combined towers make a comfortable though apparently unremarkable home, until the history is revealed. It wears its flat roof with as much aplomb as William Hague wears his baseball cap.

Idlicote

Dovecote (18th century)
SP 280 440

Just southeast of Halford, this tiny hilltop village in scenery more reminiscent of the Wiltshire plains than Warwickshire, has at Idlicote House a charming 18th-century dovecote-cum-water tower. It is octagonal and castellated, with ogival windows and spirelet roof.

King's Norton (West Midlands)

Lifford Hall Watch Tower (18th century)
SP 057 797

Lifford Hall, in the valley of the Rea at the bottom of a dip in King's Norton, has an 18th-century castellated watch tower at the end of a weakly battlemented red sandstone wall. Armed with a lawnmower and some old bits of rope, this tiny belvedere struggles feebly against the visual weight of a behemoth of an industrial complex above and behind it, manufacturing petro-chemical developments by the size of it. Firms of accountants and lawyers now infest the ancient hall it once served as a pleasure pavilion.

Leamington Spa

Obelisks (1875; 1880)
SP 320 650

The charming Jephson Gardens hold an interesting fountain of 1869, Dr Jephson's statue in a temple (statue by Peter Hollins of Birmingham, 1846, and temple built over it three years later by the Leamington architect Daniel Goodman Squirhill) and finally an obelisk of 1875 to Edward Willes 'to whom Leamington is indebted for the site of these gardens'. Mr Bob Hirons also informs us that there is another obelisk at Holly Walk, erected in 1880 and originally equipped with a drinking fountain as well—a memorial to alderman Henry Bright, 'to whose untiring exertions this town is chiefly indebted for its supply of pure water'.

Leek Wootton

Gaveston Cross (1832)
SP 289 676

This isn't a folly, but why include obelisks if we can't manage the occasional odd-looking cross, although it is not really the cross that is out of the ordinary, but its pedestal. There are four, rather rough-looking, square, stone-blocked pillars on a plinth, surmounted by the cross. It is the work of the Leamington architect John George Jackson. The inscription is thus:

> *In the Hollow of this Rock*
> *Was beheaded,*
> *On the 1st Day of July, 1312,*
> *By Barons lawless as himself,*
> *PIERS GAVESTON, Earl of Cornwall:*
> *The Minion of a hateful King:*
> *In Life and Death,*
A memorable Instance of Misrule.

Meriden (West Midlands)

Cyclists' Obelisk (20th century)
SP 238 824

West Midlands is an urban county; one must not expect countryside. There is, however, a gap in the houses between Birmingham and Coventry, and one of the little towns plugging the gap is Meriden, so called because like so many other towns it marks the geographical centre of England. The Cyclists' Association supported the town's claim by erecting an obelisk here to the memory of all the cyclists who were killed in World War II, which struck us as an utterly pointless gesture. It is the only war memorial we have included because of its *raison d'être* rather than its architecture.

Napton-on-the-Hill

The Folly (late 18th century)
SP 460 630

Even less a folly then The Folly at Halford, this pub along the canal was formerly known as the Bull and Butcher, but acquired its present name when it re-opened in 1990. This area of the village has always been known as The Folly. Why? Nobody knows.

Solihull (West Midlands)

Sir Anthony's Keep (1991)
SP 176 792

Not many successful corporations are sufficiently self-confident to boast the wilful eccentricity of Whale Tankers, Britain's leading manufacturer of sewage disposal tankers for local authorities. We will spare you the company's self-description, although those of you with a coprophiliac turn of mind may well guess—but the company shares the zest for life that permeates so many great follies. It does not come as much of a surprise to discover that it has built one of its own. Needing gravel to build a factory extension, it excavated the material from its own land, flooded the resulting pit and landscaped it to

Sir Anthony's Keep

create a lake complete with island. It looked pretty, but clearly something was lacking. After some thought, the Board decided to erect a sham castle on the island, constructed of castellated galvanized steel—in fact, an economic adaptation of the company's own product. It was named Sir Anthony's Keep after the managing director's father, who had conveniently been knighted some six months earlier. The factory grounds have now acquired a replica of a Saxon cruck house and a woodland walk, and we await further developments with interest. One can get a good view of the castle from the company's car park—you may not be shot if you dash in and out—and the plaque commemorating the construction of the car park is well worth reading.

Southam

Dispensary Monument (1823)
SP 410 620

The site of the Dispensary Cottage at Southam is marked by a wordy little plinth surmounted with an urn, each of the four sides packed with inscriptions recording the benevolence of Mr H.L. Smith, who on this site founded the first 'Self Supporting or Provident Dispensary in the Kingdom'—the first cash chemist?

Stoneleigh

Tantara Lodge (early 19th century)
SP 330 720

In Stoneleigh Abbey's park Tantara Lodge is a rather grand affair, and, indeed, it fits the abbey connection with its arched gateway, with pointed windows and buttresses. Barbara Hague suggests that it is the work of Charles S. Smith, a Warwickshire architect who busied himself with additional work at Stoneleigh in 1813 and again in the late 1830s.

Stratford-upon-Avon

Obelisk (1876)
Clopton House Tower (1844)
SP 210 560

Just north of Stratford, in the grounds of the Welcombe Hotel (not a marketing man's ploy, but the mansion's real name before it became an hotel), is a gigantic obelisk, easily the biggest in the county and one of the largest in England. It was erected in memory of Mark Philips in 1876 by his brother, Robert Needham Philips, and both brothers and their father have lengthy plaques on each side recording their great humanity and successes in business and politics. The fourth side carries the family coat of arms, and the whole granite monster cost £4,000 to build.

Just a little nearer the town, in fact one field away from it, is the pretty little Clopton House Tower, which has three storeys and is octagonal, heavily battlemented, with a higher spiral stair turret. It has been carefully converted into a private house, and a new section has been added in identical style—the same grey stone brick and the same battlements, a perfect match. The owners love it—'it's ideal for parties!'—despite falling off the top of the stair turret one Christmas while stringing lights around it and just managing to cling to the icy battlements of the main tower some 50ft above the ground until the cries for help were finally answered. It was designed as a belvedere for Clopton House, a lovely 17th-century building now sadly abandoned and decaying, and was built by Charles Thomas Warde in 1844 as either the 'smallest castle or grandest cottage in England!'

Stretton-on-Dunsmore

Departure Monument (1921)
SP 420 740

The Departure Monument is a 55ft (16.8m) obelisk now precariously perched on the central reservation of the Coventry–London road, commemorating the rally of thousands of troops who marched from here to war and death in 1915.

Sutton Coldfield (West Midlands)

Ionic Temple (19th century)
SP 134 981

A shabby little garden pavilion with an Ionic tetrastyle portico was removed from Old Moor Hall and re-erected in the grounds of the immaculate Ashfurlong Hall, on the Tamworth road. It stands hard by the

Ashfurlong Hall Temple

rhododendron-swathed drive to the Hall, which clearly is not suffering from a lack of funds, so it is hard to see why this rather beautiful garden building should have been overlooked.

Umberslade

Obelisk (1749)
SP 140 720

At Umberslade Park near Nuthurst Lord Archer had an obelisk erected in 1749 for one of three reasons: to celebrate his elevation to the peerage in 1747; to mark the burial place of a favourite horse; or because it had something to do with Archer's interest in astronomy, which sounds like the least likely reason.

Walton

Bath House (mid-18th century)
SP 280 30?

Walton Hall, south of Walton, has a mid-18th-century bath house in the appropriately named Bath Hill Wood. It contains a 'cold bath' and is built as a grotto in the classical style. It was saved by the Landmark Trust and restored in the early 1990s by William Hawkes and Diana Reynell. Sanderson Miller is believed to have been the architect.

Warwick

Spiers Lodge (1764–6)
SP 283 631

This romantic Gothick hunting lodge in the park offered broad views of Warwick Castle before heavy tree growth obscured both the lodge and its view. It was not only inspired by Timothy Lightoler's *The Gentleman and Farmer's Architect* (1762) but was in all probability adapted by Lightoler, who was working at Warwick Castle in the 1760s. It is in a rather undecided style, with Tudor elements, some earlier, some later, and fantastic chimneys. It is buried deep in the woods, as remote a house as one could imagine in the Midlands, dark and oppressively overshadowed in the forest. Although it is occupied, surely the owners can access it only by Landrover. Lightoler also designed the castellated mill at Warwick and, of course, the castle, which, with its 18th- and 19th-century additions, is all the better for it.

North of Warwick is the famous Guy's Cliffe chapel, a medieval hermitage, and its rock chambers and statue. Along the way parts of it were follified in the 18th century.

Spiers Lodge, buried deep in the woods

WILTSHIRE

Of the four Wessex counties, Wiltshire is perhaps the bleakest, with little to offer the traveller in search of scenery. The M4 cuts the head of the county off from the rest, leaving Swindon, born like Atlanta as a railway marshalling yard, soulless and vacant, an artificial city. There is only one curiosity worth seeing north of the motorway, and that is not a folly. It is Wanborough Church, which, like Ormskirk in Lancashire, has both a tower and a steeple, but here they are at opposite ends of the nave. The strangest thing about it is that no legend has grown up in explanation. South of the motorway the county wastes away into the sparse treelessness of the Marlborough Downs and Salisbury

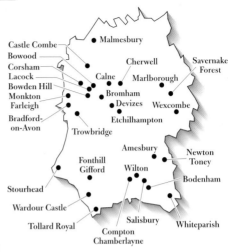

Plain, beloved of Ancient Britons, corn circles, flying saucers and the British Army, and punctuated only by Savernake Forest and the pretty Vale of Pewsey. Despite the county's unprepossessing appearance to an outsider, its moonraker people's pride is strong. Europe's most important prehistoric monuments are to be found in Wiltshire, and it is said that its very barrenness was due to the intensive agriculture carried on here in prehistoric times.

Amesbury

Grotto (c.1730)
Chinese Temple (c.1748–early 19th century)
SU 140 420

There is a grotto called the Diamond in the grounds of Amesbury Abbey, where everyone says that John Gay wrote 'The Beggar's Opera'. Why not believe it? This would mean the grotto would have been built before 1732, and therefore the ubiquitous Jos. Lane of Tisbury could not have crafted it. Polly Peachum has got her own tower, up in Yorkshire.

Chinoiserie expert Michael Cousins has found mention of the next item as early as

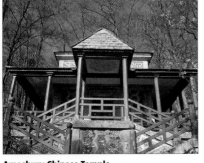

Amesbury Chinese Temple

1748: 'On the Bridge, over the River, is built a Room after the Manner of the Chinese.' It is still there, although it may have been rebuilt or in some other way altered by William Chambers in 1772—the situation is the same though, it is still a Chinese temple on a bridge. Some changes certainly occurred in the early 19th century, and the building is none the worse for it. It is square, of stone and flint, with a fretwork balustrade and a good oriental round window, a later addition. But somewhere along the way it has lost its bearings: on closer inspection it looks as if a classical bridge had plummeted through a Chinese takeaway.

Bodenham

Longford Castle (late 16th century)
SU 170 260

Longford Castle was built as a house in the late 16th century and has remained continuously inhabited for 400 years. It can scarcely be counted as a folly, yet its unusual triangular plan is shared in Britain only by the contemporary Triangular Lodge at Rushton in Northamptonshire and the rash of 18th-century folly towers germinated by Henry Flitcroft with Fort Belvedere in Windsor Great Park. Unquestionably, the builder, Sir Thomas Gorges, was a certified eccentric, but so tantalizingly little is known about him that the stories of a Swedish wife pining for her triangular castle back home and Longford being built on the booty from a Spanish galleon must stay as speculation. There is a triangular castle at Gripsholm in Sweden that dates from 1537, and a Sir Ferdinando Gorges was a contemporary naval commander who was probably a relation, but further than that we cannot go. The building, with its symbol of the Holy Trinity in the central courtyard, should be regarded in the same light as Rushton: an affirmation of faith in the Trinity. There are some interesting lines in Spenser's *Faerie Queene* about the Castle of Temperance:

> *The frame there of was partly circular*
> *And part triangular—O work divine…*

and Gorges appears to have been one of Spenser's patrons.

Bowden Hill

Gatehouses (16th century; 1796)
Grotto
Tower (19th century)
ST 950 670

There is a mysterious and wooded triangle between Devizes and Chippenham—this is Cotswold Wiltshire now; the land has softened and mellowed, the stone is more honeyed. Bowden Hill, on a back road to

Spye Park Gatehouse

Lacock, has two gatehouses standing glowering across the road at each other. One is the Tudor gateway to Spye Park House; the other, an eyecatcher, an upstart (James Wyatt, 1796), is a gateway to Bowden Park halfway down the hill, hinting perhaps of ancient rivalries. There is a grotto in Bowden Park which we have not seen. There may be more, but this is utterly private. The Spye Park gateway is not all it seems; although genuinely Tudor, it was erected here after the estate it originally graced, Old Bromham House, was destroyed by the Roundheads in 1645. The Boynton family moved in style— when they bought Spye Park they brought their gatehouse with them.

Sandridge Tower, south on the A3102, is a dour, castellated tower made into a house. No names, no dates.

Bowood

Grotto and Garden Buildings (18th century)
ST 980 700

Bowood, just beyond Calne, is open to the public in the summer. It is a place of pilgrimage for the folly-hunter because the great cascade was designed by the Hon. Charles Hamilton, who created the famous gardens at Painshill in Surrey. His work at Bowood owes much to the influence of Poussin and other romantic landscape painters. The major work is the cascade, far more impressive than his own at Painshill, largely because it still works, but there was also a grotto by the Lanes of Tisbury—as at Painshill, but virtually non-existent nowadays—a rustic stone seat, a still extant Doric temple and a superb mausoleum (kept in immaculate condition) by Robert Adam.

The towering, asymmetrical Italianate gate lodge, known as the Golden Gate, was designed for the marquess in 1834 by Sir Charles Barry at his Barrymost. It took four years to complete.

Bradford-on-Avon (Avon)

Belcombe Court Garden Buildings
(18th century)
Budbury Castle (1850)
ST 790 610

Bradford is best known for its lock-up, *née* chapel, on the old bridge over the river, and for its extremely old little church up the hill. But the follies of Bradford are more in the direction of Winsley. Belcombe Court holds a *cottage orné*, the former laundry, also known as the Gothick Cottage, a rotunda temple and a grotto decorated with ammonites.

We vaguely remember seeing Budbury Castle and dismissing it, but when Pevsner (on consulting his Wiltshire tome again) says 'folly', then it's a folly, 1850, 'with an Italianate roof'.

Bromham

Tree House (1990s)
ST 970 650

Tree houses are notoriously ephemeral, although some have been in a state of suspended animation for centuries. This one was noticed in 1994, near Mark Wilkinson's furniture showroom in Bromham. It is 30ft (9m) up on an open ladder and apparently it is fitted with nearly everything you could wish for, except a lift. Which kept us out.

Calne

Maud Heath's Column (1838)
Bremhill Follies (early 19th century)
ST 970 730

The Marquess of Lansdowne was partly responsible for a really primitive statue, which sits with a shopping basket on a column at the top of Wick Hill, northwest of Calne. It commemorates one Maud Heath, a market trader, who left money in her will when she died in 1474 to build a causeway over the often flooded land between Wick Hill and Chippenham Clift. In 1698 pillars in her honour were erected at the start and finish of the causeway, and in 1838, feeling that two pillars were not enough, came this column:

ERECTED
AT THE JOINT EXPENCE OF
HENRY MARQUESS OF LANSDOWNE
LORD OF THE LAND AND
WM. L. BOWLES VICAR OF
THE PARISH OF BREMHILL
JUSTICES
1838
Thou who dost pause on this aerial height
Where MAUD HEATH's Pathway winds in shade or light
Christian wayfarer, in this world of strife
Be still and ponder on the Path of Life.
WLB.

William Lisle Bowles's poetry could have been better—he was a friend of Wordsworth, Lamb and Thomas Moore and corresponded with many of the leading literary figures of the time. Bowles (1762–1850) was the author of *Fourteen Sonnets Written Chiefly on Picturesque Spots During a Journey* (1789), praised by Coleridge, who might be forgiven

Maud Heath's Column

as he was 17 years old at the time. Bowles resolutely refused to be measured by tailors and once failed to notice, while leading his horse on the bridle, that the animal had long since disappeared. He was known as a shy and frightened man, although that is perhaps belied by his many literary connections. An enthusiastic amateur of all things artistic, he may well have perpetrated the statue too. Bowles was devoted to the memory of William Shenstone of Leasowes fame, perhaps because, like Shenstone, he adored women but was constantly refused and remained a bachelor. So he went and created his own Leasowes at the vicarage of nearby Bremhill, of which a cave, some urns and a sham ruin appear to have survived.

Castle Combe

Bell-turret (19th century)
Arbour (19th century)
ST 840 770

Castle Combe is small and attractive and full of tourists. The Manor House is a hotel and restaurant and the grounds are out of bounds to the commoner. In 1977 we had to eat to get in. The bell-turret of the Biddestone Church, a hamlet a mile or two to the south, is placed as a garden feature, providing a Gothic seat. In the Italianate terraced garden is a polygonal open arbour in the Gothic style. Changes were made to the garden in 1857 and a wing was added to the house in 1873—the former date may be right for the arbour. The Castle Tower, a tall and slim round folly tower that looked like an Celtic round tower, was built around 1850 near the original castle remains. We didn't find a trace of it.

At nearby Yatton is a string of towerettes in the fields to disguise ventilation shafts or waterworks—one forgets.

Cherhill

Landsdowne Obelisk (1843)
SU 050 690

We catch our first glimpse of the Lansdowne Obelisk in Cherhill as we enter West Kennet. It is a straightforward obelisk, notable only for its height and site, and the attractions of West Kennet, one of the oldest human settlements in Europe, are considerably greater—the Long Barrow and the astonishing Silbury Hill, of uncertain purpose. A prehistoric folly? There is a delightful and more modern curiosity in West Kennet itself; a thatched wall on the south side of the road. The obelisk itself was built in 1843 by the Marquess of Lansdowne to commemorate his ancestor Sir William Petty. It was built on Oldbury Castle, an Iron Age fortification, and there is a chalk white horse carved in the downs below to the east.

Compton Chamberlayne

Arch (1858)
SU 040 290

West of Wilton are the two great parks of Stourhead and Fonthill; on our way we are detained briefly by an arch at Compton Chamberlayne, right on the side of the A30. It leads nowhere but to a scrubby, sapling-covered hill, and there is no trace of a drive to Compton Park, the house of the Penruddocks. A small plaque reads:

CP

FHP

1858

The embattled arch is flanked by two square towers of different sizes. In the 1990s a new and not unsympathetic house in Castle Style was added to the larger tower.

Corsham

Sham Castle Screen (mid-19th century)
ST 870 710

Corsham Court as we see it today was built in 1844–49 by Thomas Bellamy for Lord Methuen. Bellamy was a student under David Laing, who specialized in building picturesque villages and *cottages ornés*, which may explain the extraordinary edifice behind the stables, screening them from the road that leads to the house and the church. It is an enormous crinkle-crankle wall, about 60ft (18m) high and 100ft (30m) long. Evidently intended to convey an ecclesiastical air, this monstrosity was built with stones from Chippenham Abbey, including some of the window tracery. If it was meant to disguise the stables it fails magnificently; so blatant an object in this setting cries out to be investigated. Solidly, massively and very carefully built, with Gothick chimneys perched on the top apparently as afterthoughts, it is large enough to conceal small rooms in its base, which probably came in handy as hen houses. Details such as the Gothick window tracery are far more prominent on the north side of the wall, showing it was intended to be seen from the house. If not Bellamy, then Repton may have been responsible for this magnificent folly.

In and around the suave golden-and-green landscaped park are some good gates and garden buildings, most of which have in some way been embellished by bits and pieces from other buildings—the Methuens were evidently architectural magpies.

Devizes

Devizes Castle (1842)
Shane's Castle (early 19th century)
Market Cross (1814)
SU 010 620

We went down to Devizes because we had heard that there were two folly castles. Devizes Castle was originally a Norman motte and bailey fortification around which the town grew up. It fell into disrepair, was slighted by Cromwell and by 1842 it had virtually disappeared. Then William Beckford's protégé, H.E. Goodridge, 'rescued' it by building a Gothic fantasia full of louring walls and forbidding battlements, but it has now been robbed of its grimness by being turned into flats.

Shane's Castle sounded promising, but turned out to be a castellated toll cottage on the junction of the A361 and the A342.

The market cross of 1814 was built by Benjamin Dean Wyatt and paid for by Viscount Sidmouth, formerly known as Mr Addington, the Recorder of Devizes. It commemorates the fate of one Ruth Pierce from Potterne, who, on market day 25 January 1753, swore to God that she had paid her share of a sack of corn and 'wished she might drop dead if she had not'. A moment or so later she did drop dead and the money she owed was found in her hand.

Etchilhampton

Lydeway Monument (1768)
SU 030 610

Southeast of Devizes is Etchilhampton Hill, on top of which is the Lydeway Monument, an iron-tailed lion, dating from 1768 and sitting on a pedestal to commemorate a road improvement scheme. There's a custom that has died out—why no M25 Memorial?

Fonthill Gifford

Remains of Fonthill Abbey
(late 18th–early 19th century)
ST 930 330

Fonthill was the classic folly, 'the most prodigious romantic folly in England', as Pevsner described it. But there is virtually nothing to see. Gone is the vast Gothick house by Wyatt, gone is the 276ft (84m) high tower, but what captured the imagination more than either of these was the spire, towering to an incredible 450ft (137m) and overtopping the spire at Salisbury Cathedral—the tallest in Britain—by nearly 50ft (15m). The watercolour by Charles Wild that depicts it was based on a design by James Wyatt—but luckily it was never built, otherwise the tower that was to have supported it would have collapsed much sooner. Beckford's father followed the fashion of his day by employing Josiah Lane to build him a grotto, and it is said that he also built a now vanished folly tower on Stop's Hill, the start of young William's fascination with towers. The story of Fonthill and its houses is long and complicated; we need be concerned only with the Fonthill of William Beckford.

Beckford was a true child of the sixties: born in 1760, he fervently embraced Romanticism in all its forms. In addition to his early talents as a writer and his remarkable looks, he was by all accounts the richest young man in England. As such, he was the natural prey for every marriageable young woman in the country, but his sensational affair with William Courtenay, then a 12-year-old boy but later to become the Earl of Devon, soon put a stop to all that. He was married off in 1783 to Lady Margaret Gordon, by whom he had two daughters before she died three years later. In the same year, 1786, he published *Vathek*, a seminal Gothick novel, now almost unreadable but a book that influenced writers as diverse as Byron and Disraeli. The hero of the novel lived alone in a mighty tower, master of all he surveyed, possessed of an evil eye that could strike people dead with terror. Unlike other romantic writers, Beckford had the means to indulge his fantasies—he had so much money that there was no reason why he should not build a romantic tower for himself.

He began by surrounding his estate with a 12 mile long, 12ft (3.7m) high wall, behind which he could live in 'despotic seclusion' (at the time he divided his life between France, Portugal and Fonthill Splendens, the house built by his father, which had a public road running in front of it that even his wealth and influence could not close). Having secured the services of the fashionable but slapdash architect, James Wyatt because of his undoubted skill with the Gothick touch, Beckford was very specific about what he wanted, using Wyatt largely as the means of translating his ideas into stone. The original intention was to build a ruined convent on top of the hill, where Beckford could write or contemplate or entertain his catamites. Wyatt, of course, had ideas of his own, including the dumpy spire, which appears in J.M.W. Turner's watercolour of Fonthill painted in 1799. This spire collapsed in 1800. Wyatt was also enthusiastic about compo, a form of ornamental stucco or plaster, in which he encased the abbey. This lasted six years in the English climate before it deteriorated so severely that it had to be stripped off.

Legends grew up about the place—that it was a den of vice and perversity (true); that it was possible to drive a coach and six to the top of the tower (false); that building went on throughout day and night—partly true; as Beckford wrote to Franchi in 1808:

It's really stupendous, the spectacle here at night—the number of people at work, lit up by lads [sic]; the innumerable torches suspended everywhere, the immense and endless spaces, the gulph below; above, the gigantic spider's web of scaffolding—especially when, standing under the finished and numberless arches of the galleries, I listen to the reverberating voices in the stillness of the night and see immense buckets of plaster and water ascending, as if they were drawn up from the bowels of a mine, amid shouts from subterranean depths, oaths from Hell itself, and chanting from Pandemonium or the synagogue.

Beckford's relationship with Wyatt, whom he nicknamed 'Bagasse' (slang for the worthless residue left after refining sugar-cane—only a

All that remains of England's greatest folly

plantation owner would know the word), veered from adoration to exasperation, and his lamentations have a familiar ring to anyone who has ever tried to get building work done. On the actual design, Beckford was unstinting—'Wyatt merits and, I am sure, will receive the highest praise'—but as Wyatt's interest in the actual execution of his design diminished, so Beckford's frustration increased. In 1808 he expressed a desire to strangle him, and thereafter much time was spent in trying to catch Wyatt and bring him back down to Fonthill to finish the job:

Don't lose sight of him; don't let go of him until he's on his way here… The weather, everything is favourable, if only the cursed architect does not fail… If he does not wish to bring about the final ruin of the edifice, tell him to come…

One can't trust the infamous Bagasse in the slightest thing. Every day brings new proofs of his negligent apathy… I regret infinitely the fatal necessity of seeing here once more that cursed, infamous Bagasse; but come he must, and if he won't come soon, I'll send for Jeffry Wyatt [James Wyatt's nephew, later Sir Jeffry Wyatville]… Curse the infamous Bagasse a thousand and again a thousand times!… negligent and ruinous… if Bagasse doesn't come everything will go to the devil…

Sometimes everything became too much, and he vented his spleen not only on Wyatt but on architecture itself:

Would to God that he had never been born and that the Turks, Moors and Arabs had been not merely circumcised but castrated before inventing their pointed saracenic-Gothic architecture—the cause of my ruin. The devil take them.

But come he eventually did, and 'stupid, lazy Mr Wyatt' was suddenly transformed:

He works with a brio, a zeal, an energy a faith that would move the largest mountain in the Alps… He is all ardour and zeal as never before… My dear, angelic, most p-p-p-p-perfect Bagasse is killing himself with work: every hour, every moment, he adds some new beauty.

Full of admiration for Wyatt's work though Beckford may have been, he was less enthusiastic about his company: 'Certainly if I could be bored, it would be in his company. Ah my God, how slow, silent and null he is!'

Beckford's criticisms were not without foundation, unlike Wyatt's tower. During the 16 years that Wyatt sporadically worked on Fonthill there were rumblings of discontent about the quality of his construction, rumblings that were echoed elsewhere, for example at Blithfield Hall in Staffordshire, where the notorious compo cement made another appearance through the courtesy of his brother Benjamin. It seems to have been forgotten that the building was originally intended to be a sham. In 1814 Beckford's friend and companion, Gregory Franchi, wrote to the Marquess of Douglas, Beckford's son-in-law, that 'almost all that the villainous Bagasse built has been dismantled (to forestall finding ourselves buried in its rotten ruins)'. However the magnificent central tower remained, and it was still standing when Beckford's creditors finally caught up with him and he was forced to sell his beloved, uninhabitable Fonthill in 1822. It was bought for £330,000 ('very advantageously' admitted Beckford) by John Farquhar, an unkempt and eccentric gunpowder millionaire who enjoyed being mistaken for a beggar in the street.

On the night of 21 December 1825 the massive, foundationless tower could stand no more. It collapsed into a pile of rubble, watched by only one man, and brought much but not all of the rest of the abbey down with it. Farquhar died of apoplexy the following year; the subsequent disappearance of the rest of Fonthill Abbey was due to the Marquess of Westminster, who used the ruins as a quarry for his house, which was demolished in 1955, much as Beckford used Fonthill Splendens as a quarry for his abbey. All that remains of Fonthill Abbey today is the Oratory, the Sanctuary and the Lancaster Tower, together as a small private house. Meanwhile, Beckford was building another tower at Lansdown, north of Bath—which still stands. He must have the last word: 'Some people drink to forget their unhappiness. I do not drink, I build. And it ruins me.'

Lacock

Columns (18th century)
ST 920 680

Down Bowden Hill is the National Trust's Lacock, famous as much for its beauty as for being the birthplace of William Henry Fox

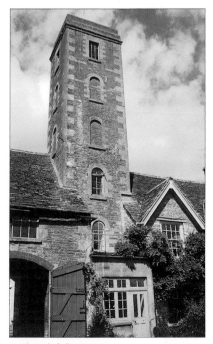

Dr Player's folly tower

Talbot, the inventor of the photographic negative, and his picture of one of Lacock Abbey's windows is the first ever to be put on a negative. There are two coupled Tuscan columns in the grounds, topped with a sphinx (by Benjamin Carter), and the Gothick gateway to the Abbey is by Sanderson Miller, as is the splendid hall of the house. Pevsner tells us that the columns formed a chimney on the house and were later taken down. But recently a watercolour of *c.*1800 of Devizes market place has come to light, showing the very same columns, only topped by what looks like a lion with his paw on a ball. Did the other set of chimneys go to Devizes or what?

Malmesbury

Tower (1819)
ST 930 870

In Cross Hayes Lane a small tower seem to spring up from two adjoining houses. It is built into the structure of one of the dwellings (hence Tower House). It is square, with partially blocked arched windows, and was built in 1819 by a Dr Player, the town's physician and keen astronomer, for star-gazing purposes. There is no evidence of any scientific apparatus ever being installed here, so he must have taken the portable. There is a very good view from the top, so the astronomy was obviously an excuse to come and sit here. The present owner, Mr André Ptaszynski, has taken to flying the Polish flag from the tower on red-letter days.

No folly, but hard to resist is Hannah Twynnoys's gravestone in the abbey churchyard, which mentions a 'Tyger fierce': she was killed in 1703 by an escaped tiger in Malmesbury's White Lion Inn. (This sort of thing seems to have been particular to Wiltshire: at Winterslow, in 1816, a lion mauled a horse of the Exeter mail coach to death.) A tiger's leap away is the Old Bell Hotel, at the back of which a rather good gazebo with remarkable windows is perched above the town walls.

Marlborough

Grotto (1720–30s)
SU 190 690

In the grounds of Marlborough College (formerly the Duke of Marlborough's house) is a grotto, recently restored by Diana Reynell, which in 1739 was judged to be better than Pope's grotto. Three small pools outside were conceived to mirror the interior of the grot.

Monkton Farleigh

Browne's Folly (1848)
ST 800 650

The escarpment at Monkton Farleigh is a Wiltshire cliff, hanging out over the county of Somerset with magnificent views of Bath. Colonel Wade Brown, who leased the manor of Monkton Farleigh in 1842, built this unexceptional tower in 1848; it had been preceded on the site by a semaphore tower. Many of the estate workers were without jobs because of the agricultural depression, so Brown set them to work on rebuilding the tower. While the scaffolding was still up, the Ordnance Survey took the opportunity to start surveying from its top. Brown had little time to waste on architectural niceties; his tower is devoid of decoration. It is square, faintly Italianate, windowless and tapering up to the top room, which is lit by four round-arched windows with balustrades underneath. The entrance is, of course, locked up, but above the door is a plaque reading:

W 1848 B

E

C 1907 H

The CH stands for Sir Charles Hobhouse, who had bought the estate and adapted the tower in 1907 as a hunting box. On some of the approaching footpaths to the tower traces can be found of what appear to be collapsed conduits and at least one man-made cave (probably a quarry, tarted up after use), and one may assume that the area around Browne's Folly was at the time a pleasure garden. Wade Brown died in 1851, leaving a village school where he had personally taught the girls. The Folly Fellowship has now taken over ownership of the tower in order to safeguard its preservation.

Newton Toney

Grottoes (18th century)
Column (1897)
SU 230 410

Wilbury House at Newton Toney has two grottoes, perhaps designed by the owner-architect of the house, the egregious William Benson (1682–1754). Talented Benson undoubtedly was, but he was also a conniving, self-seeking sycophant, who wheedled his way into the lucrative governmental position of Surveyor of the Works, displacing Sir Christopher Wren, the previous incumbent. He held the post for 15 months while he and his collaborator Colen Campbell milked it for what they could get. In 1719 he was forced to resign, having made more out of the job in one year than Wren made in 40, as Hawksmoor remarked. He sold Wilbury House in 1734 to Henry Hoare of Stourhead, so it is possible that Hoare had a hand in the grotto—but Tower Hill to the south used to be crowned by a circular brick structure known as Benson's Folly, now demolished. If he built that, then he could have built the grotto, which would make him one of our earliest folly builders. One grotto is buried in a mound below an octagonal Gothick summerhouse, while the other, larger, and almost certainly earlier one is in the wood between the house and the main road. There is also a column to commemorate Queen Victoria's Jubilee of 1897.

Salisbury

Arch (15th century–1791)
SU 150 300

James Wyatt removed an elegant 15th-century porch from Salisbury Cathedral during his restoration work in 1791, and it was re-erected in the grounds of Wyndham House, now the Council House, in Bourne Hill. The garden is now a public park abutting the Council House, and the little porch, with its polygonal roof, acts as a secular archway over one of the shady paths.

Bourne Hill Arch

Savernake Forest

Ailesbury Column (1781)
Lodge (mid-18th century)
`SU 230 670`

In the famous and ancient Savernake Forest Thomas Bruce, Earl of Ailesbury, erected a tall column by way of thanks to his uncle for leaving him his title and estates. If it is possible for a sycophant to disclose himself through one inscription, then Bruce succeeds:

*This Column was erected by Thomas
   Bruce, Earl of
Ailesbury, as a testimony of gratitude to
   his ever
honoured uncle Charles, Earl of
   Ailesbury and Elgin, who
left to him these estates, and procured for
   him the
Barony of Tottenham, and of loyalty to
   his most gracious
sovereign George the Third, who
   unsolicited conferred
upon him the honour of an earldom, but
   above all of piety
to God, first, highest, best, whose blessing
   consecrateth
every gift, and fixeth its true value.
   MDCCLXXXI.*

It must be rare to find an inscription irritating, but a hundred feet of Ionic column towering over the unsolicited earl's pious beliefs and his reverential trust in the proper order of things (1. Uncle Charles, 2. George III, 3. God) cannot be anything but annoying. The column itself is satisfying: perched on a monumental plinth, it is crowned by an urn, covered in lichen and splendidly sited on a low rise at the end of a 1½ mile avenue running from Tottenham House. Still in excellent condition, it is solidly built in an attractive dusky red stone. On the north side of the plinth the servile Bruce had another tablet inscribed:

*In commemoration of a signal instance
   of Heaven's
protecting providence over these
   kingdoms in the year
1789 by restoring to perfect health from a
   long and
afflicting disorder their excellent and
   beloved sovereign
George The Third.*

King George had spent most of the previous year in a strait-jacket out of harm's way, and despite the stony ministrations of the Earl of Ailesbury, it was not long before he returned to it permanently. But perhaps the saddest thing about the Ailesbury column is that it wasn't originally Bruce's; he bought it second-hand. It had originally been erected at La Trappe House in Hammersmith in 1760 by George Bubb Dodington in memory of his wife, and was moved to Savernake 20 years later, where it is now readily accessible on foot off a forest road.

The octagonal summerhouse in the forest, now used as a cattlefood store, was one of two designed for Bruce's uncle by Richard Boyle, Lord Burlington, together with a Banqueting Hall which was demolished in 1824.

At Forest Hill on the A4 towards Marlborough stands a delightful Gothick lodge of the middle of the 18th century. It owes much to a design by Batty Langley (*Ancient Architecture Restored and Improved*, 1741) for a 'Gothick Portico' with its whimsical pinnacled parapet. The lodge's quatrefoil windows don't figure in the design but are perfectly fine. It is alternately described as a toll house and a lodge; it was probably both.

Stourhead

Folly Group (18th century)
`ST 770 340`
Alfred's Tower (18th century)
`ST 750 350`

The garden at Stourhead is the Pole Star in the National Trust's galaxy. Of all the great 18th-century gardens—Hawkstone, Hackfall, Studley Royal, Stowe, Painshill, the Leasowes among many—Stourhead has maintained a continuity over 200 years, maturing slowly under the English summer sun, lying dormant in the changeable English winter. It is the *premier grand cru* of English

The Temple of Apollo

St. Peter's Pump

gardens, owned by the same family, the bankers Hoare, from 1715 to 1947. Henry Hoare II began the garden as we see it today in 1740, by damming the head of the River Stour to create a romantic serpentine lake. To provide some garden buildings, he employed Henry Flitcroft, a protégé of Lord Burlington's, who had designed Benjamin Hoare's Boreham House, Essex, in 1727.

Flitcroft's first essays in folly architecture were classical, and the formality of his temples contrasted sharply with the new informality in garden design pioneered by Kent and Bridgman and enthusiastically maintained by gifted amateurs like Hamilton, Shenstone and Hoare before reverting to professionals with Brown and Repton. With all the remaining classical buildings at Stourhead one should not forget that it looked substantially different: Hoare had a Turkish tent erected and contemplated building a sham mosque right in the middle of the garden. And there is also that coveted Gothic rustic cottage and its sidekick, the rustic convent, while buildings like the hermitage, the Chinese temple and ditto umbrello were demolished by Sir Richard Coalt Hoare in order to falsify Stourhead as The Great Classical Garden.

The National Trust's guidebook goes into much greater detail than we have room for here, so a short catalogue of the interesting buildings will suffice. The first,

chronologically, was the grotto of 1740, perhaps by Hoare himself, looking across the lake to St Peter's Church and the Tuscan Temple of Flora (originally the Temple of Ceres) by Flitcroft in 1744. Then came the obelisk of 1748, possibly by Francis Cartwright, to the memory of Hoare's father, then Flitcroft's Pantheon, or Temple of Hercules, from 1754. This is a domed temple with a Corinthian portico, unnaturally white in the naturally green and brown landscape. Flitcroft's last garden building was the Temple of Apollo, or the Temple of the Sun, based on the Temple at Baalbec, finished in 1767; but as this was taking shape he designed a real no-nonsense folly up west on a hill just over the Somerset border.

Alfred's Tower is one of the finest triangular folly towers in the country. It was designed by the man who gave us Wentworth Woodhouse's Hoober Stand and Fort Belvedere in Windsor Great Park, the first triangular folly tower. Alfred's Tower stands 160ft (49m) high, sheer windowless brick, unashamedly built for the view from the top—the ten tiny stair-turret windows do no more than illuminate the steps. Designed in 1765, it was completed in 1772 on the spot where:

Alfred the Great AD 870
On this summit erected his
standard against Danish
invaders. To him we owe the
origin of Juries, the establishment

of a Militia, the creation of a
Naval Force.
Alfred, the light of a
benighted age was a
philosopher and a Christian,
the father of his people,
the founder of the English.
MONARCHY and LIBERTY

The plaque is placed above the door and
below a large niche holding a statue of King
Alfred. Henry Hoare had the idea of the
tower in 1762 after reading about
Alfred in Voltaire's *Histoire
générale*, and he initially wanted
to build a replica of St Mark's
Tower in Venice. Lighter
coloured brickwork in one of
the angle turrets shows where
a de Havilland Norseman
(shades of the Danes here)
flew into the tower in
June 1944, killing all
five American
serviceman on
board. More lighter
brickwork shows a
repair carried out in
the early 1960s, after
a large part of the
wall fell away while
there were visitors at
the top of the tower.
The visitors had to
make their way
down the spiral
staircase past a
gigantic gaping hole
in the fabric of the
building. Not the
sort of thing one
would easily forget.

A little way away
is St Peter's Pump,
a 15th-century
conduit removed

from Bristol in 1768 and re-erected on a
grotto base over the spring in Six Wells
Bottom, a grassy marshy valley descending
towards the house. There is another removal
right at the head of the lake—the 1373 Bristol
High Cross, given to Henry Hoare in 1780. It
punctuates the view of the lake and the
Pantheon to perfection.

If we treat a garden as important as
Stourhead in an apparently desultory
fashion, it is because there is already such a
wealth of accurate and accessible information
about the place that little or no amplification
is needed in a work of this nature.

Tollard Royal

Larmer Tree Grounds (1880s–90s)
ST 940 180

How weird in itself is the fact that we tend
to call people who are
concerned about their
fellow men slightly dotty,
and once they start
combining diverse
interests we award them
the title of eccentricity.
Lieutenant-General
Augustus Henry Lane
Fox Pitt-Rivers
(1827–1900) is best
known for his innovations
in archaeology, but he
started his military career
by improving the
mechanics of the army
rifle. He was also an
anthropologist, endowing
a museum or two, and
once he had inherited
Rushmore at Tollard
Royal, he started
improving the minds and
bodies of his neighbours
by laying out the Larmer

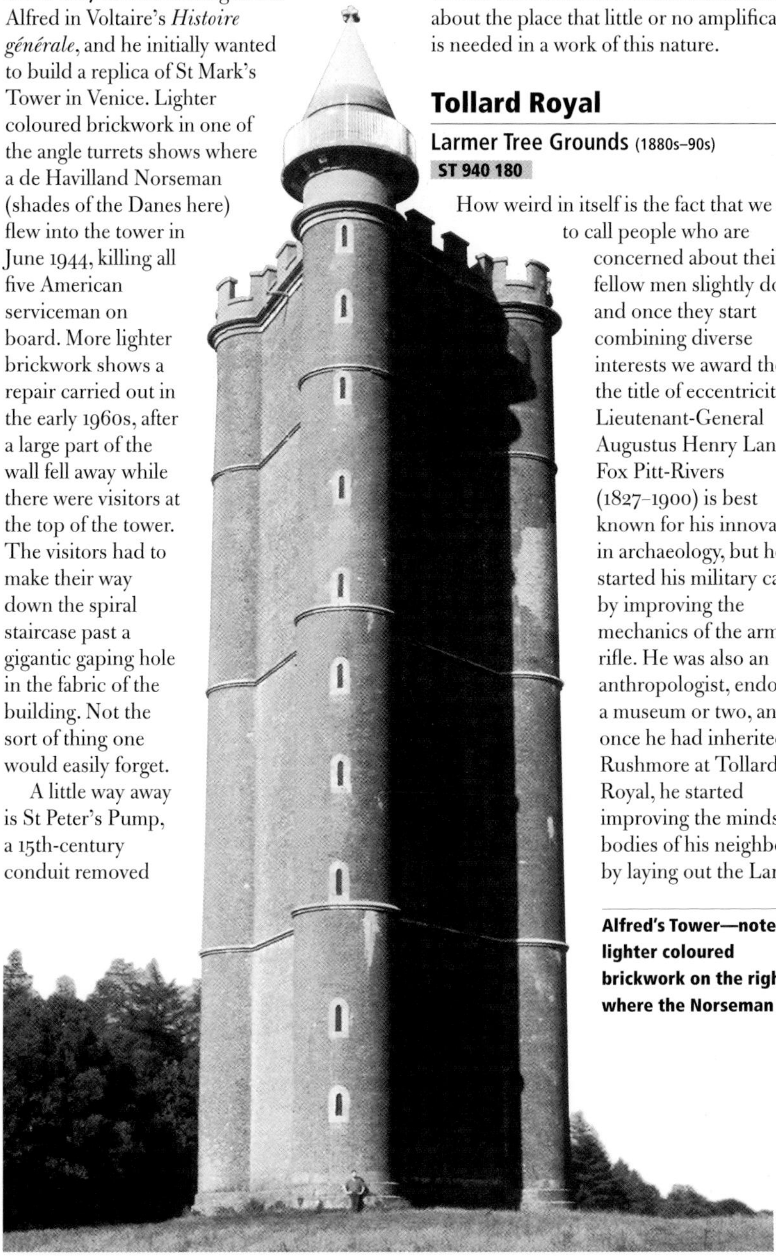

**Alfred's Tower—note the
lighter coloured
brickwork on the right
where the Norseman hit**

Tree Grounds. This park was intended for the population of Tollard Royal and surrounding villages. There was apparently no master plan for the design of the gardens, but through the years the General continually added to them.

It was, in fact, a huge picnic area (alcoholic beverages strictly forbidden though). The public were allowed in free of charge on every weekday and were especially made welcome on Sundays when a band played—they were workers from the estate, but trained by professional musicians—and on a typical Sunday the Kentucky Minstrels would sing their hearts out, or the agency of Mr T. Gannon, Hillgrove Street, Bristol, would provide a ventriloquist who could also do some juggling or, inevitably, a Punch & Judy show. It all cost a lot of money, but the General never minded. He even provided the picnickers with crockery and cutlery, and exotic animals were kept in the grounds: llamas, reindeer, parrots, peacocks, yaks and the more plebeian poultry and farm animals.

The planting of the grounds resembled an arboretum, and Pitt-Rivers saw to the buildings as well: the wooden open-air theatre still remains, and there are some rustic huts and a temple. The most attractive parts are the Quarters, originally six of them, but through the years these fell into disrepair

The Indian House at Larmer Tree Grounds

and some buildings were cannibalized in order to save others. They are (take your pick) in the Indian, Burmese or Nepalese style, and the General bought their fittings at the Indian exhibitions that were at the time constantly held in London. In 1895 one of those shows included the temporary erection of a whole Indian 'city', and it may be that he bought some items here, but Jonathan Holt has shown that Pitt-Rivers also acquired, for example, 'some old Indian carving' from Messrs Foster that originated from the 1896 Earl's Court Exhibition. A year later there

A Larmer Tree temple

followed three Burmese carved windows from a Mrs Learmont (£63) and a 'carved Indian teak doorway' from the India-China Trading Company. By 1900 work was drawing to a close, and by 1940 the work money had run out and the park was shut to make way for an evacuated prep school; but the benevolent ghost of General Pitt-Rivers is still there, as are some of the buildings.

Trowbridge

Lodges (1848)
ST 890 560

Near Trowbridge there are two splendid and heavily castellated lodge houses to the now-demolished Rood Ashton House, which had been built in 1808 by Jeffry Wyatville. Part of a wing remains, as at Fonthill, and it has been rehabilitated as a house. The lodges have all the right castellations and machicolations. Castle Lodge (of 1848, with additions later that century) is asymmetric, with a bartizan turret; Rood Ashton Lodge is built as a long straight façade, rising to a twin turreted archway.

On the other side of Trowbridge, at Trowle Common, is Longscroft Farm, the disconsolate survivor of an abandoned project, a tall, spindly, L-shaped house on the A363 originally erected in connection with the abortive plan to link Widbrook and Trowle by a branch of the Kennet and Avon Canal.

Wardour Castle

Grotto (1792)
ST 940 250

The grotto at Wardour Old Castle (a mile or so southeast of Wardour Castle, the new mansion) was built by Josiah Lane of Tisbury, the most famous grotto builder of them all. It may be thought that it was his work here and at Fonthill that drew him to the attention of a wider circle of clients than could be found within 2 miles of Tisbury, but both these grottoes would seem to have been made towards the end of his life and rank among his last commissions, after his successes throughout the rest of the country. A grotto builder is not without honour, save in his own county.

Nearby is a stone circle with two rustic alcoves, and in close proximity to the castle is also the Gothick Banqueting House, possibly by Lancelot Brown. Recently the old plans for several garden buildings have emerged from a pram (and from some 200 archive boxes) kept at Wardour Castle. These predate the other follies and were made by Richard Woods the landscape gardener, who worked here in the 1760s, but apparently they were never built. Among them are a camellia house and a sham inn—a folly not too common in Britain, although the Dutch around 1800 went in for sham rural inns in a big way (the 'jenever house' at Velserbeek still exists). The restoration of the Palladian Wardour Castle will possibly be carried out with old plans in hand, and why not erect the follies as well.

Wexcombe

Pineapple Pumping Station (1899)
SU 260 590

'We was the first village in Wiltshire to have our own pumped water,' declared a farmer at the hamlet of Wexcombe, and the local pride and joy is the village waterworks. This is a reservoir on the top of Grafton Hill, with a tiny pumping station in front, adorned (if you have a touch of imagination) with a pineapple roof. The Gift of Dr William Corrin Finch is still in working order, although nowadays the village water comes from the mains. Why the pineapple roof? 'Because the doctor liked pineapples,' answered the farmer, obviously perplexed that anyone should find it in the least bit strange. 'It's used in car rallies and the like—find a pineapple in Wiltshire and that sort of thing.' The inscription above the door of the tiny tower is in Gothic capitals, probably the most illegible typography devised by man, and records that Wexcombe Waterworks was built in 1899. The little red brick pineapple tower is enchanting.

Whiteparish

The Pepperbox or Eyre's Folly (1606)
SU 220 250

In and around Salisbury are the three oldest buildings in this chapter. Are they follies? Certainly one has been accepted as such since before follies were called follies; that is the National Trust's Pepperbox, or Eyre's Folly, on Pepperbox Hill. It is well documented, but little is known about it. Hexagonal, brick built,

Eyre's Folly

The Palladiam Bridge at Wilton

with a pyramidal roof and three low storeys, all the little windows are bricked in. At ground level it originally stood on open arches; these too have been filled in. It was built by Giles Eyre in 1606 and is generally regarded as one of the earliest follies in the country. The story—there has to be a story to justify such ancient folly—is that Eyre was envious of the tall towers of the bizarre Longford Castle and built the tower on high ground so that he could overlook Sir Thomas Gorges's strange creation. The epitaph on Eyre's tomb in Whiteparish Church describes him as a man 'much oppressed by Publick Power'. If there is a saner reason for the existence of this sensible little tower (it has no folly atmosphere), it may logically have been built as a hunting stand.

Wilton

Grotto (17th century)
Arch (c.1800)
Palladian Bridge (1737)
SU 090 310

Wilton House is open to the public, but the Old Schoolhouse in the grounds is not. It was built in 1838 using the façade of the old grotto, which had been erected in the 17th century by Isaac de Caus and was therefore one of the earliest in the country. The façade is formal, rigid in its rustication; the Italian style was still the correct approach and the eccentric, eerie, English grotto was a

hundred years away.

The Triumphal Arch of 1757 by Chambers was originally built on the hill to the south of the house, but was moved to the entrance court around 1800. And then of course there's the Palladian Bridge of 1737, by Roger Morris. But the grotto must be one of the great losses. Celia Fiennes described it around the end of the 17th century:

Grottoe is at the end of the garden… its garnished with many fine figures of Goddesses, and about 2 yards off the doore is severall pipes in a line that with a sluce spouts water up to wett the Strangers; in the middle roome is a round table, a large pipe in the midst, on which they put a crown or gun or a branch, and so its spouts the water through the carvings and poynts all round the roome at the Artists pleasure to wet the Company; there are figures at each corner of the roome that can weep water on the beholders, and by a straight pipe on the table they force up the water into the hollow carving of the rooff like a crown or coronet to appearance, but is hollow within to retaine the water forced into it in great quantetyes, that disperses in the hollow cavity over the roome and descends in a shower of raine all about the roome… and also it is so contrived in one room that it makes the melody of Nightingerlls and all sorts of birds…

WORCESTERSHIRE

The county offers lots of towers, some well known, others preferring to remain incognito. Sham ruins are the second favourite folly in Worcestershire, most owing to the existence of the county's most important landscape parks, Hagley and Croome Court. And the other forms of folly sometimes truly amaze.

The most interesting demolished folly is Ryland's Folly, Malvern, an elaborate complex containing concert hall, art gallery, baths and a grotto and rustic temples in the grounds, which was built in 1883 by W.H. Ryland at Wyche Cutting to the south of the town. The remote site and the fact that in the town the equally attractive Assembly Rooms opened were responsible for its closing just 12 years later and its subsequent demolition. Only a gate and some mosaics remain.

Abberley

Clock Tower (1883)
`SO 750 680`

Worcestershire's most bizarre folly tower is surely the clock tower at Abberley, an extraordinary piece of Scottish Baronial architecture set among the apple orchards. It is completely out of proportion and an eyecatcher for miles around. The top of the tower takes up half its height, if that makes sense—the building doesn't make any sense so why should we?—which means that visually, once the object of view has been reached, in this case the clock, towers are expected to burst out into over-florid decoration, then stop. This pinnacled pike carries on for the same height again, sprouting gargoyles, turrets and tiny lucarnes. Because of this imbalance, the tower looks gigantic when seen from the road; the mind assumes that such a mighty head must be carried by an equally massive body and one expects at least 50 metres of tower trunk beneath. It comes as quite a shock to see how small it actually is; although it is huge by any other standards, one automatically expects more.

The foundation stone was laid on 4 May 1883 by John Joseph Jones and his wife Sarah Amelia (Amy). It was designed by J.P. St Aubyn, a Victorian church architect, and was built as a bell tower in memory of Jones's father. On the entrance front, above an oriel window and just below a clock-face, is a sundial—a good example of Victorian belt and braces.

There is a much less impressive clock tower in Whitchurch to the memory of John Leech and his sisters; square, red brick, pyramidal roof and an inscription: REDEEM THE TIME. An unheeded warning?

Baughton

Tower House (early 19th century)
`SO 080 420`

Tower House was probably built as an eyecatcher to Croome Court. It stands on Baughton Hill, close to the M5. The

The Tower House at Baughton

octagonal tower has two storeys (three storeys once one finds the basement) and pointed windows and a door. It was probably always meant as a cottage. In the early 1990s permission was granted for a scheme to extend Tower House with two annexes that did not disturb the tower's original character.

Belbroughton

Castle Bourne (late 19th century)
SO 944 769

Castle Bourne is apparently a folly castle, attached by a three-arched wall to the house itself (near Bell End), with two towers, quatrefoil windows and so on. A closer inspection was impossible because the drive to the house was gated and locked; the lights were on but nobody was at home.

Bredon Hill

Bell Castle or Parson's Folly (late 18th century)
SO 960 400

Mr Parson of Kemerton Court built this one (small, square) inside a 2000-year-old fort on Bredon Hill. The views are great. It may have influenced the building of Broadway, which outshines it in every respect. The tower's height is 39ft (12m), in order to bring Bredon Hill up to its full 1000ft (305m), the official designation of a mountain in England—this is a perpetual obsession of the English, who believe that mountains have more fun than hills. It also served as a tea-house.

It may have been Bredon and not Broadway Tower (the two are almost on the same height, and Bredon is closer to Croome) that has something to do with the story about the Countess of Coventry told in our entry for Broadway, but see below.

Broadway

Tower (1794)
SP 120 360

Broadway Tower is right on the Gloucestershire border, on top of Broadway Hill at a height of exactly 1000ft (305m): a mountain, of course. In 1951 the Headley family visited it and a photograph shows Richard, Joanna and Shân Headley walking away having seen the old tower, leaving five-year-old Gwyn absolutely captivated by this extraordinary building, which didn't seem to do anything or to be used for anything. Buildings were where people lived or worked or worshipped, and Broadway Tower wasn't any of those. It was very confusing for a five-

year-old, and parents explaining that the building was called a folly and didn't have any purpose other than to look pretty was no sort of an explanation, especially when it was so honestly ugly to untutored eyes.

That brief digression explains how one of us at least got swept up into folly mania at an early age; from then on, car trips always had to have a 'folly hunt' included or there was hell to pay.

Broadway Tower—voted Most Favourite Folly by members of the Folly Fellowship

The tower itself was designed in 1794 by James Wyatt as a 'Saxon' (Norman really) tower, for the Earl of Coventry of Croome Court, of which more later, but was apparently finished only in 1800. This makes Wyatt responsible for one of Britain's best known follies, and his Fonthill would, had it remained standing, been the most famous of them all. The story behind the tower is a mixture of sense and showmanship. When Broadway Hill was first proposed as a site for a tower to be seen from Croome Court, which is 15 miles away as the crow flies, the Countess of Coventry suggested that a beacon be lit on the hill to ensure it could indeed be seen from Croome. When this had been done to her satisfaction, she called on all the local gentry to make sure the beacon could also be seen from their estates. The tower now forms the centrepiece of the Broadway Tower Country Park.

Clent

Sham Ruin (18th century)
SO 930 790

Clent Grove, near Hagley, has a sham ruin attributed to Sanderson Miller. It is a two-towered real ruin now, in the grounds of a children's home, but nothing is really known about it, and it seems unlikely that he would consent to copying his favourite formula so close to one of his major patron's estates.

Croome d'Abitot

Garden Buildings (1760s and later)
SO 080 440

Two great gardens in Worcestershire overshadow everything else in the county; Croome d'Abitot and Hagley Park. Both are linked by the dilettante genius of Sanderson Miller. In 1752 the Earl of Coventry wrote to Miller that 'it will be ungrateful not to acknowledge you the primary Author' (of Croome). Croome Court is credited to Lancelot Brown, who was not renowned as an architect, but it appears that Brown followed Miller's sketches.

Surprisingly, with Sanderson Miller and Lancelot Brown on hand, Croome Court's garden buildings were largely the work of Robert Adam. The house was sold by the Coventrys in 1948, became a Catholic school and was then bought by the Hare Krishna sect, which put it up for sale at £750,000. Most of the follies had been sadly neglected,

The Panorama Tower at Croome Court

but the Krishnas undertook a careful maintenance programme and looked after them well. Later on it was turned into a conference centre/carvery, and of late Sun Alliance, which owned most of the estate, has sponsored the National Trust to do its bit to park and buildings. The house itself was, when last heard of, still empty.

The round-domed Panorama Tower, built by Adam in 1766, still has the eyecatching effect originally intended. It looks like a professional version of Clavel's Tower at Kimmeridge in Dorset. Adam was also responsible for the

Dunstall Castle

temple near the church, which is similar to Stuart's at Hagley. Corinthian columns were used for the summerhouse by the lake, and another rotunda, open this time, has a dome coffered on the interior. There are also a Dry Bridge (signed and dated 'COADE LONDON 1797'), a pleasant three-arched grotto, the Brown monument of 1809, a park seat with Tuscan columns (known also as the Owl House) and a Gothic ruin, which does not look like much, on the other side of the motorway.

Many of the buildings at Croome, including Sanderson Miller's tremendous eyecatcher Dunstall Castle, can be seen from the M5, which cuts through Brown's carefully landscaped park. Dunstall is Miller out of El Greco: two tall, thin, round towers joined by an impossibly elongated archway; no rust here, simply decay.

Droitwich

Chateau Impney Tower (19th century)
SO 912 642

On the northern outskirts of Droitwich stands the Chateau Impney, built by a real Parisian architect for the French wife of salt manufacturer John Corbett in 1869–75. A small, tall and slender tower stands on the edge of a small wood to the left of the main drive to the Chateau, now a country house hotel. On closer inspection, the tower, more elegant than one might expect, betrays a distressing functionality for our interests. Its purpose has long passed—the oval concrete pool behind it is cracked and empty, the tower itself vacant and thin, with a rickety wooden belvedere platform perched crudely on top. Once it may have held a water tank.

Evesham

Leicester Tower (mid-19th century)
Obelisk (mid-19th century)
Ice-house (1852)
SP 031 457

Leicester Tower is in the grounds of Abbey Manor. The grounds were developed on the theme most appropriate for Evesham: the battle of 1265 and Simon de Montfort, Earl of Leicester. There is an obelisk commemorating the battle itself. Leicester Tower is dedicated to one of the battle's most famous casualties. It is a brick, polygonal and embattled tower with lots of windows, mainly small lanceted ones, but two-lighted near the top, in between its machicolations are mock medieval heads and the whole generally is very satisfying.

The ice-house (dated 1852) could have

stored Leicester's body—had it only been some six centuries older.

Great Witley

Fountains (18th century)
SO 760 640

The most impressive ruin in the county is undoubtedly Witley Court at Great Witley. The gigantic house was partly burned down in 1937, but since then it has been allowed to decay, until all that remains is a shell. The church, a magnificent example of English rococo, remains intact, but what concerns us here are the astonishing fountains by the Scottish brothers James and William Forsyth.

Inspired by Bernini's fountains in Rome, they outclass them in size and silence. Facing the east front is the Flora Fountain, an impressive enough work, but the Perseus Fountain on the south side is truly

The Perseus Fountain at Great Witley

staggering. The sculpture is said to be the largest in the British Isles, and one can well believe it. It rises 26ft (8m) above the long-vanished water level, and when it was playing the thunder of its waters could be heard all over the estate. Underneath is a high-domed chamber big enough to hold 50 people, accessed by a tunnel running the whole length of the grounds from the house. Other tunnels, containing the pipes and pressure boxes, run off this. Will these fountains ever play again?

Since we first wrote this, a restoration project has been mounted, which will see to the repair of the fountains. Work has started on the dainty—10ft (3m)—figure of Flora, which necessitated a block of Portland stone weighing 24.42 tonnes. Apparently after the disastrous fire at Witley, the fountains were coveted by both Bing Crosby and Billy

Butlin, and attempts were made to move them, resulting in Flora taking a tumble and being totally destroyed. Sculptor Steve McCarron confided that his model for the Flora statue will be a 'senior executive of English Heritage' discovered when on inspection at Witley. We are assured it is a female executive, which is nice.

Hagley

Ruinated Castle (18th century)
Hagley Park Garden Buildings (18th century)
SO 930 810

Sanderson Miller designed the house at Hagley, in similar four-square vein to Croome Court, for Lord Lyttelton in 1754, but earlier he had produced his masterpiece in sham ruins, the Ruinated Castle at Hagley. This was the very one that prompted Walpole to write his famous comment: 'There is a ruined castle built by Miller that would get him his freedom even of Strawberry, it has the true rust of the Baron's Wars.' This was a generous compliment seeing that Walpole proposed that George Lyttelton should use John Chute, the architect of Strawberry Hill. George Lyttelton wrote in his accounts book:

In the year 1747 I built the Castle and also the Cottage… In 1748 I built the Rotundo and in 1749 the half octogon seat and made the 'Haha' over against it. Mr Miller, architect of the Castle. Mr John Pitt of the Rotundo and Octogon. Sir Thomas Lyttelton paid William

Hitchcox for Building the Rotundo in Hagley Park the sum of £151.

William Hitchcox was, of course, Miller's action man, the one who executed his schemes. John Pitt was the gentleman-architect who designed his own house at Encombe in Dorset, including the famous rock arch.

Hagley seems to have been a breeding ground for new talent. After Miller's successful sham castle, it seemed as if every estate in the country had to have one, and Lyttelton followed it up in 1758 (actually only started a year later and still not finished by 1761) with an even more influential building, the Temple of Theseus. He wrote to Mrs Montagu that James Stuart was:

going to embellish one of the Hills with a true Attick building, a Portico of six Pillars, which will make a fine object to my new house, and command a most beautiful view of the country.

This Doric hexastyle temple was the first work by 'Athenian' Stuart after his return from Greece with Nicholas Revett, and it is the first Greek Revival building in Britain. As such, its importance is undeniable, and it is interesting to speculate on how many architectural styles or revivals first saw the light of day as follies or garden buildings. In spite of Lyttelton's enthusiasm, both parties seem to have regarded the building as something of an experiment, as Stuart's payment for the design was only £20. The estate also has a thin obelisk, which makes a fine eyecatcher from the A456, and a rather amusing statue of

The obelisk at Hagley

The Ruinated Castle

Frederick, Prince of Wales dressed as a Roman emperor, perched on top of a tall, thin column. As it was a gift from the prince, a friend of Lyttelton's, its erection was inevitable.

Inkberrow

Inkberrow Folly (1996)
SP 011 670

Planning permission was granted to the company that runs Orange mobile phones to build a 39ft (12m) high '18th-century folly tower' off Stonepits Lane. And up it went. The result is a very pleasing 19th- rather than 18th-century-style, four-storey, brick tower, with battlements, crenellations and blind arrowslits. Even the actual transmitters, clinging to the corner castellations, aren't that bad.

Lickey

Obelisk (1834)
SO 990 750

In Monument Lane at Lickey, on the outskirts of Birmingham, is an 1834 obelisk by John Hanson and unusually built from Anglesey marble, commemorating the 5th Earl of Plymouth.

Rous Lench

Post-boxes (late 19th century)
Tower (late 19th century)
SP 020 530

Sleepy Rous Lench, dozing with its brother villages Ab, Atch, Church and Sheriff's in the south Midland sun, has nodded off again after the shock of having Dr W.K.W. Chafy as its squarson for 40 years around the turn of the century. He built the village school, an extraordinary multicoloured Victorian brick building, banded like an armadillo; two remarkable half-timbered post-boxes, with steeply pitched tiled roofs, one in Rous and the other in Radford, a mile away (both the size of bus shelters); and a beautiful Italianate, 60ft (18m) tall, red brick tower, heavily machicolated, at the top of his topiary garden, with two white ceramic plaques on the first floor—Dr Chafy and his son?

Dr. Chafy's pillar box at Rous Lench

Spetchley

Root House (18th–19th centuries)
SO 890 530

Spetchley Park is just outside Worcester. This is a haven for horticulturalists, with a well-stocked garden centre and the sweetest smelling jasmine we have ever encountered, and just across a little canal from a lawn of rare fritillaries is a little summerhouse, built of bark and boles, knotted roots and chevroned twigs. It exudes peace, but the garden separates the M5 and the Birmingham–Bristol railway, so the buzz of traffic drowns the hum of bees. The Spetchley root house is a poor relation of Dr Jenner's hut in Berkeley and the Badminton root house.

Stourport

Rock Hermitage (medieval)
SO 820 680

There are as many rock hermitages, if not more, in this county as there are in Derbyshire, although here they all seem to

Spetchley Root House

have been used as everyday living quarters at some stage in their histories. Astley, Downton, Southstone, Stourport and Wolverley all have troglodyte dwellings. The façade of Redstone Rock at Stourport mimics Petra in having a Borromini-like recess with two columns at what would be the first floor level above the entrance—carved or through natural erosion?

Tardebigge

Water Tower (1880s)
`SP 011 682`

Hewell Grange, east of Tardebigge, near Redditch, was built in the 1880s, replacing an earlier house. It is now a Borstal, and the water tower, like a battered watch tower, leaps out from the side of the B4096 as one rounds the bend. As a watch tower it might come in handy at a Borstal. We don't know whether the famous revolving rock doorway (a megalithic entrance to the rock garden, made of enormous slabs of stone with a standing stone in the doorway that could be opened by simply pushing) still survives—surely even vandals wouldn't have been able…

Tenbury Wells

Kyre Park Follies (18th century, 1998—99)
`SO 627 636`

Kyre Park is rumoured to be a Capability Brown creation. It is a riveting spot: lots of lakes and water, cascades and cataracts, the remains of a tunnel or two and a rustic hut now being restored. But owner Jon Sellers has gone one better—he has had the audacity to improve upon the existing layout, with the assistance of folly architect Vernon Gibberd. It has worked out well.

One of the existing tunnels has been doubled in length, culminating in a circular grotto which will be adorned with a gigantic Medusa's head. The other entrance to the tunnel is spiky and rough, complete with the relief of a Green Man. At the tunnel's other end stands a two storey observation tower, rather pretty in a classic embattled style, faced with a sun in splendour, faces and water being the themes at Kyre Park.

Upper Arley

Spite Tower (1842)
`SO 770 800`

A delightful small, square battlemented tower, rather a petite castle, with a polygonal side turret, Arley Tower was built in 1842 for Lord Mountmorris. Sam Willcox of Upper Arley had refused to sell his house to Mountmorris, and to get even he built this toy castle in order to block Willcox's view, in which it succeeded.

The Spite Tower, Upper Arley

Wolverley

The Aviary and Others (18th and 19th century)
`SO 830 780`

Around Wolverley are several rock dwellings like the one near Stourport, but Wolverley itself seems to have been subjected to a mild form of follification by several of the inhabitants. We were told of the Aviary at Syon Hill House, a nursing home. The Aviary had a bark interior, now sadly gone, and is believed to have been an 18th-century summerhouse. Up the hill are two forlorn, embattled lodges, and in Wolverley proper is a sham chapel. Near Drakelow, to the north of the village, is a small obelisk 'a little up a wooded hillside'—the Baxter Memorial.

YORKSHIRE

The West Riding of Yorkshire has by any standards the greatest number of follies in the centre and north of England. It is possible to point to a concentration of follies, roughly following the River Ure and centred around the cathedral town of Ripon.

Apart from two outstanding groups, South Yorkshire is as poor in follies as North Yorkshire is rich. The urban expanses of Sheffield, Rotherham, Doncaster and dozens of industrial villages leave little space for follies, and the few that exist are dominated in quantity and quality by the buildings at Wentworth Woodhouse and Wentworth Castle. The old North Humberside—much of the East Riding—has a surprising number of good follies.

WEST RIDING

Aberford

Parlington Park Arch (1783)
SE 422 365

On the outskirts of Aberford are the remains of Parlington Park, with the Triumphal or Victory Arch, a weather-worn, three-arched conceit standing against a wood at a bend in the drive, proclaiming on both sides

LIBERTY • IN • N • AMERICA • TRIUMPHANT •
MDCCLXXXIII

It was designed by Thomas Leverton for Sir

Thomas Gascoigne in 1781, when Cornwallis's surrender brought a successful end to the American Revolution. It had been hoped to finish the arch the following year, but it was not completed until the 1783 Treaty of Versailles. Gascoigne was a Member of Parliament who was not alone in his pro-Republican stance or in going so far as to commit himself in stone to honour a rebellion against the Crown—the Duke of Norfolk built his follies at Greystoke in Cumbria for the same reason. Obviously not everyone shared their enthusiasm. In 1806 the Prince of Wales came to visit Parlington, got as far as the arch, read the inscription and immediately turned back. There is no longer a house at Parlington Park. Broadcasters who voice suckling heresies against royalty and jovially finish off declaring, 'Well, bang goes my K!' have no idea how lucky they are nowadays.

Elsewhere on the estate is said to be the crumbling base of a round tower.

Adel Cum Eccup

York Gate Garden (1986)
SE 277 402

We cannot be held responsible for Yorkshire place-names. Adel is a plush village in the process of being absorbed by Leeds. In Back Church Lane a new garden has been created at York Gate. Tiny structures are still added to it, and it is kept as neat as sixpence, whatever that may be. This has become a refuge for battered buildings, and some were used in the three garden erections: an arbour with a slate roof, a stone classical tempietto and an open, rustic coroneted construction rather grandly called The Folly. It is good to see tradition carried on.

Allerton Mauleverer

Rotunda (late 18th century)
SE 408 584

Allerton Park, at the crossroads of the A1 and A59, has a prominent Doric temple, octagonal, domed and surrounded by a colonnade. It was possibly done by Henry Holland when he worked here in 1788—it is a very large garden ornament rather than a folly—but it was a pity to see the temple in such a ruinous state. In 1993 £85,000 was raised to carry out essential repairs, and the exterior has now been restored.

Apperley Bridge

Elam's Tower (1804)
SE 198 383

Elam's Tower, in the grounds of Woodhouse Grove School in Apperley Bridge, still survives in reasonable condition, although a degree of vandalism has inevitably occurred. Robert Elam bought Lower Wortley Manor, as it was then known, in 1799, and on the hill where the tower now stands was a pagoda, probably built by the previous owners. The village unemployed were set to work to pull down the pagoda and erect the tower in its stead, and it was completed in 1804. The locals refer to it as the Old Water Tower, but it is doubtful if it was used as such.

Azerley

Tower (early 19th century)
SE 266 742

Halfway between Ripon and Grewelthorpe a tall tower appears on the skyline. The approach is to be made from the hamlet of Azerley, parking the car at a roadside lodge with amateur rough stone castellations. The astonished visitor will notice that when crossing the fields that Azerley Tower gets smaller and smaller, like something out of *Alice's Adventures in Wonderland*, until all that remains is a slender, castellated tower rising from a petite Victorian house. Stories behind it include the familiar one of the landowner surveying his labour forces from the top of the tower. It has no rooms, just a staircase winding 120 steps to the top, which makes another story a little less believable: that it was built for a cripple to watch the hunt. Even among the corrugated iron debris of what appears to have been a failed agricultural enterprise, the tower stands like a jewel in a tin setting. For years on the lawn in front of the tower stood a tiny replica of the folly, no more than 20in (50cm) high, but it vanished sometime after 1978.

Barnsley

Locke Park Tower (1877)
SE 342 051

Locke Park Tower in Barnsley is a wonderful cosmopolitan Victorian fancy—a 70ft (21m) belvedere tower consisting of a round wooden hut on top of an Italianate drum above a circular Ionic colonnade. It is very

Locke Park Tower

attractive, despite its curious stylistic blend. It was built in 1877 by an unknown architect, rumoured to be a Parisian, for Miss Sarah McCreary. Locke Park had been donated to the people of Barnsley by Phoebe Locke in memory of her husband, Joseph, a prosperous railway engineer. Phoebe died in 1866, and 11 years later her sister Sarah erected the tower as a memorial to her, a memorial within a memorial, for the initials S.M.C. are still visible on the weathervane, which argues a memorial to Sarah rather than Phoebe. The people of the town have expressed their gratitude by repeatedly vandalizing the tower, although this form of gratitude was never restricted to Barnsley, so it is now protected by a high wire fence engulfed by a hedge. This has preserved it reasonably intact, but we fear greater forces than vandalism may threaten this pretty tower—it has developed a perceptible backward tilt.

The obelisk and statue on top of Kendray Hill, a mile to the east of Locke Park, is not a folly but a monument to the 361 men and boys killed in the underground explosion at the Oaks colliery in 1866.

Deffer Wood Summer House (1791)
SE 342 051

This little summerhouse was built by Spencer Stanhope so his daughters could picnic and paint the sublime landscape (this before the industrial revolution bit hard). Restored in 1991, it received a Civic Trust commendation for the quality of the work, along with a strange request not to release the information about the award to the local media. Perhaps an attempt to keep the notorious Barnsley vandals (see above) in ignorance?

Batley

Batley Arch (1995)
SE 247 241

On Station Road in the middle of town a wonderful three-tiered arch leading into a blank wall arose on the site of an old cab stand and gentlemen's urinal. The upper two storeys are flanked by miniature replicas of Batley's satanic mills, and the topmost piers are crowned with two terracotta bats (*Batley*) affronty, wings elevated and displayed, in heraldic terms. A pleasing touch is the use of folded blankets (carved in stone, *please*) as footings for the arches, to remind us of the reason for Batley's first prosperity. It was erected by Public Arts of Wakefield with the

Batley Arch

help of £110,000 from the European Union's regional development fund and a variety of other grants, and not unsurprisingly on its erection in 1995 a poll showed that 95 per cent of the town's population thought 'it were bloody rubbish and a ruddy eyesore'. We predict they will grow to love it in time.

Bierley Woods

Grotto (1751)
SE 174 296

Bierley Hall Woods, on the outskirts of Bradford, has a dilapidated grotto—a jumble of rocks, which could be described as cavelets—and the remains of a fake stone circle in the park where Bierley Hall once stood. A father and son, both named Richard Richardson, created the park between 1720 and 1760, with four artificial ponds at different levels (the top one has drained out). The stones were chosen from nearby Wibsey for their romantic appearance. The Richardsons were avid plant collectors, with over 2000 botanical species in the grounds. They built the first glasshouse and grew the first cedars of Lebanon (the badge of the country estate) in England, so successfully that by 1850 they had to be felled because they were crowding the house. In the 1950s the house was demolished and replaced by a hospital, which, in its turn, has been torn down to make way for cheap executive homes. Of this garden glory nothing beside remains, just a desert of anglers stretching far away. Angling is a pastime as baffling to us as folly hunting must be to them.

There is nothing else of interest to see in Bradford except its answer to London's Highgate Cemetery: Undercliffe Cemetery has some remarkably fine monuments.

Birdwell

Wentworth Obelisk (1775)
SK 347 006

Birdwell, south of Barnsley, became a real muddle. While looking for a hermitage, because of a steep hill called Hermit's Hill, while finding that Lady's Folly at Tankersley had been demolished and while fruitlessly trying to find the reported 'Boston Castle', we found an obelisk standing like a mene tekel. 'Wentworth Castle 3 miles/1775' it said, trying to lure us into what promised to be an easy catch.

Boston Castle was said to have been demolished when the M1 was built, but there were unconfirmed reports that it had been reprieved. It turned out to be a case of mistaken identity. Birdwell's so-called 'Boston Castle' is not actually a folly—a pity, for to judge from an old photograph it is a remarkable eyecatcher in a curious asymmetrical design. Much confusion has arisen about this odd tower, which is still standing although we never managed to find it. It is an industrial building in the castellated style, a tower to hold the beam engine for Rockley Furnace. On this 'Boston Castle' the story had been grafted that it had been erected by the 3rd Earl of Effingham to celebrate the Boston Tea Party—there was great sympathy for the American colonies' struggle against the Crown among the Whig aristocracy—but this story actually belongs to the real Boston Castle, a square, castellated shooting box standing over the Rother valley, a mile south of Rotherham. Tea is said to have been forbidden at the house-warming in 1775, a sacrifice of sorts, as one cannot imagine the assembled lords to have been seriously incommoded by this prohibition. Yet both buildings could well have been built by the same architect, for the castellations of both the sham and the genuine Boston Castle had the same hard edge to them.

Birkenshaw

Cross Lane Windmill (1966)
SE 208 294

When you start putting water features into a garden you start spending serious money. A string of ponds in a 3 acre (1.2ha) garden needed a water supply, so this 20ft (6m) whitewashed brick windmill was constructed to supply it; then it was decorated to look like a fancy liqueur bottle. With its six stubby sails, it was always more of an eyecatcher than a practicality.

Bishopthorpe

Church Façade (1763)
Bastion
SE 598 478

South of York lies Bishopthorpe, where the Archbishop of York's palace and the gatehouse are built in Batty Langley-style Gothic. Thomas Atkinson had them built between 1763 and 1769 for Robert Hay Drummond. Archbishop Drummond was no conscious builder of follies, although he had enough taste for it. Yet there is a folly in Bishopthorpe, unintentional perhaps, but a folly it has become. When St Andrew's Church was demolished in 1899 the west front was left standing to make a superb eyecatcher, now lost in a green lane leading down by the side of the palace to the River Ouse.

There are, in fact, two follies: when we first visited we missed a circular castellated stone tower buried in the woods behind the eyecatcher, but there it lurks, defiant in its empty purpose. The Archbishop's accounts for June 1766 credit 'Thos. Atkinson, for work at the circular wall and battlement'. The employment of Atkinson is mildly surprising, as this York architect and stonemason had converted to Catholicism six years earlier. Was this an early example of

Bishopthorpe Bastion

Church of England liberalism or was Drummond a secret sympathizer?

Bradfield Moors

Boot's Folly (1927)
SK 230 900

The 20th-century folly tower is one of the rarest creatures in the book; indeed, the only one that springs readily to mind is Lord Berners's Folly in Faringdon (see Oxfordshire). But here is a pleasant surprise: a solid, four-storey tower, well sited on the edge of Strines Reservoir to the west of Sheffield, built by Charles, scion of the Henry Boot construction company. Apparently there are wonderful views to be had from the tower, but when we visited we walked round it in circles for half an hour before it loomed wetly and satisfyingly from the mist 5 metres away. Traditional folly stories resurface—it was built to provide employment, a cow climbed the tower and got stuck at the top—but we speculate that Mr Charles simply enjoyed towers, having already added a castellated one to his nearby house, Sugworth Hall. But how soon they forget—within 15 years the interior panelling had been stripped out for firewood, and the decay was irreversible. Remnants of a panelled staircase clinging to the wall 40ft (12m) up are the only indications of a once elegant interior. The top floor is still *in situ*

Boot's Folly

but probably not for long. The fine stonework of the tower was enhanced by mullioned windows taken from Nether Holes farmhouse.

Bramham Park

Gothick Temple (1750)
SE 411 418

Bramham Park, due south of Wetherby, has nothing particularly distinguished save the Gothick Temple. Most of the Bramham buildings were raised for George Fox, Lord Bingley. The provenance of the Gothick Temple, in the southern part of the park near the graves of the family's dogs, can be traced through two design books. The temple dates from 1750 and has been attributed to James Paine. If so, then Paine lifted it straight out of Batty Langley's plate number 57 in *Gothic Architecture Improved* (1747). This, in turn, was based on plates 70 and 71 in James Gibbs's *A Book of Architecture* (1729). Langley expanded on Gibbs's classical design: the pilasters were changed to buttresses, the round windows into Wankel pistons, the round-arched door and windows on the ground floor grew pointed, and a band of ogee gables with trefoils and finials was added on top of the structure. As it now stands, only very minor details were changed in Paine's final version. A classical temple near the entrance, originally an orangery designed by Paine, has been converted into a chapel. The other temples are also classical, except for a rustic house, once thatched, and an 1845 Gothic summer house to the south.

Richard Pococke's *Travels Through England*, a manuscript account of his visits to park and country houses, contains a description of Bramham. Apparently Pococke found the number and variety of temples bewildering:

> One comes round to a Dorick building like the front of a temple & then to a Gothick building not quite finished [the Langley copy] & so one descends to the water, from which there is an avenue to the house, & another up to a round Ionick Temple, something in imitation of the Temple of Hercules at Tivoli… & from [the ascent to the temple] are three or four visto's cut, one of which is terminated by a Dorick building, something like the Portico of Covent garden Church:—& to the west of the garden in the Park is a thatched house, to which the family sometimes go for variety & take some refreshments…

Pococke visited Bramham in 1750, so would

not have seen the obelisk behind the Ionick Temple, erected in 1763. In the northern part of the garden is the Four Faces, an urn on a pedestal with four faces representing the four seasons.

Bramhope

Bramhope Hall Gazebo (18th century)
SE 255 435

A new development in the former grounds of the now-demolished Bramhope Hall has placed a modern executive-style home just yards from a circular 18th-century gazebo. This is all very well for the executive, but the little temple has not taken kindly to its temporary occupation as a site office for the contractors, and there must be fears for its future. The ball finial from the domed roof lies unregarded on the ground.

Don't miss the tunnel entrance here, a mighty sham castle covered under the Otley entry.

Brighouse

Robin Hood's Grave (19th century)
SE 170 160

Kirklees Park has the most improbable epitaph we have discovered on our travels. It is affixed to Robin Hood's Grave, an enclosure with railings. While there seems to be no reason why this should not be the site of Robin's grave, the inscription is wonderfully bogus, a 19th-century precursor of seeing Elvis in K-Mart:

Hear Underneath dis laitl stean
Laz robert earl of Huntingtun
Ne'er arcir ver az hie sa geud
An pipl Kauld im robin heud
Sick utlawz az hi an iz men
Vil england nivr si agen
Obiit 24 Kal Dekembris 1247

Read it aloud for the best *Mots d'Heures, Gousses, Rames* effect.

Burghwallis

Robin Hood's Well (1711)
SE 519 119

A small squat structure is the first building on the A1 as we cross the county boundary from West Yorkshire. Near the signpost to Burghwallis the arched, square little building suddenly pops up on the left. Robin Hood's Well, as it is called, was carefully moved to this site when the A1 was widened, and now it sits at the end of the lorry-filled lay-by. Why this unassuming object should have been preserved when so many others have been lost is because it was allegedly designed by Vanbrugh in 1711. The original site marked the spot where the Bishop of Hereford was said to have been forced to dance after being robbed by Robin Hood. The folly's major claim to fame is its nomination by Wim Meulenkamp as 'Most Boring Folly in Britain'.

Cringles

The Old Tower (1855)
SE 049 487

We thought that the Old Tower, off the A6034 above Cringles on Rombalds Moor, had lost its credentials but that it could have been a hunting stand. It strongly resembles

The Old Tower at Cringles

the Hartcliff Tower at Penistone (see below), although it is not ruinous. There is a walled-up entrance, but the tower looks too slender to have been climbed, certainly by stout fellows like us. In fact, it was a strictly utilitarian and not particularly old building, erected as a survey tower for the construction of the Barden aqueduct. The part of the moors near Ilkley to the east used to have another hunting tower by the Thimble Stones, on the highest point of the moor.

Dallowgill

Grey Garth Monument (1897)
SE 185 724

Sheep and Primitive Methodism thrive on these bleak moors round Dallowgill. On top of a hillock on Swetton Moor, by the hamlet of Greygarth, stands the Grey Garth Monument, a minute, square, rough stone tower, built to commemorate Queen Victoria's Diamond Jubilee and restored in 1984. There is a little aluminium ladder that wafts you to an aluminium viewing platform, a dizzy 10ft (3m) above the moor top and from where the view is similar.

Egypt

Walls of Jericho (mid-19th century)
SE 091 341

Every English county has its share of splendid place-names, and West Yorkshire is no exception: Goose Eye, Scapegoat Hill, Triangle, California, Krumlin, Canada, Toot Hill, Catherine Slack and many others. West of Bradford is a hamlet called Egypt, where some former quarrymen built grit walls along the road, earning the stretch the rather grandiose title of the Walls of Jericho, but they have now disappeared.

Gisburn (Lancashire)

Lodges
Dog Kennels (late 18th century)
Temple
SD 823 498

The curious lodges to Gisburn Park, covered with tiny erect castellations, look as if they have been badly frightened. Unusually they bear no stylistic relation to the main house. The railway line runs just behind and below the lodges through tunnel entrances decorated with mighty turrets and frowning battlements.

Gisburn Park is now a private hospital, and its Dog Kennels are not in its ownership. Which is a pity, for this remarkable building,

The Dog Kennels at Gisburn

unique in Britain, is in urgent need of restoration. It stands among bluebells and wild garlic on the banks of the River Ribble, a monumental building on a minute scale. The classically proportioned central chamber is a double cube, no more than 18ft (5.5m) wide and vaulted on the interior with brick piers. A blank ogee arch decorates the eastern wall. Flanking this central pavilion are two circular towers with domed brick roofs to each of the two storeys. The ground-floor room in the north tower has a short flight of stone steps leading to an upper chamber. All this is ruined and overgrown, but it is not so far gone as to be hopeless. The building can and should be rescued. Its location is tranquil and beautiful, and it would not take much to restore it into a tiny holiday home.

We walked down by the side of the hospital to see the Temple, which was clearly marked on the map. On the other side of the hundred foot ravine was a heavily wooded bluff. Why don't you let us know if you can find it?

Halifax

Wainhouse's Tower (1875)
SE 078 240

Halifax can boast the best folly in the county, one of the finest in the whole country: Wainhouse's Tower, also known as Wainhouse's Folly or the Octagon Tower. John Edward Wainhouse (1817–83) was someone whose preoccupations resemble those of R.H. Watt in Knutsford, Cheshire. Both started their building activities late in life, both built a remarkable factory tower (although the Wainhouse one stands supreme), and both threw some quaintly decorated cottages into the bargain. It all started with the Smoke Abatement Act of 1870. Wainhouse owned, together with a large fortune from an inheritance, the Washer Lane

Dye Works in southern Halifax, which was run by a manager. After the Act came into force, it became necessary to build a tall chimney to carry the smoke out of the valley in which the works were built. In 1871 plans were drawn up by the architect Isaac Booth for a chimney that would be fed with the smoke from the factory by means of a pipeline. In 1874 Wainhouse sold the works to his manager, who refused to bear the tremendous costs incurred in finishing the chimney. Wainhouse decided to keep it himself and convert it into a tower, which he proposed to use as 'a general astronomical and physical observatory'. The tower was finally completed in 1875 by the architect Richard Swarbrick Dugdale at a total cost of £14,000 and in such an elaborate style that not even a pocket telescope could have been fitted in between the orgy of finials, pillars, buttresses and balustrades. The very slender tower rises 275ft (84m) high, its shaft decorated with Gothicisms and the ornate top in a perverted but well-proportioned neo-renaissance style. The result of the four years' work is a belvedere tower by a medieval watch tower out of Château Chambord.

Wainhouse's Tower is naturally linked with its owner's feud with Sir Harry Edwards, a parvenu industrialist, freemason and Justice of the Peace. From 1873 onwards one small incident quickly provoked another, and within a few months the two men were at each other's throats. After Edwards misused his position as JP, things went from bad to worse, and Wainhouse became afflicted, like so many Victorians, with the pamphleteering mania. From 1876 until he died a flood of pamphlets was penned by Wainhouse, but did not result in the anticipated responses from Edwards, as the JP seems to have been a weak correspondent. It has been suggested that Wainhouse built the tower so he could always keep an eye on Edwards's activities. Apparently Edwards abhorred chimneys, so Wainhouse's somewhat noticeable structure may well have been embellished to such an extent simply to goad—but he also abhorred white cattle or white linen hanging out to dry (strange man) and there is no record of Wainhouse taunting him in this manner. Wherever he could, Wainhouse had mottoes referring to his row with Edwards. West Air, his eccentric house—no two windows are the same—was built in 1877, also by Dugdale, and has, among others, an inscription quoting the Aeneid: *Parcere subjectis et debellare superbos* ('Spare the lowly and make war upon the proud'). Wainhouse not only

Wainhouse's Folly

spared the lowly, he took to embellishing their humble abodes. In Scarr Bottom a row of cottages was fitted out with mottoes and ornate Gothic porches.

The houses in Wainhouse Terrace had their balconies renewed and supported by a colonnade like some Mediterranean stoa. The balcony can be reached by two bridges projecting from squat, machicolated towers—sadly the houses have now been demolished, but the gallery remains.

Harden

St David's Ruin (1796)
SE 089 379

Among the ghosts of the collieries and textile mills, West Yorkshire is adorned with a fair number of follies. There is a preference for Gothick towers, most of them in the area round Bradford—J.B. Priestley and John Braine territory. A scene in Braine's *Room at the Top* is set in a fictional Gothick folly:

> *The Folly was an artificial ruin in the Gothic style. There were three turrets, sawn off, as it were, obliquely, and far too small ever to have been much use as turrets. The tallest even had two window slits. One side of the main building had a door and an aurora of stone around it, and the other had three windows ending a little too abruptly half way up. It was very solidly built… 'My great-great-great-grandpa built this,' Susan said. 'He was called Peregrine St Clair and he was terribly dissipated and used to be a friend of Byron's. Mummy told me a bit about it; he had orgies here. All of Warley practically was St Clair and he could do just what he liked.'*

Although it differs from his description, St David's Ruin overlooking the B6429 at Harden Banks, near the Malt Shovel, was the inspiration for John Braine's fictional St Clair folly. It was built for Benjamin Ferrand in 1796 (the initials and date are carved in the pointed door arch) and served as an eyecatcher to his now-demolished St Ives, built in 1759 by James Paine. The ruin was tidied up in the 1950s; the artfully damaged tower, which left one Gothick window frame intact although surrounded by crumbling masonry, was truncated into a neat cylinder with a band delineating the start of the second storey. A piece of ruined wall with a pointed arch through it stands on its own; once it was probably connected. St David's Ruin is an excellent example of the Mow Cop genre of folly: more precise and controlled than its predecessors Mow Cop and Old John, more Georgian in its atmosphere, but certainly one of the three best interpretations of this style in England.

Harrogate

Harlow Hill Tower (1829)
SE 288 541

Harrogate as a spa is largely an Edwardian invention. When John Thompson built his observatory on Harlow Hill, on the edge of

Harlow Hill Tower

Harlow Moor, the first Pump Room had yet to be built. The lintel above the door reads 'HARLOW-HILL TOWER 1829', and other than that the 90ft (27m) tower is utterly without decoration: no battlements, finials or other frills, no windows to light the stair, just one tiny pane on each side at the top. Its only purpose was to serve as an observatory, but not until 1933 was it turned into a proper observatory, complete with telescope and everything. It was already open to the public by 1900; people paid sixpence to enter. Despite local claims, Helvellyn is not visible from the tower. A renovated house is attached to the tower but is in separate ownership—once a month the stargazers of Harrogate troop up to the tower to use it as an observatory while the owner sits at home next door and seethes. The telescope dome that once topped the tower has long gone, but the fabric is immaculate.

The plump circular water tower of 1902 on the other side of the lane is a far more educated building, richly decorated with pilasters and blind windows with fine pediments, dressed, like a minor dignitary, much too pompously for its humble function.

Hazlewood

Hazlewood Castle Tower (1760s)
SE 449 398

Hazlewood Castle, a mile west of Grimston, was built in the 1760s–70s. The small, octagonal towerlet, looking rather ramshackle,

probably dates from this period. It is
castellated, with round windows on the
second floor and arches at ground level. Too
small to have served as a belvedere, it was
perhaps considered a fine spot for picnicking.

Hickleton

Bilham Belvedere (1800)
SE 484 064

The architect died in poverty, and one of his
last buildings is going the same way. This
imposing hilltop belvedere was designed by
John Rawstorne for Thomas Selwood, but
much of it has now collapsed (as has
Selwood's house)—the upper storey in the
central bayed pavilion and the flanking walls
to the sides. Hidden deep in the woods and
still with wonderful views, there must be a
chance for its salvation.

Hoyland Nether

Hoyland Lowe Stand (18th century)
SE 370 000

Near Birdwell in Hoyland Nether is another
hunting tower or folly, Hoyland Lowe Stand.
Again this is a tower with little recorded
history. There are two storeys with a higher
turret, seeming to date from the 18th century.
We could not find it, although it still stands at
the time of writing.

Huddersfield

Jubilee Tower (1897)
SE 152 140

Huddersfield itself has two folly towers, the
first of which is the Victoria Jubilee Tower of
1897, south of the town on the 900ft (275m)
Castle Hill at Almondbury. A grim, grey,

The Victoria or Jubilee Tower, Huddersfield

square, tapering tower, with a higher corner
turret and a spectacular view from the top, it
is a popular local tourist attraction, not least
because of the pub just below it. The author
of an Edwardian guidebook, hardened to the
claims made on behalf of various belvedere
towers, pointed out that: 'The Victoria
Tower commands a wide view, in which, *of
course*, York Minster is *sometimes* visible.'
Below the tower in High Lane is a new round
house, built in 1995.

Lindley Clock Tower (1902)
SE 118 181

The second tower is in the northwest
perimeter of the town, in Lindley. It is a
square clock tower with an octagonal copper
pagoda roof, originally built for the Sykes
family by the Arts and Crafts architect Edgar
Wood, and with sculptures by T. Stirling Lee:
> *This tower was erected by James Neil
> Sykes Esq JP of Field Head, Lindley for
> the benefit of his native village in 1902.*
A desire for beauty more than folly seems to
have conjured up this delectable tower, an
important contribution to the architectural
mood at the turn of this century.

Ravensknowle Park Follies (1929)
SE 175 168

The survivals in Ravensknowle Park are
perhaps more congruous with the word folly.
The park, 1½ miles to the east of the town
centre, was donated to Huddersfield as a
World War I memorial. After the Huddersfield
Cloth Hall was demolished in 1929, parts of it
were removed to Ravensknowle, where its old
clock tower was re-erected on top of a shelter
made of stones from the old Hall.

Knaresborough

Fort Montagu (18th century)
SE 351 564

Knaresborough, on the banks of the River
Nidd, is a planet to Harrogate's sun. The
riverscape, with house and churches strewn
along the river banks, gives the town a slightly
foreign look. In other ways it resembles parts
of Derbyshire, not least because of the large
number of hermit's caves. The Chapel of Our
Lady of the Crag, sometimes mistakenly called
St Robert's Chapel, is a medieval wayside
shrine with beautiful Gothic decorations;
immediately above it is Fort Montagu.
Langdale's *The Tourist's Companion* of 1822
has a few words to say on it:
> *Fort Montagu is three storeys high,
> inhabited by a family who live beneath*

Fort Montagu, Knaresborough

the rock, which has nothing artificial but part of the front. It was the work of 16 years, performed by a poor weaver and his son, which since its completion has been called FORT MONTAGU, from this poor man's kind patroness, the Dutchess of Buccleugh [Lady Elizabeth Montagu]; *having on the top a fort with cannon, a flag waving and other military appearances. The same ingenious artificer has cut a solid rock in such a way as to form a garden, with terraces, on the very acme of the cliffe. And by the labour of many years he has formed in the garden... pleasant walks, ornamented with a profusion of shrubs and flowers. Here is also a green-house and tea-room, which are much frequented by the visitors from Harrogate, &c.*

Painted on the side of the cliff, but now very faded, is the legend 'THE HOUSE IN THE ROCK'. For many years it has been owned by the nearby Catholic public school of Ampleforth, but in 1998 it decided to put it up for sale.

Leeds

Bear Pit (1840)
SE 280 350

Leeds has a surprising diversity of follies. In Cardigan Road is a Bear Pit, which was once part of the Leeds Zoological and Botanical Gardens, opened in 1840. It stands forlornly

among modern houses in the northwestern quarter of the city. The Bear Pit has a sham castle façade: two castellated turrets and a wall in between, with three barred entrances for the bears' lairs. The walls and towers are crumbling, inadvertently turning the sham castle into a sham ruin. We have to confess, however, that we are fairly useless when it comes to discovering and locating follies, unlike all our friends and colleagues, and despite slow reconnoitring up and down the length of Cardigan Road we have failed to spot this one, although others insist it still exists.

Roundhay Park Castle (early 19th century)
SE 335 384

Roundhay Park, on the northeastern edge of Leeds, has a more substantial ruin. The 800 acre (325ha) park was laid out for Thomas Nicholson in the 1820s. In 1872 it was bought by Leeds Corporation for the large sum of £140,000 and opened to the public by Prince Arthur, the royal one. Only a few amenities for visitors had to be added, the rest was already there: a rustic hermitage on the upper lake and a sham castle, curiously unnamed, near Waterloo Lake. The castle is square, with round corner towers. The front towers are the tallest, with a pointed entrance and cruciform arrowslits in between. At certain times an eerie grating, crashing, rattling noise echoes through the gate of the castle, as if an invisible portcullis were being raised by a team of ghostly knights in rusty armour, but further intrepid investigation uncovers a miniature

Roundhay Park Castle, Leeds

gauge railway running just behind the folly. The sham castle is very well done, catching the right flavour because of the rough stone out of which it was built. The same material was used for Cobble Hall, a large lodge to the east of the castle. It is also castellated with pointed windows. The 'tasteful, circular Corinthian temple presented to the borough in 1882 by the late Sir John Barran, Bart' described in the 1909 edition of Baddeley's *Yorkshire* is now known simply as the Fountain. Leeds had another sham castle in the Stonegate Road, King Alfred's Castle, but it was demolished some years ago.

Temple Mills (1837–43)
SE 296 328

Southern Leeds is the more industrialized part of town; there is little call here for suburban sham castles. Yet the area contains

buildings stranger than cardboard Camelots—an Egyptian mill, an Italian chimney, and a Moorish warehouse. The Temple Mills in Marshall Street were built by Joseph Bonomi Jr, brother of the more famous Ignatius, and James Combe, a local architect, for John Marshall. The whole Temple Mills project is alleged to have cost around £250,000. It was worth it. It was a matter of course to build the chimneys in the shape of obelisks, but it is the façade of the administration block, added in 1843, that is the real wonder. It is trapeziform with winged emblems above the entrance and a portico with huge lotus flower capitals. The grime on the building and the ignorant lettering of the firm that took over the premises are the only non-Egyptian motifs. Bonomi drew his inspiration from the temples at Edfu,

Whose name was excised?

Dendera and Philae after spending eight years in Egypt, and he left visual proof of his field studies—incised on an inner wall of the Temple of Hatshepsut at Medinet Habu in Luxor. On his return he set up practice with an almost unrivalled knowledge of Egyptian architecture, confident that it was to be the

Temple Mills Administration Block

coming thing, but apart from the spring at Hartwell House in Buckinghamshire, the Egyptian Court at the Crystal Palace and this wonderful mill, commissions were virtually non-existent.

An enlightened and considerate employer, John Marshall had his mill equipped with 66 glass domes on the flat roof in order to let daylight percolate to the factory floor. Then he conceived the idea of allowing his workers somewhere to relax, so he had the rest of the roof grassed over to provide a spacious lawn. Mowing became a problem with all the domes in the way, but Marshall hit on a brilliant solution—he hoisted up a flock of sheep, which had the dual benefit of keeping the grass cropped and providing extra wool for the mill.

Unfortunately, one of the more adventurous sheep clambered onto a glass dome and fell through, killing one of Mr Marshall's employees who was standing beneath as well as itself. Few factory workers get killed by flying sheep nowadays; the sad story is reminiscent of the old Monty Python sketch: 'Sheep don't fly, they plummet.' Despite this unfortunate accident, Marshall does appear to have had his workers' interests foremost.

Tower Works (1899)
SE 295 328

It was through the influence of Sir Robert Rawlinson, civil engineer and pamphleteer, that the Tower Works in Globe Road came to have its towers. After complaining to *The Builder* about the ugliness of the average factory chimney, Sir Robert set about remedying these ills. In 1858, a year after his article, he published 'Designs of Factory Shafts', followed some time later by 'Designs for Factory, Furnace and Other Tall Chimneys', in which the medieval and Italian Renaissance styles of tower were favourably discussed. In the Battle against the Dull Chimney Rawlinson found an ally in J.C. Loudon, the leader of contemporary opinion on matters such as landscape gardening and architecture. As a direct result of the campaign, Thomas Shaw, a Yorkshire architect, built the first of the Globe Road chimneys in 1864, inspired by the Lamberti tower in Verona, for Harding & Son, makers of pins, combs and cards for the textile industry. When a second tower was needed, a very tall copy of the Gothic campanile in Florence by Giotto was built. It was finished in 1899 by William Bakewell, together with a boiler house, which serves as a monument to those who furthered the cause of the textile

industry. The campanile still makes a welcome contribution to the Leeds skyline.

In 1995 an application for a £60 million Lottery Fund grant to remodel the Holbeck chimneys and complex was made by the Leeds Architecture and Design Initiative, and work on the taller tower is now complete. It is a splendid sight, apart from the inappropriate bronzed glass that was sadly fashionable with architects of meretricious commercial developments for a few months in 1988. Perhaps this was leftover stock, given free to the restoration fund.

Tower Works

St Paul's House (1878)
SE 296 337

In St Paul's Street in the centre of the city is a brick and terracotta Spanish/Moorish fantasy, a warehouse built by L. Ambler for Sir John Barran, the clothes manufacturer, who donated the splendid rotunda fountain in Roundhay Park to the city. It even used to have minarets on the roof, but these have now gone. The building has recently been restored as a prestige office complex, and it looks splendidly exotic, suitably celebrating the multiculturality of present-day Leeds. Unfortunately, we have another glazing problem here—the developers have opted for float glass in all the windows, perfectly flat, perfectly reflective, perfectly characterless. It looks as if the Moorish

A detail of St. Paul's House, Leeds

façade cloaks a conventional glass office block. Perhaps it does.

Lepton

Black Dick's Temple (18th century)
SE 208 171

At the turn of the last century, every *bon mot* was ascribed to Oscar Wilde; later in the 20th century Dorothy Parker received the popular credit. Huddersfield's historical equivalent was Black Dick Beaumont, an adventurer after whom this solid square masonry block of a building on Houses Hill, visible from many parts of Huddersfield, was named. Facts deny the legend; Sir Richard Beaumont, local hero or villain, depending on who you listen to, died in 1631, many years before this pleasaunce was built as a summerhouse to the long-gone Whitley Beaumont Hall. Of course, Brits of advancing years tend to forget that the epithet 'black' is no longer a synonym for evil; politically correct Huddersfield historians argue that perhaps the Beaumont family fortunes suffered during his lifetime or he 'may have been a dark-haired man of swarthy countenance'. Could he have simply been wicked?

Little Ribston

Arch and Butler (late 18th century)
SE 392 540

> *I said to Heart, 'How goes it?' Heart replied:*
> *'Right as a Ribstone Pippin!' But it lied.*

Hilaire Belloc's funny, moving little couplet is all we have in memory of a once renowned apple—surely the last thing he thought of when writing it. Ribston Hall was home of the Ribstone (with an 'e') Pippin, a winter apple no longer seen in supermarkets because it might frighten punters accustomed to the blandness of a Golden Delicious. A Gothick arch of the late 18th century standing in the park here may have been designed by John Carr of York, but if it is still standing it evaded our search. The keystone in the gate to the kitchen garden shows a Janus face, smiling one side, sticking his tongue out the other. Very apt, as Janus is the god of doors, of opening and closing, of beginning and ending. Local tradition says it has the face of a former butler, showing him while receiving and having received an order. 'Find me a Ribstone Pippin, Jeeves.'

Methley

Clumpcliffe Gazebo (1708)
SE 390 260

Southeast of Leeds stands (or did at the time of writing) the shattered remnants of a Grade II* listed gazebo or hunting tower, the central tower having collapsed into the plain, single-storey building at its base some time ago. Given its location and condition, it is unlikely that this curious, mysterious building will be rescued.

Mirfield

Dumb Steeple (1816)
SE 202 19

In the early 19th century the Luddites were wreaking havoc in the newly industrialized north. Smashing the new-fangled machines that they saw as a threat to their livelihood, they moved like flying pickets from town to town, bent on destroying the means of production. In 1812 a band of them assembled in Mirfield in order to attack Cartwright's Huddersfield mill. The attack was a failure and precipitated the downfall of the Luddite movement, but the spirit lives on. An obelisk in Mirfield, quaintly known as the Dumb Steeple, marks the assembly spot.

Newmillerdam

Boathouse (1847)
SE 335 156

Until recently the Boathouse at Kettlethorpe Hall in Newmillerdam was incongruously set with its back to 20th-century housing. It was

The remaining Kettlethorpe Boathouse

has been left standing, belonged to Sir Isaac Holden (1807–97), inventor and textile millionaire. Holden was something of a health crank, although he redeemed himself by smoking a couple of cigars a day and having the occasional drink. His mind was rather fixed on the outdoor life, but to shelter his wife on rainy days he attached a winter garden to the house. This alone was reputed to have cost him £120,000, a preposterous sum, although other sources go as low as £30,000—still not cheap, but with a Turkish bath included. The winter garden has been lost, but the park itself has deteriorated only slightly. Work was carried out between 1864 and 1874 by specially imported labourers who made the gardens into a twilight world of caves, grottoes and underpasses, using a method of iron-reinforced moulded concrete known as the *Système Monier*. The cement rustic work was carried out by the Paris firm of Aucante. Most of this bizarre decoration is still there: the rustic concrete summerhouse made to look as if it had been built of unprocessed tree, the grand cascade and the

the medieval façade of the old Bridge Chapel in Wakefield, consisting of five pointed arches and gables and a ruined second storey. The façade was re-erected here in 1847 when it was decided to renovate the chapel. Behind it a room was added on. The whole building was rather bruised, as befits a building in a public park, so much so that eventually the council decided to take it down and store it while it tried to decide what to do with it. The park also contains the ruin of a Gothick cattleshed, and the surviving boathouse on the Newmillerdam lake has a more conventional late Gothic aspect.

Norton

Obelisk (early 19th century)
SK 364 825

On the village green in Norton, now a suburb of Sheffield on the hills south of the city, an obelisk was erected to the memory of Sir Francis Leggatt Chantrey (1781–1841), the sculptor of so many busts of late Georgian members of the nobility and gentry.

Oakworth

Oakworth Park (1865)
SE 034 389

South of Keighley in the Worth valley is Oakworth Park, now Oakworth Municipal Park. The mansion, of which only the portico

Cement rustic at Oakworth Park

grottoes around three sides of the former house, with the star attraction being the sham fossil tree, which, on closer inspection, reveals a flight of steps leading to an elevated walkway round the hanging gardens. There is now a bowling green where once the house stood. This is a surprising and delightful garden, carefully tended by the local council.

Small and massive—the Bramhope Monument

Otley

Bramhope Monument (1850)
SE 201 454

In Otley churchyard is a replica of the northern entrance of the Bramhope Railway Tunnel, a tunnel folly grander than Clayton in West Sussex. The model in the churchyard was built as a memorial to the navvies who died driving the 2¼-mile tunnel under Bramhope Moor. Its façade, with one polygonal turret and a higher, round turret flanking the arched entrance, has been repeated at the other end of the monument so that it has two matching façades with a short length of tunnel in between. The structure, which looks like a large toy fort, is only about 6ft (1.8m) high, and it was paid for by James Bray, the contractor, along with his sub-contractors and the remaining workers. Curiously it does not mention how many men were killed—a staggering 23, all on different dates—but Mr Bray features prominently in the dedication. The memorial appears to be more to his greater glory than to the dead navvies. One wonders uncharitably if Mr Bray also deducted the contributions for the monument from the survivors' pay packets. The tunnel itself was built between 1845 and 1849, and the larger turret of the castle entrance was used to house railway staff before becoming a store; now it is derelict and the floors have fallen in.

Pateley Bridge

Yorke's Folly (1800)
SE 158 636

On the moor south of the village are two tall ruined pillars that, upon closer inspection, look like the arches for a cathedral nave. Yorke's Folly, or The Stoops, was built for John Yorke of Bewerly Hall. Originally there were three Stoops, dating from 1800, and built, naturally, by unemployed workmen, but one fell down in 1893. As Bewerly Hall was originally owned by the monks of Fountains Abbey, Fountains may have been the inspiration. The old chapel at Bewerly still has an inscription reading *Soli Deo Honor et Gloria,* like the chapel on How Hill at Studley Royal (see below).

Yorke's Folly, Pateley Bridge

Penistone

Hartcliff Tower (c.1851)
SE 224 018

A good mystery concerns dates and the builder of Hartcliff Tower at Bella Vista Farm in Thurlstone, near the invigoratingly named Penistone. The tower itself is simple enough: round, rough stone, windowless and plain, although we do not know what the roof was like since it was blown off in a gale. The tower has now sheared in half from top to bottom, leaving just a semicircular wall standing and lambs playing on the rubble of the remainder. The architect, or rather the head mason, was a Mr Askham from Thurlstone. 'About 1851' is the nearest we can get to a date, while a Captain Ramsden is said to be the builder. But John Ramsden, a local man who was a captain in the East India Company's mercantile fleet, died in 1841. A puzzle, but not for long, as another sharp winter or stiff breeze will bring the rest tumbling down very shortly.

Not far away, towards Cubley, was a square, battered gazebo with pointed windows on all sides and an oriental-looking roof, topped by a pike; this too has gone.

Pool

Avenue des Hirondelles Arch (c.1900)
SE 248 447

An ornate archway enigmatically inscribed 'Avenue des Hirondelles' stands on the A658 south of Pool. We swallowed our curiosity and travelled on.

Avenue des Hirondelles Arch

Rawdon

Cragg Wood Summerhouse (19th century)
SE 204 390

This is small and difficult to find. It is in Rawdon, on the way to the Leeds/Bradford airport, and it is a simple, domed retreat, a kind of elaborate summerhouse, hidden deep against a wall in Cragg Woods. Built of stone and steel, it is still in fair condition, but we do not know who built it or when.

Ripley Castle

Swiss Village (early 19th century)
SE 282 606

Immediately south of Sawley is Ripley Castle, in the valley of the Nidd. Here the estate village was deliberately rebuilt by the Ingleby family to resemble an Alsatian community. This has resulted in a typically English village with the largest house labelled 'Hotel de Ville' and a sentry box by the castle bearing the legend 'Parlez au Suisse.' The owners used to call Ripley Castle Das Schloss; the only similarity between Ripley and Alsace seems to be the inability to distinguish German from French.

Ripon

Obelisk (1781)
SE 312 713

Ripon's market place has a wonderful 90ft (27m) obelisk with an inscription reading:

MDCCLXXXI
ERECTED AT THE EXPENCE OF
WILLIAM AISLABIE ESQUIRE,
WHO REPRESENTED THIS BOROUGH
IN PARLIAMENT SIXTY YEARS.
THE MAYOR, ALDERMEN AND ASSISTANTS
OF RIPON ORDERED THIS INSCRIPTION
MDCCLXXXV
THE HONOURABLE FREDERICK ROBINSON
MAYOR

It is, in fact, a rebuilding of a 1702 obelisk by Nicholas Hawksmoor for William Aislabie's father John. The elder Aislabie had been Chancellor of the Exchequer and was implicated in the disastrous South Sea Bubble crash of the 1720s. Nationally he fell into disgrace, but locally the Aislabies remained honoured and respectable gentry.

Gazebos (18th century)

In the garden at the back of No. 9 Park Street, opposite the Ripon Baths, is a pair of exceptionally large 18th century gazebos built into the garden wall, recently fully restored.

Settle

The Folly (1679)
SD 822 636

The traveller with time to spare and an eye for a beautiful landscape will find the drive across the dales to Settle more than rewarding. Train enthusiasts agree that the Settle to Carlisle line is the loveliest in England, so catch it quick before it's closed down. This small market town has a remarkable and substantial town house set away from the main thoroughfare, called The Folly or Folly Hall, one of the earliest buildings to bear the name Folly—the lintel is dated 1679. The warm stone, three-storey house shows the characteristics of 'Gothic Survival' architecture, with the entrance porch as the most astonishing feature: tiny, double Gothic arches of an uneasy design above a doorway flanked by Gaudí-esque pillars. The main body of the house is more traditional—well lit with lovely stone mullioned windows, one of which is a round-headed arch flanked by four lights,

The curious doorway of The Folly in Settle

which could be a curious interpretation of a Venetian window but is completely original. The fenestration is the joy of this curious construction—the house deserves to be called The Folly on the strength of its highly individual decoration alone, but it seems the main reason for calling it so was because Richard Preston, the builder, ran out of capital and had to leave his knick-knack unfinished.

This is at odds with historical fact—Preston, a tanner, died in 1703 after living in Tanner Hall, as he called it, for over 20 years. It was owned by the Dawson family for 250 years, although they never lived in it, and the name of Preston's Folly was acquired in the 18th century. In the 1990s it stood empty for some time while a struggle for its ownership between a Mr Opie and a Mr Burton amused local gossips. Eventually the North Craven Building Preservation Trust acquired half the folly to convert it into a Museum of North Craven Life, but it was still empty and unattended when we reconnoitred in 1998.

Sheffield

Monuments (19th century)

In Sheffield, monuments rather than follies are thick on the ground. The Cholera Monument is a Gothic spire just east of the Midland Station in a public park off Norfolk Road. It commemorates the 400 cholera victims buried there in 1832, the year the monument was built. The Crimean War Monument, which cost £1000 to build, has now been moved from its old mid-town site to the Botanical Gardens in southwest Sheffield. A more peaceful commemoration is that of Queen Victoria's Jubilee, marked by an obelisk that stood 200 metres from the former monument in Fargate. Like its neighbour, the obelisk has forsworn the inner city and moved out to Endcliffe Park, where it is surrounded by gay lanterns.

Corner House (19th century)
SK 327 906

Relief from all these worthy monuments was provided by Mr Charles Simmons, who built a sham castle, now a children's nursery, in Wadsley Lane on the corner of Marcliffe Road in Hillsborough. Bow-fronted, castellated and practical, it has little of the folly left about it, apart from the inappropriate half-timbered extension to the rear.

Skipton Castle

Grotto Room (17th century)
SD 994 519

Lady Anne Clifford, an indefatigable builder and restorer of six castles and a dozen or so churches and chapels, made herself a grotto room inside the castle and lined it with shells. For more about the buildings of the resourceful and indefatigable Lady Anne, see Brougham in the Cumbria chapter—here we will simply point out that this is one of the earliest shell grottoes in the country (and the only one we could find in Yorkshire). Lady Anne should be commended for her advanced thinking; grottoes were not to come into fashion for another three-quarters of a century.

Stainborough

Stainborough Castle (1730)
Sun Monument (1744)
Steeple Lodge (1775)
Queen Anne Obelisk (1733)

Part of the immense Stainborough Castle folly

Argyll Monument (1743)
Gothick Temple (1759)
Tivoli Temple (1746)
Corinthian Temple (1766)
SE 315 031

Wentworth Woodhouse

Needle's Eye (1746)
Ionic Temple (1735)
Menagerie (1738)
Doric Temple (1744)
Hoober Stand (1748)
Keppel's Column (1779)
Rockingham Mausoleum (1785)
Exmill Cottage
Bean Seat
SK 396 988; SK 408 985; SK 389 948

That rivalry has sometimes been a cause for the building of follies is well illustrated in the case of the two Wentworth estates. When William Wentworth, 2nd Earl of Strafford, died childless in 1695, the earldom became extinct, and he left Wentworth Woodhouse to his relative Thomas Watson rather than to his expected heir, his next of kin Thomas Wentworth, who received the lesser title of Lord Raby.

Understandably irritated and in a permanent fit of pique, Wentworth (who 16 years later fought and succeeded in becoming the 1st Earl of Strafford of the second creation) bought the Stainborough Estate, a mere 7 miles away from his estranged kinsman's Wentworth Woodhouse. The battle of wills over, the Battle of Folly began. It was several years before Strafford

Steeple Lodge from the Barn

erected his first folly; a solid square sham castle gatehouse set on an Anglo-Saxon earthwork west of the house, called Stainborough Castle. According to Horace Walpole, it was built 'in the true style'—in other words, it conformed to contemporary ideals. What Walpole omitted to mention was its immense size: it is bigger than most genuine castles. The encircling wall is 220 yards (200m) in circumference, and there are four square towers, one on each quadrant. The four round corner towers of the Gatehouse were named after Strafford himself and his three daughters (why not his wife?), but only the two western towers are still standing. The others collapsed after a storm in 1962 that also destroyed most of the trees in Bramham Park.

A grassy rhododendron lined walk leads up to the folly from the Sun Monument, flanked by mighty bastions on one side. Stainborough was begun before 1730, remarkably early for a fully fledged sham castle, and the classic example of a man constructing his own spurious ancestry out of stone. On completion of his folly, Strafford changed the name of the estate to Wentworth Castle. Stainborough Castle is somewhat surprisingly only listed Grade II*, and need not be in such poor condition.

When Strafford died in 1739 his son William Wentworth inherited the estate and the earldom, and one of his first tasks was to erect another obelisk, called the Sun Monument, near Stainborough Castle folly. This one was dedicated

TO THE MEMORY OF THE

RT. HON LADY MARY

WORTLEY MONTAGU

WHO IN THE YEAR 1720

INTRODUCED INOCULATION

OF THE SMALL POX

INTO ENGLAND FROM TURKEY

Lady Mary, wife of the British Ambassador to Turkey, was a close neighbour. At the bottom of the grassy avenue to the obelisk is a temple façade in the form of a Venetian window, with stone so weathered that the columns resemble recently-united stalactites and stalagmites.

Near the entrance to the house is Steeple Lodge, a sham church in the form of a Gothic tower with four obelisk-like pinnacles on each corner. The adjacent castellated cottage is inhabited, so the folly is well looked after. It was for sale in 1991 for £120,000, then reduced to £105,000 in 1993. This building seems to have greatly pleased the 2nd Earl, for he then erected a copy of it at his estate at Boughton in Northamptonshire. Opposite

the lodge is a wonderful barn, an open colonnade, roofed, with a single central projecting column at each end.

To the east of Wentworth Castle, at Green Lodge, is an obelisk of 1733 dedicated to Queen Anne—Strafford owed his ascendancy to the late queen. At Boughton as well as Wentworth the new earl's building fever resulted in an great number of often very elaborate follies, spurred on by Walpole's ever favourable comments.

In 1743 a Column to Minerva in the Corinthian style was put up to commemorate the death of Wentworth's father-in-law, the 2nd Duke of Argyll. In 1756 Rockley Woodhouse followed, a classical building with an tower, of which no trace remains. Three years later the Umbrello or Gothick Temple, a copy of the famous Chichester market cross, was completed in Menagerie Wood. It had taken a long time to evolve; Walpole had already written in 1752 to Richard Bentley, his architect-protégé, that he would bring him '*a ground plot for a Gothic building which I have proposed you should draw for a little wood, but in the manner of an ancient market cross*'. The cross was very ruinous when the first edition of this book was published; now one of Bentley's best efforts has been reduced to a pile of rubble. A folly that has totally disappeared deserves a mention here, as it is often confused with Stainborough Castle, and even now people persist in quoting Walpole's 'the ruins of a

Hoober Stand

large imaginary City' with regards to the sham castle. The 'City' was, however, the ruins of fortifications built in 1765–66 on the edge of a hill on Worsborough Common, about 2 miles east of Wentworth. On nearby Blacker Common another string of fortifications was added a year later, together with a pyramid known as the Smoothing Iron. All this, including a Chinese Temple, has gone, leaving Wentworth Woodhouse predominant in South Yorkshire follies.

It had not always been this way. Walpole, after lauding Strafford ('Nobody has a better taste than this Lord') continued with a description of the pathetic rival follies at Wentworth Woodhouse:

> *Now contrast all this, and you may have some idea of Lord Rockingham's…*
> *There are temples in cornfields; and in the little wood, a windowframe mounted on a bunch of laurels, and intended for a hermitage.*

Despite Walpole's waspish comments the follies at Wentworth Woodhouse have endured and bettered their neighbour's attempts. Thomas Watson, 1st Marquess of Rockingham, built only one of the Wentworth 'specials': the impressive Hoober Stand, designed by Henry Flitcroft. It was erected in 1748 to celebrate the Pretender's defeat at Culloden, where Watson had also fought. Hoober Stand is as strange as its name, over 100ft (30m) of smoke-blackened yellowstone, triangular with rounded corners, tapering towards the top over 100ft (30m) above, with lucarne windows to light the now inaccessible staircase. From a distance it hovers over the horizon like the apparition of a crazy factory chimney, but the iron railings at the top proclaim its true function as a belvedere tower.

1748
This Pyramidal Building was Erected by his Majestys most Dutyfull Subject
THOMAS Marquess of Rockingham Etc.
In Grateful Respect to the Preserver of our Religion
Laws and Libertys
KING GEORGE The Second
Who by the blessing of God having Subdued a most Unnatural Rebellion
In Britain Anno 1746
Maintains the Ballance of Power and Settles A Just and Honourable Peace in Europe.
1748

This is a unique structure, an appendix in the history of architecture—we know of no other like it in the world—but its enchanting name turns out to have a prosaic meaning:

Hoober is a nearby hamlet, while Stand is a local name for a tower.

The 2nd Marquess of Rockingham matched his neighbour's *folie de batir*. Between 1773 and 1781 John Carr built a huge solitary Tuscan column for him, 15ft higher than Hoober Stand. It is a monument to Viscount Keppel, Rockingham's First Lord of the Admiralty, who had earlier achieved immense public popularity when he was acquitted in a court martial on five charges, including 'scandalous haste in quitting the scene of a naval engagement'. Keppel's Column stands south of the house, beside a housing estate on the A629. Again this was built as a belvedere. The entrance was sealed with a stout iron grille, which local youths

The Needle's Eye

have managed to break down; this was ineffectually replaced by a wooden panel, which has proved much less of a deterrent. Although the stairs inside were clearly visible, hugging the central brick core, we lacked the courage to make the ascent. Frankly, the column looks most unsafe. The enlargement *ad absurdum* of what is, after all, only an architectural element carries Keppel's Column beyond the boundaries of mere monument and turns it into true folly. Coincidentally, a young naval officer who, under pressure from Sir Hugh Palliser, falsified his log and testified against Admiral Keppel, had a column built to his memory near Street in Somerset—50 years later when

Rockingham Mausoleum

he had become Admiral Sir Samuel Hood.

Sometime before 1746 another unique structure appeared on the estate, north of the house in a small wood: the Needle's Eye, a slender pyramid with a tall ogee arch through it and a flamboyant urn on top. It has traditionally been ascribed to Carr, but recent research has shown that it may be over 50 years older than was thought. The most memorable factor behind this beautiful folly is the legend of how it came to be built, a story both ridiculous and credible. One night the marquess, like Tommy Osborne an excellent coach-and-four man, accepted a flattering wager that he could 'drive a carriage through the eye of a needle'. The sober dawn brought home the monstrosity of the bet and also the impossibility of failure; hence the construction of this elegant wager winner, a narrow arch just wide enough to allow a coach through and called the Needle's Eye. We will never really know the truth of these wager/folly stories—see the tales about Mad Jack Fuller in Sussex—but the marquess was known to favour the odd bet; he once staked £500 on a race between five turkeys and five geese from Norwich to London. The Grade II* listed Needle's Eye has been variously described as an obelisk and belvedere; there may have been an earlier obelisk on the same site that led to later confusion, but pedantic disputations about attributions should be set aside when confronted with such an indisputably beautiful folly. The Needle's Eye is shown on the Earl of Malton's estate map; as the earl was elevated to the Marquessate of Rockingham in 1746 this argues the folly existed earlier.

Rockingham died in 1782 and was interred in York Minster. In 1785 his heir Earl Fitzwilliam commissioned John Carr to build an eerie, three-storey mausoleum in his honour near Nether Haugh, 'not to entertain the eye, but to instruct the mind'. Now restored, it was opened to the public in 1989 for the first time in 200 years. It now entertains the eye purely as a mighty monument to Whiggery rather than a mausoleum, for Rockingham was never buried here.

There are yet more follies at Wentworth Woodhouse: first, the Round House, an embattled ex-windmill not far from the Needle's Eye, with neither date nor architect. Another windmill converted into a cottage, a little further north and therefore out of the immediate curtilage of the village, has to do without castellations. Over the road from the Round House is a garden centre, set within the remains of an early 19th-century Japanese garden. Close by is the Bear Pit, an underground tunnel with barred niches where the bears had their quarters. The two entrances to the Bear Pit are highly decorated with festoons, volutes and shields, all in the mannerist style of the early 17th century. A couple of free-standing, ill-proportioned statues probably date from the same time. The Bean Seat was recently demolished by Guy Canby, the Wentworth agent, without planning consent. It was built for Lady Fitzwilliam to feed the park deer. Conservationists need not heed the call to arms: the seat was in such a bad state that Canby had it demolished and rebuilt. It was then discovered that planning permission was required, so retrospective consent was applied for and granted.

Earl Fitzwilliam, the last private owner of this remarkable collection of monuments, donated the follies to the Wentworth Monuments Society just before his death in 1989; Keppel's Column was separately bought by Rotherham Council. This resulted in the Countryside Service Department producing a 'Follies Trail' to guide visitors round the follies, but vandalism is illogical by its nature—instead of the buildings being damaged the informative sign boards were stolen. The follies at Wentworth Woodhouse were in a very sorry state when we first encountered them, but thanks to the Wentworth Monuments Society and the Wentworth Fitzwilliam Trust restoration is making steady progress. The Mausoleum in particular has been transformed from a steel-banded, subsidence-threatened sepulchre into as majestic a building as could possibly be expected in the sodden English countryside.

Steeton

Steeton Tower (1897)
SE 039 440

This fat Diamond Jubilee tower, bigger than the normal run of such towers, with a hideous beige pebble-dashed, castellated extension at the base, is well sited as an eyecatcher from the valley steeply below. In 1997 it had been unoccupied for several years and was offered for sale for £95,000; at the time of writing the lucky new owners had the builders in. Perhaps they will strip off the pebble-dashing.

Studley Royal

Folly Group (18th century)
SE 280 690

John Aislabie used a large part of his fortune to create Studley Royal, his estate a few miles from Ripon, now a National Trust property. The garden there acts as a link between the formal French style and the new romantic landscape movement. Over a period of 20 years John Aislabie, succeeded by his son William, and their chief gardener, William Fisher, created a poetic valleyscape rivalled by only a few others in the country. They made use of the undulating valley of the Skell to lay out a series of ornamental ponds leading from a large sheet of water at the garden entrance to the focal point, the grandest eyecatcher in Britain—the genuine ruins of Fountains Abbey.

John Aislabie's buildings are all in the classical vein, among them Colen Campbell's Banqueting House of 1729, the Temple of Piety and the Octagon Tower. After his father's death in 1742, William Aislabie finally took over and from then on the Studley gardens were fitted out with follies. The craggy west side of the valley on which the Octagon Tower stands may represent a kind of political landscape, perhaps in reference to William Aislabie's unpublished 'Essay upon some Particulars of the Ancient and Modern Government, Conventions and Parliament of England, treating of politics from the Saxons until Edward I'. The Octagon Tower, originally a classical pavilion, was altered by William in 1738 into a Gothic belvedere that had to be approached by a tunnel cut into the hillside. It has all recently been most carefully restored. Next to the tower is a small construction, which could well be England's first barbecue. Walking south along the ridge we come across the ruins of a pillar, referred to as a Column to Liberty. Next is the rotondo Temple of Fame and finally Anne Boleyn's Seat in carpenter's Gothick. This seat provides the famous Surprise View of Fountain's Abbey. One is not supposed to cheat—the undergrowth along the side of the walk is supposed to be a little thicker—so keep your eyes straight ahead. The surprise view is spectacular even when anticipated.

From here a path through the back of the wood leads to Mackershaw Lodge, a Greek-fronted eyecatcher visible from the Pillar and the site of the now-demolished house. The outer parts of Studley are follywise at least as interesting as the garden itself. From the Lodge a wooded walk leads to Mackershaw Trough and the Chinese Wood. By now one has entered what is known as the Valley of the Seven Bridges, or Mackershaw Valley, also a National Trust property. The rustic bridges, which are all in the same style, were built by William Aislabie when he made Mackershaw into a sub-Studley. The site is much rougher and less artificial than Studley, reflecting the younger Aislabie's avant-garde taste for the Picturesque and the Chinese. A view *c.*1750 by Balthasar Nebot, who painted all of Aislabie's possessions, shows an open Chinese building, more Tartar than Cantonese, on a steep cliff in Mackershaw and in the distance a small white building, possibly the entrance to Mann's Cave. Only the curiously formed foundations of the Chinese building remain, together with two rustic gateposts, which give entrance to a small copse. According to a bill, work was carried out on 'ye Cheineys Building &… Pillers &c in South scrarr' from December 1744 until October 1745. The Belvedere, a few hundred yards from the site of the Chinese building, has also disappeared, but a little further off the Roman Pill Box guards the valley's proper entrance from Studley. This simple, square building was dedicated to the Roman legend of the three Horatii, another political reference.

From here one can return to Studley or have a look at the twin fishing tabernacles and the Gothic Studley Lodge at the park's main entrance. Above Studley the drive, aligned with Ripon Cathedral, starts at solitary St Mary's Church. Behind this Burges church the obelisk is hidden, built in 1815 in place of William Aislabie's Stowe-inspired pyramid. Re-entering Studley and following the High Walk along the west ridge one encounters a small neglected Greek seat, and finally, in the valley again, arrives at the area called Quebec. This encompasses a rustic bridge and a pond with the Quebec Monument in the middle, in memory of General Wolfe who died in the battle for the Heights of Abraham in 1759. Through the woods the Temple of Fame can be seen on the east crag, intended as a celebration of Wolfe's fame. Opposite the monument a small rustic grotto has been cut into the hillside. Some yards south of Quebec is Tent Hill, upon which an oriental building formerly stood. This was the original site of the Temple of Venus, moved in 1758. In the late 1990s restoration was being carried out here by the National Gardens Scheme, and time will tell if the Bedouin tent will be reinstated. Turning the corner towards the ruins of Fountains Abbey, the rubble of the Gothic Rustic Lodge can be found in Bank Wood.

To the south of the park, superbly sited on How Hill like St Michael's on Glastonbury Tor, is the Chapel of St Michael de Monte. The site has been associated with the court of a Saxon king. The medieval chapel that stood here fell into ruins after the Dissolution, and two years after John Aislabie inherited Studley Royal in 1716 he rebuilt it, making it into a quasi-chapel, classical, but with a cross on top and incorporating the original Gothic inscription *Soli Deo Honor et Gloria*. No matter how politically inspired Studley and its surroundings may have been, the religious aspect should not be overestimated: in 1737 gaming tables were installed in the How Hill 'chapel'.

The Temple of Piety at Studley Royal

Lund's Tower

Sutton Moor

Lund's Tower (1897)
SD 993 431
Wainman's Pinnacle (1816)
SD 984 429

On Sutton Moor west of Keighley, above the villages of Sutton and Cowling, a square castellated tower and a companion obelisk hide their history from the casual visitor. Lund's Tower, or Ethel Tower, was built by James Lund of Malsis Hall either to celebrate Queen Victoria's Golden Jubilee in 1897 or to celebrate his daughter Ethel's 21st birthday. Given the traditional canniness of the Yorkshireman, we suggest both reasons. There is a spiral staircase with a small viewing platform at the top to celebrate the jubilant views.

The nearby inscriptionless obelisk is unconnected. It is said to have been erected in memory of the son of Richard Wainman, killed in the Napoleonic Wars, or to commemorate Waterloo or a Wainman killed in the Civil War—no one seems quite sure.

Tadcaster

Grimston Park Tower (mid-19th century)
SE 492 409

Near Tadcaster is Grimston Park, the 19th-century house of Sir John Hobart Caradoc, 2nd Baron Howden, and his wife Catherina Skravonsky. Howden was a diplomat whose appointments carried him all over the world, never allowing him a long stay at Grimston. He must have set his mind on a beautiful home, however, for as soon as his father died in 1839 building started under Decimus Burton, and Grimston was created while Howden was in South America. The tower near the house reflects Howden's (and Burton's) cosmopolitanism: it is of the type loosely called Italianate, a style that never succeeds in suppressing other influences—

Grimston Park Tower

the battered plinth on which the tower stands and the entrance surrounds are distinctly Egyptian in feel and treatment. The tapering shaft is lit by tall, round-arched windows on each side, capped with *oeil-de-boeuf* lights. On top of the balustrade is an open octagonal tempietto somewhat resembling the Choragic Monument at Alton Towers.

Todmorden

Stoodley Pike (1856)
SD 973 241

The most conspicuous folly in the area is the obelisk called Stoodley Pike, 2 miles east of Todmorden. In 1814, after Paris had surrendered, it was decided by the local gentry to erect a commemorative obelisk. Public subscription was to pay for the monument, the building of which was stopped when word reached Todmorden that Napoleon had escaped from Elba. Work started again when word reached Todmorden of the triumph at Waterloo. It turned out to be a weird structure, a base with a fat column on it topped by a tall cone. On 8 February 1854, however, the obelisk collapsed. The *Halifax Guardian* commented on the 'evil omen' as this had also been the day when word reached Todmorden that the Russian Ambassador had left England prior to the outbreak of the Crimean War. The prominent burgesses of the town decided to build a new obelisk, and by 1 June plans for a new monument were submitted. The new obelisk, the same height—120ft (37m)—as the old one but a different design, was ready in time to celebrate the peace treaty between Britain and Russia. The monument's architect was a local man, James Green, and the building contractor was a Mr Lewis Crabtree. Wise after the event, they prudently surrounded the new obelisk with eight heavy buttresses upon which a balustrade was erected, with the obelisk proper towering above. It cost £812, and the momentous occasion was feted by the Todmorden poet, J. Barnes:

> *...like the fabled Phoenix, thou*
> *From thy ashes rose*
> *Thy friends were firmer, greater, now,*
> *Than had been all thy foes;*
> *Again they raised they heavenward sign–*
> *And may it long remain,*
> *A Monument of Peace benign,*
> *On Langfield's moorland plain.*

The inscription on the obelisk reads

STOODLEY PIKE

A PEACE MONUMENT

ERECTED BY PUBLIC SUBSCRIPTION

Commenced in 1814 to commemorate the surrender of Paris to the Allies and finished after the Battle of Waterloo when peace was established in 1815. By a strange coincidence the Pike fell on the day the Russian Ambassador left London before the declaration of war with Russia in 1854, and it was rebuilt when peace was proclaimed in 1856. Repaired and lightning conductor fixed 1889.

Curiously, the obelisk has remained standing, despite 1914, 1939, 1982, and even 1999. It is so solid that probably only a nuclear blast would topple it.

Wakefield

Walton Hall Follies (mid-18th century)
SE 364 165

Walton Hall, now a hotel, was once the residence of one of Britain's greatest eccentrics, the traveller, naturalist, taxidermist and devout Catholic squire

Stoodley Pike

Charles Waterton. It is an elegant country house, blissfully sited on an island in a lake and accessible only by footbridge. The lake was originally a moat; Waterson had it enlarged to attract birdlife and in the process attracted pure sharawaggi.

Waterton was far too practical to bother with any deliberate follies, but in the course of his long life some ornamentation was added to his house and grounds that may be considered eligible. Early on he turned his estate into a nature reserve, keeping poachers out by means of a 3-mile wall. Most of his buildings reflected his concern for animals—a couple of stone pigsties, an intrusion-proof tower for the birds—but he was also no stranger to mottomania: he placed a millstone round a tree and inscribed it 'The National Debt'. The smaller buildings at Walton Hall were designed and erected by Jack Ogden, a former mason and poacher turned keeper. Unlike many animal lovers, Waterton quite liked humans as well, and he regularly opened the grounds and even the house to visitors. According to *Charles Waterton: His Home, Habits and Handiwork* written by his friend Richard Hobson, he even constructed a 'Chair-swing, of truly noble dimensions and of extensive sweep, in which many a buxom country girl has joyously received the swinging attentions of her devoted swain'.

The entrance to the house still surprises visitors with its two door-knockers: the one in the form of a welcoming face is a fake, while the other one works and makes a face appropriate to the occasion. In the grounds was a rough stone grotto, sometimes put to good use:

> the hundred lunatics, from the Wakefield Asylum, who were wont to be kindly permitted by Mr Waterton to have their harmless and frolicsome merriment—their dancing, and their dinner, within the grotto—were always delighted, and even tranquillized, so as to temporarily forget their pitiable and frequently unhappy condition, and one and all to declare the grotto to be an elysium.

An old Water Gate, now completely cloaked in ivy, which, together with a swivel cannon, held off Cromwell's troops, was embellished by Waterton with a cross. Some years earlier a cross was erected, on top of a temple near the grotto, which was held by Waterton to have been the first cross to be erected in public view in England since the Reformation. Round the park were six small towers, which Waterton used for observing wildlife—precursors of the twitchers' hides perhaps.

Wentworth Woodhouse
See **Stainborough**

Wetherby
Gazebo (1930)
SE 405 485

At Wetherby in the northeastern tip of West Yorkshire is a garden containing a gazebo brought over in the 1930s from Ferriby Hall in Humberside. It is simply a square room with a pyramidal roof topped by an urn, dating from the second half of the 18th century.

Wragby
Nostell Pyramid (1776)
SE 405 185

Nostell Priory is a National Trust property 3 miles east of Walton. It was built for the Winn family by James Paine, with Robert Adam adding a wing in 1766. Adam also would seem to have been responsible for the remarkable Pyramid Lodge pierced by an arch at the far north of the property, also known as the Needle's Eye—the more famous Needle's Eye at Wentworth Woodhouse is only 25 miles away. The top of this strange and bizarre pyramid has collapsed, and as there is no other building in Britain remotely like this, it urgently needs to be saved. Access to it is discouraged. In the park are several Gothick fabrics, among them an arched seat and the Menagerie, which was the keeper's cottage. This, too, has been ascribed to Adam, but it is not one of his finer works. It is polygonal, with pointed windows and doors and rather weak castellations.

NORTH RIDING

Aske Hall
Aske Hall Temple (mid-18th century)
NZ 177 035

Aske Hall Temple, one of the largest Gothic follies in Britain, was probably used as a banqueting house. The base is formed by an arcade with a central projecting entrance and half-round end bays. On top of this is a two-storey central block, castellated, with two half-round turrets at the flanks, also castellated. This is typical façade architecture, with only a staircase at the back, supposedly to allow bawds from the town to enter unobserved into the Temple. Bawds? In Richmond, Yorkshire? In all probability the staircase was put at the back only so as not to interfere with the overall concept of the design. Lancelot Brown did a bridge for Sir Lawrence Dundas in 1779, but the Temple has been convincingly attributed by Peter Leach to Daniel Garrett.

Oliver Duckett (late 18th century)
NZ 184 030

Another even more intriguing though less grand folly is Oliver Duckett, on the other side of the road and further south. One of the few follies to have been named after a person, it acquired its name because at one time it was the site of the home of Mr Oliver Duckett. Sir Conyers Darcy took the building, once an outpost for Richmond Castle, a medieval pillbox, and 'restored' it into a thoroughly martial folly, with a high projecting and virtually unassailable base, and a round bastion tower with ample gunports and a pointed door and window. There is absolutely no entrance in the base; the only access could have been by ladder.

Aysgarth

Swinithwaite Temple (1792)
SE 033 891

Wensleydale is famous far beyond Yorkshire for its beauty and its cheese. There's little enough cheese to be found there now, but its beauty remains. Beyond Swinithwaite on the A684 to Aysgarth lies Temple Farm, and on the north side of the road, hidden among the trees behind a high wall, was a dilapidated but still beautiful temple by John Foss. It

Swinithwaite Temple

consists of a rusticated octagonal base with blocked arches and the bas-relief of a dog above the door. The staircase runs between the outer and inner walls, leading to a balcony around a smaller domed octagonal room on the first floor, and we are pleased to note that it has now been restored and is let out for holidays. It was built for nearby Swinithwaite Hall, together with a belvedere, which we failed to find.

Sorrel Sykes Follies (early 20th century)
SE 024 883

Near the famous Aysgarth Falls is Sorrell Sykes Park, the home of a set of particularly quaint follies, variously ascribed to a Mrs Hutton in the 19th or early 20th century. As an entrée, a tall chimney stands in the garden of a farmhouse to the east of Sorrell Sykes Farm. The chimney was bought by a major some years ago and transported from the Home Counties to Yorkshire in two army trucks. The Sorrell Sykes Farm is a weird amalgam of building styles. The façade towards the road only has a series of farmhouses to show for itself, except for a west wing of 1921 with huge classical windows. The park façade, however, is that of a Palladian mansion of about 1750. The park is essentially a lawn bounded by a steep ridge, with a great variation of heights in between. On the lawn stood a column with an eagle on top, until in 1980 a tractor accidentally knocked it down. The base is still there, as for some years was the eagle, regretfully eyeing the rubble of its perch, but the sculpture was too attractive to remain lying around in full view and it has now disappeared.

Halfway along the ridge stood a sham ruin, built to hide the site where earlier in the 18th century there had been a lead mine, but it was downed by a storm in 1992. An old gully still leads down to the lawn where lead deposits form a few hillocks. The centre of the ruin consisted of a blank arch, above which was an *oeil-de-boeuf* window and a small pediment. The flanking walls, which have small pointed arches and windows, are in danger of becoming genuine ruins. To the east the sham ruin screen is mirrored on the other side of the valley by Bolton Castle. From the screen one walks down to a field with a strictly vernacular barn, but along the edge are three follies in a neat row.

First, a cone like a spinning top, a large smoke hole, constructed from rough stone in 1921, then a tiny gate consisting of two cones with a bend stone for an arch, too small for anyone to enter the field through. The last folly is the Rocket Ship, as it is locally known:

The Rocket Ship at Sorrel Sykes

a cone rising from a square base with a room inside. Buttresses are placed against the base, probably because the local builder was afraid the cone wouldn't stand on its own. It is the buttresses that give the folly a startling resemblance to Dan Dare-style rockets from 1950s comic strips. In 1993 a grant from the Yorkshire Dales National Park Committee enabled this weirdly compelling little group of follies to be consolidated, rather than restored—alas too late for the sham ruin.

Folly Rock Garden (1903)
SE 018 883

We chanced upon this one late one summer's evening, taking a stroll down Aysgarth's main (and only) street. At the last house of the village a small enclosure is fenced off by iron rails and bizarre rock formations tower over it. A sign on the little gate said 'PRIVATE ROCK GARDEN', and that was all we could see in the dark. In the early light of morning the garden presented itself rather less mysteriously: it consists of narrow walkways through miniature chasms, planted very agreeably with all manner of plants and shrubs and flowers. Two or three rock arches are crammed in, as well as the beginnings of a tiny grot or two. The site is extremely claustrophobic and looks like a dwarf's idea of the sublime. It belongs to the Victorian Heather Cottage across the road, itself fronted by a good cast iron veranda with some left-over rock-work in the garden. The Rock Garden itself is usually open on bank holidays and despite its prettiness (or because of) we would have hesitated to call it a folly if the locals hadn't done it for us: they refer to it as The Folly Rock Garden and claim it was built in 1903 to relieve local unemployment. The only thing one misses is a hermit—he should be there, coughing a hesitant serenade to tuberculosis.

Castle Howard

At Castle Howard we move not just into a different league, but a different stratosphere, starting with its self-deprecatory name—this is nothing so commonplace or utilitarian as a castle. This is a palace. It defines the word.

Howsham is the best vantage point for the southern approach to this spectacular house, which was built for the interminably rich but otherwise nondescript 3rd Earl of Carlisle, Charles Howard, by the soldier and playwright Sir John Vanbrugh. Vanbrugh gave the Earl the sumptuous baroque palace he so desperately wanted, but indulged his own preferences for battlements in the walls and outbuildings. The extraordinary thing about this commission is that when Vanbrugh was approached by Howard, he was a military man just embarking on a remarkably successful second career as a popular playwright, and as far as is known he had never before shown the slightest inclination towards architecture. Yet he was incontrovertibly appointed the architect for Castle Howard, and even if he was aided by Nicholas Hawksmoor it seems that the designs were his.

Howard Monument (1870)
SE 715 671

Before reaching Vanbrugh's fortified walls, the visitor encounters the column on Bulmer Hill near Welburn, at the southern boundary of the Howard Estate, erected to the memory of George William Frederick Howard, the 7th Earl. The column was designed by S.P. Cockerell.

Carrmire Gate (1725)
SE 713 680

From the Howard Monument the avenue undulates 2 miles straight as a die to the Carrmire Gate, a rusticated arch with broken pediment and six small capped brick pyramids on piers clustered either side, running off into castellated walls and actually designed by Hawksmoor.

Pyramid Gate (1719)
SE 711 694

After some 2000ft (610m) of wall, a tall gate with side pavilions and a vast pyramid roof provides the main entrance to the estate. The

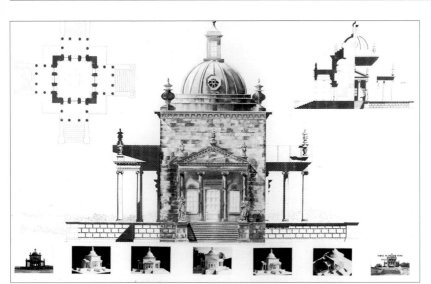

The Temple of the Four Winds—an entry for the Folly Fellowship's Measured Drawings Award

gate was designed by Vanbrugh, but it is the castellated wall with a total of 11 different Gothick bastions that shows his hand at its best. Some of the bastions are square, others round or hexagonal, all harking back to Vanbrugh's Blackheath Castle and the Claremont Belvedere, which he had built since first starting on Castle Howard in 1699. All the park buildings here are listed Grade I.

Obelisk (1714)
SE 710 699

Further north, on the crossing of the two drives, stands a 100ft (30m) obelisk, making it his first folly here as it dates from 1714. There is a Latin inscription to the Duke of Marlborough, but on the other side is a later inscription:

IF TO PERFECTION THESE PLANTATIONS RISE
IF THEY AGREEABLY MY HEIRS SURPRISE
THIS FAITHFUL PILLAR WILL THEIR AGE
DECLARE
AS LONG AS TIME THESE CHARACTERS WILL
SPARE
HERE THEN WITH KIND REMEMBRANCE READ HIS
NAME
WHO FOR POSTERITY PERFORM'D THE SAME.
CHARLES THE III EARL OF CARLISLE
OF THE FAMILY OF THE HOWARDS
ERECTED A CASTLE WHERE THE OLD CASTLE OF
HENDERSKELFE STOOD, AND CALL'D IT CASTLE-
HOWARD.
HE LIKEWISE MADE THE PLANTATIONS IN THIS
PARK
AND ALL THE OUT-WORKS, MONUMENTS AND
OTHER
PLANTATIONS BELONGING TO THE SAID SEAT.

HE BEGAN THESE WORKS
IN THE YEAR MDCCII
ANNO D:MDCCXXX

An apt illustration of the principle that he who provides the money gets the credit, although the awareness of his responsibility to posterity and the passage of time reads pleasantly nowadays.

Temple of the Four Winds (1724)
SE 723 700

East of the palace is the Temple of the Four Winds by Vanbrugh, a shoot from Palladio's Villa Rotonda. From here, one takes in the carefully composed Claude-like picture of Sion Wood to the left, the New River bridge in the middle distance and, as a focal point, Hawksmoor's gigantic mausoleum.

Mausoleum (1731–42)
SE 728 696

This is shaped like a domed Greek tholos, round, with pillars carrying a frieze. The 3rd Earl of Carlisle is buried here. Around it Daniel Garrett later added the fortified wall, square with semicircular projections on each side.

Hawksmoor Pyramid (1728)
SE 719 692

From the mausoleum one can see the tall Hawksmoor pyramid to the southwest. Further to the southeast is Pretty Wood, hiding another Hawksmoor pyramid, this one in a truly dreadful condition, and a column called the Four Face (quatre faces—Carfax); the same name serves the large vase with four heads on each side at Bramham Park.

Constable Burton

Akebar Caravan Park (1981)
`SE 189 906`

Towards the east of Leyburn, between
Constable Burton and Patrick Brompton
(two villages that sound more like a charge
sheet) is the Akebar Caravan Park, the shop
of which takes the unexpected form of a
castle farm. It consists mainly of its own
façade, leaving the tourists little space for
squeezing their rain-tanned bodies through
the supermarket's turnstiles. The façade is
about 100 yards long and faces Constable
Burton. It is superbly asymmetrical; one end
has a vernacular house, the other a sham
ruined tower with a small corner outcrop. In
between is a rough wall, partly ruined, with
an ogee gate with pediment and finials. The
façade looked like the fulfilment of a long-
held dream. The construction workers told
us that the owner doesn't like it to be called a
folly because he just wanted it to blend with
the surroundings. As its immediate
surroundings consist of acres of parked
caravans, the shop is a prime example of
what a modern-day folly can be, as opposed
to the studied retrogression of Quinlan Terry
and Peter Foster. It was built by a Mr
Ellwood, the owner of the caravan park, who
strongly objected to its description as a folly
in the first edition of this book. More recently
he quoted the description in a caravanning
magazine with evident delight, and confessed
when people mistake it for an antique
building: 'I get a bit mischievous and don't
always let on.'

Two miles northwest, above Constable
Burton Hall, the Grotto clearly marked on
the Ordnance Survey map turns out to be a
plain little lodge with a seductive name.

Crayke

Crayke Castle (15th century)
`SE 560 707`

In a county that has converted entire religious
foundations into garden features—Rievaulx,
Fountains—the preservation of a small service
wing of a minor castle as a garden ornament is

Part of the Akebar Caravan Park

hardly the headline news it would be in, say Leicestershire, but nevertheless this is a Grade I listed Ancient Monument, which has been promoted to the status of a real 'sham' ruin in a landscaped garden.

East Hauxwell

Wellhead Folly (18th century)
`SE 162 932`

Close to Hauxwell Hall is a small folly made to look like a wellhead, but without a well. It is a circular assembly of recycled mullions from redundant windows, capped with a small stone dome. To the south stands an obelisk.

East Witton

Slobbering Sal (1821)
Tilsey Folly
`SE 139 851`

Slobbering Sal is a female head, rather like the heads on medieval capitals, attached to a large structure like a grotto entrance, spouting a gentle but never-ending stream of water from her mouth, even in the dryest summers. High in the woods above East Witton, on Witton Fell, it is marked on older maps as Castaway Well. The arch above the re-roofed grotto entrance is inscribed

Mqfs of A
1821

for the Marquess of Ailesbury.

Tilsey Folly, also noted nearby on local maps, is a barn incorporating a few medieval fragments.

Ebberston

Aelfrid's Memorial (1790)
`SE 898 833`

Near Colen Campbell's tiny, elegant Ebberston Lodge, above the A170, is King Aelfrid's Cave, where the Northumbrian king is supposed to have succumbed to mortal wounds received in battle. Above the cave towers a sham tumulus, erected as a memorial to King Aelfrid, who is otherwise totally forgotten.

Eston Nab (Cleveland)

ICI Beacon (1956)
`NZ 570 184`

The brightest light in the sky round these parts is the eternal flame at the Billingham petrochemical works, built for the chemical giant ICI. The pillar on Eston Nab, a rocky headland, or nab, overlooking the works,

replaces a signal station built by Thomas Jackson of Lazenby, which dated from the Napoleonic Wars and had become a prominent local landmark. It was demolished by ICI and could be read as just another example of rampant capitalism except that the company had honestly tried to maintain the building but lost the fight to vandalism. So eventually the old ruin had to go, but its function as an eyecatcher was carried on by the new rectangular column built, using stones from the original building, by ICI in 1956. The *raison d'être* of the new eyecatcher is to commemorate the old signal station—one tries to imagine the shareholder's meeting where the ICI directors announced that they had built a folly. The little pillar is now dwarfed by the telecommunications masts surrounding it.

Great Ayton

Cook Obelisk (1827)
`NZ 590 101`

On Easby Moor, in the northernmost part of the county, stands a tall obelisk erected in 1827 to commemorate Captain Cook. His cottage in Ayton was sold and transported to Melbourne, Australia, in 1934. In return, another obelisk marks the site of his cottage. Yet another Cook obelisk can be found in Hawaii, marking the spot where the great explorer was killed by the erroneously named Friendly Islanders. Gisborne in New Zealand has no obelisk, but does possess part of Marton Church, from the village in Cleveland where Cook was born.

Grewelthorpe

Hackfall (1750)
`SE 235 770`

Although William Aislabie had Mackershaw Valley to experiment with, he was surely torn by the dichotomy faced by all planners with a respect for the past: the need to conserve his father's garden at Studley, which he properly realized to be a masterpiece, although hopelessly old-fashioned by 1750, and the desire to see his own schemes and designs laid out. On the look-out for new terrain, he came across the steep and remote Ure valley near Grewelthorpe, another Aislabie property. In 1750 planting and building started in the woods at Hackfall.

Hackfall became one of the first and perhaps the greatest 'romantick' gardens in England. With its hanging woods, wild river and rocky cliffs, only Hawkstone in

Hackfall in the eighteenth century

Shropshire can rival it. The centrepiece at Hackfall was, however, formed by the Fountain Plain, a formal arrangement reminiscent of designs in Batty Langley's *New Principles of Gardening* (1728). The garden—calling it a garden is like calling Buckingham Palace a house—became a Yorkshire showcase for the next century and a half; even in the early 20th century charabancs from Harrogate arrived at the entrance, where the tourists paid a small fee and proceeded on foot, stopping to take tea in the Graeco-Roman folly at Mowbray Point. The gardens at Hackfall have now fallen completely into decay, and it is difficult to tell that there was even a plan, until one stumbles across a folly in the undergrowth. Most of the trees were felled in the 1930s, and the buildings have been set fire to or otherwise slighted. The restoration of Hackfall will be a massive and costly operation, but there is enough information and contemporary accounts through the encomia of distinguished 18th-century travellers such as William Gilpin, Arthur Young and Thomas Pennant to make it feasible.

Near the entrance are the ruins of what must have been a covered stone and tufa seat, reverently called Kent's Seat (Kent was a hero of Aislabie's), facing the Alumn Cascade, which still trickles feebly down the mossy stones. A little further on is Fisher's Hall, named after John Aislabie's chief gardener who died in 1743 and who also worked for William. The roof of this octagonal lancet-windowed grotto room set on a little mound has long ago come down, but the inside walls still show the remains of shells and pieces of glass. Above the door is a tablet inscribed 'W.A. 1750'. Fisher's Hall seems to owe something to a design of Robert Morris, but as his *Architectural Remembrancer* was published in 1751, it may have been the other way round. Walking down the slippery steps to the River Ure, one comes to the scanty remains of what must have been a storeroom for fishing tackle and/or wine, or perhaps it was a barbecue like the one at Studley Royal.

To the north is the Fountain Plain, where the formal layout has now disappeared into the undergrowth, the pond now only a stagnant sheet of water with a small peninsula on which was formerly a 'Fountain throwing Water to a great height'. Near the pond are the ruins of a grotto, situated in front of a cascade that falls 40ft (12m), and the Rustic Temple, a simple enough folly, made of huge boulders. In one of its walls is a niche for a statuette. Still further to the north one can find the remains of the Sand Bed Hut and a small obelisk, broken in two and probably dating from Victorian times when Lord Ripon owned Hackfall.

The two most important follies are each on the edge of the cliffs that form the natural boundary of the estate. Mowbray Castle, which towers high above the river to the south, is visible from the other side of the garden. The view towards Mowbray Castle was painted by Turner in 1816. The castle is a

Mowbray Castle

In rural pride, transported fancy flies.
Oh! Bear me, Goddess to these sylvan
plains,
Where all around unlaboured beauties
rise.

There is now hope for Hackfall: it has been acquired by the Woodland Trust. Naturally its priority is the trees, but one hopes it will spare some attention to the follies. The Landmark Trust, English Heritage, the Woodland Trust, the local authority, English Nature, the Hackfall Trust—all worthy bodies, all working to rescue the park, each to its own agenda. One is irresistibly reminded of a camel.

In the church in Masham a painting by John Blakey shows the Madonna and Child stepping out into the world from the Rustic Temple at Hackfall.

Hartforth

Hartforth Hall Archway (mid-18th century)
NZ 170 065

An embattled cottage and an archway to Hartforth Hall, assembled out of the bric-à-brac of a demolished medieval church. One of the estate farms has a sharply pointed and castellated gable to serve as an eyecatcher—perhaps the inspiration for the Sedbury Park buildings?

Helmsley

Duncombe Park Temples (1730)
SE 606 831; SE 578 844

West of Helmsley is Duncombe Park, with Duncombe Terrace, a drive flanked by two temples: an Ionic Temple of *c.*1730, which has been attributed to Vanbrugh, and a slightly later Tuscan temple. The column shafts of the Grade I listed Ionic Temple are badly decayed and in need of repair.

Like the Aislabies, the Duncombes were fortunate in having the ruins of a genuine abbey, Rievaulx, in their grounds. In about 1758 a second terrace was made, directly overlooking the abbey ruins, and at intervals trees on the steep bank were cut away so that a series of carefully composed views of the abbey ruins revealed themselves to promenaders. This astonishingly beautiful ½-mile walk along Rievaulx Terrace (a National Trust property) starts from the Tuscan Temple and moves towards the Ionic Temple, which contains some startlingly ugly furniture by William Kent. There have been plans to link both terraces so that the resulting drive would be about 3 miles long.

sham ruined tower, meant to be seen from both sides. Great care has been taken to detail the building with sham features, even on the inside, although it was never more than an empty shell. It received its name from the De Mowbrays, fierce medieval knights who lived near here, and the romance was augmented by the fact that almost all of them died violent deaths.

Above Fountain Plain stands the Mowbray Point Banqueting House, with a ruined Gothic servant's hall not far away. Mowbray Point has two distinct façades, one turned towards the fields and showing an Elysian Greek front (or back). The other faces the great expanse of land beyond Hackfall itself. This façade represents a fake Roman ruin: there are three arches of crumbling sandstone, looking like a minor edition of the Caracalla Baths in Rome and perhaps inspired by the engravings of sham Roman ruins in Langley's 1728 publication.

For the first edition of this book it took us five separate visits to check all the sites of the follies at Hackfall—or perhaps we were just looking for excuses to revisit the place; desolate as it was, it still retained a powerful fascination, especially on a bleak winter's morning when the place seems to be haunted by Aislabie's ghost inspecting the grounds. The writer of an 1822 guide book caught the place at a happier moment:

To Hackfall's calm retreats, where
nature reigns

Kirkleatham (Cleveland)

Turner Mausoleum (1740)
Gatehouse Arch and Bastions (18th century)
Fortresses (18th century)
NZ 598 217

Marwood Turner of Kirkleatham Hall, now a museum run by the local council, died on the Grand Tour in 1739; he may well have been travelling with John Hall Stevenson of nearby Skelton Castle. The remarkable octagonal (heptagonal if one discounts the church) Turner Mausoleum, with its pyramidal stone roof, built by the great Tory architect James Gibbs in 1740, stands attached to Kirkleatham Church, but that scarcely hints at its monumentality—it utterly dominates the church, which is reduced to the status of a bystander.

> THIS MAUSOLEUM
> WAS ERECTED 1740
> TO THE MEMORY OF
> MARWOOD WILLIAM
> TURNER ESQUIRE

and then hidden round the back:

> THE BEST OF SONS

Much of the facing of the mausoleum, including part of the inscription, has been sensitively restored, but it remains at risk.

Another member of the family, Sir Charles Turner, had a couple of castellated round bastions erected flanking the ha-ha beyond the Hall. These decaying bastions, and the Gothick gatehouse arch now stripped of its crenellations, may have been built by either

The Turner Mausoleum

A tiny fortress at Turner's Hospital

John Carr or William Chambers, both of whom had also worked at Skelton. The bastions and arch, to the east of the main house beyond the palatial stable block, were built about the same time as the publication of Stevenson's 'Crazy Tales', but time and vandalism have accelerated their decay—the elegant and unguarded dressed stone has proved too tempting for local builders.

Some years later two mighty little square fortresses were added to complete the arcades at Turner's Hospital, the nearby almshouse. These are beautifully designed toy forts no more than 12ft (3.6m) high, with battered battlemented turrets squeezing the hint of a central round tower. Who was the architect? Their position in full view of the road has saved them from the fate of the unguarded bastions, for apart from these tiny forts, all the council-owned Grade II* garden buildings on the Kirkleatham Estate have been 'named and shamed' in a 1998 English Heritage Buildings at Risk report.

Levisham

Skelton Tower (1819)
SE 821 930

The Rev. Robert Skelton was an enthusiast for grouse shooting, so keen, in fact, that he built himself a square, two-storey hunting box to save himself the arduous journey to and from the moor from Levisham village. Being mildly romantic, he decorated it with lancet-arched windows and tiny castellations, and so it survived, its original purpose long forgotten, until it was restored in 1978 to commemorate the silver jubilee of the North Yorkshire Moors National Park. It stands high above the North Yorkshire Moors Railway in Newton Dale.

Leyburn

Middleham Castellated Bridge (1829)
SE 119 888
Sham Castle (early 19th century)
SE 110 905

Along the A6108 to Leyburn the road crosses
the Ure by means of a converted suspension
bridge at Middleham. The original
suspension bridge was built in 1829, but
when it was converted to an ordinary bridge
the pylons were medievalized by adding
castellations and blind arrowslits.

Another example of this style is the sham
castle at the back of Thornborough Hall, now
the Rural District Offices. The Hall was built
in 1863 by Joseph Aloysius Hansom, inventor
of the hansom cab and builder of Middleham
Bridge, in partnership with Edward Welch.
The sham castle, hard against a cliff in its
Victorian garden with a small, rustic bridge,
looks several score years earlier than the
mansion, perhaps nearer the date of the
bridge. It consists of a centre block guarded by
two round towers with another shorter tower
on the upper level. The back of the little castle,
just big enough to house the rusting remains
of a Leyburn-built hand mangle, is the cliff
face, and to reach the next storey one has to
walk to the end of the garden and turn back
along an upper path. The council has barred
access to the folly pending restoration work.

Masham Moor

Arnagill Tower (1824)
SE 153 757

Southwest of the Druid's Temple on
Masham Moor is a tiny sham ruined tower,
another Gothic mood piece. It is dated 1824.
Although no further information is available,
the date and situation do suggest William
Danby as the builder.

Middleton Tyas

Tempest's Folly (1990)
NZ 225 055

A folly story rather than a folly—the designer
of the superb Forbidden Corner at Tupgill
built a detached three-storey house in a new
residential development in the shape of a
dovecote, and with no internal walls so the
buyer could specify his own layout. It seems
eminently practical to us, but it was quickly
christened Tempest's Folly. 'I don't see why
everything should be bland and rational,'
complained architect Malcolm Tempest.
Quite so.

Oldstead Tower

Oldstead

Oldstead Tower (1838)
SE 537 804

Just north of the ruins of nearby Byland
Abbey is a belvedere tower, built in the year
that Victoria ascended to the throne by J.
Dodds for John Wormald, a partner in
Child's Bank and father of the famous
surgeon Thomas Wormald. The square
tower is rather austere, with ash railings on
the top and small plain windows. Wormald
correctly felt optimistic about the young
queen's forthcoming reign; a poem above the
door to the tower reads:

> *Here hills and waving groves a scene*
> *display*
> *And part admit and part exclude the day*
> *See rich industry smiling on the plains*
> *And peace and plenty tell VICTORIA*
> *reigns!*
> *Happy the MAN to who these shades*
> *retires*
> *Whom NATURE charms, and whom the*
> *muse inspires*
> *Who wandering thoughtful in this silent*
> *wood*
> *Amends the duties of the wise and good*
> *To observe a mean, being himself a*
> *friend*
> *To follow NATURE and regard his end.*

At the back of the tower:

> *JOHN WORMALD*
> *IN THE FIRST YEAR OF THE*
> *REIGN OF*

QUEEN VICTORIA
CAUSED THIS OBSERVATORY TO
BE ERECTED
J. DODDS BUILDER

Today the use of the word observatory has been restricted to star-viewing chambers, but then it simply meant an outlook tower or belvedere.

Richmond

Culloden Tower (1747)
Obelisk (1771)
NZ 172 100

In the northern part of the beautiful country town of Richmond is Temple Lodge, a Gothic castellated mansion built in 1769 for John Yorke—perhaps the nephew of the Pateley Bridge John Yorke. In the grounds is a glorious Gothic contraption, an octagonal tower on a square base, with an outside staircase, pinnacles and Gothic windows. The Culloden Tower was built in 1747, immediately after the battle, and commemorated the strong involvement of the Yorke family. Joseph Yorke fought at Culloden, while Charles and Philip Yorke were both responsible for legislation concerning the Pretender and his fellow-travellers. Unlike the great majority of follies, the interior of Culloden Tower is sumptuously decorated in the rococo style; even more unlike most follies the decoration is in excellent repair and is likely to remain so, since the tower has been bought by the Landmark Trust. The architect is supposed

to be Daniel Garrett, and the same goes for the Temple at Aske Hall, a mile or so north of the Culloden Tower.

Richmond also has a rather curious obelisk in its market place. It stands on a hexagonal base with niches all round for decoration. The shaft is an elongated sugar loaf shape, topped with a ball finial, like an 18th century ice cream cornet. It was built in 1771, but is the re-erection of an earlier obelisk.

Fyling Hall Pigsty

Robin Hood's Bay

Fyling Hall Pigsty (1883)
NZ 936 042

The romantically named Robin Hood's Bay is so called because the outlaw is supposed to have had ships laid ready here for any necessary escapes. Hidden among the narrow, vertiginous lanes is a palatial pigsty screened by a classical façade, built in 1883 by Squire Barry of Fyling Hall, who was undoubtedly an inspiration and precursor for Wodehouse's Lord Emsworth. It took three men two years to build, because of the squire's constant dithering.

Here the Empresses of Fyling (large whites, for the porcophiles among us) luxuriously wallowed in glorious mud, admiring the tremendous view to the south, until death or loss of interest led to its inevitable dereliction and decay. In 1990 it was cleverly restored and converted by the Landmark Trust into a holiday cottage, replacing four of the six squat, wooden Doric pillars of the façade. The trapezoid windows at the back of the building lend it a distinctly Egyptian air.

Culloden Tower

Saltburn-by-the-Sea (Cleveland)

Albert Memorial (mid-19th century)
NZ 666 217

When Henry Pease, railway promoter, MP for South Durham and member of the Peace Society, brought the railway to the coast in the 1860s, the grim holiday town of Saltburn-by-the-Sea was conceived. It had been Pease's idea to build the town out of white brick 'so that the new resort would gleam like the celestial city', but he was not to foresee that white bricks were soon to become the favoured material of builders of public lavatories. The original celestial city was built from chalcedony, chrysolite, sardonyx and sapphire, while Saltburn makes do with Emerald, Coral, Diamond and Pearl Streets. It still has all the trappings of a successful seaside town—plenty of hotels, a municipal park with a miniature railway running up the dene—but somehow it never caught on, although it is currently billed as the Windsurfing Capital of the North. Presumably the windsurfers wear dry suits.

The Albert Memorial in the Valley Gardens is a brave but now disgusting attempt to brighten a bleak holiday, which even the best folly could not save. This classical portico was the façade to Barnard Castle railway station—did Pease want to preserve a favourite building or was he merely economizing? Whatever his motives, the motives of the late 20th century are more clearly read: spend as little as possible on maintenance and then abandon the structure to druggies and smackheads. Broken glass, needles and discarded rubbers make visiting the site more dangerous than sublime.

Scarborough

Baron Albert's Tower (1842)
Peaseholme Park Pagoda (1929)
TA 036 894

Do not be misled by the 75ft (23m) obelisk on the summit of Oliver's Mount, from where the sea and surrounding countryside provide spectacular views. It is a war memorial. South of the town is Baron Albert's Tower of 1842, a ruin, though never meant as such. The tower takes its name from the builder, Albert Denison, 1st Baron Londesborough, who as President of the British Archaeological Association was very much interested in Saxon tumuli. In the 1990s it was proposed to make the site of the tower a focus of a council-sponsored Round Scarborough Walk, but a curious objection

Peasholme Park Pagoda

was raised by a local resident, the Ministry of Defence, which was worried that publicity for the folly would draw attention to the nearby top secret Composite Signals Operations Station at Irton Moor.

Just inland from North Bay is one of Scarborough's many public gardens, Peasholme Park. This japonesque park was begun at the height of the fashion, in Edwardian times. It's all here—a glen, miniature lakes, a cascade tumbling down the cliff from the pagoda and two islands in the main lake, artfully improved from the natural beauty of the dene. Its setting recalls the Parc du Buttes-Chaumont in Paris, but with more fun. The buildings, a floating bandstand, a café and the *pièce de résistance*, the Pagoda, are all in the Japanese style. The colourful, two-storey, 30ft (9m) high pagoda was designed by George W. Alderson as late as 1929. At night during the season the large waterfall is illuminated, and, to add to all these pleasures, mock naval battles are fought on the lake twice a week between May and September; a pleasant revival of a popular folly pastime. The park is tremendously popular, always crowded.

Scotch Corner

Sedbury Park Watch Tower (1795)
NZ 200 005

Spaghetti Junction and Scotch Corner are perhaps the only nationally known crossroads; here the Scotch traffic heading north turned off to Carlisle and Dumfries, while Watling Street continues north to Durham and Northumberland. At Sedbury Park nearby there is a little watch tower, exquisitely sited on an outcrop of rock, which was built for Sir Robert D'Arcy Hildyard by the Richmond architect John Foss. The splendidly castellated farm buildings on the estate are earlier, and may have been designed by the prolific John Carr who worked here in 1770.

Skelton (Cleveland)

Wellhead (mid-18th century)
Grotto (19th century)
NZ 650 193

A hundred years or so before its venture into tourism, the Saltburn beach saw a helter-skelter chariot race. One chariot was driven by the Rev. Laurence Sterne, and the other by John Hall Stevenson, squire of Skelton Castle, Sterne's cousin by choice and a lesser known writer of facetious books. In between beach races at Saltburn, sojourns at Scarborough and 'fact-finding' trips to London, Stevenson resided at Skelton Castle, a mile or two south of Saltburn. He had a fortune to spend and professed that his only aim in life was enjoyment. After some years of steady application to this self-imposed task, he had become a drunkard and a near bankrupt. He started his career as a rake by leaving Cambridge without a degree, but not before first becoming Sterne's bosom pal. Italy awaited him, so Stevenson set off on his Grand Tour in 1738. He returned safe and spoilt, and some years later inherited Skelton Castle. South of the house he had a souvenir of his Grand Tour erected—a classical rusticated wellhead temple, supplying the mansion with water. Under some medallions with inscriptions in Latin a plaque reads:

> *Leap from thy cavern'd mossy bed,*
> *Hither thy prattling waters bring.*
> *Blandusia's Muse shall crown thy head*
> *And make thee too a sacred Spring.*

Skelton Castle itself, heavily castellated, was used by the Hell Fire-type 'club of demoniacks', founded by Stevenson, Sterne and other libertines for convivial evenings. They probably also had the run of Stevenson's large pornographic library. The 'demoniacks' referred to Skelton as Crazy Castle, the name it also took in Stevenson's *Crazy Tales* (1762). It is doubtful whether the club met as well in the grotto situated in the bank of the castle's moat, for that appears to be 19th century. The castle is now guarded by keypad entry gates, so casual visitors are discouraged.

Sneaton Moor

Falling Foss Hermitage (1790)
NZ 888 035

The 45ft (14m) Falling Foss (or Force) in a valley on Sneaton Moor is an impressive waterfall for England, not a country abundant in real cascades. In the vicinity of the aptly named Midge Hall in Newton Woods is a hermitage hollowed out of the solid rock. A pointed entrance leads into a room where up to 20 people can be seated. The rock itself is inscribed '*The Hermitage*' and '*G + C 1790*'. Newton Hall, not far away, has an obelisk to the memory of James Brown who 'made the moor blossom like a rose'.

Swinton

Classical Dovecote (18th century)
SE 731 788

Masham is home of the famous Old Peculier beer, named after the Peculier of Masham, a medieval official. Just south of the town a signpost on the right points to Nutwith Cote Farm, a small mansion also known as Old Swinton Hall. Until recently it contained a Chinese wallpapered room. One of the outbuildings stands on a base where beehives have been spaced out, one of only two such arrangements in the country. Past the house is a ruined classical dovecote on a little knoll, still looking austere and dignified. In former times Nutwith was a resting place for monks on their way from Rievaulx to Fountains. There is local talk of an ancient tunnel, used by the monks in order to pass under the River Ure, which flows through the Nutwith Estate.

Druid's Temple (1800)
SE 175 787

New Swinton Hall is only a mile or so to the west, near Ilton. It was built by the owner himself, William Danby (1752–1833), with a little help from James Wyatt, John Foss and Robert Lugar. Building went on for a remarkable 50 years, well into the 1820s, and Swinton's central tower, by Lugar, can almost be counted as a folly in its own right. Danby was a good example of the English eccentric. From the Hall he saw several of his literary works published, mostly written in his old age. They consist of four illuminating volumes of Thoughts: *Travelling Thoughts*, *Thoughts chiefly on Serious Subjects*, *Thoughts on Various Subjects and Ideas and Realities*, with an additional *Extracts from Young's Night Thoughts, with Observations upon them*, which was published a year before his death. It wasn't only his literary ambitions that flowered late; by the time Danby took to crenellating his mansion his thoughts also turned on relieving the unemployment in the area.

The first project was the labour-intensive work of creating another Stonehenge, with a shilling a day paid to the workers. No common or garden stone circle this. Like a true Yorkshireman, Mr Danby believed that a job had to be done properly if it was to be done at all. An enormous oval of altars, menhirs, dolmens, sarsens and other phallic and neo-Druidical paraphernalia was raised on the Yorkshire moors. Several solitary standing stones lined a ceremonial avenue leading to the temple. It is well preserved in the middle of Forestry Commission land, an unnatural object unnaturally surrounded by gloomy evergreens and popular with picnickers. Vandals come off second best

A sham cromlech at the Druid's Temple

against these massive monoliths, but make their presence known in other ways. Baroness Masham has led a campaign to change the name of the Druid's Temple, on the grounds that it attracted the wrong sort of visitor—in June 1993 a severed pig's head was discovered on the main altar stone. Now that the more famous Stonehenge is off-limits to everyone bar bureaucrats, the attention of the solstice seeker has been drawn to this lesser circle, with inevitable consequences.

That new name—how about Shamhenge?

A 1910 guide to the district repeats the old hermit story, claiming that the builder of the temple offered to provide any individual with food, and a subsequent annuity, providing he would reside in the temple for seven years, living the primitive life, speaking to no one and allowing his beard and hair to grow. It is claimed that one man underwent this self-imposed infliction for four-and-a-half years, at the end of which he was compelled to admit defeat. Several others made the attempt but gave up. If this is true, this is by far the longest tenure we have come across in any of the hermit stories. Visiting the Druid's Temple on a windy January afternoon we were astonished that anyone could have lasted four and a half minutes, let alone four and a half years there. Towards the west through the trees a view has been left open towards Leighton Reservoir, lying far below in the valley.

The Mount (1830)
SE 202 795

When writing his observations upon Young's *Night Thoughts*, Danby undertook another enterprise: the building of Quarry Gill Bridge, south of Swinton. This is a Gothic bridge, designed by Foss, forming an ensemble with The Mount, the nearby seat from where Danby could watch the deer sauntering in the lowlands. The Mount, a castellated half-hexagonal room over open arcading, served as viewpoint, eyecatcher and screen for a farm cottage, and allowed Danby to be left to his own night thoughts when the sun set and the damp filtered through the blankets covering his body. A year later he was dead, aged 81. Robert Southey, who visited him some time before his death, thought much of Danby, and so did his villagers. They lost a benevolent employer and a considerate landlord, who happily opened his private grounds to the public.

Thirsk

Pattison's Folly (1920)
SE 430 821

A trifle: a jeweller's shop in Castlegate was outfitted by Mr Thomas Stokes with tiny castellations in the 1920s. This was scarcely worth noting until an extension was needed in the 1980s, and sensing that the building may have been built on part of the earthworks for Thirsk Castle, torn down by Henry II in 1184, the owners decided to continue the castellations. Work on the new extension revealed foundations 10ft (3m) below the presbytery garden next door, which led the owner to infer the Thirsk Castle theory may have been true. 'I was a bit sceptical about creating a bigger folly than the one that was already there, but the design symbolizes Thirsk Castle,' said Charles Pattison defensively.

Tupgill

The Forbidden Corner (1990 to date)
SE 090 865

The door through which you entered the room has slammed shut. It cannot be reopened. You are surrounded by eight identical doors. You cannot go back. You must go on. Start walking around the pool in the middle of this octagonal room and you quickly lose any sense of orientation. This door opens into an oak-panelled and richly carpeted staircase. This door… is locked. This door opens on to a blank wall. A corridor leads away behind this door. Which to choose? Calmly now, count the doors. Eliminate the impossible, and what remains must be the possible. Right, let's leave a marker here by this locked door and we'll try each of the others in turn. That done, here's the marker. But the door is now unlocked. Has the marker moved? Has the marker been moved? Are we quite alone? Choose one of the doors at random, quickly, and scuttle down the corridor to another much smaller circular room, lighter yet more oppressive.

A rustic Corinthian corner

Just six doors to choose from here. While you decide, the doors seem to move in front of your face. Steady now—no, it's the floor of the room. It is actually turning, slowly, slowly as you puzzle over which door to take. Stand still and make your selection. Every path leads to a rediscovered childhood.

This extraordinary private fantasy 2 miles southwest of Middleham in the wilds of the

The Glass Pyramid at The Forbidden Corner

North Yorkshire dales has the ability to reverse the ageing process. Octogenarians emerge as eight-year-olds, teenagers as judges; there are places that are physically accessible only by the very small. As you push deeper into its secrets, you begin to suspect that the builder may quietly have overturned the law of gravity, and soon you will be walking—no, prancing—among the ceilings and pinnacles of this fantastick garden. Because this is a garden; we have no other word to describe what has been created here. On a larger, loucher, commercial scale this would be a theme park, but here tawdriness and profit have been forbidden

A welcoming face at The Forbidden Corner

entry and only magic penetrates. It is a garden, a pure folly garden.

It would be invidious to deconstruct this astonishing and delightful paradise, to take you through it step by step and reveal all its hidden treasures. Better by far is for you to go and experience it for yourself, because you can and must go. The owner, Colin Armstrong, allows the public to visit it most summer Sundays, and if you have a taste for the strange and the curious, if you have read *Tristram Shandy* and *Through the Looking-Glass* and can recite *The Jabberwocky* by heart, it will be like coming home. Just a few words of advice: check everything you see before walking through to the next stage of the garden, because there's no going back. As we said at the beginning, the doors close behind you, and they cannot be reopened. Malcolm Tempest, the creator of this

unrivalled reverie for Mr Armstrong, is too practical and commonsensical to propose a metaphysical theory for his dream garden, but even the simplest mind will grasp that this is a metaphor for life, its perils, pleasures and mysteries. There's no turning back—but whatever you do, you must follow the stepping stones.

Around the 4 acre (1.6ha) garden the same coat of arms is occasionally discovered, and as a gilded weathervane it proudly tops the stable block. Rather gruesomely it consists of a mailed fist clutching a severed leg gouting blood. Was this a feared and ancient heraldic device of the Armstrong family, we wondered? 'No,' came Tempest's blunt reply. 'It's just that this whole place has cost an arm and a leg.'

West Witton

Polly Peachum's Tower (c.1750)
Bolton Hall Tower (19th century)
`SE 085 882`

On top of Capple Bank, a hill between West Witton and Agglethorpe in Wensleydale, stands the ruin of a square, classical, two-storey tower, built of rough stone but with dressed quoins. The ruin can be seen from the road and a short climb from the side up the slope brings you to it. Sheep now inhabit it and have some of the best views in Wensleydale. It has a romantic story attached to it, which for once may even be true. The house directly opposite, on the other side of the valley, is Bolton Hall, once belonging to Charles Paulet, 3rd Duke of Bolton. In or before 1728 Paulet started an affair with the celebrated actress and singer Lavinia Fenton, who was all the rage for her role as Polly Peachum in John Gay's *The Beggar's Opera*. Hogarth painted the scene, with the duke in one of the boxes. By this time Paulet had separated from his wife, and la Fenton was to bear him three children. In 1751, his wife having died, he married the actress. It may have been around this time (if they were discreet, which we are assured they were) that he could build her this summer pavilion, and Lavinia Paulet was indeed extremely pleased with the little folly, admiring the views from it whenever she was in Yorkshire. Of course, there is a variant to this story: the duke built her this small tower so that she could rehearse her singing there undisturbed, and one author uncharitably asserts 'the tower is miles from anywhere—she must have had a lousy voice!' No, she didn't.

As we looked out towards Bolton Hall (nearer to Wensley than to West Witton) and the ridge above it, we appeared to begin to suffer from mirages—in this case aroused by a rare medical condition known as folly fatigue. It can't have been the climb, even we could manage that. Across the valley, set in the woodlands surrounding the Hall we could see a grey-whitish tower. We focused our binoculars but couldn't get a very good view even then, although it was surely a tall, free-standing tower. And further from Bolton Hall, on the ridge itself, in the meadows and with a backdrop of trees we could see another item—indefinable, more broad than high—an ornamental cascade and temple? But what was it doing there? We couldn't find the latter folly, and mirage it must have been, nor could we find the Bolton tower—we encircled the private woods via a wheatfield and the sloping grasslands almost until we had reached the bottom of the valley again—surely this tower ought to be visible from here. In the end we gave up, and on consulting Pevsner found he doesn't mention a tower at Bolton, so that's all right then. A week later we heard someone mention the tower at Bolton Hall: 'Have you seen that? I know some people who have. Apparently it's marvellous. Tall, large, light coloured stonework, can't miss it once you're there. Can't miss it. It was in that Wilkie Collins TV play, *The Woman In White*. Didn't you see it?' Grr.

Yarm (Cleveland)

Yarm Castle (1882)
NZ 420 120

Yarm Castle by Commondale House in West Street was built by 18-year-old David Doughty. He spent much of his youth in creating the castle, which towers up to 2ft (60cm) high on the top of a garden wall, safely out of Yarm's way. He decorated the castle, which is said to represent the real but long-vanished Yarm Castle, with over 800 windows, coloured to represent all the known gemstones at the time (David was also ardent about minerals). Next to it is a model of the Town Hall, which still stands in the middle of Yarm's broad and delightful high street. Further down in the garden are a couple of churches, some sham fragments and two armoured knights made of concrete. They have survived since the 19th century, a rare longevity in gnomic circles. Doughty grew up to head the Yarm Gas Company, a change of direction as he had originally planned to light the interior of his castle with electric light so all the colours in the windows would shine clearly out. Was this ever done?

Yarm Castle

EAST RIDING

Brough

Palmer Obelisk (1873)
SE 938 273

In the grounds of a house in Cave Road stands a large obelisk, a memorial to Brigadier-General Thomas Palmer, who died in 1854. It was erected 19 years after his death by his cousin, Thomas William Palmer of Brough House.

Carnaby

Carnaby Temple (1770)
TA 141 666

Just outside Bridlington is one of the great East Riding follies, Carnaby Temple. It is a self-willed reworking by John Carr of the Temple of the Winds in Athens, splendidly sited in the open, amid fields that stretch for miles until they disappear into the sea. We first visited it on a hot, breathless day in early summer; it was rare for there not to be a sharp little breeze, but the air was fat and humid. In addition, we had attacked it from the wrong side, having no map, and had walked for 20 minutes with hope diminishing before catching a glimpse of it 2 miles away. The descriptions of its condition were wrong; work had recently been done on it to preserve it from the whims of weather and the more determined vandal. Octagonal, brick-built, two-storeyed with an ogee roof with the motif repeated on the lantern above, it had its roof tarred and its windows sealed up; there was also evidence of some repointing work on the bricks. It was obviously intended for preservation. An outhouse was stuck on a mound at the back when the tower was lived in, but curiously it did not detract from the elegance of the structure.

Carnaby Temple was built for Sir George Strickland of Boynton Hall, who also had a late medieval summerhouse Gothicized at the same time. When we visited it again after a gap of some 20 years it appeared to be in an identical condition. The dome inside is still plastered and most of the coving remains, as does a short rotten wooden staircase emerging through a yard of bird droppings up to the few pieces of planking which make up the main floor. This could yet make another Landmark Trust holiday cottage. Early photographs show it surrounded by an orchard, with other buildings in the vicinity, but nothing of these remains above ground. It was last used as a Home Guard look-out in World War II, but one of its prime uses before then had apparently been to act as a look-out for the 'chucker' from boats entering Bridlington Harbour. This was contraband thrown overboard by smugglers before the excise check, its position noted so it could be retrieved later.

Cottingham

Thompson's Folly or
Castle Hill Tower (1825)
TA 023 322

In the grounds of Castle Hill Hospital at Cottingham is a 40ft (12m) Gothic octagonal

Castle Hill Tower, Cottingham

tower of pale cream brick. It was built as an eyecatcher for Cottingham Castle, completed in 1816 but now demolished. The tower was a belvedere for viewing the River Humber and 'the lovely land on every side'. At the top was a topograph to identify the visible landmarks, with edifying quotations from poets such as Cowper and Goldsmith. Folly and castle were owned by the banker and Member of Parliament Thomas Thompson, father of the Benthamite General Thomas Perrouet Thompson, whose real claim to fame was as the inventor of the 'Enharmonic Guitar'.

Carnaby Temple

Elloughton Castle

Perhaps the folly was built as a music room to keep the noise of the inventor's creation at a civilized distance from the house. Roofless and hollow, the tower stands on a little nettle-covered mound in a strip of woodland by the A164.

Elloughton

The Castle (1886)
SE 942 278

Elloughton has one of those confusing edifices called the Castle, where a passing reference in an old guidebook can start a wild-goose chase, which more often than not ends at a bungalow with flowerpots spaced along the roof. A 'castle' can range from a humble lodge to a megalomaniac pile of Fonthillian dimensions. This one is in-between and late—a substantial white stuccoed 1886 villa bordering a golf course at the end of Mill Lane, amply justifying its name with its thicket of castellations.

Grimston

Grimston Garth (1781–86)
TA 283 351

Ten miles south of Hornsea is Grimston Garth, a large, triangular house built by John Carr for Thomas Grimston in the 1780s, at the height of fashion for triangular buildings. The triangle, with three castellated round towers at its apices, thrusts southwards, with a

lower service courtyard, also castellated, behind it to the north. The centre tower contains both a Gothick and a Chinese room. Around 1812 the Gatehouse was added: battlements, turrets and a portcullis, a particularly true-to-history embellishment, which was to become so popular through J.C. Loudon's engravings of gateways. John Earle, a mason from Hull, worked on the gatehouse, but it is not clear whether he was the architect or not. The house is in splendid condition, superbly looked after and beautifully decorated. It is ingeniously kept that way by preventing access to casual visitors, who have to negotiate a secure factory complex with gates, floodlights and guards before reaching the drive to the house.

Grimston Garth

Halsham

Constable Mausoleum (1794–1802)
TA 270 279

We keep feeling that mausoleums should not be included in books that celebrate the follies of mankind, but then we discover another splendid example of horrendously expensive 18th-century architecture that has been abandoned and ignored by the dynasty it was supposed to glorify. Here, at the end of an avenue of yews off what is now the B1362, Edward Constable of Burton Constable Hall employed the elderly Catholic architect Thomas Atkinson to construct a beautiful, circular, blind-arcaded building with a stone domed roof, very crisp dressed white ashlar, very Soanian, standing on a large plinth with a fine double staircase rising to it—Atkinson's last building, completed after his death. It took eight years to build and 200 years to forget. As its function fails, it falls into folly. The mausoleum carries its years gracefully, and unusually it has resisted the attentions of graffiti artists—not a single uninvited carving or daub of paint disfigures its noble visage. Atkinson was also responsible for the folly bastion at Bishopthorpe for the Archbishop of York.

Hornsea

Bettison's Folly (1844)
TA 203 474

Hornsea, famous for its pottery, has a 50ft (15m) castellated, round, brick tower called Bettison's Folly, engulfed and topped by trees, dark brown brick enlivened with knobs of protruding, burned, misshapen bricks, making it look a little like a charred and chewed corn on the cob. These are locally called honey bricks, normally useless for building as they have been overcooked and distorted by heat in the kiln. The tower was erected by Mr Bettison for the purposes of carriage-watching; the idea was that servants should try to sight their master's gig coming up the Hull road so that they could serve dinner the moment he burst into the house demanding food. The story of how it got its name is so ordinary as to be almost certainly true: shortly after it was built, a young sailor shinned up it and hung a piece of cardboard from the top, proclaiming it to be Bettison's Folly. It is one of the two follies in the country we have discovered to have a retractable flagpole, the other being the ruined Powderham Belvedere in Devon. At Bettison's Folly the flagpole rises the whole height of the tower (how did they get it in?), capped on the roof by a piece of plastic piping. A winch on the second storey raises it the height of two full floors above the parapets, and it is held in place with a mighty cotter pin. The English flag is flown on St George's Day, fortunately before all the leaves on the surrounding trees conspire to conceal the tower. Bettison's own house has long disappeared to be replaced by a drab 1960s old people's home, which will itself shortly disappear to make way for a new housing estate.

Hunmanby

Arch (1809)
TA 099 768

The sporting squire Humphrey Osbaldeston lived in Hunmanby Hall, near the coast. His more famous brother, George, lived a few miles away at Hutton Bushel. Humphrey built himself an 'Early English' gateway to the hall, using stones from the Filey Brigg cliff. People protested, but the squire paid no heed, continuing his work until the ruined gateway was complete to his satisfaction. Inevitably, coastal erosion was accelerated and continues to this day. One can scarcely blame a folly for losing a few acres of prime Yorkshire land to the North Sea, but it certainly was a contributing factor. Nevertheless it makes a pretty sham ruin, with the pointed windows on both sides of the arch covered in creeper. Hunmanby Gate is supposed to have been erected in 1809, although Thomas Allen in his *History of the County of York* (1831), asserts that the date is 1829.

Hull

Wilberforce Column (1834)
TA 093 284

Hull was the birthplace of the slave emancipator William Wilberforce and consequently has the Doric 90ft (27m) Wilberforce Column in Queen's Gardens. It was put up with funds provided by public subscription the year after the great man's death in 1833. The Humber Bridge, briefly the world's longest suspension bridge, is the least likely place in Britain to find a traffic jam.

North Cave

Castle Farm (early 19th century)
SE 907 333

Castle Farm is a large and comfortable house, which once served as an eyecatcher to

Hotham Hall. Now its castellations have been removed, and little folly feeling remains other than the open arcade supporting the first-floor bay window, topped by a curious double-ridged roof.

North Grimston

Horseshoe Piles (mid-20th century)
SE 843 677

Scarrington in Nottinghamshire has the most famous and best-documented horseshoe pile in the country, but everything in Yorkshire is bigger and better, so here we have not one, not two but three tall horseshoe piles, not quite as high as the Scarrington one but cumulatively much bigger. As one might expect.

Horseshoe piles at North Grimston

Riccall

Gothic Folly (mid-19th century)
SE 622 376

Riccall Hall, the 18th-century seat of the Wormley family, was torn down in 1951. The servant's wing was retained, converted into a smaller house and assumed the name. An estate agent, advertising a development opportunity called Beckwith Hall Drive on part of the site in 1994, mentioned the house, stables, four building plots and a Gothic folly. This turned out to be a three-arched alcove, probably left over from some mid-Victorian extension to the house, whitewashed and of no discernible interest.

Scampston

Deer House (late 18th century)
SE 865 766

Scampston Hall is on the A64 leading towards the coast. Capability Brown worked here in 1772–75 for Sir William St Quintin. The classical bridge with pavilion near the house, at the edge of the lake, was built to Brown's specifications. At the back of the pavilion is a tiny cascade with a wooden rustic bridge spanning it, probably of the same period. Further to the south is the Deer House, which is Gothick—for some reason most of them are. It is a castellated 'cottage'— six bedrooms, three bathrooms, 20 acres (8ha)—and was sold separately from the Hall for nearly £300,000 in 1992. One of the conditions of English Heritage funding in 1997 means that Scampston Hall has had to be opened to the public for the first time in 300 years.

Seaton

Mushroom Cottage (1812)
TA 171 466

At Wassand Hall, Seaton, a little inland from Hornsea, is Mushroom Cottage, a *cottage orné* with just the right ingredients: thatched roof supported by rustic pillars and Gothic windows. It was built by Thomas Cundy in 1812–14, the same time as the Hall.

Sledmere

Sykes's Follies (mid-19th century)
SE 933 646

The major folly group in the East Riding is at Sledmere, home of the Sykes family. A century and a half of sustained folly building by that remarkable clan, stretching from the last quarter of the 18th century to World War I, has left a confusion of monuments, memorials and eyecatchers. Two Marks, two Tattons and two Christophers were responsible, but patience and a steady hand will reveal the provenance of the follies.

It starts with Sir Christopher Sykes, the 2nd Baronet, a great agricultural improver, expressing an aptitude that runs in the family. Castle Farm, thought by many (but not us) to be the best folly in the group, serves as an eyecatcher in Lancelot Brown's landscape, after the park had been enclosed in 1776. The building was originally intended as a dower house, but Mother preferred to stay in the main house. Although Sir Christopher designed many of the farm buildings himself,

Tatton Sykes Monument

around this time, but there is no record of the architect or when it was built.

Sir Christopher eventually got his memorial in 1840, 39 years after his death. The village well was given a classical rotunda as a canopy by Sir Tatton Sykes, a famous sportsman and stockbreeder. It was his son, also named Tatton, who became the family's true eccentric. He inherited in 1863 and straightway donned the mantle of autocrat.

Soon after his mother, who adored flowers and gardens, died, Sir Tatton had the lawns and flowerbeds ploughed up, forbidding the villagers to grow the 'nasty, untidy things' around their cottages. 'If they have to grow flowers,' he rumbled, 'let them grow cauliflowers.' Another bewildering measure was to forbid his tenants the use of their front doors; newly erected houses were given *trompe l'oeil* front doors. As a builder Sir Tatton was enthusiastic, to say the least. He decided to repair and restore the churches in this part of the East Riding, and together with the architect Temple Moore he tackled quite a number of them, developing the Tatton style as he went along and disbursing over £2,000,000 in the process.

In 1865 there appeared on Garton Hill, 3 miles south of the house, the finest folly in Humberside and one of the best in Britain. The Sir Tatton Sykes Memorial Tower by J. Gibbs (not the famous one) probably had more to do with the warmth of local remembrance for the old squire than with the not so very fond memories the younger Tatton had of his father, who habitually sent his son on long voyages so as not to have to endure him at home. It was 'Erected to the memory of Sir Tatton Sykes Bart by those who loved him as a friend and honoured as a landlord'. The memorial consists of a 120ft (36.6m) pyramidal Gothic tower with bas-relief plaques round the base—one showing old Sir Tatton on horseback, another decorated with agricultural emblems—and inscriptions such as *The Memory of the Just Is Blessed* running as a frieze round the four sides of the structure. The main features of this horrific and utterly compelling monument are hardly describable: they constitute a full frontal attack on the rules of architecture and taste as anybody has ever known them. Nevertheless, it undeniably fulfils the primary function of a monument—that is, to draw attention to itself—and it has remained standing in a very exposed position for 120 years.

Sir Tatton and Temple Moore later erected their own monument in 1895, the

Castle Farm was almost certainly designed by John Carr. It was intended to resemble a gatehouse and provides a competent façade for hiding the house itself, although there is no record of it actually being used as a farm building until 1895. There is a highly personal architectural touch between the two sturdy towers flanking the 'gateway'—tall castellations pierced alternately with arches and quatrefoils. The individuality of the building's architecture has led to its being attributed to Brown himself or even Joseph Rose, a plasterer who worked for the Wyatts. Another eyecatcher, a pedimented arch on a hilltop near the B1251, probably dates from

A detail of the Waggoners' Memorial

Eleanor Cross just outside the walls of the park, a copy of the Northampton cross. Not surprisingly, there was no memorial for this Sir Tatton when he died in 1913, but there was to be yet another—the Wagonners' Memorial. Sir Mark Sykes, the heir, was something of a traveller, probably in his turn running away from a stifling parent. He had been to the Middle East several times and had installed a Turkish Room in the house. In 1912 he raised a company of Yorkshire Wagonners. He occupied himself during the war by designing their memorial, a squat column decorated with rural and then battle scenes, the basic impression being that of the Trajan Column inside a highly ornamented wine press and squeezed to the point of bursting. The monument was erected immediately after Sir Mark's own death in 1919, the last of a long line of memorials at Sledmere. David Hockney painted the Wagonners' Memorial in a series of Yorkshire landscapes he produced in 1997.

South Cave

Cave Castle Gatehouse (1875)
SE 922 315

Cave Castle is a square Gothic concoction with four corner towers, built for B. Barnard by Henry Hakewill in 1804. Hakewill's forte was Gothic, especially Tudor Gothic, castles. Parts of the house were demolished in the 1930s, the building already having been tampered with in 1875, and now it is converted

into an hotel and golf course there has been an unfortunate single-storey extension to the entrance front. The Castle was not beautiful to begin with, and this hasn't helped. The over-ambitious gateway on the A1034 is flanked by two bears gardant. The drive they guard so menacingly no longer leads to the house, but to a separate housing estate.

A bear on Cave Castle Gateway

Glossary

acroterion (*pl.* **acroteria**): lit. highpoint, generally referring to statues on plinths placed on the parapet of a building

architrave: the lintel supporting the pediment on top of a column

arrowslit (window): a narrow window allowing an archer both protection and a field of fire

bartizan: a turret usually corbelled out from and supported by a corner wall

batter/battered: a wall sloping inwards as it rises from a base

belvedere: from the Italian for beautiful view; a tower or room with a pleasing aspect or vista

chattri: from the Hindu, meaning a memorial

chinoiserie: decorative elements in a Chinese style, fashionable in the 18th century as China was being opened up to Europe

compo: a composition mixture of cement and lime used as a render, not always having the intended adhesive properties

cottage orné: from the French for ornamental cottage, where a building's picturesque quality was more important than its function

diocletian (window): a semi-circular window usually emphasised with two thick mullions at 30 and 150 degrees

distyle: a portico with two columns in front

doocot: the Scots term for a dovecote

exedra: a semi-circular wall

ferme ornée: from the French for ornamental farm, where a building's picturesque quality was more important than its function

feuillée: (French for leafed, leafy) a copse or grove on a hilltop; a word used by the Normans and mutated by Anglo-Saxons into 'folly'. Hence 'Folly Farm', 'Folly Hill' when no such building existed.

flambeau: a decorative carving or moulding representing a torch of burning flames

gloriette: a colonnaded loggia or walkway, usually on a prominent mound or hillock; sometimes on top of a building

harled: a Scottish rendering similar to pebbledash

helix (*pl.* **helices**): the spiral form of a nautilus or uncurled fern, used as volutes in Ionic and Corinthian capitals

hood moulds: projecting ledges over windows and doors originally to protect them from water damage, later used ornamentally

hexastyle: with six columns in front

lucarne: a tiny dormer window usually used to admit light into a spire or other steeply pitched roof

lunette: a little moon, a small half moon window

machicolations: holes in a projecting parapet for pouring boiling oil on attackers

modillion: small ornamental bracket under a cornice

monopteros: from the Greek, a circular single colonnaded temple

oeil-de-boeuf: from the French for bull's eye, a small but prominent round window

ogee: an arch which curves first one way and then the other

palmette: a decorative carving or moulding representing a palm leaf

pargeting: ornamental patterning in exterior plaster work, popular in East Anglia

pediment: the triangular end of a roof above a colonnaded portico

pilaster: a column-like motif usually flat against a building's wall

quatrefoil: a pattern, moulding or window in the shape of a four-leafed clover

reredos: literally rear back wall; the screen in a church which separates the choir from the nave

Romanesque: in a Roman style, usually involving round-headed arches

rusticated: stone blocks carefully fashioned to look unfinished or rough-hewn

sharawaggi: an English word dating from *c.* 1670, said to derive from a Chinese or Japanese dialect word meaning the felicitous placement of objects and structures in a landscape, a kind of outdoor feng-shui

souterrain: underground

spandrel: the triangle formed at the intersection of the ribs of a vault

spirelet: a little spire

tempietto: a little temple, particularly Italian in style

tetralithon: literally 'four stones', a cromlech

tetrastyle: having four columns at the front

tholos: a round building, a dome or cupola

tympanum (*pl.* **tympana**): literally a drum; the space bounded by a pediment

vermiculated: a pattern in rusticated stone giving the appearance of worm casts

Bibliography

The following is a comprehensive listing of reference material consulted in the preparation of this volume, but we should point out that we do not include the numerous eighteenth- and nineteenth-century county histories, old tourist guides and guidebooks to gardens and/or follies, or articles and books concerning one specific folly or architect. Because of the bulk of material in *Country Life*, articles from that magazine have not been specified here either. Extensively used were the volumes of *The Royal Commission on Historical Monuments*, *The Victoria County Histories*, *The Shell County Guides*, Arthur Mee's *The King's England* series, *Garden History: the Journal of the Garden History Society* and *The Journal of Garden History*. Most references for this new edition have been gleaned from the now indispensable quarterly *Follies: The International Magazine for Follies, Grottoes and Garden Buildings*, and some more information came from its sister-publication for the Netherlands and Belgium: the *Nieuwsbrief De DonderbergGroep*. For reasons of space we were not able to list articles in all the afore-mentioned magazines either. We should also like to acknowledge our special debt to Barbara Jones's *Follies and Grottoes*, Nikolaus Pevsner's *The Buildings of England, Scotland and Wales* series, the many volumes of the *Dictionary of National Biography* and Howard Colvin's *Biographical Dictionary of British Architects: 1600—1840*.

Julia Abel Smith, *Pavilions in Peril*, London, 1987

A. Aikman, *Treehouses*, London, 1989

M. Aldrich, *Gothic Revival*, London, 1994

J.J.C. Andrews, *The Well-Built Elephant and Other Roadside Attractions*, New York, 1984

Anon., *Decorations for Parks and Gardens*, London, 1790

Anon., *The Rise and Progress of the Present Taste in Planting Parks, Pleasure Grounds, Gardens, &c.*, London, 1767 (reprinted Newcastle-upon-Tyne, 1970)

J. Alexander, 'Follies', *Lincolnshire & Humberside Arts Diary*, 1977

B.J. Archer, *Follies: architecture for the late twentieth-century landscape*, New York, 1983

M. Archer, *Indian Architecture and the British*, Feltham, 1968

C. Aslet, 'Pavilioned in Extravagant Splendour', *The Times*, 1983

P. Atterbury and C. Wainwright, *Pugin: a gothic passion*, New Haven and London, 1994

W.A. Bagley, 'Some Sussex Follies', *Sussex County Magazine*, 1937

R.C. Bald, 'Sir William Chambers and the Chinese Garden', *Journal of the History of Ideas*, 1950

J. Baltrusaitis, *Aberrations: quatre essais sur la legende des formes*, Paris, 1987

— 'Jardins et pays d'illusion', *Traverses*, 1976

F. Barker and R. Hyde, *London As It Might Have Been*, London, 1982

N. Barlow and S. Sample Aall, *Follies and Fantasies: Germany and Austria*, New York, 1994

Mavis Batey and David Lambert, *The English Garden Tour: a view into the past*, London, 1990

J. Beardsley, *Gardens of Revelation: environments by visionary artists*, New York, 1995

N. Beautheac and F.-X. Bouchart, *L'Europe exotique*, Paris, 1985

W. Beckford (ed. Boyd Alexander), *Life at Fonthill*, London, 1957

A. Beckles Willson, *Strawberry Hill: a history of the neighbourhood*, Richmond, 1995

J.S. Berrall, *The Garden: An Illustrated History*, Harmondsworth, 1978

P. Bicknell, *Beauty, Horror and Immensity: Picturesque Landscapes in Britain, 1650—1850*, Cambridge, 1981

M. Binney and A. Hills, *Elysian Gardens*, London, 1979

J. Brown, *The Art and Architecture of English Gardens*, New York, 1989

E. Burke, *A Philosophical Enquiry into the Origin of Our Ideas of the Sublime and the Beautiful*, London, 1773 (ed. princ., 1756)

A. Burton, *The Shell Book of Curious Britain*, Newton Abbot, 1982

T. Buxbaum, *Scottish Garden Buildings: from food to folly*, Edinburgh, 1989

Enid Byford, *Somerset Curiosities*, Stanbridge , 1987

R.G. Carrott, *The Egyptian Revival: its sources, monuments and meanings, 1808—58*, Berkeley, Calif., 1979

G. Carter, P. Goode and L. Kedrun, *Humphrey Repton: Landscape Gardener, 1752—1818*, London, 1982

Sir Hugh Casson (ed.), *Follies*, London, 1963

— *Monuments*, London, 1963

D. Chambers, *The Planters of the English Landscape Garden*, New Haven and London, 1993

W. Chambers, *Designs of Chinese Buildings*, London, 1757

— *Dissertation on Oriental Gardening*, London, 1772

H.F. Clark, 'Eighteenth-century Elysiums: the role of association in the landscape movement', *Journal of the Warburg and Courtauld Institutes*, 1943

— *The English Landscape Garden*, Gloucester, 1980 (ed. princ., London, 1948)

K. Clark, *The Gothic Revival*, London, 1975 (ed. princ., 1928)

G. Clarke, *Prior Park: a compleat landscape*, Bath, 1987

D. Clifford, *A History of Garden Design*, London, 1962

T.H. Cocke, 'Pre-Nineteenth-century Attitudes in England to Romanesque Architecture', *Journal of the British Archaeological Association*, 1973

— 'Rediscovery of the Romanesque', in *English Romanesque Art 1066—1200*, London, 1984.

D.R. Coffin, *The English Garden: meditation and memorial*, Princeton, 1994

H. Colvin, *A Biographical Dictionary of British Architects: 1600—1840*, London, 1978 (ed. princ., 1954)

H. Colvin and J. Harris (eds.), *The English Country Seat*, London, 1970

P. Conner, *Oriental Architecture in the West*, London, 1979

N. Cooper, 'Indian Influence in England: 1780—1830', *Apollo*, 1970

D. Cox, *Odd & Unusual Bedfordshire*, s.l. 1982

J. S. Curl, *The Egyptian Revival*, London, 1982

J. Curling, 'Castles in the Air', *Lilliput*, 1948

R. A. Curtis (ed.), *Monumental Follies*, Worthing, 1972

A. Dale, *James Wyatt*, Oxford, 1956

G. Darley, *The Idea of the Village*, s.a., 1976

T. Davis, *John Nash: The Prince Regent's Architect*, Newton Abbot, 1973

— *The Gothick Taste*, Norwich, 1974

T.D.W. Dearn, *Designs for Lodges and Entrances to Parks, Paddocks, and Pleasure-Grounds, in the Gothic, Cottage and Fancy Styles*, London, 1823 (ed. princ., 1811)

P. Decker, Chinese Architecture, London, 1759 (reprinted Farnborough, 1968)

— *Gothic Architecture Decorated*, London, 1759 (reprinted Farnborough, 1968)

R. Desmond, *Bibliography of British Gardens*, Winchester, 1984

R. Dixon, *Cotswold Curiosities*, Stanbridge, 1988

R. Dixon and S. Muthesius, *Victorian Architecture*, London, 1978

J. Dobai, *Die Kunstliteratur des Klassizismus und der Romantik in England*, Bern, 1974—77

C. Dupavillon and F. Lacloche, *Le triomphe des arcs*, Paris, 1989

R. Dutton, *The English Garden*, London, 1945

J. Elffers and M. Schuyt, *Fantastic Architecture*, London, 1980

R. Elsam, *An Essay on Rural Architecture*, London, 1803 (reprinted Farnborough, 1972)

E. Erdberg, *Chinese Influence on European Garden Structures*, Cambridge, Mass., 1936

D. Erwin, 'A Picturesque Experience: the Hermitage at Dunkeld', *The Connoisseur*, 1974

K.A. Esdaile, 'The Small House and its Amenities in the Architectural Handbooks: 1749—1847', *Transactions of the Bibliographical Society*, 1917—19

R. Fedden and R. Joekes (eds), *The National Trust Guide*, London, 1984 (3rd edn)

M. Felmingham and R. Graham, *Ruins*, Feltham, 1972

H. Fenwick, 'Features and Follies', *Scots Magazine*, 1965

F.D. Fergusson, *The Neo-Classical Architecture of James Wyatt*, unpublished PhD thesis, Harvard, 1973

M. Fischer, *Katalog der Architektur- und Ornamentstichsammlung der Kunstbibliothek Berlin, I, Baukunst England*, Berlin, 1977

J. Fleming, *Robert Adam and his Circle*, London, 1962

— 'Adam Gothick', *The Connoisseur*, 1968

L. Fleming and A. Gore, *The English Garden*, London, 1979

O.S. Fowler, *The Octagon house: a home for all*, New York, 1853 (reprinted New York, 1973)

P. Frankl, *The Gothic: literary sources and interpretations through eight centuries*, Princeton, NJ, 1960

G.E. Fussell, 'Natural Ice', *Architectural Review*, 1952

J. Gandy, *The Rural Architect*, London, 1805

J. Gaus, 'Die Urhütte: über ein Model der Baukunst und ein Motiv in der bildenden Kunst', *Wallraf-Richartz Jahrbuch*, 1971

G. Germann, *Gothic Revival in Europe and Britain: sources, influences and ideas*, London, 1972

W. Gilpin, *Essays in Picturesque Beauty: on picturesque travel and on sketching landscape*, London, 1794

S. Girardet and others, *Architectures fantastiques*, Paris, 1986

M. Girouard, *The Victorian Country House*, London, 1978

— *Life in the English Country House*, London, 1979

J. Gloag, *Georgian Grace: a social history of design, 1660—1830*, London, 1956

— *Mr. Loudon's England*, Newcastle-upon-Tyne, 1970

R.H. Goodsall, 'Follies and Gazebos', *A Second Kentish Patchwork*, 1968

M. Grant, 'Full Circle at the Folly', *Country Fair*, 1967

L. Greeves (ed.), *The National Trust Atlas*, London 1981

Mrs D. Guinness, 'The Deliberate Follies of Ireland', *Ireland of the Welcomes*, 1972

R. Gunnis, *Dictionary of British Sculptors: 1660—1851*, London, 1968 (ed. princ., 1953)

J. Hadfield (ed.), *The Saturday Book 27: The Oriental Dream*, London, 1967

— *The Shell Guide to England*, London, 1977

M. Hadfield, *The English Landscape Garden*, Aylesbury, 1977

M. Hadfield, R. Harling and L. Highton, *British Gardeners: a biographical dictionary*, London, 1980

W. Halfpenny, *New Designs for Chinese Temples, etc.*, London, 1750

W. and J. Halfpenny, Rural Architecture in the Chinese Taste, London, 1752

— *Rural Architecture in the Gothic Taste*, London 1752

J. Hall, *Essay on the Origin, History and Principles of Gothic Architecture*, London, 1813

R. Harbison, *Eccentric Spaces*, New York, 1977

E. Harris, 'Burke and Chambers on the Sublime and Beautiful', *Essays in the History of Architecture presented to Rudof Wittkower*, London, 1967

— 'False speranze e vani desideri: progetti di Thomas Wright', *Arte illustrata*, 1973

— 'Batty Langley: a tutor to freemasons (1696—1751)', *The Burlington Magazine*, 1977

J. Harris, 'Exoticism at Kew', *Apollo*, 1963

— 'The Dundas Empire', *Apollo*, 1967

— *Sir William Chambers: Knight of the Polar Star*, London, 1970

— *The Artist and the Country House: a history of country house and garden view painting in Britain, 1540—1870*, London, 1979

— 'William Kent's Gothick', *A Gothick Symposium*, London, 1983

G.F. Hartlaub, *Der Gartenzwerg und seine Ahnen*, Heidelberg, 1962

G. Hartmann, *Die Ruine im Landschaftsgarten*, Worms 1981

W. Hawkes, 'The Gothic Architectural Work of Sanderson Miller', *A Gothick Symposium*, London, 1983

Raymond Head, *The Indian Style*, London, 1986

G. Headley, *Architectural Follies in America*, New York, 1996

— 'The Follies of Dorset', *Dorset Arts Magazine*, 1984

J. Heely, *Letters on the Beauties of Hagley, Envil and The Leasowes*, London, 1777

A. Hellyer, *The Shell Guide to Gardens*, London, 1977

R. Hewlings, 'Ripon's Forum Populi', *Architectural History*, 1981

W. Hipple, *The Beautiful, the Sublime and the Picturesque in Eighteenth-century British Aesthetic Theory*, Carbondale, 1957

G. Hogg, *Odd Aspects of England*, Newton Abbott, 1968

A.M. Holcomb, 'The Bridge in the Middle Distance: symbolic elements in the Romantic landscape', *The Art Quarterly*, 1974

H. Honour, *Chinoiserie: the vision of Cathay*, London, 1961

J. Howley, *The Follies and Garden Buildings of Ireland*, New Haven and London, 1993

J.-M. Humbert, *L'égyptomanie dans l'art occidental*, Paris, 1989

J. D. Hunt, 'Emblem and Expression in the Eighteenth-century Landscape Garden', *Eighteenth-century Studies*, 1971

— *The Figure in the Landscape: poetry, painting and gardening during the eighteenth century*, Baltimore, Md, 1976

J.D. Hunt and P. Willis (eds), *The Genius of the Place: the English landscape garden, 1620—1820*, London, 1975

P. Hunt, *The Book of Garden Ornament*, London, 1974

C. Hussey, *The Picturesque*, London, 1927

— *English Gardens and Landscapes: 1700—1750*, London, 1970

E. Hyams, *Capability Brown and Humphrey Repton*, London, 1971

O. Impey, *Chinoiserie: the impact of Oriental styles on Western art and decoration*, London, 1977

G. Jackson-Stops, *An English Arcadia 1600—1990*, Washington, 1991

D. Jacques, *Georgian Gardens: the reign of nature*, London, 1983

E. Jameson, *1,000 Curiosities of Britain*, London, 1947

J. Jarratt, *Ivory Towers and Dressed Stones: exploring the follies, prospect towers & other curiosities of northern England*, Milnthorpe, 1994

D. Jarrett, *The English Landscape Garden*, London, 1978

C. Jencks, *Bizarre Architecture*, London, 1979

F.I. Jenkins, 'Harbingers of the Eiffel Tower', *Journal of the Society of Architectural Historians*, 1957

— 'Some Nineteenth-century Towers', *RIBA Journal*, 1958

— 'John Foulston and his Public Buildings in Plymouth, Stonehouse and Devonport', *Journal of the Society of Architectural Historians*, 1968

G.W. Johnson, *A History of English Gardening*, London, 1829 (reprinted New York, 1982)

B. Jones, 'Beside the Sea', *Architectural Review*, 1947

— *Follies and Grottoes*, London, 1953

— *Follies and Grottoes*, London, 1974 (new edn)

M. Jourdain, *The Work of William Kent*, London, 1948

E. Kaufmann, *Architecture in the Age of Reason*, New York, 1968 (*ed. princ.*, 1955)

A. Kelly, 'Coade Stone at National Trust Houses', *National Trust Studies 1980*, London, 1979

P. Kidson, P. Murray and P. Thompson, *A History of English Architecture*, Harmondsworth, 1979

R.A. Kindler, 'Periodical Criticism 1815—40: originality in architecture', *Architectural History*, 1974

N. and B. Kitz, *Painshill Park: Hamilton and his picturesque landscape*, London, 1984

R.P. Knight, *The Landscape: a didactic poem*, London, 1794

— *An Analytical Inquiry into the Principles of Taste*, London 1805

S. Koppelkamm, *Der imaginäre Orient: exotische Bauten des achtzehnten und neunzehnten Jahrhunderts in Europa*, Berlin, 1987

D. Lambin, 'Notes on Space and Space Perception in Eighteenth-century Parks and Gardens', *Kunst und Kunsttheorie des XVIII. Jahrhunderts in England*, Hildesheim, 1979

L. Lambton, *An Album of Curious Houses*, London, 1988

— *Beastly Buildings: the National Trust book of architecture for animals*, London, 1985

C. Lancaster, *Architectural Follies in America or Hammer, Saw, Tooth and Nail*, Rutland, Vt, 1960

S. Lang, 'The Principles of the Gothic Revival in England', *Journal of the Society of Architectural Historians*, 1966

S. Lang and N. Pevsner, 'Sir William Temple and Sharawaggi', *Architectural Review*, 1949

B. and T. Langley, *New Principles of Gardening*, London, 1728

— *Gothic Architecture Improved*, London, 1747 (reprinted Farnborough, 1967)

F. Laske, *Der Ostasiatische Einfluss auf die Baukunst des Abendlandes*, Berlin 1909

S. Lasdun, *The English Park*, London, 1991

B. Lassus, *Jardins imaginaires*, Paris, 1977

J. Lees-Milne, *The National Trust: a record of fifty years' achievement*, London, 1945

— *Earls of Creation*, London, 1962

— *William Beckford*, Tisbury, 1976

C.H. Liebs, *Main Street to Miracle Mile: American roadside architecture*, Boston, 1985

T. Lightoler, *The Gentleman and Farmer's Architect*, London, 1774 (*ed. princ.*, 1762; reprinted Farnborough, 1968)

C.J.E. Prince de Ligne, *Coup d'oeil sur Beloeil; et sur une grande partie de l'Europe*, Paris, 1922 (*ed. princ.*, 1781)

I.G. Lindsay and M. Cosh, *Inveraray and the Dukes of Argyll*, Edinburgh, 1973

J.C. Loudon, *An Encyclopaedia of Gardening*, London, 1822

— *An Encyclopaedia of Cottage, Farm and Villa Architecture and Furniture*, London, 1833

— *In Search of English Gardens: the travels of John Claudius Loudon and his wife Jane*, London, 1990

A.O. Lovejoy, *Essays in the History of Ideas*, Baltimore, Md, 1961

'M. Lucan and D. Gray' [= A. Martin and J. Fletcher], *The Decadent Gardener*, Sawtry, 1996

J. Macaulay, *The Gothic Revival 1745—1845*, Glasgow, 1975

R. Macaulay, *Pleasure of Ruins*, London, 1953

M. McCarthy, 'Sir Thomas Robinson: an original English Palladian', *Architectura*, 1980

— *The Origins of the Gothic Revival*, New Haven and London, 1987

R. F. Maccubin and P. Martin (eds), 'Special issue: British and American gardens', *Eighteenth-century Life*, 1983

M. McMordie, 'Picturesque Patternbooks and Pre-Victorian Designers', *Architectural History*, 1975

E. Malins, *English Landscaping and Literature: 1660—1840*, London, 1966

E. Malins and the Knight of Glin, *Lost Demesnes: Irish landscape gardening, 1660—1845*, London, 1976

E. Malnic, *Folies de jardin: art et architecture des fabriques de jardin du XVIIIe siècle à nos jours*, Paris, 1996

E. Manwaring, *Italian Landscape in Eighteenth-century England*, New York, 1925

J. Margolis, *The End of the Road: vanishing highway architecture in America*, Harmondsworth, 1981

C. Marriott, 'The Necessity of Follies', *Architectural Review*, 1950

S. Marsden and D. McLaren, *In Ruins: the once great homes of Ireland*, London, 1980

J.P. Martinon, 'Les espaces corrigés', *Traverses*, 1976

G. Mason, *An Essay on Design in Gardening*, London, 1795

W. Mason, *The English Garden*, London, 1777—81

J. Massey and S. Maxwell, *Gothic Revival*, London, 1994

C. Meeks, 'Picturesque Eclecticism', *Art Bulletin*, 1950

— 'Creative Eclecticism', *Journal of the Society of Architectural Historians*, 1953

U.M. Mehrtens, *Folly in Groot Brittannië: aanzet en ordening aan de hand van een bronnenonderzoek*, unpublished PhD thesis, Utrecht, 1980

H.C. Mettin, *Furst Pückler reist nach England*, Berlin, 1938

W. Meulenkamp, *Follies: bizarre bouwsels in Nederland en België*, Amsterdam, 1995

— '*Fuller hath done a very great thing*': '*Mad Jack*' *Fuller and his follies*, unpublished PhD thesis, Utrecht, 1980

— 'Portfolio Follies: journaal van een reis naar Engeland, etc.', *Maatstaf*, 1978

— *Verloren land: drie eeuwen non-conformisme*, Nieuwegein, 1996

C. Middleton, *Decorations in Parks and Gardens*, London, 1800

N. Miller, *Heavenly Caves: reflections on the garden grotto*, London, 1982

S.H. Monk, *The Sublime*, Ann Arbor, Mich., 1960 (*ed. princ.*, 1935)

J. Mordaunt Crook, *The Greek Revival*, Feltham, 1968

— 'The Pre-Victorian Architect: professionalism and patronage', *Architectural History*, 1969

— Introduction to C. Eastlake, *A History of the Gothic Revival*, London, 1872 (reprinted New York, 1970)

— *The Greek Revival: neo-classical attitudes in British architecture 1760—1870*, London, 1972

C. Morris (ed.), *The Illustrated Journeys of Celia Fiennes c.1682—c.1712*, London, 1982

R. Morris, *The Art of Architecture: a poem*, London, 1742

— *Rural Architecture*, London, 1750

— *The Architectural Remembrancer*, London, 1752 (reprinted Farnborough, 1971)

M. Mosser and G. Teyssot (eds.), *The History of Garden Design*, London, 1991

G. Mott and S. Sample Aall, *Follies and Pleasure Pavilions*, New York, 1989

T. Mowl, 'The Evolution of the Park Gate Lodge as a Building Type', *Architectural History*, 1984

T. Mowl and B. Earnshaw, *Trumpet at a Distant Gate: the lodge as prelude to the country house*, London, 1985

K. Murawska, 'An Image of Mysterious Wisdom Won by Toil: the tower as symbol of thoughtful isolation in English art and literature from Milton to Yeats', *Artibus et historiae: rivista intemazionale di arti visive e cinema*, 1982

C.W. Nachmani, 'The Early English Cottage Book', *Marsyas*, 1968

P.J. Neville Havins, *The Spas of England*, London, 1976

E. Newby and D. Petry, *Wonders of Britain*, London, 1968

A. Nuijten, *Op de valreep beschouwd: Hackfall, een tuin en zijn gebouwen*, unpublished PhD thesis, Utrecht, 1983

A.-L. Nyreröd, *Lusthus: och bruks och till syns*, Stockholm, 1979

P. Oppé, 'Robert Adam's Picturesque Compositions', *The Burlington Magazine*, 1942

C. Over, *Ornamental Architecture in the Gothic, Chinese and Modern Taste*, London, 1758

T.C. Overton, *Original Designs of Temples (The Temple Builder's Most Useful Companion)*, London, 1766

J. Owen, *Eccentric Gardens*, London, 1990

J.B. Papworth, *Rural Residences*, London, 1818 (reprinted Farnborough, 1971)

A. Parreaux and M. Plaisant (eds), *Jardins et paysages: le style anglais*, Lille, 1977

R. Paulson, *Emblem and Expression: meaning in English art of the eighteenth century*, London, 1975

N. Pevsner, 'The Other Chambers', *Architectural Review*, 1947

— 'Good King James's Gothic', *Architectural Review*, 1950

— (ed.), *The Picturesque Garden and its Influence Outside the British Isles*, Dumbarton Oaks, 1974

N. Pevsner and S. Lang, 'The Egyptian Revival', *Architectural Review*, 1956

J. Piper, 'Pleasing Decay', *Architectural Review*, 1947

J. Plaw, *Ferme ornée; or Rural Improvements*, London, 1795

W.F. Pocock, *Architectural Designs for Rustic Cottages*, London, 1807 (reprinted Farnborough, 1972)

M. Praz, 'Costume 14: Follies', *Bellezza e bizzarria*, Milan, 1960

E. Preston, *Curious England*, Aylesbury, 1977

U. Price, *An Essay on the Picturesque*, London, 1794

M. Racine, *Architecture rustique des rocailleurs*, Paris, 1981

J. Raspi Serra (ed.), *La fortuna di Paestum e la memoria moderna del dorico, 1750—1830*, Florence, 1986

J. Rees, *Das Capriccio als Kunstprinzip*, Milan 1996

A.W. Reinink and J. Vermeulen, *Ijskelders*, Nieuwkoop, 1981

H. Repton, *Observations on the Theory and Practice of Landscape Gardening*, London, 1803

O. Reutensvard, *The Neo-Classic Temple of Virility and the Buildings with a Phallic-shaped Ground Plan*, Lund, 1971

M. Revesz-Alexander, *Der Turm als Symbol und Erlebnis*, The Hague, 1953

RIBA, *Catalogue of the Drawings Collection of the Royal Institute of British Architects*, London, 1969—76

A.E. Richardson, *Robert Mylne*, London, 1955

D.S. Richardson, *Gothic Revival Architecture in Ireland*, unpublished PhD thesis, Yale, 1971

S. Roberts, *Bird-keeping and Birdcages: a history*, New York, 1973

J. M. Robinson, 'Model Farm Buildings of the Age of Improvement', *Architectural History*, 1976

— *The Wyatts: an architectural dynasty*, Oxford, 1979

— *Georgian Model Farms*, Oxford, 1983

— *The Latest Country Houses*, London, 1984

J. Rory (ed.), *Adam de la Halle: le jeu de la feuilée*, Paris, 1977

G. le Rouge, *Détails des nouveaux jardins à la mode (Jardins anglo-chinoise à la mode)*, Paris, 1776—88

A. Rowan, *Garden Buildings*, Feltham, 1968

— 'Gothick Restoration at Raby Castle', *Architectural History*, 1972

— 'Batty Langley's Gothic', *Studies in Memory of David Talbot Rice*, Edinburgh, 1975

P. de la Ruffinière du Prey, 'John Soane, Philip Yorke and their Quest for Primitive Architecture', *National Trust Studies 1979*, London, 1978

— *John Soane: the making of an architect*, Chicago, 1982

J. Rykwert, *On Adam's House in Paradise: the idea of the primitive hut in architectural history*, New York, 1972

— *The First Moderns: the architects of the eighteenth century*, Cambridge, Mass., 1980

W. Shenstone, *The Works in Verse and Prose*, London, 1766 (*ed. princ.*, 1764)

J. Shirley Hibberd, *Rustic Adornments for Homes of Taste*, London, 1856

J. Simmen, *Ruinen-Faszination in der Graphik vom 16. Jahrhundert bis in die Gegenwart*, Dortmund, 1980

D. Simpson, *Gothick: 1720—1840*, Brighton, 1975

O. Sirén, *China and the Gardens of Europe*, New York, 1950

J. Smith (ed.), *The Landmark Handbook*, Shottesbrooke, 1977

South Yorkshire County Council, *Follies & Monuments of South Yorkshire*, Gainsborough, 1977

P. Stanton, *Pugin*, London, 1971

J. Steegman, *The Rule of Taste from George I to George IV*, London, 1968 (*ed. princ.*, 1936)

K. Stempel, *Geschichtsbilder im frühen englischen Garten*, Munster, 1982

S.H. Stephenson, *Rustic Furniture*, New York, 1979

K. Stromberg, 'Von Göttern und Gartenzwergen: die bewohnte Natur als Kunst und Kunstkammer', *Kunst & Antiquitäten*, 1981

D. Stroud, *Humphrey Repton*, London, 1963

— *Capability Brown*, London, 1975

D.C. Stuart, *Georgian Gardens*, London, 1979

R. Sühnel, *Der Park als Gesamtkunstwerk des englischen Klassizismus am Beispiel von Stourhead*, Heidelberg, 1977

J. Summerson, *The Unromantic Castle, and other essays*, London, 1990

— 'The Vision of J. M. Gandy', *Heavenly Mansions*, New York, 1963

— *Architecture in Britain: 1530—1830*, Harmondsworth, 1970 (*ed. princ.*, 1953)

D. Sutton (ed.), 'The Splendours of Stowe', *Apollo*, 1973

A.A. Tait, *The Landscape Garden in Scotland: 1735—1835*, Edinburgh, 1980

N. Temple, *John Nash and the Village Picturesque*, Gloucester, 1979

C. Thacker, *Masters of the Grotto: Joseph and Josiah Lane*, Tisbury, 1976

G.S. Thomas, *Gardens of the National Trust*, London, 1979

P. Toynbee (ed.), 'Horace Walpole's Journals of Visits to Country Seats, &c.' *Walpole Society*, 1928

A. Vidler, 'The Architecture of Lodges: ritual form and associational life in the late Enlightenment', *Oppositions*, 1976

H. Vogel, 'Agyptisierende Baukunst des Klassizismus', *Zeitschrift für bildende Kunst*, 1928—29

H. Walpole, *Works*, London, 1798—1825

D. Watkin, *Thomas Hope and the Neo-Classical Idea*, London, 1968

— *The English Vision*, London, 1982

I. Weibezahn, *Geschichte und Funktion des Monopteros*, Hildesheim, 1965

R. White (ed.), *Georgian Arcadia: Architecture for the Park and Garden*, London, 1987

— 'The Influence of Batty Langley', *A Gothick Symposium*, London, 1983

J. Whitelaw, *Follies*, Aylesbury, 1982

D. Wiebenson, 'Greek, Gothic and Nature: 1750—1820', *Essays in Honour of Walter Friedlaender*, Glückstadt, 1965

— *Sources of Greek Revival Architecture*, London, 1969

Sir Clough Williams-Ellis, *Architect errant*, London, 1971

P. Willis (ed.), *Furor hortensis: essays on the history of the English landscape garden in memory of H. F. Clark*, Edinburgh, 1974

M.I. Wilson, *William Kent: architect, designer, painter, gardener: 1685—1748*, London, 1984

J. Wilton-Ely, 'Beckford the Builder', *William Beckford Exhibition 1976*, Tisbury, 1976

R. Wittkower, 'English Neo-Palladianism, the Landscape Garden, China, and the Enlightenment', *L'arte*, 1979

C. Wolsdorff, 'Englische Publikationen des 18. Jahrhunderts zu "Architecture" und "Building"', *Kunst und Kunsttheorie des XVIII. Jahrhunderts in England*, Hildesheim, 1969

A.C. Wood and W. Hawkes, 'Sanderson Miller of Radway/Miller's Work at Wroxton/The Architectural Work of Sanderson Miller', *Cake and Cockhorse*, 1969

T.E.B. Wood, *The Word 'Sublime' and its Context*, The Hague/Paris, 1972

K. Woodbridge, *Landscape and Antiquity*, Oxford, 1971

— 'Kent's Gardening: the Rousham letters', *Apollo*, 1974

— *The Stourhead Landscape*, s.l. 1974

M. Woods, *Visions of Arcadia: European gardens from renaissance to rococo*, London, 1996

G. Worsley, *Classical Architecture in Britain: the heroic age*, New Haven and London, 1995

T. Wright, *Arbours and Grottos: a facsimile of the two parts of 'Universal architecture' (1755 and 1758)*, London, 1979

W. Wrighte, *Grotesque Architecture*, London, 1790 (*ed. princ.*, 1767)

P. Wrightson, *The Small English House*, London, 1977

B. Zijlstra, *De folly en haar ontwerp in de 18e en vroeg 19e eeuwse architectonische handboeken*, unpublished PhD thesis, Utrecht, 1980

Index